CHINA
IN THE ERA OF
DENG XIAOPING

Studies on Contemporary China

Studies on Contemporary China

CHINA IN THE ERA OF DENG XIAOPING

A DECADE OF REFORM

MICHAEL YING-MAO KAU
SUSAN H. MARSH
editors

Yevgeniy Afanasyev
Hungdah Chiu
Robert F. Dernberger
Lowell Dittmer
June Teufel Dreyer
Kimio Fujita
Merle Goldman
Harold C. Hinton

Nicholas R. Lardy
Hong Yung Lee
Li Luye
Suzanne Pepper
Jonathan D. Pollack
J. Stapleton Roy
Stuart R. Schram
Kungchia Yeh

An East Gate Book

M.E. Sharpe
Armonk, New York
London, England

An East Gate Book

Library of Congress Cataloging-in-Publication Data

China in the era of Deng Xiaoping: a decade of reform / edited by
Michael Ying-Mao Kau and Susan H. Marsh.
p.   cm.—(Studies on contemporary China)
Includes index
ISBN 1-56324-277-X
1. China—Politics and government—1976–.
2. Teng, Hsiao-p'ing, 1904–.
I. Kau, Michael Y. M., 1934–.
II. Marsh, Susan H., 1926–.
III. Series.
DS779.26.C473512   1993
93–31395
CIP

Printed in the United States of America

The paper used in this publication meets the minimum requirements of
American National Standard for Information Sciences—
Permanence of Paper for Printed Library Materials,
ANSI Z 39.48-1984.

BM (c)   10   9   8   7   6   5   4   3   2   1
BM (p)   10   9   8   7   6   5   4   3   2   1

CONTENTS

PREFACE

THE YEAR 1987 marked a decade of sustained reform under the leadership of Deng Xiaoping. In the years following the Third Plenum of the Eleventh Central Committee of the Chinese Communist Party in December 1978, Deng and his close associates reversed the course of the Maoist model of revolution and introduced reforms of historic significance in virtually every sector of China's internal and external development. The decade epitomized the rise of the Deng Xiaoping line of building "socialism with Chinese characteristics."

Existing scholarly works and journalistic accounts have well documented the various aspects of the dramatic phenomena of post-Mao reforms. There is, however, insufficient analysis and assessment of the basic nature and long-term significance of the post-Mao developments. What precisely does "socialism with Chinese characteristics" mean? Is Deng genuinely engaged in a gradual process of "de-revolutionizing" China? What is the significance of Deng's "second revolution" of the 1980s in comparison with Mao's "first revolution" of the 1950s? What are the sources of support for and resistance against further development of the "Dengist model"? Moreover, what are the implications of Deng's "pragmatism" and reforms for the future of China, in particular, and of Marxism-Leninism, in general? Finally, what has been the impact of Deng's reforms on China's relations with its neighbors and with the superpowers, and on the redefinition of China's role in the world arena? Answers to these questions are essential not only for advancing our own knowledge of China's political development and social change, but also for formulating appropriate foreign and economic policies toward China.

Hence, the idea for a conference to examine "A Decade of Reform Under Deng Xiaoping" was conceived in 1986. The intellectual strength of the Chinese Studies community was mobilized to carry out a comprehensive analysis and assessment of the nature, pattern, and trend of Deng's reforms. With the generous support of the Institute for International Studies at Brown University and the Chinese Studies Program of the Wang Institute of Graduate Studies, a major international academic conference was convened at Brown University during the period of November 4–7, 1987. The conference brought together sixty leading scholars and senior policymakers from various parts of the world.

The conference was conducted in two consecutive phases. During the first phase, a senior government official from Beijing gave a presentation outlining the reforms of the post-Mao period. Officials from Tokyo, Moscow, and Washington followed with their assessments of the policy implications of Deng's reforms, from the perspectives of their respective countries. The second phase of the conference centered on the presentation and discussion of twelve research papers by leading Western scholars. Two participants were assigned to critique each paper and lead off general discussion. While the presentations by the policymakers were open to the entire Brown community of faculty and students, the discussion of research papers took place in a seminar setting limited to invited participants.

The two-phase conference format was specially designed to serve a dual educational and scholarly objective. The public lectures gave the university community a rare opportunity to benefit from the perspectives of leading policymakers from the four powers. The closed seminar offered scholars and specialists a setting conducive to in-depth discussion of papers and ideas.

This volume is essentially the collective intellectual product of the conference, based on the research papers, policy speeches, and critical commentaries that were presented. The tedious organizational and editorial tasks of shaping the conference proceedings into a conference volume turned out, as usual, to protract much longer than originally anticipated. The dramatic development of the Democracy Movement and the bloody Tiananmen suppression in the spring and summer of 1989 further complicated our editing and publishing schedule. The tragic event prompted some authors to reevaluate their arguments and analytical frameworks. Some even argued for postponing the publication schedule in order to observe how the Tiananmen Square massacre would affect the direction and momentum of Deng's reforms. With the hindsight of the post-Tiananmen developments, we are relieved and convinced that Deng has managed successfully to keep his reform program intact and stay on course.

This conference volume owes its inception to the intellectual leadership and moral support rendered by the Institute for International Studies (IIS) at Brown University and the Chinese Studies Program of the Wang Institute. On the Brown University side, we are particularly grateful to the late President Howard R. Swearer, Provost Maurice Glicksman, and Professor Abbott Gleason (then acting director of the IIS). On the Wang Institute side, we are deeply indebted to the late chairman An Wang, President Edmund T. Cranch, and members of its National Advisory Committee (Samuel C. Chu, Kuang-chih Chang, William T. de Barry, Michael Y. M. Kau, Rhoads Murphey, and William S. Y. Yang).

We wish to take this opportunity to express our deepest appreciation to each and every conference participant—senior government officials, paper writers, and paper discussants—whose direct contributions constitute the very base of this volume. As the names of these individuals already appear in various parts of the book, it would be redundant to mention them here. We are very fortunate to have received, at different stages of the project, the superb administrative support from the staff of the two institutions involved, especially Margaret C. Fung, Julia Emlen, William Slack, and Eric Broudy.

For the tasks of copyediting and computer formatting, we are most appreciative of the excellent job done by Rita L. Bernhard and Jo Allsopp. The acknowledgment of our appreciation cannot be complete without a word of special thanks to Douglas Merwin, Asian studies editor at M. E. Sharpe. His unfailing support and patience are always a source of encouragement and morale to the scholarly community of Chinese Studies.

Michael Ying-mao Kau
Brown University

Susan H. Marsh
Providence College

CONTRIBUTORS

Hungdah Chiu is Professor of Law at the University of Maryland School of Law. He received the S.J.D. degree from Harvard Law School in 1965. Among his many publications are *People's China and International Law: A Documentary Study* (Princeton University Press, 1974); *Criminal Justice in Post-Mao China* (State University of New York Press, 1985); and *The Future of Hong Kong* (Greenwood, 1987). In 1976 he was awarded a Certificate of Merit by the American Society of International Law.

Robert F. Dernberger has been Professor of Economics at the University of Michigan since 1967, serving as Director of the Center for Chinese Studies in 1983–85. He received his education in Chinese studies at the University of Michigan (M.A., 1958) and in economics at Harvard (Ph.D., 1965). He has taught at the University of Chicago and has served as editor of *Economic Development and Cultural Change* and as president of the Association for Comparative Economic Systems. Professor Dernberger has written more than fifty articles and books on economic development and comparative economic systems, with special reference to China.

Lowell Dittmer (Ph.D., University of Chicago, 1971) taught at the State University of New York at Buffalo and at the University of Michigan before joining the Political Science Department at the University of California at Berkeley in 1978. His principal works include *Liu Shao-ch'i and the Chinese Cultural Revolution* (California, 1974); *China's Continuous Revolution* (California, 1986); and *Sino-Soviet Normalization and Its International Implications* (University of Washington Press, 1991). He is now engaged in a study of the Chinese reforms.

June Teufel Dreyer (Ph.D., Harvard University, 1973) is Professor of Political Science and Director of East Asian Programs at the University of Miami, Coral Gables, Florida. She is a member of the International Institute of Strategic Studies

(London), has written extensively on the Chinese military and related topics, and has held many consultantships. She was the editor and a contributor to *Chinese Defense and Foreign Policy* (Paragon House, 1989) and *Asian Pacific Regional Security* (Washington Institute Press, 1990). She is currently working on two book-length manuscripts: "The Party and the Gun: Civil-Military Relations in the People's Republic of China" and "Chinese Politics: The Search for Modernity Within Tradition."

Merle Goldman is Professor of History at Boston University. She received her Ph.D. in history and Far Eastern languages from Harvard University in 1972. Her publications include *Literary Dissent in Communist China* (Harvard University Press, 1967) and *China's Intellectuals: Advise and Dissent* (Harvard University Press, 1981); four volumes of which she served as editor or coeditor; and numerous articles. Receiver of the Radcliffe Graduate Medal for Distinguished Achievement in June 1981; and a Guggenheim Fellow in 1987–88, she is currently working on a book, "The Sprouts of Democracy in Post-Mao China."

Harold C. Hinton is professor of Political Science and International Affairs at the George Washington University. Since receiving his doctorate at Harvard University in 1951, he has traveled extensively in East Asia and has published numerous books and articles on comparative and international politics, including *Communist China in World Politics* (1966) and "China as an Asian Power," in a symposium volume published by Oxford University Press.

Michael Ying-mao Kau (Ph.D. Cornell University) is professor of Political Science and director of the Mao's Writings Project and the East Asian Security Project at Brown University. The editor of *Chinese Law and Government*, his books include *The People's Liberation Army and China's Nation-Building, The Lin Piao Affair, The Writings of Mao Zedong 1949–76, Critical Issues Facing Taiwan's Current Reform* (in Chinese), *In Search of the Way: Taiwan in a Time of Transition, Comparing Development Experiences of Taiwan and Mainland China* (in Chinese), and *Taiwan: Beyond the Economic Miracle.*

Nicholas R. Lardy is Professor of International Studies at the Henry M. Jackson School of International Studies at the University of Washington. He is the author of *Economic Growth and Distribution in China* (Cambridge University Press, 1978); *Agriculture in China's Modern Equipment Development* (Cambridge University Press, 1983) *China's Entry into the World Economy* (University Press of America, 1987); *and Foreign Trade and Economic Reform in China* (Cambridge University Press, 1991).

Hong Yung Lee is Professor of Political Science at the University of California at Berkeley and Research Associate at the East-West Center, the University of Hawaii. He is the author of *The Politics of the Chinese Cultural Revolution* (University of California Press); *From Revolutionary Cadres to Party Tech-*

nocrats in Socialist China (University of California Press); and *Research Guide to Red Guard Publications* (M. E. Sharpe, forthcoming).

Susan H. Marsh is Professor of Political Science at Providence College. She was born in China and educated at St. John's University (Shanghai) and the University of Chicago. She taught at Stanford, Columbia, Cornell, and Brown Universities before joining the faculty of Providence College in 1977.

Suzanne Pepper received her Ph.D. in political science in 1972 from the University of California at Berkeley. A long-time resident of Hong Kong, she lectured on Chinese politics as the East Asia Associate of the American-based Universities Field Staff International during 1985–87. She is the author of *Civil War in China: The Political Struggle, 1945–49* (University of California Press, 1978). Her publications on post-1949 Chinese education include the relevant chapters in the *Cambridge History of China*, vols. 14 and 15, and *China's Education Reform in the 1980s: Policies, Issues, and Historical Perspectives*, A China Research Monograph, published by the Institute of East Asian Studies of the University of California at Berkeley, 1990.

Jonathan D. Pollack is Corporate Research Manager for International Policy at RAND, Santa Monica, California. His recent publications include *U.S. Strategic Alternatives in the Changing Pacific* (1990) and *Into the Vortex: China, the Sino-Soviet Alliance, and the Korean War* (1991).

Stuart R. Schram (Ph.D., Columbia University, 1954) was Professor of Politics at the School of Oriental and African Studies of the University of London from 1967 to 1989, when he became Professor Emeritus. From 1968 to 1972, he was concurrently Head of the Contemporary China Institute. Since 1989 he has been Visiting Scholar at Harvard University in charge of the preparation for publication of a complete English translation of Mao Zedong's writings down to 1949. He has published some twenty books and sixty articles, including *Marxism and Asia*, in collaboration with Hélène Carrère d'Encausse (London, 1969); *Mao Zedong: A Preliminary Reassessment* (Hong Kong, 1983); *Foundations and Limits of State Power in China*, edited with a contribution (London and Hong Kong, 1987); and *The Thought of Mao Tse-tung* (Cambridge, 1989).

Kungchia Yeh, senior economist at the RAND Corporation, received his L.L.B from the National Tsing Hua University in Beijing and Ph.D. from Columbia University. He was Visiting Lecturer at the University of California at Berkeley and Chung Hua Institution of Economic Research, Taipei, and a consultant to the World Bank and Bechtel Corporation. His recent publications include *The Changing Asian Economic Environment and U.S.-Japan Relations* (1990) and *Lessons of Asian Development and Alternative Development Strategies for Hainan* (1991).

INTRODUCTION

Susan H. Marsh
Michael Ying-mao Kau

I

AT THE THIRD PLENUM of the Tenth Party Central Committee in July 1977, Deng Xiaoping emerged from political disgrace for a second time and began to aggressively reassert his leadership. When the historic Third Plenum of the Eleventh Central Committee convened in December 1978, Deng declared reform and opening up as the new party line. In the ensuing years, he skillfully outmaneuvered his political opponents by systematically purging the supporters of the Gang of Four and other Maoist radicals, while gently pushing thousands of aging senior leaders upstairs to "honorable" retirement. By the time Deng called a special Party Conference in September 1986, he and his close associates—Hu Yaobang and Zhao Ziyang—had successfully installed their protégés and supporters in more than three-fourths of the top party, government, and military leadership positions (in such organs as the Central Committee, the State Council, and the Military Commission). Remarkably, the new leadership achieved this dramatic transformation of power all in the name of reforming the administration and rejuvenating the cadres.

The decade under Deng leadership has also witnessed dramatic changes in China's ideological and policy orientations. In contrast to Mao's pursuit of the fanatic political goals of "continuous revolution" and utopian egalitarianism, the new leadership stressed the pragmatic goals of the "Four Modernizations" and economic development. According to Deng, the "principle contradiction" of society resided in the material and technological bases of production rather than in the social relations of production, as Mao emphasized. Hence, Deng's reinterpretations required fundamental changes in China's party line and policy direction.

In the countryside, the persistent Maoist push for continuous socialist transformations was reversed by Deng's policy of "decollectivization." The people's communes were abandoned in favor of a "household responsibility system," which legitimized personal initiatives and material rewards. Once attacked by

Mao, the "revisionist" practices of tolerating "three freedoms" (free enterprise, free market, and free private plots) and setting production quotas at the household level became promoted as the official policy of the day.

In the urban industrial sector, rigid bureaucratic centralization and political control loosened its grip on the entire planning and management system. The concept of "command economy" yielded to the new principle of "guidance economy," thereby recognizing and legitimizing the efficacy of the market mechanism. Under the new "enterprise responsibility system," the manager enjoyed an unprecedented degree of autonomy in matters related to investments, marketing, pricing, wages, man-power control, and profit distribution. In addition, small-scale private businesses were promoted nationally to stimulate production and absorb unemployed labor. Equally significant were the far-reaching reforms instituted by Deng in the areas of education, law, and cultural life.

Under Deng's leadership, China's economic relations with the outside world also changed dramatically. The Maoist obsession with "self-reliance" was replaced by an aggressive open-door policy to foster international trade and technology transfers. A variety of special economic and technology zones were created along China's coastal regions in order to attract joint ventures and foreign investments.

While Deng's ideas for changing China's basic domestic policy were unmistakably clear throughout the 1980s, the direction of Beijing's foreign policy and security strategy remained somewhat ambiguous and uncertain. China's strategic and economic ties with the West had developed in the past decade to the point where Beijing could not afford to make any major shifts without jeopardizing the nation's central commitment to the "Four Modernizations" and reform.

However, as Mikhail Gorbachev continued to move the Soviet Union down the "road of *perestroika*," Beijing also began a new policy of relaxation and normalization with Moscow. As the world witnessed the emergence of a new international order, China declared its pursuit of an "independent" foreign policy of peace and of opening up. Yet at the same time, China's concrete regional and global roles remained undefined. The course that China elects for its external economic and security relations in the 1990s will clearly have far-reaching effects on the West's strategic interests, as well as on the global balance of power.

II

Reversing the order of the conference proceedings, Part I of this volume begins with the twelve analytical papers and their accompanying comments prepared by the scholars who participated in the conference. Part II contains the four policy speeches delivered by senior policymakers from Beijing, Tokyo, Moscow, and Washington. Comments by scholars on the policy speeches are also included.

The book opens with Lowell Dittmer's paper on the theory and practice of the post-Mao reforms. He analyzes the structure of communism, the cyclical patterns of the political movement, and the secularization trend of the modernizing Chinese society. Dittmer traces the genesis of Deng's reforms to the period of New Democracy and Socialist Construction in the 1950s and to Liu Shaoqi's theoretical works.

Dittmer states that Mao had earlier discovered that at certain historical junctures the relations of production were more important than the forces of production and that the superstructure held sway over the economic base. Now under Deng, the development of material forces is stressed as the crucial determinant of the character of society. Whereas Mao and the Gang of Four overemphasized class struggle as the motive force in historical development, now the development of production forces was primary. Socialism aims to end poverty, even if in doing so China would have to retreat from an "advanced" form of economic organization. Dittmer predicts that since ideology in the Chinese Communist Party (CCP) serves to consolidate the regime, in the future there will be strenuous efforts to reinterpret ideology so as to serve the needs of the new political leadership.

In examining the changing party leadership and bureaucracy in the People's Republic of China (PRC), Hong Yung Lee has combed through numerous sources and compiled tables of the numbers and divisions of party and government personnel in the PRC. He states that the CCP and the state bureaucracy on the eve of Deng's reforms were inefficient, politicized, factionalized, and demoralized. A major cause of such a sorry state of affairs was the anti-intellectual bias that had culminated in the Cultural Revolution, when experts were equated with the undesirable bourgeois class.

Although Deng's administrative reforms have succeeded in reducing the number, lowering the ages, and raising the educational levels of the cadres, Professor Lee argues that reform has failed to address some fundamental structural problems. The bureaucracy is larger than ever now and is supported by a much higher percentage of the national budget. Rampant corruption allows li-xiu cadres to carry their exalted status and benefits into retirement, while the offspring of top leaders entrench themselves in profitable enterprises or positions in the state and party bureaucracy.

Hungdah Chiu offers a comprehensive discussion on the PRC's efforts to institute a new legal system. The impetus for such measures was the legacy of the 1949–1978 period, when laws and constitutions were made but woefully disregarded. Currently, the basic rights outlined in the 1982 Constitution of the PRC may be legally curtailed in the name of state and public security. The so-called anticrime campaigns in 1981–1985 ignored the procedural safeguards provided under the criminal law. In the Tiananmen Square massacre of 1989, the Chinese authorities justified their use of lethal forces by designating the democracy movements as a "counterrevolutionary rebellion." Party officials seriously compromise judicial independence by constant interference in the duties performed by the judicial organs. Torture and labor camps continue to exist.

Chiu concludes that legal reform in China remains limited due to the leaders' insistence on operating the legal system within the confines of the "Four Basic Principles," and to the transformation of Chinese society into a strict class society since 1949.

Nicholas Lardy, in examining the structural reform of agriculture and industry in the PRC, argues that China's economic reform seems far more successful than other centrally planned economies, especially in the agricultural sector. However, Lardy does not think that this rapid growth in the agricultural sector can be sustained. The failure of urban industrial reform can be traced to various factors, including the relative lack of competition in the industrial sector, inefficiency in manufacturing as reflected in the segmented markets, a low level of development of the labor market, and the differing costs of capital in the two sectors.

Reviewing the scenario of China's reform since 1978, Lardy believes that the best opportunity for addressing the fundamental issues of China's reform has passed. While agreeing with Lardy's essential points, Professor Louis Putterman has a less pessimistic evaluation of China's economic progress in his comments on Lardy's paper.

K. C. Yeh's paper seeks to answer three questions. What has happened to China's foreign trade, capital inflow, and technology transfer since the implementation of the open-door policy? What major problems must China face in continuing an open-door policy? To what extent has the open-door policy contributed to economic growth in recent years?

The phenomenal expansion of foreign trade since 1979 has led to the emergence of trade deficits and a shift from trading predominantly with the communist bloc countries to trading with the West. China currently earns large trade surpluses through Hong Kong and Singapore to offset the trade deficits. Yeh argues that China must change the management of its overall trade balance by promoting exports to the Western countries from which it imports technology and equipment. Foreign capital flow is desirable and recognized as beneficial. However, the size of China's current debt, as well as China's ability to service its loans, are important questions that remain. With regard to technology transfer there does not seem to be a problem of absorption. Yeh concludes that had China closed its doors in the past decade, its economic growth probably would not have been as rapid as it has been.

Based on available statistics, Robert Dernberger, in his paper on the PRC's drive for economic modernization, characterizes the Deng economy as a growth economy. Rich in resources, China will have a high rate of growth with proper investment, regardless of whether such a strategy is efficient. Dernberger finds that the economy continues to be inefficient and faces new problems that are directly attributable to reform: unemployment, inflation, balance of payment, and budget deficit. Dernberger believes that the success of reform depends on clearly articulating the objectives, proposing a strategy, and establishing a timetable. He is pessimistic because when it comes to economic reforms, the Chinese find virtue in stepping on stones and feeling their way across the river.

Suzanne Pepper's paper on educational reform is richly endowed with insights, succinct reasoning, and abundant documentation. She argues that to understand the significance of post-Mao educational reforms it is necessary to reexamine China's educational issues in the past five decades. Limited resources have contributed to the struggle between regularization and popularization that characterizes the development of educational policy. The excesses of the Cultural Revolution and a realization of China's backwardness fueled the movement for educational reform in the post-Mao era.

Pepper believes that in its eagerness to achieve stable progress and catch up with the more advanced countries of the world, the new educational program is elitist and favors the children of well-placed Chinese families. The inequality generated by the new educational system will ultimately pose a serious political and ideological challenge to the PRC's official claim of adherence to the four cardinal principles.

In her paper, "The Intellectuals of the Deng Era," Merle Goldman aptly identifies the similarities and differences between the treatment of intellectuals in the Mao and in the Deng eras. Goldman also examines how the intellectuals themselves have differentiated and have changed in their treatment of one another. Yet, just as in the Mao era, the oscillations in policy toward intellectuals under Deng were determined by political factors, factional maneuverings, and power struggles in the top leadership.

Professor Goldman divides the intellectuals into three groups for separate analyses: the scientific, the nonscientific, and the critical intellectuals. Goldman compares the critical intellectuals to their literati predecessors. Goldman believes that the critical intellectuals of the Deng period are different from those of traditional times and of the Maoist period because the ideas they propose are self-effacing. That is, the traditional role of the intellectuals as the spokesmen for the people would be rendered obsolete, should the democratic institutions they advocate be realized.

June Dreyer describes the reorganization of the People's Liberation Army (PLA) after 1949 in her paper "Reorganizing and Modernizing the Military." Dreyer observes that the military model espoused by Deng contains certain aspects of both the classic Maoist and the functional specificity models, combined in new and different ways. She states that Deng's remedies for certain perceived deficiencies in the PLA, together with reforms in other areas of society, will lead to the introduction of new strategic concepts and weapons, a streamlining and reorganization of the military, and a redefinition of the relationship between the military and Chinese society.

Jonathan Pollack, in his paper on China's search for a security strategy, credits Deng with recasting the framework of China's national security policy and shifting Beijing's calculations of external threat. Superseding Maoist convictions about the struggles between imperialist and anti-imperialist forces, Deng deemphasized the immediacy of military threat, and has tried to reshape opinions in the West about China's importance and strategic value. As the pace and scope of economic development are accelerated, however, new problems emerge. Failure to cope with these problems leads to tragedies such as the Tiananmen Square massacre.

Harold C. Hinton's paper, "Reorienting China's Foreign Policy: China and the World," documents the changes in China's foreign policy under Deng's leadership. The ideological drive and the eagerness for confrontation that were conspicuous under Mao have declined. With the emergence of modernization as a clear priority, Chinese political activism in the Third World, previously encouraged by Mao, has declined as well. "World revolution" as an operational goal of Beijing's foreign policy is no longer mentioned. One of the most constructive and potentially most important features of China's external relations under Deng has been the increasingly close, fruitful, and responsible interactions with major international economic agencies, such as the World Bank and the International Monetary Fund.

Finally, Stuart Schram discusses modernization with "Chinese characteristics" and the future of Marxism-Leninism. He reasons that the enunciation of the "Four Basic Principles" in 1979, the campaign against Bai Hua in 1981, the movement against spiritual pollution in 1983, the overthrow of Hu Yaobang in the name of opposing bourgeois liberalization in 1987, and ultimately the massacre at Tiananmen Square in June 1989 are all developments that "mark not so much Deng's return to Marxist orthodoxy as a return to the dogmatic attitudes of an earlier period in the history of Chinese communism, of which the roots are not necessarily or entirely Marxist." Schram's analysis stresses the continuing influence of the Chinese tradition.

According to Schram, Deng is closer to Marx than Mao ever was because Deng believes that true socialism can only be built on a highly developed economy. But Deng's determination to ensure an orderly transformation of the Chinese political system under party control means that Leninism is the only valid interpretation of Marxism at the present time. "Thus the central feature of the ongoing reform process is the paradox that the quest for the institutionalization of the reform has to be maintained and guaranteed primarily by the authority of one old man."

Part II of the book covers the policy addresses delivered by senior government officials from the major powers. Li Luye, the PRC Ambassador to the United Nations, is the first speaker of the open sessions. He describes the essential elements of Deng's reforms in the context of China's geopolitics and party history, and characterizes the reform program as a self-improvement process of the country's socialist system. Citing the impressive gains achieved in the areas of urban and rural industrialization, Li pronounces that the achievements made in the agricultural sector would be irreversible. Li also cautions that further changes in the political structure are necessary to keep pace with China's economic progress. Adhering to official CCP lines on essential points, Li optimistically declares that China has found a suitable strategy for reform and modernization.

Kimio Fujita, Director General of the Asian Affairs Bureau of the Ministry of Foreign Affairs of Japan, delivers an address that is a veritable scholarly treatise on Japan-PRC relations. He stresses the positive efforts on the part of Japan, especially that of Prime Ministers Ohira and Nakasone, to build official and unofficial bridges between the two countries. Fujita discusses with candor the PRC's inadequacies in competing with other developing nations, especially with the ASEAN, for credit and investment capital, and calls on China to improve its economic climate.

Ambassador Fujita also points out that Japan simply does not have a "China Card" to play because of the restraints placed on the country by Article IX of its Constitution. Nor would Japan adopt a "Gaullist" policy to go at it alone because Japan wants the assurance that her friendly relations with China is compatible with the spirit of the U.S.-Japan Security Treaty.

Yevgeniy V. Afanasyev, Counselor of the Embassy of the USSR in Washington D.C., attended this conference in place of E. A. Konovalov of the Institute of the Far East, USSR, who had submitted a paper on the "Reform of the Price-Making System in the PRC" but was unable to come in person. After summarizing Konovalov's paper briefly, Afanasyev discusses his views regarding the Soviet perspective of Deng's reforms. He acknowledges that the Soviets are paying close attention to reforms in China and comparing their own *perestroika* to China's experiences.

Citing similarities and differences in the two countries' reforms, Afanasyev stresses Soviet hopes for China's success in reform and for peaceful coexistence and stability in Sino-Soviet relations. Afanasyev recognizes that sharing the longest international borders in the world would inevitably lead to problems and emphasizes that any differences can be resolved on the basis of mutual respect and cooperation. Finally he advises that economic success requires not only structural changes in policy, but also a genuine commitment to long-term reform.

J. Stapleton Roy, now U.S. ambassador to China, discusses the foreign policy of the PRC and the impact of Deng's reforms on U.S.-PRC relations. He extols the healthy pragmatism exhibited by PRC leaders in reorienting their foreign policy according to the changing international environment. Roy also observes that the United States and the PRC both share a coldly realistic assessment of Soviet policies and "have developed mutual confidence and are less concerned with being manipulated by the Soviet Union within the great power triangle."

While praising Deng, Roy cautions against excessive optimism regarding China's reforms. The key question he asks is whether China's current reformers can succeed where earlier reformers have failed. He concludes by stressing that the Chinese people, now living in a more open and prosperous society, have everything to lose should reform efforts be interrupted. Taking account of the events of 1989, Roy suggests in the revised version of his paper that in the case of the Deng leadership, "pragmatism" can also lead to the suppression of liberalizing tendencies.

III

Most of the papers presented at the conference indicate that China achieved a great deal of economic progress during the decade of Deng's leadership. Some consider the improvements to be merely cosmetic and unsustainable without further political liberalization. Others view the material improvements within the context of increasing inequality and flagrant abuse of human rights. Recent newspapers report that well-worn practices for indoctrinating the younger generation, such as upholding Lei Feng as a model or conducting tours to Mao's birthplace, continue to be employed. Since the 1989 Tiananmen Square massacre, there appears to be a widened gap between the so-called conservative reformers, headed by Deng and Yang Shangkun, and the student generation, in terms of their respective perspectives and aspirations.

Can we now regard Deng's reform program as having failed, with respect to politics? Or do the recent developments constitute merely a minor setback in an overall record of progress? If we regard Deng's reforms as a failure, we can explain it in terms of history and China's traditions. We can also explain the 1989 suppression of the student activists at Tiananmen Square in terms of political necessity from the standpoint of those who are in power. It is the consensus among the reform leaders that economic progress should be sought in an environment of stability and order, but liberalization on the political and social fronts is another matter. To them, liberalization certainly will entail their loss of control, and they cannot conceive of a regime based on true democracy without their helmsmanship, especially when they and their families have reaped the highest profit in the economic reform under their control.

Chinese social scientists who studied the West and Japan after 1978 have provided the "conservative" leaders with the necessary tools to formulate their own theory and strategy of reform. On the one hand, they can point to Japan during the Meiji Restoration and under General Douglas MacArthur, Bismarck's Germany, Taiwan under Chiang Kai-shek and Chiang Ching-kuo, South Korea under Park Chung Hee, and Singapore under Lee Kuan Yew to justify the need for authoritarian rule to create a stable environment for attracting the trade and investments of capitalists. On the other hand, the Chinese leadership also defends its suppression of liberalizing tendencies by accusing the West of social chaos and moral decline. While the conference did not address the crucial question of whether incremental democratization should be preceded by industrialization under an authoritarian regime, the experiences of many Asian NICs seem to support this theory.

As Professor Andrew Nathan points out, when Deng came to power, the victims of the Cultural Revolution and of the Gang of Four were rehabilitated on the basis of their obedience to the party. The party did not uphold the freedom of speech of these people, but instead praised them for having voiced "correct" opinions. Just as the late Qing reformers could not transcend the framework of Confucian mentality, Deng and his associates cannot escape the confines of Marxism-Leninism and Mao Zedong Thought as they have defined it in the last several decades. Deng does have a better understanding of modernization, which was never Mao's priority. Deng has a program of reform but lacks a coherent policy and ideology. When the program generates political outcomes beyond his expectations, Deng can only react by stressing the need for stability and the maintenance of party leadership in the political arena.

The debates over whether China is in the "primary stage" of socialism or in other stages of socialism are moot. If China cannot declare Chinese socialism to be superior to capitalism, then why should it insist on the socialist road? China continues to emphasize "socialism with Chinese characteristics," even though such characteristics embody traits that, as the Chinese have conceded, are dysfunctional to modernization. The four cardinal principles of Deng's reform have left party dictatorship intact, while economic expansion erodes the integrity of the party and the government.

Discussants at the conference agree that the regime's treatment of intellectuals will have bearing on its success or failure of the "Four Modernizations." The educational system is responsible for training the future leaders in all sectors of society. The inequality of educational opportunities in the PRC today is nothing unusual. Such inequality has always existed in China in fact, if not in theory. What is unusual today is the failure to cultivate a meritocracy, which has traditionally inspired the educated. After the 1989 Tiananmen Square incident, a growing percentage of college students have become restless. Students study primarily to find opportunities to go abroad. Even the students with good academic records are pessimistic about their prospects in China because they know that the better positions have already been claimed by those with connections.

The enormity of the problems faced by China is self-evident. The sheer size of China—its population and geographical extent—is already mind-boggling. In the modern period, Chinese patriots invariably point to the country's disunity as the causal factor of China's problems. National unity has been regarded as the panacea to all problems in China. The achievement of national unity has justified all kinds of autocratic measures.

Throughout the history of mankind, one can rarely find the germination of democracy in countries of continental proportions. Only in city states and small political entities has democracy as a political process taken root. Perhaps the future of China, ironically, will depend on disunity, with parts of China spinning off like another Taiwan, gradually modernizing and democratizing on their own. Or de facto decentralization could give regions authentic freedom to manage their own affairs. Perhaps the future of China does not lie in a culture cum nation, but in the establishment of several political entities grounded more or less in the same Chinese culture but each free to strive forth economically and politically.

For now, insistence on a continental empire will enable China to enjoy big power status internationally. But like the USSR, democracy and welfare will elude the people. If we consider the decentralization of the USSR as the first step to democratization in that big country, we can also consider the possibility of a decentralized China as a means of achieving democracy in that country. Each province can fully explore its opportunities for economic and political development without having to contend with a bureaucratic state and the problems of leveling down. Since all the papers and discussion at the conference seem to presuppose a unified enormous China as the starting point of their analysis, we are offering this unorthodox view as an alternative perspective.

Realistically, the struggle for power and reform in the PRC today is ultimately linked with the succession to Deng. It is not simply sheer coincidence that Deng, as the supreme leader, has also decimated his number two man, not once, but twice, just as Mao had done before him. In this regard, the lessons of CCP history and politics have taught us that chaos and suppression often follow closely on the heels of reform efforts. Therefore, a definitive evaluation of Deng's reforms is a task we may have to postpone until a later date.

PART I:
ANALYTICAL PAPERS
AND COMMENTS

1

CHINESE REFORM SOCIALISM UNDER DENG XIAOPING: Theory and Practice

Lowell Dittmer

THE DENG XIAOPING model of developmental socialism is much more tentative and pragmatic than its forerunner, stepping gingerly from stone to stone in a stream (to use a Chinese metaphor)[1] rather than leaping forward, giving it a protean quality difficult to pin down. This remains true despite the amplified information and improved access to sources available to contemporary China scholars. Whereas Mao's theory of continuing revolution under the dictatorship of the proletariat seemed to have been constructed a priori, in response to the logical imperatives of doctrine, the thinking behind the post-Mao reforms seems to have arisen a posteriori; it is not coincidental that Western accounts of late Maoism have often been theoretically "supply-side," whereas accounts of the Deng model have tended to deemphasize the impact of theory, placing it in the position of a dependent variable when it is considered at all.[2] Though such a distinction involves considerable oversimplification, in the sense that Maoism at its most radical was still shaped by political-economic exigencies just as the policies of Deng Xiaoping are also undergirded by theoretical assumptions, there is some truth to it.

It is thus fitting that we begin with an examination of the Deng model in practice. This examination begins, not with the Third Plenum of the Eleventh Central Committee that marks the advent of Deng's political hegemony, but back in the period of New Democracy and Socialist Construction, where indications of a theoretical divergence between what later became known as Mao Zedong Thought and the "revisionist" thinking of Liu Shaoqi and Deng Xiaoping made their first appearance. This survey of the prehistory of Deng's thought will be partial and superficial rather than comprehensive, and unabashedly tendentious, selecting for special attention those incidents that hindsight reveals to have anticipated the genesis of the reform package. It will be followed by a "phenomenological" reconstruction (i.e., without critical commentary) of the theoretical arguments implied by, and sometimes articulated in defense of, reform policy innovations. In the second section this picture of the reformist policy "line"—and the imminent theory formulated in its wake— will be confronted by externally generated queries, comparisons, and theoretical schema.

The Practice of Reform

Origins

The first indications of sharp policy conflict within the leadership did not emerge until the mid-1950s, in the course of the completion of collectivization, but as early as 1951 there was already preliminary evidence of disagreement between Mao and Liu Shaoqi, with whom Deng seems to have been closely associated at the time.[3] In the fifth volume of his *Selected Works*, Mao criticized Liu in sharp, explicit terms:

> In July 1951, Liu Shaoqi turned his back on Comrade Mao Zedong and the party center to personally write a commentary recklessly criticizing a report submitted by the Shanxi Provincial Party Committee on the development of mutual aid and cooperativization in agricultural production, moreover distributing [the commentary] to every locality. In his commentary Liu Shaoqi opposed Comrade Mao Zedong's line on the socialist transformation of agriculture, insulting it as being a "mistaken, dangerous, utopian idea of agricultural socialism."[4]

It is now possible to verify the accuracy of Mao's quotation and to put it into the context of the original document.[5] The thrust of Liu's criticism of the Shanxi Party Committee report was that precipitate speed in the implementation of cooperativization would outpace the financial wherewithal of the freshly established cooperative organizations to ensure their prosperous future—the same concern that was to animate Deng Zihui (who then chaired the Rural Work Department) when he, in a meeting chaired by Liu, moved to dissolve twenty thousand Agricultural Production Cooperatives that in his judgment could not meet such criteria of financial soundness in 1955.[6] Mao again expressed ire at the foot-dragging tactics of the "old women with bound feet" who had opposed him, imposing self-criticisms and demotions to punish them.[7]

On the surface, this seems to have been no more than a tactical disagreement concerning the scope and pace at which collectivization would be implemented. That it was, but in light of subsequent developments, it seems also to have signaled a more fundamental strategic divergence concerning the necessary preconditions for socialization of the means of production. To Mao, these preconditions seem to have been essentially political: could sufficient peasant enthusiasm be mobilized to achieve decisive collective action? If so, the party should strike while the iron was hot. Further material preconditions need not be supplied—let alone state investment in the movement—for the economies of scale achieved in the new socialist units offered the capability of vastly increasing outputs without additional inputs. To Mao, improved "relations of production," to use the Marxist terminology (the more efficient collective organization, the emancipated productive enthusiasm of the peasantry), were of decisive importance. To his opponents, the "forces of production" were still decisive; implicitly discounting the advantages of higher economies of scale, they assumed that any improvement of output would require additional material inputs—meaning specifically (in this case) that the period of family farming should last until industrialization produced the farm machinery that would make larger collective units more efficient. Implicit in this contretempts were at least three issues: the relative importance of material versus ideal motivations, economic growth versus redistribution, and organization versus mass participation. On each issue Mao accorded priority to the latter, while his opponents tilted toward the former.

Suggestive as such reconstructions of the historical record may be, it would probably be erroneous to press them too far. Whereas Mao's putative opponents did have their differences with Mao, their objections seem to have been relatively tentative at this stage, for they promptly reversed course when Mao chastised them, made self-criticisms, and expedited the timetable for collectivization. All this suggests that their reservations did not yet rest on deeply felt or theoretically elaborated convictions; they were acting more on the basis of pragmatic than principled considerations; so when Mao was able to demonstrate that accelerated collectivization was compatible with continued increases in agricultural production, they yielded. Indeed, both Liu Shaoqi and Deng Xiaoping subsequently became enthusiastic supporters of the Great Leap Forward, which reenacted the errors of overhasty collectivization in spades. Only after the Leap had failed decisively did Mao's opponents gain sufficient confidence in their own alternative policy preferences and theoretical assumptions to put these into effect in a relatively systematic way, in the context of economic reconstruction. But before looking at what came through the reform "window" of the early 1960s, one other incident of the late 1950s deserves momentary consideration.

The so-called double hundred ("Let a hundred flowers bloom, let a hundred schools of thought contend ") warrants mention because it illustrates the attitude of these proleptic reformers to "public opinion" and elite-mass relations. Clearly they were not "liberals," to judge from MacFarquhar's analysis of the intra-elite cleavage that preceded the decision;[8] Deng Xiaoping himself seems to have led the antirightist movement that suppressed outspoken critics of the regime in the fall of 1957. Yet they also expressed certain subsequent misgivings about the severity of the antirightist movement, and Deng Xiaoping sanctioned the rehabilitation of some 200,000 "rightists" in 1977. During the early 1960s, they also sponsored a somewhat pallid revival of the double hundred, in which professional or academic expertise was meant to function as a gatekeeper to "blooming." When this too nonetheless got out of hand, resulting in the airing of Aesopian criticisms of Mao's personality cult, *inter alia*, it was their desire to limit the official reaction to "gentle breeze and mild rain" that overtaxed Mao's patience and eventually triggered his resort to extramural rectification techniques in the Cultural Revolution.

During the early 1960s, the reform package soon to be denounced as "revisionism" was articulated systematically, as the reformers took advantage of Mao's retreat to theoretical concerns and their own promotion to the "first front" of policy-making to present a relatively comprehensive platform (while still avoiding any frontal ideological confrontation with Mao). In the wake of Sun Yefang's and others' theoretical mooting of the "law of value," free market activity was expanded in the countryside, peasant private plots enlarged, and in certain provinces hit particularly hard by the post-Leap depression, land was reassigned to peasant families in a revival of the production responsibility system of the mid-1950s. In industry, there was greater emphasis on economic efficiency, including an attempt to detach the party committees from control and devolve authority to factory management, greater reliance on piece-rate and performance-gauged incentives, professionalized accounting, and the introduction of horizontally integrated complexes ("trusts"). Liu was even quoted in support of reviving the stock market and permitting a substantial private sector to survive socialization of industry. Education became more elitist and meritocratic, with clear qualitative distinctions between full-time and part-time schooling.

Politics and ideology were almost completely untouched, tacitly conceding Mao's hegemony in these areas. Yet during the Cultural Revolution, Mao himself claimed he could find the ideological precursors of what he dubbed "revisionism" in the theoretical writings of Liu Shaoqi—the only other party leader besides himself to have made a significant contribution to the party classics. It is perhaps not coincidental that Liu's *Collected Works* were republished following Mao's political eclipse (and Liu's own posthumous rehabilitation) and have been circulated relatively intensively in connection with party rectification, indicating they have regained canonical status under reform auspices. Though now superseded by the publication of the *Collected Works* of Deng Xiaoping and Chen Yun, Liu's works remain philosophically richer than these more politically topical (and clearly written) companion volumes. In my judgment, Mao was essentially correct in tracing the roots of reform socialism to Liu's theoretical contributions, which provide an articulate, internally consistent grounding for the policies introduced in the early 1960s. And I would argue that there is a direct line of descent between these limited experiments and the reforms implemented on a far grander scale in the post-Mao period. The same general posture toward innovation seems to have reemerged, for example, consisting of open-minded eclecticism with regard to political economy, but a much more cautious approach to ideological or political innovation. Certainly in the area of party life and ethics, Liu's contributions remain definitive. Because Liu's ideological framework continues to inform Deng's reform efforts, a brief synopsis seems appropriate.

Liu's worldview was characterized by moral elitism, a conviction that the party leadership in particular was morally superior to the masses it led. The contrast with Mao's populist emphasis on the masses as the ultimate source of truth and virtue could not be more striking. The basis of the party elite's superiority was its synoptic vision: ordinary people could discern and pursue their individual and group interests, but only the elite were able to rise to the appropriate level of abstraction to understand the interests of the people as a whole; only the party elite had the moral self-discipline to renounce personal advantage on behalf of public interest. Such self-discipline had to be "cultivated" through constant study and self-criticism. Thus, the party was conceived to constitute a hierarchy of moral efficiency in which those able to serve the interests of the whole and abnegate short-term self-interest would rise to the top. For the party was so arranged that the interests of the dedicated party members "merged" with those of the party—hence the nation—as a whole.

Epistemologically, Liu blended monism regarding essentials with pluralism concerning nonessentials. The essentials were political, over which the party had a monopoly of truth. Economics was also important, for economic desires were after all universal—people everywhere always needed to eat, sleep, and clothe themselves. Yet political truths were more important and "higher" than economic questions, because they encompassed a wide range of discrete interests. Thus, "all the economic demands of the masses must be integrated with political and cultural demands. When the masses begin to take action on one simple demand, we must lead the masses in fields related to their action on this simple demand so they can better understand a series of problems and further push their actions to a still higher stage." Thus, the masses might be eventually brought to a "higher" conception of their interests (i.e., one that would take into account the interests of others). Only the party fully grasped these interests, which was why it retained a monopoly of power and virtue.

This had at least two important implications: On the one hand, it entailed a hermetic isolation of the party from the surrounding environment in order to protect and cultivate its special subculture. A "line of demarcation" had to be drawn, and it was strictly forbidden to allow social or commercial interest to intrude into the magic circle; party discussions and disciplinary proceedings (where Liu was coincidentally a real martinet) must remain strictly "inner-party." On the other hand, it also implied a relatively generous latitudinarianism with regard to those areas of life and truth defined as nonessential. For Liu esteemed the division of labor as an attribute of modernization, and supported a considerable range of functional subsystem autonomy: in economics, economic professionals should hold sway (to run the economy on political principles, he once said, was "feudalism"); the press should operate according to sound journalistic principles (bylines, investigative reporting, features, and so forth); academics and scientists should have jurisdiction in the educational-cultural sphere. Only over politics (Liu was thoroughly Maoist in the priority he accorded politics) must the party hold uncontested sway to apply the higher principles of Marxism. In other functional realms, pragmatism was the rule—with which Deng's famous "black cat, white cat" quip is perfectly consistent. (The boundary-maintenance question of which issues are "political" and which matters of functional expertise also remained within the party's discretion.)

The final episode that figured importantly in the evolution of reform thinking is the Cultural Revolution itself, ten years dedicated to the complete eradication of reform ("revisionist") ideas. As an alternative to continuous revolution, reformist meliorism was revealed to be damnable per se, a temptation to evade necessary struggle and passively ally with the forces of the status quo. To keep revolutionary values alive, redistribution must be given priority over economic growth, the superstructure and the relations of production over the forces of production, zealous mass participation over efficient organization. The impact of the Cultural Revolution can be seen in both personal terms, as it affected leading members of the reform group, and in national terms, as it affected participants and observers. The impact on the "revisionists" was to subject them to ten years of "criticism" and "struggle," including status degradation, labor stints, dismemberment of families, and other hardships. In the short run, to judge from available interview data, the attempt to achieve thought reform through such less-than-subtle forms of coercion usually proved ineffective, resulting only in expedient confessions that soon proved "insincere." Over the longer term, the political positions of such prominent Cultural Revolution survivors as Deng Xiaoping, Li Xiannian, Ye Jianying, Hu Yaobang, and Peng Zhen have varied on any number of dimensions, but they have been united by their opposition to the Cultural Revolution and the "proletarian revolutionary line"—for a number of years, this tie created a solidaristic and effective political coalition.

As far as the impact on the nation as a whole was concerned, the data are impressionistic and somewhat more ambiguous. Economically the experience was disruptive during the first three years of spontaneous mass mobilization, but the available statistics do not indicate a catastrophic impact if this ten-year period is compared with the previous decade.[9] The negative verdict on the experience, which available interview data suggest was widely and fervently shared,[10] must hence be based on its political rather than economic impact. Most telling here was not that there were so many victims but that there were so few beneficiaries. As the movement whiplashed back and forth from left to right, nearly everyone seems to have become ensnared sooner or later in the coils of self-criticism. After breaking the back of institutionalized revisionism in the initial breakthrough period, the movement found itself unable to surge forward to the communist utopia because of internal contradictions among radical factions (such as between military and cultural radicals) and among radical tenets (such as between the desire for rapid economic growth and the taboo against materialism). Maoist radicalism seemed to have reached a stalemate contrived by its own internal contradictions. This state of affairs encouraged those who wished to lead the country in a new direction (preferably as different as possible)—which meant, first of all, an end to endless mass movements that led nowhere.

Although the overall impact of the Cultural Revolution on subsequent reform efforts was thus ironic and reflexive, some of its consequences have been lasting and consistent with its original intentions. Particularly in its early phases, the movement seems to have tapped a reservoir of unmet needs. One of these that has recurrently emerged in interview protocols is a vague but real yearning for greater personal liberty, or democracy. Any alleged popular interest in democracy in China has typically met with skepticism, as informed observers point out that the Chinese historical experience with democracy has been miniscule and on the whole unfortunate. Be that as it may, the Cultural Revolution did provide brief opportunities to experience democracy of a relatively primitive, anarchic form, marked by unprecedented freedom of speech, organization, and personal mobility; those who had this exultant experience never forgot it.[11] A second deeply rooted popular theme is resentment of cadre privilege and the "steep" bureaucratic hierarchy, which has been prone to explode whenever conditions permit: it propelled not only the "movement to seize power" in the winter of 1966–67, but a series of anti-elitist movements thereafter, such as the "against the current" (fan chaoliu) of 1972–73, the critique of the "back door" in 1974, of "bourgeois right" in early 1975, and the Tiananmen protest of 1976. Both these themes seem to have survived the repudiation of the Cultural Revolution more or less intact, and have exerted recurrent influence on the reform movement—most notably during the student protest movements of 1985–89.

The Reform Experience

The Hua Guofeng period, which lasted from Mao's death in September 1976 until the Third Plenum, represented transition to reform. Hua's personal commitment to Mao, whose blessing alone legitimized his succession ("With you in charge, I am at ease."), entailed continuing lip service to Maoism. Nevertheless, Hua took several important steps in the direction of reform. First, through his arrest and repudiation of the Gang of Four, he underlined the point (in action if not yet in words) that the Cultural Revolution was over and that radicalism was not a feasible approach to government. Second, he did a great deal to reconsolidate and bolster the party-state apparatus, whose morale was sagging after years of recurrent criticism: he called for "great order under heaven," he tried (in his famous "two whatevers") to restore some discipline to the hierarchical command structure, he began to convene cadre meetings of various types on a more regular basis, he accelerated the rehabilitation of purged cadres (already initiated on a piecemeal and conditional basis under Mao), and he introduced policies designed to appeal to the bureaucracy and mobilize their support (N.B., the ambitious ten-year plan introduced at the Fourth National People's Congress [NCP]). Third, though he could not claim credit for this for fear of deviating from Mao's Thought, he in fact shifted the operational priorities of the regime from the pursuit of socialism and communism to the realization of economic modernization. His intention may have been to implement the Four Modernizations within the framework of continuing the revolution under the dictatorship of the proletariat,[12] but the rhetoric of the latter lost credibility in light of its growing irrelevance to concrete policies. Among the more glaring instances of this irrelevance was Hua's "foreign leap forward" (so nicknamed because of its heavy reliance on the purchase of turnkey plants and other equipment from abroad), which flew in the face of the Maoist doctrine of "self-reliance."

The Deng Xiaoping reform period is conventionally dated from the Third Plenum of the Eleventh Central Committee in December 1978, for it was at this meeting that the Hua-Deng struggle for control of the Politburo was resolved in Deng's favor; despite his personal integrity and political moderation, Hua's reform stance had been hopelessly compromised by his ties to Mao. For the sake of analytical convenience, the reform period may be divided into two stages, the first lasting until the fall of 1984, the second lasting through the summer of 1988. Each period is in turn subdivided into cyclical oscillations between waves of cultural relaxation, *fang*, and retrenchment, *shou*. Most recently (June 1989 to June 1990), there has been a slackening of reform momentum whose ultimate significance remains unclear at this writing. We proceed in stages, providing a brief purview of the major economic and political changes during each period.

In addition to confirming such reform processes as "de-Maoization," the rehabilitation of cadres purged in the Cultural Revolution, and the calibration of material incentives to productive outputs rather than labor inputs, the reshuffled Chinese Communist Party (CCP) leadership of the Third Plenum undertook a number of important new policy departures. Probably most significant was the introduction of legislation initiating the shift to the household responsibility system in agriculture, which would result in the de facto decollectivization of farmland under continuing de jure public ownership (via the contractual device of leaseholds, lasting fifteen or even thirty years). Along with the subsequent elimination of the communes, this reform reduced the party's presence in the countryside and unleashed peasant initiative, dramatically increasing yields without bringing additional land under cultivation. The policy of opening the country to the outside world is usually traced to the Third Plenum, though it did not really begin to gather momentum until July 1979, when legislation authorizing joint ventures with foreign firms and the establishment of "special economic zones" (with particularly favorable conditions for foreign investment) was passed by the Standing Committee of the National People's Congress. In addition to Chinese involvement in the world market and the tourist influx, the policy of opening resulted in the massive outflow of China's most promising young people to Western universities. Though industry was not in focus at the Third Plenum (the ill-conceived ten-year plan was soon abandoned in favor of "adjustment"), experiments with the decentralization of control from central ministries to enterprise management were authorized in Sichuan and Anhui provinces that would eventually be generalized to the rest of the country. Small rural markets proliferated, enlivening the commercial sector and for the first time also penetrating urban areas. The emerging problem of unemployment that accompanied liberalization of the *xiaxiang* policy (sending urban youth to work in the countryside) was to some extent alleviated by the encouragement of collective industry and private firms: the number of private firms numbered only about 100,000 in 1978, growing to 5.8 million (with 7.5 million employees) by the end of 1983, to 17 million in 1985. By the end of June 1983, some 3.2 million more people were employed in urban collectives than in 1978. These were initially small firms in the repair and service sector, including small merchants, traders, restauranteurs, and, more recently, doctors and other professionals; by the late 1980s they had grown larger, sometimes employing several hundred workers.

The leadership was much more chary about introducing political reforms, although such reforms had strong popular backing in the form of various protest movements. The first important political demarche was Deng's introduction of the "Four Cardinal Principles," to provide a criterion for acceptable political participation and repress those who failed to meet it. The statement made at the Third Plenum denouncing disruptive mass movements seems to have been addressed primarily to the democracy activists. Later, in 1980 and 1981, the regime endeavored (with modest effect) to provide a legitimate outlet for participatory zeal in the form of electoral reform permitting more than one candidate to run for the same seat at county as well as local levels.[13] Probably the major watershed in political reform at this stage was not the Third Plenum, but Deng's August 1980 speech on governmental reorganization, which focused on political renewal— i.e., there should be fixed terms of office at least in government posts, aged leaders should be encouraged to retire or at least move to nonvoting "counselor" posts or to the Central Advisory Commission, and younger cadres should be recruited on the basis of professional expertise in addition to political merit. The reforms sketched by Deng, and later elaborated on by Liao Gailong, also featured a functional division of powers: the separation of party from government, the creation of a Central Disciplinary Commission and Central Advisory Commission to function beside the Central Committee, the subsequent revival of the General Secretariat to operate in tandem with the Politburo. Most of these reforms were formally sanctioned in the 1982 Constitution of the Twelfth Party Congress and the Fifth National People's Congress. The Twelfth Party Congress also marked the advent of China's "independent" foreign policy of peace and bloc de-alignment.[14]

The second stage of reform was inaugurated by the important economic laws in the fall of 1984; but during this stage many of the reforms actually introduced were implemented on a partial or trial basis without legislative sanction (which could not easily be obtained from the conservative NPC), and in retrospect seem to have lacked leadership consensus. The reason for this lack of support has to do first with the unintended problematic consequences of previous reforms (e.g., loss of fiscal control, budget deficits, imbalance of trade, and inflation), and second with the nature of the second-stage reforms themselves, which often seem to have been borrowed from Western capitalist systems.

Agricultural reform during the second stage consisted essentially of universalization of policies introduced during the first stage rather than the innovation of major new departures: universal application of the most radical form of the *bao chan dao hu* system, the increasing shift of the work force from agriculture to rural collective industry, and the shift from grain to cash crops. The major successful reform introduced during this stage (actually in 1982) was the advent of the "specialized household," consisting of peasant families whose economic activities (usually dairy farming, industrial raw materials, commerce) seem to be completely extra-plan; by 1985, an estimated 4–7 percent of the farm population were "specialized." There was also an attempt to substitute contractual for compulsory crop deliveries, but implementation seems to have bogged down in the face of peasant resistance, with a resulting recourse to compulsory procurements.

Urban industry became the main focus of reform during the second stage, featuring a multipronged effort including enterprise management law, price reform, tax-for-profit legislation (*li gai shui*), a contract labor system, bankruptcy legislation, and experiments with new ownership arrangements. Although the results have been mixed, the urban industrial reform package at this writing appears to have been unsuccessful. Enterprise management legislation designed to separate party from government functions was stymied until 1988 in the NPC Standing Committee, together with national bankruptcy legislation (designed to permit unprofitable state enterprises to fold); passage of these reforms was followed so quickly by the retrenchment introduced after experiments with price reform unleashed a high rate of inflation in the summer of 1988 that they have not been systematically implemented. A contract labor system (similar to the system that prevailed in the early 1960s) designed to break the "iron rice bowl" and permit greater labor mobility was approved in 1986 to apply to entry-level workers; veteran workers have been able to contain their enthusiasm. A three-tiered Hungarian-style price system was introduced (with fixed prices, prices free to fluctuate within a specified range, and free prices), but this precipitated price inflation, beginning at around 7 percent in 1984–85 and jumping to more than 20 percent (in official statistics) in the summer of 1988, and price reform gave way at the Third Plenum of the Thirteenth Central Committee (October 1988) to a three-year retrenchment period. Joint stock ownership systems and even a small stock market in five major cities were introduced (amid considerable fanfare in the Western press), but implementation was more circumspect than theoretical projections and seems to have stalled in the post-Tiananmen retrenchment. With regard to political and cultural reform it seems to have been impossible to mobilize an effective consensus to move beyond the prohibitions of the Four Cardinal Principles. Hu Yaobang succeeded in pushing political rejuvenation (with the implied forced retirement of veteran cadres) further at the September 1985 special Party Congress, only at the cost of vindictive conservative opposition. Hu Qili issued a guarantee of creative freedom in late 1984,[15] only to have Hu Yaobang decree that the media should function as the mouthpiece of the party. The minimal next step in political reform on which a consensus might be reached would seem to involve separation of the party from the government, but because of the 1986–87 and 1989 conservative backlashes to populist demands for more rapid reform, this too was deferred.

Reform in Theory

The Hua Guofeng regime, based as it was on Mao's "feudal" designation of a personal successor, had a vested interest in perpetuating popular allegiance to Mao Zedong Thought. Yet because the policies Hua introduced in his attempt to appeal to a bureaucratic base were in effect moderate reform policies, ideology gradually shifted in the same direction. This could be seen, for example, in the gradual reconceptualization of the "crimes" of the Gang of Four: for two years after their arrest, they were arrayed with Liu, Deng, and Lin Biao as members of the rightist "bourgeois reactionary line,"[16] but by the fall of 1978 they had been recategorized as "ultra-leftists"—reflexively shifting political orthodoxy to the right. With the passage of time, Mao's reputation faded rather quickly, as measured in newspaper quotations and references; though his works were republished to forestall this, there was an increasing tendency to skip the Cultural Revolution decade and resort to the more moderate writings of the 1950s and early 1960s.[17] A nationwide intellectual discussion of the "criterion of truth" was initiated by Deng's supporters in June 1978, which contended (based on quotations of Chairman Mao) that practice alone—not "dogma"—was the only valid criterion. Although this campaign redounded to Hua's political disadvantage, as the chief defender and beneficiary of the thesis of Mao's infallibility, he did not publicly oppose it. Indeed, at the Third Plenum, he himself repudiated Mao's personality cult (which he had previously tried to appropriate) in the name of collective leadership. It was also under Hua that classes and class struggle began to be conceptualized in a less exclusive and more conciliatory manner, resulting in the removal of most former rightists' pejorative labels (*maozi*) by November 1978, and the relegation of class struggle to a no longer "principal" form of contradiction in that socialist society, to be carried out by the police and the courts. With the neutralization of class categories, economic modernization gradually became somewhat more detached from political considerations; Hu

Qiaomu and others abetted this tendency in the summer of 1978 by relating the Four Modernizations to objective economic laws.[18]

Ideologically speaking, the Third Plenum did not represent a sharp break, but rather the formal confirmation of new ideological positions undertaken over the last six months and tentative approval of continued intellectual exploration. This exploration tended to ramify into various directions and move slowly forward until it ran up against an ideological taboo, which usually took the form of a movement (e.g., anti-spiritual pollution), a critical barrage in the press, or a denunciation from a senior cadre, whereupon exploration would temporarily cease, manuscripts would go into desk drawers, and "ten thousand horses would stand mute," as the Chinese put it. There is apparently no prepublication censorship in post-Mao China, so there is a certain lag-time between the point when an intellectual "wave" begins and the point when the authorities move to counter it; if the new wave generates too much popular support, it may prove too expensive politically to suppress (depending on the "atmosphere"). For all the discounting of "theory," policy reforms tend to be anticipated by theoretical advances. But theoretical discussions, like fiscal policy, could be controlled only imperfectly from the center. Without pretending to be exhaustive, let us look at some of the more prominent themes bruited during this stage.

Encouraged by the criterion-of-truth debate and by the Third Plenum decisions, intellectuals pursued some of the implications of this argument: if practice was the sole criterion, the class nature of truth so dear to the Maoists was in trouble. The Maoists had been radical relativists—in the sense that they were convinced that all truth is relative to class standing—although they were also convinced that some classes were right and some wrong. The reformers argued that truth was simply the correct "reflection" of objective events and their lawful relationships, irrespective of the subjective wishes of particular classes. The "Maoist" conservatives insisted that class status could still override any pretense of objectivity. Both sides resorted to quotations from Mao's works—"Where do correct ideas come from? . . . from social practice, and from it alone" quoted one side, while the other said, "In class society everyone . . . and every kind of thinking, without exception, is stamped with the brand of a particular class."[19] The temporary upshot was that although the natural sciences (and perhaps even economics) might be "objective,"[20] the social sciences have remained relative to class interest, particularly after Tiananmen, when new educational policies dealt the social sciences a severe setback.[21] Yet the reformers continued their quest for "objectivity," which linked them to an international scientific community that recognized a truth without class or national distinction.

Second, some of the basic assumptions of historical materialism began to be reconsidered. Among Mao's most important doctrinal innovations had been his discovery that at certain historical junctures the relations of production were more important than the forces of production and the superstructure held sway over the economic base.[22] During the first stage of reform, this innovation was challenged.

Paradoxically aligning themselves with Stalin, the reformers asserted that the production forces were the most active and revolutionary factor, and human society "is determined by the development of material forces, e.g., production forces"—just as the superstructure essentially reflected the economic base.[23] Whereas Mao and the Gang of Four had overemphasized class struggle as the motivating force in historical development, to the reformers the development of the forces of production was primary; whether class struggle plays a role in society is determined by whether it can liberate the productive forces.[24] Echoing the formulation arrived at by the Eighth Party Congress, the reformers considered the basic contradiction in Chinese society to be, not class struggle, but the contradiction between advanced production relations and backward production forces. This implied the need for a crash program to develop production forces, and that (given the discrepancy) it was permissible to retreat from one form of economic organization to a previous form without "changing color." Such policies as dissolution of the commune or decollectivization could be seen as an "ample retreat" from "an abnormal form of development to a more rational structure."[25] This was also consistent with a revisionist perspective on previous forced-draft collectivization drives, whose economic and human costs are now emphasized.

As for the purpose of development, the reformers stated clearly that it was the improvement of material living standards. Mao had never denied this; for example, he dangled the prospect of future prosperity before peasants during the early Great Leap, but the Leap's failure seemed to sour his outlook toward material prosperity. Now he began mocking Khrushchev's "goulash communism." During the Cultural Revolution, the Red Guards thus raided suspect households, triumphantly displaying items of conspicuous consumption as sufficient proof of bad class background. In a generalization of the ethos Liu had previously preached to the party elite, China's worker and peasant masses were now expected to live a pure, spiritual, and selfless life; any economic policy that used material incentives to stimulate greater initiative was pandering to bourgeois inclinations. In refutation, Stalin is quoted: "People do not produce for the sake of production, but produce to satisfy their own needs. The goal of socialist production is people and their need."[26]

On no other point of doctrine is there so clear a distinction between Maoists and reformers. Deng himself made clear that "Socialism is to put an end to poverty. Poverty is not socialism, nor is it communism."[27] To get rich through labor was good for not only the individual worker but for the collective, and it was openly conceded that some would prosper sooner than others. Just as the Maoist ethos of self-abnegation implied a "Stalinist" growth strategy emphasizing high state accumulation and investment in heavy industry, the reform strategy implied a shift from heavy to light industry, in order to produce the consumer goods necessary to motivate the work force: light industry's proportion of the gross value of industrial output hence climbed from 42.7 percent in 1978 to 46.6 percent in 1985.[28]

Marxist historiography also came under reconsideration to explain the suddenly diminished interest in, and objective prospects for, completing the transition to the communist utopia soon following the shift of priorities to economic modernization. Whereas for Mao, socialism had been only a brief and contentious transition from capitalism to communism, socialism now became a separate "mode of production," which is characterized by three factors: public ownership of the means of production, distribution according to labor, and regulation of production primarily by the law of value. A distinct mode of production is a more stable arrangement than a mere phase of transition, reducing the perceived danger of capitalist restoration. Su Shaozhi used Zeller's recently discovered testimony[29] to argue that socialism must indeed go through several stages before approaching utopia. From capitalism to communism there are now three stages: first, a transitional stage from captalism to socialism (which is in turn divided into two substages), then a "developed" socialist stage, and finally the communist stage. Since completion of its transition (New Democracy, from 1949–1956), China has remained in the undeveloped, "initial stage of socialism."[30] Like the Soviet Union before it, China indefinitely deferred the communist utopia in pursuit of more immediately achievable material progress.

Chinese theorists also took considerable interest in the Asiatic mode of production, an anomalous stage Marx coined specifically to explain the apparent failure of India and China to pass through the five stages of Western economic development. This theory appealed to the Chinese propensity to see their own national experience as unique, and promised to explain several troublesome features of Chinese socialism, such as the "feudal" tendency to heroize individual leaders, the recurrent "leveling" or egalitarian tendencies ("agrarian socialism") of the Chinese peasantry, and the utopian radicalism of the petit bourgeoisie or small producers.[31] It has never been officially embraced by the CCP leadership, probably because it makes China's developmental experience irrelevant to the rest of the world (not to mention potentially stagnant). Yet references to "feudal socialism" and "agrarian socialism" have appeared quite frequently in social science journals.

Last but not least, there was great and sustained interest in democracy, fostered by a friendly rapport and some intellectual exchange between certain leading intellectuals and some members of the Democracy Wall movement (before the movement was suppressed, which tended to scare off establishment intellectuals). Countless articles on democracy appeared in 1978 and 1979, offering emotional criticisms of despotism and enthusiastic praise of democracy, but exhibiting little understanding of the inner workings of parliamentary democracy. Beyond vague notions that officials should be the servants of the people rather than their masters (probably derived from Mao's well-known admonition "to serve the people," they contained no definition of democracy. An article in *Chinese Youth Daily* (which consistently featured this topic) states:

> A very important principle of the Paris Commune is . . . to prevent the state and state organs from turning from social servants to social masters. Only when this is achieved can socialist democracy be realized, and it can truly be

said that the real goal of proletarian dictatorship has been achieved. In order to reach this point, Engels said that "The commune adopted two methods. First, it gave all positions of executive, judicial, and national education to those who were elected by universal suffrage at any time and decreed that the electors had the right to recall the elected. Second, the wages paid to all government officials, whatever their positions, was the same as that paid to other workers.[32]

Another frequent argument was based on the need to avoid social problems and disorder (such as the Cultural Revolution) by dint of popular feedback.[33] The "rule of law" was often discussed in direct connection with democracy, with little attempt to disguise the Western origins of the conceptual framework: "independent jurisdiction," "equality before the law," "presumption of innocence," "human rights," and so forth. Chinese understanding of these ideas seems to have been fairly rudimentary at this stage; for example, in Western political philosophy, human rights are based on the concept of natural right, but Chinese intellectuals typically used "human rights" as an abstract term without clear definition.

The discussion of "alienation" and "humanism" represents an (ultimately unsuccessful) attempt to place the interest in democracy within an orthodox Marxist framework. The discussion of alienation began with the appearance of an article by Wang Ruoshui, then chief editor of the *People's Daily* (the article was actually first written in 1963–64, but first published in 1979). Wang's article introduced the concept of alienation, and an "internal" (but widely circulated) speech Wang gave in 1980 then applied the concept of alienation to socialist society. This extension of Marx's concept by analogy was controversial and soon ran afoul of conservative resistance, but its broad impact suggests that it responded to a widespread sense of passivity, fecklessness, of being completely under the control of "alien" forces—the same feelings that invoked the yearning for democracy. The equally celebrated debate about "humanism" spoke to the same needs. The rhetoric of the Cultural Revolution had, under the pretext of class struggle, relegated whole categories of people to subhuman status, and there was hence widespread interest in more inclusive concepts of humanity that would preclude such ostracism, social pressure, even physical torture. Humanism implied a duty "to respect the human value of the individual." Many intellectuals attempted to reconcile humanism with Marxism:

> Humanity and human nature are the criteria for history. . . . Whether humanity itself becomes the real goal of any social activity is the most reliable criterion to judge whether a social system is a socialist system. . . . Human history is the history of the alienation and recovery of human nature.[34]

The ideas of "alienation" and "humanism" seemed to challenge the socialist claim to a monopoly of truth (by implying that socialism was also vulnerable to corruption), and they were officially repudiated after strenuous debate in the campaign against "spiritual pollution." Hu Qiaomu's well-reasoned refutation, which accepted humanism as a constituent part of Marxism but not the reverse, ended public debate without really settling the matter.[35]

Many of these discussions were continued or resumed during the second stage of reform that began in late 1984, but there were also significant new departures. Just as the concrete policies introduced during this period transcended elite consensus, intellectual exploration became even bolder than before. Inasmuch as this would be a period for the construction of "socialism with Chinese characteristics," and no one knew exactly what that denoted, open discussion seemed inevitable. The announcement that this meant a "socialist commodity economy" simply touched off a debate over the correct proportion of plan and market. "We cannot ask that the works of Marx and Lenin written for their time be able to solve the problems we have today," announced the *People's Daily* on December 7, quickly amending this the following day to say: "solve all the problems we have today."[36] This proclamation of open-mindedness (and hasty qualification) set the tone for the period: bold, yet nervous.

Among the many themes explored during this period, two seem particularly prominent. One was an attempt to gain an orientation to the nation's past and future. The other was a search for values, suggesting dissatisfaction with officially sponsored conventional values.

The search for roots resulted in what the Chinese call a cultural wave or "fever" (*wenhua re*), which seemed to reach its peak in 1986. As one intellectual put it, "The 'cultural fever' that is recently rising in our country is a very complicated intellectual movement with many causes and rich connotations."[37] In 1982, prominent scholar Li Zihou of the Chinese Academy of Social Sciences published his *Mei de licheng* (The development of aesthetics), an essay in intellectual history that relies heavily on "cultural-psychological structure" to explain Chinese aesthetic development. Since that time, Chinese intellectuals resorted increasingly to cultural causal explanations, turning to Chinese tradition to discover the source of the nation's current political plight. The reason for the "fever" has been attributed to easier contact with foreign culture (which provided an external reference point for Chinese to reevaluate their own culture), the rapid change of economic, social, and ultimately cultural conditions under modernization, and a confusion of values stemming from the Cultural Revolution. Yet cultural investigations were more often critical than reaffirming. For example, the concept of *li* (rites), which regulates human relationships according to the Confucian ethic, was alleged to eliminate the character of the subject and the individual in its overemphasis of the group, making the individual seem other-directed and passive, lacking an active nature. *Li* makes the adult a child and builds a "slave" character. Confucianism is humanistic, but in a different sense from Western humanism. Western humanism champions the human being as an individual; Chinese humanism regards a human as part of a group, occupant of a role in the social structure. Thus, Western humanists feel that the Chinese have no respect for the individual whereas Chinese fault Westerners for rejecting the collective social aspects of society. Western humanism emphasizes freedom, equality, and rights, while Chinese humanism emphasizes harmony, duty, and the individual's contribution to the collective. Yet Chinese attitudes toward Chinese humanism varied widely: some believed that "practical rationalism" was the core spirit of Chinese culture, while others stated that "typical idealism" is the core. Most writers concurred that Chinese tradition, a "static culture of an agrarian society," was not conducive to modernization and would have to be reformed, though a minority defended it.[38]

If the past was regarded critically, the future aroused great expectations—and it tended to have a Western cast, particularly during the euphoric revival of the "double hundred" policy in the spring of 1986. Vice Premier Wan Li seems to have sanctioned discussion of the use of advanced social science theories in the building of socialism in a speech on "soft science" (ruan koxue) given in July,[39] which prompted widespread discussions and suggestions of how the "three theories"—systems theory, communications theory, and cybernetics—could facilitate various facets of modernization. For example, Qian Xuesen, a former Chinese-American astrophysicist who made major contributions to the Chinese rocket program, suggested that the People's Republic of China (PRC) "establish systems engineering of the legal system and law enforcement," and also apply systems theory to the quantitative study of history.[40] Many of the characters in popular fiction talked of systems theory.[41] These techniques were not viewed as mere means to an end, but as having substantive philosophical claims worth consideration (which were, rather facilely, assumed to be compatible with Marxism-Leninism).[42] Popular Western technological determinism made its appearance in the form of Chinese translations of Naisbitt's Megatrends and Toffler's The Third Wave,[43] which had an enormous eclat in China. Zhao Ziyang cited Megatrends in a 1984 speech,[44] and articles and seminars concerning the two books appeared everywhere. The reason for the enthusiasm with technology in general and with these books in particular seems fairly obvious: they were thought to be scientifically based and hence prestigious, and although neither Toffler nor Naisbitt were Marxists, they shared the assumption that the future is determined by the linear extrapolation of immutable historical laws (Toffler even had a three-stage theory of history) and that material forces—indeed, forces of production—determined each stage.

The strong attraction to Western intellectual trends that characterized Chinese technological utopianism is also apparent in the further development of reformed political thought. In following the further discussion of democracy, for example, one finds more structurally elaborated descriptions, which often incorporate Western concepts, such as Yan Jiaqi's important article emphasizing the "separation of powers," or the latest incarnation of a proposal for a bicameral legislature (embracing both the National People's Congress and the People's Political Consultative Conference).[45] Whereas such discussions had previously been inhibited by the Maoist doctrine that democracy is a means rather than an end, or that only socialist and not "bourgeois" democracy may be applied to China, in 1986 the liberals countered that democracy was a valued end in itself as well as a means, or that one might also learn from the bourgeois democratic experience in constructing socialist democracy without being irremediably tainted. The ideological conservatives were hampered in that they had no positive ideas to offer themselves, clinging instead to a set of theories that had emerged from the revolutionary war and manifested serious problems in their application to modernization. In sum, progress was tacitly identified with the West, reaction with China's "long-standing feudal, despotic tradition."[46]

A second noteworthy ideological tendency could be traced to the search for values for the individual Chinese to orient his or her life. This search was symptomatic of the decline in credibility of Marxism-Leninism in filling this need, as Hu Yaobang himself recognized in an important 1986 speech, and suggested a considerable de facto growth of individualism in the context of growing social mobility, differentiated life-styles, and rapid change. Whereas during the first stage such discussions were at least oriented around recognizably Marxist concepts, they now began to transcend this framework. The search for value was exhibited, for example, in the interest in existentialism, in certain non-Marxist Western philosophers such as Nietzsche, who discussed the need for a reevaluation of values, and in Freud and psychoanalysis.

The interest in existentialism was originally occasioned by *soi-distant* Marxist Jean-Paul Sartre's death in 1980, which was commemorated by the publication of a volume of his writings in Chinese, which seems to have had a considerable impact on Chinese youth. As one of them later confessed:

> Among the modern Western philosophies, existentialism had a relatively great impact on our youths' thinking. . . . When I first had contact with existentialism, I was inspired, and thought that existentialism was very deep and expressed the truth of life with philosophical languages. Existentialism believes that people spend their lives in anxiety. More than ten years before the collapse of the Gang of Four, people didn't have anxiety in their lives. Society split up, families collapsed, family members left, friends became enemies, everyone worried about himself, none knew what would happen tomorrow. All of this caused anxiety. I was also attracted to the existentialist idea that the goal of life is complete freedom. During the ten years of turmoil, the socialist legal system was destroyed and people's democratic rights became luxuries that could only be seen but not touched. Under such circumstances many people longed for individual freedom! [47]

There were not many articles published explicitly discussing existentialism, but a sort of existentialist attitude was sometimes discernible in certain literary works.[48] Conservative literary authorities certainly took the problem seriously, as an article written during the first campaign against "bourgeois liberalization" remonstrated:

A literary school guided by existentialism has emerged. . . . The common character of these works is the philosophy that reality is absurd and people are free; in the subjective world, they assert the self-perfection of human nature; they attempt to substitute universal human nature and humanism for a Marxist outlook. . . . After the Cultural Revolution, young people suffered from spiritual depression and could not find their futures. They have a feeling of being cheated and abandoned, and have lost their confidence in socialism. Existentialism, therefore, is very well suited to their mood.[49]

The interest in Freud and psychoanalysis first emerged in 1982, thence coming under attack in the anti-spiritual pollution campaign of 1983. The *Red Flag* categorized psychoanalytic thought as "bourgeois ideology in an imperialistic period," contending that Freud "denies the effect of human consciousness and actually lumps together people and animals."[50] Yet interest in psychoanalysis nevertheless continued to wax, becoming another "fever" by 1986, causing psychology books to become best-sellers.[51] The reason for their popularity may have to do with Freud's frank focus on sex, surely as strictly repressed in socialist China as in the Confucian (or Victorian) eras. In attempting to explain the chaotic developments of the Cultural Revolution, the resort to irrational, unconscious motives seems also to have been appealing. In early 1987 a "Nietzsche fever" arose, as some of his books were translated and became best-sellers. Other fevers also appeared during the same period, according to the *People's Daily*: "methodology fever," "new idea fever," "modernist ideology fever," and so forth.[52]

Since the repression of the democracy movement at Tiananmen Square in June 1989, the period of relatively uninhibited intellectual "blooming and contending" that began in the summer of 1986 has of course been brought to a sanguinary end. The post-Tiananmen period has not hitherto been characterized by new ideas, either in the theory or the practice of reform. Into the intellectual void thereby created the regime has sought to introduce a selection of ideas ironically revived from the defunct Mao Zedong Thought—the immortality of class struggle, the unceasing struggle between capitalism and socialism, the tempting threat of the "capitalist road" (now refered to as "peaceful degeneration"), a suspicion of outside cultural influences (implicitly targeted as "spiritual pollution," but not explicitly mentioned because of increasing reliance on foreign trade, loan, and investment). The regime apparently hopes to use late Maoism in a purely defensive capacity, without allowing true Maoists to push this ideology to its ultimate logical conclusions either. In the course of its existence, the CCP leadership has progressed from ideological "true believers" to virtuoso interpreters of a repertoire of nuanced ideological rhetoric.

Reform Socialism in Perspective

Despite the fact that CCP ideology has served as the functional equivalent of a regime constitution, its content has been highly versatile, shifting via tortured reinterpretation to meet the needs of the political leadership at any given histori-cal stage. If CCP ideology at any given time might be said to be arbitrary or inflexible, if one has time to wait it will surely change, like the weather to which it is frequently compared. Indeed, the greatest difficulty in characterizing CCP ideology over any extended period is to find generalizations that can consistently apply, *mutatis mutandis.*

One aspect of the Marxist legacy shared by post-Liberation Maoism, Deng's reform regime, and even the pre-Liberation CCP ideological tradition, is the removal of the concept of "class" structures from their orthodox Marxist-Lenin-ist framework: in China, what is decisive for the definition of class is no longer the question of the conditionality of social structures and states of awareness on economic factors, as in Soviet or "classical" Marxism, but rather whether the individual himself subjectively shows his willingness to participate in the na-tional task of building a "wealthy and powerful" nation-state. This may be traced back to Li Dazhao's subjectification of the concept of class, translating the term into a moral decision by the individual to adopt a certain attitude or "class standpoint," as well as to the nationalization of the concept in the form of the "proletarian nation." If the conclusion that Mao drew from this was that political priority should be given to the creation of a "new man" through psychocultural transformation of the individual's awareness (thought reform, cultural revolu-tion), in the context of the more realistic picture of human nature held by today's reformers it is interpreted to mean two things: On the one hand, it means that measures geared toward efficiency and economic growth can be evaluated inde-pendently of their impact on the class structure, narrowly interpreted; on the other hand, it means that changes in the area of political culture are regarded with misgivings, and that they should be brought under control—*ergo* calling for the development of "socialist material and spiritual civilization." Despite such significant changes, class remains throughout subjective and "political" rather than objective and economic.

A second constant in CCP ideology has been the concept of the "united front"—which is, in a sense, a logical extension of the CCP concept of class. Just as the subjectivization and nationalization of class permits people of different social backgrounds to unite in pursuit of common political goals, the united front permits heterogeneous classes—or, in its international context, nation-states—to be brought together in pursuit of common political objectives. The concept of the united front seems to have faded in the reform era because of the lack of erst-while exclusive categories (such as class, or an impermeable friend-foe distinc-tion). There are, for example, no real enemies on the international scene for the first time in CCP history.

The ideology of the CCP has been otherwise extremely variable. Bearing this mutability in mind, reform ideology represents a relatively decisive departure from Maoism accompanied by a reluctance to foreclose a return to it under unforeseen circumstances. This seems to have given rise to a sense of ideological homelessness and nostalgia among the more ideologically fixated members of the leadership and to nightmares of a recurrence of the Cultural Revolution among those committed to the success of the reforms, with an unresolved tug-of-war between the two. For example, collective ownership was abandoned to the extent that collective farmlands were redivided into family plots, but the state retains ownership and has adamently refused to forswear eventual resumption of control, despite the chronic insecurity this arouses among peasants. Since Tiananmen, the regime has endorsed a "voluntary" movement toward re-cooperativization, albeit with neither popular response nor great political determination. Class struggle has been foresworn, but only in its "violent, turbulent" form, with the important proviso (repeatedly invoked since Tiananmen) that enemy class remnants and the struggle against them will continue indefinitely. Mass movements have been renounced, but the regime continues to launch campaigns. The departure from antimaterialistic asceticism has been similarly ambivalent, with emphasis on consumerism and "getting rich first" alternating with campaigns for thrift, self-sacrifice, and the emulation of Lei Feng. Even the shift from productive relations and productive forces and from the superstructure to the base seems to have been at least partially superseded by the introduction of the ideal of "socialist spiritual civilization." The attitude toward traditional Chinese culture betrays a similar ambivalence. The campaign against the residual influence of Confucianism has continued, now being embraced, however, by the Right rather than the Left, who see in China's past the origins of dogmatism, the personality cult, and a pattern of submission to authoritarian figures; the orthodox left, for its part, seems to have assimilated both Mao and Confucius to the nation's patriotic heritage, tracing the seeds of "bourgeois liberalization" and other unhealthy tendencies to the opening to the outside world.[53]

How can the modernization ideals of the reformers be reconciled with the classical Marxist-Leninist vision of the socialist utopia? This difficult question has been somewhat clarified since the issuance of the October 1984 Resolution, particularly in the theory of the "initial stage of socialism" mentioned above. The sparse prognoses of Marx, Engels, and others concerning the configuration of the future socialist economy (which have historically provided the doctrinal underpinnings for the command economy) are herewith dismissed as irrelevant to the problems of reform in China. Of much more significance are the analyses in *Capital* which were originally conceived as a description of the universally valid laws governing any commodity economy—that is, any economy operating under conditions of shortage. These laws, which have had their hitherto best-known application to that form of commodity economy known as "capitalism," are theoretically no less applicable to undeveloped socialist systems. The "socialist commodity economy" is thus no longer radically distinct from capitalism, but rather a subtype of the type of "commodity economies" of which capitalism is the other major subtype. The decisive difference between the two seems to be that socialism is still based on de jure common ownership and at least partially steered by central planning (the "cage" for Chen Yun's "bird"), though there is still unresolved controversy (at this point frozen) over how much privatization and how much marketization is permissible while still retaining a socialist identity.

What may be said from the perspective of comparative communism about the prospects for this modernization effort to succeed? According to one distinguished exponent of comparative communist theories of change, there are three schools of thought concerning the prognosis for reform.[54] According to the first, the theory of "totalitarianism," as represented by such theorists as Friedrich and Brzezinski, Hannah Arendt, Nathan Leites, and, more recently, Richard Pipes, the prospects for essential change are nil. Whether totalitarianism consists of some short list of stigmata, as suggested by Friedrich and Brzezinski, or is essentially a cultural system or subculture that perpetuates its worldview and operational code via various recruitment and socialization mechanisms, as suggested by Pipes or Leites, it is essentially an ultrastable (or stagnant) system with little prospect for change. Members of this school hence devote little attention to that prospect, except perhaps to expose illusions of change that might otherwise mislead the gullible.

The other two schools of thought take the prospect of change quite seriously. The "devolutionists," including such scholars as Barrington Moore, Samuel Huntington, and Robert Tucker, are descendants of Max Weber, who perceive change in communist systems in terms of the routinization of charisma, representing a descent from high drama to the everyday. On the other hand, the "evolutionists," whom Lowenthal refers to as the school of "bureaucratic enlightenment," including Cyril Black, Kautsky, Jowitt, Meyer, and Ludz, view the modernization prospect as one of institutionalization and rationalization.[55]

If we dismiss the first school as irrelevant to our divinatory purposes, the other two may be collapsed into one, resulting in predictions of surprising unanimity. According to this consensus, reform socialism in China is likely to proceed from its present half-reformed, amphibian form toward a corporation form of market socialism, probably at least initially under authoritarian auspices. The Eastern European route of instantaneous democracy through a spontaneous mass upheaval can probably be discounted in China because of the presence of a strong and loyal indigenous army and the absence of partisan or sectarian traditions around which opposition forces might coalesce. It also seems unlikely that a Gorbachev might arise within the next generation of leadership because of the setback suffered by reform elites in the wake of the Tiananmen massacre. China and the other communist-ruled Asian powers seem more likely to experience an evolutionary form of change. Exactly what this will look like remains to be seen. Over time and amid periodic crises and regressions, it seems likely that the hiatus between elites and masses will be bridged, as the masses' sense of political efficacy rises with their living standards and the role of elites changes with a shift of their legitimating competence from ideology to various occupational or technical specializations. The role of ideology will thus continue to fade, to the extent that "domestic policy disputes no longer involve ideology, but conflict between the goal of economic modernization and the tendency toward bureaucratic stagnation."[56] Finally, there will be an increasingly intricate functional division of labor, as in all modern industrial systems, with a shift from "extensive" to "intensive" development, implying greater reliance on science and technology to improve productivity and less reliance on forced-draft mobilization of the primary factors of production (land, capital, and, particularly, labor) to fuel growth, as well as a shift of investment priorities from heavy to light industry.[57] This implies a rise in status of functional elites, including intellectuals of all sorts, as Fang Lizhi has correctly (but indiscreetly) predicted. What is distinctive about the Chinese case in this regard is that the imperative for such a shift does not arise from factory shortages, as in the USSR or Eastern Europe (areas that face labor and possibly material supply/energy shortfalls), but rather from consumer quality demands in Western markets—given the PRC's apparent intention to pursue an export-promotion growth strategy, à la the Asian NICs (newly industrialized countries).

Having arrived at this generally agreed on forecast, we should note that it includes a number of lacunae and unresolved tensions. For example, the question of the relationship between political and economic reform remains problematic. Most discussions of change in communist systems focus on economic developmental strategies and their impact on society. Politcs is usually ignored or relegated to the status of a dependent variable. Among Marxist theories (as well as among certain Western scholars, such as Fisher or Ludz), politics dissolves into the administration of things, resulting in an enormous but rationalized and relatively efficient bureaucracy. Certainly that approximates the official Chinese version of the future, unruly protests having been forbidden, the "fifth modernization" driven abroad.

In my judgment, this is an unlikely prospect. The Chinese will continue to have "politics"—struggles for power, policies, position—as opposed to administration so long as there are conflicts concerning the identity or future direction of the leadership. Politics will continue to surface, for example, during succession disputes (Tiananmen is only the latest reminder), for China has succeeded no more than any other communist system in institutionalizing succession arrangements. Another issue likely to provoke politics is that of the future of the party. The process of "inclusion" has indeed been taking place in China, but it poses some unpleasant dilemmas.[58] As the brief review of Liu Shaoqi's theories of party-building indicated, it has always been deemed essential for the party to insulate itself from its environment in order to preserve its own subculture and sense of mission. The problem has always been that this tends to create a sense of alienation and resentment between elites and masses, inhibiting communication and fostering polarization during periods of strain. The value system being propagated among the masses under the aegis of reform is one of getting rich through hard work and innovative business practices. That is utterly inconsistent with the elite ethos of selfless sacrifice for the public interest. Party elites are being instructed to foster economic growth without personally engaging in business, to be "in" the world but not "of" the world. That this is an extremely difficult line to toe is indicated by the proliferation of cases of economic corruption. If elites take advantage of their positions and connections to engage in business, this is of course viewed as corruption; it is also corrupt for them to render services in exchange for consideration. Yet if elites strictly avoid defiling involvement in business activities, they risk becoming irrelevant to the modernization effort (*bao chan dao hu, bu yong ganbu*) or so resentful of nouveau riches entrepreneurs that they become fodder in a war against spiritual pollution. The appropriate ethos and role requirements for party cadres have yet to be worked out.

Political competition between groups not standing in a hierarchical relation to one another is also likely. In the Maoist period, "unified leadership" precluded the possibility of any group not standing in hierarchical relationship to other groups; only when formal organization fell into disarray (as during the Cultural Revolution) could political conflict erupt between vertically integrated informal groups, or factions. Factional alignments have, to some degree, continued to exist throughout society in the post-Mao period. Increasingly, as the formal institutionalization and the functional division of labor take effect, and as informal groups are dispersed through skilled personnel management (such as the periodic rotation of the PLA [People's Liberation Army] Military Region commanders) the focus of political affiliation seems likely to shift from primordial ties to current bureaucratic connections. This change is already discernible in elite purge patterns: since the fall of the so-called small gang of four in 1981, conflicts among the top-level elite have not revolved around factional alignments based on old solidarities, but functional interests. Thus, the "petroleum faction" consisted of those with interests in the heavy industrial ministries, whereas the cultural conservatives who have been most reluctant about further reform tend to be concentrated in the propaganda and security departments (the PLA, CAC, and Party Propaganda Department). The purges following the 1986–87 and 1989 crackdowns defined targets on a combination of behavioral and ideological criteria. This tendency seems likely to continue with modernization, perhaps giving rise to a sort of "cryptopolitics" similar to that associated with the Soviet Union.

Notes

1. So far as I know, Deng coined the expression, now widely cited without acknowledgment, of taking one step and then looking around before taking another [*zou yibu, kan yibu*] *Renmin ribao*, June 30, 1985, p. 1.

2. E.g., *vide*. John Bryan Starr, *Continuing the Revolution: The Political Thought of Mao* (Princeton: Princeton University Press, 1979); Brantly Womack, "Chinese Political Economy: Reversing the Polarity," *Pacific Affairs* 54:1 (Spring 1981), pp. 57–82, respectively.

3. Deng was paired with Liu in Red Guard polemics during the Cultural Revolution as the "number two party person in authority taking the capitalist road," and also purged with Liu at the Twelfth Plenum of the Eighth Central Committee in October 1968. Clearly, the Maoists considered Deng a top member of the "bourgeois reactionary headquarters." Deng implicitly conceded the accuracy of this pairing: unlike other targets of Red Guard criticism, such as Zhou Enlai or Peng Dehuai, he never repudiated Liu nor sought to distance himself from him in his public self-criticisms, despite indications that he might have thereby improved his own chances of political survival. That Liu was posthumously rehabilitated in 1981, despite evidence of elite dissent by Ye Jianying and others (and little indication of widespread public enthusiasm for the act), may be attributed chiefly to Deng's efforts on his behalf.

4. Mao Zedong, *Xuanji* (Beijing: People's Publishers, 1977), 5:59; see also anon., *Wuo guo nongye de shehuizhuyi gaizao* (The socialist transformation of agriculture in China) (Shanghai: People's Publishers, 1977), p. 47.

5. See Liu Shaoqi, "Zai zhonggong shanxi shengwei guanyu 'Ba laoqu huzhuzu shi tigao yi ba' baogaozong de piyu" (Commentary on the Report "Further Strengthening the Organization of Mutual Aid Teams in the Old Liberated Areas" prepared by the Shansi Provincial Party Committee), in *Liu Shaoqi wenti ziliao zhuan ji* (Complete collection of materials on the question of Liu Shaoqi) (Taipei: Institute for the Study of Chinese Communist Problems, 1970), pp. 245–46. See also Yang Junshi, *Xiandaihua yu Zhongguo gongchanzhuyi* (Modernization and Chinese communism) (Hong Kong: Chinese University Press, 1987), pp. 65–67.

6. Cf. Yan Ling, "The Necessity, Possibility, and Realization of Socialist Transformation of China's Agriculture," *Social Sciences in China* 3:1 (March 1982), pp. 94–123; see also Thomas Bernstein, "Stalinism, Famine, and Chinese Peasants: Grain Procurements during the Great Leap Forward," *Theory and Society* 13:3 (May 1984), pp. 339–77.

7. Cf. Vivienne Shue, *Peasant China in Transition: The Dynamics of Development Toward Socialism, 1949–1956* (Berkeley: University of California Press, 1980), pp. 281–92.

8. See Roderick MacFarquhar, *Origins of the Cultural Revolution; I. Contradictions among the People, 1956–1957* (London: Oxford University Press, 1974).

9. See Carl Riskin, *China's Political Economy: The Quest for Development since 1949* (Oxford: Oxford University Press, 1987).

10. See, for example, B. Michael Frolic, *Mao's China: Sixteen Portraits of Life in Revolutionary China* (Cambridge: Harvard University Press, 1980), and Anne Thurston, *Enemies of the People* (New York: Knopf, 1987).

11. See the following memoirs by former participants: Gordon A. Bennett and Ronald A. Montaperto, *Red Guard: The Political Biography of Dai Hsiao-ai* (Garden City, NY: Doubleday, 1971); Ken Ling, *The Revenge of Heaven: Journal of A Young Chinese* (New York: G. P. Putnam's Sons, 1972); Liang Heng and Judith Shapiro, *Son of the Revolution* (New York: Knopf, 1983).

12. See Michael Sullivan, "The Ideology of the Chinese Communist Party since the Third Plenum," in Bill Brugger, ed., *Chinese Marxism in Flux, 1978–1984: Essays on Epistemology, Ideology, and Political Economy* (Armonk, NY: M. E. Sharpe, 1985), pp. 67–97.

13. See Brantly Womack, "The 1980 County-level Elections in China: Experiments in Democratic Modernization," *Asian Survey* 22:3 (May 1984), pp. 417–41. The immediate upshot of the changes seemed to have been routine implementation in most places (with little change of past procedures) and lively controversy in a few urban areas (particularly those containing large numbers of educated youth, as on a university campus). The latter so upset the authorities that electoral procedures seem to have been modified to reduce popular input into the nominating process.

14. See Michael Oksenberg, "China's Confident Nationalism," *Foreign Affairs*, Fall 1986.

15. *Renmin ribao*, December 30, 1984.

16. E.g., in early March a triple editorial appeared entitled "Transform China in the Spirit of the Foolish Old Man Who Moved the Mountains: Hailing the Successful First Session of the 5th NPC," which criticized "the radicals, Liu Shaoqi, and the bourgeoisie." *Hongqi*, March 2, 1978, pp. 70–72.

17. See Helmut Martin, *Cult and Canon: The Origins and Development of State Maoism* (Armonk, NY: M. E. Sharpe, 1982).

18. Hu Qiaomu, "Act According to Economic Laws, Accelerate the Four Modernizations," published (after a three-month delay) in *Renmin Ribao*, October 6, 1978.

19. Mao Zedong, "Where Do Correct Ideas Come From?" in *Selected Readings from the Works of Mao Zedong* (Beijing: Foreign Languages Press, 1965), p. 1; Mao, "On Practice," *Selected Works of Mao Zedong*, vol. 1 (Beijing: Foreign Languages Press, 1965), p. 296.

20. This possible application was cautiously raised by Hu Qiaomu in the article cited above, but not until the second stage of reform was the functional autonomy of economics explicitly demanded, notably in the controversial article by Song Lungxiang (pseud. Ma Ding), "Ten Major Changes in China's Study of Economics," *Beijing Review*, no. 49 (December 9, 1985), pp. 17–20. In this article, Song bluntly deplored the lack of empirical economic research, as opposed to finding doctrinal justification for economic policies of the day, and called for the application of advanced quantitative techniques from the West. The article was highly controversial, precipitating a public cleavage between defenders of Marxist orthodoxy and supporters of academic professionalization.

21. See Yu Heng, "Kuan yu zhenli you meiyou jiejixing wenti de taolun" (The discussion on "Does truth have a class nature?") *Xinhua wenzhai*, January 1979, pp. 24–25.

22. See Tang Tsou, *The Cultural Revolution and Post-Mao Reform: A Historical Perspective* (Chicago: University of Chicago Press, 1986), pp. 112–44.

23. *Xue lilun* Editorial Department, "Shehuizhuyi zui gebende renwu jiushi fazhan shengchanli" (The most basic task of socialism is the development of production forces), *Xue lilun* (Learning theory) 218 (1984), p. 22. Also Zhang Yonghui and Cheng Peng, "Makesizhuyi shi jiefang he fazhan shengchanli de kexue" (Marxism is the science of emancipating and developing production forces) *Zhongguo Shehui Kexueyuan Yanjiushengyuan xuebao* (Journal of the Faculty of Graduate Studies of the CASS) 25 (1985), pp. 22–29.

24. Dong Zhuping, "Shengchanli shi lishi fazhan de jiben dongli" (The productive forces are the basic dynamic of historical development), *Xinhua wenzhai*, January 1980, p. 43.

25. *Beijing ribao*, June 15, 1981, trans. in *Joint Publications Research Service* [JPRS], no. 78709 (August 10, 1981), p. 35; as quoted in Sullivan, "Ideology," p. 85.

26. Su Shaozhi, "Shehui zhuyi shengchan de mudi shi manzu renmin de xuyao" (The purpose of socialist production is to satisfy the people's needs), *Xinhua wenzhai*, January 1980, p. 72.

27. Deng Xiaoping, *Jianshe Zhongguo tese de shehuizhuyi* (Building socialism with Chinese characteristics) (Shanghai: People's Publishers, 1984), p. 36.

28. This represents an increase of slightly more than nine percent. Jurgen Domes, "China auf dem Wege zu einem 'marktwirtschaftlichen' Sozialismus? Entwicklungen, bisherige Ergebnisse und Zukunftsperspektiven der Politik der Wirtschaftsreformen in der Volksrepublik China," *Zeitschrift fuer Politik* 33:4 (1986), p. 363.

29. Zeller reported that Marx repeated many times from the winter of 1849 through 1850 that there had to be several stages before communist society could be established:

the socialist republic would emerge after a petit bourgeois revolution succeeded in seizing political power, then a social communist republic would be established, and finally a pure communist republic. Su Shaozhi and Feng Lanrui, "Wuchanjieji qude zhengquan hou de shehui fazhan jieduan wenti" (The problem of the stage of social development after the proletariat gains political power), *Xinhua wenzhai,* October 1979, p. 26.

30. The concept of an "initial stage of socialism" appeared for the first time in the resolution on party history adopted at the Sixth Plenum of the Eleventh Central Committee in June 1981, which stated that China had reached the stage of socialism, but was still in its early phase of development. The same notion was articulated in Hu Yaobang's report to the Twelfth Party Congress in September 1982. The idea then went into eclipse for four years, probably because of conservative opposition. Not until after Gorbachev introduced the notion that the Soviet Union was not "developed" but "developing" socialism (in February 1986) did the "initial stage" concept make a comeback (at the Sixth Plenum of the Twelfth Central Committee in September 1986). The concept was then sanctified in Zhao Ziyang's report to the Thirteenth Party Congress (October 25, 1987).

31. See Wu Dakun, "The Significance of the Asiatic Mode of Production in the Study of World History and Chinese History," *Xinhua wenzhai,* April 1981, pp. 88–91; Lin Ganquan, "The Asiatic Mode of Production and Ancient Chinese Society," ibid., April 1981, pp. 92–95; Wang Xiaoqian, "Critique of Agricultural Socialism," ibid., May 1980, p. 7.

32. Wang Zisong, "Servant and Master," ibid., April 1979, p. 8.

33. Li Hongling, "Answers to the Question About Democracy and Order," ibid., April 1979, p. 5.

34. He Zhi, "Ren de wenti, rendao zhuyi wenti shi bushi Makesizhuyi de zhongxin?" (Are the problems of man and humanism the core of Marxism?), ibid., March 1982, p. 29.

35. See Hu Qiaomu's official response, "Guanyu rendaozhuyi ho yihua wenti" (Concerning the problems of humanism and alienation), ibid., January 1984, pp. 6–7.

36. See also the *Hongqi* editorial on December 1, which emphasizes the need to develop Marxism to fit current conditions. "For example, Marx wrote of class struggle, these ideas are not appropriate for current practice." Marxism is more than just knowing Marx; even Marx studied the work of others. "Some Questions on the Reform of Courses in Marxist Ideological Theory," *Hongqi,* December 1, 1985, pp. 8–13.

37. Wang He, "Chuantong wenhua ho xiandaihua" (Traditional culture and modernization), *Xinhua wenzhai,* July 1986, p. 188.

38. E.g., Wang He, ibid., pp. 188–91.

39. See Chen Chujia and Wu Ming, "Wan Li Addresses National Soft Science Symposium," *Xinhua* (Beijing), July 31, 1986, as cited in FBIS-China, August 26, p. K27.

40. Qian Xuesen and Wu Shihuan, "Shehuizhuyi fazhi he fazhixue, xiandai koxue jishu" (Socialist legal system, modern science and technology), *Xinhua wenzhai,* March 1984, p, 17; also Qian Xuesen, Shen Dade, and Wu Tianjia, "Yong jishu koxue fangfa zuo lishi koxue xitonghua" (Quantify history with the method of systems theory), ibid., December 1986, pp. 60–63.

41. One example is in the novel *Xin xing* (New star), by Ko Yunlu, p. 517.

42. E.g., "From the viewpoint of ontology: systems exist objectively, everywhere and at all times; the character of a system is a general phenomenon in nature, society, and human thinking. The concept of 'systems' reflects objective dialectics." Chen Yiyuan, "Xitonghua fengfu zhexue dan bu neng dai zhexue" (Systems theory enriches philosophy but cannot replace philosophy), *Xinhua wenzhai,* May 1982, p. 32; see also Su Shaozhi, "Zhengzhi zhuanzhi gaige dangyi" (Random thoughts on the reform of the political system), ibid., September 1986, p. 13.

43. Alvin Toffler, *The Third Wave* (New York: Morrow, 1980); John Naisbitt,

Megatrends: Ten New Directions Transforming Our Lives (New York: Warner Books, 1982).

44. Wen Yuankai, "Xinzi jiushi ziyuan, rencai jiushi ziben" (Information is resource, talent is capital), *Xinhua wenzhai*, September 1984, p. 10.

45. Dai Qing, "Tan zhongguo zhengzhi zhuanzhi gaige: fang Yan Jiaji" (Discussing China's political system reform: a talk with Yan Jiaqi), ibid., September 1986, pp. 9–10.

46. Feng Shujun, "Reforming the Political System Should Aim at Doing Away with Overconcentration of Power as the General Root Cause of Bureaucratism," *Guangming ribao*, September 22, 1986, p. 3; in FBIS-China, October 9, 1986, p. K2.

47. Chen Zhongya, "Wuo gaobie zunzaizhuyi" (I bid farewell to existentialism), *Zhongguo qingnian*, October 1982, p. 30.

48. The novels *Fluctuate* by Zhao Zhenkai and *When the Glow of the Sunset Disappears* by Li Peng attracted the most criticism from the conservatives.

49. Yi Yan, "On *Fluctuate* and others," *Wen yi bao*, April 1982, p. 40.

50. Zhao Biru, "Pingyu Fu-luo-de de xinlifenxikoxue" (On Freud's psychoanalysis), *Xinhua wenzhai*, November 1983, pp. 28–31.

51. *Renmin ribao* (overseas ed.), May 30, 1987, p. 8; July 16, 1987, p. 8; July 27, 1987, p. 8.

52. Ibid.

53. For a historically extended analysis of the xenophobic impulse in Chinese politics, see Kuang-sheng Liao, *Antiforeignism and Modernization in China, 1860–1980* (Hong Kong: Chinese University Press, 1986).

54. Andrew C. Janos, *Politics and Paradigms: Changing Theories of Change in Social Science* (Palo Alto: Stanford University Press, 1986), pp. 97–127.

55. Richard Lowenthal, "The Ruling Party in a Mature Society," in Mark G. Field, ed., *Social Consequences of Modernization in Communist Societies* (Baltimore, MD: Johns Hopkins University Press, 1976), pp. 81–118.

56. Lowenthal, "The Ruling Party."

57. Bill Brugger, "Undeveloped Socialism and Intensive Development," in Brugger, *Marxist Theory*, pp. 102–11.

58. See Kenneth Jowitt, "Inclusion and Mobilization in European Leninist Regimes," *World Politics* 28:1 (October 1975), pp. 69–97.

Comments by Parris Chang

Lowell's paper is well written and makes use of many sources. I shall ask questions and raise alternative viewpoints for discussion. The political report of the Thirteenth Party Congress contains interesting new material. For example, the following new idea on the primary stage of socialism: In Lowell's discussion on the sources of reform, he talks about the period of New Democracy, social construction, the Great Leap Forward, the Cultural Revolution, and so on; how great a part does the Soviet experience play in the thinking of Chinese planners in the past and in the future? Certainly this idea of the primary stage of socialism dates back to Leninism; then are we in the New Economic Plan (NEP) in China?

Lowell speaks of Western impact and Western sources. Are these reference points? How do the Chinese in the government and in the Academy of Social Sciences view the experience in Korea, Taiwan, and Japan, and the Meiji Restoration? They do not necessarily imitate what these countries have done, but these countries do provide useful reference points for them to look at. Recently the following question was raised: If the Soviet reform should fail, what would be the impact on China? I believe if the Soviet reform should fail, the Chinese reformers would be propelled to look more seriously to the West. Until now, Chinese leadership, including those who have been trained in the Soviet Union, have tended to view the Soviet experience with sympathy; if Gorbachev failed, I think the Chinese leadership would have no choice but to view the West more seriously. Until now, some leaders have had reservations about learning too much from the West; they feel the Soviet experience is the legitimate source for new learning.

I have a number of questions regarding Deng's reform theory. One concerns pragmatism. Deng has been very pragmatic [*zou-i-bu, kan-i-bu*], but this has been a dilemma for the reformers because in China theory and ideology are closely related. Until now, reformers have been able to point to ideological justifications for what they have tried to do. With this primary stage of socialism, they also need to spell out ideological justifications for China and for what China will do in the future. Until now, talk of socialism with Chinese characteristics does not tell one much. This primary stage of socialism, however, could perhaps carry with it programs for the Chinese reform.

Returning to a noteworthy point Lowell made: the Chinese fascination with Toffler's idea of future shock. Why are the Chinese fascinated by the idea? They try to telescope time, to cut short the time for development. In my view, however, their fascination with this notion has subsided. By now most Chinese have realized there is no free lunch; one cannot cut back necessary input. Until now, the Chinese leadership (that is, the eight hundred) has admitted they do not have experience in economic reform; so they improvise, they zig-zag and make mistakes, and they grope for magic formulas for modernization. I think they will continue to do so. It is not possible to follow a coherent strategy considering China's divergent conditions, so the leadership must continue to improvise.

Regarding political reform, until now the Chinese have been talking about *dang-zheng feng-kai* [separation of party and government]. Earlier in 1980 Deng talked about reforming the leadership system. I think that is the extent of China's understanding of what it takes for political reform. That is certainly not sufficient. Last night Prof. Li Miao talked about a more independent critical press; perhaps that is one more step China should take. Beyond that, the Chinese leaders may in fact not understand what it takes to deal with the problems of the past, with bureaucracy, and those who are involved in academic fields may be able to make some useful suggestions to the leaders as to exactly what they must do to get started on political reform.

Finally, when we study Chinese politics and Chinese reform, what are our best sources in addition to written materials? At this conference are a number of people involved in the actual planning of the reform: Prof. Xiong Xing-mei of Nankai University and Profs. Li Miao and Wang Huning of Futan University. Perhaps we could learn from them how the Chinese leaders think. I also want to call attention to the Chinese novel, which provides much insight. I have learned a great deal, for example, by reading a work called *New Star* by Ko Yunlu. This is an important novel regarding the thinking of reformers, opposition to reform, and how the political elite thinks in general.

Comments by Lynn T. White

The well springs of Deng's reformism, as Lowell has shown, turn out to be very old. He follows this stream from those springs down the river to the present. He tackles this huge topic first as a history, then as a phenomenology—not quite Gertz, but almost, then as a systems approach, taking the crystal and holding it up to various lights.

A dichotomy running through the paper pits the ideas of Mao against those of Deng and Liu Shaoqi. In a sense I think this relates to what Stuart Schram is saying [in his paper in this volume] and I agree with it. The Mao versus Liu-Deng is about Mao putting socialism first and development second, theory a priori, as Lowell says. And Liu-Deng, putting development first, and then socialism later in time; theory a posteriori, as Lowell says—Mao stressing the relations of production as the lever of history and Liu and Deng stressing the forces of production. But if someone like Doris Solinger were here, she would show that Deng isn't in all respects the new Liu Shaoqi. Deng is for more of an elitism, of a party separate from the masses. Both Lowell's and Stuart's papers have interesting new sources from Deng Xiaoping on that. But Deng may well not be as consistent on this point as Liu Shaoqi was. For a while, Deng was even like Hu Yaobang. Lowell refers to a "moral efficiency," a curious term, I think, that tries to bring together the two aspects of what is being discussed together here, but I think there is a lot of efficiency that strains against a lot of morals. The history Lowell offers is rich, and there is no hope of saying all the positive things I would like to say about the paper in the time available.

I think many of the most interesting aspects of Lowell's paper relate not to the consciousness of a few top leaders but to the consciousness of the leaders of very large social groups. He makes the unusual statement that the Cultural Revolution had a positive legacy for the present. Most people would not say those things, but you know he is right. He talks about a legacy of resentment of cadre privileges, which is obvious in politics since 1978, and a legacy of a primitive sort of anarchic democray. There is another point: he gives a fine and precise description, actually of the difficulty of implementing economic reforms: price reform leads to inflation, that leads to demonstrations on the streets, and that, through the political system, leads to the end of reform—a syndrome, well, even an equilibrium; but for political equilibrium, not for raising production or efficiency in any other sense.

In general, what is wrong with Liuism, as well as Maoism, that the current period under Deng is trying to correct is that large social groups, not just top leaders, see the revolution as having put itself in a rather ambiguous position. The revolution itself does not have an ambiguous reputation now; it has pushed people around too much. I don't need to detail for this audience the occasions when this has happened. It has scared people. As Lowell says, the moral elite party insulates itself to lead a revolution, but this breeds resentment among the masses. So I conclude, look also at groups other than the party and at "isms," the ideas of people whose names never get "ism" attached to them. The sense that this is a problem emerges where Lowell points out that there is no convincing definition of democracy in China today; the discussions of the rule of law and alienation and humanism in China, though interesting, are somewhat inconclusive because those terms aren't clear, and also because they obviously don't fit a Leninist framework even though they may well be Marxist—more Marxist, in fact, than the party in many cases.

Ideology is less important in China today because it is now in such an intellectual mess. Lowell mentions that Wan Li, in one mood, sanctioned the use of soft science [*ruan ko-xue*] by which of course he meant social science, systems theory, communications theory, surveys, to help development. I must mention something about Su Shaozhi because I think I succeeded in making myself misunderstood yesterday—the official party has stolen Su's idea, I think, and Stuart Schram mentioned this to me yesterday and I agree with him. Without acknowledgment it's been stolen, and it now becomes the new idea of the initial stage of socialism. But that idea now in the official line is embedded in sentences, implying a much greater guiding role for the party than Su wanted. Whether Su is still in the party is something I received completely different reports on from different people yesterday, and I wish someone could clear up that matter. He really represents a kind of *wen-hua re*, a political kind really, as does Liu Bingyan, or even Wei Jingsheng. The real Marxists in China are mostly not in the party, because development, not theory, is the main aim now. And as Lowell suggests [in his oral presentation], Chinese theory is in a mess.

Comments by Roderick MacFarquhar

I believe there is a problem in the association that Lowell makes between Liu Shaoqi and Deng Xiaoping. Lowell is not the only one to make this association and it is a problem not just relevant to history. I am not going to argue the nuts and bolts of it. Fundamentally, it causes us to underestimate the extent of what is happening today. If we think the sprouts of Deng were visible in the 1950s, and even in the early 1960s, there is no question, as Lowell points out, some of the reforms, the actual reforming of how the agriculture is run, were tried briefly in the early 1960s. All the leaders, not just the Liu-Deng group but Zhou Enlai and all the others, were associated with this, and Mao knew well enough not to interfere. To suggest that what is happening today is simply a continuation interrupted by ten years of the Cultural Revolution is to underestimate the magnitude of what is going on.

2

POLITICAL AND ADMINISTRATIVE REFORMS OF 1982–86: The Changing Party Leadership and State Bureaucracy

Hong Yung Lee

Historical Legacy

WHEN the Chinese Communist Party (CCP) made the historic decision to shift its main goal from revolution to economic construction in the later part of 1978, the Chinese bureaucracy was ill-equipped for the new goal. Its structure was cumbersome and top heavy, an "upside-down pyramid" with numerous redundant offices and ill-defined authority, function, and responsibilities. Its personnel was gigantic, with 21 million cadres, 39 percent (8.8 million) of whom were "responsible leaders."[1] In addition, the leading cadres were old and their educational level was very low. The existing cadre corps was politicized, factionalized, and demoralized. Having been the ruling elite that had not only created but also manned the new ruling structures since 1949, the cadre corps had vested interests in the existing economic and political systems. Deng Xiaoping, however, had nothing but this inefficient bureaucracy with which to lead China in a new direction.

The bureaucracy consisted of several layers of cadres recruited at different times for different tasks. At the top was the Long March generation, estimated to number around three thousand, occupying the top echelon of the bureaucracy. The second layer was the anti-Japanese war generation, many of whom had reached the level of ministers and vice ministers and secretaries on the provincial level. The third layer was the civil war generation, entrenched in the middle-level bureaucracy. The total number of "old cadres," those who joined the revolution before 1949 and who are entitled to the special retirement benefits of *li xiu*, is reportedly around 2.2 million, most of them occupying higher positions than the administrative ranks of the eighteenth grade. Most "old cadres" were recruited from the peasants—particularly from the poorest rural groups with minimal formal education—for the guerrilla war was initially against the Japanese and then against the Nationalists, although the anti-Japanese war generation included some highly educated intellectuals.

The Maoists' emphasis on class struggle and permanent revolution compelled the CCP to continue to base its recruitment on political loyalty rather than functional competency and other abilities even after 1949. Consequently, most of the post-Liberation cadres also largely came from the rural poor. Particularly, the land reform and collectivization generations were made up of poor peasants who had proven their activism in the socialist transformation. Not only did the CCP recruit its cadres from social groups that were ill equipped to act as "proctors," it also failed to train them in the complexities of economic development and management in modern society. This anti-intellectual bias continued, reaching its peak during the Cultural Revolution, and often equating "experts" with the often denounced bourgeois class.

During the ten years of the Cultural Revolution, approximately 5.4 million people entered the cadre ranks, making up about a fourth of the entire cadre corps. The former victims/now rehabilitated top leaders suspected the political loyalty of these people, however, because they were beneficiaries of the Cultural Revolution whose ideology was contaminated by the leftist view. Consequently, they were subjected to careful investigation and some were purged as the "three types of people" during the 1983–86 party rectification. For a distribution of cadres by generation, see Table 1.

Generally speaking, the generations of cadres parallel the bureaucratic hierarchy. This was largely because of the absence of a retirement system, as well as an emphasis on seniority in personnel management. Consequently, all those who had previously become officials remained in the bureaucracy. Only death or purges removed some from office.[2] When Deng Xiaoping returned to power in 1977, all the victims of previous political purges were rehabilitated, thus further aggravating an already serious overstaffing problem. The seniority system helped cadres (presumably with little ability or tangible achievements) to move up further in the hierarchy.

The overall educational level of the bureaucracy was quite low; 40 percent of twenty-one million cadres reportedly had the educational level of junior high school or below, whereas only 6 percent of those employed in the party-state organs had a college-level education (although China had six million college graduates as of 1982).[3] Furthermore, the senior ranking cadres had even less formal education than the junior generation, because, as shown in Table 2, the old-age group had fewer college graduates than the younger-age group in the population as a whole.

Table 1

Distribution of Cadres by Generation

Generation	No. of cadres
Long March	3,000
Anti-Japanese War	230,000
Civil war	2 million
Land reform	4.6 million
Collectivization	4.1 million
Cultural Revolution	5.4 million
Post-Mao	2–3 million

Source: Shehui kexueyuan yanjiu cankao ziliao (Sichuan), 21 February 1985.

Although the need to make the bureaucracy efficient was apparent to everyone, any effort to reorganize it was bound to offend the political interests of some elite groups. That was why Deng Xiaoping moved to tackle the troublesome question only in 1982 when his power base was successfully consolidated.

Leadership Changes: Process and Results

Officially labeled as a "revolution in administrative structure: but not against any persons," the bureaucratic reforms had two ostensive and one hidden objective.[4] The first was to upgrade the quality of the cadre corps by making them "revolutionized, better educated, professionally competent and younger in age"—the "Four Transformations"—so that it could lead China toward the "Four Modernizations." Another objective was to streamline the unruly bureaucracy by reducing the size of the cadres, devising rational division of works, and clearly defining the authority, responsibility, and task of each unit. The hidden agenda was to insure the continuity of Deng Xiaoping's reform line by promoting to key political positions those cadres whose personal interests were tied to the reforms.

The actual process of administrative reform reveals an interesting sequence:

1. changing the ministers and vice ministers of the central government in May 1982;

2. readjusting the leadership of the functional departments of the Central Committee—such as the Organizational Department and Propaganda Department—in the summer of 1982;

3. appointing a large number of new members to the Twelfth Central Committee in September 1982;

4. reshuffling provincial leadership in 1983;

5. adjusting leading bodies at the district and municipal levels (completed in December 1983);

Table 2

Rate of College Graduates by Age Group

Age groups	Population (millions)	Intellectuals (nos.)	% of (% of pop.)	Intellectuals % of intellectuals	Females (%)	Illiterates (%)
60+	76.6	241,460	.31	4.0	14.6	79.4
55–60	33.9	213,080	.63	3.5	15.7	67.9
50–54	40.8	386,710	.95	6.4	18.8	61.7
45–49	47.3	762,590	1.00	12.7	21.3	52.1
40–44	48.3	1,061,830	2.20	17.6	24.9	38.7
35–39	54.2	773,930	1.40	12.9	28.3	28.0
30–34	72.9	567,470	.77	9.4	28.7	26.2
25–29	92.5	755,250	.81	12.5	30.1	22.4
20–24	74.3	656,340	.88	10.9	28.7	14.3
15–19	125.3	601,870	.48	10.0	26.4	9.4
Total	666.0	6,020,530[a]	.9	100.0	25.7	

Sources: Xinhua wenzhai, no. 8 (1984), 6–7. For illiterates, *Zhonghua Renmin Gongheguo Ziliao Shouce* (Beijing: Shehui Kexue Wenxian chubanshe, 1986), 308.
Note: A criterion used here to define an intellectual was one who had received a college-level education; [a]another source reports that the total number of college graduates as of 1982 was 4,417,110, 0.4% of the total population.

6. changing leadership at the county level (completed in September 1984);

7. reorganizing leadership at the enterprise levels;

8. initiating the party rectification campaign, removing former Cultural Revolution rebels from cadre positions;

9. preparing lists of the third echelon of cadres; and

10. carrying out the second-round readjustment of leadership at the central and provincial levels in 1985.

As demonstrated by this sequence, Deng Xiaoping employed a bureaucratic approach toward bureaucratic problems. The regime moved slowly but firmly, step by step, level by level, and area by area. Instead of aiming at the ambitious and risky goal of replacing all older cadres at once, the regime placed them batch by batch, dividing its potential political adversaries, and dealing with them one by one. It first reorganized the central government, and then brought a large number of government cadres into the Central Committee. As members of the Central Committee they probably supervised the reorganization of party and government units at the provincial level.

The central authority limited the number of provincial secretaries to four or five, barring anyone over sixty-five from becoming First Secretary and requiring new leading groups to include various specialists familiar with the works of industry, agriculture, culture, education, and science and technology.[5] To supervise the provincial leadership change, the center organized a "Small Group to Lead Leadership Change at the Provincial Level" with Song Renqiong as its head. Each province drew up its own reorganization plan which was then submitted to the center. The pilot project was carried out in Sichuan and its exemplary results were sent to other provinces as an example.[6]

The newly organized provincial leadership, in turn, carried out leadership adjustments in their subordinate units according to the specific guidelines set up by the center. The central guidelines specified that the number of municipal secretaries should be limited to between three and five, that more than 50 percent of each leadership group should have an educational level higher than that of senior high school and that they should be younger than fifty years old, and that no one older than sixty should be included.[7]

A similar procedure was adopted for leadership reorganization at the county level. The central authority stipulated that the average age of the new county-level leadership be around forty-five, and that a third of them have a college-level education.[8] Each newly appointed provincial leadership organized "inspection teams"—drawn from the cadres in the personnel field and retired senior cadres—to supervise reforms at the lower levels. For example, the Guizhou provincial party committee dispatched about 60 inspection teams that allegedly interviewed 3,000 potential candidates and surveyed 24,500 people's opinions about the candidates.[9]

The results of the administrative reforms are tabulated in Tables 3 and 4. The reforms succeeded in reducing the number of leading cadres, and lowering their ages, while improving their educational levels. The number of ministers and vice ministers was trimmed by 77 percent and the number of provincial leaders by 35 percent. Even county-level leadership was trimmed by 25 percent. The percentage of college graduates increased substantially: from 38 percent to 59 percent among the central government leaders, from 20 percent to 44 percent among the provincial leaders, and from a mere 14 percent to 44 percent among lower-level leaders. The drastic improvement in the educational quality of lower-level leaders was possible because, as we noted in Table 2, the age group between forty and fifty had the highest percentage of college graduates. The average age of the leadership was reduced by approximately eight to five years. In terms of generations, those who had graduated from college around 1949 entered ministerial-level leadership, and those who had graduated from college just before the Cultural Revolution moved up to municipal leadership positions.

By relying on an incremental approach, Deng Xiaoping achieved what Mao had failed to achieve through mass mobilization in the Cultural Revolution. Table 5 (p. 43). examines the rates of personnel changes. Only 43 percent of the Eleventh Central Committee members made it into the Twelfth Central Committee—a slightly higher portion than that of the Eighth Central Committee who bore the brunt of the Cultural Revolution, but lower than the number of Ninth Central Committee and Tenth Central Committee members who made it to succeeding central committees. Twenty-seven percent of the incumbent provincial party secretaries survived the reform, whereas only 10 percent of the ministers and vice ministers managed to retain their positions.

Table 3

Reduction of Bureaucracy during the 1982–84 Reforms

Position	Before	After	Percentage of reduction
State council			
Offices	98	52	57
Ministers and vice ministers	1,000	300	77
Directors and deputy directors	5,000	2,500	50
Personnel in the state council	49,000	32,000	35
All cadres at the central level	600,000	400,000	44
Central party organs			
Offices			17
Directors and deputy directors			40
Heads and deputy heads of offices			14
Provincial level			
Secretaries, members of standing committees, governors, vice governors	698	463	34
Heads of bureaus[a]	16,658	10,604	
Municipal level			
Leaders			36
District level			
Leaders			29
County level			
Leaders[a]			25

[a]Includes all bureau-level offices of provinces, districts, and municipalities.
Sources: Collected from various Chinese official publications, including *Dangshi Ziliao Suju Tongxun*, March 1986.

After the reorganization, newly promoted cadres made up 62 percent in the central government, 56 percent in the Central Committee, 51 percent in the provincial secretariat, 50 percent in the district- and municipal-level leadership, and 53 percent among the county-level leadership. Heilongjiang reported that 60 percent of all leadership at various levels in the provinces were newly appointed. In spite of the overall reduction of the number of positions, the Deng group managed to promote many cadres of their choice.

Table 4

Age and Percentage of College Educated after the 1982–84 Reforms

	Average age		% of College educated	
	Before	After	Before	After
Ministers and vice ministers	64	58	38	59
Directors and deputy directors of the State Council	59	54	35	52
Directors and deputy directors of central party organs	66	62	43	53
Heads and deputies of bureaus of central party organs	60	54	50	56
Provincial secretaries, governors, and vice governors	62	55	20	44
Directors and deputy directors of provincial bureaus	62	55	14	51
Municipal leaders	58	50	14	44
District leaders	57	50		37
County leaders	48	42	14	47
Township		39		10
Village		35		1
Industrial enterprises National District[a] County[a]		45 52 47		89 40 35
Business units District[a] County[a]		52 47		84 60

Sources: Collected by the author from various official Chinese publications; [a]From Guizhou provincial figures, *Guizhou Nianjian* (Guizhou: Guizhou Renmin chubanshe, 1985).

Table 5

Scope of Changes in the Central Committee, Provincial Leadership, and Central Ministries

	Total number before the reforms	Total number after the reforms	Rate of survival	Percentage of new cadres
Members of the Central Committee (CC)	(11th CC) 354	(12th CC) 341	43% (151 out of 354)	56% (190 out of 341)
Provincial party secretaries	229	137 (reduced by 50%)	27% (66 out 229)	51% (71 out 137)
Ministers and vice ministers	474	143 (reduced by 70%)	10% (49 out of 474)	65% (94 out of 143)

Source: Collected by the author from various official Chinese publications
Note: The first column in the table does not include the heads and deputy heads of commissions.

To induce old cadres to step down, the regime developed the attractive retirement (*li xiu*) package that allowed veteran cadres to enjoy all the financial and political perks of their position even after their retirement. Indeed, the regime showed great flexibility in dealing with old revolutionaries, respecting to a certain extent their individual preferences on the matter of retirement. This flexibility, along with the opportunity to retire with honor and privileges, made personnel changes politically palatable to the old guard. By 1986, almost 54 percent of the "old cadres" had retired from active duty. (See Table 6).

The age factor played a crucial role in determining whether one would be removed or promoted. The age differences between those who were removed and those who were newly promoted were significant: fourteen years among the Central Committee members, seven years among the ministers, and two years among the provincial party secretaries. These aggregate figures, however, do not do justice to individual cases. Some cadres with the "right" ages lost their positions if their political loyalty was suspected. Mostly, the cadres who had enjoyed rapid promotion before the ascendancy of Deng Xiaoping belonged to this category. For example, the average age of the Eleventh Central Committee members who had failed to make it into the Twelfth Central Committee (sixty-three for full members and fifty-four for alternate members) was lower than that of the group who did (seventy for full members and fifty-four for alternate members). Those who entered the Ninth Central Committee had fewer chances at surviving the reorganization than those who were first appointed to the central committee in the Tenth or Eleventh Central Committee.

Table 6

Distribution of Retirees by Years

Date	No. of retirees	% (a)
1982	7,260	0.3
September 1983	470,000	21.3
March 1984	870,000	39.5
1985	1,000,000	45.4
1986	1,200,000	54.5
Not retired	1,000,000	

Source: Deborah Davis, "Unequal Chances, Unequal Outcomes, Pension Reforms and Urban Unequality," *China Quarterly* 114 (January 1988), 231.

There is no way of measuring the political attitudes of various categories of cadres, nor is it possible to operationalize the term "revolutionized." In the official definition, however, "revolutionized" was often equated with support for the policy line of the Third Plenum. In addition, one's performance in the Cultural Revolution was used as a criterion for inferring "revolutionized." The cadres who enjoyed rapid promotion during the Gang of Four period failed to pass the test of "revolutionized," despite their appropriate ages and probable professional competence. On the other hand, those who had not been deeply involved easily passed the political test and were promoted in the reform. In other words, the political requirement for promotion in the administrative reform was not positive proof of loyalty to the present leadership, but instead a negative sign indicating they were not loyal to former radical leaders.

In terms of career background, more than half the ministers and vice ministers promoted during the 1982 reform had started their careers in the functional positions of basic units, finally becoming directors and deputy directors of government ministries (58 percent). In addition, 18 percent of these can be classified as professionals. Even though we do not have complete information concerning their educational backgrounds, their career backgrounds lead us to conclude that the majority of the government leaders were competent in their respective functional areas. More than 60 percent of the ministers and vice ministers were identified as having work experience in production fields—industry, agriculture, finance, and transportation. The majority of them have experience in production rather than planning—for example, economic management—and surprisingly few people have work experience in the agricultural field. In contrast, only 5 percent have career backgrounds as party secretaries.[10]

The functional competency of the provincial leaders, although substantially improved, was not as high as that of the government leaders. Of the new provincial leaders, 37 percent had once served as directors or deputy director of functional departments, whereas 29 percent were from secretarial positions at the lower levels. A high percentage (42 percent) of provincial party secretaries had career backgrounds exclusively in political fields—such as secretariats, organizational departments, Secretary General offices, and the party committees at the lower levels. The differences between the career backgrounds of the government and the provincial leaders, however, narrowed substantially by 1986.

Apparently, after reviewing the results of the administrative reforms, the Deng regime carried out second-round readjustments at the central and provincial government level in April 1984. Instead of across-the-board readjustment, the regime replaced only those who had survived the first readjustment of 1982–83 with 126 younger cadres. Sixty-three percent of the newly promoted cadres are under fifty, and 80 percent have a college-level education.[11] As a result, the new leadership within each office formed a "ladder-shaped" structure by including those in their sixties, fifties, and forties. The average age was lowered to fifty-three and the educational level improved drastically: the number of leading cadres at the central and provincial levels with college-level educations grew from 43 to 60 percent.[12]

At the Fourth Plenary Session of the Twelfth Party Congress (convened in September 1985), 54 full members and 10 alternate members of the Twelfth Central Committee (out of the 341 elected in 1982) resigned.[13] Age seemed to have been the most important factor for this. Twenty-eight of the fifty-two senior leaders who were in their seventies had retired, whereas only six out of twenty-two who were in their sixties had. The average age of the retired members was seventy-five. Age was not the only factor, however, deciding who would resign and who would stay. Among the thirty-five senior cadres who had entered the Central Committee at the Eighth Party Congress (all of them are over seventy), only eighteen retired, whereas seventeen stayed. Political factors also seemed to be operative. Eight of the twelve leaders who had survived the Cultural Revolution have retired, whereas only ten of the twenty-three rehabilitated senior leaders have resigned. This means that Deng Xiaoping has been skillfully using the issue of retirement to force the senior cadres with personal ties to Mao and to Hua Guofeng to retire, while allowing a large number of his own political allies to remain in power.

After removing the old cadres, about sixty new ones were added to the Central Committee. Most of the new members were promoted to key party, government, and military posts before the Central Committee meetings and then moved into the Central Committee when the meeting was convened. The regime also replaced some ministers and provincial leaders in 1985 and 1986.

Tables 7 and 8 analyze the characteristics of the Central Committee members added in September 1985, all ministers, provincial party secretaries—the first party secretary system has been abolished—and governors as of 1986. They are key decision makers in the Chinese bureaucracy. Several observations can be drawn from the tables.

First, the group that entered the Central Committee in September 1985 represents a new generation of leaders, with fifty-seven as the average age and fifty-

Table 7

Age Structure of the Leadership as of 1987

	Ministers	Secretaries	Governors	Central Committee members added
Average age	59 (35)	56 (20)	56 (20	57 (32)
Median age	59 (35)	56 (20)	55 (20)	55 (32)

Source: Collected by the author from various official Chinese publications.
Note: The numbers in parentheses are the numbers of cases.

five the median age as of 1987. Most of them have college degree—thirty-one out of the sixty were positively identified as having a college-level education—and twenty-two have engineering titles.

Second, all ministers, provincial party secretaries, and governors have seats in the Central Committee. Unlike the radicals whom the Gang of Four promoted to the Central Committee in the Ninth and Tenth Party Congresses, the current Central Committee leaders have solid power bases in the formal bureaucracies of the central and provincial organs. Although their prestige among subordinates and their informal power bases are not known, that they concurrently hold positions in the Central Committee, as well as in other power organs, shows they can exert substantial political influence.

Third, the average age of the new leaders entrenched in power organs by 1986 indicates that most of them had joined the revolutionary works in the latter part of the civil war or around the time of Liberation. In contrast, except for the few still remaining in government positions, usually as chiefs of the central government commissions, the Anti-Japanese War generation has been largely removed from active duties. By and large, the majority of the top political elite (who were twenty-three years old in 1949) belong to the post-Liberation generation. Some might have joined the revolutionary works in the latter stage of civil war, but those who have college degrees would still have been students at the time.

Fourth, the average age of the four groups are similar, indicating that the regime's effort to upgrade the age at the top level has succeeded. Particularly amazing is that the average age of the provincial secretaries is only fifty-six years, lower than even the government ministers. Except in the early stages of the 1950s when the CCP was setting up its institutional structures, they have never been younger.

Fifth, their level of education appears to be quite high although information is incomplete. It is likely that most of them have college-level educations, although only twenty-six Central Committee members, sixteen provincial party secretaries and governors, and eighteen ministers have been positively identified as such. The new leaders are from the best-educated groups in China.

Sixth, 45 percent of ministers, 25 percent of provincial party secretaries, and

Table 8

Leaders' Work Experience as of 1987

Work experience	Year	Ministers No.	Ministers %	Secretaries No.	Secretaries %	Governors No.	Governors %	Central Committee members No.	Central Committee members %
Engineering	1987	17	45	7	25	8	33	34	26
	1982	1[a]	2	0	0	0	0	4[b]	2[c]
Economics and management	1987	9	24	2	7	4	16	10	7
	1982	2	5	0	0	1	4	6	3
Functional Bureau	1987	8	21	3	11	2	8	18	13
	1982	11	26	2	7	1	4	11	6
Secretary and politics	1987	2	5	10	36	7	30	38	29
	1982	26	60	24	83	23	84	91	48
Communist Youth League	1987	1	3	6	21	3	13	13	10
	1982	0	0	1	3	1	4	1	1
Military	1987	1	3	0	0	0	0	20	15
	1982	3	7	2	7	1	4	48	26
Mass organizations	1987	0	0	0	0	0	0	0	0
	1982	0	0	0	0	0	0	29	14
Total	1987	38	100	28	100	24	100	133	100
	1982	43	100	29	100	27	100	190	100

Sources: Compiled by the author from biographical information;
[a] based on figures prior to the 1982 bureaucratic reform;
[b] the Eleventh Central Committee;
[c] the Twelfth Central Committee.

33 percent of governors are engineers. If one adds the people with experience in economics and management, the number of those whose speciality is production increases to 70 percent of the ministers, 32 percent of the party secretaries, and 50 percent of the governors. This represents the greatest change from the Maoist era. In contrast, there are only a few cadres with experience in overall political leadership—5 percent of the ministers, 36 percent of the secretaries, and 21 percent of the governors. Virtually none of the leaders examined here have had any in-depth experience in the propaganda field. This graphically illustrates the lessening importance of a political career as the required background for promotion to top leadership positions.

Seventh, only one person among eighty top leaders has any career background in the military. He is Zhang Aiping, the minister of defense. This indicates probable difficulties for the new leaders in dealing with the military in coming years.

Eighth, it is believed that the vice ministers, deputy secretaries, and vice governors, although not included in Table 8, are already younger and better educated—hence presumably functionally more competent—than the groups they are replacing.

The preceding discussion allows us to draw a composite file of China's new leaders. They are, by and large, the post-1949 generation who graduated from college about the time the People's Republic of China (PRC) was established. The majority studied natural science and started their careers in technical posts at basic units, moving up along the bureaucratic hierarchy for the past forty years. They would probably have learned politics on the job while trying to survive and succeed in a bureaucratic setting. Unlike the retiring veteran cadres, these new leaders do not have any experience with guerrilla warfare. As their careers largely evolved in an urban setting, their understanding of and sympathy for the peasants appears to be minimal. As such, they are pragmatic and oriented toward problem solving. Their concern with political ideology appears to be much less than that of the veteran leaders they are succeeding.

The leadership changes are not limited to the group examined above. According to an official source, about 200,000 young cadres—those "under fifty-five years of age and with abundant specialized knowledge and long work experience"—entered into leadership positions above the county level. More than 1.08 million young people have been recruited into the cadre ranks.[14] Consequently, "after two years of structural reforms, the age, knowledge, and specialty structure of the leading bodies at various levels have improved substantially."[15]

In addition, the regime prepared the third echelon of cadres who would move into leadership positions as the older groups in the present leadership retire. About 100,000 cadres have reportedly been selected for the third echelon: approximately 1,000 for provincial and ministerial leadership positions, 20,000 for the jobs at the bureau and district level, and the rest for county-level positions.

As shown in Table 9, each province and ministry prepared lists of candidates for key leadership positions at different levels. The total number of the third

Table 9

Number of Cadres Selected for the Third Echelon, as of 1984

Unit	Total	Provinces	Districts	Bureaus
Tianjin	1,693	18	418	2,517
Beijing	3,000			
Henan	2,919	30	797	2,108
Shandong	5,896	34	437	5,425
Shanghai	1,500			
Liaoning		25	333	
Ministry of Railways	10,877	11 (ministry level)		

Sources: Renmin ribao, 5 November 1984; 29 October 1984; 20 April 1984; 11 September 1984; 24 February 1984.

echelon at each level approximates the number of incumbents—which is probably fixed by regulations. Reserve cadres are selected even for the directorship of provincial bureaus.[16]

Table 10 indicates that most of the cadres who made it into the third echelon are below 45 years of age. For example, the average age of twenty-five provincial-level cadres in Liaoning is 45.[17] Shandong reports that 45 is also the average age of thirty-four nominees for provincial leadership; 40, for the district- and bureau-level positions; and 35, for the county level jobs.[18] Similarly, Tianjin reveals that the majority of the cadres slated for department- and county-level positions are about 35 to 40 years old.[19]

As far as the level of education is concerned, most of the cadres in the third echelon appear to have had a college-level education. For example, all 25 persons selected for provincial leadership positions in Liaoning had college degrees; the group, 4 of whom are women, includes researchers, associate doctors, associate professors, and two nonparty persons.[20] In Tianjin, 17 out of 18 provincial-level candidates have had a college-level education; of 418 persons nominated for positions on the department- and district-levels, 335 (80 percent) were college educated.[21] In the 121 enterprises under the Ministry of Coal, 387 cadres were selected for the third echelon: 86 percent of these are below forty-five years of age, and 75 percent had a college-level education—69 percent with professional titles.[22] Likewise, Shanghai reports that 90 percent of the 1,500 reserve cadres has had a college-level education and 70 percent also had career backgrounds as professionals and specialists.[23] The third echelons are largely from the

Table 10

Characteristics of the Third Echelon

Unit	No. and position	Average age (%)	College educated (%)	Specialized knowledge (%)
Henan	137 for county		89	45
Shanghai	1,500 for all	42	90	70
Sichuan	173 for province	39	90	54
Gansu	for district (diqu) for county	40 37	94 80	
Beijing	3,000 for all	96% below 45	85	
Liaoning	25 for province	45	76	70
Tianjin	18 for municipality 418 for district (qu)	76% bet. 35-45	94 80	
A Ministry	452 for all	85% below 45	76	70
Ministry of Railway	1,087 for all	45	77	67
Ministry of Coal	452 for enterprise	86% below 45	76	70
Loyang municipality	1,964 for all	68% below 45	67	74
Textile Bureau of Liaoning	4 at bureau level 24 at division level	40 37	100 50	

Sources: Renmin ribao, 5 November 1984; 29 October 1984; 20 April 1984; 11 September 1984; 24 February 1984.

Cultural Revolution and the post-Cultural Revolution generations. The land reform generation and collectivization generation have been skipped over by the younger generation. Although the present leaders and the third echelon cadres are parted by two generations, they share some common characteristics: they are technocrats who built their political careers in a bureaucratic setting. The term most appropriate for this group is "bureaucratic technocrats."

Unresolved Structural Problems

The overall results of the 1980s bureaucratic reforms is mixed. On the one hand, the efforts succeeded in replacing the old revolutionary cadres, who in spite of their low educational level had founded the People's Republic of China and thereafter dominated Chinese political process for almost thirty years, with a younger and better educated generation. The new leaders are selected largely on the basis of such objective and universal criteria as age, educational level, and professional competency. The use of nonpolitical criteria for the selection of top-level leaders marks a decisive break with past practices, representing and reinforcing the CCP's commitment to the Four Modernizations. Although initially compelled by the imperatives of industrialization, the achievement-oriented criteria, once officially adopted for personnel management, will remain permanent.

On the other hand, the reforms have not resolved some persisting problems of the Chinese bureaucracy. First, the regime's change of criteria for personnel management from the political to more task-oriented ones did not have much impact on the age and educational structure of the entire cadre corps, simply because of the limited resources of the educated persons. It seems the revolutionary cadres still constitute a large portion of the present cadre corps. Second, China paid a high price for inducing the old cadres to retire through the *li xiu* system.[24] The system increased the regime's administrative expenditure and set up the ironic precedent that one can earn more when retired. Worse still, it has allowed the retiring cadres to take their bureaucratic ranks and status into society, thus further contributing to possible stratification of society along the lines of the bureaucratic hierarchy.

Third, the administrative reform has failed to resolve the structural problems of bureaucracy. The effort to make the bureaucracy slimmer ended in "total failure"; after the reforms the cadre size increased, particularly at the provincial level and below, pushing up the administrative expenditure from 4.2 percent of the total government budget in 1978 to 6.8 percent in 1982, 7 percent in 1982, and 8 percent in 1985.[25] Nor did the reform change the tendency for each organization to maintain itself as a self-contained unit with a large support staff, virtually "owning the cadres" and workers, and practicing the "life tenure" system.[26] Overstaffed offices continued to "stand like trees in a forest," forming numerous layers. The phenomenon of "documents and conferences forming mountains and seas" persists. Many cadres still "spend half a day drinking a cup of tea, smoking a cigarette, and reading a paper of internal circulation."[27]

Fourth, despite the limited effort to rationalize the personnel management system, the system by and large remains intact. Any reform of the system requires simultaneous changes of many different components. For example, to induce the cadres to work efficiently, the regime needs a rational incentive system, which in turn touches not only on the question of the wage and bonus system, but also on how to evaluate job performance. Any evaluation system presupposes a "postresponsibility system." But to develop a postresponsibility system, the regime has to come out with a comprehensive scheme to classify the entire cadre corps.[28] In turn, the classification of the cadres in China is predicated by a clear differentiation of the political from the administrative cadres, and the administrative cadres from the technical ones. In other words, a precondition for classifying the bureaucrats is to extract the party from day-to-day administration and economic management by separating one from the other. This cannot, however, be achieved without clearly defining what roles the party, particularly the basic party committees, should assume, when the party regards economic development and reforms, rather than the class struggle, as its main task. Yet the party is not prepared to give up its political prerogative. Consequently, the regime's feeble attempt at separating the party from the government without resolving the fundamental question only aggravated the bureaucratic labyrinth even before the 1989 Tiananmen Square massacre.[29] With the bloody suppression of the democratic movement, even public discussion of political reforms has disappeared in China's mass media.

Last and most important, the bureaucratic technocrats are still not completely free from interference from the old veteran cadres. Although formally removed from official positions, the retired revolutionaries, some on active duty and others entrenched in advisory commissions at various levels, frequently interfered with the work of the new leaders. As a result, the bureaucratic technocrats occupy all the important official positions, but the senior revolutionary cadres still make crucial decisions behind the scenes. The old guard's political muscle was dramatically demonstrated in the dismissal of Hu Yaobang from the general secretaryship, the ruthless suppression of the students' democratic movement, and the fall of Zhao Ziyang.

Having experienced purges during the Cultural Revolution and then having been rehabilitated after Mao's death, the old revolutionaries initially favored reforms and the cultivation of the successors when they were reinstated. But as the reforms progressed to the extent of threatening the very ideology of socialism, they turned conservative. They were particularly concerned with what they called "bourgeois liberalism." "Bourgeois liberalism," however, cannot be blamed on the bureaucratic technocrats. It reflects the Leninist party's ideological dilemma when it tries to liberalize society and the economy for the sake of economic development. Given the historical changes in all socialist systems, it is unrealistic to expect that China's new leaders will be able to balance political and ideological requirements of the Leninist party with the prerequisites of economic development.

Despite the retreat from the previous reform effort, the process for the bureaucratic technocrats to rise to the top political positions continues even after the Tiananmen Square tragedy. This may indicate that the incident did not shake the old revolutioary leaders' confidence in the bureaucratic technocrats. Or perhaps the old revolutionary leaders, even if they wanted to, may not have enough power to undo what they have been doing since 1982. Many of the new leaders, moreover, are the children of high-ranking cadres. Within a few years, the first generation of revolutionaries will pass away and China will be left to a new generation of cadres.

A long-term implication of the elite transformation for China is apparent. For the first time since the disapperance of the Confucian-gentry-scholar elites at the turn of the century, the leaders of the state are being recruited from the best-educated sector of society. Unlike the traditional elites trained in the humanities, the rising bureaucratic technocrats are mostly engineers and specialists in the "hard sciences." This is largely due to the shortage of trained experts in "soft sciences" and to the present stage of China's industrialization, where increasing production is still the major concern. Compared to the retiring old guards, the new leaders have a better understanding of and better qualifications to deal with such prerequisites of industrialized society as functional specialization, coordination of various areas, rational decision making, and problem solving, whereas their concern with political ideology appears to have lessened. Being "intelligentsia" rather than intellectuals, the bureaucratic technocrats are likely to utilize their expertise to improve and maintain rather than innovate and change the existing system.[30] It is therefore unlikely that the new leaders will lead China in a new direction, particularly toward a Western type of democracy. Instead, it is likely China will move toward a more authoritarian regime, while cautiously carrying out economic reform.

Yet China's short-term future is unpredictable. Probably when the remaining senior revolutionary leaders, now working as centripetal forces, pass away, China may experience another political turmoil. How well China will be able to deal with an almost unavoidable succession crisis largely depends on two factors. First, whether the new generation of leaders will achieve unity among themselves. Because the process of selecting future leaders involved a fair amount of nepotism and corruption, further weakening the central authority of the party, there are obviously many different groups within the new leaders owing their rise to groups of senior leaders, and with different ideological perspectives. One cannot, therefore, be too optimistic that the new generation of cadres will be able to manage their differences while effectively leading a billion people, when the remaining senior leaders disappear.

Another factor is whether the new group leaders have the ability and political acumen to lead China through the multitude of contradictions that reforms are bound to produce. This is largely dependent on the extent to which the specialized knowledge of the new leaders will help them in acquiring political wisdom and insight, and how they will combine their political leadership with their speciality.

Notes

1. For the definition of "responsible person," see *Zhiye fenlei biaozhun* (Standard classification of occupations) (Beijing, Zhufa tongji ju, 1982).

2. Michel Oksenberg, "The Exit Patterns of Chinese Politics and Its Implications," *The China Quarterly*, no. 67 (September 1976), pp. 501–18.

3. *Renkuo bucha 10 percent chuyang ziliao* (Beijing, Guowuyuan renkuo bangongzhi, 1982).

4. *Daily Report*, 9 March 1982, p. 4.

5. *Jiaoxue cankao* (Library of Anhui party school), 20 July 1983, p. 21.

6. Ibid.

7. Cao Zhi, ed., *Zhonghua renmin gongheguo renshi zidu* (Beijing: Beijing daxue chubanshe, 1985), p. 225.

8. Ibid.

9. *Guizhou nianjian* (Guizhou: Guizhou Renmin chubanshe, 1985), p. 292.

10. For a detailed discussion on this point, see Hong Yung Lee, "Evaluation of China's Bureaucratic Reforms," *Annals of the American Academy of Political and Social Science*, November 1984, pp. 34–47.

11. *Renmin ribao*, 8 September 1985.

12. Ibid., 9 September 1984; 5 October 1985.

13. Ibid., 17 September 1985.

14. *Jiushi niandai*, September 1985.

15. *Renmin ribao*, 10 April 1984; 20 October 1984.

16. Textile Bureau of Liaoning selected four reserve cadres for bureau directors and twenty-six for chu level positions. Gansu has selected twenty-five for municipal-level and eighty-two for county-level leadership positions. Ibid.

17. *Renmin ribao*, 20 April 1984; 11 September 1984.

18. Ibid., 14 January 1985.

19. Ibid., 15 November 1984.

20. Ibid., 20 April 1984.

21. Ibid., 15 November 1984.

22. Ibid., 20 October 1984.

23. Ibid., 19 September 1984.

24. For *li xiu* system, see Chao Zhi, ed., *Zhonghua renmin gongheguo renshi zhidu*.

25. *Jiao yan cankao*, 15 April 1985; *Renmin ribao*, 7 March 1985.

26. *Jingji fazhan yu tizhi gaige*, no. 7 (1986), pp. 7–12.

27. *Zhongguo xingzheng guanli*, no. 2 (1978), p. 5.

28. For the postresponsibility system, see *Shehui kexuyuan* (Liaoning), no. 33 (1984), p. 5.

29. For the effort, see Zhang Dailun, *Changzhang fuze zhi* (Beijing, Jingji kexue chubanshe, 1985). Before the reform, for example, the county-level authorities had only two systems—the party committees and the government organizations. But now there are five different sources of authority: the party committees, the government, the National People's Congress, the Political Consultative Conference, and the Disciplinary committees.

30. Alvin Gouldner, *The Future of Intellectuals and the Rise of the New Class* (New York: Seabury Press, 1979).

Comments by Ilpyong Kim

Parris Chang remarked that if the Soviet reform should fail, then China might turn to the West. How about China turning to the East following the South Korean model of development or the Taiwanese or East Asian models of development? I think Hong Yung Lee's paper provides a fine analysis of the structural changes of the administrative and bureaucratic cadres that took place under Deng Xiaoping's leadership in the past five years, from 1982 to 1987. The paper's thesis seems to be that Deng Xiaoping had to replace the old cadres, who had become cumbersome, top heavy, and inefficient, with the new generation of cadres in order to execute the economic reforms. He gives an excellent portrait of the old cadres from the Long March generation to the anti-Japanese cadres to the Cultural Revolution cadres and up to the more recent ones.

I detect contradictions in Lee's arguments, however, when he says the newly promoted cadres owe their new success to Deng and that therefore their future careers are tied to the success of Deng's reforms. I believe he argued in an earlier section of his paper that the administrative and bureaucratic reforms were carried out on the basis of professional competence and managerial efficiency. He then later changes this view. If the CCP continues the reform, will it allow the new generation of cadres to express their diverse viewpoints? Or will it sustain the institutional viewpoints as outlined by Deng? Are the young and different generations of cadres likely to continue the reform when they are entrenched in leadership positions at the top level? The age factor was considered in the replacement of the old cadres, but the educational factor has not been clearly or succinctly analyzed, especially when Lee mentioned in his presentation that engineers or those with an engineering education may limit their perspectives and views, and therefore Lee is pessimistic about the continuation of the reform. We must also look, however, at those who are physicists or natural scientists, or engineers who in the past have been good administrators at the universities or at the local levels. Can we really rule out those with an engineering background as being limited in administrative and managerial skills?

Lee assumes that changes of old cadres with the young generation predictably assures the continuation of the reform program. Therefore, we need to know more about the education and the policy outlook of a particular generation to find out the policy perspectives and policy output. Further research and analysis of the educational factor is needed to establish a correlation between the level of education and its impact on the policy output of the new generation of cadres if we are to be able to understand and predict the continuity and change of the reform program. The latest generation of cadres who have received a college education seems to have a wider range of viewpoints and a more diverse outlook. Would the CCP allow these ideas to be expressed and channeled through the policy-making process when these newly promoted cadres are entrenched in leadership positions? Would it be possible to identify the relations between the level of education and diversity of views among the new generation of cadres and their likely impact on the future of the reform program? Moreover, we have heard a great deal about *dang-zheng feng-kai*, but we don't know very much about the process by which such a program is being implemented even at the top-level leadership positions, including the Central Committee and the Standing Committee of the Politburo. From Lee's analysis of the changes in the administrative and bureaucratic cadres, can we really predict the outcome of *dang-zheng feng-kai*?

Comments by Roderick MacFarquhar

The tremendous turnover at this [Thirteenth Party] Congress, and indeed at the 1985 Conference, and because so many gave up so much for so little in return, should make us sit back and try to grasp the extent of this revolution. In my view, that is what this is about. Hong Yung Lee has said, "What can physicists think about politics?" Well, the Soviet revolution also has leaders, Gorbachev and others, who are largely trained in some form of natural or applied science, yet Gorbachev is able to grasp that something big is needed and that one must be brave enough to do it and take a good segment of the elite along with him. Simply put, if we look too far back and try to pin down the roots, we would underestimate the incredible nature of the revolution that Deng Xiaoping has been engineering, and with which presumably he is reasonably satisfied, otherwise he might not have retired at this stage.

Comments by Lynn T. White

Lowell Dittmer ends his paper with a prediction, with which I agree, that elite-mass relations are improving mainly because of recruitment, and this projection is already interjected into Hong Yung's paper. I must disagree, however, with both Lowell and Hong Yung on the inevitability of bureaucratic stagnation.

The Chinese elite is diversifying rather quickly now and the revolution might not devolve into a dull bureaucratic monstrosity, such as we have seen in the USSR, because Mao, unlike Stalin, did not succeed in killing off everyone who had different ideas than he. Moreover, China now has many theorists: some in jail; some in enterprises, offices, hospitals, and universities; some in the party and some out of the party. Hong Yung deals with the change in leadership, now the most important subject in China, and he presents hard quantitative data and carefully sticks to the data. I might add he is admirable in the Yale tradition of closely relating conclusions to data. He is not responsible, therefore, for some of the thoughts I conclude from the data he presents.

The Chinese state was captured in 1949 by a limited elite that tried to run China alone. At the time they had few expert cadres; now they need more of them to achieve their original nationalistic patriotic purposes. But this means a need for younger college-educated vocational cadres. In social terms, this means more ex-bourgeois people. Even "to revolutionize," as Hong Yung's paper says, means supporting the Third Plenum policies, especially not having become too involved in the Cultural Revolution. Most of the radical cadres are not the revolutionized ones. In the past Central Committee, as Hong Yung says, nearly half the members were engineers. How will this affect political decisions? It may rationalize them, make them dull, but we do not really know yet what the effect of having engineers run China will be. As Hong Yung points out, only one of the top eighty members of the Central Committee is a soldier. The whole Korean War generation, people who were young soldiers, twenty years old in 1950, will be sixty years old in 1990; these people seem to have been left out. Whether that will remain permanent is an important question. It might.

One of the big changes Hung Yung points out is the reduction of the top-level bureaucracy. I want to emphasize "top-level." Seventy-seven percent of the ministers and vice ministers from the past Central Committee are out, but as one looks at the tables Hung Yung presents, the farther down the administrative level, the less streamlining there has been; when one gets below the county level, the suggestive evidence is that in fact there has been additional recruitment. People in low-level offices have accepted the new policies and said, "Great, we can hire more people for our units." An example of "gigantism," a characteristic of Chinese organizations, not just communist ones, absorbing resources and searching for new functions. There are really three groups that emerge from Hong Yung's paper: (1) the land reform civil war group—older leaders who generally do not have college degrees; (2) a large group that received university certification, if not a very good education, in the five or six years surrounding the leap of 1958; and (3) the young group—the revolutionaries, fifties graduates and the new eighties graduates. What does this signify? I believe it clearly means more diversity; the oldest group is old and for actuarial reasons will die out; much of what happens is actuarial.

Hong Yung, like Lowell, therefore expects bureaucratic authoritarianism, especially among the 1950s-educated people, which would lead to a rather dull, stagnant situation. Perhaps. But this Chinese revolution is not necessarily going exactly the way of the Russian one. The party's role is so unclear now that we do not know the extent to which the party will remain a party in the future in the usual Leninist sense. We have other revolutions to compare China with. Those of the English and the French, for example. There are now many groups of local leaders in China with many theories. The party is presumably only a large propaganda team now. It is supposed to pull out of management work, yet it is staffed almost entirely with engineers and managers with no experience, as Hong Yung says, in propaganda. They do have ideas, however. What ideas? We don't know nearly enough about that yet.

3

INSTITUTIONALIZING A NEW LEGAL SYSTEM IN DENG'S CHINA

Hungdah Chiu

Impetus for Legal Reform: The Legacy
of the Cultural Revolution and Before

ONE of the major reforms of the post-Mao leadership in the People's Republic of China (PRC) is to rebuild and strengthen the legal system. Since 1977, not a single day has passed without articles or reports on law appearing in the newspapers and other publications or in the media in the PRC. This is in sharp contrast with the Maoist era, especially during the period of the Cultural Revolution between 1966 and 1976, when PRC leaders and the general public paid almost no attention to law. To understand why the PRC has changed its attitude toward law in the post-Mao period, a review of the legal developments between 1949 and 1976 is needed. Generally, legal developments in the PRC, as viewed by Chinese scholars, may be divided into four stages:[1]

The Period of the Establishment
of the Legal System (1949–1953)[2]

The primary role of the PRC state with respect to law and justice during the period from 1949 to 1953 was to demolish the old legal system and establish a new socialist legal system along the Soviet model.

Early in February 1949, before the Communists had captured the whole mainland, the Chinese Communist Party (CCP) issued the "Directive Regarding the Abolition of the Guomindang's *Complete Book of Six Codes*" and the "Affirmation of the Legal Principles in the Liberated Areas." This directive was later incorporated into Article 17 of the Common Program, adopted in late September 1949 by the Chinese People's Political Consultative Conference (CPPCC), which served as an interim constitution until the adoption of a formal constitution on September 20, 1954. The CPPCC was intended to serve as the provisional legislature of the country; but in fact it only exercised limited legislative functions. From 1949 to September 20, 1954, when legislative functions were taken over by the National People's Congress (NPC) under the 1954 Constitution, the CPPCC and the Central People's Government Council under it only adopted fifty-one laws and decrees. If one includes decrees issued by the Government Administrative Council, the total number of important laws and regulations adopted during 1949–53 was only 148. Moreover, among the laws, regulations, and decrees adopted in this period, there were no criminal, criminal procedure, civil, and civil procedure codes. The only important legislation enacted was the Act for the Punishment of Counter-Revolutionaries of the PRC, promulgated on February 21, 1951. This act applied retroactively to pre-1949 activities, permitted the use of analogy, and was vaguely drafted for flexible use.

In 1951, the PRC set up a three-level, two-trial (one appeal) system of people's courts: county people's courts, provincial people's courts, and the Supreme People's Court. All the people's courts were organic parts of the people's governments of the corresponding levels. A people's procuratorate was also established on a level corresponding with each people's court; the procuratorate was at the same time a component of the people's government at the same level. As a result, both the courts and the procuratorate were, in law and in fact, under the control of administrative organs and there was no separation of power among them. At first, because of the insufficient numbers of legally trained Communist personnel, many former Nationalist legal personnel were retained to serve the people's judiciary. In 1952, however, a Judicial Reform Mass Movement was launched against "old" legal principles, such as "judicial independence," "no punishment without preexisting law," or "law has no class character"; the movement was intended to strengthen the Communist party's leadership over judicial work. As a result of this movement, most former Guomindang judicial personnel were dismissed from office or even condemned as counterrevolutionaries. Their positions were taken over by communist cadres who had received little or no legal training.

In fact, legal training was not essential to implementing the people's law and justice, as the judiciary was frequently instructed to follow orders or policies of the government or of the party in cases not covered by existing laws. In addition, the courts were neither required nor expected to cite the applicable provisions of law in rendering their judgments. Moreover, the dynamics of the Chinese mass movement included a disregard of law as an ordering force in society.

The Period of the Development of the Legal System[3]

On September 20, 1954, the PRC promulgated a formal constitution incorporating provisions concerning a judiciary and people's rights that indicated a tendency to follow the Soviet model of establishing a stable legal order and a permanent judicial structure. Among the four chapters of the Constitution, Chapter IV (Articles 85 to 103) is entirely devoted to the "Fundamental Rights and Duties of Citizens." This chapter guarantees, among other freedoms, equality before the law and freedom of speech, of the press, of association, of demonstration, and of religion, as well as the right to work, to leisure, to education, and to social assistance. Article 89 of the Constitution specifically provides protection against arbitrary arrest: "Freedom of the person of citizens of the People's Republic of China is inviolable. No citizen may be arrested except by decision of a people's court or with the sanction of a people's procuratorate." To implement this article, on December 20, 1954, an Arrest and Detention Act of the People's Republic was promulgated.

The Constitution also provided in Articles 73 to 84 the basic organizational structure of the people's court and the people's procuratorate. On September 28, 1954, the PRC promulgated organic laws governing the people's courts and people's procuratorates. The Constitution and the Organic Laws gave the PRC judicial system a permanent structure. Under the National People's Congress and its Standing Committee, two separate but interlocking hierarchies were established. The people's courts, headed by the Supreme People's Court, were given the sole authority to administer justice. The people's procuratorates, culminating in the Supreme People's Procuratorate, were to exercise the supervisory power over the execution of the law. Below the Supreme People's Court, local courts were divided into higher people's courts, intermediate people's courts, and basic people's courts. In 1962, it was reported that there were thirty higher courts, two hundred intermediate courts, and more than two or three thousand basic courts.

The Period When the Legal System Construction Was Subject to Interference and Ceased to Develop (1957–1965)[4]

During 1956–57, the PRC launched the movement of "letting a hundred flowers bloom and a hundred schools of thought content." Many jurists and scholars took this opportunity to criticize the government for the lack of basic laws and the defective administration of justice. Alarmed at the strong criticism evoked by the "Blooming and Contending" Movement, the PRC launched an anti-rightist movement in the summer of 1957 to silence its critics. So far as law and justice were concerned, this meant a serious setback for the development of a stable and less arbitrary system of justice. Two years later, in 1959, another movement against "rightist opportunism" was launched within the party, further undermining the efforts to establish a stable legal system.

The declining trend toward legality was also reflected in the number of laws, decrees, and other documents adopted by the National People's Congress or its Standing Committee in each year. In 1957, 108 items were adopted and in 1965 the number was down to 11. During this period, the PRC's judiciary gradually regressed to its earlier practice, with the public security (police) organs playing a growing role at the expense of the procuratorate and the courts. The defense lawyers system was also gradually phased out with the reduction of the number of lawyers to a few, primarily to serve foreigners.

The Period When the Legal System Was Severely Undermined (1966–1976)[5]

Although law and the justice system were not among the major revolutionary targets at the beginning of the Cultural Revolution in 1966, they were no exception from the ensuing destruction of the "establishment." The formal legal structure received serious blows during the Cultural Revolution. To achieve the transformation of political-legal organs, Mao proceeded to have a large number of cadres purged without resort to any formal process, including the President of the People's Republic of China, President of the Supreme People's Court, the Chief Procurator, and the First Deputy Minister of Public Security. The procuratorate was abolished and the courts functioned only sparingly and were placed under the supervision of the military. It was only between 1970 and 1973 that military control over law enforcement gradually receded, though the pace varied from region to region and from agency to agency. The 1975 Chinese Constitution confirmed the trend of downgrading the legal system by subjecting the people's courts to the control of local government (the revolutionary committees) at corresponding levels and the application of the mass line as the operational principle for procuratorial (assigned to the police) and trial work. During this period the system of defense lawyers was abolished.

Most offenses and disputes in China were handled by extrajudicial institutions led by party committees and the police. The courts often played a subsidiary or ceremonial role in judicial proceedings. Moreover, during the mass movement or campaign, legal procedures were often totally disregarded and ad hoc procedures were set up to arrest, investigate, and detain offenders for indefinite periods of time.[6] A clear provision of law on a given subject could be repealed by party policy.[7] Persons in one of the five categories—former landlords, former rich peasants, counterrevolutionaries, rightists, and bad elements—or their descendants, were discriminated against in an administration of justice that rejected the principle of equality of all persons before the law. Members of the Communist Party of China, if they belonged to a faction in power, would receive preferential treatment before the law. The party secretaries at different levels, in fact, made decisions on the arrest, prosecution, and sentencing of the accused, despite the formal separation of powers of the public security, procuratorate (1951–69), and the courts.[8] At trial, torture was frequently used to extract confessions. Judges, most of whom received no formal legal training at all, were only interested in accepting evidence proving the guilty charge of an accused and rejecting evidence favorable to an accused.[9] An accused could be detained for a long period until he confessed his crime or when the authorities decided to conclude the case.[10]

Under such an irrational, ruthless, and unpredictable legal system, the post-Mao PRC leaders were confronted with a population demoralized and frightened by years of chaos, abuses, and uncertainty; this was especially true with regard to the intellectuals who suffered most in the period of the Cultural Revolution. To carry out an ambitious modernization program, launched by the post-Mao PRC leaders, it was obvious that the Chinese legal system, severely disrupted and undermined by the Cultural Revolution, had to be rebuilt and strengthened so as to provide an orderly, predictable, and secure environment for economic and social development.

Strategy and Process of Legal Reform

The communiqué of the Third Plenary Session of the Eleventh Central Committee of the Communist Party of China (December 18 and 22, 1978) set the goals of China's legal reform as follows:

> To safeguard people's democracy, it is imperative to strengthen the socialist legal system so that democracy is systematized and written into law in such a way as to ensure the stability, continuity, and full authority of this democratic system and these laws; there must be laws for people to follow, these laws must be observed, their enforcement must be strict, and law breakers must be dealt with. From now on, legislative work should have an important place on the agenda of the National People's Congress and its Standing Committee. Procuratorial and judicial organizations must maintain their independence as is appropriate; they must faithfully abide by the laws, rules, and regulations, serve the people's interests, and keep to the facts; they must guarantee the equality of all people before the people's laws and deny anyone the privilege of being above the law.[11]

The goal as set in the above communiqué was to introduce a certain degree of democracy to the Chinese political system through law and to provide a stable and predictable legal system for the Chinese people.

When the PRC began its ambitious Four Modernizations program (in agriculture, industry, national defense, and science and technology) in 1979 and allowed the people more economic freedoms, the goal of law reform announced in the above communiqué soon became inadequate. With a more rapid growth of the economy, there was the need for various economic laws, regulations, and rules to regulate economic and commercial relations among the people and various organs of the society. Moreover, the PRC wanted to expand its trade, import advanced technology, and attract foreign investments to develop the Chinese economy; thus, it was necessary for it to enact laws and regulations to govern these economic activities involving foreigners, especially in areas of patents, trademarks, taxation, and technology transfer.

Internationally, the post-Mao PRC has ended its self-imposed isolation policy and has actively increased its contacts with the outside world; this policy has prompted it to take a positive attitude toward international law and to participate in many international conventions, especially those relating to trade, investment, and maritime matters.[12] Once the PRC participates in an international convention, it may be necessary to enact or revise its domestic law and regulations in order to implement its treaty obligations. Thus, participation in international conventions by the PRC also puts some pressure on the PRC's domestic legal reform.

To implement the policy of legal reform, the PRC has taken a series of steps: first, to enact the necessary laws and regulations; second, to make the necessary structural reorganization of its judicial system; third, to restore and expand legal education so as to staff its judicial organs with competent personnel and develop its legal research so as to deal with many current and future problems of law; and, finally, to publicize laws and promote the concept of legality among the officials and the people.

Before the PRC could take any steps to implement its goal of legal reform, however, it was necessary to resolve the basic issue of whether to retain the 1975 Constitution[13] enacted by the so-called Gang of Four (Zhang Chunqiao, Yao Wenyuan, Wang Hongwen, and Mao's wife, Jiang Qing), who were overthrown in a coup in October 1976. It was decided that a new constitution should be enacted to replace the 1975 Constitution, and it was done in 1978.[14] With Deng Xiaoping emerging as the dominant figure among Chinese leaders in 1980, he and his associates soon found the 1978 Constitution unsatisfactory, so a new constitution was enacted in late 1982, which has been in force since then.[15]

In the following sections, measures of the PRC's legal reform will be summarized; substantive problems incurred by the legal reform will be discussed later.

Legislative Activities

The lack of applicable law is a serious problem in the PRC, so the government has accelerated its legislative activities since 1978. Up to 1988 the National People's Congress and its Standing Committee has enacted sixty-seven laws and adopted sixty-three resolutions to supplement or to amend the laws. The State Council issued more than five hundred regulations. The people's congresses and their standing committees of the provinces, autonomous regions, and municipalities, which were under direct central government control, enacted more than seven hundred laws.[16] Major laws, decisions, and regulations are listed as follows:[17]

1978:
March 5: Constitution

1979:
February 23: Forestry Law (Trial Implementation)
February 23: Arrest and Detention Act (Revised)

July 1:

1. Organic Law of the Local People's Congress and Local People's Government at Various Levels (Revised)

2. Electoral Law for the National People's Congress and the Local People's Congress at Various Levels (Revised)

3. Organic Law of the People's Courts (Revised)

4. Organic Law of the People's Procuratorates (Revised)

5. Criminal Law

6. Criminal Procedure Law

7. Law on the Joint Ventures Using Chinese and Foreign Investment

8. Resolution of the National People's Congress on Amending Certain Provisions in the Constitution

September 16: Environmental Protection Law (Trial Implementation)

November 29:

1. Decision of the Standing Committee of the National People's Congress on the Question of Validity of the Laws and Decrees Enacted since the Founding of the People's Republic of China.

2. Supplementary Regulations on Reeducation Through Labor (Promulgated by the State Council and Approved by the Standing Committee of the National People's Congress)

1980:

August 26: Provisional Act on Lawyers

September 10:

1. Nationality Law

2. Marriage Law (Amendment)

3. Resolution of the National People's Congress on Amending Article 45 of the Constitution

1981:

June 10:

1. Provisional Act on Punishing Dereliction of Duties of Military Personnel

2. Resolution of the Standing Committee of the National People's Congress on Strengthening the Work of Interpretation of Laws.

3. Decision of the Standing Committee of the National People's Congress on the Question of Approving Death Sentences

4. Decision of the Standing Committee on the National People's Congress on Handling Reform-through-Labor Criminals or Reeducation-through-Labor Personnel Who Have Escaped or Committed Criminal Offenses Again

December 13:

1. Economic Contract Law

2. Joint Venture Income Tax Law

1982:

March 8:

1. Decision of the Standing Committee of the National People's Congress on Severely Punishing Criminals Who Have Severely Undermined the Economy

2. Civil Procedure Law (Trial Implementation)
April 14: Act on Public Notary (Issued by the State Council)
August 23:
    1. Maritime Environmental Protection Law
    2. Trademarks Law
November 19:
    1. Law on the Protection of Cultural Materials
    2. Food Sanitation Law (Trial Implementation)
December 4: Constitution
December 10:
    1. Organic Law of the National People's Congress
    2. Organic Law of the State Council
    3. Organic Law of the Local People's Congress and the Local People's Government at Various Levels (Revised)
    4. Electoral Law for the National People's Congress and the Local People's Congress at Various Levels (Revised)

1983:
March 12: Provisional Regulations on Control of Some Cutting Tools (Promulgated by the Ministry of Public Security with the Approval of the State Council)
September 2:
    1. Decision of the Standing Committee of the National People's Congress on Severely Punishing Criminals Who Have Gravely Endangered the Public Security of the Society
    2. Decision of the Standing Committee of the National People's Congress on the Procedure to Swiftly Try Criminals Who Have Gravely Endangered the Public Security of the Society.
    3. Decision of the Standing Committee on the Revision of the Organic Law of the People's Courts
    4. Decision of the Standing Committee of the National People's Congress on the Revision of the Organic Law of the People's Procuratorates
    5. Decision of the Standing Committee of the National People's Congress on the Exercise by the State Security Organ [Ministry of State Security] of the Functions and Powers of Public Security Organs in Conducting Investigations, Detentions, Pre-trial Hearings, and Arrests.
    6. Law on the Safety of Maritime Traffic
September 20: Regulations on the Implementation of the Law on Joint Ventures Using Chinese and Foreign Investment (Promulgated by the State Council)

1984:
March 12: Patent Law
May 11: Law on the Prevention of Water Pollution
May 31:
    1. Law on Self-Government of National [Minority] Regions
    2. Military Service Law
September 20:
    1. Forestry Law

2. Law Governing Drugs
1985:
January 21: Accounting Law
March 21: Foreign Economic Contract Law
April 10: Law on Inheritance
June 18: Law on Grasslands
September 6:
    1. Law on Measurement
    2. Act on Identity Cards of Residents
November 22:
    1. Law Governing the Entry and Exit of Foreigners
    2. Law Governing the Entry and Exit of Citizens

1986:
January 20: Fishery Law
March 19: Mineral Resources Law
April 12: General Principles of Civil Law
June 25: Law Governing Land [Use]
September 5:
    1. Act on Diplomatic Privileges and Immunities
    2. Security Administration and Punishment Act (Revised)
December 2:
    1. Law on Enterprise Bankruptcy (Trial Implementation)
    2. Law on Border Sanitation and Quarantine
    3. Postal Administration Law
    4. Election Law for National People's Congress and Local People's Congresses at Different Levels (Amendment)
    5. Organic Law on Local People's Congresses and Local People's Governments at Various Levels (Amendment)
    6. Decision of the Standing Committee of the National People's Congress on Establishing the Ministry of Supervision

1987:
January 20: Customs Law
June 23: Technology Contract Law
September 5: Law on the Prevention of Air Pollution
November 24:
    1. Organic Law on Village Committee (Trial Implementation)
    2. Procedural Rules of the Standing Committee of the National People's Congress

1988:
January 21: Water Law
April 12: Amendment to Articles 10 and 11 of the Constitution
April 13:
    1. Law on Industrial Enterprises Owned by the Whole People
    2. Law on Chinese-Foreign Cooperative Joint Ventures
September 5: Law on Guarding State Secrets
November 8: Law on the Protection of Wild Animals

One important law the PRC has not yet completely enacted is a Civil Law. In 1949 the PRC abolished all laws of the Republic of China, including the Civil Code. In 1982 the PRC abandoned the idea of enacting a comprehensive civil law and decided to draft a general collection of basic principles.[18] On April 12, 1986, the General Principles of Civil Law was promulgated.[19] But, unlike the Civil Law of other countries, there are no special parts (obligation, property, family law, succession, and so forth) to follow the general principles.

The chairman of the drafting committee, Wang Hanbin, in presenting the draft to the National People's Congress, stated that the lack of special parts would be compensated for to a certain extent by other special laws on civil matters such as the Economic Contract Law, the Foreign Economic Contract Law, the Trademarks Law, the Patent Law, the Marriage Law, and the Inheritance Law. The gaps would just have to remain for a time.[20] As pointed out, however, by an American specialist on Chinese law:

> The difficulty with this is the extent of the gaps. There is almost nothing on property except for the two types of intellectual property. The question of how authorized interests in land are to be conveyed is not treated. Nor is there any provision on the transfer of chattels (movables). Indeed, movables and immovables are not even defined or differentiated. The economic Contracts Law is fairly complete, but it does not apply to noneconomic contracts, and it would require considerable work to factor out the general principles of contracts law from it (formation, for instance). The provisions on juristic persons in the General Provisions make constant reference to laws that do not yet exist. The result is that it will not be possible to use this act as it stands. It can only be used by means of supplementary statutes, regulations, and treaties, or, of course, precedents if they are available. In other words, the enactment of this statute did not change Chinese civil law much.[21]

Despite the extensive legislative activities in the post-Mao period, the PRC still lacks many important laws and regulations; therefore, one major item in the PRC's Seventh Five-Year Plan (1987–92) is enacting more laws and regulations. According to an interview with the Deputy Director of the Legal Bureau of the State Council, Wang Shirong, in April 1987 the Bureau plans to draft fifty laws and three hundred administrative regulations in the next five years,[22] covering eleven areas: financial planning and economic supervision; natural and economic resources; labor, urban, and rural reconstruction and environmental protection; external economic relations; science and technology, education, health, and family planning; public security; judicial administration; civil affairs; national defense; and foreign affairs. Most laws and regulations will be in the areas relating to economics. Moreover, the Bureau plans to screen more than three thousand administrative regulations or documents of a regulatory nature promulgated between 1949 and 1984 to abrogate those that are no longer needed or are outdated.[23]

Structural Reorganization of the Judicial System

The 1978 Constitution revived the people's procuratorates, which had been abolished by the 1975 Constitution (Article 43); it also abolished the provisions on placing courts under the control of the administrative organ at the same level provided in the 1975 Constitution (Article 25). The 1982 Constitution further strengthened the position of the procuratorate by providing that "the people's procuratorates shall, in accordance with the law, exercise procuratorial power independently and are not subject to interference by administrative organs, public organizations, or individuals" (Article 131).

In 1979, the Ministry of Justice, which had been abolished in 1959, was restored to take charge of the judicial administrative work, compilation of laws, and legal research.[24]

Both the 1978 Constitution (Article 41, paragraph 3) and the 1979 Criminal Procedure Law (Article 26) explicitly recognize the right of an accused to defend himself; and the 1979 law also recognizes the right to hire a lawyer to defend one's case. In 1980, the Provisional Act on Lawyers was enacted, formally restoring the lawyer system that had been virtually abolished after 1957. The 1982 Constitution also provides that "the accused has the right of defense" (Article 125).

With respect to the structure of the public security organ (police), the 1979 Criminal Procedure Law and the revised Act on Arrest and Detention have placed restrictions on police powers regarding arrest, investigation, and search.[25] Moreover, the 1957 Security Adminstration and Punishment Act was revised on September 5, 1986.[26] Under this revised Act, any fine (up to 5,000 *renminbi* [people's dollar], approximately U.S. $1,350), detention (up to fifteen days) or compensation to the injured party imposed by a public security organ is now subject to judicial review. Formerly, the decision of a public security organ was final and could not be appealed to a court.[27] A public security organ, however, can still send a person to "reeducation through labor," i.e., to a labor camp, up to four years without judicial review.[28] Formerly, there was no time limit for "education through labor," and some remained in a labor camp for "reeducation" for as long as twenty years.

In June 1983, the PRC established a new Ministry of State Security to "ensure the security of the state and strengthen counterespionage work."[29] While the regular police work remains under the Ministry of Public Security, the new Ministry is to control the People's Armed Police Force, which was established in early 1983 to include the PRC's border guards and special units that guard government buildings, embassies, and residence compounds set aside for foreigners. This new ministry is similar to the KGB of the Soviet Union.[30]

Restoring and Expanding Legal Education and Research

Legal education was virtually suspended during the Cultural Revolution period. Although in 1974 the Law Department of Beijing University reopened on a limited basis with about sixty students for a three-year program,[31] the students are selected on the basis of their class and political backgrounds rather than their academic competence. In 1977, the PRC restored the system of nationwide university entrance examinations for high school graduates, replacing the admission of students based primarily on political background as instituted during the Cultural Revolution period. In the same year the Beijing University expanded its educational program to four years, including law. In the fall of 1980, about 230 additional law students were enrolled, bringing the total number of law students enrolled to 570.[32]

Since 1977, law departments that had existed prior to the Cultural Revolution have begun to reopen, and new law departments have been formed. Similarly, the political-legal institutes that were suspended during the Cultural Revolution have also been reopened. There are in 1987 some thirty-five departments of law at the universities in the PRC, one China University of Political Science and Law, and four institutes of Political Science and Law, with a total enrollment of more than twenty-five thousand.[33] In addition, the Ministry of Justice has established twenty-eight judicial schools, twenty-seven cadre schools on political science and law, and other ad hoc short-term institutes for judicial personnel. Each year, more than twenty thousand cadres have been given basic legal education.[34]

Legal research was totally suspended during the Cultural Revolution and the only academic association for law, the Chinese Association of Political Science and Law, was in fact dissolved. Virtually no scholarly law books and articles were published during that period. Things began to change after the death of Mao.

In 1977, the Philosophy and Social Science Division of the Chinese Academy of Sciences was separated from the Academy and reorganized as the Chinese Academy of Social Sciences. An Institute of Law was established under the Academy. The Institute soon sponsored a ten-day Conference on Legal Research Planning that was held on March 21–31, 1979. It set forth an outline for a seven-year legal research plan.[35] The Institute, law departments of universities, and institutes of political science and law also began to translate foreign legal works and to publish studies on various subjects of law.

Legal journal publications were resumed and expanded. The following are some important ones now in circulation:

Faxue yanjiu (Studies in law), bimonthly, 1979– (Institute of Law of the Chinese Academy of Social Sciences).

Minzhu yu fazhi (Democracy and the legal system), now translated as Democracy and legality), monthly, 1979– (Shanghai Law Association and East China Institute of Political Science and law). This is probably the largest circulated law journal in the world, with a million copies printed for each issue.

Faxue yi cong (Law translation series), bimonthly, 1980– (Institute of Law of the Chinese Academy of Social Sciences).

Guowai faxue (Foreign law), bimonthly, 1980– (Department of Law, Beijing University).

Faxue (Legal science), monthly, 1981– (East China Institute of Political Science and Law). This journal had begun publication in 1957, but was suspended in the early 1960s.

Zhengfa luntan (Tribune of political science and law), bimonthly, 1985– (China University of Political Science and Law).

Zhongguo faxue (Law of China), at first published quarterly, now bimonthly, 1984– (China Law Society).

Faxue pinglun (Law review), bimonthly, 1983– (Department of Law, Wuhan University).

Faxue zazhi (Law magazine), bimonthly, 1980—

Fazhi jianshe (Law and order), bimonthly, 1984– (Ministry of Justice).

Zhengshi yu falu (Political science and law), bimonthly, 1982– (Institute of Law of the Shanghai Academy of Social Sciences).

Zhongguo guojifa niankan (Chinese yearbook of international law), 1982– (Chinese Society of International Law).

In addition to professional journals, increasing numbers of scholarly legal articles have been published in university academic journals on humanities or social sciences.

In 1980 the PRC government resumed its two important official gazettes that contain legal matters: *Quanguo renmin daibiao dahui changwu weiyuanhui gongbao* (Gazette of the Standing Committee of the National People's Congress) and *Zhonghua renmin gongheguo guowuyuan gongbao* (Gazette of the State Council of the People's Republic of China). In 1985, for the first time in the PRC's legal development, a quarterly publication *Zhonghua renmin gongheguo zuigao renmin fayuan gongbao* (Gazette of the Supreme People's Court of the People's Republic of China) began to appear, which publishes some court judgments, replies by the Supreme People's Court to questions of law submitted by local courts, and other related matters. Since 1979, a number of scholarly conferences on various subjects of law have been held, Chinese lawyers have been sent to visit foreign legal institutes or judicial organs; foreign lawyers, judges, or prosecutors have also been invited to China.

In 1982, the China Law Society was founded. It has branch law societies in provinces or municipalities under the direct administration of the State Council. It also set up branches to study different subjects of law, such as constitutional law, civil law, and others. It has 2,500 individual members, 29 group members, and 74 local branches, with a total membership of more than 10,000.[36] In 1982, the Chinese Society of International Law was founded and it now has several hundred members.

Publicizing Law and Legality among the Officials and the People

The chaos and lawless situation of the Cultural Revolution have caused both officials and the people to disregard and disrespect law, order, and legality. To deal with this situation, the PRC has launched a massive legal education campaign to familiarize people with the substance of the Criminal Law and Criminal Precedure Law. Also, because of the increase in juvenile crimes, the PRC has conducted campaigns in universities, colleges, and high schools on the observance of law. All college and university students, since the fall semester of 1979, must complete either a special course on the legal system or a general course on politics with a strong emphasis on law. A popular newspaper on law—*Zhongguo fazhi bao* (China legal news)—began publication in 1980 to promote general legal education. Furthermore, traditional operas and contemporary plays with the theme of law and justice are being performed on television and onstage.

At a national conference on law propagation and education held in June 1985 by the Ministry of Justice and the Propaganda Department of the Communist Party of China, a Five-Year Plan for Spreading Basic Legal Knowledge among All Citizens was formulated. It is reported that more than 200,000 people have been trained to explain the law to the people. Many popular books on law were also published for use by workers, peasants, and soldiers.[37] On November 22, 1985, the Standing Committee of the National People's Congress adopted the "Resolution of the NPC Standing Committee on Basically Popularizing General Knowledge of Law among Citizens." This movement was scheduled to begin in 1986 and is to continue on a regular basis for "the next five years or so" and be "gradually institutionalized." The main targets of the movement are cadres and young people; the latter are to be reached primarily through the schools.[38]

Participation in International Conventions

Since the death of Mao, the PRC has participated in many international conventions, several primarily related to human rights, such as conventions on genocide, refugees, and racial or sex discrimination.[39] These particular conventions, however, have limited impact on China's domestic legal system.

The PRC has not yet signed the International Covenant on Economic, Social, and Cultural Rights and the International Covenant on Civil and Political Rights adopted by the General Assembly of the United Nations in 1966. In the 1984 Sino-British Joint Declaration on the Question of Hong Kong,[40] Annex 1, Article 13, paragraph 4, however, it is provided that "the provisions of the International Covenant on Civil and Political Rights and the International Covenant on Economic, Social, and Cultural Rights as applied to Hong Kong [now by the British Government][41] should remain in force" for a period of fifty years after 1997, the year specified in the Joint Declaration when the PRC is to assume control of Hong Kong. This arrangement would create a strange situation because only part of China [Hong Kong] would be subject to both covenants. In view of this contradiction, there were indications that the PRC intended to participate in the covenants after the Hong Kong agreement. On November 24, 1986, the Agence France-Press (AFP) reported from Beijing that the PRC was likely to sign both covenants soon.[42] At the time of this writing [October 1989], however, the PRC has not signed either covenant. While one can only speculate as to the reasons for the PRC's failure to do so, it seems reasonable to assume that the PRC appears to be concerned about the educational and promotional consequences in the PRC of both covenants. This concern may be strengthened by the outbreak of student demonstrations, demanding more freedoms and democracy, in various Chinese cities between December 1986 and January 1987,[43] as well as the student demonstration between April and June 1989 at Tiananmen Square in Beijing that resulted in the massacre of students by the PRC military forces on June 4, 1989, and the mass arrest of students and others afterward.[44] Moreover, some Chinese domestic laws, regulations, and practices are not consistent with the standards provided in the 1948 Universal Declaration of Human Rights and the two covenants to implement and expand the rights provided in the Declaration.[45]

Salient Issues and Problems

Despite the reform of the legal system as summarized in the previous section, there are certain basic issues that the present reforms are unable or unwilling to overcome. The PRC has made it clear that its legal system is subject to the so-called Four Basic Principles—namely, keeping the socialist road, upholding the dictatorship of the proletariat, party leadership, and Marxism-Leninism-Mao Zedong thought. These principles were also incorporated in the Preamble of the 1982 Constitution. Moreover, Article 1 of the Constitution states that the PRC is "a socialist state under the people's democratic dictatorship led by the working class and based on the alliance of workers and peasants." It also provides that the "socialist system is the basic system" and "sabotage of the socialist system by any organization or individual is prohibited." Article 3 states that "the state organs of the People's Republic of China apply the principle of democratic centralism." These provisions make it clear that the PRC is essentially a totalitarian system where no challenge to its socialist system is allowed and that the decision-making process is in the hands of a few in the name of "centralism." The following is a concise analysis of certain basic issues of the Chinese legal system and the limit of its reform.

Constitutional Guarantee for Citizens' Rights [46]

Generally speaking, except for the missing stipulation on freedom of residence,[47] the 1982 Constitution restores or expands the provisions on individual rights and freedoms in the 1954 Constitution. The most notable provision is for equality before the law for all citizens of the People's Republic of China (Article 33). In religious freedom, the Constitution drops the right to propagate atheism as contained in the 1978 Constitution. It states that "the state protects normal religious activities" but adds that no religious affairs may be "subject to any foreign domination" (Article 36). The Constitution guarantees the "freedoms and privacy of correspondence" and at the same time permits public security units of procuratorial organs to censor correspondence in accordance with the procedures prescribed by law "to meet the needs of state security or of investigation into criminal offenses" (Article 40).

Among the major new additions of the Constitution is the provision that the "personal dignity of citizens of the People's Republic of China is inviolable. Insult, libel, false charges, or slander against citizens by any means is prohibited" (Article 38). There is also an added statement on the freedom of the person: "Unlawful deprivation or restriction of citizens' freedom of the person by detention or other means is prohibited; unlawful search of the person of citizens is prohibited" (Article 37). The Constitution specifically stresses that the rights of citizens are inseparable from their duties (Article 33). The Chinese people not only have the right but also the obligation to work (Article 42) and to receive education (Article 46). Added to the list of citizens' duties are to safeguard state secrets (Article 54) and to refrain from infringing "upon the interests of the state, of society, and of the collective or upon the lawful freedoms and rights of other citizens" when exercising their freedoms and rights (Article 51). These vaguely phrased provisions can be invoked by the authorities to restrict the citizens' freedoms stated in the Constitution.

The Constitution provides in Article 41 the right of citizens to criticize and to file complaints with state organs and establishes the principle of state compensation for infringing on the civil rights of citizens.

Besides the provisions contained in chapter 2 of the Constitution, there are other provisions closely related to the implementation of citizens' rights and duties under the Constitution. Chapter 1, Article 5, of the Constitution establishes the principle of supremacy of the Constitution. There was no comparable article in any previous PRC constitutions. Therefore, the inclusion of this article in the 1982 Constitution clearly demonstrates that the leadership in 1982 was more serious about enhancing the status of the Constitution in the PRC.

Moreover, the 1982 Constitution restores the provisions of the 1954 Constitution on judicial and procuratorial independence in Articles 126 and 131 of chapter 3 of the Constitution.

Despite the listing of many rights of Chinese citizens in the Constitution, there appears to have been no effective mechanism created in the Constitution to prevent the legislative and administrative organs from curtailing such rights and increasing the citizens' duties in disregard of the constitutional provisions.

Theoretically, the Constitution of the PRC is the supreme legal instrument, and according to Article 5, paragraph 2, "no law or administrative or local rules and regulations shall contravene the Constitution." The so-called basic statutes (laws) rank second in the hierarchy of legal order, and they can only be enacted and amended by the National People's Congress (Article 62, paragraph 3). Next in binding force are statutes enacted by the Standing Committee of the National People's Congress (Article 67, paragraph 2).

The State Council can, however, exercise the power "to adopt administrative measures, enact administrative rules, and issue decisions and orders in accordance with the Constitution and the statutes" (Article 89, paragraph 1). Although under Article 67, paragraph 7, of the Constitution, the Standing Committee of the NPC can exercise the power to annul those administrative rules and regulations, decisions, or orders of the State Council that contravene the Constitution or the statute, so far no such case has ever arisen. Moreover, there is no procedure for an individual to challenge the legality of administrative rules issued by the State Council.

In accordance with Article 5, paragraph 2, of the Constitution, the laws enacted by the NPC should not contravene the Constitution. In reality, however, the NPC can enact any laws it wishes in disregard of the spirit and letter of the Constitution. This is because the Constitution has given the power to interpret the Constitution to the NPC's Standing Committee (Article 67, paragraph 1). It is beyond imagination that this subordinate organ would interpret a law enacted by its parent organ, i.e., the NPC, as "unconstitutional."

Moreover, despite the fact that the Constitution restricts the NPC Standing Committee's power only "to enact, when the National People's Congress is not in session, partial supplements and amendments to statutes enacted by the National People's Congress provided that they do not contravene the basic principles of these statutes" (Article 67, paragraph 3), in fact the Standing Committee can do as it pleases, with respect to the statutes enacted by the NPC, because it has the power to interpret statutes (Article 67, paragraph 4). It is beyond imagination that the Standing Committee would interpret its supplement or amendment to an NPC statute as contravening the basic principles of that statute.

Party Control and Judicial Independence

Despite the fact that the 1954 Constitution and the Organic Law of the People's Court all provide for judicial independence, legal scholars and practitioners who took this provision seriously were branded in 1957 as "rightists" challenging party leadership. In practice, there was no judicial independence, and the party dominated all judicial work throughout the system of the so-called *Shuji pian* ("approving cases by the [party] secretary").[48]

In August 1980, Jiang Hua, then President of the Supreme People's Court, announced that the party decided to abolish this system. In spite of this announcement, there is evidence that party officials have continued to interfere in the performance of adjudication functions by the judicial organs, as some cases reported in the authoritative *Renmin ribao* (People's daily) have indicated.[49]

Moreover, abolishing the practice of "approving cases by the secretary" does not mean the party would totally relinquish its control over the judiciary. In his address given in November 1981, Jiang Hua said that the courts should take the initiative to report to and seek instructions from the party committee over significant policy questions and the handling of important and complicated cases. The court should also regularly keep the party committees informed of the conditions of judicial work. In fact, judicial cadres in China today still find it prudent, as in the past, to secure advice and consent from party committees in dealing with many criminal cases. Sometimes it takes direct intervention from party committees to settle cases of a controversial or political nature.

Furthermore, there is no legal sanction against a party committee's interference with judicial independence. A party committee in a county of Henan ordered the court there to sentence an innocent person to imprisonment. When the president of the court refused the request, he was dismissed and the party committee appointed an acting president to render the decision. On appeal, the case was reversed. No sanction was imposed on the county party committee except that it "accepted the reprimand" of its superior organ.[50]

Vagueness and Flexibility of Chinese Legal Provisions

Despite the PRC's effort to establish a stable legal system, it has retained some of its vaguely drafted earlier laws and regulations, and, in the post-Mao legislation, it has also included vague, flexible provisions in major laws. Several laws containing such provisions are explained below:

1. In 1951, the PRC promulgated the Provisional Act on Guarding State Secrets.[51] Article 2 includes almost all information not officially made public as "state secrets" and a "catchall" provision on "all other state affairs which should be kept secret." This law was republished in the authoritative *Renmin ribao* on April 11, 1980, to warn the public.[52]

On September 5, 1988, the Law on Guarding State Secrets was enacted and entered into force on May 1, 1989.[53] This law replaces the 1951 Provisional Act. It is more specific in defining the scope of state secrets and sets a time limit and procedure for releasing certain secrets. Article 8, after listing six items of state secrets, contains a catchall provision by authorizing the authorities in charge of guarding state secrets to designate other items as state secrets. Article 10, paragraph 3 provides that the concrete scope of state secrets should be announced. This is an improvement over the 1951 Act, which treated all materials or information not officially published as state secrets. In fact, however, this law expands the scope of punishment for leaking state secrets. According to Article 13 of the 1951 Act, only when a person is selling or leaking state secrets to a domestic or foreign enemy, or selling or leaking secrets to a domestic or foreign unscrupulous merchant (*jianshang*) can he be held responsible for a counterrevolutionary offense. Similarly, Article 97 of the 1979 Criminal Law provides that only when a person is supplying information to an enemy, or joining an enemy secret service or espionage organization, or receiving orders from an enemy, can he be charged with a counterrevolutionary offense. Therefore, a citizen passing or leaking secrets to a foreigner or corporation from a country having diplomatic relations with the PRC cannot be charged with a counterrevolutionary offense; he can only be charged with committing a malfeasance under Article 186 of the Criminal Law for divulging "important state secrets and the situation is serious." The maximum punishment for this offense is seven years fixed term imprisonment, whereas the maximum punishment for a counterrevolutionary offense under Article 97 is life imprisonment or death.[54] If the state secret leaked is "not" important and the situation "not" serious, a citizen cannot even be charged under Article 186. Article 31 of the new State Secret Law makes all leaking of state secrets (*not* limited to "important state secrets"), if the situation is "serious," subject to the punishment prescribed in Article 186 of the Criminal Law. Moreover, the Standing Committee of the National People's Congress also adopted a resolution on September 5, 1988, to amend the Criminal Law as follows:

> A person who steals, detects, purchases or illegally provides state secrets to an organ, organization, or personnel outside our country shall be sentenced to a fixed-term imprisonment between five and ten years; if the situation is minor, he shall be sentenced to no more than five years, detention, or deprivation of political rights; if the situation is serious, he shall be sentenced to imprisonment for more than ten years, life imprisonment or death and deprivation of political rights.[55]

2. The administrative sanction of "reeducation through labor," formerly adopted by the State Council in 1957,[56] is retained. Under this system, a public security organ (police) can send a person to a labor camp for up to four years[57] without judicial review for one or more of the following reasons:

a. Those who do not engage in proper employment, those who behave like hooligans, and those who, although they steal, swindle, or engage in other such acts, are not pursued for criminal responsibility, who violate security administration and whom repeated education fails to change.

b. Those counterrevolutionaries and antisocialist reactionaries who, because their crimes are minor, are not pursued for criminal responsibility, who receive the sanction of expulsion from an organ, organization, enterprise, school, or other such unit, and who are without a way of earning a living.

c. Those persons who have the capacity to labor but who for a long period refuse to labor or who destroy discipline and interfere with public order, and who [thus] receive the sanction of expulsion from an organ, organization, enterprise, school, or other such unit and who have no way of earning a living.

d. Those who do not obey work assignments or arrangements for getting them employment or for transferring them to other employment, or those who do not accept the admonition to engage in labor and production, who ceaselessly and unreasonably make trouble and interfere with public affairs and whom repeated education fails to change.

Although the PRC does not consider this to be criminal sanctions, an Amnesty International report indicates: "The work required of and the discipline imposed on offenders [in this category and those criminals sentenced to reform through labor] are similar. Both categories have to work very hard for an average of eight to ten hours a day and the stigma attached to both punishments is said to be practically the same."[58] Moreover, an internal (unpublished) regulation enacted in 1982 by the Ministry of Public Security expands the scope of persons subject to reeducation through labor by including "anti-[Communist] party elements."[59]

Another type of administrative sanction is the so-called shelter and investigation (*Shourong shen-cha*) imposed by the police. The measure is based on an unpublished "Notice Concerning the Incorporation of the Forced Labor and the Shelter and Investigation into Reeducation Through Labor," issued by the State Council, although the date of the document is not clear.[60] According to a published article, people who commit minor offenses and whose identities, addresses, or backgrounds are unclear, or who are suspected of having roamed from place to place committing crimes or forming criminal gangs may be subjected to "shelter and investigation" by the police in a period of one to three months.[61]

The legal basis for this type of detention is not clear. According to another published article, among the many problems created by this measure are the lack of strict and rigorous approval procedures in subjecting a person to shelter and investigation, imposing corporal punishment and torture on the detainees to extract confessions, exceeding the time limit for holding a person in detention, and poor health and sanitation conditions in the places of detention.[62]

3. During the Maoist period, judges were only interested in accepting evidence to prove the guilty charge of an accused and rejecting evidence favorable to an accused.[63] The 1979 Criminal Procedure Law attempts to correct this attitude in Article 32, which provides: "The adjudicating, procuratorial, and investigative personnel must, in accordance with the legal process, collect various kinds of evidence to prove whether the defendant is guilty or innocent, or the degree of seriousness of the offense committed." This law still does not establish the principle of presumption of innocence in criminal trials, however. In fact, courts assume the guilt of any person brought to trial.[64]

4. According to Article 5 of the revised 1979 Arrest and Detention Act, in carrying out an apprehension or in making an arrest, the police must produce a warrant. The family of the detainee or the arrested should be notified of the reason for the action and the place of confinement within twenty-four hours, "unless in a situation *where investigation may be hampered* or notification is impossible." The escape clause authorizes the PRC authorities to hold a person incommunicado indefinitely, from several days to more than a year. A Hong Kong Chinese Hansen Huang was arrested in early 1982, but his mother did not hear from him until two years later when the PRC's Ministry of Justice announced his sentence of fifteen years' imprisonment on a charge of espionage.[65] On January 11, 1987, a Chinese student, Yang Wei, was detained in Shanghai

after taking part in the student demonstration there for free speech and democracy,[66] but the notice of detention was issued retroactively on May 15, 1987.[67]

On November 7, 1987, a public prosecution for counterrevolutionary activities was filed against Yang. According to Article 92 of the 1979 Criminal Procedure Law, the maximum detention period for a suspect is three months, unless the Standing Committee of the National People's Congress approves the extension of detention. Yang was detained for almost ten months before he was indicted. During that period, his parents were not allowed to visit him for several months.[68] There was no indication of approval of his extended detention by the NPC's Standing Committee. On December 21, 1987, a court sentenced Yang to two years' imprisonment for inciting unrest and spreading propaganda for the New York-based Chinese Alliance for Democracy during the student demonstration and protests in Shanghai in late December 1986 and early 1987.[69]

5. The 1979 Chinese Criminal Law does not recognize the principle of "no punishment without preexisting law making the act a crime" (*nullum crimen, nulla poena sine lege*). Article 79 of the Law provides that: "A person who commits a crime not explicitly defined in the specific parts of the Criminal Law may be convicted and sentenced, after obtaining the approval of the Supreme People's Court, according to the most similar article in this Law."[70]

Moreover, many provisions of Chinese Criminal Law referred to "according to circumstances," "minor circumstances," "serious circumstances," or "harm to country and people"; the length of imprisonment or even the death penalty depends on such vague definitions.[71]

Internal (Unpublished) Rules, Regulations, or Decrees

Although the post-Mao PRC has made official efforts to publish laws and regulations so as to make them available to the general public and foreigners, there are thousands of administrative rules, regulations, or decrees that the PRC considers *neibu* (internal) documents and these are neither published nor available to the people and foreigners.[72] Thus, in dealing with the PRC authorities, one is always in a "no-win" position. As explained earlier, there is no legal procedure for a person to challenge the PRC's administrative rules, regulations, or decrees on the grounds of their violations of the Constitution, laws, or published regulations.[73] Even if one could get a copy of internal rules, regulations, or decrees of an administrative agency, one cannot use that document to challenge the decision of that agency, because the mere fact of acquiring an internal document may be in violation of the 1951 Provisional Act on Guarding State Secrets, or after May 1, 1989, the Law on Guarding State Secrets.[74]

After Western reporters in Tibet reported disturbances there in early October 1987,[75] PRC authorities ordered them to leave Tibet within forty-eight hours on the ground that they were violating reporting regulations issued last year concerning foreign news coverage in China. The PRC officials in the Tibetan Foreign Affairs

Office invoked Article 16 of the alleged regulations which provides that foreign reporters wishing to cover news outside Beijing must apply ten days in advance with the local foreign affairs office. Their requests are subject to approval by local officials. Western reporters argued that they had never seen the regulations, and they asked why, if their presence there was illegal, some officials in the office had met with them earlier for interviews. The Chinese officials replied that the regulations were secret.[76]

Torture

In view of the widespread use of torture and reliance on confessions in criminal trials in the Maoist period, the 1979 Criminal Procedure Law specifically provides in Article 32 that "it is strictly forbidden to exhort confessions by torture or under duress and to collect evidence by threat, enticement, deceit, or other 'illegal means.' " Despite this prohibition, according to a recent Amnesty International report[77] that is based primarily on published Chinese sources and interviews with past prisoners, widespread torture persists in the PRC and the government efforts to curb it are being thwarted by the public security (police) and Communist party officials.

Most victims are criminal suspects who are beaten or whipped and hung up by the arms, assaulted with electric batons, subject to the tightening of handcuffs so they cut to the bones, around-the-clock interrogation, and kicking and hair pulling to force them to confess. Convicted prisoners are sometimes severely ill treated for breaches of prison discipline. Some have been held in solitary confinement for years with no contact with their families or fellow inmates, and some of these have lost their minds.

It does not appear that the officials responsible for torturing innocent people, suspects, or prisoners have been punished according to law. A deputy Party Secretary of a town in Hunan Province named Huang Chongfu, who had "frequently bound and beaten" nine innocent people in August and September 1983, was sentenced to a year imprisonment after the victims persistently complained, but the sentence was suspended in 1986.[78]

The official efforts to stop torture have focused on the work of the procuracies. Since 1986, the procuracies have been instructed to give a high priority to the investigation of cases of torture and other abuses by officials. In many cases, local Communist party officials obstructed the investigation. Some local people's congresses have also paid attention to this problem by issuing instructions to the procuracies or making investigation of turture cases themselves. It is not clear whether these measures are effective in dealing with the torture situation.[79]

After the June 4, 1989, Tiananmen Square massacre of students by the PRC military forces, the PRC authorities have engaged in mass arrest of prodemocracy protesters. It is reported that the protesters have been severely beaten by the police and the soldiers, and it is feared that detainees may be put under strong pressures, including torture, to confess to crimes or to denounce others involved in the protests.[80]

The Problem of Implementing Court Decisions in Economic Cases

With more economic freedoms granted to the people and increased economic acitivites, the number of cases of economic dispute has increased rapidly. According to the Work Report of the Supreme People's Court presented to the Fifth Meeting of the Sixth National People's Congress on April 6, 1987, Chinese courts accepted 322,000 cases on economic disputes in 1986, an increase of 42.11 percent over the previous year. Ninety percent of these cases relate to economic contract disputes.[81] There has been increasing failure, however, to carry out decisions on economic cases.

Using the figure supplied by the Supreme People's Court, a Chinese newspaper *Economic News* said that 20 percent of the courts' decisions on economic dispute could not be implemented. In Henan Province, for example, 4,148 (23.5 percent) of 18,106 economic case decisions were not implemented in 1986. There are several reasons for the failure to implement the courts' decisions. First, many debtors are unable to pay the court-assessed compensation or damages. Second, some cadres tend to protect the losing parties in their own areas by undermining the implementation of the courts' decisions. For example, some cadres ordered the banks not to cooperate with the courts when they were ordered to transfer the money from the losing party to the winning party. Third, some courts did not pay sufficient attention to the problem of implementation of the courts' decisions. Fourth, the courts lack sufficient personnel to see that court decisions are fully implemented. There are now 3,400 courts of various levels in China, but they have only 1,301 people among them to enforce decisions in economic disputes.[82]

The Shortage of Lawyers and Lack of Respect for Lawyers

The PRC had more than twenty thousand lawyers in 1985[83] and the number is expected to reach fifty thousand by 1990.[84] Among the twenty thousand lawyers, one-third are full-time, one-third have not yet acquired the certificates of law, and the remaining third are part-time lawyers. There are thirty-eight counties in the country that do not have law officers.[85] According to a PRC Vice Minister of Justice, among all cases handled by the courts only 6 percent are represented by lawyers; for criminal cases, only 20 percent are represented by lawyers.[86]

Despite the severe shortage of lawyers, many lawyers decide to quit the profession and thus further aggravate the situation. Two major factors make law practice unattractive to law graduates. First, many people consider lawyers as "those who speak for criminals" and some officials regard the defense prepared by a lawyer as a challenge to their authority. According to the PRC's press reports, government and party officials sometimes expel lawyers from courts, arrest or detain them, and even persecute them. Judges also harbor a negative attitude toward lawyers and, in one case, a lawyer was handcuffed to a tree for eighty minutes.[87] Second, lawyers' salaries are low and their working conditions poor. Some lawyers' offices have no typewriters, copiers, tape recorders, or cameras.[88]

In Jilin Province, one-third of the lawyers have quit since 1984. Thus, in 1985 only 8.6 percent of criminal cases and 8.1 percent of civil cases in the province were represented by lawyers.[89] At present, it does not appear that the PRC is taking any effective measures to improve the social status of lawyers, their working conditions, or their salaries.

The Anticrime Campaign in 1981–1985

Since the PRC began to allow more economic freedom and to exert less control on the movement of people, the crime rate has risen significantly. The high unemployment rate among youth is a main cause of increasing crime. The crime rate continued to rise in 1981 and on June 10, 1981, the NPC Standing Committee adopted two resolutions to deal with the problem. The first granted to higher people's courts, for the period of 1981–83, the right to approve death sentences for murderers, robbers, rapists, bomb throwers, arsonists, and saboteurs.[90] Under the Criminal Procedure Law, however, a death sentence must be approved by the Supreme Court. The second resolution provided for heavier penalties for escapees who are undergoing reform or reeducation through labor.[91] A nationwide campaign against crime was then launched.

During the campaign, the Chinese press frequently reported mass meetings to pronounce death sentences and the immediate execution of the accused after the meeting. Despite the existence of all procedural safeguards provided in the Criminal Procedure Law, Chinese judicial authorities apparently paid little attention to them. For example, on June 23, 1981, the Nanjing Municipal Intermediate People's Court convened a mass rally, attended by ten thousand, where a murderer named Luo received the death penalty and was immediately executed. It took only eight days for the entire legal process to transpire, from the arrest of Luo to his execution, including police investigation, prosecution, trial, sentencing, and his appeal to the Provincial Higher Court.[92]

Under China's Criminal Procedure Law, a copy of the indictment must be delivered to a defendant at least seven days before the court hearing. After receiving a court's judgment, the defendant can file his or her appeal within ten days. How the case of Luo was handled within eight days was not explained.

The anticrime campaign was intensified in 1983 and 1984. On September 2,

1983, the NPC Standing Committee adopted a resolution to amend Article 13 of the Organic Law of the People's Courts, enacted by the NPC, to allow the Supreme People's Court to delegate the authority to approve death sentences to the provincial-level higher people's courts in cases of murder, rape, robbery, the use of explosives, and other serious offenses.[93] Another resolution of the NPC Standing Commitee removed practically all guarantees of due process provided in the Criminal Procedural Law for persons accused of murder, rape, armed robbery, and other violent crimes.[94]

This resolution made ineffective Article 110 of the Criminal Procedure Law, which requires that the defendant must receive a copy of the indictment at least seven days before the trial in order to prepare his defense. It also shortened the time limit for appeals to three days instead of the ten days stipulated in Article 131 of the Criminal Procedure Law. In another resolution adopted on the same day, the NPC Standing Committee revised the Criminal Law, enacted by the NPC.[95] The revision increased sharply the number of capital offenses to cover virtually any serious crime, and ordered the courts to impose stiffer penalties, including execution, on persons convicted of violent crimes.

Under the amended Criminal Law and Criminal Procedure Law, a person charged with one of the violent or serious crimes could be executed within eight days or so from arrest, investigation, prosecution, sentencing, and appeal to execution.[96] Condemned offenders are usually paraded in public before execution and humiliated in other ways. For example, they are forced to keep their heads bowed and wear placards proclaiming their crimes. They are frequently executed in public, despite Article 155 of the Criminal Procedure Law that states: "the condemned should not be exposed to the public."

Despite the existence of a Criminal Procedure Law that provides for conducting "trials in public" (Article 8), little is known about the procedure followed at the trials of people sentenced to death, except the occasional release of scanty information on trials by the press or in legal periodicals. Public notices summarizing the cases of condemned offenders are usually posted outside the buildings of the court that has passed the sentences. The notices include biographical data about the condemned offenders, but they usually give almost no information about the procedures followed at the trials. According to various sources, such proceedings are very brief. Because the Chinese courts seek to conclude criminal cases quickly, it is almost impossible for the accused to exercise effectively his or her right of defense.[97]

A recent Chinese article revealed that during the anticrime campaign some Legal Adviser Offices, where Chinese lawyers are required to practice, were reluctant to accept cases for accused criminals. Some courts even rendered sentences before the trials, and a judgment was written up before the case was heard.[98] Since the Criminal Procedure Law refuses to adopt the principle of presumption of innocence, once a person is arrested he or she is almost certain to receive a criminal sanction.

The Tiananmen Square Massacre of June 4, 1989, and Subsequent Mass Arrest and Execution

In mid-April 1989, students began to protest and demonstrate at Tiananmen Square in Beijing, demanding an end to official corruption and calling for political and democratic reform. Their demands evoked widespread popular support and the protests developed into a prodemocracy movement. The movement soon spread to other major cities in China. Their protests and demonstrations were peaceful and in good order.[99] On May 20, 1989, the PRC authorities imposed martial law in Beijing.[100] In early June, the number of students gathered at Tiananmen Square decreased significantly. On June 4, 1989, however, the authorities used tanks and military forces to open fire against the students who remained there, resulting in at least several thousand casualties.[101] At least three hundred people are also reported to have been killed by PRC regular or security forces in Chengdu, the capital of Sichuan Province, following student protests there.[102] A number of civilians are reported to have been killed by security forces in Lanzhou, capital of Gansu Province.[103] The Chinese Communist government later justified its use of lethal forces by characterizing the democratic movement as a "counterrevolutionary rebellion" and even denied that a massacre ever occurred.[104] Since the massive military massacre in early June, at least four thousand people are officially reported to have been arrested throughout China in connection with the prodemocracy movement. Many believe the true number of detainees to be much higher. They include students, workers, peasants, teachers, writers, journalists, artists, academics, government officials, military officers, and unemployed people. The charges under which they are held include involvement in "counterrevolutionary activities," disrupting traffic or public order, attacking soldiers or military vehicles, sabotage, and looting. Those arrested are believed to be held incommunicado, without access to relatives or lawyers. Some are reported to have been severely beaten by police or soldiers and it is feared that detainees may still be subject to strong pressure—including the use of torture—to confess to crimes or to denounce others involved in the protests. Some have been executed after summary and unfair trials; many more executions than those officially reported are believed to have been carried out.[105]

In giving the order to massacre the students and in the subsequent arrest and execution of the students, the PRC authorities paid almost no attention to the Constitution and other relevant laws on arrest, detention, and the criminal procedure in the PRC.

Chinese Law and Foreign Trade and Investments

Before 1979, the PRC had practically no laws or regulations on economic activities relating to foreigners or foreign countries. In the past ten years, the NPC and its Standing Committee and the State Council have enacted more than seventy laws and regulations in this respect. Local people's congresses and their standing committees and local governments, however, have also enacted many local laws and regulations relating to foreign trade and investment. Internationally, the PRC has adhered to several international conventions and concluded bilateral treaties with various countries relating to international economic and trade relations.[106] The following is a list of major laws and regulations.[107]

Foreign Direct Investment

The National People's Congress has enacted the Law on Joint Ventures Using Chinese and Foreign Investment, the Foreign Investment Enterprise Law, the Income Tax Law on Joint Ventures Using Chinese and Foreign Investment, and the Income Tax Law on Foreign Investment Enterprises. The State Council has enacted an Implementing Act of the Law on Joint Ventures Using Chinese and Foreign Investment, Labor Administration Regulations for Joint Ventures Using Chinese and Foreign Investment, Provisional Act Governing Foreign Exchange, and regulations on labor, taxation, finance, land use, and others. In 1986, the State Council enacted Regulations Concerning Encouragement of Foreign Investment.

Foreign Economics and Trade

Foreign Economic Contract Law, Act on Inspection of Import and Export Commodities, Provisional Act on Licensing of Import and Export Goods, and others were enacted.

Sino-Foreign Economic and Technical Cooperation

Patent Law, Trademark Law, Act Governing Contracts to Import Technology, Measures Reviewing Contracts on Technology Transfer, and others were enacted.

Customs Administration

Customs Law, Regulations on Supervision for Tax Exemption of Imports and Exports of Goods Concerning Joint Ventures Using Chinese and Foreign Investment, and others were enacted.

Legislation Enacted for Special Economic Zones and Coastal Areas

The Standing Committee of the NPC adopted the Resolution on Delegating Authority to People's Congresses and Their Standing Committees of Fujian and Guangdong Provinces to Enact Various Economic Regulations in Their Special

Economic Zones. Shanghai and Tianjin Municipalities also enacted local regulations relating to foreign investments.

International Agreements

The PRC has adhered to the Convention Revising the Paris Convention of March 20, 1983, for the Protection of Industrial Property, enacted on July 14, 1976,[108] and the United Nations Convention on Contracts for the International Sale of Goods, enacted on April 11, 1980.[109] It concluded investment protection or avoidance of double taxation agreements with the United States, the United Kingdom, France, the Federal Republic of Germany, Austria, Singapore, and other countries.

According to Chinese authorities, up to July 1988, the PRC had given approval to 12,161 foreign firms to invest in China with a total value of U.S. $25 billion, of which 9.8 billion has already been invested.[110] But foreigners have many complaints about the investment and business environments in the PRC; many are increasingly doubtful that their dream of gaining access to vast Chinese markets will ever materialize. Western businessmen and diplomats recently pointed out that there was a 50 percent drop in foreign investment in the PRC in 1986 as evidence of the harsh environment.[111] All but a handful remain, plagued with problems of foreign exchange controls, disputes over contract interpretation, an inflexible bureaucracy, and high costs for business operations. These complaints relating to law are discussed as follows:[112]

First, it is evident that the laws on economic activities are inadequate and that the Chinese authorities make constant recourse to internal (unpublished) rules that are unknown to foreign investors and businessmen. A Chinese writer acknowledges this problem by pointing out that there are too many internal (unpublished) rules that are difficult for foreign businessmen to know about. Moreover, some important laws relating to foriegn economic relations, such as a Foreign Trade Law, have not been enacted.

Second, the extraordinary costs of doing business in China result from the Chinese authorities' arbitrarily setting a high price for foreign businessmen. Many are paying rents of $90,000 a year for a three-bedroom apartment, and proportionate amounts for office space. One American company was asked to pay $9,000 a month for a Chinese-trained high-technology specialist, more than ten times the specialist's take-home pay for one year. Foreigners have to pay substantially higher prices for airplane and railway tickets, for telephone use, and for hotel accommodations. Foreigners in all these areas have been marked for discrimination.

Third, primarily because of the PRC's low foreign exchange reserves, foreign firms have difficulty in repatriating their profits abroad.

Fourth, there is the problem of interference by Chinese officials in the operation of joint ventures.

Fifth, a hostile tax structure and tax administration often prevent foreign investors from evaluating the profitability of a proposed project.

Sixth, as a Chinese writer has pointed out, there are loopholes and contradictions among economic laws and regulations themselves and between those and other laws and regulations. There are also local laws and regulations that cannot be accommodated to the central legislation.[113]

Seventh, the most serious problem is contract negotiation. According to several American lawyers with extensive experience in dealing with the PRC, Chinese negotiators often refuse to permit foreign companies to write detailed contracts to protect their interests. Even after contracts are signed, it is common for the Chinese to insist on renegotiation. Sometimes Chinese government agencies will directly interfere with the performance of the contract by imposing new rules, conditions, or fees that affect the profitability of the foreign enterprise.[114]

It was reported that in view of the seriousness of the complaints of foreign investors in China the Chinese authorities were taking steps in 1988 to improve the investment environment in China in the following ways:[115]

1. enacting additional laws and regulations on external economic relations, for example, allowing foreign enterprises to use their own accounting systems in compliance with certain principles prescribed by the PRC Ministry of Finance;

2. reducing the tax burden of foreign enterprises (authorities are currently enacting a unified law on income tax for foreign enterprises);

3. encouraging foreign businessmen to manage their enterprises directly, including those joint or cooperative ventures between Chinese and foreigners;

4. reforming the foreign trade system; and

5. expanding the authority of coastal areas to approve direct foreign investments.

Despite the Chinese authorities' efforts to improve the investment environment in China, there was no sign of any significant improvement in early 1989, as the whole economy was encountering such problems as high inflation, corruption among officials dealing with economic matters, domestic trade barriers imposed by local authorities, an inefficient work force, an international trade deficit, and a shortage of foreign exchange.

The brutal and bloody suppression of China's democracy movement on June 4, 1989, and the subsequent arrest and execution of dissidents dealt a severe blow to the flow of foreign loans and investments to China as foreign bankers and businessmen sensed political instability in China.[116] Moreover, the United States and Western European countries also imposed economic sanctions on China after the suppression.[117]

In response to the above situations, the Chinese government has taken austere measures to conserve its scarce foreign exchange, thus sharply reducing its imports and causing an inordinate number of contract defaults by China's national trading companies.[118]

The June 4, 1989, brutal suppression also undercut the confidence foreign businessmen had in the Chinese legal system because the Chinese government, in its suppression of the democracy movement, acted in total disregard of its own Constitution and relevant laws.

Overall Assessment and Future Prospects

In the PRC, the state policy toward the legal system in the pre-1977 period was not only inconsistent but also subject to several radical fluctuations. It was not until after Mao's death and the emergence of a new leadership under Deng Xiaoping in the late 1970s that the government realized that a stable and modern legal system is a prerequisite for development and modernization; only then did the PRC begin to build a stable and modern legal system. The present goal of the PRC's effort for legal reform is still limited, however, as revealed by its insistence on operating the legal system within the Four Basic Principles. Even within that limited framework, however, whether the PRC will eventually succeed in its efforts remains questionable.

On the positive side, the present leadership appears to understand fully that the Chinese legal system must be strengthened and perfected so as to provide an orderly, predictable environment for the national modernization program. Moreover, during the turmoil of the Cultural Revolution, the lack of discipline among the poeple, workers, and peasants seriously affected production on various levels; there were also serious problems, including inefficiency, corruption, and waste, in the operation of state enterprises. To put its house in order, it will also be necessary to reestablish social discipline and order and to put the operation of state enterprises in order through the mechanism of law. Furthermore, the experience of the Cultural Revolution, in which the present leadership and their followers were also victims, seems to have taught the present leaders that the creation of a more stable and less repressive legal system is not only for the benefit of the great majority of the Chinese people but also for the benefit of the leaders themselves and their followers. Finally, without a stable legal system it is not possible to attract foreign investment and to promote foreign trade, both essential to the PRC's modernization program.

On the other hand, one must realize certain important negative elements concerning the establishment of a modern legal system in the PRC. The modern type of legal system with a separation of powers among the police (public security), procuratorates, and the courts was unknown to traditional China. Decades of communist rule have not weakened that tradition.

Second, Chinese society, instead of practicing the egalitarianism that some China scholars ascribed to the PRC, has been a strict class society since 1949. A higher rank in the party, government, or military units provides greater access to the amenities of life, which cannot be purchased by money. Moreover, since the open-door policy of 1978, there has been greater opportunity for corruption in the form of receiving gifts, money, or other benefits. Also, the higher one's position, the greater one's privileges and immunities. These privileges and immunities also extend to one's children, relatives, and close friends. Because the PRC relies on the loyalty of this privileged class to control the people, it would be difficult for the leadership to enforce the principle of universal equality before the law. This also explains why the party committees, despite official prohibition, have continued to interfere with the administration of justice.

Third, a modern legal system cannot function without a sufficient number of lawyers. With a low salary scale set by the state, poor working conditions, and official and public bias against lawyers, law practice is not an attractive career. This will pose a serious problem for the PRC's legal reform which is already confronted with a severe shortage of lawyers.

Fourth, when compared with previous PRC Constitutions, the 1982 Constitution is the most liberal, but how the Standing Committee of the NPC is to exercise its role of supervising the implementation of the Constitution is not clear. Referring to the experience of the 1954 Constitution, a Chinese scholar has pinpointed the problem as follows:

> Although the 1954 Constitution provided that the Standing Committee of the National People's Congress has the authority "to annul decisions and orders of the State Council which contravene the Constitution, laws or decrees" and "to revise or annul inappropriate decisions issued by the government authorities of provinces, autonomous regions, and municipalities directly under the central authority," there is, however, no implementing regulation to govern how the Standing Committee of the National People's Congress is to exercise this authority, [including] the procedure to exercise it and the organ assigned to handle these cases. It is clear that the organ and the form of supervising the implementation of the Constitution in our country is inadequate. This has caused the provisions on supervising the implementation of the Constitution to remain merely a formality and thus there is no important guarantee to implement the whole Constitution. This situation has resulted in a phenomenon of paying little attention to the Constitution or disregarding the Constitution in our country's political life.[119]

At present, the PRC does not seem to be responding to the problem of supervising the implementation of the Constitution raised by this scholar. Similarly, there appears to be no effective procedure available to individual citizens to challenge the unconstitutional legislation, illegal administrative rules issued by administrative organs, and interference by the party committees at different levels and party officials in the administration of justice.

Fifth, the Chinese leaders have paid sparse attention to legal procedures to carry out their policies. They appear to consider that the ends can justify the means. The anticrime campaign is an example. In carrying out this campaign, the Chinese leaders paid almost no attention to proper procedures prescribed by law. They intended a "quick fix" and thus dispensed with legal procedures. The June 4, 1989, Tiananmen Square massacre further proves that the Chinese leaders lack basic common sense on the rule of law. When necessary, they are willing to disregard the Constitution and relevant laws in order to maintain their power ruthlessly.

With such an attitude toward law, even a limited degree of the rule of law will be difficult to take root. After the mid-1989 Tiananmen Square massacre, high officials in the Ministry of Public Security, the Supreme People's Court, and the Supreme People's Procuratorate have again emphasized the theory of class struggle as the guideline for judicial work. The Supreme People's Precuratorate even complained that too few people were sentenced for counterrevolutionary offenses.[120] It appears, therefore, that for the foreseeable future the criminal justice system will be somewhat politicized, thus further deviating from even a limited rule of law that the leadership has attempted to establish in the last decade.

Sixth, prospects for building a modern legal system in China are necessarily tied to the PRC's political stability. The 1989 Tiananmen Square massacre and the removal of Chinese Communist Party's General Secretary Zhao Ziyang clearly indicate the lack of political stability in China. Deng Xiaoping is now eighty-five years old, and a power struggle is most likely to break out after his passing.

Finally, one must realize that the goal of the Chinese legal reform is to establish a stable and modern legal system within the Four Basic Principles, similar to the Soviet concept of socialist legality and socialist democracy, that is, legality and democracy conditioned by the needs of socialism as defined by the Communist party. Consequently, no principle, however normatively stated, in the Constitution or law, is permitted to conflict with the policy needs of the Communist party. Although these two concepts do contain the potential for instability and lack of predictability in the legal system, the Soviet experience has demonstrated that its legal system still maintains a substantial degree of stability and predictability, except in the limited areas of special Communist party concerns, such as the security of the regime and the integrity of the Communist system. At present, the Chinese legal system is far from achieving even the standards attained by the Soviet justice system.

Notes

1. The division of periods of development is based on Chen Shouyi, Liu Shengping, and Zhao Zhenjiang, "Woguo fazhi jianshe sanshinian" (Thirty years of the building up of our legal system), *Faxue yanjiu* (Studies in law), no. 1 (1979), p. 1.
2. Unless otherwise indicated, this part is summarized from Shao-chuan Leng and Hungdah Chiu, *Criminal Justice in Post-Mao China: Analysis and Documents* (Albany, NY: State University of New York Press, 1985), pp. 11–13.
3. Ibid., pp. 13–16.
4. Ibid., pp. 16–17.
5. Ibid., pp. 17–20.
6. See "Beijing zhengfa xueyuan susong fa jiaoyan shi" (Teaching and research office

on procedural law of Beijing), in *Zhonghua renmin gongheguo xinshi susong fa jianghua* (Talks on the criminal procedural law of the People's Republic of China), ed. Institute of Political Science and Law (Beijing: Qunzhong chubanshe, 1979), p. 20.

7. Yu Haocheng, "Cong xin hunyinfa de banbu tandao yifa banshi" (The promulgation of the new marriage law and handling cases according to law)," *Minzhu yu fazhi* (Democracy and the legal system), no. 4 (1980), p. 11.

8. This is referred to as "shuji pian" (deciding a case by the secretary) in the PRC, that is, "Whether the facts of a case are clear, the evidence is convincing; the defendant should be subject to criminal sanction and the criminal punishment that should be imposed on the defendant should be sent to the secretary in charge of political-legal affairs of the local party committee at the same level for review and approval." See Liao Jungchang, "Duli shenpan yu shujipian" (The independence of trial and [the system of] deciding a case by the secretary), *Xinan zhengfa xueyuan xuebao* (Journal of the Southwest Institute of Political Science and Law), no. 1 (1979), p. 7.

9. *Talks on the Criminal Procedural Law*, see note 6 above, p. 22.

10. Amnesty International, *Political Imprisonment in the People's Republic of China* (London: Amnesty International, 1978), p. 49.

11. "Quarterly Chronicle and Documentation (October–December 1978)," *The China Quarterly*, no. 77 (March 1979), p. 172.

12. See Hungdah Chiu, "Chinese Attitude Toward International Law in the Post-Mao Era, 1978–1987," *International Lawyer* 21 (1987), pp. 1127–66.

13. English translation in Michael Lindsay, ed., *The New Constitution of Communist China, Comparative Analysis* (Taipei: Institute of International Relations, 1976), pp. 328–36.

14. English translation in *Beijing Review* XXI:11 (March 17, 1978), pp. 5–14.

15. English translation in ibid., XXV:52 (December 27, 1982), pp. 10–29.

16. The numbers of laws and regulations up to September 1986 is from Zhang Youyu, "Yige bixu renzhen yanjiu, tansuo de wenti—guanyu jinyibu kuoda shehui zhuyi minzhu, jianguan shehuizhuyi fazhi he zhengzhi tizhi gaige de wenti" (A problem researched seriously—problems on taking a step further to develop socialist democracy, to strengthen the socialist legal system, and to restructure the political system), *Zhongguo faxue* (Law of China), no. 3 (1987), p. 8; the numbers between October 1986 and December 1988 are taken from *Zhonghua Renmin Gongheguo falu huipian, 1979–1984* (Collection of laws of the People's Republic of China, 1979–1984) (Beijing: Renmin chubanshe, 1985); ibid., 1985 (1986) and ibid., 1986 (1987); ibid., 1987 (1988); *Zhonghua Renmin Gongheguo xin fagui huipian 1988, Diyiji* (Collection of new laws and regulations of the People's Republic of China, 1988, series 1) (Beijing: Xinhua chubanshe, 1988) and *Zhonghua Renmin Gongheguo guowuyuan gongbau* (Gazette of the State Council of the People's Republic of China), nos. 1–29 (1987); and *Zhonghua Renmin Gongheguo quanguo renmin daibiao dahui changwu weiyuanhui gongbao* (Gazette of the Standing Committee of the National People's Congress), nos. 4–7 (1988).

17. For the text of these laws, see several collections mentioned in note 16. For English translations of these laws, see the Legislative Affairs Commission of the Standing Committee of the National People's Congress, ed., *The Laws of the People's Republic of China*, vol. 1 (1979–82) and vol. 2 (1983–86) (Beijing: Foreign Languages Press, 1987).

18. See William Jones, "Some Questions Regarding the Significance of the General Provisions of Civil Law of the People's Republic of China," *Harvard International Law Journal* XXVIII:2 (Spring 1987), p. 309.

19. Text in *Gazette of the Standing Committee of the National People's Congress*, no. 4 (May 30, 1986), pp. 3–25.

20. Jones, "Civil Law," see note 18 above, p. 311.

21. Ibid., pp. 311–12.

22. Different ministries and agencies altogether requested the enactment of more than 150 laws and 1,400 regulations between 1987 and 1992, but the Legal Bureau considered that it was unrealistic to implement such a huge legislative plan in five years. See Shi Chaoxu, " 'Qiwu' qijian de Zhongguo fazhi jianshe—fang Guowuyuan Fazhi Ju Fujuzhang Wang Shirong" (China's legal construction in the Seventh Five-Year Plan—an interview with the Deputy Director of the Legal Bureau of the State Council Wong Shirong), *Liao-wang* (The outlook), no. 14 (April 6, 1987), p. 14.

23. Shih Chaoxu, ibid., p. 13. The legislative plan of the State Council for 1988 requires that its Legal Bureau draft 37 laws and 174 administrative regulations. See Zhao Qingpei, "Guowuyuan jinnian lifa zhanwan" (Outlook on legislation of the State Council this year), *Liao-wang* (The outlook), no. 13 (March 28, 1988), pp. 16–17.

24. See "New Ministry of Justice Interviewed," *Beijing Review* XXII:42 (October 19, 1979), pp. 3–4.

25. See Leng and Chiu, *Criminal Justice*, see note 1 above, pp. 87–89.

26. Text in *Zhongguo fazhi bao* (China legal news), September 6, 1987, p. 2.

27. Article 39 of the Act. On March 16, 1987, a district people's court at Lianshui County overruled a decision of the detention ruling of Huaiyang County Public Security. This is the first case of judicial review over the decision of a public security bureau. See *Democracy and the Legal System*, no. 5 (May 1987), 17.

28. See notes 52–55, below, and accompanying text.

29. "Ministry of State Security Established," *Beijing Review* XXVI:27 (July 4, 1983), p. 6.

30. Christopher S. Wren, "Peking to Create New Security Unit," *New York Times*, June 7, 1983.

31. Timothy A. Gelatt and Frederick E. Snyder, "Legal Education in China: Training for a New Era," *China Law Reporter* IL 2 (Fall 1980), p. 4.

32. Ibid., pp. 44–45.

33. Information provided by Professor Shao-chuan Leng of the University of Virginia from his interview with visiting Chinese lawyers in July 1987.

34. *China Legal News*, December 25, 1985, p. 1.

35. *Zhongguo baike nianjian 1980* (Yearbook of the encyclopedia of China 1980) (Beijing/Shanghai: Zhongguo dabaike quanshu chubanshe, 1981), pp. 444–45.

36. Tao-tai Hsia and Wendy I. Zeldin, "Recent Legal Developments in the People's Republic of China," *Harvard International Law Journal* XXVIII:2 (Spring 1987), p. 275.

37. "Leaders Attend National Legal Conference," *Foreign Broadcast Information Service* (hereinafter cited as FBIS), *China*, June 10, 1985, p. K17.

38. *Gazette of the Standing Committee of the National People's Congress*, no. 6 (December 10, 1985), pp. 23–24.

39. Convention on the Prevention and Punishment of the Crime of Genocide, done on December 8, 1948 (UNTS 78:11), entered into force for the PRC on July 17, 1983; Convention Relating to the State of Refugees, done on July 28, 1951 (UNTS 189:137), entered into force for the PRC on December 23, 1982; Protocol Relating to the Status of Refugees, done on January 31, 1967 (UNTS 606:267), entered into force for the PRC on September 24, 1982; International Convention on the Elimination of All Forms of Racial Discrimination, done on March 7, 1966 (UNTS 660:195), entered into force for the PRC on January 28, 1982; International Convention on the Suppression and Punishment of the Crime of Apartheid, done on November 30, 1973 (UNTS 1015:244), entered into force for the PRC on May 18, 1983 and Convention on the Elimination of All Forms of Discrimination Against Women, done on December 18, 1979 (U.N. Doc. A/RES/34/180) and entered into force for the PRC on December 4, 1980). See *Shijie*

zhishi nianjian 1984 (1984 yearbook of world knowledge) (Beijing: Shijie zhishishe, 1984), pp. 471–79.

40. Text reprinted in *International Legal Materials* XXIII:6, (November 1984), pp. 1371–87.

41. On May 20, 1976, the United Kingdom declared that its ratification of both covenants is applicable to Hong Kong. See *Multilateral Treaties Deposited with the Secretary-General, Status as of 31 December 1984* (New York: The United Nations, 1985), pp. 121, 141.

42. See "PRC Likely to Sign UN Human Rights Conventions," FBIS, China, November 28, 1986, pp. A1–A3.

43. E.g., see Edward A. Gargan, "Thousands Stage Rally in Shanghai Demanding Rights," *The New York Times*, December 21, 1986, pp. 1, 19 and "China Denounces Student Protests as 'Illegal Acts,' " ibid., December 22, 1986, pp. A1, A14.

44. There are numerous news reports on the student demonstration, to mention just a few: "State of Siege, with Tiananmen Square the Epicenter, a Political Quake Convulses China," *Time*, May 29, 1989, pp. 36–45; "Deng Strikes Back," *Newsweek*, June 5, 1989, pp. 31–34; "Despair and Death in a Beijing Square," *Time*, June 12, 1989, pp. 24–27; "Reign of Terror," *Newsweek*, June 19, 1989, 14–23. For a more complete summary of the June 4, 1989 massacre and subsequent arrest and execution of demonstrators, see *People's Republic of China, Preliminary Findings on the Killing of Unarmed Civilians, Arbitrary Arrests, and Summary Executions since 3 June 1989* (London: Amnesty International, August 1989).

45. E.g., Article 79 of the Chinese Criminal Law allows the use of analogy, see note 70 above, violates Article 15(1) of the International Covenant of Civil and Political Rights that provides that "no one shall be held guilty of any criminal offense on account of any act or omission which did not constitute a criminal offense, under national or international law, at the time it was committed." The Chinese Criminal Procedural Law does not include the principle of presumption of innocence in criminal trial as required by Article 14(2) of the Covenant.

46. For an analysis of this problem, see Hungdah Chiu, "The 1982 Chinese Constitution and the Rule of Law," *Review of Socialist Law* XI (1985), pp. 143–60.

47. The PRC strictly restricts a person's freedom of movement and right to change residence. Rural area residents are not allowed to move to the city without special permission.

48. See note 8 above.

49. See Leng and Chiu, *Criminal Justice*, see note 1 above, pp. 100–101.

50. Liu Ningshu, "Xianfa de chongfenshixian shi fazhi de zuigao jiazhi" (The highest value of the legal system is the full implementation of the Constitution)," *Shanghai fazhibao* (Shanghai legal news), December 8, 1986, p. 6.

51. English translation in Leng and Chiu, *Criminal Justice*, see note 1 above, pp. 182–87.

52. This law can be invoked against any Chinese who provides unfavorable information to foreigners. In January 1987, a Chinese student was arrested for passing "intelligence" to a reporter of Agence France-Presse. No details have yet been released. Edward A. Gargan, "China Arrests Student as Spy," *The New York Times*, January 26, 1987, p. 3.

53. *Gazette of the Standing Committee of the National People's Congress*, 1986, no. 6 (October 15), pp. 3–8.

54. Zhang Wenshou, "Kuanyu 'Zhonghua Renmin Gongheguo Baoshou Guojia Mimi fa (casan)' " (Explanation concerning 'the law on guarding state secrets of the People's Republic of China (draft),' " *Gazette of the Standing Committee of the National People's Congress*, no. 6 (October 15, 1988), p. 11.

55. *Gazette of the Standing Committee of the National People's Congress*, no. 6 (October 15, 1988), p. 17.

56. English translation in Leng and Chiu, *Criminal Process*, see note 1 above, pp. 249–51.

57. Before 1979, there was no time limit for "reeducation through labor."

58. *Political Imprisonment*, see note 10 above, p. 90.

59. See Fu Ge, "Laodong jiaoyang lifa de lilun yu shiji" (The theory and practice of the legislation on reeducation through labor), *Faxue* (Law science), no. 7 (1987), pp. 44–45.

60. Wang Jian, "Shourong shencha shi shenmoshi?" (What is shelter and investigation?), *China Legal News*, August 30, 1986, p. 1.

61. Ibid.

62. Yuan Shida, "Shourong shencha gonzuo jidai lifa" (It is urgent to legislate on shelter and investigation), *Faxue* (Law science), no. 3 (1987), p. 52.

63. *Talks on Criminal Procedure*, see note 5 above, p. 22.

64. See *Country Reports on Human Rights Practices for 1986* (Washington, D.C.: U.S. Government Printing Office, 1987), 686 and *Country Reports . . . for 1987* (1988), 664. In the Report of the Supreme People's Court to the Fifth Meeting of the Sixth National People's Congress, April 6, 1987, it is disclosed that only 0.7 percent of the criminal suspects prosecuted were acquitted. *Gazette of the Supreme People's Court*, no. 2 (1987), p. 4.

65. See "China Confirms Jailing of an Ex-U.S. Lawyer," *New York Times*, February 2, 1984, p. A7; Frank Ching, "Lawyer Who Worked at American Firms Imprisoned in China as Spy for the U.S.," *Asian Wall Street Journal Weekly*, January 23, 1984, p. 3; and "PRC Upholds Ten-Year Sentence for Hong Kong Man," FBIS, China, September 9, 1983, p. W1.

66. Lena H. Sun, "Chinese Student Is to Face Trial, Graduate of U.S. University Demonstrated for Democracy," *The Washington Post*, June 2, 1987, p. A26.

67. A photocopy of the detention notice is available at the University of Maryland Law School, East Asian Legal Studies Library. At the right bottom corner, the notice stated that it was issued on May 15, 1987, although the official date of the notice is January 10, 1987.

68. See "Cong Yang Wei an de jinkuang kan zhongquo dalu de fazhi" (Looking at the rule of law in Chinese mainland from recent development of the Yang Wei case), *Zhongquo zhi chun* (China spring), no. 53 (November 1987), pp. 19–20.

69. "Student Found Guilty," *Beijing Review*, vol. 30, no. 52 (December 28, 1987), pp. 12–13; English translation of the complete text of the judgment may be found in "Court Verdict on Yang Wei," *China Spring Digest*, vol. 2, no. 1 (January/February, 1988), pp. 11–12.

70. Leng and Chiu, *Criminal Justice*, see note 1 above, p. 203.

71. See Werner Pfennig, "Political Aspects of Modernization and Judicial Reform in the People's Republic of China," *Journal of Chinese Studies*, vol. 1, no. 1 (February 1984), pp. 92–93.

72. See Edward A. Gargan, "Investing in China: Still Hard," *The New York Times*, June 16, 1987, p. D5; and "Zhonggong fazhi: qingkuang yipian huanluan, faguei zhiding buquan, qie wei quanmian gongbu" (The situation of the Chinese Communists' legal system is in total chaos, laws and regulations are not only incomplete but also not published in their entirety), *Huayu kuaibao* (Sino-daily express), June 22, 1987, p. 7.

73. See Subsection 1. of this section.

74. See notes 51 and 52 above and accompanying text.

75. E.g., Edward A. Gargan, "Chinese Report Protest By Lamas to Free Tibet," *The*

New York Times, October 1, 1987, p. A8; and his "Tibetan Protest for Independence Becomes Violent, Six Are Killed in a Clash," ibid., October 3, 1987, pp. 1, 5.

76. "Western Reporters Ordered Out of Tibet, Chinese Officials Cite Rule Violations," *The Sun*, October 9, 1987, p. 9A.

77. Amnesty International, *China, Torture and Ill-Treatment of Prisoners* (London: Amnesty International, September 1987). See also, "Rights Unit Tells of China Torture," *The New York Times*, September 9, 1987, p. A10; and "China's Meager Effort to End Torture," *The Asian Wall Street Journal Weekly*, September 21, 1987, p. 16.

78. *China, Torture*, see note 77 above, p. 42.

79. Ibid., pp. 40, 42.

80. *People's Republic of China, Preliminary Findings*, see note 44 above, p. 38.

81. *Gazette of the Supreme People's Court*, no. 2 (1987), pp. 7–8.

82. "Implement Law Courts Decisions," *China Daily*, July 16, 1987, p. 4.

83. Minister of Justice Zou Yu revealed these statistics at the National Legal Conference held on June 9, 1985. "Leaders Attend National Legal Conference," FBIS, China, June 10, 1985, p. K17.

84. *People's Daily*, July 7, 1986, p. 4.

85. *Zhongbao* (Central daily news), July 29, 1987, p. 16.

86. *People's Daily*, July 11, 1986, p. 4.

87. Ibid., August 27, 1986, p. 4.

88. *Central Daily News*, July 29, 1987, p. 16.

89. *China Daily*, November 29, 1986, p. 3.

90. *People's Daily*, June 11, 1981, p. 1.

91. Ibid.

92. *China Daily*, June 26, 1981, p. 3.

93. *People's Daily*, September 3, 1983, p. 3.

94. English translation in Leng and Chiu, *Criminal Justice*, see note 1 above, pp. 232–33.

95. Ibid., pp. 211–14.

96. Amnesty International, *China, Violation of Human Rights, Prisoners of Conscience and the Death Penalty in the People's Republic of China* (London: Amnesty International, 1984), p. 69.

97. Ibid., p. 65.

98. A. Zhang, "Rouqing shishui zhuangzhi rugang—yiwei lushi de beihuan" (The tender feelings of a lover just like water and the lofty ambition just like steel—the sorrow and joy of a lawyer), *Democracy and Legal System*, no. 2 (1985), p. 16.

99. Numerous news reports were published relating to student movements in various newspapers or magazines, to cite just a few: "Upheaval in China," *Newsweek*, May 29, 1989, pp. 16–28; and Tu Jih-huei, "A Chronology of the Student Movement at Tiananmen Square," *Sinorama*, August 1989, pp. 19–21.

100. John Schidlovsky, "China Sets Martial Law to Quell Beijing Protests," *The Sun*, Baltimore, May 20, 1989, pp. 1A, 4A.

101. E.g., see "Beijing Bloodbath," *Newsweek*, June 12, 1989, pp. 24–29; "Despair and Death in a Beijing Square," *Time*, June 12, 1989, pp. 24–27; and "What I Saw Is Bodies, Bodies, Bodies, Eyewitness Accounts of the Battle of Beijing," *Newsweek*, June 19, 1989, pp. 22–23.

102. *People's Republic of China, Preliminary Findings*, see note 44 above, p. 1.

103. Ibid.

104. E.g., see "Deng's Big Lie, the Hard-liners Rewrite History to Justify Arrests and Bury Democrary," *Time*, June 26, 1989, pp. 32–34.

105. E.g., see Paul Lewis, "China Is Said to Execute Some in Secret," *New York*

Times, August 31, 1989, p. A3; and *People's Republic of China, Preliminary Findings*, see note 44 above, p. 3.

106. Yuan Jianquo, "Zhongguo shewai jingji lifa de huigu yu qianzhan" (Review and prospect of China's economic legislation—involving foreign countries)," *The Outlook*, no. 36 (September 1987), p. 8.

107. Ibid. For an overall survey of Chinese law of foreign trade and investment, see Michael J. Moser, ed., *Foreign Trade, Investment, and the Law in the People's Republic of China*, 2d ed. (Oxford, New York, and Hong Kong: Oxford University Press, 1987); and Henry R. Zheng, *China's Civil and Commercial Law* (Singapore: Butterworths, 1988).

108. *Yearbook of Encyclopedia of China 1985* (1986), p. 133.

109. *International Legal Materials* XXVI (1987), p. 595.

110. Zhang Shangtang, "The Laws and Regulations Regarding Approval of Foreign Investment," *Sixth U.S.-China Joint Legal Seminar* (Washington, D.C.: U.S. Department of Commerce, Office of the General Counsel, November 1988), p. 15. Through June 1988, the United States has 493 investment projects in China with a total value of 3.2 billion U.S. dollars. See Yuan Zhenmin, "China's Economic Reforms and Improvement of Conditions for Foreign Investment in China," *Sixth U.S.-China Joint Legal Seminar*, p. 1.

111. Gargan, "Investing in China," see note 72 above.

112. Based on ibid., and John F. Burns, "Why Investors Are Sour on China," *The New York Times*, June 8, 1986, p. F7.

113. Yuan Jianquo, "China's Economic Legislation," see note 106, p. 8.

114. Gargan, "Investing in China," see note 72 above.

115. See Li Dahong and Wang Peiyu, "Zhongguo yunniang guli waishang touzi di xin cuoshi" (China is deliberating new measures to encourage foreign investment), *The Outlook*, no. 19 (May 9, 1988), pp. 13–14; and Zhang Shangtung, "The Laws and Regulations Regarding Approval of Foreign Investment," *Sixth U.S. China Legal Seminar*, see note 110 above, pp. 15–19.

116. E.g., see "Beijing Troubles Could Hurt the Flow of Foreign Capital, Technology to China," *The Asian Wall Street Journal Weekly*, June 12, 1989, p. 2.

117. See "Senate OKs Tougher China Sanctions," *The Sun*, Baltimore, July 15, 1989, p. 2A; and Karen Hosler, "Summit Urges China to End Repression," ibid., July 16, 1989, pp. 1A, 6A.

118. Julia Leung, "Foreign Companies Brace for Plunge in Trade with China," *The Asian Wall Street Journal Weekly*, October 9, 1989, pp. 1, 2.

119. Zhang Chen and Tie Song, "Lun xianfa de shishi" (On the implementation of the Constitution)," in Zhang Youyu et al., eds., *Xianfa lunwenji* (Collected essays on the Constitution), vol. 2 (Beijing: Quanzhon chubanshe, 1982), p. 297.

120. *Shihjie jihpao* (World journal), October 28, 1989, p. 31.

Comments by William C. Jones

I have one comment on an area of legal life that has been passed over, namely, legal education in China. As a result of the history of Chinese law since 1949, legal education in China is terrible; the standard of teaching is poor. Professors are not well prepared and the legal books are not well written. The material published in Chinese legal periodicals is a joke. When I say such things, I sound patronizing as if I have nothing but contempt for the Chinese. That isn't true at all. I have a great deal of sympathy but, since 1949, it's no fun to be a lawyer in China. If China is going to join the international legal community, we must tell it like it is. I might add that the younger law students do not present a problem. They seem quite aware of the difficulties in the system and are not adverse to discussing them, at least privately. The older Chinese law teachers I have known do not seem to like to talk about them at all. I certainly understand that, too.

In any event, it is correct to say, as Professor Chiu has said, that the Chinese have not established a modern legal system. What would the situation be like if they had established such a system? My own bottom line in the criminal system is to see that people are acquitted. In China people are not acquitted. It seems to me that unless people go free, including those one thinks are guilty but who have not been proven guilty according to procedural rules, a trial is phony. I myself have not seen any evidence, before or after Deng, of any Chinese criminal proceedings I would characterize as a trial. Although many proceedings are labeled trials, I would not characterize them as trials.

I would like to pose a hypothetical case. Suppose that after ten years of Deng Xiaoping and a new legal system, the Flying Pigeon Bicycle Company wants to open a branch factory and a distribution center throughout China. It wishes to open one in Wuhan; so it goes to its lawyer who examines its corporate charters and laws to see if it can be done, and to see if the financing plan works. Then he studies the Wuhan and Hupei provincial regulations, all of which are available in the Shanghai Law Library, or in a recently published leaflet, "How to Open Up a Branch Factory in China." Appropriate memos and documents are then prepared by the law offices. Local lawyers in Wuhan will acquire local permits. Should a permit be denied, the person denying it must provide a reason based on a statute, and this action is subject to review by independent tribunals that will examine the reasons given in light of objective standards and the evidence cited in support of the decisions. Although this is what would happen in any European legal system, it is not what happens in China. That is the problem. What China has been purporting to install is essentially a European legal system, one constructed primarily on the German model, which has no Chinese roots. It is true that in the middle and later parts of the Nationalist regime a group of codes drafted on the German model were promulgated, but these never took root because of the political situation. When the PRC repealed the Nationalist codes in 1949, it was not in fact repealing anything very real. Nor is it surprising that the new government of China has not enacted a Western legal system with Marxist modifications and based on the Soviet model because almost none of the leaders had legal training, and none had ever lived in a society where Western law operated. Consequently, the Chinese have failed to enact any Western-style legal system. It would be surprising if they had. The real puzzle is why they are trying so hard to do so. As Victor Li said, "Every time you train a lawyer, you don't train an agronomist." It seems a rather curious set of values to me.

I can understand why the Japanese enacted the German codes of law as they did; they were trying to get rid of extraterritoriality. With the existence of the German codes and the building of a good navy, the Western countries were all willing to admit that Western values were being maintained in Japan, and so they got out. Once that happened, of course, the Japanese paid no attention to the Western codes and carried on according to their old ways. That's perfectly understandable. That is not China's problem.

I can also see why, after the Cultural Revolution, people who had been treated as other people were in the 1950s had the notion that they would not have been so treated had they had some rule of law. Not that anyone who matters in China has the remotest notion of what is meant by this term. There is no way they could, given their educational background. I can also see why they might want a system of law to make American businessmen happy. American businessmen are unhappy when they are not accompanied by their lawyers; the lawyers are unhappy when they cannot look at bodies of law. So most Asian businessmen have provided these crutches to Americans to keep them happy, although they themselves, I am told, normally do not use lawyers in their own internal transactions. This is not because they did not have a legal system. Perhaps, this is not the time to go into the legal system but it seems to me that the legal system has two essential elements, one of which has been referred to by Professor Chiu and Professor Leng in their recent book. All legal systems are influenced by policy. If one wants the 55-mile-per-hour speed limit, this is policy. In China, policy is law; the new institution of land tenure in the countryside is an example of that. The long-term leases that are essentially what the peasants had until recently have now in effect become ownership, and this ownership can be transferred. The word "ownership" is not used, and the word "property" is not used. This kind of legal transfer of landed interest has already taken place. So what happens when the legislation is enacted? If it is enacted, will it be confirmed? This happens over and over again in the development of the land law since the founding of the PRC.

Another aspect of the system is that it is rigidly regulated, even during the most violent years of the Cultural Revolution. Trains continued to run, electricity was produced and distributed, crops were sown, and salaries were calculated and paid. All these activities required rules that had to be followed, or the system would break down. One must assume these rules were rigidly enforced. I have been convinced from talking to refugees that there were in fact in China, and still are, manuals for the management of prisons, similar to what we called the navy brick manual, in which instructions were given on the kinds of penalties to give.

These aspects of law continue to exist. The plan also constitutes law because it determines people's rights and interests. The campaign is very much a part of the Chinese legal system, certainly prior to the Deng years. It was said this morning that the campaign no longer exists; I question that. Perhaps it does not exist in the violent sense, but how would you characterize the birth control program? It seems to me to be very much a campaign. Professor Chiu referred to the anticrime campaigns. These are big ones. There are smaller-scale campaigns all the time: campaigns to stop smuggling, to stop pornography, and so forth. At the moment, there is a "stop defective goods" campaign, with an exhibition of defective goods in Beijing. So it seems the pre-Deng legal system is alive and well. It has not changed very much.

I agree with what Professor Chiu has said, with one exception. I am not sure whether the Soviet model really works in China, because Russia is a European country with a European tradition. Lenin had studied law, and it is easy to reestablish the European system. China is different. Maybe the area where the Western legal system is permitted to function has to be much more regulated than in the Soviet Union. One final example, the bankruptcy act, is not a bankruptcy act in the Western sense. The proceedings and procedures contemplated are highly supervised in China. The company concerned would first be put on probation, and then put out of business, a gentle maneuver by American standards. That is a mix of Western ideas and Chinese supervision, which might be the way Chinese law can develop.

Comments by Shao-chuan Leng

This is a well-researched and carefully written paper. I tend to be more optimistic, however, than two of my colleagues. I think our differences may be in degree, not in kind. Let me quickly comment on what has emerged from China's legal system. Here we should talk about the legal system, not the rule of law, because in terms of law China has a long way to go to achieve the rule of law.

China does currently have something of a legal system, referred to by the Chinese as socialist legality with Chinese characteristics. The phrase is as ambiguous as speaking of socialism with Chinese characteristics. But I will try to outline some of the features that are peculiar to the Chinese.

First, in line with China's *li-fa* tradition alongside China's judicial tradition, there are in China public security organs and other judicial institutions that continue to play important roles in maintaining peace and order, imposing administrative sanction, and settling disputes.

Second, in criminal cases Chinese laws appear to be much more generally moralistic than are Soviet laws, for example, the frequent use by the Chinese of circumstances in determining penalties and the practice of combining punishment with education in its penal policy.

Third, the principles of the general civil law published in 1986 also contain features peculiar to the Chinese in that they protect the property rights of the state, collectives, and individuals, which is peculiar to the Chinese socialist economy and also supportive of Deng's open-door policy.

The traditional preference of settling disputes through mediation is also manifested both in law and practice in the PRC today. But of course problems are quite numerous in Chinese civil law precedure, in economic contract law, and in China's trade grievances with foreign countries. Hungdah has already outlined some of these problems. The famous jurist in China, Zhang Yuyu, stated that the problem facing China is not the lack of laws, but failure to improve them. So official abuses of power continue to occur in terms of illegal arrest, unlawful detention, and interference with judicial work. The Chief Procurator Yang Icheng stated that in 1986 there were thirty-two thousand cases of infringement on people's rights.

Nevertheless, the people's courts continue to seek the guidance of the party committees on policy matters and on important complicated cases. In the early 1980s the anticrime drive was launched by the political and legal committee of the Central Committee of the CCP, which resorted to mass arrest, publicized executions, and the removal of procedural guarantees from certain felonies. The ongoing drive in the PRC against corruption and economic crimes has been criticized for not attacking tigers but only flies. Occasionally, children of senior party cadres have been severely punished, even executed, only after Deng Xiaoping's personal intervention. There was a famous case in 1986 involving Yeh Zifang, the daughter of General Yeh Fei, as principal offender of an alleged sale of state secrets to foreigners. She was sentenced to seventeen years' imprisonment. Her accomplices, however, received lighter sentences. This raised the question of judicial independence. Hungdah refers to the term "state secrets," which can mean anything, including Mao Zedong's mental state. During the Cultural Revolution, a man called Mao a mad man; the verbal attacker was sentenced to fifteen years' imprisonment for insulting the Chairman and given another fifteen years for revealing a state secret.

This practice has problems, of course, but I am still hopeful. The problems we have discussed here have been openly discussed in the PRC. This is quite a change from the past. Moreover, the Chinese leaders appear to be aware of these problems and are making efforts to alleviate the situation. In 1986, when they launched a five-year universal legal education drive, the leaders, including Hu Yaobang, Hu Qiaomu, and others, even attended a special class in Zhongnanhai to study law. Furthermore, some of the classical legal concepts of Marx, including the class nature of the law, have been openly challenged in legal circles in China and in some legal journals.

Finally, the reform policy as confirmed by the Thirteenth Party Congress, in my view, is likely to strengthen the legal system, and vice versa. Of course it would be naive to think that the rule of law is taking root in China. It is possible, however, that the emergence of a regularized legal system with sufficient functional autonomy and professional competence will help institutionalize the fruits of reform and provide Chinese people with a secure environment. I think this incremental progress, probably in the long run, along with other factors, will contribute to a significant change in China's legal system.

4

RECASTING OF THE ECONOMIC SYSTEM: Structural Reform of Agriculture and Industry

Nicholas R. Lardy

CHINA'S post-Mao economic reform program is arguably more successful than that of any other socialist country. This success is evident in terms of both an acceleration of the rate of expansion of national output and China's opening of its economy to the outside world. Between 1978, when the reform began, and the end of 1988, China's national income more than doubled in real terms.[1] In percentage terms the average compound rate of growth was 9 percent, more than 50 percent greater than the long-term rate achieved in the two-and-one-half decades from the beginning of 1953 through 1978.

This is more than six times the recent average annual rate of growth in Eastern Europe as a whole and more than four times the growth of the most rapidly expanding economy in the region, Romania. It is a distinctly superior record of economic reform. In Hungary the rate of growth of gross national product actually has declined significantly since the introduction of the New Economic Mechanism in 1968 and has averaged just 1 percent in 1980–84.[2] China's economic performance in the first decade of reform not only vastly surpassed that of the most successful reformers in Eastern Europe but actually approached that of the most rapidly developing countries in East Asia where the average annual rate of growth of Japan over approximately the same period was 4 percent; of South Korea, 8 percent; of Taiwan, 6 percent; of Singapore, 7 percent; and of Hong Kong, 7 percent.[3]

China has also been relatively more successful than other socialist countries in opening its economy to the outside world. China's relative success is evident in several measures of trade and investment performance. First, China's growth of total trade turnover has been far more rapid, increasing more than fivefold from less than $15 billion in 1977 to more than $100 billion in 1988.[4] Morevoer, because most of this growth has been with market economies China's hard currency trade has grown far more rapidly than that of the countries of Eastern Europe. Again, the contrast with Hungary is instructive. In the first half of the 1980s Hungary's trade with the nonsocialist world was actually shrinking while its barter trade with the Soviet Union was growing rapidly.[5] China's trade growth has been so rapid and so overwhelmingly with market economies that by the mid-1980s its hard currency trade surpassed both that of the Soviet Union and of Eastern Europe taken as a whole. Although some of China's trade growth has been financed by borrowing, the growth of exports between 1978 and 1988 averaged about 15 percent annually, substantially in excess of the performance of any of the countries of Eastern Europe or of the Soviet Union. This, and China's unusual ability to attract foreign investment (discussed below) has meant that China's growth of external debt relative to its hard currency export earnings has been far more modest than in Eastern Europe. China contracted approximately $40 billion foreign debt by the end of 1988.[6] Although this is the same order of magnitude of the most heavily indebted East European state, Poland, the disparity in their relative positions is made clear by examining the ratio of debt to annual hard currency export earnings. Poland's hard currency exports in 1983 were just more than $5 billion, about a fifth of its net debt. China's hard currency exports in 1988, about $45 billion, were roughly equal to its net debt. China's position is more favorable than that of Hungary where annual hard currency exports are about two-thirds of net external debt.[7]

In its ability to attract foreign investment China has vastly surpassed all other socialist states and indeed compares favorably with the most successful developing market economies. While the Soviet Union and several Eastern European economies have sought to acquire Western technology through licensing agreements and the other forms of technology transfer, the development of the legal and administrative framework for attracting direct foreign investment is still in the very early stages. By contrast, since the promulgation of China's Foreign Investment Law in 1978, direct foreign investment has grown steadily. During the first four years (1979–1982) total direct foreign investment in China, inclusive of foreign funds committed in equity joint ventures, contractual joint ventures, cooperative resource exploitation, wholly foreign-owned firms, and in compensation trade averaged $440 million. In 1983, 1984, 1985, and 1986 the actual inflow rose significantly to $916 million, $1,419 million, $1,959 million, and $2,244 million, respectively.[8] By 1985–86, the inflow of direct foreign investment to China exceeded that of all other developing countries. And even though China's direct foreign investment program was relatively new, by the end of 1986 the cumulative amount of direct foreign investment (exclusive of contracted projects that have not yet been undertaken) had surpassed that of Indonesia, Argentina, Hong Kong, Venezuela, Taiwan, South Korea, and the Philippines to rank fifth or sixth among developing countries. The flows to China continued to expand in 1987 and 1988, reaching $2,620 million in the latter year.[9]

While China's performance in the first decade of reform may be the envy both of the socialist world and of most of the developing world, it is not clear whether the reform of China's basic institutional structure in manufacturing and in farming is sufficiently far-reaching to sustain China's initial transition away from a Soviet-type economy toward market socialism. The experience of reform programs in Eastern Europe suggests that there is a natural and perhaps inevitable tendency for an erosion of the institutional reforms made in each reform impetus and that a succession of major efforts is needed to sustain economic reform. In the remainder of this paper I will examine the restructuring that has occurred to date in agriculture and industry with a view to examining the sustainability of the reform program in the two sectors.

Agricultural Restructuring

The general pattern of restructuring in agricultrue is so well known that a detailed treatment is unnecessary. Reform in agriculture had three major components: a return to a traditional household-based farming system in place of the Maoist collective structure; a substantial improvement in the prices received by farmers for the sale of their products; and a greatly expanded role of private markets for agricultural goods, including cereals, in both rural and urban areas.

Collective ownership arrangements that had prevailed since the mid-1950s had been replaced by the mid-1980s with a system of long-term land contracts in which the operational and allocational unit was the farm household rather than a collective organization. Thus China's present land system has more in common with the fixed rent contracts and tenancy arrangements characteristic of the private land ownership system of the pre-1949 era than with the collective arrangments of the Maoist era. The most salient characteristic of the present system is that about 95 percent of all farm households operate under a form of the responsibility system known as contracting to the household in which peasants having long-term contracts (a minimum of fifteen years) for specific parcels of land in exchange for delivery of specified quantities of agricultural products at fixed prices and fixed payments that include an agricultural tax and other fees.

Even as the state substantially altered the ownership and production arrangements in the collective farm sector it introduced an equally far-reaching set of changes in pricing and marketing policies. After more than a decade of fixed farmgate prices, the state began to overhaul procurement prices systematically beginning in 1977. The state raised average farmgate prices substantially relative to industrial product prices, systematically altered relative prices of various agricultural products to stimulate a change in the mix of output, and introduced a revamped system of premium prices to provide additional incentives for increased marketing through state channels.

Simultaneously, the state eased long-standing prohibitions on the sale of cereal crops on rural markets as part of a policy of encouraging increased specialization to promote productivity growth. The state made explicit commitments to supply food grains to producers of nongrain crops to encourage specialized production. Moreover, the state removed institutional barriers to private long-distance interregional marketing of cereals and other crops, again to facilitate increased specialization.

The initial response to these reforms was spectacular. Between 1978 and 1984 the value of farm output (measured in constant prices) grew at almost three times the long-term historic rate achieved between 1957 and 1978. Grain output rose from 305 to 407 million metric tons, an average annual increase of almost 5 percent, well over twice the historic rate of just more than 2 percent achieved between 1957 and 1978. At the same time, growth of nongrain crops was even more rapid. After two decades of indifferent performance, soybeans, cotton, and edible vegetable oils all posted stunning advances. Output of cotton, traditionally China's second most important crop category after cereals, almost tripled between 1978 and 1984. The output of oilseed crops more than doubled. The output of minor crops, such as sugarcane and sugar beets, also accelerated markedly. Nonfood crops, such as tea and tobacco, achieved notably higher growth rates. Production of pork, beef, and mutton exceeded 15 million metric tons by 1984, up about 80 percent over 1978.

Indeed it is remarkable that with the single exception of aquatic products, the levels of agricultural output achieved by the end of 1984 far surpassed the targeted levels for 1985 established by the Central Committee of the Chinese Communist Party at the time of its historic decisions on agrarian reform at the Third Plenum of the Eleventh Central Committee in December 1978. Oilseed production was 50 percent ahead of the 1985 plan, cotton 70 percent, and meat more than 100 percent, suggesting that the central leadership substantially underestimated the spurt of growth that would be stimulated by the package of pricing, marketing, and institutional reforms.

Equally remarkable as this spurt of output growth is the large role played by increased productivity. When agricultural reform began in 1978, it was predicated on the need for a substantial increase in state resources flowing to agriculture—both current expenditures and investment. An excessively penurious state policy toward agriculture, reflected in a low allocation of state funds and high indirect taxes levied on agriculture through unfavorable state-manipulated terms of trade, was believed to be a primary cause of the low rate of agricultural growth. The Decision on Accelerating Agricultural Development, adopted in draft form by the Central Committee of the Chinese Communist Party in 1978, called for a fundamental change in the allocation of state resources. Most notably, the share of state investment outlays allocated for agriculture was to rise within a period of a few years from its then current 11 percent to a level of 18 percent. The Central Committee also endorsed an increase in the share of state budgetary expenditures allocated for noninvestment expenditures, mainly current outlays for water conservancy, state farms, fisheries, meteorological services, and support for collective agriculture. Moreover, the initial Central Committee directives on agricultural reform envisaged increased mechanization as a major source of output growth.

As increased privatization of land-holding arrangements proceeded, however, and farmers responded with alacrity to improved price incentives and marketing opportunities, the state actually curtailed the flow of funds to agriculture. State budgetary expenditures for farming, state investment in agriculture, and state bank credit extended to agriculture declined after 1979. By 1984 the share of state investment allocated to farming had shrunk to 5 percent, the lowest level in the entire post-1949 period. Moreover, collective investment in farming fell by half compared to the late 1970s, and expanding private rural income was allocated overwhelmingly to increased consumption and housing investment. Little was left for private farming investment.

In short, about half the growth of farm output in the early years of reform appears to be accounted for by increased productivity—more units of output being produced by each unit of input.[10]

The record since 1984, however, suggests that a large share of the increased output and productivity in farming achieved in the early 1980s represented one-time gains, not a transition to a permanently higher trend of growth. As I have argued elsewhere, China is not likely to be able to simultaneously sustain rapid growth, minimize the commitment of the state's resources to farm investment, and preserve some degree of collective ownership in farming.[11] The evolution of policy reflects compromises among the three conflicting goals. The state has had to accept a significantly lower rate of growth of farm output since 1984, has accepted a greater degree of privatization of farming than initially envisaged, and has had to allocate modestly increased state investment for agriculture (although as measured by the share of state investment agriculture's priority continued to fall through 1989).

The most alarming development has been in the production of grain. Output in four consecutive years (1985–88) fell below the peak of 1984, leading to new calls for more restrictions on individual farm household decisions on cropping patterns.

Industrial Restructuring

In contrast to farming, the growth of manufacturing output has not accelerated and, although there are some uncertainties in the data, it appears there has been little if any increase in productivity, at least in state-owned firms that in the mid-1980s still produced more than two-thirds of the gross value of industrial output. In state-owned enterprises there has continued to be a massive accumulation of fixed assets, a phenomenon familiar to students of centrally planned economies, rather than a transition to a regime in which enterprise managers seek to weigh the costs of additional machinery and equipment against the benefits to be derived therefrom. For the years 1978–83, estimates published by the World Bank show manufacturing productivity in the state-owned sector declining at an annual rate of 1.2 percent.[12] Using the same basic framework to extend the analysis through 1985 shows a smaller rate of decline, 0.3 percent per annum.[13]

The Causal Factors

In my view there are four fundamental factors explaing the different performance of industry and agriculture since 1978: the differing role of prices in the two sectors, the relative lack of competition in the industrial sector—a long-term problem that has been aggravated by the combination of administrative and market-oriented reform underway since 1978, the limited development of a labor market in the modern sector, and the differing costs of capital in the two sectors.

The Price Environment

Agricultural prices differ fundamentally from those in industry in several aspects. First, and most important, agricultural production units, whether the collectives of 1955–80 or the households of the early 1950s and the 1980s, have not been subsidized by the state and thus have retained substantial sensitivity to the prices of the products they sell and the inputs they purchase. In short, the incomes of farmers have depended on their success in maximizing the difference between the value of their outputs and the cost of their inputs. The prices they faced in both output and input markets were, of course, not market determined in most periods. But farmers did try to maximize profits subject to the prices set parametrically by the state and subject to various other state-imposed conditions.

Second, the state periodically has adjusted upward the prices it pays for farm output so that they cover average production costs. Acute crises have occurred when this has not been true, for example, in the mid-1970s. These crises have led to rapid remedial action, as in the case of the major adjustment of agricultural procurement prices begun in 1977.

Third, the state has adjusted the relative prices of various agricultural products to induce the desired output mix. That was most obvious in the early 1950s, the early 1960s, and since the mid-1970s. Only in 1966–77 did the state forgo the adjustment of relative prices and rely almost exclusively on bureaucratic commands to influence the output mix.

Finally, since the reform of the procurement system in the mid-1980s the number of products subject to compulsory procurement has been reduced. Thus, for many farm products the relevant price for farmers is the market price.

In industry, by contrast, the price structure was fixed in the early to mid-1950s without consideration for its effect on resource allocation. Raw materials and intermediate goods were assigned low prices so that the profits of state-owned enterprises, the source of more than 90 percent of state fiscal revenues, would be concentrated in the final stages of the production process. Raw materials and intermediate goods increasingly were distributed through the system of material balances so that underpricing did not necessarily lead to excess demand. Particularly after the completion of the socialist transformation in the mid-1950s the output mix of final goods was determined by the annual planning process, not by the decision of profit-maximizing enterprise managers.

Second, once the fixed price structure was in place there were few subsequent adjustments. Reform of the industrial price structure was attempted in the mid-1950s, in the mid-1960s, and again in the 1980s but with very modest results.[14] As a consequence of the initially distorted price structure and the subsequent rise in costs, in the late 1970s as the industrial reform was getting underway more than a quarter of all state-owned industrial enterprises could not cover their operating costs from their current revenues and depended on state budgetary subsidies to remain in operation.[15] Obviously in this environment the state did not adjust relative product prices to influence the output mix of state-owned enterprises but relied on changing physical output targets.

The introduction in the early 1980s of a dual pricing structure in which a declining share of major producer goods is allocated by the state at fixed prices and a significant and rising share is sold on parallel markets, is the most significant innovation of the current reform.[16] In that system the fixed-price structure is not adjusted, except for a few commodities, but firms are allowed to sell their over quota production on the open market. Moreover, many enterprises are not able to acquire all their inputs through state allocations at fixed prices but must purchase some share of their needs on the open market.

In theory, if firms behave according to profit maximizing principles the widespread existence of parallel markets would compel a rational allocation of resources. The availability of some fixed quantity of inputs at a state, below-market price would be the equivalent of a lump sum subsidy of the firm but would not affect their choice on levels of input usage. If managers were profit maximizers, that choice would be made by comparing the marginal cost (i.e., market price) of the additional inputs and the marginal revenues that could be gained from selling the resulting additional outputs.

Whether reality corresponds to theory is not clear. Several factors tend to undermine the hypothesized advantage of the dual price structure. First, although a significant share of many goods are distributed in parallel markets, some inputs, notably electricity and other energy sources, remain almost entirely subject to state bureaucratic distribution. Second, the degree of price flexibility on parallel markets appears to be inhibited by state regulations. For some products there are regulations limiting the market price to a range of plus or minus 20 percent from the state fixed price.[17] The share of producer goods that are distributed through the most marketlike channels, the so-called producer goods trade centers, was only 10 percent in 1985.[18] Third, many high-priority large state factories may still get all their inputs through the state-controlled materials allocation system and thus are not forced to economize on state raw materials and other inputs. It appears to be primarily collective and private firms that purchase inputs on the market. That sector is the most rapidly growing and, one might hypothesize, a potentially significant source of productivity growth. Fourth, it is not clear the extent to which the managers of state-owned firms really have adopted profit-maximizing decision rules.[19] Three or more decades of output-maximizing behavior may have engrained alternative decision rules that are not readily overthrown. Finally the persistence of the dual price structure over a period of time inevitably gave rise to widespread corruption that has undermined support for reform. The huge profits that can be made by illicitly reselling state allocated goods on the free market, at prices up to several times those paid to the state, has led to a widespread diversion of inputs to unplanned uses. While one can argue that those reallocations are economically efficient, they have given rise to huge income disparities and thus have undermined popular support for urban reform.

In short, in contrast to agriculture, the fixed-price structure in which state-owned industrial firms operate does not appear to provide the basis for rational decentralized decision-making. Most industrial prices do not reflect opportunity costs. The price structure discourages enterprise managers from expanding the output of many products whose production entails a financial loss, but that are highly valuable from society's point of view. Concomitantly, the price structure encourages enterprise managers to excessive production of overpriced goods that are financially profitable, but whose real value to society may be low or even negative.

Finally, because managerial rewards are unrelated to profits and the flow of government budgetary subsidies and bank loans to money-losing enterprises is seemingly unlimited, there are no sustained incentives for enterprise managers to reduce costs. Thus, even if state-owned firms operated increasingly in parallel markets or if the fixed-price structure could be magically corrected overnight, there is no assurance that managers would respond in the appropriate fashion.

The Competitive Environment

Limited competition in state-owned industry is a second fundamental factor inhibiting improvements in efficiency in manufacturing. Limits on competition are reflected in segmented markets for many products caused by barriers to internal trade and the absence of systematic rules for exit via bankruptcy.

In Eastern European nations competition in many product lines is limited by the small size of the domestic market. Thus, except to the extent that firms in these countries must compete with foreign producers, barriers to entry frequently inhibit the development of competition. In this regard, China, with a vast internal market, is much more favorably positioned. With a population roughly ten times that of all of the Eastern European countries combined, in virtually every sector the market is sufficiently large to support several, if not many firms. The aggregate figures reflect the contrast. In 1981 Hungary had only 714 state-owned industrial enterprises, China more than 80,000.[20]

Moreover, there are few formal barriers to entry in many lines of business in China. Machinery and many raw materials can be acquired on the open market, and the profusion of distribution channels now available makes reliance on the state commercial sector unnecessary for many products. This is borne out by the steady expansion in the number of state-owned industrial enterprises in China since the reform began. In 1978 there were 82,100 state-owned firms, by 1983 this number had expanded to 87,100, and by 1986 to 96,800.[21] By contrast, the number of enterprises in Hungary has fallen continuously since the introduction of the New Economic Mechanism and the degree of industrial concentration has increased.

While the data on the growing numbers of state-owned firms in China suggest increased competitive pressures that in theory should lead to a more efficient allocation of resources, many of the newly created firms may be seeking out the high financial return available in product lines where state-fixed prices are quite high. As suggested in the discussion above of China's price structure, high prices for some products do not reflect scarcity value but are a reflection of the fact that provincial and local governments can enact trade barriers and establish new firms to produce goods for which there is no real shortage of supply.

The result is a surprisingly low degree of specialization in production. Rather than produce a few products for a regional or even national market many localities attempt to be relatively self-sufficient in manufactured goods. The result is many small plants, producing at far less than optimum scale. While costs of local producers may be higher and quality lower, a local market is frequently assured by a blockade on products from other, more efficient regions.

The drive for local self-sufficiency is hardly new. During the First Five-Year Plan national economic planners attempted to capture economies of scale by enforcing a considerable degree of regional specialization in production. But these efforts were vastly reduced during the Great Leap Forward and were further eroded during the Cultural Revolution. But the trend toward local self-sufficiency appears to have been given a new impetus by the fiscal reforms that have accompanied industrial reform.[22]

China's post-1978 reforms have sought simultaneously to enhance the power of enterprise managers and of provincial and local governments. The experience of other socialist systems and of China in earlier reform periods suggests that this combination may lead to increased inefficiency, in part because in the absence of price reform it provides increased incentives for local protectionism. The expansion of the revenue-sharing system in particular has provided incentives for local governments to capture industries that generate significant "profits" which, under new revenue-sharing schemes, may be retained to finance local government expenditures. That type of rent seeking, a source of inefficiency whenever government regulations such as trade restrictions or price controls give rise to economic rents,[23] is particularly acute in China because the government-imposed price structure has created enormous disparities in rates of "profitability" of different branches of manufacturing. The rate of return on fixed assets in different subsectors of industry in 1982 varied from as high as 91 percent in food processing and 81 percent in textiles to as low as 3 percent in coal mining.[24] The scope for local initiative in starting new state enterprises is greatest in processing agricultural products since the inputs are less subject to central control than those, for example, used in petroleum refining.

Some regions that once shipped their raw materials elsewhere have sought to build their own processing facilities in recent years, particularly when they are allowed to retain a substantial share of the "profits" that invariably are generated when the final goods are somewhat overpriced and the major raw materials, agricultural goods, still somewhat underpriced. This has created significant difficulties for a municipality such as Shanghai, China's single most important industrial city, but one that is obviously heavily dependent on the flow of cotton, wool, animal hides, tobacco, and other agricultural raw materials for its processing industries. In the early years of reform the supplies of agricultural raw material distributed to the city fell by 32 percent.[25]

One example of this type is cigarette manufacturing, one of the activities included within the scope of the "food processing" industry. Although no tobacco is grown in the outlying counties that fall within the municipality, Shanghai historically has been a major manufacturer of cigarettes. When control of investment decisions was decentralized in the late 1970s, however, local authorities in tobacco-growing regions began to build up their own cigarette plants. The reason was not hard to find—the financial returns were unsurpassed. In 1982, for every 100 yuan of fixed assets the cigarette industry annually generated 667 yuan in profits and taxes. That was thirty-one times the average for all industry and ten times the next closest competitor, salt manufacturing.[26] On average during the Sixth Five-Year Plan the industry, which accounts for only about 5 percent of all retail sales in China, generated an excess of 10 billion yuan annually in profits, almost 10 percent of the fiscal revenues of all levels of government.

The establishment of additional cigarette factories outside Shanghai led to unutilized capacity in the industry in Shanghai and thus increased inefficiency in the use of capital. This problem was ultimately addressed by a directive prohibiting local governments in tobacco-producing regions from building additional cigarette factories; continuing complaints from Shanghai about the shortages of tobacco suggest the central government has had difficulty enforcing the restriction.[27]

Rent seeking via local protectionism occurs in the production of consumer durables and some producer goods as well. Rising domestic demand for bicycles, which followed from the sharp increase in real personal income after 1978, was met largely through an expansion in the number of firms in the industry. But the new entrants were small-scale, high-cost producers. The break-even point was about 300,000 to 500,000 units annually, a level reached by only 11 of the 140 bicycle factories in 1982.[28] The ability of new entrants to sell high-cost, frequently inferior products in local markets was assured by local protectionism. Sale of bicycles and other goods produced at lower cost but by more distant existing plants frequently was prohibited via trade barriers imposed by local commercial bureaus.[29]

The phenomenon of localized rent seeking is recognized as a flaw in the current institutional arrangements, but there is no clear strategy yet developed to address this problem. Zhao Ziyang's "Report on the Seventh Five-Year Plan," presented in the spring of 1986 at the fourth session of the Sixth National People's Congress was particularly revealing on this problem. The sharply rising investment rate of 1984–85, with its attendant shortages and inefficiencies, was said to be the result of the "random launching of new projects by localities and departments," a trend that if continued would make it "difficult to continue the ongoing reform of the economic structure." Localities were implored to "have the nation's interests in mind" and "strictly abide by and implement the state's macroeconomic policy decisions."[30] More recently, the failure to let competitive forces break down the barriers of local protectionism is evident in a new state directive that attempts to control the proliferation of inefficient small-scale manufacturing enterprises by establishing a minimum scale of capacity for new factories in power generation, iron and steel, nonferrous metals, chemicals, petrochemicals, building materials, motor vehicles, and light and textile industries.[31] If small-scale, high-cost producers were subject to competition from more efficient, lower-cost producers, such norms would not be necessary.

The contrast with agriculture is sharp. Under the present system in rural China, households, which hold long-term land leases, have considerable freedom to change their mix of output in response to changing prices and market demands. This is evident in the changes that have occurred annually since 1978 in the allocation of land to alternative crops and the reallocation of other factor inputs. Competition has intensified as restrictions on private marketing activity have been eased. Initially when rural markets were reopened in the late 1970s many restrictions applied. Marketing could only be undertaken by producers; middlemen were discouraged. Producers were restricted by regulations that limited both the physical quantities and spatial dimensions of their marketing activities. Certain farm crops, such as cotton, could still not be sold in rural markets. Marketing beyond one's closest market was prohibited and quantities were limited to what could be carried, pushed, or pulled by hand. By 1983 private rural ownership of trucks was sanctioned and long-distance, large-scale private marketing began in earnest.[32] The state, too, stepped up its own long-distance marketing of key agricultural crops. By 1983 interregional marketing of grain was ten times the prereform levels.[33]

Increased marketing both reflects and facilitates increased interregional specialization. High-cost local production of agricultural commodities for restricted markets increasingly has been replaced by specialized production in comparative advantage regions where farmers are now frequently producing for national markets. High-cost producers of these crops are forced to shift their cropping patterns, except to the extent high transport costs continue to provide them with a certain degree of natural protection. In manufacturing such competitive pressures are more limited.

In market economies efficiency in resource allocation depends not only on entry of firms into fields where rates of return are above average, but also the exit of firms where productivity is so low that they are unable to cover their marginal costs. But in China, exit of inefficient producers is so rare as to be practically nonexistent. China's reformers, recognizing that breaking the so-called iron rice bowl required both the possibility of individuals losing their jobs and the possibility of individual enterprises failing, began to discuss the concept of "socialist bankruptcy" in the early 1980s. Bankruptcy was placed on the legislative agenda at the second session of the Sixth National People's Congress in 1984. The State Council took the lead in drafting the legislation, a process that consumed two full years. The bankruptcy law, however, was not approved when submitted to the sixteenth meeting of the Standing Committee of the Sixth National People's Congress in June of 1986, but was sent back to the State Council for further revisions. Toward the end of the year the Standing Committee approved a watered down version of the law for "trial implementation."[34] The law was enacted by the Sixth National People's Congress at its fifth session, convened in late March 1987.[35]

But "trial implementation" of the law in selected localities was made conditional on approval of an "enterprise law" that was to establish the independence of state-owned enterprises and the primacy of the enterprise managers rather than the party committees within the firms. But Peng Zhen, the conservative president of the NPC, mobilized his forces and defeated the enterprise law in the eighteenth meeting of the Standing Committee of the NPC in December 1986, and thus it was sent back to the State Council for redrafting. Quite conspicuously, the law was not passed at the subsequent meeting of the Standing Committee in the spring of 1987, reportedly because of continuing disagreements over the appropriate role of the party in state firms.

Thus, while the draft bankruptcy law has been promulgated for trial implementation it is effectively in limbo. Moreover, unless the price formation process is reformed, even after the enterprise law is finally approved, it can only be implemented bureaucratically. A detailed investigation will be necessary to discover the cause of financial losses in each money-losing enterprise. Many money-losing enterprises may be burdened with artificially low prices for their final products. Others may be grossly mismanaged.

But both types of enterprises appear to be equally insulated from the possibility of bankruptcy by the present system that provides a growing volume of government subsidies. During the years the bankruptcy law has been under discussion the value of state subsidies has grown enormously. In 1981 subsidies to money-losing enterprises (as distinguished from price subsidies for urban consumption of grain, vegetables, and meat) amounted to 10 billion yuan. By 1987 the budgeted amount for this purpose had soared to 36 billion yuan.[36]

Labor Markets

A third element inhibiting productivity growth in manufacturing is the low level of development of the labor market in China's modern sector. Although technical and skilled manpower is in especially short supply it does not appear to be well allocated. Most school leavers are assigned permanent jobs and subsequent turnover is minimal. As David Granick has pointed out, compared to the Soviet Union, inter-enterprise competition for labor is virtually nonexistent in China. In contrast to the Soviet industrial enterprise where the annual quit rate is 17–20 percent, the Chinese enterprise has virtually no quits, is frequently constrained to replace retiring workers with one of his or her children, and faces severe administrative constraints on its choice of new recruits.[37] Since the state wage structure is quite compressed and the differential wage paid to highly skilled and technically trained workers as compared to unskilled labor is modest by international standards, enterprises have inadequate incentives to utilize skilled workers and technical personnel efficiently.

The Cost of Capital

At the outset of the reform it was widely recognized that underpricing of capital was a major source of inefficiency, encouraging firms to utilize machinery and equipment inefficiently. It was the root cause both of what Kornai calls the hunger for investment at the firm level and the periodic inability of the center to control adequately the aggregate rate of investment. Assets could be acquired at little or no cost to enterprises since their acquisition was financed by interest-free grants from the state budget. New construction projects could be initiated even if there was little prospect of completing them on a timely basis since there was little cost of tying up huge amounts of capital in such projects.

While the incentive to use capital wastefully had existed since the early 1950s in China, the incentive for waste was substantially enhanced in a little-noticed reform initiated in 1967.[38] Beginning that year provincial and municipal governments were allowed to retain the depreciation funds of locally controlled enterprises. Moreover, the monies were treated as extrabudgetary funds that increased the degree of discretion local governments could exercise in their use. Earlier these funds, which were determined as a fixed percent of the original value of fixed assets, were remitted in their entirety (along with enterprise profits) to the state treasury. Because enterprises that are losing money were allowed to treat these retained depreciation funds as a cost item covered by subsidies from the state treasury, the incentive for an enterprise to expand its assets was substantial. This incentive to hold assets was broadened in 1971 when the retention of depreciation funds was generalized to all industrial enterprises.

Since reform began, an increasing share of industrial investment has been financed by bank loans and by enterprise retained earnings. Although complete reliance on budgetary grants is a thing of the past, it is not clear that this has increased the cost of capital to firms to anything approaching its scarcity value. Banks, for example, are not independent organs and are frequently compelled to lend funds to support the projects favored by the local party secretary, even when the prospects for amortizing the loan are bleak.

In principle, state-owned enterprises might treat retained funds as a scarce resource to be allocated according to economic criteria. Given the very incipient stage of development of capital markets, however, firms and local governments cannot weigh the trade-off between returns on internal versus external invest-ments. In many cases the only feasible use of retained funds is to expand further the fixed assets under the direct control of the locality. Even if the social value of the incremental output is very low the investment will generate a financial return to the enterprise and locality into the indefinite future. In short, even in the current reformed system, enterprises and local governments still appear to follow an asset maximizing strategy. Fixed assets come to them below cost and then generate a permanent cash flow in the form of retained depreciation funds that are in no way connected with profits or with meeting goals for cost-reduction targets.

The contrast between industry and agriculture is striking. State funds for large-scale water conservancy investments and for mechanization of state farms are modest, and peasants finance the largest share of farm investment from their disposable incomes.

Summary

As measured by conventional performance criteria China's economic reforms seem far more successful than those of other centrally planned economies. Com-pared to socialist states in Eastern Europe, however, China is at a substantially lower level of economic development and the farm sector is far more important in terms of its contribution to national income. In short, China by conventional measures has done quite well both because of the revolutionary nature of the reforms in farming and because of the critical importance of that sector in a relatively low-income country. But China's gains in agriculture have already begun to slow significantly and to date the reforms in manufacturing do not appear to have been sufficient to induce a significant improvement in productivity.

There are several respects in which the manufacturing sector has not been fundamentally recast. Although prices for a small number of specific products have been rationalized somewhat and flexible prices have been introduced for above-quota production of some products, there has been no fundamental reform of the price formation process in manufacturing. The hierarchical structure through which enterprises are controlled similarly has been changed little. Indeed, in some ways the transfer of power to intermediate levels of political authority has increased the degree of supervision of production units. Moreover, these same intermediate levels of authority increasingly have used their enhanced administrative power to create local segmented markets in which inefficient small-scale local producers are insulated from competitive pressures. Finally, labor and capital markets are at such a primitive stage of development that the bureaucratic allocation of these resources is almost inevitable, reducing the prospect for increased efficiency of resource use.

While China's reformers may still overcome these difficulties, it appears in retrospect that the best opportunity for addressing these fundamental issues has passed. In the first half of the 1980s, there was a confluence of events that was highly favorable for more far-reaching urban reforms. At the time agriculture was growing rapidly, providing for increased levels of consumption without significant inflationary pressure. Imports were growing rapidly helping to meet rising consumption demand and serving as an important source of new technologies for manufacturing. Rapid import growth was possible for three reasons. China in 1984–85 was able to sell a sharply rising quantity of petroleum and refined products into a relatively strong international oil market. China also could draw down its foreign exchange reserves and utilize an increasing flow of direct foreign investment and loan funds.

In the latter half of the 1980s, there was less cushion to absorb the transitional disruptions and costs urban reforms necessarily entail. Farm output growth was down significantly and, as a consequence, food prices in 1987 and 1988 increased more rapidly than at any other period since the famine of the early 1960s. The reformers have conceded that the rise in consumer prices has reduced the real income of a significant portion of the urban population, and they have been forced to impose increased price controls and defer some additional planned price reform measures. Foreign exchange reserves are now somewhat smaller relative to imports and the increasing flow of foreign investment imperiled by the perception that China does not provide a hospitable environment for joint ventures or wholly foreign-owned firms. Moreover, the world oil market has softened, shifting the terms of trade against the Chinese. Thus, China found it necessary in 1986–87 to curtail drastically the growth of its imports. These developments pose a substantial additional challenge to China's pro-reform coalition.

Notes

1. State Statistical Bureau, *Chinese Statistical Abstract 1988*, p. 6; "Communique on China's Social and Economic Development in 1988," *Economic Daily*, March 1, 1989.

2. John P. Hardt and Richard F. Kaufman, "Policy Highlights: A Regional Economic Assessment of Eastern Europe," in *Eastern European Economies: Slow Growth in the 1980s*, Selected Papers Submitted to the Joint Economic Committee, U.S. Congress (Washington, D.C.: U.S. Government Printing Office, 1985), pp. viii–ix.

3. Internantional Bank for Reconstruction and Development, *World Development Report 1988* (New York: Oxford University Press, 1988), pp. 224–25.

4. Nicholas R. Lardy, *China's Entry into the World Economy* (New York: The Asia Society and Lanham, MD: University Press of America, 1987), p. 4; State Statistical Bureau, "1988 Communique."

5. Jan Vanous, "Macroeconomic Adjustment in Eastern Europe in 1981–83: Response to Western Credit Squeeze and Deteriorating Terms of Trade with the Soviet Union," in *Eastern European Economies*, pp. 28, 32–33.

6. Yuan Zhou, "Clamp Put on Foreign Borrowing," *China Daily*, April 24, 1989.

7. Vanous, "Macroeconomic Adjustment," pp. 28–29.

8. Nicholas R. Lardy, *China's Entry into the World Economy*, 37; State Statistical Bureau, *Chinese Statistical Abstract 1987*, p. 93.

9. Statistical Bureau, "1988 Communique."

10. D. Gale Johnson, "The Agriculture of the USSR and China: A Contrast in Reform," unpublished manuscript, September 1985.

11. Nicholas R. Lardy, "Prospects and Some Policy Problems of Agricultural Development in China," *American Journal of Agricultural Economics*, vol. 68, no. 2 (May 1986), pp. 451–57.

12. Gene Tidrick, *Productivity Growth and Technical Change in Chinese Industry*, World Bank Staff Working Paper Number 761 (Washington, D.C.: International Bank for Reconstruction and Development, 1986), p. 4.

13. Nicholas R. Lardy, "Technical Change and Economic Reform in China," unpublished paper, June 1987. There are many uncertainties surrounding the estimates—particularly the procedures used by the Chinese to construct the time series data for industrial fixed assets. The Chinese data are compiled in current prices that would result in an upward or downward bias in the index if prices of machinery and equipment and construction costs were rising or falling, respectively. Thomas Rawski, after attempting to correct for biases, argues that factor productivity in state-owned industry actually has increased since 1978.

14. Nicholas R. Lardy, "Dilemmas in the Pattern of Resource Allocation in China, 1978–1985," in Victor Nee and David Stark, eds., *Remaking the Economic Institutions of Socialism: China and Eastern Europe* (Stanford, CA: Stanford University Press, 1989), pp. 288–302.

15. Ibid., p. 291.

16. William Byrd, "The Impact of the Two-Tier Plan/Market System in Chinese Industry," *Journal of Comparative Economics*, vol. 11, no. 3 (September 1987), pp. 295–308.

17. Zhang Hongming, "Where Is the Dual-Track System of Producer Goods Headed?" *Wuzi jingji* (Commodity economics), no. 2 (1986), pp. 31–33, reprinted in *Shehui kexue* (Social science), no. 2 (1986), pp. 50–52.

18. In 1985 only 10.5 billion yuan in producer goods was distributed through producer goods trade centers, the unrestricted market for machinery, raw materials, and other producer goods. Above-quota output may be sold on these markets. State Statistical

Bureau, "Statistical Report on Economic and Social Development in 1985," *People's Daily*, March 2, 1985. The modest volume of these sales is confirmed in Shanghai where, in the first five years such sales were allowed, they totaled only 1.1 billion yuan. Xinhua, *China Daily*, January 21, 1986. By comparison, total producer goods output over these five years was in excess of 145 billion yuan. Shanghai Municipal Statistical Bureau, *Shanghai Statistical Yearbook 1983* (Shanghai: People's Publishing House, 1984), p. 81.

19. Dwight H. Perkins, "Reforming China's Economic System," *Journal of Economic Literature*, vol. 26, no. 2 (June 1988), pp. 615–19.

20. *Hungary: Economic Developments and Reforms* (Washington, D.C: International Bank for Reconstruction and Development, 1986), p. 86.

21. State Statistical Bureau, *Chinese Statistical Yearbook 1983*, 193; *Chinese Statistical Abstract 1987*, p. 38.

22. Michael Oksenberg and James Tong, "The Evolution of Central-Provincial Fiscal Relations in China, 1950–1983," unpublished manuscript, 1987.

23. The classic article on this topic is Anne O. Krueger, "The Political Economy of the Rent-Seeking Society," *American Economic Review*, vol. 64, no. 3 (June 1974), pp. 291–303. Jagdish N. Bhagwati refers to the same category of activities as directly unproductive, profit-seeking activities. He points out that while the activities provide income to the factors employed in them, their effect is to contract the available set of consumption possibilities of the economy as a whole. Jagdish N. Bhagwati, "Directly Unproductive, Profit-Seeking (DUP) Activities," *Journal of Political Economy*, vol. 90, no. 5 (October 1982), 988–1002.

24. World Bank, *China: Long Term Development Issues and Options*, p. 74.

25. Zhou Xiqiao, "A Preliminary Discussion of the Changing Trend and Rational Adjustment of the Prices of Industrial Raw Materials," *Finance and Economic Research*, no. 2 (1984), p. 30.

26. State Statistical Bureau, *Chinese Statistical Yearbook 1984*, pp. 267–68.

27. Xie Songxin, "State's Cigarette Profits Light Up," *China Daily*, December 30, 1985.

28. Gene Tidrick, *Productivity Growth and Technical Change*, p. 13.

29. World Bank, *China: Long-Term Development Issues and Options*, p. 74.

30. Zhao Ziyang, "Report on the Seventh Five-Year Plan," *Beijing Review*, no. 16 (1986), pp. VII, XI.

31. "State Issues Production Capacity Norms," *China Daily*, August 1, 1987.

32. Nicholas R. Lardy, "Agricultural Reform in China," a background paper prepared for the 1986 World Development Report.

33. Nicholas R. Lardy, "Grain Marketing and Import Demand in the People's Republic of China," unpublished manuscript, June 1985.

34. "China's Enterprise Bankruptcy Law (for trial implementation), *Economic Daily*, December 3, 1987.

35. "The Sixth National People's Congress Enacts Twenty-nine Laws," *People's Daily*, March 30, 1987.

36. *China: Long-Term Development Issues and Options*, 148. Wang Bingqian, "Report on the Implementation of the State Budget for 1986 and on the Draft State Budget for 1987," *Beijing Review*, April 27, 1987, p. VII.

37. David Granick, "Prices and the Behavior of Chinese State Industrial Enterprises: Focus on the Multi-Price System," unpublished manuscript, 1986.

38. Barry Naughton, "Savings and Investment in China," unpublished Ph.D. dissertation, Yale University, 1986, pp. 182–84.

Comments by Louis Putterman

Professor Lardy's paper provides an insightful and quite valuable analysis of the economics of the first post-Mao decade in China. Beginning with an aptly rosy depiction of the achievements, he concludes that the easy gains of the reforms are probably now behind China and that the prospect for the future are not merely uncertain but affirmatively dim, or at least dimmer than the recent past. I find the logic of his argument and the power of his illustration compelling. Much of what I can say by way of criticism must therefore be as a devil's advocate, rather than as someone convinced that the details of Lardy's arguments are wrong.

The central point of Lardy's paper, as I understand it, is that China's superior economic performance during the past decade, especially as compared with Eastern Europe, can be explained by the early successes of its agricultural reforms, and by the larger relative importance of agriculture to China as a more backward economy, and that industrial reform has thus far failed to achieve very significant results. Because the main effects of the agricultural reforms are likely to represent a one-time shifting upward of the agricultural growth path (a point also developed in Professor Dernberger's paper), because these gains are now mostly in the past, and because industrial reform continues to be a hard nut to crack, the prospect for continued reform and continued high growth are limited. That the recent decline in agricultural growth followed earlier predictions and warnings (e.g., by Lardy himself), that this could be expected is striking. The problems of industrial reform and the severity of the remaining inefficiencies of the state sector identified in the paper are also quite sobering.

While I agree with the basics of this analysis, I am less pessimistic about the prospects for economic growth, which I believe may not be quite so dependent on system change as Lardy's argument implies. A good place to begin discussing this point is with a statement in Professor Dernberger's paper [presented at this conference]. "That China's economy is a high growth economy," he writes, "is to be seen in the fact that the economy has achieved high growth rates since 1949 under a variety of policy regimes, including the 'ten terrible years' of the Cultural Revolution." Most economists do not disagree that China's per capita output grew at somewhat more than 4 percent per annum during the period in question, which was far better than the average low-income economy and somewhat above average for the less-developed countries as a whole. Although much of the *increase* in the overall growth rate in the Deng era can be attributed to the change in the rate of agricultural growth, the nature of that change is that *the rate of agricultural growth for the first time approached the growth rate of industry, which remained high.* Even if growth in the farm sector proper slows again—but note that much rural growth has of late come from rural industry, which has shown no sign of slowing down—overall economic growth can be expected to remain substantial.

The bottom line of my argument is that even though output at each point in time, and perhaps also the rate of growth in output over time, can be expected to be higher when resource allocation is efficient than when it is not, *inefficient* economies can also grow. Among the causes of China's broadly favorable economic performance since 1949 that are *not* systemic in nature can be listed as follows: (1) its positive base of cultural and individual human capital (the second of which has seen significant upgrading during the period in question); (2) its generous endowment of previously undeveloped natural resources; (3) the very low level of economic development that obtained at the beginning of the period; and (4) the achievement of relative political unification and stability after a long period when these were absent. The low level of dvelopment cannot be overemphasized as an explanation of the high growth rate to date, and a predictor of high growth in the future, assuming the continued presence of the other factors. This applies not only because of the greater importance of the rural sector (pointed out by Lardy), but also because of the arithmetic of industrial growth from a small base (mentioned by Dernberger), and the general backlog of technological and resource exploitation possibilities waiting to be tapped by such an economy. Geographic and cultural proximity to the most economically dynamic nations in the world is a complementary factor rendered operational by China's greater openness since 1978. (It also helps explain why that openness came about in the first place, i.e., through the "demonstration effect.")

Although *maximum* exploitation of these potentials may require that the economy operate on efficient principles, much of their effects may well be felt despite great inefficiencies. This is especially the case when the desire for economic growth, which may be associated with the nationalistic strand in the Chinese revolution, has risen to a new level of importance in the minds of China's leaders and educated personnel at both national and provincial levels. One can go further and suggest that certain institutional features that appear to be inefficient from the perspective of standard economics may well have their functional sides. For example, centralized allocation of resources, which has been associated with success in the *intensive* growth phase in the Soviet Union and the less-developed Eastern European countries, seems to have played a similar role in Chinese industrialization. Collective control over labor and other resources in the countryside had some positive effects in China, too: the development of irrigation, improvement of farmland, fostering of an indigenous green revolution, and beginnings of rural industrialization all took place under the Maoist regime and laid the groundwork for much of the growth spurt that began in 1978. In the countryside, at least, one is tempted to speak of a phase of "socialist primitive accumulation," during 1958 to 1978, that has paid large dividends in the era of liberalization.

Beyond this, there may even be some positive effects of the regional autarchy that Lardy quite correctly associates with very substantial efficiency losses. The idea here is similar to the dissent on free trade associated with the "dependencia" school and with China's old philosophy of "self-reliance." This approach urges a country to break out of the existing international division of labor by rejecting its inherited comparative advantage, and to achieve the transition to industrialization through a coordinated set of government interventions. Although the import-substitution thrust associated with these arguments has been significantly discredited in recent years, the benefits of at least partial self-isolation from the world economy have arguably been demonstrated by Japan in the nineteenth century and perhaps by China itself in the decades prior to 1978. Increasingly, too, students of business, political economy, and economic history are noting the role of strong states and massive government intervention in the pre-export growth phases of the South Korean and Taiwanese economies. That Shanghai is unable to dominate all of China in sales of many manufactured goods because of barriers to trade has both advantages and disadvantages from the standpoint of developing China as a whole.

Moreover, while as an economist I must agree with Lardy that such barriers should be used far more selectively than they have historically been and are presently being applied in China, I also cannot help but be impressed by the sheer entrepreneurial energy and urge to growth exhibited by governments at provincial, municipal, and county levels almost throughout the country. In many respects, China's decentralization is based on regional and local administrative units, rather than on enterprises. China's complement of growth-oriented political entrepreneurs is the kind of asset that must be envied by much of the economically more stagnant Third World.

With regard to reform as such, my disagreement with Professor Lardy is probably narrower. I agree entirely with the list of obstacles he cites, and do not mean to suggest that I see some idealized market-socialist economy as being just around the corner. I have greater faith than Lardy, however, that even enterprise managers emerging from decades of slothful existence in a nonmarket world would adopt profit-oriented behavior if only the requisite institutional changes—giving them the opportunity to generate profits and the right to claim benefits from them—occur. But more centrally, my *relative* optimism on reform stems from my belief that some of the most important changes in the Chinese economy are occurring in the sphere of rural (and suburban) industrialization, where the rules of the game are already far more competitive, although the entrepreneur is, as I just mentioned, often more a committee of local czars than a partnership of businessmen in the usual sense. As rural industrialization proceeds apace, the likely slowdown in agricultural growth will be offset in terms of overall growth in the countryside, and the state-sector's share of nonfarm output will decline.

Let me conclude on the question of political will. My own opinion here is undoubtedly worth no more than the next scholar's simple gut feeling. But I attach enormous importance to two factors: namely, the reemergence of nationalism as the most important surviving ideology in the present Chinese revolution, and the demonstration effect and close proximity of Asian economic powerhouses. The door has been opened to allow both populace and leaders to have a clear sense of how much further China has to go along the road to standing up, in an economic sense, in the rapidly changing modern world. The romantic appeal of extreme leftism has most likely been destroyed as an effective force in China. It is therefore difficult for me to imagine that Chinese leaders over the next decades will turn away from economic growth as a priority objective. Especially if reform winds continue to blow strongly in the Soviet Union, if the deficiencies of traditional socialist economic institutions with regard to the current information and bio-technological revolutions continue to be manifest, and if industrializing Asia completes the process of closing its gap in living standards with the earlier industrialized nations of Europe and North America by adhering to a market-centered economic model, it appears probable (although by no means certain) to me that even if reform is displaced from the Chinese agenda for brief periods, it will reemerge more or less of its own accord.

5

FOREIGN TRADE, CAPITAL INFLOW, AND TECHNOLOGY TRANSFER UNDER THE OPEN-DOOR POLICY

Kungchia Yeh

IN 1978 the Chinese leadership under Deng Xiaoping launched a new development program to modernize the Chinese economy. A major component of this program is the policy of opening China's economy to the outside world. In the subsequent decade, profound changes in China's foreign economic relations have taken place as a consequence of this policy. Not only has China's foreign trade increased by leaps and bounds, technology imports have also accelerated and foreign capital inflow has expanded on a scale unprecedented in the history of the People's Republic. This paper outlines the major trends in these developments, particularly those that are distinctly different from the past, examines the constraints and options for China to continue pursuing the open policy in the future, and concludes with some preliminary observations on the effect of the open policy on economic growth.

Trends and the Pattern of Foreign Trade since 1978

The most dramatic change in China's foreign trade is its rapid growth since 1978. Table 1 compares the nominal and real growth rates of the last decade with those prior to 1978. The first subperiod, 1952–57, covers the years immediately before the launching of the First Five-Year Plan and the period of the plan itself. It represented a unique phase of development under Soviet-type centralized planning. Some features of the development policy for this period were similar to those of the current open policy, such as the heavy reliance on foreign technology, sending students abroad, and foreign borrowing. Even though the door was open, however, it was open mainly to the Soviet Union and other

Table 1

Average Annual Growth Rates of Exports and Imports, 1952–1987
(Percent)

	1952–57	1957–70	1970–78	1978–87
In current prices				
Exports	14.2	2.7	20.0	15.2
Imports	6.1	3.4	21.3	13.3
In constant prices				
Exports	—	—	7.8	14.8
Imports	—	—	12.9	12.2

Source: Growth of exports and imports in current prices are based on totals from the *1988 Trade Yearbook*, p. 351. Those in constant prices are based on data from the *1984 Trade Yearbook*, pp. IV–5, and the *1988 Trade Yearbook*, p. 355. The price weights for the series in constant prices are not known. Presumably they were 1970 prices. It should be noted that the trade statistics are those compiled by the Ministry of Foreign Economic Relations and Trade, which are somewhat different from those given by the Customs Office. The latter, however, are available only for the period since 1979. For an explanation of the differences, see *Jingji ribao* (Economic Daily), March 4, 1986, p. 2.

communist countries. In part, this was because of the trade embargo imposed by Western countries during the Korean War. Nevertheless, exports grew at a rapid rate of 14 percent per year, and imports at 6 percent during this period.

The second subperiod, 1957–70, witnessed a sharp turn toward autarky by the leadership. It was the period when China experimented with the Great Leap and failed, Sino-Soviet relations sharply deteriorated, and the political upheaval during the Cultural Revolution profoundly disrupted economic growth. The leadership's desire for self-reliance and self-sufficiency was particularly strong. The importance of foreign technology was downgraded. China prided itself as being the only major country in the world without internal or external debts. In short, economic blockades by East and West closed the door from outside and China's self-imposed isolation closed it from the inside. As a result, foreign trade stagnated.

In the third subperiod, 1970–78, the leadership turned slightly outward as China joined the United Nations and U.S.-PRC relations started to thaw. The economy and hence its export capacity continued to grow at a moderate pace during this period. China began to import turnkey plants from the West. The rate of growth of both exports and imports was very rapid, about 20 percent per year.

In the period of the open policy, 1978–87, exports and imports both expanded at phenomenal rates, 15 and 13 percent, respectively. They were higher than those in the 1950s and 1960s but lower than in the 1970s. China's growth of foreign trade in the 1970s, however, was unusual, in part because of the low level in the aftermath of the Cultural Revolution, but mainly because of the sharp rise in world prices following the global energy crisis. A comparison of the growth of trade in constant prices for the period after 1970 shows that the real growth rate of exports in 1978–87 was much higher than in 1970–78, whereas that of imports remained about the same.

A major consequence of the rapid growth of exports and imports is China's increasing share of imports and exports in GNP, as shown in Table 2. First, in the period from 1952 to 1978, exports and imports as percentages of GNP remained more or less unchanged at about 5 percent. The open policy has now raised these ratios to more than twice the preceding levels, indicating a much stronger link to the world economy than ever before. Second, the rising average imports to GNP ratio since 1978 implies that the elasticity of imports with respect to GNP was greater than one. The high sensitivity of import demand to GNP growth has important implications for import projections. Third, China's share in world exports had declined during 1957–58, but since 1978 the trend has been sharply upward and by 1988 China had regained the lost ground.

Another distinctive feature of the recent development in foreign trade is that in 1978–88, China had a sizable deficit, in contrast to a more or less balanced trade prior to 1978.[1] To some degree, the current trade gap is related to changes in the direction of trade in recent years. The first notable change is the dramatic swing from trading primarily with communist countries in the late 1950s to predominantly with noncommunist countries in the 1980s. In 1957 the share of trade with communist countries was 59 percent of China's total trade. The swing began in the 1960s. By 1978 the share dwindled to 14 percent, and, under the open policy, it further declined to 9 percent in 1987.[2] Correspondingly, the share of China's trade with noncommunist countries reached 91 percent in 1988, far exceeding the share of communist trade even at the peak of the Sino-Soviet alliance.

It is noteworthy that the decline in the share of trade with communist countries in 1978–87 was not the result of a drop, but of an increase in the absolute volume at a rate slower than the growth of China's total trade. Unlike in the 1950s when the door was closed to the United States, it was open in the 1980s to both the Soviet Union and the United States. Indeed, Sino-Soviet trade in 1978–87 grew at a very rapid rate of 20 percent per year. By 1987, the Soviet Union was the fifth most important trading partner in China. According to the Sino-Soviet trade agreement, bilateral trade is expected to increase from 4.6 billion Swiss francs in 1985 to 9 billion Swiss francs in 1990, or at an annual rate of 14 percent.[3] The expansion in Sino-Soviet trade was not without an economic basis. Bilateral trade is conducted in barter terms so that there is no need for hard currency. Furthermore, China could export to the Soviet Union agricultural products and textiles that are difficult to sell on the world market in exchange for raw materials such as timber, steel, and cement. Then, China could obtain the Soviet equipment to renovate the 156 industrial projects imported from the Soviet Union in the 1950s. An agreement has already been reached for the Soviet Union to assist China in refurbishing 17 projects and building 7 new projects.

Table 2

Ratios of Imports and Exports to GNP in China

	1952	1957 (percent)	1978
Exports/GNP	4.0	5.2	4.7
Imports/GNP	5.5	4.7	5.2
PRC exports/world exports	1.0	1.4	0.7

Sources: 1. For exports and imports in 1952, 1957, and 1978, see State Statistical Bureau, *Zhongguo tongji nianjian* (China statistical yearbook 1981), p. 353. Those for 1988 are taken from *International Financial Statistics Yearbook 1989* (International Monetary Fund, 1989), p. 291. For GNP, see *Tongji* (Statistics), no. 6 (Beijing, 1985), p. 4 and Li Chengrui, "Only Socialism Can Develop China," *Beijing Review*, October 2–8, 1989, pp. 20–29. For the percentage of China's exports in world exports, see Editorial Board of the Almanac of China's Foreign Economic Relations and Trade, *Zhongguo duiwai jingji maoyi nianjian 1986* (1986 yearbook of China's foreign economic relations and trade), China Resources Trade Consulting Co., Ltd, Hong Kong, n.d., p. 950, and Editorial Board of the Almanac of China's Foreign Economic Relations and Trade, *Zhongguo duiwai jingji maoyi nianjian 1988* (1988 yearbook of China's foreign economic relations and trade); China Advertising Corporation, Hong Kong, n.d., p. 356.

The upward trend in Sino-Soviet trade, however, is not likely to alter the overall pattern characterized by the dominant position of the industrialized Western countries and the high degree of concentration of China's trade among a few Western partners. The shares of China's trade with its top five trading partners in 1957, 1978, and 1988 are shown in Table 3.

Although the degree of geographical concentration remains rather high, China has abandoned its former policy of leaning heavily on a single country. In 1988, trade with Hong Kong, the most important trading partner, accounted for 29 percent, substantially lower than the share of Sino-Soviet trade in 1957. Indeed, China has opened its door to virtually all countries of the world. Indirect trade with Taiwan rose sharply in recent years, and for the first time since 1949 China began trading with South Korea.

Another important change in the direction of China's foreign trade occurred in the overall balance of trade with key Western countries. Table 4 shows China's trade balances with countries grouped into four categories in 1957, 1978, and 1988. The first group includes six countries from which China imports mainly technology, equipment, and industrial materials. The second group includes four countries supplying grain to China. The third group includes three regions with which China maintains a large trade surplus. Trade with these thirteen countries in 1978 accounted for 63 percent of China's total exports and 66 percent of its total imports. The fourth category includes all other countries. The grouping is intended to show the changing characteristics of China's balance of trade in the 1950s, 1970s, and 1980s. In the 1950s China's trade was largely with the communist countries and conducted mainly on a bilateral balance basis

Table 3

China's Trade Shares with Top Trading Partners

1957		1978		1988	
Soviet Union	43.9	Japan	23.4	Hong Kong	29.4
Hong Kong	6.4	Hong Kong	13.3	Japan	18.5
East Germany	5.2	West Germany	6.6	United States	9.7
Czechoslovakia	5.0	United States	4.8	West Germany	4.8
Japan	3.7	Australia	4.0	Soviet Union	3.2
Subtotal	65.2	Subtotal	52.1	Subtotal	65.6
Total (5)	100.0		100.0		100.0
Total (U.S. $ billion)	3.11		20.64		102.79

Sources: Same sources as Table 2.

so that any imbalances that emerged were relatively small. The swing to trading with Western countries since then changed that and created a problem of hard currency to finance deficits in multilateral trade. The pattern in 1978 depicted in Table 4 shows how China used to deal with the problem before the open policy was adopted. China acquired machinery and grain from the Western nations and incurred a sizable deficit. To a large extent these deficits were covered by China's trade surplus with Hong Kong and Singapore. Trade with all other countries was kept more or less balanced so that the net balance with the first three groups of countries virtually represented China's trade balance.

In the decade since 1978, China continued to import technology and equipment from the Western countries but on a much larger scale than before. Similarly, grain imports increased sharply. China still earned substantial foreign exchange from Hong Kong and Singapore. Its imports from Hong Kong also increased rapidly, however, so that the export surplus could cover only a smaller portion of the deficit with the technology and grain suppliers. Consequently, China had a huge trade deficit in 1988. In its attempt to solve this problem, China has reoriented its major export effort toward the Western and the Third World countries. This brings us to the question of what China has been exporting to these countries.

A comparison of the commodity structures by broad categories of SITC classification in 1979 and 1988 shows some interesting changes (Table 5, p. 130).

Up to 1979, the overall pattern remains one of rather heavy dependence on the export of primary products to finance the imports of manufactured products. Since then, the share of manufactures exports has been rising, from 46 percent in 1979 to 70 percent in 1988. The change signifies the rapid growth of China's capability to compete in the world market for manufactures. It also suggests possible frictions with domestic manufactures in the major markets.

To examine the commodity structure at a less aggregate level, Table 6 (p. 131) compares the shares of the ten most important exports and imports in 1987,

Table 4

China's Trade with Major Country Groups, 1957, 1978, and 1988
(million U.S. $)

	1957			1978			1988		
	Exports	Imports	Balance	Exports	Imports	Balance	Exports	Imports	Balance
Technology suppliers	131	196	−65	3,033	5,591	−2,558	14,704	24,556	−9,852
Grain and food suppliers	3	19	−16	231	1,444	−1,213	797	3,785	−2,988
Foreign exchange suppliers	175	25	150	2,915	121	2,794	20,196	13,138	7,057
Subtotal	309	240	69	6,179	7,155	−963	35,696	41,479	−5,783
Others	1,291	1,270	21	3,566	3,738	−172	11,844	13,771	−1,927
Total	1,600	1,510	90	9,745	10,893	−1,148	47,540	55,251	−7,710

Source: China Statistical Yearbook 81; 1984 Trade Yearbook; China Trade Report, August 1989, pp. 14-15. Technology suppliers include the United States, Japan, West Germany, the United Kingdom, France, and Italy. Grain and food suppliers include Canada, Australia, New Zealand, and Argentina. Foreign exchange suppliers include Hong Kong, Macao, and Singapore. Subitems do not necessarily add up to totals because of rounding.

Table 5

Commodity Structures by Broad Categories of SITC Classification

	1979 (%)	1988 (%)
Exports:		
Primary products	53.6	30.4
Manufactured products	46.4	69.6
Imports:		
Primary products	28.2	18.2
Manufactured products	71.8	81.8

Sources: Editorial Board of the Almanac of China's Foreign Economic Relations and Trade, *Zhongguo duiwai jingji maoyi nianjian 1984* (1984 yearbook of China's foreign economic relations and trade) (Beijing: China's Foreign Economic Relations and Foreign Trade Publishing House, 1984), pp. iv–11; *Zhongguo duiwai jingji maoyi nianjian 1988*, pp. 35962; and *China Trade Report* (July 1989), p. 15.

classified by the two-digit SITC system, with those in 1978. The first notable feature about China's export structure in 1987 is its high degree of commodity concentration. The top three commodities (textile yarn and fabrics, petroleum and petroleum products, and clothing) remained on top in 1987 as in 1978, accounting for 39 percent of total exports. The rather high degree of export concentration indicates that, if and when external conditions relating to these few commodities change, the effect on China's total exports would be quite profound. The drop in world oil prices and the rise of protectionism against textiles in the advanced countries in recent years are cases in point.

The most significant change since 1978 was the sharp increase in the relative importance of key manufactured products (clothing, arms, electrical machinery, and travel goods) in total exports. Arms exports were particularly notable, increasing from U.S. $7 million in 1978 to U.S. $2,389 million in 1987, a 241-fold increase in nine years.[4] Meanwhile, the relative shares of exports of primary products (fish, vegetables and fruit, and petroleum) declined.

On the import side, there has been a sharp rise in the shares of electrical and nonelectrical machinery, textile yarn, plastic materials, and precision instruments. The major items that declined in importance include iron and steel, textile fibers and wastes, cereals, and transport equipment.

To recapitulate, China has stepped up the import of equipment and other manufactured products. China still depends heavily on a few product groups to finance these imports. In the 1950s the most important item was agricultural products. From the 1960s on, textiles became prominent. By the 1970s, crude oil exports joined the other two. In the 1980s, the list included also military equipment. The crucial question for the future is whether the growth of these exports can keep pace with the growth of imports, and, if not, what options are open in order to keep the open policy viable?

Table 6

Major Exports and Imports of China, 1978 and 1987
(Percent)

	1978	1987
Exports:		
Clothing	7.1	16.5
Textile yarn and fabrics	16.9	14.3
Petroleum and petroleum products	12.6	8.4
Military firearms	0.1	5.0
Electrical machinery	1.4	4.6
Textile fibers	3.9	3.5
Vegetable and fruits	6.1	3.3
Chemical elements	1.4	2.5
Travel goods	0.5	2.4
Fish and fish preparations	2.8	2.0
Subtotal	52.7	62.5
Total	100.0	100.0
Imports:		
Machinery	8.6	18.1
Electrical machinery	2.2	12.4
Iron and Steel	28.9	10.9
Textile yarn	1.9	8.2
Transport equipment	9.0	6.1
Plastic materials	1.3	4.2
Cereals	9.0	3.6
Textile fibers	8.7	3.5
Chemical elements	3.6	3.3
Precision instruments	1.2	2.8
Subtotal	74.6	73.0
Total	100.0	100.0

Source: Estimates are based on SITC two-digit totals given in *China: International Trade, Annual Statistical Supplement*, Central Intelligence Agency, 1984 and 1989. Both exports and imports are FOB. Items do not necessarily add up because of rounding.

To assess China's foreign trade prospects, it will be convenient to begin with a simple framework relating imports to aggregate income. We have noted earlier that China's income elasticity of demand for imports in the 1980s was rather high. At the same time, China's projected GNP growth is also quite high, 7.2 percent per year in the next decade or so. If China's GNP growth is higher and its elasticity of imports no lower than those of the major countries importing from China, then China's trade deficit is likely to be a long-term one. Barring serious political upheavals in the future, China's GNP growth is likely to exceed those of its major trading partners, with the possible exception of Hong Kong.

China's income elasticity of imports is also likely to remain high because of increasing dependence on imported machinery and industrial raw materials. Hence, viewed from the perspective of comparative GNP growth, a long-term trade imbalance is quite plausible.

The real world, however, is more complicated. Much depends also on the price elasticities of China's exports and China's ability to expand its share of the market, particularly for its agricultural and energy products, the internal constraints are likely to be more important. China's agricultural production has had phenomenal growth since 1978, due partly to the replacing of the commune system with household farming, partly to sharp increases in the procurement prices of agricultural products and in the supply of chemical fertilizers, and partly to the opening of rural markets. The effects of these changes, however, appeared to be leveling off. Meanwhile, new problems emerged, such as the neglect of the maintenance of irrigation systems, reduction in the cultivated acreage, the peasants' lack of incentive to invest in farmland, and a decline both in the absolute and relative size of state investment in agriculture. If a slowdown in agricultural growth should occur, not only will export growth be adversely affected but imports of such products as grain, vegetable oils, and chemical fertilizers may have to be increased, thus worsening the trade balance.

Similarly, there are some uncertainties concerning China's capacity to increase its energy exports. China today is facing an acute shortage of energy. The domestic demand for energy is likely to accelerate because of rapid growth of such energy-consuming sectors as transportation, synthetic fibers, and metallurgy, rising rural demand for commercial energy, and rapid urbanization. Meanwhile, output in the two decades after 1980 is projected to grow at only 3.5 percent per year. Energy conservation will have to fill a good part of the gap. But even allowing for considerable improvements in conservation, according to the State Council's research group, the energy gap in the year 2000 will widen to 15–20 percent of projected output in that year.[5] Under the circumstances, rapid growth of energy exports is still feasible, but only at a very high cost to the domestic economy. If the energy shortage should constrain GNP growth, the leadership might decide to cut oil exports. Of course, the discovery and development of a large onshore or offshore oilfield would change the picture. But no such discovery has been reported thus far.[6] Efforts have been made in recent years to increase coal exports with notable results. Also, large-scale developments in hydroelectric power are being planned, and, if realized, they could enhance China's export capacity by releasing other primary energy products for export. Of course, China must still face the uncertainty of the world prices of coal and oil.

The factors constraining the growth of textile exports are mainly external, including most restrictions by the advanced countries and competition from other developing countries. Because most of China's fabrics and clothing exports are medium- or low-grade products, any significant growth would require a shift to exporting high-grade products.[7] It will not be an easy task for an industry that had thrived in a seller's market and under the planner's sovereignty in the last three decades. The Chinese, however, had been able to increase their total textile exports rapidly and continuously since 1978. It remains to be seen whether the momentum can be sustained.

An important step taken by China to deal with antidumping charges or discriminatory restrictions on China's textile or other exports is its recent attempt to join the General Agreement on Tariffs and Trade (GATT). After China joins GATT, a signatory cannot take unilateral action against China for charges of dumping of subsidies and must handle the matter according to the GATT provisions. Furthermore, China, as a signatory of GATT, will be eligible for tariff reduction in the United States under the generalized system of preference. The preferential treatment will considerably enhance China's competitive position relative to countries like Taiwan and South Korea in the U.S. market.

Little can be said about the potential for China's arms exports. The market seems vast, particularly for the relatively low-priced equipment made by China. At present, China's defense industries apparently have sizable excess capacities because of the leadership's decision to postpone large-scale weapon modernization until some years later. There should be no serious restrictions on the supply side. Nevertheless, there may be political constraints, as in the case of selling missiles to Iran, and possible competition from other suppliers, such as the Soviet Union.

The Chinese planners are obviously aware of all these problems and uncertainties, as evidenced by the vigorous effort to achieve breakthroughs in new directions. Four important policy measures in the connection deserve note.

The first is the policy of utilizing imports to develop exports.[8] One such measure is to import raw materials to be processed for exports, such as importing cotton, wool, and jute and exporting clothes and gunny sacks. Another form is to import parts for assembling in China and export the finished products. Examples are the exports of watches, motorcycles, and recorders made with imported parts. A third way to promote exports through imports is compensation trade, which simply means payment for imports in the form of Chinese goods. In 1982, exports directly linked to imports constituted approximately 40 percent of the total.[9] More significant, great emphasis has been placed on the import of technology to facilitate the technological transformation of export industries.[10] For example, based on imported technology, China's television industry is now producing sets with sufficiently high quality to edge into the international market.[11] In sum, one important aspect of the open policy relates to the reorientation of imports. In the 1950s, imports were to support domestic economic construction. Hence, the 156 Soviet aid projects were almost totally unrelated to China's export capacity. In the 1960s and 1970s, imports were mainly to support China's policy of import substitution. For example, the purchase of chemical fertilizer plants from abroad was intended to reduce China's dependence on the import of fertilizers and grain. In the 1980s, the goal of imports was broadened to include export promotion, as illustrated by the acquisition of foreign technology in off-shore oil exploration and coal mining.

Another important feature of the current policy is to develop vigorously new exportable goods and services. Potential in three areas is particularly noteworthy. The first is the direct export of labor in the form of construction service abroad. Prior to 1978, sending Chinese laborers abroad would have been ideologically unthinkable, except to socialist countries. But now such practices are being promoted.[12] During the years 1980 to 1985, China had contracted for more than 2,800 projects worth U.S. $5.1 billion in eighty-eight countries, and so far U.S. $2.5 billion has been received from the completed projects.[13] A third area is technology exports. In recent years China began exporting technology in the fields of medicine, electronics, and metallurgy, to such countries as Japan, Switzerland, and Luxembourg.[14] During the period from 1979 to mid-1987, China exported eighty-four items amounting to U.S. $109 million.[15] The interesting feature is that some of the technology exported were quite advanced by world standards. Examples are new material KTP crystal (potassium titanium oxide phosphoric acid), exported to Vacuum Technology of Japan, and the two-stage fermentation technology to manufacture vitamin C, exported to Hoffman-Laroche of Switzerland. A more striking example is China's satellite launching service for foreign commercial customers. Each of these steps is a small one in terms of the amount of foreign exchange earned, but together they signify the entrepreneurial spirit that is vital to successful implementation of the open policy.

A third novel development is the creation of experimental special economic zones (SEZs). In 1979 the leadership decided to establish four SEZs in Shenzhen, Zhuhai, and Shantou in Guangdong Province and Xiamen in Fukien Province. What is special about these zones is the preferential tax treatment of foreign investment and foreign trade, and the liberal policies toward enterprises in these zones. The SEZ was intended to be a multipurpose experiment, where the promotion of exports was not the only nor the most important objective. Originally the planners had two main objectives. One was to promote economic relations with foreign countries to attract and absorb foreign technology, management techniques, and capital. The other was to experiment with various measures of economic and management reform. The SEZ would serve as a case study of how entrepreneurs might operate in a quasi-socialist setting.[16]

The concept of the SEZ seemed so promising that the government decided in 1984 to open fourteen coastal cities and Hainan Island to foreign investment, and in 1985 extended the opening to three regions: the Zhujiang Delta, the Changjiang Delta, and the Minnan Delta. These cities and regions are actually in a better position to attract foreign capital than the four SEZs because of their well-developed infrastructure and industrial system. But before any significant progress could be made, numerous problems emerged in the SEZs, setting off a debate at the high levels over the role of the zones.[17] The state had invested an enormous amount of money in the zones. Yet they attracted little advanced technology. Most foreign investments concentrated in services rather than industrial production. Corruption became rampant. Worse still, the enterprises in the zones sold more on the domestic market than on the world market so that the zones could not balance their international payments.[18]

By the end of 1985, the debate over the future of the SEZs was apparently resolved. The purpose of the zones has been redefined to emphasize outward orientation, industrial development, and high technology. It is yet too early to tell if the new policy has an effect on exports.

In the meantime, the Tiananmen massacre has made the future uncertain. According to the Chinese, apart from temporary disruptions during and immediately after the incident, there had been virtually no adverse effect on China's exports.[19] Imports of technology had been affected to some extent by the economic sanctions imposed by Western countries restricting transfer of military technology and suspending government loans to China. Clearly, the Chinese have grossly underestimated the negative effects of the recent turmoil on China's foreign exchange earnings the shortage of which seriously constrains imports. In the first nine months of 1989, the trade deficit already totaled U.S. $6.5 billion.[20] As a direct consequence of the incident, revenue from tourism is expected to lose U.S. $1.3 billion in 1989.[21] The squeeze on China's foreign exchange reserves is further tightened by the suspension of loans by the World Bank. The risks of political stability and uncertainties about the future of economic reform also have a deterring effect on commercial lending to China.

By October 1989, the effect of foreign exchange shortage was already evident. Imports of not only consumer goods but also critically needed raw materials, such as steel, chemical fertilizer, and plastics, were being cut.[22] Because many imported materials were used directly or indirectly to produce exportable products, curtailing imports eventually will also adversely affect China's exports.

Another impact of the Tiananmen massacre was the decision by the GATT shortly after June to postpone a meeting that was to consider a bid by China to join the trade forum.[23] Whatever potential advantage in foreign trade that China might derive from joining the GATT has thus been delayed. At the same time, the suspension of reform by the Chinese leadership may raise new doubts in the minds of the GATT members about the compatibility of China's current policy orientation with the GATT's general principles based on free market economies.

Utilizing Foreign Capital

Apart from rapid expansion of foreign trade, another important change under the open policy is the large influx of foreign capital since 1978. The main purposes of China's promoting capital inflow are the following: to supplement domestic savings, to augment the supply of foreign exchange, and to bring in new technology and management techniques along with foreign capital. The foreign funds sought by China can be divided into two categories: foreign investments and loans. Table 7 presents the amounts of foreign funds China received in the period from 1979 to 1988. The record shows that total capital inflow increased from an annual average of U.S. $3 billion in 1979–81 to about U.S. $10 billion in 1988. In the decade since the implementation of the open policy, China mobilized $47 billion, substantially more than the total foreign loans and investments in the three decades prior to 1979.[24]

From the planners' viewpoint, however, the structure of foreign capital was less than ideal. First, the Chinese planners generally prefer foreign investments to loans, partly because direct investments facilitate technology transfer, partly because provisions for repatriation of capital and earnings are less rigid than in the case of foreign loans, and partly because foreign investors often have well-developed marketing channels and management experience, an area in which the Chinese lack expertise. Cumulative foreign investments in 1979–88, however, accounted for only 14 percent of the total.

Second, by far the largest share of total foreign investments in 1979–88 came from Hong Kong.[25] The United States and Japan were the second and third most important sources. The pattern suggests that, during this period, the overseas Chinese were the largest investors. American and Japanese manufacturers have not yet played any significant role.

Third, the allocation of foreign investments in 1979–85 was somewhat lopsided, as shown in Table 8 (page 138).

About half of all the investments in joint ventures and cooperative joint ventures went into real estate construction, including hotels, commercial buildings, and apartments. A substantial share of the investments in joint ventures was in light industry and textiles. In short, most of the investments were not in high-technology industries as the Chinese planners had hoped. Since 1985, the situation improved somewhat. In 1985, 70 percent of the contracts were for investment in "productive" sectors, rising to 85 percent in 1988.[26]

Even before the June 4 massacre occurred, China had some problems in its attempt to attract foreign investment. Apparently, the poor investment environment, limited access to the domestic market, and difficulty in converting profits in domestic currency into foreign currency have been the key factors deterring new investment. The poor investment climate is the product of the economic system now being reformed. A basic characteristic of this system is the highly centralized decision-making tradition and the hierarchical administrative structure that gives rise to red tape and bureaucratic practices confronting foreign investors. Another characteristic is that, in a command economy that operates on the basis of planners' sovereignty, the legal system is inevitably underdeveloped, taxes and levies arbitrary, and the interpretation of existing laws cryptic. The direct allocation system of distributing key materials such as cement, steel, and electric power makes it difficult for domestic and foreign enterprises alike to ensure adequate supply of raw materials as the need arises. Prolonged neglect of

Table 7

Foreign Loans and Investment, 1979–1988
(million U.S. $)

	1979–81	1982	1983	1984	1985	1986	1987	1988
Total	10,211	2,432	1,980	2,705	4,462	7,258	8,452	9,840
A. Foreign loans	9,090	1,783	1,065	1,286	2,506	5,014	5,805	6,577
Government loans	925	553	716	723	486	841	798	—
International organizations	932	3	73	183	604	1,342	715	—
Buyers' credit	206	188	106	133	126	178	473	—
Foreign banks	6,700	860	—	122	526	1,495	2,580	—
Bond issues and shares	328	178	170	124	762	1,159	1,239	—
B. Foreign investments	738	430	636	1,258	1,659	1,874	2,313	2,678
Joint ventures	65	34	74	255	580	804	1,486	—
Contractual joint ventures	353	178	227	465	585	794	620	—
Joint exploration	318	178	291	523	481	260	183	—
Foreign-owned enterprises	1	39	43	15	13	16	24	—
C. Commercial credit	383	219	280	161	297	369	323	647
Compensation trade	282	122	197	98	168	181	222	—
Leasing and processing	101	97	83	63	129	188	111	—

Source: Trade Yearbook (TY) 84, pp. iv–183, 184; *TY86*, p. 1212; *TY87*, p. 618; *TY88*, p. 592; *SSB 1989*, pp. 22–23.
Note: Data missing from the table were not available.

Table 8
Allocation of Foreign Investments, 1979–1985

	Joint Venture	Cooperative Venture (%)	Foreign-owned
Real estate	48.5	50.0	—
Machinery and electrical equipment	17.5	2.0	50.0
Light industry and textiles	20.0	5.0	30.0
Energy	10.0	20.0	—
Agriculture	—	8.0	—
Materials	—	10.0	—
Others	4.0	5.0	20.0
Total	100.0	100.0	100.0

Source: Chu Baotai, "China's Use of Foreign Capital in Recent Years," Wen huibao (August 5, 1986), p. 9.

science and technology in the past has created a shortage of technical manpower which the foreign investors must develop for themselves. And decades of a local self-reliance policy have left the transportation system totally unprepared for an open economy. In short, the poor investment environment is part and parcel of the economic system, and, as such, it can improve significantly only if the entire system improves. The implication is that improvements in the investment climate will be slow.

The foreign investors are attracted by China's cheap labor, natural resources, and the domestic market. Chinese labor is not as cheap as it appears, however. A comparison of the investment costs in Shenzhen and Hong Kong in 1986 reveals that the average wage and welfare benefits of an ordinary worker in the SEZ would be 87 percent of that in Hong Kong; that of a technical worker, 80 percent; and that of a managerial worker, 90 percent.[27] The comparative advantage in labor costs is often offset by higher costs of other items, such as electricity, machine repairs, costs due to delays, and miscellaneous fees. Not surprisingly, it costs Nike more to make shoes in China than in Maine, and Peugeot more to make trucks in China than in France.[28] At the same time, no major oil fields have been discovered by the foreign firms involved in joint exploration, and the low world price of oil has provided no incentive for more exploration. About the only new project of any significant scale in energy development is the Pingshou coal mine.

The huge potential market in China is perhaps the most important incentive for foreign investment. The problem is that the Chinese government generally keeps the domestic market off limits to foreign investors, partly to protect domestic industry and partly to urge the joint ventures to sell the products abroad and earn foreign exchange. The conflict of objectives could be resolved if the products are competitive in quality and price in the world market. But most products produced by the joint ventures are not.[29] The problem of foreign exchange shortage is further compounded by the need of some joint ventures to import raw materials or parts not available in China, and by the need of foreign investors to convert their accumulated Chinese currency into foreign exchange. The problem of foreign exchange is illustrated by the sizable trade gap of these enterprises in 1985. Total imports of these enterprises amounted to U.S. $1,495 million and exports, U.S. $466 million, leaving a gap of U.S. $1,029 million, roughly 11 percent of the trade deficit for the nation as a whole.[30]

In 1986, China planned to import U.S. $40 billion of foreign capital during 1986–90.[31] Of this total, two-thirds would be foreign loans, the rest being foreign investment. If this plan is to be realized, China would need U.S. $15 billion of foreign capital in 1989–90. What are the prospects of achieving this goal in the aftermath of the political turmoil in June 1989? According to the Chinese officials, the future is not as bleak as it seems. In 1988, most of the foreign-funded enterprises reportedly showed profits and their net foreign exchange earnings have improved.[32] Indeed, even the Tiananmen Square incident did not deter foreign investors. In the first three quarters of 1989, new foreign investment totaled U.S. $2 billion, an increase of 29 percent over the same period last year.[33] Of the 4,281 new foreign-funded enterprises during the January-September period, 1,249 were approved in the third quarter.[34]

In sharp contrast to the optimistic assessment of the Chinese officials, the Western media reported a loss of foreign investors' confidence after the June massacre.[35] Their main concerns were the stability of the new leadership and the prospects of economic reform. Because of the uncertainties, some investors have suspended their plans for new investment in China.[36] Others began to look elsewhere for investment outlets.[37]

Whatever the prospects for foreign investment, China will need substantial foreign loans in the future. The crucial question is China's capacity to borrow, which depends on the growth of external debts and exports. Table 9 shows estimates of China's foreign debts in 1982–88. The International Monetary Fund (IMF) estimates are considerably higher than the official ones. Nevertheless, both series indicate the same rapidly rising trend. In six years (1982–88) the total debt jumped almost sixfold, increasing at an average annual rate of 37 percent, three times the growth rate of exports over the same period.[38]

The sharp rise in foreign borrowing had caused some concern among Western bankers even before the June massacre occurred, for the following reasons. First, the proportion of short-term debt in China's loan portfolio is rather high, about 33 percent in 1987, higher than what is generally considered normal (25–30 percent). Furthermore, long-term commercial debt in 1987 stood at U.S. $14 billion, or 57 percent of China's total long-term debt.[39] This means that the debt service is heavier than if the share is smaller, because interest rates on commercial loans are generally higher than those for government or World Bank loans. The second concern is the high proportion of yen-dominated loans in China's

Table 9

China's Foreign Debt, 1982–1988
(year-end totals in U.S. $ million)

China's official estimates

Medium and long term	6,058	6,397	5,861	9,406	16,700	24,500	32,700
Short term	*	*	1,373	6,419	4,800	5,700	7,300
Total	6,058	6,397	7,234	15,825	21,500	30,200	40,000

International Monetary Fund (IMF) estimates

Medium and long term	NA	5,624	6,485	10,877	17,900	24,300	NA
Short term	NA	3,984	5,600	9,007	8,700	12,000	NA
Total	NA	9,608	12,085	19,884	26,600	37,300	47,000

*Negligible; NA: Not available.
Source: 1982–85 : *Far Eastern Economic Review*, March 26, 1987, p. 53; 1986–88: *People's Daily*, October 7, 1989, p. 1; *Far Eastern Economic Review*, November 2, 1989, p. 48; and *International Monetary Fund*.

total debt. The bulk of the yen debt was contracted at a time when the value of the yen was low in terms of the U.S. dollar. Because China's exports earn mostly U.S. dollars, the appreciation of the yen increases China's real debt burden substantially. Third, China's debt payments are expected to rise sharply from U.S. $4.5 billion in 1988 to a peak of U.S. $10 billion in 1992.[40] Chinese officials have repeatedly stated that China will have no problem in repaying its debt, and that the debt service ratio will reach only 5 to 10 percent by 1992.[41] Still, China's Vice Finance Minister announced that China would take out new loans to repay old ones over the next two years when facing a debt repayment peak.[42] If and when that happens China will find new borrowing more difficult and more costly than before because of the Tiananmen Square incident. At present, foreign lending has virtually stopped, as the World Bank, the Asian Development Bank, and some Western governments held up negotiations for new loans to China as part of the economic sanctions against China. Some commercial banks have also suspended plans for lending to China, although others have been quietly making small and short-term loans to China.[43] But even if these institutions and governments should resume lending in the future, commercial banks will probably charge higher interest rates than before because of higher political risks.[44]

In addition to political risks, economic risks are also mounting. As noted earlier, there has been a sharp drop in tourist income in the wake of the Tiananmen massacre. Loans outstanding to China's hotel and real estate sector amounted to 15 to 20 percent of China's total debt, and this sector is now in trouble.[45] More generally, continued delay in economic reforms is likely to see further deterioration in China's confidence which, shattered by the June 4 incident, cannot be rebuilt overnight. In the meantime, the possibility of a liquidity crisis looms on the horizon.

Technology Transfer

China's vigorous effort to attract foreign investment and borrow abroad is related to its need for foreign technology. An enormous gap exists today between China's technological level and that of the advanced countries. To narrow this gap China has set ambitious goals for its science and technological development in the next decade. By 2000, China's technological capacity will reach the levels of the developed countries in the 1970s and early 1980s. Achieving these goals is crucial to the attainment of the grand objective of quadrupling the 1980 GNP by the year 2000, because such a high rate of economic growth cannot be sustained by increasing capital and labor inputs alone, and total factor productivity must be raised essentially through technological advancement. In this process, technology transfer can upgrade technological levels, enhance China's ability to develop new products, introduce management and marketing techniques, improve quality, reduce costs, and boost China's competitiveness in international markets.

Not unexpectedly, the volume of technology imports reached an unprecedented scale since the implementation of the open policy, as the following data show: average annual imports, in million U.S. $, in 1950–60 was 245; in 1962–68, 37; in 1973–78, 1,158; and in 1979–88, 2,100.[46] Technology imports as defined here refer to the acquisition of licenses, patents, technical services, and technology-embodied equipment. If we define technology imports more broadly to include the transfer of technical knowledge through training, scholarly exchanges, and so forth, the contrast between recent and past developments would have been even more striking.

As the volume of imports increased, there have also been notable changes in the structure of imports. First, about 70 percent of the technology imports were from the United States, Japan, West Germany, Britain, and France, in contrast to the situation in the 1950s when the Soviet Union was virtually the sole supplier. Among the Western suppliers, the United States is the most important for good reasons. The United States has the largest technical-industrial complex in the world and is at the forefront in a number of fields of great interest to the Chinese, such as supercomputers, microbiology, and materials sciences. In the last two decades, the United States has attracted many high-powered scientists from all over the world to settle in the country. Among them is a large congregation of Chinese scientific manpower with which China has made great efforts to establish a close relationship. Most American businessmen are eager to sell technology to China. The U.S. government has also made use of technology transfer to strengthen Sino-U.S. relations. But the United States is only one of the forty suppliers. There appears to be a deliberate effort for China to diversify the sources of supply among countries and among manufacturers within a country. The intent is to put China in a better bargaining position among many sellers. Partly for this purpose, the Chinese are also importing technology from the Soviet Union and from Eastern European countries.

Another notable change in China's acquisition pattern is the shift of emphasis from buying turnkey plants to buying key components, and from buying machinery and equipment to buying technical know-how. In terms of industrial users of imported technology, the priority sectors used to be machine-building, metallurgy, and the heavy industries. Now many other industries are importing technology, including energy, transport and communications, textile, and light industries.[47]

A third notable policy shift includes the change from importing technology for new plants to importing technology for the technological transformation of existing enterprises, from acquiring technology for import substitution to technology for export promotion, and from insistence on state-of-the-art technology to used plants and equipment.[48] All these changes indicate a more pragmatic, cost-effective approach to technology imports than previously.

Fourth, China has greatly increased the number of students sent abroad since 1978, making extensive use of this particular channel of technology transfer. In the brief period from 1976 to 1989, fifty-eight thousand students studied abroad, compared to only twelve thousand during the twenty-seven years from 1949 to 1976.[49]

There can be little doubt that China would continue to acquire foreign technology on a sizable scale. There may, however, be some external and internal constraints blocking the future trend. On the part of foreign businessmen, a major concern is inadequate protection of technical information, despite the enactment of China's patent law. Another concern is that China may become a competitor on the world market. Then, technologies China wants to buy may be subject to controls by foreign governments and the Coordinating Committee on Multilateral Export Controls. Although restrictions on technology exports to China have been easing since the 1970s, some high technology is still under strict control. The restrictions may even be tightened, as was the case when the United States recently decided to curb high technology exports to China in response to China's refusal to acknowledge shipping missiles to Iran. The Tiananmen massacre has made matters worse. The Western countries not only suspended all sales of military technology to China, they also permitted the Chinese students to extend their stay, thus disrupting the inflow of some key technologies.

Internally, the principal constraint is China's foreign exchange reserves. There had been a sharp cutback in technology imports following China's overspending abroad in 1978. Technology imports surged forward in 1985 after three consecutive years of trade surplus in 1982–84. Looking ahead, a Chinese official from the State Administration of Exchange Control anticipated a shortage in foreign exchange reserves for a long time to come.[50] If indeed a shortage persists, the growth of technology imports will be limited by China's own buying power, even if there is no restriction on the supply of technology.

The Open Policy and Economic Growth

To what extent have the profound changes under the open policy contributed to economic growth? We shall only present some preliminary observations, in part because the complexity of the problem demands a more elaborate analysis than is feasible here, and in part because some of the long-term effects have yet to unfold.

In general, the growth of exports affects economic growth through its impact on output and employment of the export or export-related industries, and on domestic productivity because of scale and external economies. In China's case, both the static and dynamic gains seem significant. China benefited from its natural endowment and exported on a relatively large scale crude oil, coal, nonferrous metal ores (tungsten and bauxite), and processed or unprocessed agricultural products (silk, cotton, animal hair, soy beans, oil seeds, vegetables, and hogs). The rapid growth of exports of manufactured products is also important because industry provides more scope than agriculture for internal economies of scale and extends economic benefits to the rest of the economy. For several decades China's industry had been developed to become self-sufficient whether they were large- or small-scale industries. The result was that benefits from specialization and economies of scale were sacrificed. Opening the channels for exports helps to recapture some of these economic gains. Furthermore, putting the Chinese products to the test of competition in world markets pressures the Chinese producers to focus on quality improvement, cost control, and marketing techniques, all of which have long been neglected and caused immeasurable waste in a command economy.

The contributions of imports are more obvious. The industrial materials that China imported on a large scale were products in critically short supply, such as steel, iron ore, chemical fertilizer, raw timber, copper, aluminum, zinc, wool, and synthetic fibers. Their imports had the effect of relieving bottlenecks. Although the imports of grain and sugar resulted in financial losses to the state because of subsidized selling prices, they helped improve the standard of living of the population, particularly that in the coastal cities. Imports of machinery and equipment have been an important part of the investment program. For example, imports in 1984 constituted about 25 percent of the machinery and equipment in total investment in 1985.[51] The machinery imports also conferred a substantial economic benefit by virtue of the modern technology they carried.

The contributions of foreign capital in narrowing the savings and foreign exchange gaps are also considerable. The percentage share of foreign capital inflow in total savings and the ratios of net capital inflow to the net balance on current accounts in 1985 were 13.0 and 78.6, respectively, and in 1986 were 7.2 and 84.5, respectively.[52] For the period 1979–88, foreign capital amounted to 10.3 percent of domestic investment in state-owned enterprises and government organizations.[53]

The effects of technology transfer are less clear. There are numerous reports that technology imports have yielded positive results.[54] But there are obviously many problems, such as overlapping imports and choosing technically or economically inappropriate technologies.[55] The most serious is that the Chinese industrial enterprises have often failed to absorb effectively the foreign technology because of China's rather weak R&D capability.[56] There are indications, however, that the Chinese are learning from their past mistakes.

By and large, it seems fair to say that if the Chinese economy had been closed or half-closed to the outside world as before, economic growth would probably have been much less rapid. To the extent this assessment is correct, China's economy may well be heading toward difficulties because, although the door remains open, outsiders may stay away for some time to come. As one astute observer points out, "Business will be reduced simply because the business environment—inward-looking, tightly controlled, and centrally planned—is unattractive."[57]

Notes

1. For the period 1982–88, China's balance of payments statistics show a deficit of U.S. $23 billion, statistics of the Ministry of Foreign Economic Relations and Trade show a deficit of only $5.3 billion, and the Customs report a deficit of $36 billion. See *Beijing Review*, September 7, 1982, p. 29; October 17–23, 1988, p. 30; and October 2–8, 1989, p. 10; *China Daily Business Weekly*, August 28, 1989, p. 3; Editorial Board of the Almanac of China's Foreign Economic Relations and Trade, *Zhongguo duiwai jingji maoyi nianjian 1988* (1988 yearbook of China's foreign economic relations and trade) (cited later as *TY 88*), p. 351; State Statistical Bureau, *Zhongguo tongji zheyao 1988* (Statistical abstract of China 1988) (cited later as *1988 Abstract*) (Beijing: China Statistical Publishing House, 1988), p. 85; *Renmin ribao (People's daily)*, March 1, 1989, p. 2.

2. *TY 88*, p. 363.

3. *China Statistical Yearbook 81* (*SY 81*), pp. 353–67; *China Trade Report* (August 1989), pp. 14–15.

4. See Table 6. Exports in 1988 increased further to U.S. $3,100 million. *Wenhui bao*, August 9, 1989, p. 1.

5. Lin Hanxiong and Wang Qingyi, "China's Energy Sources in the Year 2000," *Jingji ribao* (Economic daily), November 9, 1985, p. 3.

6. The Chinese remain optimistic. A recent estimate put China's oil reserves at 78.75 billion tons. *Wenhui bao* (Wenhui daily), Overseas edition, San Francisco, September 2, 1987, p. 10.

7. One indicator of the low quality is the average unit price of the cloth exported by China in 1985, $35.4 per dozen, compared to $62 for manufactures from Hong Kong, and

$57 for products from South Korea. *Liaowang* (Outlook), Hong Kong, July 21, 1986.

8. Liu Guoen, "Current Status and Development of the Practice of Utilizing Imports to Support Exports," *Guoji maoyi* (International trade), no. 3 (1982), pp. 5–8; and Zheng Tuobin, "China's Foreign Trade Policy," *Beijing Review*, October 16–22, 1989, pp. 10–11.

9. He Xinhao, "Utilizing Imports to Service Exports Is a Strategic Policy for the Development of China's Foreign Trade," *Guoji maoyi* (International trade), no. 11 (1983), p. 30.

10. For the rationale of this policy, see Du Qiang, "The Strategy of Technology Imports and Exports Promotion," *Guoji maoyi* (International trade), no. 6 (1986), pp. 22, 23.

11. *China Daily*, August 4, 1987, p. 2. The introduction of new technology is important in traditional export industries such as textiles. See, for example, the case cited in *Beijing Review*, October 12, 1987, pp. 28–29.

12. Li Hongbo and Yan Kalin, "New Trends in World Service Trade and Implications for China," *Xinhua wenzhe* (New China digest), No. 12 (1985), pp. 54–56.

13. *China Daily*, July 18, 1987, p. 1.

14. JPRS-CST–87–008, March 6, 1987, pp. 9–11.

15. *Wenhui bao*, September 24, 1987, p. 9.

16. Liu Guoguang, "Certain Problems Relating to the Strategy for the Development of the Special Economic Zones," *Caimao jingji* (Finance and trede Economics), no. 2 (1987), pp. 1–6.

17. For an interesting account of the debate, see Joseph Fewsmith, "Special Economic Zones in the PRC," *Problems of Communism*, November–December 1986, pp. 78–85.

18. Huan Guocang, "China's Opening to the World," *Problems of Communism*, November–December, 1986, p. 60.

19. Zheng Tuobin, "China's Foreign Trade: Past Development and Future Prospects," *Liaowang* (Outlook), No. 39 (1989), p. 9.

20. *Renmin ribao*, October 21, 1989, p. 2.

21. Estimated by Liu Yi, Director of the State Tourism Bureau, *Wenhui bao*, September 19, 1989, p. 2.

22. *Asian Wall Street Journal*, October 5, 1989, pp. 1, 6.

23. Ibid., July 6, 1989, p. 4.

24. For the use of foreign funds prior to 1979, see Long Chucai, "Review of Foreign Capital Use since the Founding of New China," *Guoji maoyi*, no. 9 (1984), pp. 5–7.

25. *Wenhui bao*, November 14, 1989, p. 12.

26. State Statistical Bureau, "The Utilization of Foreign Capital: 1979–88," *Beijing Review*, March 6–12, 1989, p. 23.

27. Tan Xiaozhang, "A Comparison of Investment Costs in Shenzhen and Hong Kong," *Wenhui bao*, July 21, 1986, p. 9.

28. *Wall Street Journal*, July 17, 1986, p. 16.

29. The Jardine Schindler recently lost a bid to provide elevators for the New Bank of China building in Hong Kong to a Japanese firm presumably for this reason. Another example is the joint venture producing the Santana automobile which had to stop production in 1989 because cost per car amounted to U.S. $14,000, compared to the price of the same car of U.S. $9,000 exported by Brazil. *Wenhui bao*, October 22, 1989, p. 2.

30. *Wenhui bao*, July 17, 1986, p. 1.

31. *Wenhui bao*, August 8, 1986, p. 2.

32. State Statistical Bureau, "The Utilization of Foreign Capital: 1979–88," p. 24.

33. *Renmin ribao*, November 7, 1989, p. 1.

34. FBIS-CHI–89–209, October 31, 1989, p. 33.

35. See, for example, reports in *Asian Wall Street Journal*, August 3, 1989, pp. 1, 8; *Hong Kong Standard*, August 25, 1989, p. 2; and *Far Eastern Economic Review*, September 21, 1989, p. 25.

36. For example, Peugeot S.A. and Pepsi Company have postponed expanding their separate joint ventures in China. A group of investors from Hong Kong, Taiwan, and the United States has suspended implementation of their proposed industrial estate projects worth U.S. $5 billion in Fujian and Guangdong. Elec and Eltek has canceled a U.S. $76 million investment plan in Shenzhen. *Asian Wall Street Journal*, August 3, 1989, p. 8; *Hong Kong Standards*, August 24, 1989, p. 12; October 23, 1989, p. 1.

37. *Asian Wall Street Journal*, October 14, 1989, pp. 1, 10.

38. For growth of exports, see *1988 Abstract*, p. 85, and *Renmin ribao*, March 1, 1989, p. 2. As a result, the debt service ratio is rising.

39. *Far Eastern Economic Review*, May 25, 1989, p. 64.

40. *Sankei Shimbum*, July 2, 1989, p. 1. Estimates of debt service for 1992 vary widely, ranging from U.S. $4.2 billion to U.S. $12 billion, mainly because of statistical coverage. See *New York Times*, August 14, 1989, p. C4, *Wenhui bao*, August 31, 1988, p. 10. The estimate by the Ministry of Foreign Economic Relations and Trade, U.S. $10 billion, is perhaps more reliable. *China Daily*, Beijing, October 7, 1989, p. 1.

41. *China Daily*, October 7, 1989, p. 1. Note, however, an unofficial estimate of 19 percent reported in *Wenhui bao*, August 31, 1988, p. 10.

42. *Xinhua*, October 26, 1989, reported in FBIS-CHI–89–207, October 27, 1989, p. 1.

43. *Far Eastern Economic Review*, November 2, 1989, pp. 48–49.

44. The higher risks are reflected in the downgrading of China's credit rating from A3 to Baa by Moody's Investors Service in November 1989. *New York Times*, November 10, 1989, p. C2. The higher lending cost is estimated to range from a fourth to a half a percentage point more than the usual spread above the London Interbank Offered Rate, or between a half and one percentage point more than the spread above the Hong Kong Interbank Offered Rate. *New York Times*, August 14, 1989, p. C4, and *Asian Wall Street Journal*, September 25, 1989, p. 3.

45. *Asian Wall Street Journal*, September 25, 1989, p. 1.

46. Liu Hu, "Technology Import Reaches New High," *Beijing Review*, no. 10 (1986), pp. 23–24; *China Daily Business Weekly*, April 15, 1987, p. 1; *China Business Review*, May–June, 1987, p. 34; State Statistical Bureau, "The Utilization of Foreign Capital: 1979–88," p. 25.

47. In 1980–87, imported technology and equipment for the light and textile industries accounted for 41 percent ot the total; machinery and electronics industries, 38 percent; and raw materials and energy industries, 21 percent. *China Daily*, March 30, 1989, p. 2.

48. The use of imported technology to enhance export capability is illustrated by China's exports of military equipment that embodies foreign technology. See *China Trade Report*, November 1988, p. 13.

49. *Renmin ribao*, September 16, 1989, p. 5.

50. *Ta Kung Pao* (English edition), February 6, 1986, p. 5.

51. For sources, see State Statistical Bureau, *Zhongguo tongji nianjian 1986* (China Statistical Yearbook 1986) (Beijing: China Statistics Publishing House, 1986), pp. 442, 580; and *China: International Trade* (1986), p. 53.

52. For the percentage share of total savings, see *Jingji yanjiu* (Economic research), no. 8 (1987), p. 28. For data on balance of payments, see *Beijing Review*, no. 36 (1987), p. 28.

53. State Statistical Bureau, "The Utilization of Foreign Capital: 1979–88," p. 25.

54. See, for example, Bai Yiyan, "Open Policy Boosts Technical Growth," *Beijing Review*, no. 29 (1987), pp. 18–22; *Xinhua*, Beijing, February 26, May 4, and May 15,

1987, reported in JPRS-CEA-87-039, April 30, 1987, pp. 35–36; JPRS-CEA-87-047, May 26, 1987, pp. 19–20; JPRS-CAR-87-003, June 9, 1987, p. 78; and *China Daily*, August 29, 1989, p. 1.

55. *Jiefang ribao*, May 11, 1989, p. 3; *Renmin ribao*, May 18, 1989, p. 6.

56. Dennis F. Simon, "China's Capacity to Assimilate Foreign Technology: An Assessment," Joint Economic Committee, U.S. Congress, *China under the Four Modernizations* (Washington, D.C.: Government Printing Office, 1982), pp. 514–52.

57. Roger Sullivan, *Asian Wall Street Journal*, November 3–4, 1989, p. 10.

Comments by Timothy Gellat

As one who spends most of his time negotiating investments and contracts with China, I was asked to give my perspective on Professor Yeh's paper. We have heard a good overview of the general trends, and I can offer some impressions of what is going on in today's climate. First, let me say a few words on the legal system as it affects the subject that Professor Yeh's paper addresses. I think, since 1979, one could certainly say, as the paper correctly points out, that the system could be called underdeveloped. China has made impressive progress in developing a legal system for the kinds of transactions discussed in this paper, particularly technology transfer and joint ventures of various kinds; some areas are obviously better regulated than others. In the early days of 1979 and 1980, when China only had a sketchy joint venture law, foreign companies complained about going into China because they said there was no law; now companies are heard to complain that things are not as flexible as in the old days because now they have all these regulations to worry about. You can't please everyone.

Generally, the development has been positive, and not only have the laws become more complete—regulating tax, labor, land issues, and a host of other areas—but also, as the paper alludes to, interpretation has improved. No longer is it true that the law is written one way and one has no idea how it is interpreted in practice. Now we have a body of experience, some of which has been published, and the Chinese are becoming more forthcoming about publishing case examples, particularly in the tax areas, for example, publishing rulings quite as the IRS does about how particular cases were treated. So when one entered into negotiations in the early 1980s, it was extremely common to see the Chinese negotiator sitting across the room with a paper under the table on his lap. When you asked what that was, you were told, "Land regulations on joint ventures." Because you happened to be discussing the land clause at the moment, you, the foreign companies, might quite logically say, "Can we see what it says?" They would say, "Oh, no, they are internal regulations; only the Chinese side can refer to them." As ludicrous as this sounds, it is sad but true. Many companies are discouraged by the so-called legal system everyone was talking about; it existed only for the benefit of one side. Nor was that phenomenon eliminated in the domestic Chinese legal system or in the foreign investment system. But it is diminishing; China is getting more forthcoming about publishing regulations more rapidly; not only the regulations themselves, but the interpretive documents that explain what the regulations really mean. This is a positive step, and facilitates the negotiations.

Another question that is an ongoing concern to companies is how the laws that have not yet come out (and there will be many) will affect the contracts being signed and negotiated today, particularly in regard to contractual joint ventures, a somewhat bizarre phenomenon that no one in China, including the lawmakers, really understand. When I asked Liu Qiu, head of the Treaties and

Law Section, when the laws were going to come out, he said that first we had to figure out what collaborative venture was and then we could develop a law for it. That is a hybrid type of partnership arrangment. There is no concrete legislation that governs how it is to be structured and how it is to be negotiated. The virtue of this is that negotiations are flexible: one can kind of make one's deal every time. The question is what happens when the law does come out and says something different from what your contract says today. This is something companies try to protect themselves against by negotiating what the Chinese call "freezing clauses" into their contracts. To their unjustified surprise, no one would accept it, including the United States. The Chinese never accepted the clause that said [their] future laws would not affect this contract. They have begun to take some steps, however, including provisions in the foreign economic contract law as well as ad hoc rulings, to some extent. They are not doing so as quickly as foreign companies would like, but at least they are showing that they are sensitive to the problem of having to protect preexisting contracts against subsequent legislation, if that subsequent legislation is inferior. Sometimes the law is subsequently better, sometimes it improves incentives. In that case, they have generally given the benefit of the new improvement to earlier projects. In many respects there is much to be done, but the legal framework has taken many steps forward.

The investment environment clearly has many problems, as Professor Yeh has pointed out, and the Chinese have begun to take that into account. The year 1986 was a bad one; everyone went to the press with sob stories. The biggest one concerned the American Motor Company projects. As is commonly known, American Motors, which was the largest joint venture in China at the time (because of the foreign exchange problem, about which I will say a few words later), had the problem of not being able to import the assembly kits they needed to put their vehicles together. So they had to stop production. Moreover, they had the problem of high labor costs, and companies were getting taxed in what they considered an arbitrary manner. Everyone was complaining, giving China considerable bad publicity. Then, in October 1986, the so-called Twenty-two Articles, regulations to encourage foreign investment, were put out. I think these regulations were effective less because of what they actually said on paper than because of the changing attitudes they exemplified. China has since come out with many more detailed regulations, lowering tax rates and lowering land rates. I think the very top levels are becoming aware that they must have an attractive investment environment and must make it competitive; they cannot expect foreigners to come to China just for the privilege of doing business with China, which is still the attitude of many Chinese negotiators and officials. That attitude is slow to change, but I think it is slowly being rubbed off in negotiations.

Finally, I would like to comment on the foreign exchange problem; one cannot really talk about foreign investment law without mentioning it. It affects negotiations. This is the greatest problem in almost every joint venture. Unless one's product is obviously exportable, or is a hotel venture, which the paper points out is on the wane now, the problem is how the foreign investor is going to get his money out. A market of a billion consumers is a great attraction, but this attraction is lost if everyone pays in RMB. China is beginning to cope with this. The Chinese just came out with the import substitution regulations, which already have been experimented with at the local level. This would allow selected products produced by joint ventures, that is, products that are on priority lists China is putting out on the national and provincial level, to be sold at least in part for foreign exchange on the domestic market. We hope this will essentially, although the administrative mechanism is yet to be developed, force Chinese units to purchase from joint ventures by denying them import licenses to purchase these products on the international market. This would thereby curb the natural tendency to buy abroad wherever possible, rather than from a Chinese enterprise, even though it may be a joint venture with foreign technology. People's assumption is always that a product must be better if it comes from abroad. The Chinese have to fight against this tendency. These regulations will be a big help not necessarily for consumer products but for products in the high-technology area, an area of high priority in China. Other mechanisms are also being developed.

A company must realize that when it goes into China it is not going to receive a guarantee from the Chinese government of repatriation of its currency. By the same token, China must realize that foreign companies are not going to come in if they cannot get their profits out. Therefore, they must continue to develop mechanisms to deal with this problem.

Comments by Dennis F. Simon

I want to pick up where Professor Yeh left off when he talked about the interrelationship between what has been going on in the Chinese economy and what is going on in foreign trade, because ultimately we want to ask two questions on China's foreign trade:

First, to what extent will China actually become a trading nation? Will it be to the extent that trade will indeed be an important catalyst in its economic development? Professor Yeh suggests that China has started to have a role, but the extent to which it will play a major role, like Taiwan and Korea, is somewhere on the horizon; whether China will ever reach that level remains to be seen.

The second question is broader: If China indeed becomes a trading nation, how important a trading nation will it become? Will it play a major role in the world economy?

I will argue, as Professor Yeh does, that one must look at three sets of factors when one examines China's foreign trade. Here we look at foreign trade broadly defined as foreign trader relations, foreign investments, and technology imports, which are a part of the domestic factors of the economy at large, everything from price reform to centralization and decentralization. I would argue they are also a part of two external factors. One is what I would call competitive factors, that is, competition in China, not in terms of products but in terms of attracting foreign investment and foreign technology. Then there is a set of political factors. We've touched on some of these, such as export controls. I would also argue that in all three of these areas things would have to be worked out in a unique way if China is indeed to play a major role.

One subject I wish Professor Yeh had addressed in his paper is to link some of these macroeconomic data in terms of trade performance with what is really going on at the microeconomic level. If we really want to understand China's trade potential, we need to understand these reforms and structural changes and to understand whether the economy is actually moving in a direction supportive of trade expansion and greater interaction with the outside world or not. On the plus side, we have seen a number of things going on. First, in sections like textiles, which are big, there are many support mechanisms—technical transformations of enterprises, hardware and software, and improvement of factories. We just visited ten textile factories during the summer. There is a massive amount of imported equipment coming in from Europe and Japan, and there is a whole sector there that is being revitalized. The managers running the textile industries and the factories are improving. They are more sensitive to the quality, the style, the design, and the product niches. In that sense, one sees things improving in the textile area. In other sectors, we also see improvement. Again, it is only the beginning, but still it is a hopeful sign. We see work going on in terms of the production responsibility system. We know that in industry it has been moving along rather slowly, but we also see positive shifts. In the import of technology, for example, one sees a shift in the system away from grants to a system of bank loans. Bank loans are designed to give people more responsibility for the outcome of technology imports. One has a new sleuth of paper work now that is the responsibility of the manager in terms of the feasibility studies; they must show they have exhausted all kinds of analyses as to who can provide the technology, why they pick partner A or partner B, to show their project is indeed feasible so that the money will not be wasted, and all these loans will have to be paid back. And if foreign exchange quotas are involved, then indeed they would require projects that are being exported, and therefore it would be important that the project succeed. A third factor that seems supportive of this trade growth is the expansion of the network of organizations that have been developed within China and around the world to support the bilateral trade.

One sees trading companies all over. In Hong Kong, for example, every province has set up its trading company for import and export purposes. In the United States, one sees a proliferation of Chinese organizations both visiting and in places designed to facilitate trade. All these are bringing information to the Chinese economy, about product design and about packaging. One begins to see an economy somewhat sensitive to the requirements of being a trading nation.

I would argue, however, that a number of disincentives are at work, as well as a number of problems limiting trade on the domestic front. First is the price reform problem. During the summer, for example, we interviewed workers at the Shanghai Beer Factory. The Shanghai Foreign Trade Corporation gave this factory a big push to export, yet the factory manager said that was the last thing they wanted to do. They sell to the Foreign Trade Corporation at the wholesale price, which means they get less direct profit. In fact, they would rather sell on the retail market domestically where demand is much greater than supply, and where they always sell out their product. They basically don't want to export, much as they are admonished to do so. This raises another interesting question in the area of technology import. *In all this work I have been doing on technology import I have found that the biggest impetus to technology import is not export, but indeed to serve the domestic market.* Most Chinese managers would rather deal with internal competition than with the problems of external competition. It is easier to deal with the Chinese market, which is much less demanding. Generally, consumer demand exceeds supply and therefore it is an easy market to serve. People are more cognizant of internal dynamics and establish a product in line with the market instead of getting into the world economy. We should realize the incentive structure that makes the managers view the world that way.

Other problems to consider include the Chinese tendency regarding the import of technology, the talk levels, and, ultimately, buying on price. Obviously, because of foreign exchange constraints, when Chinese buy on price they package the technology imports, which means they leave out many support services, the assistance needed to implement the projects effectively. A Japanese manager once told me that the only way his company could fulfill the contract was literally to cheat the Chinese because they had forced the price down so low; often the only option was to leave something out.

In the West, trade, politics, and technology transfer will all ultimately be linked. As Professor Yeh mentioned, there are problems of protectionism. A delegation from the State Economic Commission coming to Boston was supposed to visit a General Motors plant that had just been closed down two days earlier. We received a call from the union; the union refused to have the Chinese come in. The last thing the union wanted was a group of Asians visiting their factory. Again, this is the kind of sensitivity we are starting to see.

On the competitive side, I believe the question is not whether Chinese products are going to be competitive but in fact whether anyone wants to play the game with the Chinese. Does anyone really want to link up with the Chinese economy other than to serve its domestic market? Professor Yeh cites many of these problems, with various reasons why companies do not want to come in. A lot of problems are not just on the Chinese side, but on the corporate side. People were told not to have unrealistic expectations when they got in. The problem is that the world economy is changing. Consider the automobile industry. The Chinese want to be big players. Manufacturing processes are converging, and labor components are decreasing. China's reservoirs of so-called cheap labor is really not going to be the attraction (although the Chinese thought it would be); the labor reservoir may become increasingly irrelevant. Chinese talk of becoming a player in the world of the automobile industry and other industries. The question is with whom are they going to team up. In a world economy looking for high value, high quality, high volume, and low cost, the Chinese really do not have much to offer.

The question is where are they going to make their mark. I offer two possibilities. One is in the area of China as a technology exporter. This may sound ironic. I would argue, however, that China's problem is that there is a lot of art going on, but not much deed; a lot of research, but not much development. In reality, it is possible that U.S. industries or other foreign industries could actually plug into China and Chinese research. We have seen Japanese firms plugging into the Chinese software industry, an emerging industry. The other possibility is that China could serve as an intermediate zone to enter other markets that might be difficult to enter. This idea comes from comments made by Ju Yongji, the individual on the Economic Commission responsible for technology import. In discussing MacDonald Douglas and their project in China, he said that China might use this project as a way for the United States and China to forge an alliance to sell to the Third World and to socialist country markets. Something that could emerge from the MacDonald Douglas deal is that the Soviet Union might buy U.S. planes built in China that they might not otherwise buy directly from the United States if the planes were built for political reasons, as long as the Soviet Union could be sure they were up to U.S. quality. Indeed, the socialist bloc could serve as an intermediate zone for China to develop an economy of scale and to raise its quality. China could then be better prepared to enter the Western markets.

6

THE DRIVE FOR ECONOMIC MODERNIZATION AND GROWTH: Performance and Trends*

Robert F. Dernberger

IT IS ONLY natural for each generation to interpret contemporary political events and personages as exceptionally important in determining the course of history. Even more so for journalists who like to believe that they are witnessing and reporting on events of momentous importance. Obviously, the post-Mao program of economic reforms carried out in China under the leadership of Deng Xiaoping in the decade after 1978 is much more than an episodic aberration that will merit little more than a footnote in some later historian's account of China in the twentieth century. Nor is the Deng era likely to be a mere interim between China under Mao and China under a yet-to-emerge successor to Deng, with his or her own ideological and economic policy to solve the problems of China's economic modernization. The Third Plenum, which marked the emergence of the Deng leadership, also led to the eventual rejection of the Maoist economic policy solution to the problems of China's economic modernization. It also launched the program of experimental economic reforms that eventually resulted in significant changes in China's economic system, development strategy, economic policies, and even values and behavior. Thus, whatever the eventual result, the Third Plenum and the decade that followed mark an obvious watershed in the history of China's economic modernization.

*Some early portions of this paper are considerably revised, expanded, and updated segments from my essay, "The Chinese Economy in the New Era: Continuity and Change," presented at the Third Congress of the Professors World Peace Academy in Manila in August 1987, and published in Ilpyong J. Kim and Bruce L. Reynolds, eds., *Chinese Economic Policy* (New York: Paragon House Publishers, 1989), pp. 89–135. I wish to thank Professors Nicholas Lardy and Louis Putterman for their thoughtful and helpful comments on an earlier draft of this essay.

Some observers see this decade as the transition from the generation of "utopian" revolutionaries to a reliance on those leaders whose objectives are developmental, and the outcome of the current reform program is to be a new model of "socialism with Chinese characteristics." Others see the current changes as a period of "restoration" of more traditional Chinese economic behavior and trends. Still others, including this author, see the current mix of plan and market, decentralization and central control, state and private ownership as part of a long period of cyclical institution and policy evolution, falling somewhere well inside the two extremes of a traditional Soviet-type economy and market socialism, as that latter system is described by its founders.[1] This still leaves a wide spectrum of institutions, strategy, and policy choices to be made in formulating a "socialist economy with Chinese characteristics." The mixed economy eventually created, however, will undoubtedly include continuities from the past as well as new innovations as a result of the decade of economic reform.

The problem in assessing the extent to which the economic institutions, strategies, and policies represent a mix of old and new at any point in time, such as the present, is that the process of economic reform is still unfolding and is not following any master plan or copying any existing model. Inasmuch as the pace and extent of the reforms depend greatly on political developments, the political "crisis" of mid-1989 and consequences make any attempt to forecast the future fate of the economic reform program a mere speculation. Furthermore, as in the past, any such speculation would only reflect the particular observer's biases and intuition, often involving arguments over whether the glass of water is half-empty or half-full. The Hungarian economic reforms were adopted more or less as a complete package in 1968, a decade before the introduction of China's economic reform program, and included the outright abolition of many features of the traditional Soviet-type economy that the Chinese still retain. Nevertheless, although admitting that many changes have been achieved, Hungarian economist Janos Kornai, in his thorough evaluation of the Hungarian reforms, argues that in reality the Hungarian economy still falls well short of the reform objective of a market socialist economy.[2] He raises the question as to whether or not there are limits to economic reform in any socialist economy, as long as the bureaucracy is unwilling to observe a voluntary restraint from its interference in the economy. Kornai claims, *and we agree*, that this question "cannot be answered by speculation, only by historical experience,"[3] and he advises we must wait and see what will be revealed by the Hungarian or Yugoslav or Chinese experience to have the answer.

Without attempting to speculate as to the possible outcome of the current economic reform program, however, it is possible to evaluate the impact of a decade of Deng's leadership and economic policies on the Chinese economy.[4] In addition, in light of empirically oriented analyses, it is also reasonable and important to attempt to describe the economic policies of the Deng era, to evaluate the strengths and weaknesses of those policies, and to conclude with a few speculations about the future. That is our objective in what follows.

The first draft of this essay was written in 1987 and in making the evaluation of the Deng era economy in the sections that follow we accepted the statistics then available, i.e., for the years 1978–85 or 1986, as representative of what we refer to in the essay as the Deng era, i.e., 1978–88. More important, on the basis of the statistics then available and due to limits of both time and space, the Deng era was evaluated as a distinct and discrete period of time, i.e., a decade, and not as a continuous sequence of individual years. In other words, we asked how—on average—can we best describe and evaluate these years as a whole and, as a result of this approach, came to a rather favorable evaluation of the Deng era. Now that the statistics for 1987 and 1988 are available to us, we must acknowledge readily that a more pessimistic picture would result if we had followed the chronological approach, concentrating on the trend and not on the average in evaluating the economy over this decade. The decade begins with a most impressive and hopeful record and ends with severe economic problems and retrenchment. Furthermore, the political "crisis" of mid-1989 has led to a very unstable realignment of political leadership in China, which obviously will have a significant impact on the pace and extent of economic reform and economic performance in the future.

Hindsight always tends to make us wiser, but in this case I feel fortunate in that I do not believe it necessary to write a new and completely different essay for inclusion in this volume; my original essay has not been made out of date or hopelessly misleading by events in the past two or three years. The Deng era was a distinct and discrete period in China's history and is likely to be judged by later observers both in China and abroad much as I have evaluated it in this essay, even if that decade ended on a most sour note, with the Chinese facing a possible recession in the near term and most uncertain economic future over the coming decade. Nevertheless, certain revisions were necessary. Thus, although the statistics for 1987 and 1988 have not been incorporated in the analysis in the text, where available, they have been included in the tables as an addendum.[5] Moreover, the tragic events at Tiananmen Square in the summer of 1989 are also acknowledged and have required revisions at a few points in the body of the text and more significant changes in the conclusion. Nevertheless, the Deng era remains one of the more hopeful and promising eras in China's post-1949 history and this essay tells the story of that decade. It indeed is a tragedy that developments in the past year or so have cast a dark shadow on the hopes and promises of the Deng era.

In the first part, ("The Economy in the Deng Era"), the economy during the Deng era is described and evaluated in the context of the evolution of China's economic development during the twentieth century, and in comparison with economic developments in the other socialist economies and the nonsocialist developing economies. This first part concludes with an attempt to identify the major explanation for the record of growth during the Deng era. This summary analysis of the important macroeconomic statistics for the Deng era economy is supplemented and qualified in the second part of the paper ("The Economic Policy Regime of the Deng Leadership"), first by the review of additional macroeconomic features of the Deng era economy that can be identified as characteristics specifically related to the economic policy regime of the Deng era, and then by briefly identifying the major strengths and weaknesses of that economic policy regime. A few of the major options in the realm of economic strategy and the policy choices facing China's leaders in the remaining decade of the twentieth century are assessed in the conclusion.

The Economy in the Deng Era

The Characteristics of the Deng Era Economy

The best way to evaluate the impact of the economic reform program on the economy, especially in the attempt to characterize that program, and to identify its strengths and weaknesses, is to look at the rate of growth, the structure of growth, and the quality of growth over the past decade.

The Rate of Growth

No attempt is made here to evaluate accurately the impact of the economic reforms on China's economic performance, while holding other factors causing changes in that performance constant, i.e., removing the impact of these other factors. The impressions of the Chinese policymakers and public, however, are based to a large extent on their intuitive reading of the macroeconomic results, whether what they presently accept as the "impact of the reforms" ultimately proves to be statistically significant or not. In this sense, the widespread belief that the economic reforms have had a significant and positive impact on China's growth performance is borne out by the annual rate of growth since 1978. In current prices, the average annual rate of growth of national income in 1979–86 was 12.6 percent; removing the effects of price increases by measuring it in what the Chinese call "comparable prices," the rate of growth remains exceptionally high at 8.7 percent a year (Table 1).[6]

There is an obvious cyclical pattern in the real rate of growth since 1979, with a trough in 1981 and a peak in 1984. Yet using the traditional statistical tests to show how scattered and distorted the distributions of the annual growth rates for the period are when compared to the average growth rate for the period as a whole, the annual rate of growth in 1979–86 has a standard deviation of 3.04 percentage points, a moment coefficient of skewness of 0.50, and a moment coefficient of kurtosis of 1.94, all showing improvement when compared to the period of 1952–78.[7] These statistical tests clearly indicate that not only was the rate of growth relatively high, it was also rather stable with five of the eight growth rates thus far observed since 1978 falling within the bounds of 6 to 10

Table 1

Growth of National Income
(in percent)

	In current prices	In comparable prices
1979	11.3	7.0
1980	10.1	6.4
1981	6.8	4.9
1982	8.2	8.3
1983	11.0	9.8
1984	19.5	13.5
1985	24.0	12.7
1986	11.2	7.4
1979–86	12.6	8.7
Addendum		
1987	18.5	10.2
1988	25.7	11.1
1979–88	14.6	9.2

Sources: Growth rates in Table 1 were calculated on the basis of absolute annual values for national income in current prices and the index number for national income in comparable prices presented in State Statistical Bureau, PRC, *Zhongguo Tongji Zhaiyao, 1987* (Statistical Abstract of China, 1987) (Beijing, Chinese Statistics Publishers, 1987), p. 7; Addendum: State Statistical Bureau, PRC, *Fenjinde Sishinian* (Forty years of progress) (Beijing: Chinese Statistics Publishers, 1989), pp. 340–41.

Notes: National income, as defined in Chinese statistics, is the sum of the net output value in agriculture, industry, construction, transport, and commerce, obtained by subtracting the value of material consumption in those sectors from their gross value of output.

Values in comparable prices, as defined in Chinese statistics, are obtained either by multiplying changes in physical output by a constant price or by dividing changes in the value of output by a constant price or by dividing changes in the value of output by a price index.

percent. Is this relatively high growth rate a general result of high growth in all sectors or has the economic reform program had a differential impact such that there have been significant structural changes in China's economy over the past decade?

Structural Changes

By the mid-1970s, the level of output was well below its production possibilities frontier, especially in the agricultural sector, as a result of poor and misguided economic policies and strategies. The decisions made at the Third Plenum singled out the agricultural sector as the starting point and focus, immediately calling for a significant increase in the prices received by producers in that sector.[8] Ultimately, the economic reforms in the agricultural sector have produced the most significant and dramatic systemic changes in China's economy.

Yet even though the average annual rate of growth in the agricultural sector in

1979–85 was 8.1 percent, an exceedingly high growth rate for agricultural sector output over an eight-year period, and that sector's share of national income had increased from 35.4 percent in 1978 to 44.3 percent in 1983, its share had fallen back to 41.4 percent by 1985 (Table 2). Thus, even though the reforms in the other sectors may have started later and their impact on the individual sectoral growth rates have been much more erratic than on the growth rate for the economy as a whole, the average annual growth rates for industry, construction, and commerce in 1979–85 were still higher than in agriculture. Nevertheless, the economic reform did have an observable impact on the structure of the Chinese economy in 1979–85 in that there had occurred a slight decline in industry's share of national income and a slight increase in the share of agriculture and construction.[9]

This change has been brought about largely as a result of the "restructuring" of production in the economy on the demand for producers goods and the declines in output as industries in that sector adjusted their production to meet these changes in demand. Following this initial period of readjustment in the output mix of producers goods, however, the industrial sector resumed its role as the leading growth sector in China's economy. For example, in 1979–81, the average annual rate of growth of gross industrial output (at comparable prices) was 14 percent in light industry, but only 1.3 percent in heavy industry; in 1982–85, however, these average annual rates of growth were 11.5 percent and 13.5 percent, respectively.[10]

On balance, the impact of the economic reforms have been much more significant in maintaining high growth rates in all sectors of the economy than in fostering a significant restructuring of the economy. Thus, while the impact of the change in priorities in favor of agriculture and light industry in the economic reform program is recognizable in the statistics for 1979–85, these changes fall far short of a restructuring of the economy and the major impact of the economic reforms in restructuring the economy most certainly will be a matter of much longer-term, cumulative changes.

The attempt to alter the structure of the economy in the short run, however, may have been much more successful than the statistics in Table 2 indicate. One of the major objectives of the economic reforms has been to remove the serious bottlenecks to the flow of goods in the economy by giving greater priority to the service sector, correcting for past neglect and the severe constraints placed on growth by this sector. The statistics in Table 2 show a decline in the share of national income accounted for by the service sector, i.e., construction, transportation, and commerce, between 1978 and 1985, from 17.8 percent of national income to 17.1 percent of national income.[11] Of course, statistics for national income in the Soviet-type economies, such as China, exclude many service activities. Thus, to obtain a better estimate of the sectoral structure of economic activity in China, we can rely on statistics for the structure of employment. Only about one out of ten members of the total work force was employed in

Table 2

Sectoral Growth Rates and Shares of National Income
(growth rates and shares in percent, with shares in parentheses)

	Agriculture		Industry		Construction		Transportation		Commerce	
1978	4.8	(35.4)	17.1	(46.8)	-0.9	(4.1)	11.3	(3.9)	22.5	(9.8)
1979	7.2	(39.3)	7.6	(45.9)	1.8	(3.9)	2.5	(3.6)	6.9	(7.3)
1980	0.6	(39.1)	10.1	(45.8)	29.7	(5.0)	4.1	(3.4)	0.6	(6.7)
1981	7.5	(41.6)	1.1	(43.4)	1.6	(4.9)	3.2	(3.3)	19.0	(6.8)
1982	11.6	(43.9)	5.7	(42.3)	4.8	(4.9)	15.4	(3.5)	4.8	(5.4)
1983	9.6	(44.3)	8.8	(41.4)	18.3	(5.5)	6.7	(3.4)	13.0	(5.4)
1984	14.5	(44.1)	13.6	(40.6)	10.7	(5.4)	9.4	(3.6)	11.2	(6.3)
1985	6.4	(41.4)	17.5	(41.5)	14.0	(5.5)	13.1	(3.5)	14.5	(8.1)
Average annual rate of growth[a]										
1979–85	8.1		9.1		11.2		7.7		9.8	
Addendum										
1986	3.0	(34.4)	9.6	(45.2)	17.5	(6.5)	11.3	(4.1)	7.2	(9.8)
1987	4.5	(33.7)	13.0	(45.5)	13.3	(6.8)	11.4	(3.9)	12.4	(10.1)
1988	2.3	(32.4)	17.4	(46.2)	8.0	(6.7)	11.3	(3.7)	6.3	(11.0)
Average annual rate of growth										
1979–88	5.7		11.0		12.6		10.0		9.9	

Sources: State Statistical Bureau, PRC, *Statistical Yearbook of China, 1986* (Hong Kong: Economic Information & Agency, 1986), pp. 42–43; Addendum: State Statistical Bureau, PRC, *Fenjinde Sishinian* (Forty years of progress) (Beijing: Chinese Statistics Publishers, 1989), pp. 340–41.

[a] Annual rates of growth are for net value of output in comparable prices; sectoral shares of national income are computed in current prices.

the service sector in 1978, but one of every three new entrants to the labor force between 1978 and 1986 was employed in this sector (Table 3). This favorable impact of the economic reform program, however, is only a promising beginning as the service sector has been a serious bottleneck. The removal of this problem by means of restructuring the economy also will be possible only in the long run.

The allocation of national income between consumption and accumulation was another serious imbalance in China's economy that the new post-Mao leadership hoped to resolve in the short run. In their reliance on the Soviet-type economy for the mobilization of "forced savings" for investment in a program of extensive development, the Chinese were achieving a very high rate of accumulation by the mid-1970s (36.5 percent of national income in 1978), and were devoting a major share of those savings to investments in fixed assets and in production facilities (72 percent and 71.8 percent of total accumulation, respectively, in 1978). A major share of the investment in fixed assets was going to state enterprises (64 percent in 1978), and the major share of those investments in fixed assets in state enterprises was financed by "forced savings" (83.3 percent on the investment in fixed assets in state enterprises was financed by unilateral budget gains in 1978).[12] See Table 4 (page 164).

The attempts to foster "consumerism" and cut the rate of investment as part of the economic reform program did succeed in reducing the rate of accumulation from 36.5 percent in 1978 to 28.3 percent in 1981; but this drop occurred as the output mix of the producers goods sector was being modified to facilitate a restructuring of the economy. With the restoration of rapid growth in the industrial sector, especially the heavy industrial sector, and with local-level enterprises and units of government engaging in out-of-plan investment with self-provided funds as a result of the decentralization introduced by the economic reform program, the rate of accumulation grew rapidly to regain a relatively high level of 35.3 percent in 1985. Thus, rather than becoming a more balanced or consumer-oriented economy, insofar as the disposal of national income is concerned, the Chinese economy has remained very accumulation oriented.

Whereas "consumerism" is reflected in the statistics for savings, investment is in the very dramatic reduction in the use of "forced savings" to finance investment.[13] Because of the lack of data for the late 1970s, this shift is not fully revealed in the statistics in Table 4, but by 1985 only two-thirds of the total investment in fixed assets were in state-owned units and almost three-fourths of this investment were financed by loans, foreign investment, and by self-provided financing. These trends continued in 1986–88 (Table 4, Addendum).

Not terribly successful in trying to lower the rate of accumulation, the attempt to achieve greater balance within the allocation of investment to meet consumer needs (housing) better, remove bottlenecks (infrastructure), and achieve greater efficiency (modernizing existing facilities) was somewhat successful in the early 1980s; but these efforts could not be sustained throughout the remainder of the 1980s (Table 4).

Table 3

Structure of Employment
(annual rate of growth of sector employment
and share of total employment; share of total in parentheses)

	Agriculture		Industry		Services	
1978		(73.8)		(15.2)		(11.0)
1980		(72.1)		(16.3)		(11.6)
1981	3.2	(72.0)	3.7	(16.3)	3.6	(11.7)
1982	2.7	(71.6)	2.8	(16.3)	7.6	(12.1)
1983	1.6	(70.7)	3.2	(16.3)	10.5	(13.0)
1984	0.1	(68.3)	9.2	(17.2)	14.6	(14.5)
1985	−4.1	(62.5)	28.5	(21.1)	18.8	(16.4)
1986	0.4	(61.1)	7.9	(22.1)	5.5	(16.8)

Average Annual Growth:

1979–86	0.8		8.1		8.9	

			Addendum			
1987	1.3	(60.1)	4.5	(22.5)	6.7	(17.4)
1988	1.9	(59.5)	3.6	(22.6)	5.8	(17.9)

Average Annual Growth:

1979–88	1.3		5.7		7.5	

Sources: State Statistical Bureau, PRC, *Zhongguo Tongji Zaiyao, 1989* (Statistical abstract of China, 1989) (Beijing: Chinese Statistics Publisher, 1989), p. 17.
Notes: Statistics in this table are based on the absolute level of annual employment in Department One, Department Two, and Department Three. The sum of the three adds up to the total labor force, and employment in Departments One and Two are identical to employment totals given for agriculture and industry in earlier statistical yearbooks.

Nonproductive investments (housing and infrastructure) as a share of total accumulation became larger than productive investments, but with the resumption of rapid industrial growth, nonproductive investment now accounts for only a third of the total investment, as it did in the late 1970s. Within investment in state-owned units, technical updating expenditures increased from one out of every four dollars to one out of every three dollars of capital construction expenditures between 1980 and 1984; but with the dynamic growth of local and out-of-plan investments, technical updating expenditures declined to less than 20 percent of capital construction expenditures. Finally, in total investments on capital construction within the state sector, investments on the expansion or reconstruction of existing enterprises versus investments on new construction increased from slightly more than one-third of the total at the end of the 1970s to about one-half of the total by 1985, but the share of these investments in the total declined after 1985.[14]

Table 4

Savings and Investment

	Accumulation as % of national income	Share of accumulation devoted to:			
		Productive investment	Nonproductive Investment	Fixed capital	Circulating capital
1978	36.5	71.8	28.2	72.0	28.0
1979	34.6	64.1	35.9	72.2	27.8
1980	31.5	54.5	45.5	76.7	23.3
1981	28.3	46.8	53.2	70.6	29.7
1982	28.2	46.4	53.6	78.4	21.6
1983	29.7	52.5	47.5	79.2	20.8
1984	31.5*	58.6	41.4	82.3	17.7
1985	35.3*	57.7	42.3	81.5	18.5
		Addendum			
1986	34.7	64.1	35.9	76.2	23.8
1987	34.2	65.1	34.9	81.5	18.5
1988	34.1	66.2	33.8	n.a.	n.a.

Investment in Fixed Assets in State-owned Units

	Share in capital construction	Share of capital construction from state budget	Share in technical updating, transformation, other
1978	74.9	83.3	25.1
1979	74.9	80.0	25.1
1980	74.9	62.5	25.1
1981	66.4	56.8	33.6
1982	65.7	49.8	34.3
1983	62.4	58.2	37.6
1984	62.7	54.4	37.3
1985	63.9	39.2	36.1
	Addendum		
1986	59.4	32.5	40.6
1987	58.4	27.4	41.6
1988	57.3	23.0	42.7

The attempt to restructure investment to give greater priority to the modernization of existing facilities and to building up China's infrastructure were promising changes in the allocation of investment being realized during the early

Total Investment in Fixed Assets

	Ownership			Source of financing for state-owned investment		
	State	Collective	Individual	Budget	Loan	Self-Provided
					Domestic Foreign	
1982				36.6	16.2 1.9	45.3
1983	69.5	11.4	19.1	40.6	14.3 1.7	43.4
1984	64.7	13.0	22.3	39.0	15.4 2.2	43.4
1985	66.1	12.9	21.1	26.4	23.1 2.8	47.7
			Addendum			
1986	65.5	13.0	21.5	14.6	21.1 4.4	59.9
1987	63.1	15.0	21.9	13.1	23.0 4.8	59.1
1988	61.4	15.8	22.7	9.1	20.6 5.7	64.7

Source of Financing for Total Investment in Fixed Assets, 1985

	State-owned Units	Collectives	Individuals
State budget	26.4	1.5	
Loans	23.1	37.6	
Foreign investment	2.8	0.9	
Self-provided	47.7	60.0	100.0

Sources: First panel, from State Statistical Bureau, *Statistical Yearbook of China 1986*, pp. 49, 54. Statistics with * are from SSB, *Abstract, 1987*, p. 7; second panel, estimated from data presented in SSB, *Yearbook, 1986*, p. 370; third panel, State Statistical Bureau, PRC, *Statistical Yearbook of China, 1984*, pp. 299, 302; SSB, *Yearbook, 1985*, pp. 413, 417; SSB, *Yearbook, 1986*, pp. 365, 371; and SSB, *Abstract, 1987*, p. 59; fourth panel, SSB, *Yearbook, 1986*, p. 366; Addendum: first panel, SSB, *Abstract, 1989*, p. 8; SSB, *Forty Years*, p. 342; and State Statistical Bureau, PRC, *Zhongguo Tongji Nianjian, 1988* (Statistical yearbook of China, 1988) (Beijing: Chinese Statistics Publishers, 1988), p. 66; second panel: SSB, *Abstract, 1989*, pp. 8, 55, 73; third panel, SSB, *Forty Years*, p. 353.
Notes: All figures are percentages; the second and third columns of the top panel add up to 100, as does the sum of the fourth and fifth column; the first and third columns of the second panel add up to 100; the three columns under Ownership in the third panel add up to 100, as do the four columns under Source of Financing; the rows for the four different sources under each of the types of ownership in the fourth panel add up to 100.

1980s, but the failure to sustain these changes in the last half of the 1980s means that removing the problems caused by past neglect in these regards can only be achieved in the long run. In general, a major feature of China's economy during the Deng era of economic reform, as in the preceding period, was a very high rate of investment, with a large share of that investment going to investment in fixed assets in productive capacity.

A major restructuring of the economy requires, of course, major changes in the sectoral allocation of investment. According to policy statements regarding the desire to readjust the economy so as to restore greater balance and remove bottlenecks, the sectors to be given priority in the 1980s were agriculture, light industry, energy, and transportation. Just as the statistics for the structure of total output fail to show a dramatic restructuring of the economy, the statistics for the allocation of investment also fail to reveal a dramatic change (Table 5). In fact, agriculture's share of the total has declined significantly and, after rising notice-ably in the early 1980s, the share of light industry in total capital construction investment has fallen back to account for only a slightly larger share than in 1978, being sustained at this level only because of the very dynamic growth of local and out-of-plan investment in 1986–88. While the share of heavy industry has fallen to about 10 percentage points below its level in 1978, it remains the dominant recipient of investment funds for investment in fixed assets. While not revealing a dramatic restructuring of the economy within the material product sectors, the statistics for the allocation of investment do reflect the increasing importance of the service sectors that was also revealed in the statistics for employment. For example, investment in capital construction in the commerce, education and research, public health, social welfare, and public utilities sectors increased from 10.5 percent of total capital construction investment in 1978 to 25.5 percent in 1986. By 1988, however, capital construction investment in these sectors had declined to 20.9 percent of the total.[15]

Perhaps the most dramatic and important structural change achieved over the past decade is the increase in China's integration into the international economic system with a very rapid increase in China's foreign trade dependency rate (Table 6, page 168). As a result of the autarchic development strategy pursued in implementing the Maoist economic principles during the 1960s, China's foreign trade dependency ratio was falling to an abnormally low level during that de-cade. Under the leadership of Zhou Enlai and a rehabilitated Deng Xiaoping, China's foreign trade dependency rebounded to a level of approximately 10 percent during 1971–77.[16] Deng's advocacy of an open economic policy had led to his expulsion from positions of power in the past, but it is the one economic reform policy he has consistently and explicitly advocated. As such, it was one of the first changes in economic policy introduced after his return to power and is one of the two economic principles (along with the four political principles) that are to be upheld by all Communist party members. Thus, the statistics for China's foreign trade participation ratio show that the increase in this ratio is one of the most dramatic changes in China's economy as a result of the economic reform program.[17]

In fact, the Chinese also have changed their policy in regard to foreign invest-ment to relieve the foreign exchange constraints on the growth of foreign trade

Table 5

The Allocation of Investment in Capital Construction
(as a percent of the total)

	Agriculture	Light industry	Heavy industry	Of which: Energy	Transportation and commerce	Construction
1978	10.6	5.8	48.7	22.9	13.6	1.8
1979	11.1	5.9	43.2	21.1	13.6	2.2
1980	9.3	9.1	40.2	20.7	11.2	2.0
1981	6.6	9.8	39.0	21.4	9.1	2.1
1982	6.1	8.4	38.5	18.4	10.3	1.9
1983	6.0	6.5	41.0	21.5	13.1	1.8
1984	5.0	5.7	40.3	22.3	14.6	1.6
1985	3.4	5.9	35.7	19.1	15.9	2.1
1986	3.3	6.3	37.8	20.6	15.3	1.9
			Addendum			
1987	3.1	7.4	43.5	25.3	14.1	1.1
1988	2.9	6.4	37.5	24.0	14.1	1.2

Sources: State Statistical Bureau, *Yearbook, 1986,* pp. 375, 376; SSB, *Abstract, 1987,* pp. 64, 66; Addendum: SSB, *Abstract, 1989,* pp. 60, 62.

under the Deng leadership. From 1979 through the end of 1985, China had utilized 21.787 billion U.S. dollars in foreign capital, 15.727 billion from foreign loans, and 6.060 billion from direct foreign investment; by the end of 1988, China's total debt had accumulated to a level of 40 billion U.S. dollars.[18] Had it not been for the foreign exchange constraint, China's foreign trade probably would have increased even faster than it actually did.

Two other significant changes in the structure of China's economy as a result of the economic reform program have been the change in ownership and the complementary change in the share of economic activity that takes place within the market sector, as against that which takes place within the planned sector. The statistics presented in Table 7, panel A, (page 170) for the share of the labor force employed in the state, collective, and individual sectors can only serve as a rough indication of the very important changes that have taken place in the ownership of economic units in China's economy. For example, the statistics for employment in 1978 show that less than 20 percent of the labor force was employed in the state sector, while almost all of the remaining labor force was employed in urban and rural collectives. These collectives, however, were really economic units that were directly controlled and administered by state-appointed cadres.

Thus, although the relative shares of employment claimed by the state, collective, and individual sectors do not change very much between 1978 and 1986, there is a big change in the meaning of each of these categories of ownership between these two years. For example, although comparable statistics are not

Table 6

Foreign Trade Participation Ratio

	Exports	Imports	Balance	Total	Participation ratio[a]	
		(in billion current U.S. $)			Yuan	U.S. $
1978	9.75	10.89	−1.14	20.64	11.8	—
1979	13.66	15.67	−2.01	29.33	13.6	—
1980	18.27	19.55	−1.28	37.82	15.3	—
1981	22.01	22.01	0	44.02	18.7	19.1
1982	22.35	19.28	3.07	41.63	18.1	18.5
1983	22.23	21.39	0.84	43.62	18.2	18.2
1984	26.14	27.41	−1.27	53.55	21.3	22.1
1985	27.36	42.25	−14.89	69.61	30.3	29.2
1986	30.94	42.92	−9.98	73.86	33.1	32.7
			Addendum			
1987	39.44	43.21	-3.77	82.65	33.0	32.9
1988	47.54	55.25	-7.71	102.79	33.1	33.2

Sources: State Statistical Bureau, *Yearbook, 1986*, pp. 40 and 481. SSB, *Abstract, 1987*, pp. 7 and 89; Addendum: SSB, *Abstract, 1989*, pp. 8, 83, and 86.
[a]Participation ratio: imports plus exports, divided by national income, times 100.
Note: After 1980, foreign trade data was issued by the Chinese Customs and was based on foreign prices, whether reported in U.S. dollars or in yuan. National income data are based on domestic prices and reported in yuan. In other words, China's foreign trade data and domestic data are based on incomparable prices and the use of official exchange rates to convert the foreign trade data into yuan values to estimate the foreign trade dependence ratio reported under the heading yuan in Table 6, or to convert the national income data into U.S. dollars to estimate the foreign trade dependency ratio reported under the heading U.S. dollars in Table 6, both result in overestimates of the true foreign trade dependency ratio. If the rate of exchange established in the market in Shanghai, where joint-ventures with a surplus in their foreign exchange balances can sell foreign exchange to those joint ventures with a deficit in their foreign exchange balances, can be accepted as a better indicator of a true purchasing power parity exchange rate than the official exchange rate, the use of this "market" rate would reduce our estimate of the foreign trade dependency ratios by 40 percent.

available to show the extent to which a change of employment within state-owned enterprise has occurred, employment in small-scale, local state enterprises must have increased rapidly as a share of total employment in state-owned enterprises.[19] As for the urban collective sector, in negating the Maoist attack on the "vestiges of capitalism," the Deng leadership has not only recognized the private and collective sectors as legitimate sectors in a socialist commodity economy at China's level of economic development, but has encouraged the restoration of decision-making powers to its members, i.e., making it a true cooperative economic unit. This change is recognized in the statistics presented in Table 7, panel B (page 170), where the retail trade of the supply and market-ing cooperatives is included as part of the state sector retail trade in 1978–83, but is included as part of the collective sector's retail trade in 1984–86.

In agriculture, the commune system has been abandoned and, while most peasants technically still belong to a collective unit, basic production and income distribution decisions are made by the households under the household contract responsibility system.[20] Some households have been allowed to specialize in commodity production and sell their output on markets, while others have been allowed to leave farming and take up trades or become workers in the rapidly growing small-scale enterprise sector in local villages or towns. Thus, the revival of the individual sector in cities and urban centers may account for only about 1 percent of the labor force in 1986, but it amounts to almost 5 million workers, compared to the 150,000 so employed in the urban areas in 1977. As for the approximately 75 percent of the work force employed in the "collective" sector in 1986, many could accurately be termed "individual workers" and those who remain "technically" working within the collective sector are much less under the control of the economic bureaucracy and the planners in 1988 than was true ten years earlier.

The statistics in Table 7, panel B, also can only serve as rough indicators of the complementary change from a planned economy to a mixed economy with a significant market sector. In 1978, 90 percent of the retail trade was carried out by state-owned units and most of the remainder was carried out by cooperatives directly under the control of the state. Under the economic reform program, cooperatives and private traders are allowed, and even encouraged, to compete with the state trading network so as to free up the severely restricted channels of domestic trade. By 1986, cooperatives accounted for a market share almost as large as that of state enterprises, while individual merchants and peasants accounted for one out of every five yuan in retail sales. Much of this retail trade by cooperatives, individuals, and peasants is carried out in the market sector, and most agricultural production is carried out by households responding to market prices. The state trade and supply network no longer obtains the agricultural products it needs by assigning fixed quotas on the producer according to a plan, but negotiates directly with the peasants the quantity of output to be delivered and the price to be paid at harvest time by means of "advanced purchase contracts." State enterprises still produce to meet their assigned quotas under the plan, transferring that output to the state at administered prices and buying their inputs at similar prices. But even state enterprises now produce above-quota output for sale on the market, and also use the market to acquire inputs to produce that output. Almost every industrial commodity in China today has a market price (the marginal price), a negotiated price (usually part of a barter transaction with other enterprises), and an administered price (the state's purchase and wholesale price).

An attempt to determine the extent to which China's Soviet-type economy (which always included a planned sector, a barter sector, and a market sector) has been changed to become a "mixed economy" with the flow of resources and commodities in the economy being determined approximately equally by the

Table 7

Structure of Ownership

A. By Share of Employment
(as a percent of total employment)

	State	Joint	Individual	Collective Urban	Rural
1978	18.7		0.04	5.1	76.1
1979	19.0		0.1	5.6	74.4
1980	19.1		0.2	5.8	74.9
1981	19.3		0.3	5.9	74.6
1982	19.3		0.3	5.9	74.4
1983	19.1		0.5	6.0	74.5
1984	18.2	0.08	0.7	6.8	74.3
1985	18.0	0.09	0.9	6.7	74.3
1986	18.2	0.1	0.9	6.7	74.1

Addendum

	State	Joint	Individual	Collective Urban	Rural
1987	18.3	0.1	1.0	6.6	73.9
1988	18.4	n.a.	1.2	6.5	73.7

B. By Share of Retail Sales
(as a percent of total retail sales)

	State	Joint	Individual	Collectives	Peasants
1978	90.5		0.1	7.4	2.0
1979	88.3		0.2	8.9	2.6
1980	84.0	0.02	0.7	12.1	3.2
1981	80.0	0.1	1.6	14.5	3.8
1982	76.6	0.1	2.9	16.1	4.3
1983	72.1	0.1	6.5	16.6	4.7
1984	45.6	0.2	9.6	39.6	5.0
1985	40.4	0.3	15.4	37.2	6.8
1986	39.4	0.3	16.3	36.4	7.6

Addendum

	State	Joint	Individual	Collectives	Peasants
1987	38.6	0.3	17.4	35.7	7.9
1988	39.5	0.4	17.8	34.4	8.0

Sources: State Statistical Bureau, *Yearbook, 1986,* pp. 92 and 446. State Statistical Bureau, *Abstract, 1987,* pp. 17 and 82; Addendum: State Statistical Bureau, *Abstract, 1989,* pp. 16 and 76. State Statistical Bureau, *Yearbook, 1988,* p. 153.

Notes: Employment in urban collectives includes employment in township and village enterprises; employment in rural collectives includes individuals and specialized households in the rural area.

Peasant retail sales are sales by peasants to nonagricultural households. Retail sales by supply and marketing cooperatives are considered as retail sales by state-owned units before 1984, but are included as retail sales by collectives in 1984 and thereafter.

planned targets and market forces is one of the most important, but difficult, research questions concerning China's contemporary economy. One survey of 429 industrial enterprises in the state sector in 1985 found that slightly fewer than a third of the enterprises secured more than 40 percent of their inputs in the market sector, while slightly more than half of them marketed more than 40 percent of their output.[21] Another source cites the decline in the number of commodities handled by the state's unified distribution system (the planned allocation of inputs) from 256 commodities in 1978 to only 20 in 1986, and the decline of the state's unilateral budget grants for local-level investments from 76.6 percent in 1978 to 31.6 percent in 1986.[22] Finally, this same source claims that commodities traded according to prices fixed by the state account for 35 percent of agricultural products, 45 percent of industrial consumer goods, and 60 percent of industrial raw materials. These statistics do indicate that the Chinese economy has changed in the decade after 1978 from a Soviet-type economy, totally dominated by state ownership and control, with central planning guiding the allocation of resources and commodities, to a mixed economy with a much greater private and cooperative sector and a larger role played by markets. While the debate continues over how far those changes have gone or are likely to go in the future under a more conservative leadership, few could deny that significant changes in China's economic system did occur in 1978–88, so that a mixed economy, among the various terms traditionally used for that purpose, serves best to describe the Chinese economic system at the end of the 1980s.

The Quality of Growth

The major objective of the economic reform program was to recognize the need to provide material incentives if local initiative and efforts were relied on to achieve greater efficiency and productivity. In addition, the need to have consumers share in the fruits of economic development was put forward by the economic reformers as a fundamental objective of socialism. Thus, one of the greatest and most dramatic economic consequences that can be directly traced to the economic reform programs is the large increase in per capita incomes, even though the rate of accumulation has not declined significantly, as a result of these policies of "consumerism." Offsetting some of the gains in per capita incomes was another result of the program of economic reform, i.e., inflation; but urban workers were given subsidies to partially offset the higher prices for foodstuffs and necessities. In current prices, per capita consumption of the peasants increased at an average annual rate of 13 percent a year between 1978 and 1986, while that for nonagricultural residents increased by 10.7 percent (Table 8, panel A, page 174). Despite the inflationary price rises over this same period, real per capita consumption of the peasants increased by 8.7 percent a year in 1979–86, while the rate of growth for nonagricultural residents—despite the subsidies—was significantly lower at 5.8 percent a year. Although the pace of inflation increased dramatically in 1986–88, real per capita consumption continued to increase in those years.

More meaningful than the rise in average per capita consumption to the consumer was the increase in the per capita consumption of basic foodstuffs (Table 8, panel C, page 175). Between 1978 and 1985, per capita grain consumption increased by 3.8 percent a year and this increase in the level of per capita consumption included a nutritionally significant shift in the pattern of grain consumption from the poorer grains to the richer grains, i.e., rice and wheat.[23] The annual average increase in the per capita consumption of edible vegetable oil, meat, sugar, and cloth between 1978 and 1985 was 18.1 percent, 9.6 percent, 7.4 percent, and 5.5 percent, respectively. Stagnation in grain production at the end of the 1980s, however, did result in a slight decline in per capita grain consumption in 1987 and 1988. Even so, per capita grain consumption in 1988 was still more than 25 percent higher than it had been in 1978.

The differential impact of the economic reforms tended to narrow the ratio of real per capita consumption of the peasants to that of the nonagricultural residents (Table 8, panel B, page 174). Nevertheless, this ratio remained large and it would take a long time for the peasants' real per capital consumption level to approach that of the urban worker.[24] On the other hand, the economic reforms did lead to two changes that favored the peasants as against the urban residents that were observable to all. The peasants have used their new freedoms and increased incomes to increase rapidly their available living space, by 8.9 percent a year between 1978 and 1985 (Table 8, panel D, page 175). Although the housing space per urban dweller has also increased after 1978 (by 6.9 percent a year), by 1985 it was still less than half that of a member of the rural population. [25] Housing is said to be the worst problem facing the typical resident of Shanghai today.[26]

The second change favoring the peasants, contributing to the belief by the urban workers that they are falling behind as a result of the reforms, is the growth of rural savings. Not only did the peasants' real per capita consumption increase 50 percent faster than that of the nonagricultural population between 1978 and 1985, rural savings per capita over the same period were growing two-and-one-half times faster than the per capita savings of the average urban resident (Table 8, panel D). In 1978, the per capita urban savings were more than ten times that of the typical rural resident, but were only slightly more than two times larger in 1988. Although still smaller in per capita terms, the total pool of rural savings was larger than that of the urban population and was being used by the peasants for investment projects—including apartment and hotel buildings in the suburbs of large urban centers.

This concern of the urban workers as to their relative gains from the economic reform program, despite the improvement in their absolute level of consumption and savings, points to a very important aspect of any economy and its performance—perceptions of economic conditions by both the leadership and the general population. Thus, not only are changes in the average level of per capita incomes important, but changes in income distribution or the distribution about the mean can be even more important to the individual. The two major objectives of the economic reforms, i.e., to achieve greater efficiency and productivity and a higher standard of living, both led to a decentralization of control over the allocation of resources and incomes. Thus, local areas, enterprises, and individuals were given greater freedom to mobilize their own resources and produce for the market, while material incentives were to relate income earned with skill and effort of work performed. Logic tells us that these reforms would lead to a worsening of the distribution of income, at least regionally; better endowed areas in terms of resources, infrastructure, and markets would be better able to take advantage of the reforms. Yet if the economy in the mid-1970s was operating well within its production possibilities frontier, it should be possible, for a period of time at least, for everyone to become better off as a result of the economic reform policies with an indeterminant result so far as the distribution of personal income is concerned.

Explanations for the Record of Growth

Limits of time and space preclude any attempt to estimate changes in the distribution of income for China over the past decade. Yet the statistics published for the sample surveys carried out by the Chinese do indicate that the economic reforms indeed have made everyone (or almost everyone) better off in an absolute sense (Table 9, pages 178–79). Whether the rich are getting richer faster than the poor are getting less poor is an important question, and the answer to that question may have important consequences on popular support for the reforms. Nevertheless, the statistics in Table 9 clearly signal that incomes for a sizable portion of the poor have increased significantly over the 1980s. For those who believe the "needs" test is the most meaningful for evaluating the results of economic development programs, the evolution of China's economy under the Deng leadership marks a major turning point for the better in China's economic development efforts.

This concludes our summary statistical description and assessment of the Chinese economy in 1978–88 under the Deng leadership's program of economic reforms. To understand the true importance and unique features of the impact of the economic reform program on the Chinese economy, however, it is necessary to place China's economy during this decade in its historical and comparative perspectives.

The Deng Era Economy in Historical Perspective

One of the most significant characteristics of the Chinese economy during the 1980s has been its very high growth rate: 8.7 percent a year in 1979–88 (Table 10, pages 182–85). This is impressive, but the record of economic growth in the twentieth

Table 8

Standard of Living

A. Per Capita Consumption
(in yuan)

| | Peasants | | Nonagricultural residents | |
	Current prices	Constant 1952 Prices	Current Prices	Constant 1952 Prices
1978	132	98	383	316
1979	152	104	406	329
1980	173	115	468	352
1981	194	125	487	358
1982	212	135	500	360
1983	235	147	523	369
1984	268	164	592	407
1985	324	185	754	463
1986	352	191	865	497
		Addendum		
1987	394	201	979	518
1988	482	216	1,238	544

B. Nonagricultural Resident Consumption
(as a multiple of peasant per capita consumption)

	Current prices	Constant 1952 prices
1978	2.9	3.2
1979	2.7	3.2
1980	2.7	3.1
1981	2.5	2.9
1982	2.4	2.7
1983	2.2	2.5
1984	2.2	2.5
1985	2.3	2.5
1986	2.5	2.6
	Addendum	
1987	2.5	2.6
1988	2.6	2.5

C. Per Capita Consumption of Selected Consumer Goods

	Grain (kg.)	Edible veg. oil (kg.)	Meat (kg.)	Sugar (kg.)	Cloth (meters)
1978	195.5	1.6	8.9	3.4	8.0
1979	207.0	2.0	11.1	3.6	9.0
1980	213.8	2.3	12.8	3.8	10.0
1981	219.2	2.9	12.8	4.1	10.3
1982	225.5	3.5	13.8	4.4	10.0
1983	232.2	4.0	14.6	4.5	10.3
1984	251.3	4.7	15.6	4.9	10.8
1985	254.4	5.1	16.9	5.6	11.7
			Addendum		
1986	255.9	5.2	17.4	6.1	12.4
1987	251.4	5.7	17.6	6.7	12.5
1988	249.1	5.9	18.3	6.3	13.4

D. Per Capita Housing Space and Savings

	Housing (living space in sp. meters)		Savings (in current RMB)	
	Urban	Rural	Urban	Rural
1978	4.2	8.1	89.8	7.0
1979	4.4	8.4	109.5	9.9
1980	5.0	9.4	147.6	14.7
1981	5.3	10.2	175.5	21.2
1982	5.6	10.7	211.4	28.4
1983	5.9	11.6	237.3	40.8
1984	6.3	13.6	235.3	62.2
1985	6.7	14.7	276.6	85.2
		Addendum		
1986	8.0	15.3	334	123
1987	8.5	16.0	411	174
1988	8.8	16.6	473	214

Sources: Panel A: State Statistical Bureau, *Abstract, 1987,* p. 98; panel C: SSB, *Yearbook, 1986,* p. 596; panel D: SSB, *Yearbook, 1986,* pp. 71, 595, 599; Addendum: panel A: SSB, *Abstract, 1989,* p. 92; panel C: SSB, *Forty Years,* p. 460; panel D: SSB, *Forty Years,* pp. 459, 464, 466; SSB, Abstract, 1989, p. 14.

Notes: Consumption includes self-provided consumption; per capita consumption in 1952 prices estimated by multiplying per capita consumption in 1952 times index of per capita consumption in comparable prices with 1952 equal to one. Estimates in panel B calculated directly from statistics presented in panel A. Per capita consumption of meat includes pork, beef, mutton, and poultry. Consumption of cloth includes cotton, blended, and chemical fabrics. Consumption of individual commodities and housing estimates based on sample survey of staff and workers and peasants households. Per capita savings are estimated on basis of total rural and urban savings and total urban and rural populations.

century clearly indicates the Chinese economy, with its rich resource endowment, is quite capable of very high growth rates. According to the estimates of Dwight Perkins, China's GNP grew by only 1.4 percent a year from 1914–18 to 1933.[27] This rate of growth yields a slight decline in per capita output and cannot compare with the rate of growth under the Deng leadership after 1978. Yet an index carefully constructed for the output of fifteen industrial commodities (representing 40 percent of total industrial output by value) yields a rate of growth of industrial output of 9.4 percent a year in 1911 and 1936.[28] This is consistent with a 1.4 percent rate of growth for the economy as a whole because the industrial sector was such a small share of the total in the early twentieth century, i.e., less than 10 percent in 1933. By growing at 9.4 percent a year, however, that sector would double in size every eight years and, because of the arithmetic of growth rates, the growth rate of the whole economy would eventually approach that of this sector, rather than reflect the low rate of growth in the agricultural sector. Moreover, there is good evidence that rapid industrial growth also spills over to induce a more rapid rate of growth in all other sectors. Even though it is possible to argue that the Chinese economy was displaying signs of rapid growth in the early twentieth century, especially in the modern/urban sectors, that period of growth was brought to an end by World War II and the Civil War. Following 1949, however, with a change in China's economic system to a Soviet-type economy and the pursuit of a big-push development policy, the industrial sector of the Chinese economy resumed its very high growth record. That China's economy is a high-growth economy is to be seen in the fact that the economy has achieved high growth rates since 1949 under a variety of policy regimes, including the "ten terrible years" of the Cultural Revolution (1966–76), when China's rate of growth was 6 percent a year.

For the period 1952–78 as a whole, a general statistical description of China's rate of growth would be an average rate of 7.2 percent a year that was declining over time (had a downward trend) and followed a very cyclical path with troughs centered on 1961, 1967, and 1976. Thus, the major impact of the Deng economic reform program on China's rate of growth has been to improve on China's record as a growth economy, but, even more important, to have eliminated the downward trend in the rate of growth and to have greatly increased the stability in the rate of growth. In fact, a most noteworthy attribute of the Deng era economy is to show that very high growth rates are compatible with stable growth rates, at least a more stable growth record than China's economy exhibited in the early twentieth century and in the first three decades of communist rule.

One explanation for the unstable growth in the pre-1978 period was the major structural imbalances involved in the Stalinist or big-push development strategy that was pursued: excessive rates of accumulation, concentration of investment on creation of new production facilities and in heavy industry, the neglect of agriculture, infrastructure, and the services sector. The economic reform program has as one of its objectives the restructuring of the economy so as to correct for these imbalances. Yet the observed results show that these attempts have not been terribly successful during the 1980s, although changes on the margin are occurring and these current trends may portend a more significant restructuring of the economy in the long run. In essence, the Communists achieved a major restructuring of the economy after 1949, and the post-Mao economy has not deviated significantly from that basic restructuring of the economy insofar as the rate of investment, allocation of investment, and even structure of production are concerned. While the changes achieved in the structure of sectoral output, employment, and investment have not been impressive, the reformers were successful in shifting other investment priorities, allocating a greater share of investment to building infrastructure (nonproductive investments), in modernizing existing facilities (rather than building new ones), and in reducing excessive reliance on involuntary savings mobilized in the budget and allocated to investment.

Changes that do distinguish the Deng era economy from both that of the post-1949 period and the pre-1949 period are the important changes in ownership that occurred under the economic reform program. Unlike the pre-1949 period, state ownership dominates the industrial sector; unlike the post-1949 period, agriculture is dominated by private household units of production and income distribution. In the service sector, cooperatives and private enterprises are of major importance. Thus, the Chinese economy has become a mixed economy more than at any time in the past in terms of ownership and in terms of plan versus market, even though the state sector and the plan or central authorities have continued to dominate the economy. It is true that in the last few years of the 1980s the state's control over the economy was seriously weakened and threatened, but the more conservative reformers—as a consequence of this threat—have been able to increase their role in economic policy making and administration of the economy and impose more effective constraints on the private and market sectors of the economy.

The most distinctive or unique feature of the Deng era economy, compared to the Chinese economy during any other period in the twentieth century, is its integration into the world economy. Both during the 1920s and the 1950s, China's reliance on foreign imports and foreign investment was important but somewhat limited even for a country of China's size and level of development, i.e., exports plus imports were about 10 percent of China's national income.[29] As a result of the economic policy regime of the 1980s, however, China achieved a foreign trade participation ratio that, when estimated by relying on official exchange rates to convert national income estimates based on domestic prices and foreign trade estimates based on foreign prices, may be as large as one-third of China's national income. A much more realistic purchasing power parity exchange rate would probably indicate a foreign trade participation ratio, i.e., total exports and imports divided by national income, of about one-fifth.[30] In terms of opening the economy to foreign investment, the Deng era economy contrasts

Table 9

Distribution of Income
(in percent of households in urban or peasant sector)

	1981	1982	1983	1984	1985
Urban households with annual per capita income available of:					
RMB 240 and below	2.1	0.9	0.6	1.7	0.9
RMB 240-300	5.5	3.7	3.0		
RMB 300-420	31.8	25.6	20.3	10.5	4.3
RMB 420-600	42.3	45.4	46.6	38.9	22.2
RMB 600-720	11.9	14.2	16.4	22.7	20.9
RMB 720 and over	6.5	10.2	13.1	26.2	51.6

	Addendum		
	1986	1987	1988
RMB 600 and below	20.5	15.9	8.3
RMB 600-840	34.0	29.1	17.9
RMB 840-1080	25.1	26.7	25.0
RMB 1080-1440	15.1	18.9	28.4
RMB 1440 and over	5.4	9.4	20.5

Peasant households with per capita income of:

	1981	1982	1983	1984	1985	1986
RMB 100 and below	4.7	2.7	1.4	0.8	1.0	1.1
RMB 100-150	14.9	8.1	6.2	3.8	3.4	3.2
RMB 150-200	23.0	16.0	13.1	9.4	7.9	7.0
RMB 200-300	34.8	37.0	32.9	29.2	25.6	21.8
RMB 300-400	14.4	20.8	22.9	24.5	24.0	21.7
RMB 400-500	5.0	8.7	11.6	14.1	15.8	16.5
RMB 500 and over	3.2	6.7	11.9	18.2	22.3	28.7

Addendum

	1987	1988
RMB 100 and below	0.9	0.5
RMB 100-150	2.4	1.5
RMB 150-200	5.0	3.3
RMB 200-300	17.5	13.5
RMB 300-400	21.3	17.5
RMB 400-500	17.2	16.7
RMB 500 and over	35.7	47.0

Sources: State Statistical Bureau, *Yearbook, 1986,* pp. 576 and 582; Addendum: Urban households from SSB, *Yearbook, 1988,* p. 806; and SSB, *Forty Years,* p. 462. Due to the rapid and significant increase in the level of average urban household incomes, beginning in 1955 the statistics for income distribution in the sample of urban households collected by the State Statistical Bureau were reported according to incomes per month with a larger number of income categories. These have been converted to incomes per year in the same number of income categories as in the pre-1986 period for the purpose of presenting these statistics in this table. For peasant households, SSB, *Yearbook, 1988,* p. 822; and SSB, *Forty Years,* p. 465.

sharply with the post-1949 economy that preceded it, but falls considerably short of the penetration of foreign investment during the 1920s and 1930s.[31] On balance, however, the Deng era economy represents a greater involvement in the world economy than any previous period in China's history.

Finally, perhaps the most distinguishing feature of the Deng era economy is that the Chinese population is now enjoying their highest standard of living at any time in modern history. While the attempt to reduce the rate of accumulation to promote "consumerism" was not terribly successful, the rapid rate of growth in the production of agricultural and light industrial products far outpaced the rate of population growth, and the increase in per capita money incomes outpaced the rate of price increases throughout most of the 1980s. In 1987 and 1988, the growth trend in real per capita consumption was considerably dampened by stagnation in the growth of grain output and by a more rapid pace of inflation.

While some estimates for the 1930s show per capita grain consumption ranging between 150 and 300 kilograms per year, these estimates are usually derived from output statistics and in unprocessed grain.[32] The statistics for grain consumption in Tables 8 (page 175) and 10 (page 182) are for actual consumption of processed grain. Furthermore, the distribution about the mean in the 1980s must have been considerably narrower than in the 1930s, while the consumption of light industrial products per capita must have been significantly higher. Comparing the per capita consumption of key agricultural and processed agricultural products in the 1980s with the levels of per capita consumption statistics for the period 1952–78 shows the extent to which the Deng era economy deserves considerable credit for improving the lot of the average Chinese.

Furthermore, the comparison of the rates of increase in per capita consumption during the 1980s as against the gains made in 1952–78 clearly show the superiority of the Deng era economy: 8.7 percent a year increases versus 1.8 percent for peasants, and 5.8 percent a year versus 3.0 percent for the nonagricultural residents. Yet those statistics fail to show the full extent of the benefits to consumers in the latter versus the former period. For example, in 1952 through 1978, there was a considerable increase in the labor force participation rate and a reduction in unemployment. In other words, even with a constant income per worker, the decline in the number of dependents per worker would lead to an increase in per capita incomes. Thus, the increase in the labor force participation ratio from 36.1 percent in 1952 to 46.8 percent in 1978 and the decline in the unemployment rate from 13.2 percent to 1.3 percent over the same period yields a 50 percent increase in per capita incomes with no increase in the annual incomes of those actually working.[33] There can be no doubt that this process helps explain the increase in per capita incomes before 1978, while the increase in the incomes of those actually working is a much more important contributing factor during the 1980s.

While the record of "consumerism," i.e., increases in the standard of living, has been a most impressive feature of the Deng era economy, two aspects of these increases in the absolute level of consumption must be noted by way of qualification. As shown in Table 8, the urban-rural gap in favor of the urban dweller has been reduced in regard to the levels of per capita consumption and savings, and the urban-rural gap in favor of the peasants has been further widened in the case of per capita housing. Yet the urban-rural gap in favor of the urban dweller in per capita consumption remains somewhat greater than was true in the 1950s, and even if the differential rates of growth in per capita consumption in 1978–86 continued to hold, i.e., 8.7 percent a year for peasants and 5.8 percent a year for the nonagricultural population, a highly unlikely assumption, it would still be the year 2020 before the peasants caught up. Nevertheless, as mentioned earlier, based on the rate of change over the past few years, it is the urban workers who believe they are falling behind as a result of the reform program.[34]

In a similar manner, despite the very significant increase in almost everyone's standard of living during the economic reform program, both logic and widely held perceptions about the results of these reforms lead us to believe that they have worsened the distribution of income—largely because of very substantial increases in the incomes received by those in the upper tail of the income distribution.[35] With the change in the economic system and ownership, certainly income distribution in China today is more equitable than was true in the 1930s. Whether or not the income distribution of the 1980s is less equitable than it was during the Cultural Revolution in the late 1960s and early 1970s, when the principles of shared poverty and equality were stressed, is far from certain. Thus, it may be wise to wait until the necessary data are available before arguing that income distribution in the Deng era economy has become less equitable than in the pre-1978 period.[36]

While there are several important empirical questions that could be raised about the Deng era economy, the above discussion of the statistical record available to us should be sufficient to show why the impact of the economic reform program in the decade after 1978 generally has been perceived by the Deng leadership, the Chinese people, and outside observers to have been very successful and why even the new post-Tiananmen Square and more conservative reform leadership remains committed to continuing the economic reform program in the future. The above discussion also serves to indicate the clear features of the Deng era economy that set it off from any other period of modern Chinese economic history. China is a growth economy and has enjoyed various brief periods of rapid growth during the twentieth century; the Deng era economy has improved on the record of those other periods by achieving higher and more stable growth. Furthermore, although the program of inviting foreign investment still falls short of the relative level of foreign investment that was "forced" on China during the age of Imperialism, China's involvement in foreign trade goes far beyond the level of foreign trade dependency in any previous period in the twentieth century. For the first time in history, in fact, China is a major participant in the world economy. Finally, after three decades of very dedicated effort and hard work, with a small hope of claiming a share of the results of those efforts, the Chinese peasant and worker are being rewarded with material benefits. In so far as the empirical record of economic development under the reform program in 1978–88 is concerned, the Deng era economy has achieved a unique period of growth, has dramatically changed China's development strategy and joined the world economy, and has provided consumers with greater material benefits than in any previous period in China's modern history. Do those same features distinguish the Deng era economy when they are compared with the other socialist economies and the other developing economies?

The Deng Era Economy in Comparative Perspective

Comparing the record of the Deng era economy with other Soviet-type economies and other developing economies clearly shows that the Deng leadership has accomplished an impressive record of economic growth. Even though statistical indicators for national income in the socialist countries are not comparable with those for the nonsocialist countries, most countries that had Soviet-type economies achieved relatively high growth rates during the period 1965–80. Yet the Chinese not only maintained a record of growth over this period that was slightly better than that for the East European countries, especially over the last half of the 1970s, but also significantly better than the growth record of the Soviet Union, the industrialized market economies, and the other low-income countries in the Third World. Quite simply, the Chinese used the Soviet-type economic

Table 10

The Deng Era Economy in Historical Perspective

	1952–78	1979–85 or 86
Rate of growth	7.2	8.8 (86)
Time trend	–0.14	+0.73 (86)
Std. deviation	11.52	3.04 (86)
Coefficient of variation	159.64	34.75 (86)
Rate of Accumulation	29.2	32.2 (86)
	1970–78 = 32.4	
Structure of Output:		
Agriculture	41.1	42.1 (85)
	1970–78 = 39.0	
Industry	38.1	42.7 (85)
	1970–78 = 43.5	
Construction	4.2	5.1 (85)
	1970–78 = 4.4	
Transport	4.0	3.5 (85)
	1970–78 = 3.9	
Commerce	12.6	6.6 (85)
	1970–78 = 9.3	
Structure of Employment:		
Agriculture	1952 = 83.5	
	1965 = 81.6	1980–86 = 67.5
	1978 = 73.8	
Industry	1952 = 7.4	
	1965 = 8.4	1980–86 = 18.7
	1978 = 15.2	
Services	1952 = 9.1	
	1965 = 10.0	1980–86 = 13.8
	1978 = 11.0	
Share of total investment in fixed assets in state–owned units:		
Invested in tech. innovation and transformation	1953–78 = 18.7	33.7 (85)
Financed by state budget	1953–78 = 71.5	40.3 (85)
Share of capital construction investment:		
Invested in productive construction	1953–78 = 81.0	43.6 (85)
Invested in new facilities	1953–78 = 55.4	48.1 (85)
Sectoral structure of investment in capital construction:		
Agriculture	1953–78 = 10.7	6.3 (85)
Light Industry	1953–78 = 5.7	7.0 (85)
Heavy Industry	1953–78 = 49.2	39.3 (85)
Of which: Energy	17.2	20.5

	1952–78	1979–85 or 86
Transport and communications	1953–78 = 15.3	13.0 (85)
Construction	1953–78 = 1.8	1.9 (85)
Foreign Trade Participation Ratio	1953–57 = 12.1	
	1958–62 = 10.6	
	1963–65 = 8.5	22.9* (86)
	1966–70 = 9.4	
	1971–78 = 10.1	

Structure of ownership:
  By Employment:

State	1952 = 7.7	
	1957 = 13.1	
	1965 = 17.3	25.0(86)
	1970 = 18.1	
	1975 = 21.5	
	1978 = 23.8	
Joint	1952 = 0.1	
	1957 = 0.0	
	1965 = 0.0	0.1(86)
	1970 = 0.0	
	1975 = 0.0	
	1978 = 0.0	
Individual	1952 = 4.3	
	1957 = 0.4	
	1965 = 0.6	0.9(86)
	1970 = 0.3	
	1975 = 0.1	
	1978 = 0.0	

Structure of ownership:
  By Employment:
  Collectives:

Urban	1952 = 0.1	
	1957 = 2.7	
	1965 = 4.3	6.7(86)
	1970 = 4.1	
	1975 = 4.6	
	1978 = 5.1	
Rural	1952 = 88.0	
	1957 = 86.5	
	1965 = 82.1	74.1(86)
	1970 = 81.7	
	1975 = 78.5	
	1978 = 76.1	

Structure of ownership:
  By retail sales:

State	1952 = 34.4	
	1957 = 62.1	
	1965 = 83.3	39.4(86)
	1975 = 90.2	
	1978 = 90.5	

	1952–78	1979–85 or 86
Joint	1952 = 0.4	
	1957 = 16.0	
	1965 = 0.0	0.3(86)
	1975 = 0.0	
	1978 = 0.0	
Individual	1952 = 60.9	
	1957 = 2.7	
	1965 = 1.9	16.3(86)
	1975 = 0.1	
	1978 = 0.1	
Collective	1952 = 0.0	
	1957 = 16.4	
	1965 = 12.9	36.4(86)
	1975 = 7.7	
	1978 = 7.4	
Structure of Ownership: By Retail Sales: Peasants	1952 = 11.8	
	1957 = 13.2	
	1965 = 13.0	7.6(86)
	1975 = 2.0	
	1978 = 2.0	
Standard of Living: Rate of growth in per capita consumption: Peasants	1953–57 = 3.2	
	1958–65 = 0.9	
	1966–78 = 1.8	
	1953–78 = 1.8	8.7(86)
Nonagr. residents	1953–57 = 4.8	
	1958–65 = 1.0	
	1966–78 = 3.5	
	1953–78 = 3.0	5.8(86)
Standard of living: Per capita consumption of: Grain (kg.)	1952 = 197.7	
	1957 = 203.1	
	1965 = 182.8	254.4(85)
	1970 = 187.2	
	1975 = 190.5	
	1978 = 195.5	
Edible veg. oil (kg.)	1952 = 2.1	
	1957 = 2.4	
	1965 = 1.7	5.1(85)
	1970 = 1.6	
	1975 = 1.7	
	1978 = 1.6	
Meat (kg.)	1952 = 7.3	
	1957 = 6.7	
	1965 = 7.7	16.9(85)
	1970 = 7.2	
	1975 = 8.7	
	1978 = 8.9	

	1952–78	1979–85 or 86
Standard of Living:		
Per capita consumption of:		
Sugar (kg.)	1952 = 0.9	
	1957 = 1.5	
	1965 = 1.7	5.6(85)
	1970 = 2.1	
	1975 = 2.3	
	1978 = 3.4	
Cloth (meters)	1952 = 5.7	
	1957 = 6.8	
	1965 = 6.2	11.7(85)
	1970 = 8.1	
	1975 = 7.6	
	1978 = 8.0	

Sources: Rate of growth, time trend, standard deviation, and coefficient of variation are calculated from annual growth rates based on index of national income in comparable prices (1952 = 100); State Statistical Bureau, *Yearbook, 1986,* p. 41 and SSB, *Abstract, 1987,* p. 7. Rate of accumulation is based on sums of national incomes and accumulation in current prices over relevant periods; SSB, *Yearbook, 1986,* p. 49 and SSB, *Abstract, 1987,* p. 7. Annual accumulation 1979–86 determined by multiplying national income in current prices by annual rate of accumulation. Structure of output is calculated from sums of national income and sums of annual sectoral output in current prices. SSB, *Yearbook, 1986,* p. 40. Structure of employment is calculated from total employment and employment in the first, second, and third departments in 1952, 1965, 1978, and annually in 1980–86; SSB, *Abstract, 1987,* p. 19. Share of total investment in fixed assets in state–owned units invested in technical innovation and transformation and financed by state budget calculated from annual totals in each category in current prices, with share financed by state budget including both investment in capital construction and investment in technical innovation and transformation; SSB, *Yearbook, 1986,* p. 370. Share of capital construction investment invested in productive construction and in new facilities calculated from totals in each category in current prices for periods 1953–57, 1958–62, 1963–65, 1966–70, 1971–75, and 1976–80 and annual totals from 1978 through 1985; SSB, *Yearbook, 1986,* p. 373. Sectoral structure of investment in capital construction calculated from totals in each category in current prices for periods 1953–57, 1958–62, 1963–65, 1966–70, 1971–75, and 1976–80 and annual totals for 1978 through 1985; SSB, *Yearbook, 1986,* pp. 375–76. Foreign trade participation ratio calculated from annual values for national income and total exports and imports, in current RMB; SSB, *Yearbook, 1986,* pp. 40, 481, and SSB, *Abstract, 1987,* pp. 7 and 89; Structure of ownership by employment calculated from annual totals for total labor force and for employment under each form of ownership in relevant years; SSB, *Yearbook, 1986,* p. 92 and SSB, *Abstract, 1987,* p. 17. Structure of ownership by retail sales calculated from annual total retail sales and retail sales under each form of ownership in relevant years; SSB, *Yearbook, 1986,* p. 446 and SSB, *Abstract, 1987,* p. 82. Relevant percentages are also given in latter source, except for 1975, on page cited; Rate of growth in per capita consumption for peasants and for nonagricultural residents include self–provided consumption and are calculated from the index of per capita consumption for these two groups in "comparable prices" with 1952 = 100; SSB, *Abstract, 1987,* p. 98. This source also presents annual rates of growth for each five year plan period and for 1953–78, but the rate of growth for the nonagricultural residents in 1953–78 is a typo, i.e., should be 3.0 percent instead of 5.0 percent. Per capita consumption of various commodities are taken directly from SSB, *Yearbook, 1986,* p. 596. Meat includes pork, beef, mutton, and poultry, and cloth includes cotton, blended, and chemical fabrics.

*See Explanatory Note under "Participation Ratio," in table 6.

system to mobilize resources for the purpose of development to a greater extent than in the other socialist countries.

The unique achievements of the Deng era economy, however, are to be found in the comparison for the 1980s. Statistical analyses of the socialist economies have found that these economies exhibit relatively high growth rates, but that these growth rates are rather unstable, i.e., have cycles, with a downward trend.[37] As can be seen from Table 11, panel A (page 188), this downward trend in growth was not only pronounced for the socialist countries in the 1980s, but, with the important exception of India, was also experienced by the nonsocialist world as well, especially the middle-income countries. Thus, by not only increasing the pace of growth in an already rapidly growing economy, but also by greatly reducing the amplitude of the cyclical behavior of that growth, the Chinese accomplished a record of growth that stands out not only in comparison with the past, but also in comparison with other countries of the world.

One of the explanations for China's impressive record of growth, of course, is the very high rates of accumulation in China's economy. The analysis of the Deng era economy in historical perspective showed that only marginal gains had been made in the reformers' attempt to achieve greater balance in the structure of the economy by reducing the rate of accumulation, but that more impressive gains had been made in reviving service sector activities. When we place these changes in comparison with other countries we see how insignificant these gains are and how much remains to be done to remedy these imbalances (Table 11, panels B, C, and D, pages 188–89). After a decade of economic reforms, China still had one of the highest rates of accumulation in the world, even well above that in the other Soviet-type economies, except Romania. In terms of the structure of the economy, China still had one of the smallest service sectors, in a relative sense, of any economy in the world, again even including other Soviet-type economies. In addition, partly because of China's level of economic development, but being somewhat exceptional for a poor country as a result of rigid controls over migration, China has an exceptionally large share of both output and employment in the agricultural sector. In other words, from a comparative perspective, the reformers had not been able to make significant headway in "restructuring" the economy.

Whereas the Chinese pursuit of the open economic policy has had rather dramatic results and is a distinguishing feature of the Deng era economy in historical perspective, it remains an important, but less dramatic feature when viewed in a comparative perspective. China's foreign trade dependency ratio is not exceptional for other developing countries in Asia and is significantly lower than that for those East European economies (Hungary and Yugoslavia) that have also pursued an open economic policy. Our estimates of China's foreign trade dependency ratio, however, while significantly higher than that for other large continental economies (India, the USSR, and the United States), undoubtedly is seriously biased upward and a more accurate estimate may be in the range of 20 percent. Nevertheless, China's foreign trade in an absolute sense is now larger than that of any East European economy and larger than that of any low-income and lower middle-income country in the world.

Finally, the increase in per capita income and consumption also emerged from our analysis of the Deng era economy in historical perspective as a very distinctive feature of that economy. Yet when subjected to a comparative perspective, the fact that China remains a lower-income developing country clearly emerges. According to the *World Development Report, 1987*, the Chinese did maintain the most rapid increase in per capita GNP for any of the low-income countries by a wide margin. Yet, China's per capita income and consumption still fall well within the upper bound of those indicators for the low-income countries and well below the U.S. $820 per capita GNP for the lower middle-income countries. Thus, while the Deng era economy established an impressive record of growth, started the process of opening to the outside world, and made significant gains in improving the standard of living of the Chinese people, this can only be identified as a most promising decade in the early stages of what will be the very long process of economic modernization of China.

The Sources of Growth in the Deng Era Economy

A most important aspect of the economic reform program was the attempt to shift from a strategy of extensive growth to one of intensive growth, and from achieving increases in outputs by increases in production facilities and in the quantity of inputs used to achieving increases in output to technological innovations, increases in efficiency and productivity, and the modernization of existing production facilities. In an economy as large as China's, the sweeping and intense development program in the three decades after 1949 obviously involved productivity gains and technological innovation in some sectors over varying periods of time. Yet most attempts—some crude and some very sophisticated— to obtain a macroeconomic estimate of the sources of growth in China's economy in 1952 through the 1970s all show the same result. China's economic development over this period is a classic example of extensive economic growth: a rapid increase in output obtained by means of a proportionately rapid increase in the quantity of inputs used and new production facilities.

Perhaps the crudest attempt to estimate the sources of growth for China's post-1949 economic development is my own.[38] In that estimate, a single measure for the increase in inputs was obtained by adding together the increase in labor and the increase in fixed assets according to a fixed set of weights, comparing this increase in inputs with the increase in national income, and assuming that any difference between the rate of growth of inputs and outputs (which obviously could be the result of a host of factors) was totally due to the change in productivity of the inputs. For the period 1953–80, our results showed that when labor is given a weight of 40 percent (capital, a weight of 60 percent) the average

Table 11

The Deng Era Economy in Comparative Perspective

A. Rates of Growth

	1965–70	1970–75	1975–80	1980–85
China (NY)	8.3	5.5	6.0	9.7
USSR (GNP)	5.2	3.7	2.7	3.5
Bulgaria (NMP)	8.5	7.8	6.1	3.7
Czechoslovakia (NMP)	6.8	5.7	3.7	1.7
East Germany (NMP)	5.2	5.4	4.2	4.6
Hungary (NMP)	6.8	6.3	3.6	1.6
Poland (NMP)	6.0	10.0	1.4	–0.8
Romania (NMP)	7.6	11.2	5.0	4.3

	1965–80	1980–85
India (GDP)	3.8	5.2
Low–income countries (GDP)	3.2	2.8
Middle–income countries (GDP)	6.5	1.7
Industrial market economies (GDP)	3.7	2.3

B. Economic Structure: Investment

	Rate of Accumulation
China (1986)	34.3
USSR (1984)	27.2
Bulgaria (1984)	24.3
Czechoslovakia (1984)	20.1
East Germany (1984)	18.9
Hungary (1984)	11.3
Poland (1984)	24.7
Romania (1976–80)	35.3

	Gross Domestic Savings Rate
India (1985)	25.0
Low–income countries (1985)	6.0
Middle–income countries (1985)	23.0
Industrial market economies (1985)	21.0

C. Economic Structure: Production
(in percent of total)

	Agr.	Ind.	Con.	Trns.	Comm.
China (1985)	41.4	41.5	5.5	3.5	8.1
USSR (1984)	19.9	46.0	10.7	6.0	17.4
Bulgaria (1984)	18.5	58.1	9.5	5.8	7.7
Czechoslovakia (1984)	8.8	60.0	11.1	16.4	4.1
East Germany (1984)	12.7	62.2	6.9	9.1	6.1
Hungary (1984)	18.1	46.6	11.4	13.6	8.9
Poland (1984)	17.5	49.6	11.6	13.7	5.9
Romania (1984)	16.4	61.6	8.0	7.8	6.2

	Agriculture	Industry	Services
India (1985)	31.0	27.0	41.0
Low–income countries (1985)	36.0	19.0	45.0
Middle–income countries (1985)	14.0	34.0	52.0
Industrial market econ. (1985)	3.0	36.0	61.0

D. Economic Structure: Employment in 1984
(in percent of total)

	Agr.	Ind.	Con.	Trns.	Comm.	Other
China	69	13	4	2	5	7
USSR	19	29	9	8	10	25
Bulgaria	22	35	9	9	7	18
Czechoslovakia	14	38	8	11	7	22
East Germany	4	45	7	11	8	25
Hungary (1983)	23	32	7	10	8	20
Poland	31	29	7	8	8	17
Romania	29	37	7	5	6	16
Brazil (1982)	30	16	7	4	10	33
Burma	66	9	2	3	10	10
India (1981)	69	—14—			—17—	
Indonesia (1978)	61	8	2	2	15	12
Pakistan	52	15	5	12	5	11
Philippines	50	10	4	5	13	18
Thailand (1982)	68	9	2	9	2	10
France	8	25	8	7	16	36
Germany	6	34	7	6	15	32
Japan	9	26	9	6	23	27
United States	4	22	6	6	21	41

E. Economic Structure: Foreign Trade Participation Ratios

	Exports and Imports/National Income
China (1986)	33.1*
India (/GDP; 1984)	13.8
USSR (1984)	21.1
United States (/GDP; 1984)	15.4
Hungary (/GDP; 1984)	82.6
Poland (/GDP; 1984)	29.6
Yugoslavia (/GDP; 1984)	54.8
Burma (/GDP; 1984)	9.0
Indonesia (/GDP; 1984)	27.2
Pakistan (/GDP; 1984)	30.6
Philippines (/GDP; 1984)	34.7
Thailand (/GDP; 1984)	42.5

*See explanatory note under "Participation Ratio," Table 6.

F. Standard of Living (in current U.S. $):

	Per capita GNP	Per capita consumption
China (1985)	256.70	137.01
USSR (1984)	3,080.03	2,242.26
Hungary (1985)	1,950.00	1,228.50
Poland (1985)	2,050.00	1,271.00
Yugoslavia (1985)	2,070.00	952.20
Burma (1985)	190.00	138.70
India (1985)	270.00	180.90
Indonesia (1985)	530.00	296.80
Pakistan (1985)	380.00	315.40
Philippines (1985)	580.00	464.00
Thailand (1985)	800.00	520.00
Low–income economies (1985)	200.00	164.00
Middle–income economies (1985)	1,290.00	838.50
Hong Kong (1985)	6,230.00	4,049.50
Singapore (1985)	7,420.00	3,339.00
South Korea (1985)	2,150.00	1,268.50
France (1985)	9,540.00	6,201.00
West Germany (1985)	10,940.00	6,235.80
Japan (1985)	11,300.00	6,554.00
United States (1985)	16,690.00	10,848.50

Sources and explanations: Panel A: USSR in 1965–70, 1970–75, and 1975–80 from Herbert S. Levine, "Possible Causes of The Deterioration of Soviet Productivity Growth in the Period 1976–80," in Joing Economic Committee, U.S. Congress, *Soviet Economy in the 1980s: Problems and Prospects*, Part 1 (Washington, D. C.: U.S. Government Printing Office, 1982), p. 154. For 1980–85 SSB, *Yearbook, 1986*, p. 715. For Eastern Europe in 1965–70, 1970–75, and 1975–80 from Thad P. Alton, "East European GNPs: Origins of Product, Final Uses, Rates of Growth, and International Comparisons," in Joint Economic Committee, U.S. Congress, *East European Economies; Slow Growth in the 1980s*, vol. 1. *Economic Performance and Policy*

(Washington, D.C.: U.S. Government Printing Office, 1985), pp. 120–121. For 1980–85 from SSB, *Yearbook, 1986*, p. 715. For the non–Soviet type economies, World Bank, *World Development Report, 1987* (New York: Oxford University Press, 1978), pp. 204–205.

Panel B: For China, Table 4 and SSB, *Abstract, 1987*, p. 7. For USSR and Eastern European economies, SSB, *Yearbook, 1986*, p. 715. For non–Soviet type economies, *World Development Report, 1987*, pp. 210–211.

Panel C: For China, SSB, *Yearbook, 1986*, p. 43 and SSB, *Abstract, 1987*, p. 19. For USSR and Eastern European economies, SSB, *Yearbook, 1986*, p. 715. For the non–Soviet type economies, *World Development Report, 1987*, p. 206–207.

Panel D: In percent of total labor force, SSB, *Yearbook, 1986*, p. 714.

Panel E: China, estimated from annual absolute value of national income and exports and imports, in current prices, SSB, *Abstract, 1987*, pp. 7 and 89. USSR, estimated from annual absolute value of national income and exports and imports, in current values, SSB, *Yearbook, 1986*, pp. 715 and 730. All other countries, estimates from annual absolute value of gross domestic product and exports and imports, in current prices, World Bank, *World Development Report, 1986* (New York: Oxford University Press, 1986), pp. 184–85 and 196–97.

Panel F: For China, absolute value of gross national product and personal consumption, in current RMB, converted into current U.S. dollars by means of the average between the buying and selling rate of the Bank of China; divided by year-end total population, SSB, *Yearbook, 1986*, pp. 15, 51, and 498. For USSR, 1984 national income in rubles converted to current U.S. dollars by means of an exchange rate of 1.5 U.S. dollars = 1 ruble. Total personal consumption equals rate of consumption times total national income. Per capita figures obtained by dividing total national income and total consumption by total population at mid–year in 1984, SSB, *Yearbook, 1986*, pp. 711 and 715. For all other countries, per capita GNP in current dollars in 1985 given in source and per capita personal consumption is obtained by multiplying the rate of personal consumption times per capita GNP; *World Development Report, 1987*, pp. 202–203 and 210–211.

annual change in total factor productivity was –1.8 percent, and when capital is given a weight of 40 percent (labor, a weight of 60 percent) total factor productivity remains almost constant over this long period.

The most dynamic growth sector in China after 1949 was industry, but even if we restricted the analysis of the sources of growth to the industrial sector, estimates produced by the World Bank do not show strong productivity growth.[39] When labor is given a weight of 40 percent, total factor productivity in industry increases by 0.6 percent a year in 1952–82; when capital is given a weight of 40 percent, the average annual rate of increase becomes 1.5 percent. A much more sophisticated methodology requires the specification of an equation for the production function and the use of econometric analysis to estimate the various parameters of that function. Gregory Chow has used this method to analyze the available data for outputs and inputs in the industrial sector, concluding that industrial output in 1952–81 increased in China mainly as a result of the increase of capital assets, rather than an improvement in productivity or technology.[40]

Gerald Meier claims that only half the explanation of economic growth in the successfully developing countries in Asia can be explained by the increase in inputs over time, while half of the growth "must be attributed to technical progress, improved quality of labor, and better management that combines the inputs more effectively."[41] Thus, the Chinese were attempting to shift an excessive reliance on investment and increases in inputs as the source of growth to an emulation of the more typical pattern experienced by the successfully developing countries in Asia, i.e., where increases in factor productivity accounts for approximately half of the rate of growth.

No attempt can be made here to adequately evaluate the extent to which the Chinese economic reform program succeeded in achieving this objective. Yet some evidence can be brought forward to suggest that they have been only partly successful and that the results are mixed, at best. For example, the most successful results of the economic reform program have been observed in agriculture. Yet Justin Yifu Lin, who has analyzed the sources of growth in the agricultural sector following the introduction of the household responsibility system, shows that the reform policies can account for about 45 percent of the growth in agricultural output in 1980–83, good weather can take credit for 5 percent, while the increase in inputs still accounts for half of the increase of outputs.[42] More important, the increase in productivity due to the economic reforms occurred mostly in the initial years the reforms were introduced and the importance of this source of growth has decreased over time.

In the period after that studied by Lin, i.e., the years 1984 to 1986, crop production accounted for only 11.2 percent of the increase in agricultural production, and other traditional agricultural activities such as forestry, animal husbandry, and fishing combined to account for only another 16.6 percent of the increase.[43] More than 70 percent of the growth in agricultural output after 1983 was accounted for by "sideline" activities, the most important of which was small-scale industry; village industrial enterprises accounted for 84 percent of rural "sideline" activities in 1986. These rural, small-scale enterprises, owned and operated by local government, cooperatives, or private entrepreneurs, became the most dynamic and rapidly growing sector in China's entire economy by 1989 and, therefore, must have come to dominate the sources of growth in agriculture after 1983.

The growth of the local, small-scale enterprise sector is largely explained by the rapid growth of self-provided investment in the creation of these enterprises. For example, fixed assets in township and village enterprises—not just industrial—increased by 58 percent between 1983 and the end of 1985, while employment in township and village enterprises had grown to 44 million by 1986.[44] In light of the above arguments, productivity gains and innovation obviously contributed to the remarkable record of growth in the agricultural sector, especially in the early years after 1977. That contribution, however, may well have been concentrated in a one-time shift in factor productivity, while increases in investment and inputs continue to be able to explain well over half the increases in outputs, especially after 1983.

In industry, more data are now available so that we can base our estimates for total factor productivity on inputs and outputs for the same enterprises (state-owned industries) and use the net market value of capital stock rather than the book values of capital stock. According to the estimates in Table 12, panel A (page 194), the rate of increase in the net value of fixed assets was less than the rate of increase in the gross value of industrial output in 1978–85, whereas it had been higher in the period 1953–77. Not only was the rate of growth of total factor productivity in industry greater after 1978, but it also accounted for a significantly larger share of the growth of output. Productivity growth accounted for only 16 to 23 percent of the rate of growth of output in 1953–77, but accounted for 39 to 51 percent of the rate of growth of output in 1978–85. If accurate, these estimates would be a most significant argument for the successful impact of the program of economic reforms.[45]

Factor productivity measures the rate at which the basic factors of production (land, labor, and capital) are converted into outputs; efficiency measures the rate at which all inputs (i.e., including energy, metals, raw materials, and all other elements of operating costs) are converted into outputs. Although total factor productivity gains may have become an important source of growth in the Chinese economy as a result of the economic reform program, other evidence for the Deng era economy indicate there has been no similar breakthrough in the efficiency of industrial production, i.e., increased productivity in the use of current inputs. Material consumption per unit of output increased, output per unit of capital declined, costs per unit of sales rose, and, although prices were increasing rapidly, the amount of profits and taxes per unit of capital increased only slowly (Table 12, panel B, page 194).

The Economic Policy Regime of the Deng Leadership

The review of the macroeconomic indicators of the Deng era economy given in the first part of this paper produces a most favorable conclusion as to the results of the economic reform program when judged not only from a historical perspective, but also from a comparative perspective. This conclusion obviously must be qualified by recognizing other developments in the Deng era economy that present a much less favorable picture. These developments are readily identified as caused by the economic reform program and they led to a political crisis and realignment in the political leadership, with its support for a more conservative and cautious version of the economic reform program and an end to the Deng era economy as described above.

From the very beginning of the economic reform program in 1978, the Chinese leadership had been united behind a program of economic reforms, but had different beliefs as to what that reform program should be. At one end of the spectrum were the traditional communist reformers, found throughout the socialist world. They believe the inefficiencies of the traditional Soviet-type economic system can best be cured, while saving the essence of the system, by decentralizing decisions and reforming the planning system and enterprise management. Market forces, the role of market prices in decision making, and private economic activity are to be allowed and even encouraged, but only as a supplement

Table 12

Productivity and Efficiency

A. Sources of Growth: State-owned Industry
(average annual rates of growth, in percent)

	Gross value of output	Net value of fixed assets	Employment	Total factor productivity	
				(1)	(2)
1953–57	24.2	24.4	8.0	6.4	9.6
1958–65	14.6	16.2	6.5	2.3	4.2
1966–70	11.4	5.6	9.6	4.2	3.4
1971–77	4.8	7.4	6.3	-2.2	-1.9
1953–77	12.9	13.1	7.4	2.1	3.0
1978–55	8.8	7.5	2.2	3.4	4.5

Weights in total inputs: (1) Employment, 40 percent; fixed assets, 60 percent; (2) Employment, 60 percent; fixed assets, 40 percent.

B. Indicators of Efficiency: State-owned Industry

	(1)	(2)	(3)	(4)	(5)
1952	66.9	134	14.1	37.0	69.9
1957	63.5	139	16.9	47.7	68.1
1962	67.1	71	12.5	20.5	76.5
1965	64.0	98	21.3	39.8	69.0
1970	62.9	117	18.2	45.7	69.6
1975	64.4	105	14.2	34.0	73.6
1977	66.8	99	13.5	31.5	74.1
1978	65.4	103	15.5	35.5	72.5
1979	65.7	103	15.8	36.3	72.4
1980	65.5	101	15.5	35.9	73.7
1981	66.6	96	15.0	34.1	74.6
1982	67.3	95	14.4	33.4	75.4
1983	67.8	95	14.1	32.7	75.8
1984	67.5	96	14.2	34.0	75.7
1985	67.7	95	n.a.	33.5	n.a.

(1) Proportion of material consumption to gross output value in all industry, not just state-owned industry (state-ind).
(2) Gross output value per RMB 100 of original value of fixed assets in state-ind.
(3) Profits per RMB 100 of gross output value in state-ind.
(4) Profits and taxes per RMB 100 of net value of fixed assets in state-ind.
(5) Costs per RMB 100 revenue from sales of state-ind.
Sources: Panel A: Gross value of output, net value of fixed assets, and employment in state-owned industry estimated from annual values or rates of growth in State Statistical Bureau, *Yearbook, 1986,* pp. 21, 92, and 224.
Panel B: SSB, *Yearbook, 1985,* p. 375 and SSB, *Yearbook, 1986,* pp. 47 and 271.

to the planned and state-administered sector. More radical reformers throughout the socialist world believe the privatization and marketization reforms must be more extensive, so much so that the economy is a truly mixed system. The Chinese never resolved the differences between these two points of view, but the more radical reformers were steadily gaining control through the 1980s until 1988, after initially receiving support from Deng Xiaoping in the early 1980s. There is no need to trace the chronological history of this period; our purpose here is to identify the several economic problems that emerged as a result of the economic reform program of the Deng era economy. Despite the record of success described above, the more radical reformers showed no promise of being able to solve these problems, and as they grew more serious in 1988, Zhao Ziyang and the more radical reformers associated with him lost considerable power over economic policy, while Li Peng, Yao Yilin, and other more conservative followers of Chen Yun gained control at their expense.

Taking the Deng era economy as a discrete decade in China's contemporary economic history, our discussion here will emphasize the major themes or general principles that ran throughout the many individual policy, strategy, and institutional changes that made up the economic reform program of the Deng era economy. These major themes and general principles are sufficient to illustrate and identify the various economic problems caused by the economic reform program and also serve to indicate the major strengths and weaknesses of that program.

Characteristics of the Deng Era Economic Reform

From the beginning, the Deng leadership's economic reform program has been guided by a few basic principles, supported by both conservative and radical reformers alike. Finding fault with the Soviet-type economic system, the Stalinist development strategy, and the Maoist economic principles they inherited, the Deng era reform coalition attempted to reduce, and in some cases eliminate, the network of excessive administrative controls and the bureaucratic apparatus that dominated the allocation of resources, goods, and services in China's economy. These efforts cumulatively became a widespread attempt to decentralize economic decisions to the local level for the sake of greater initiative and efficiency. It was emphasized on many occasions, especially by the more conservative reformers, that this decentralization was to be within the limits of a socialist economy, i.e., leaving the central authorities in ultimate control over the economy. The economic reform program proceeded, however, without a clear political agreement among the various reform groups on what was meant by "leaving the central authorities in ultimate control over the economy."

In addition to the extensive process of decentralization, another facet of the reform program involved the reformers' rejection of Mao's economic principles for the socialist economy, while formulating and adopting their own. The Maoist principles consisted of a long list of prohibitions, i.e., "thou shall not engage in intra- and interregional domestic and international trade, private economic activities, the creation of unequal incomes, or allow private ownership of units of production." These prohibitions were removed and material incentives, unequal incomes, private economic activity and ownership were allowed and even encouraged, especially by the more radical reformers. Again, the limits to be imposed on these institutions and activities were never clearly determined in a political consensus among the various reform groups, but the economic reform program did remove the Maoist prohibitions and relaxed the restrictions on the prohibited institutions and activities to a considerable extent. In other words, the themes of decontrolling, decentralizing, and removing prohibitions were dominant themes in the economic reform program. As such, this freeing up of the economy and economic activity is a major explanation of the rapid growth and economic successes reported in the first part of this paper.

Unfortunately, these same characteristics of the economic reform program also were responsible for the creation of several serious economic problems. Before 1978, the Chinese leadership frequently cited full employment, a balanced budget, price stability, and a balance of commodity trade as indicators of the "superiority" of Chinese socialism, especially in comparison with the Chinese economy before 1949, but in comparison with the developed capitalist economies as well. Indeed, along with a more equitable distribution of income, outside observers often cited these same successes on behalf of "Mao's China." Soon after 1978, the process of decentralization and readjustment of the economy created a serious problem of unemployment, while the policy of the state being responsible for finding everyone a job was abandoned as inconsistent with the attempt to achieve greater efficiency and productivity in the economy. The return of rapid growth to the industrial sector as a result of the economic reforms, however, allowed for a rather impressive reduction in the "official" rate of unemployment of the urban work force from more than 5 percent in 1978 to about 2 percent in the last half of the 1980s, about two thirds of the new jobs being in the state sector (Table 13, panel A). Nevertheless, the economic reforms have considerably changed the policy, strategy and institutions in regard to employment of the labor force so that open unemployment, disguised unemployment, and the threat of unemployment have become serious problems.

Foremost of these changes was the mere allowing the problem to exist and making the individuals responsible for finding their own jobs. Many were able to do so in the state sector, but about 5 million members of the urban work force a year were unable to do so. Almost half did find jobs in the collective or individual sectors, but at lower wages, with less favorable fringe benefits and job security. In addition, some of these workers forced to find jobs in the non-state sector were working at low- productivity and low-income jobs that can only be described as "disguised unemployment." As for those who were successful in finding jobs in the state sector, many were not given job security, being given

Table 13
Economic Problems of the Deng Era Economy: The Macro-Economic Statistics

A. Employment (100,000 individuals)

	Labor force without jobs		Unemployment rate	New Jobs		% of new jobs in state-owned units
	Total	Youth		Total	Youth	
1978	53.0	24.9	5.3	54.4	3.8	72.0
1979				90.3	3.3	62.9
1980	54.2	38.3	4.9	90.0	8.0	63.6
1981	44.0	34.3	3.8	82.0	10.8	63.5
1982	37.9	29.4	3.2	66.5	11.7	61.6
1983	27.1	22.2	2.3	62.8	9.3	59.5
1984	23.6	19.6	1.9	72.2	8.2	57.6
1985	23.9	19.7	1.8	81.4	8.9	61.3
1986	26.4	20.9	2.0	79.3	9.9	67.6
			Addendum			
1987	27.7	23.5	2.0			

B. Balance of Trade (billion U.S. dollars)

	Exports	Imports	Balance	Net capital inflows		Increase in reserves
				Short-Term	Long-Term	
1978	9.75	10.89	−1.14			
1979	13.66	15.67	−2.01			
1980	18.27	19.55	−1.28			
1981	22.01	22.01	0			
1982	21.13	16.88	+4.25	−0.05	+0.39	6.35
1983	20.71	18.72	+1.99	−0.28	+0.05	3.22
1984	23.91	23.89	+0.02	−0.89	−0.11	0.08
1985	25.11	38.23	−13.12	+2.27	+6.70	−2.50
1986	25.76	34.90	−9.14	−2.30	+8.24	−1.40
			Addendum			
1987	39.44	43.21	−3.77	+0.9	+7.8	4.72
1988	47.54	55.25	−7.71	+1.6	+8.2	2.31

C. Budget Deficit (billion RMB)

	Expenditures	Revenue			Deficit
		Enterprise income	Taxes	Total	
1978	111.1	57.20	51.93	109.1	2.0
1979	127.4	49.29	53.78	103.1	24.3
1980	121.3	43.52	57.17	100.7	20.6
1981	111.5	35.37	62.99	98.4	13.1
1982	115.3	29.65	70.00	99.7	15.6
1983	129.3	24.05	77.56	101.6	27.7
1984	154.6	27.68	94.74	122.4	32.2
1985	184.5	4.38	204.08	186.6	−2.2

Addendum

1986	233.1	4.20	209.07	226.0	7.1
1987	244.9	4.29	214.04	236.9	8.0
1988	266.8	4.87	237.48	258.8	8.1

	Subsidies	Debt (Borrowing)			Currency in Circulation	
		Domestic	Foreign	Total	Level	%+
1978	9.39	—	—	—	—	—
1979	18.07	0	3.53	3.53	26.77	
1980	24.21	0	4.31	4.31	34.62	+29.3
1981	32.77	0	7.31	7.31	39.63	+14.5
1982	31.84	4.38	4.00	8.38	43.91	+10.9
1983	34.17	4.16	3.78	7.94	52.98	+20.7
1984	37.00	4.25	3.48	7.73	79.21	+49.5
1985	48.25	6.06	2.92	8.99	98.78	+24.7

Addendum

1986	56.45	6.25	7.57	13.83	121.8	+23.3
1987	66.96	6.29	10.30	16.59	145.5	+19.5
1988	76.28	13.10	13.00	26.10	213.4	+46.7

D. Price Increases (percent increase over previous year)

	Retail Prices	Urban Cost of Living	Market Price of Consumer Goods
1978	0.7	0.7	−6.6
1979	2.0	1.9	−4.5
1980	6.0	7.5	1.9
1981	2.4	2.5	5.8
1982	1.9	2.0	3.3
1983	1.5	2.0	4.2
1984	2.8	2.7	−0.4
1985	8.8	11.9	17.2
1986	6.0	7.0	

Sources and explanations: Panel A: State Statistical Bureau, Statistical Yearbook of China, 1989, p. 104; SSB, Abstract, 1987, p. 22.

Addendum: SSB, Yearbook, 1988, p. 175.

Panel B: Statistics for exports, imports, and balance of trade in 1978–81 incomparable with those for 1982–86; former compiled by Ministry of Foreign Economic Relations, latter by Chinese Customs; SSB, Yearbook, 1986, p. 481; "China's Balance of Payments in 1982–86," Beijing Review, September 7, 1987, p. 28; SSB, Yearbook, 1988, p. 769.

Addendum: Although both series were compiled by Chinese Customs, statistics for exports, imports, and balance of trade in 1987–88 are not comparable with those in 1982–1986 as source reporting former includes upwardly revised statistics for the latter. Capital flow statistics presented here are the annual change in the year end net foreign debt. SSB, Abstract, 1989, pp. 83, 75; "China Announces Foreign Debts for the First Time," Beijing Review, vol. 32, no. 44, (Oct. 30–Nov. 5, 1989), p. 40.

Panel C: The Chinese include borrowing as part of revenue, but revenue in this table excludes net borrowing and subsidies (the latter also excluded from net revenue by the Chinese) before 1985. Before 1985, therefore, reported revenue from enterprise income and taxes add up to the total reported budget revenue. With the change to the new system whereby most enterprise profits were retained by the enterprise, which now paid a profits tax, this no longer remained true; reported net total revenue in 1985 being less than reported revenue from enterprise income and taxes. This result may be due to subsidies for losses of state enterprises having been deducted from enterprise incomes, which were reported only net of these subsidies as budget revenue before 1955, and deducted from total budget revenue, which was reported net of these deductions in 1985. SSB, Yearbook, 1986, pp. 509, 511, 524–24, and 530; SSB, Yearbook, 1988, p. 749; Wang Bingqian, "Report on the Implementation of the State Budget for 1985 and on the Draft State Budget for 1986 (in Chinese), Xue Muchiao, ed., Zhongguo Jingji Nianjian, 1986 (Chinese Economic Yearbook, 1986) (Beijing: Economic Management Publishers, 1986), p. i–81; SSB, Yearbook, 1988, 762.

Addendum: Subsidies are the sum of two different categories, losses of state enterprises and subsidies paid to units and individuals to offset price increases. The former are subtracted from budget revenues before those revenues are reported net in the state budget report, but the budget report includes the losses of state enterprises that have been deducted from gross revenues. The latter subsidies are included in the budget as a line item on the expenditure side of the budget. Wang Bingqian, "Report on the Implementation of the State Budget for 1986 and on the Draft State Budget for 1987," Beijing Review, vol. 30, no. 17, (April 27, 1987), p. v (centerfold); Wang Bingqian, "Report on the Implementation of the State Budget for 1987 and on the Draft State Budget for 1988," Beijing Review, vol. 31, no. 20, (May 16–22, 1988), pp. 37–38; Wang Bingqian, "Report on the Implementation of the State Budget for 1988 and on the Draft State Budget for 1989," Beijing Review, vol. 32, no. 18, (May 1–7, 1989), p. xi (centerfold); SSB, Yearbook, 1988, p. 762; "Economic Structural Imbalance: Its Causes and Correction," Beijing Review, vol. 32, no. 36, (Sept. 4–10, 1989), p. 26

Panel D: SSB, Yearbook, 1986, pp. 535, 544; SSB, Abstract, 1987, p. 95; SSB, Forty Years, p. 413.

Addendum: SSB, Forty Years, pp. 406, 412, 413.

---

contracts for fixed terms. Finally, while the rate of unemployment was reduced during the 1980s, the problem of outright unemployment among urban workers was shifted to fall almost entirely on the youth of China; youth made up three-fourths of the unemployed urban workers, while the number of youth looking for jobs increased to almost 2.5 million in 1987.

As a result of the economic reforms, therefore, full employment of the nonagricultural labor force is no longer assured, and job security for those who do have jobs is much less secure than in the past (and will be even more so if the Bankruptcy Law is effectively implemented). These problems have been concentrated on the youth in China's urban areas, and limited strides have been made to create the necessary schemes to alleviate the problems of job insecurity the reforms have created. With relaxed controls over migration, also a result of the economic reforms, the urban work force finds itself competing for work with a significant and growing "floating" population of migrant workers from rural areas. In addition, when the conservative reformers were successful in getting restrictions imposed on bank credits to fight the inflation by the end of 1988 (see discussion below), the resulting widespread closing of the large number of very inefficient and unneeded town and village enterprises in rural areas led to the widespread unemployment of rural workers who had left the fields to find work in these enterprises. Thus, the serious economic, social, and political problems of unemployment, floating groups of job seekers, and insecure workers who have jobs in both the rural and urban areas are obvious costs of the economic reform program.

Opening the Chinese economy and seeking a greater involvement in the world economy have been key features of China's economic reform program from the very beginning of the post-Mao period, and the attempt to decontrol and decentralize decision making in the economy has included the foreign trade sector. With a seriously distorted domestic price structure and an exchange rate that overvalued the yuan by a considerable margin, however, imports grew much faster than exports. In fact, as a result of being isolated under a Soviet-type economic and development strategy regime for two decades, there was an almost unlimited demand for imports and a limited capacity, as well as few incentives, for exports; with the exception of a few raw materials and textiles, the Chinese had an absolute comparative advantage in almost nothing! Thus, during those periods of decentralization—the late 1970s, mid-1980s, and late 1980s—large import surpluses were generated (Table 13, panel B, page 197). These periods of disequilibrium in China's balance of payments would lead to the reimposition of controls over imports and the use of foreign exchange.

China's balance of payments problems in the 1980s, like the problem of unemployment, may not be as serious as those same problems experienced in some other underdeveloped countries or even in some industrialized countries, and China's current balance of payments problems also are nothing like those China experienced in the 1930s and 1940s. Yet in the absence of central controls, these problems have become more worrisome and threatening over time. In fact, China's balance of payments has been kept in balance by relying on long-term capital flows from abroad, especially loans and bond sales. This policy change clearly represents the political will and courage of the Chinese reformers in pursuing the economic reforms. Yet these and other unfavorable results of the reform policies placed the reform program in political jeopardy, ultimately leading to the more conservative reformers gaining control over the reform process by the end of the 1980s. Imports of foreign technology and capital goods, let alone consumer's durables, stand in obvious contrast to the ingrained desire for self-sufficiency by the Chinese. Paying for these imports with exports of raw materials and foreign loans only stimulated support for those opposing the pace of the econommic reform and even questioned the benefits of the reform program. By the end of the 1980s, therefore, to avoid the problem of large import surpluses and the need to finance them by means of foreign loans, the Chinese have resorted to the imposition of administrative controls, while still trying to stimulate exports to pay for imports of technology, i.e., pursuing a more conservative version of the open economic reform policy of the 1980s.

Another unfavorable consequence of the economic reform program has been a significant increase in purchasing power outside the control of the central authorities. To make the decentralization process and new incentives effective, a much greater share of revenue has been left in the hands of local units, greater prices have been paid to producers in the agricultural sector, and a greater share of profits allocated to increases in wages and bonuses for the workers. Poor results of the economic reforms in the state industrial sector and rising labor costs, not offset by growing productivity, meant that—after deducting the explicit price subsidies granted by state enterprises in the low domestic selling prices maintained for certain consumer goods (i.e., grain), agricultural producer's goods (i.e., energy), and on five important import commodities—enterprise income transferred to the budget as revenue declined steadily after 1978 (Table 13, panel C, page 198). The increase in taxes, as national income grew, was only sufficient to keep total revenue somewhat stable at about 100 billion RMB in the early 1980s, while the not entirely successful implementation of controls imposed on budget expenditures kept the level of the deficit between 15 and 25 billion RMB in 1979–83. Control over expenditures slipped considerably in 1984 and the deficit increased to more than 30 billion RMB. Although Chinese practice includes both domestic and foreign borrowing as revenues, those borrowings were far from sufficient to finance the deficit and a considerable increase in currency in circulation occurred.

These budget deficits were the return of an economic problem claimed to have been solved by the Communists, a problem often used by the Communists to illustrate the incompetence of the Nationalist regime, other developing countries, and the capitalist industrialized countries. Obviously, these budget deficits were the direct result of the effort to decontrol, decentralize, and free up the economy before the necessary monetary and fiscal institutions and instruments were in place to control the economy by indirect rather than direct administrative means. In reaction to this problem, China's economic reformers implemented a bold new reform in revenue collection in 1985; state enterprises were made responsible for their own profits, being able to retain and utilize those profits after paying a new profits tax. As a result, taxes more than doubled in 1985 and, even after adjusting taxes to account for subsidies still paid to enterprises, a small budget surplus (when domestic and foreign borrowing is included as revenue) was recorded for 1985. Nevertheless, the inability of the administrative controls over expenditures to limit them to the planned level below the rate of growth in revenues, the continued rapid growth of subsidies, and the need to rely more heavily on borrowing and increases in the money supply to keep the official budget deficit to less than 10 billion RMB in 1986–88 were creating a more serious debt problem and ever severer inflationary pressures by the end of the 1980s. These budget problems were clearly brought on by the economic reform program.

Finally, stopping the Chinese inflation of 1936–49 soon after they came to power was one of the greatest economic accomplishments of the new regime, earning them much respect among the Chinese population and from foreigners as well. During the 1980s, however, increases in labor incomes significantly beyond the growth in productivity, price subsidies used to give higher incomes to peasants, and tremendous increases in out-of-plan and out-of-budget investment have meant that demand has grown faster than supply. With the authority granted enterprises for marketing a portion of their output, nonstate transportation and trade being allowed, and the very large increase in the money supply as a result of the budget deficits that makes the greater demand effective, the inflationary pressures have resulted in actual price increases, quite unlike the inflationary pressures that were repressed and controlled at stable prices under the policy regimes in the past. The commodities included and the weights given them in the various price indexes presented in Table 13, panel D (page 198), are not an unbiased sample, while the same is probably true of the prices identified for the commodities included in the sample. Thus, the indexes presented here, undoubtedly underestimate the extent to which prices are actually rising in China, or would be rising if inflationary pressures were not suppressed by means of price controls by the authorities. Nevertheless, the indexes in panel D of Table 13 do reflect the same cyclical behavior of the other economic problems discussed in this section: a peak in 1979–80 as a result of the first wave of decontrol, decentralization, and a freeing up of the economy, followed by a reduced problem as some administrative controls were reimposed; then a second peak in 1985, much severer than the first peak, but followed swiftly by the reimposition of controls with mixed success; finally, before they had regained control over the economy, the more radical reformers under Zhao Ziyang were successful in stepping up the pace of reform, resulting in a considerable worsening of the economic problems associated with the reforms in the late 1980s.

Obviously, the economic problems of inflation, instability, budget deficits, domestic and foreign debts, balance of payments, disequilibrium, and open and disguised unemployment are of much more immediate concern to China's political leaders than the long-run benefits of the economic reform program identified and analyzed in the earlier part of this essay. Moreover, the annual gains in the long-run benefits appeared to be declining over time, while the seriousness of the economic problems was becoming worse. In these circumstances, Zhao Ziyang was removed from day-to-day control over economic policy implementation, while Li Peng, Yao Yilin, and other more conservative reformers were put in charge and began implementing greater administrative controls in the latter half of 1988 and early 1989 to try to stabilize the economy and regain control over economic developments before pursuing the long-run goals of the economic reform program at a somewhat slower pace sometime in the future.

It is most unfortunate that such a dynamic and positive period of Chinese economic development should end with the unresolved economic policy problems being answered by the use of military force in the central square of Beijing in mid-1989. Before this political crisis resolved the issue, for the time being at least, most members of the leadership group had formed a consensus in support of the reform program. They differed considerably, however, as to the pace and extent of the reforms to be implemented. In the last half of the 1980s, there appeared to be three major groupings among the reformers.[46]

The most conservative group would not turn the clock back to the mid-1950s, but does believe the attempt to reform the economic system has gone quite far and the attempt to continue with further reforms would threaten the basic principles of a socialist economy. They are willing to have a mixed economy, but privatization and marketization had gone too far and too fast under Zhao and his followers. In fact, the reforms were threatening to overthrow the socialist system.

A second group of reformers wished to move ahead with the reforms, but believed in the need to stabilize the economy by eliminating the many imbalances that continue to exist. Their priorities included removing budget deficits, import surpluses, and inflationary pressures. They also argued for a better planning of reform strategy, without the wavelike fits and starts of the past. Dedicated to the need for reform, they are very concerned that the reformers may be their own worst enemy by acting too hastily and without appreciating the consequences of their actions before they occur, often to the detriment of the economic reform program. They tend to be well aware of the political constraints on economic reforms.

Finally, there are those who have been most frequently quoted by outside observers as spokesmen for the "reformers" and are now labeled as the "radical" reformers by China's present conservative consensus leadership group. This group was dedicated to economic reforms to such an extent that they were often impatient with the wavelike character of the reform movement in the past. Their argument was that the period of transition was bound to be painful and involve costs, but these should not discourage the Chinese or cause them to retreat and reimpose controls. These people had hoped that the Chinese economy would "grow out of the planned economy" as a result of the reforms and achieve something close to a market-socialist economy.[47]

In the effort to restore stability and regain control over the economy at the end of 1988, the shift in control over the reform process essentially involved a reduced role for the third group of reformers and a greatly enhanced role for the first two groups. The demands and open demonstrations for a more open political system, greater individual freedoms, and a free press were viewed by the conservatives as but a complement to the rapid growth in the nonstate, unplanned, and market economic activities in the radical reformers' counterrevolutionary attempts to overthrow the socialist system. With the full support of Deng Xiaoping, the conservatives were able to resort to military force to end the demonstrations, remove Zhao Ziyang and other leaders of the radical reform group from their positions of power, arresting or detaining some of them, and isolating and silencing others. Again with the support of Deng Xiaoping, the conservatives were able to formulate a new, more conservative consensus leadership group, consisting largely of representatives of the first two groups of reformers, soon after the tragic events in Tiananmen Square in June of 1989. The future of the economic reforms and economic developments in China under this new leadership group will be reflected upon in the conclusion.

The demise of the radical reformers, which began well before the tragic events of mid-1989, possibly can be explained as their being the victims of a preordained fate: predictable and unfavorable economic and political developments (i.e., any meaningful economic reform of a Soviet-type economy will produce an inflation and face the hostile opposition of the old guard, which holds tremendous power at the top of the political system), opposition and betrayal by large segments of the bureaucracy and population, or by a large number of exogenous and unpredictable events that affect any economy in the world (droughts, changes in exchange rates, and so forth). In other words, the radical reformers displayed great vision and courage in fighting a brave fight, but the odds were against them and their demise was inevitable.

One cannot deny that the major strengths of the economic reform program was largely the result of the widespread recognition and acceptance of the serious problems associated with the inherited set of economic policies, strategies, and institutions, the very strong political will and courage in seeking new policies, strategies, and institutions to solve those problems, the search for those solutions within the general guidelines of greater decentralization and a greater reliance on markets, allowing for material incentives, unequal incomes, and a flourishing private sector, and a desire to allow for foreign trade ties and capital flows. This is a remarkable revolutionary change for the better in terms of economic policy, strategy, and institutions compared with the pre-1978 period; the change led to the significant improvement in economic performance described earlier in this paper. As in any such reform policy regime, the reform policies create several economic problems, such as those identified above, but the Chinese were facing these problems by implementing policies to restore stability and regain control over the economy, promising to return to the economic reform process in the near future. Thus, the events of the summer of 1989 were indeed a tragedy, bringing an unnecessary end to the benefits achieved in the Deng era economy and the promises of more to come in the future as a result of the economic reform process.

Before offering some opinions as to the future of the economic reform process in the post-Deng era, i.e., the 1990s, it is necessary to present a somewhat different interpretation of the reform program of the Deng era economy than that given above. Quite simply, far from a visionary program correctly recognizing existing economic problems and presenting effective means for correcting those problems, the economic reform program had many weaknesses, inconsistencies, and just plain errors in assumptions and design. In fact, these features of the economic reform program can be argued to have rendered the program fatally flawed. These flaws of the economic reform program itself, now built into China's economic system, must be considered at least as equally important as the social and political opposition to the reforms in making any forecast of their fate and impact in the future.

Weaknesses of the Deng Era Economic Reforms

Major reform movements in any society rarely succeed unless they are provided with a window of opportunity by an exogenous shock that leads to a change in political leadership;[48] in China, the exogenous shock was the death of Mao and the ensuing emergence of a new reform consensus leadership under Deng Xiaoping. Economic reform movements always involve the political process, i.e., political as well as economic in nature, and this was to be especially true in the case of China; under the Soviet-type economic system, which had merged the central control of the Leninist party structure and a bureaucratic administration of the economy, the economy being reformed was highly politicized. In addition, from the very beginning, the conservative reformers and Deng himself had set and repeatedly emphasized the political constraints of the reform movement, essentially that the party would retain control over the economy, the economy would remain "socialist," and the state sector and planning would dominate.

The political will with which the more radical reformers pursued the economic reform program has to be one of that program's great strengths, but, at the same time, their failure to appreciate the political constraints on the pace and extent of reform, i.e., the political reality of the situation, was a fatal flaw in their reform program. When they tried to cope with the problems being created by the reforms by pursuing more extensive reforms, ultimately supporting and even joining the demonstrations for political reforms as a necessary complement to their economic reforms, they easily allowed their powerful political opponents to argue that they were not reforming but trying to overthrow China's economic and political systems. There should have been no doubt in the minds of the reformers, if they were to have any hope of success, that they must create and hold support among the consensus leadership under Deng. They failed to do so, and Deng has been forced to search for a third self-chosen successor among the members of a more conservative consensus leadership group, the leadership group that will control the reform process in the immediate future. Any would-be reformer in the future would do well to learn this lesson of the past; any economic reform program will be a hostage to China's existing political system and must have and keep the support of the consensus leadership group at the top. Otherwise, political reform is a necessity prior to economic reform.

The economic reformers in China did little better in appreciating the social and cultural problems they faced. A major thrust of the economic reform program was the decentralization of decision making and creating material incentives so that the lure of greater incomes would greatly increase innovation, effort, and productivity throughout the economy. The Chinese have proven their cultural traits as entrepreneurs both within and outside China's borders throughout history and they lost no time in reacting to the economic reforms that provided them with fresh opportunities. As a result, some got rich quickly, while others fell behind—many of those who got richer did so by taking advantage of their position in or ties to the bureaucracy, i.e., access to resources. Local units of government jumped at the opportunity to invest in small-scale industries and enterprises to earn incomes in protected markets or tax revenue while producing at a low level of efficiency. Quite simply, the sum of the decisions made and activities undertaken in response to the economic reforms led to rapid growth in output and incomes, claimed as the reform's successful result, but also led to instability, inefficiency, corruption, and inflation—the many problems of the economic reforms that ultimately led to the stalling of the reform process as the Chinese tried to stabilize and regain control over the economy.

The reformers, of course, did not blame their reforms for these problems. Rather, individuals were blamed for their corrupt behavior, and local cadres and officials for their using the reforms for the purpose of circumventing the purpose of the reforms. But did the economic reformers expect them to react any differently? These individuals and units of government would have made the desired decisions if the prices they faced had reflected true scarcities, if property rights and contract laws had been spelled out and enforced to reward those engaging in desired acts and penalizing those engaged in corruption or antisocial acts, and if fiscal (taxes) and monetary (credit) policies had been developed and implemented to stimulate the desired behavior and constrain the undesired behavior. Yet, the Chinese reformers rushed ahead with the moves to decentralize decision making and encourage local entrepreneurial activity in the absence of any of these three essential conditions for the success of their reforms.

In fact, the reformers even made a virtue of their strategy of creeping experimentation, but—without a clear plan of what type of economic system they ultimately hope to achieve[49]—the reformers were actually moving ahead rapidly in the area of removing controls and constraints on individuals and local levels of government, while not creating a viable and rational price system to direct low-level decision making, not defining and enforcing property rights and laws that place limits on low-level decisions, and not developing a proper fiscal and monetary system that creates the indirect levers that serve to control and direct the economy in the absence of direct, administrative controls. In short, the economic system being created by the Chinese economic reformers was hard to describe as an economic system; the Chinese were "growing out" of their Soviet-type economic system (inefficient, but well defined) into a very chaotic and poorly defined economic system. Calling it a mixed system or "socialism with Chinese characteristics" did not make it work any better or preclude the need to reimpose central controls.

Finally, the reform process had some fatal flaws. A major objective of the economic reform program was to reduce the area of resource allocation and the distribution of goods and services that takes place according to plan, while enlarging that area subject to market forces. Yet, as was true in so many other areas of the reform program, "markets" took on a sort of magical meaning: a buzz word without any real substance. The reason for enlarging the scope of resources and goods allocated by markets is that doing so has benefits: markets produce scarcity prices that can be used as parameters in rational decision making throughout the economy, involve competition among buyers and sellers that generates lower costs, better quality, new products, and the elimination of buyers with lower priority demands and inefficient sellers who cannot meet the competition. For all the introduction and expansion of markets in China's economy as a result of the economic reforms, few of these benefits have been obtained. As for prices, there are market prices, but there are also multiple prices and much effort is expended in gaining access to buying on the low price market and selling on a high price market, i.e., in activities more akin to "rent seeking" than in producing economic value. Any serious price reform, i.e., how relative prices are determined, has been continually delayed as the loss in control over prices has allowed repressed inflationary pressures to become an inflationary rise in the level of all prices. The matter of price reform is a very complicated problem, with serious consequences to various significant interest groups. But a major benefit of relying on markets is that transactions take place at market prices and many of the benefits of markets are lost if they do not take place at market prices.

As for competition on the buyers' and sellers' sides of the market, most enterprises in China still buy and sell their inputs and outputs in protected markets, i.e., where transport costs, access to trading channels, and outright bureaucratic interference "protect" the traditional sources of inputs and markets for outputs from outside competition. Furthermore, with the continued existence of significant excess demand and subsidies for losses, why search for cost-cutting innovations or develop new product lines? As for the closing of enterprises that are inefficient and even wasteful of resources, the many delays in adopting a bankruptcy law and the weak version of the law that was finally adopted means that no large-scale inefficient state enterprise has been closed down. In addition, the many small scale and inefficient local enterprises created as a result of the economic reforms have their market protected from outside competition by local officials. In fact, the tight credit and money regime of administrative controls imposed by the conservative reformers at the end of 1988 has done more to eliminate inefficiency by closing the most inefficient of these new local enterprises—created by the economic reform program—than all the attempts of the economic reform program to eliminate inefficiencies in the enterprises inherited from the past.

The economic reformers, of course, were aware of each of these problems; they have written extensively about them, and have called for the desired results in many policy speeches. Yet in the changes actually introduced in China's economic system, the failure to carry out a true reform of the price system, the failure to develop an effective fiscal and monetary policy, and the failure to create markets that function as markets illustrate how the economic reforms were flawed on the grounds of political, social, and cultural considerations. It is hoped that the reform process to be carried out in the future under the new, more conservative and cautious consensus leadership will do better.

Conclusion

The Deng era economy identifies a very unique and discrete period in the economic history of modern China, the decade from the Third Plenum of the Eleventh Central Committee at the end of 1978 to the Fifth Plenum of the Thirteenth Central Committee at the end of 1989. Rejecting or seeking to modify the Maoist economic policies, the Stalinist development strategy, and the Soviet-type economic system they inherited, the new reform-minded consensus leadership under Deng Xiaoping pursued an economic reform process that was truly remarkable. This process moved forward in a wavelike fashion and involved a fragmented experimental search for the resolution of obstacles to China's modernization. Without a blueprint to the future, that future remains uncertain. This essay, however, has presented the record of accomplishments achieved and problems created by the economic reform process in the decade, both of which clearly mark off the Deng era economy from that of the Maoist era economy that preceded it. Each observer can weigh the costs and benefits, but it is hard to believe that, except for those most loyal to the Stalinist development strategy or Maoist socialist economic principles, he or she would not conclude that the Deng era economy comes out well on the plus side of the ledger.

Unfortunately, as we also have tried to argue in this essay, the economic reform process, largely under the control of Zhao Ziyang and his more radical reform followers until late 1988, contained the seeds of its own destruction—as an economic reform program it was rapidly becoming inconsistent, irrational, and unworkable. It is most likely that economic developments in the late 1980s would have spawned a conservative backlash and attempt to regain control over the economy, putting the economic reforms on hold while retrenchment was imposed for the sake of restoring stability to the economy, even in the absence of the political crisis that brought the struggle between the conservative reformers under Chen Yun, Li Peng, and Yao Yilin and the radical reformers under Zhao Ziyang to a head. As a result of this crisis, Deng Xiaoping threw his support behind the conservative reformers; Zhao and his network of radical reform followers lost their power in determining economic policy in China. Given these dramatic, rapidly unfolding, and fairly unexpected events taking place in Chinese politics, it is rather foolish to engage in forecasts of the future of the economic reform program at this time. The results of the Fifth Plenum that was to determine China's economic policy over the next few years resulted in a broadening and deepening of the retrenchment that is already breaking the back of the inflation, leading to absolute declines in the light industry and local small-scale industry sector output.[50] There are threats to impose greater controls over the private and market sectors and even calls for increasing the role of planning and supply allocation by the state, i.e., increasing the number of commodities included in the plan and allocated by the material supply bureaus. On the other hand, the new consensus leadership has frequently reaffirmed its dedication to continue the reforms, officially declared to be placed on hold for two more years.

The retrenchment, although creating a recession in the short run, may well have positive results insofar as the economic reform process is concerned, if the retrenchment helps restructure the economy so as to reduce many bottlenecks as well as reduce the rate of growth in aggregate demand. If so, the reformers then would be in a much better position to pursue an economic reform process in the future.

As long as the current conservative and moderate (middle-of-the-road) reform consensus in the leadership remains, the reform process in the future would undoubtedly place major emphasis on trying to reform the planning system, enterprise management system, the credit system, and the fiscal and monetary policy mechanism. The move to greater privatization and marketization involved in the Deng era reforms will not be rejected, but will be placed under greater control and severer constraints. In addition, there will be a significant shift away from the freedom given the coastal areas, as the center reasserts its ultimate control over the economy and addresses the needs of the interior provinces and raw material and heavy industry bases. All of these forecasts are well within the limited hints the new consensus leadership has told us are its intentions. Yet much of this will represent an inevitable and necessary period of pause, retrenchment, and realignment following the Deng era economy, a sort of interregnum between the Deng era economy and the era that will follow.

As there has been no attempt to move the purge beyond the close associates of Zhao Ziyang or those who actively supported and were involved in the student demonstrations, my friends among the ranks of the radical reformers seem to think their role in designing and implementing the reform of China's economy is not over. For the present, several subjects are taboo and many suggestions would be reckless to make and unacceptable. But after a few years, when the economy has been stabilized and some of the senior members of the leadership have finally gone to meet Marx, the Chinese will turn again to the search for China's modernization. As current events in Eastern Europe indicate, they then will discover they have not only lost more ground to the capitalist countries, but have fallen behind many of their socialist friends who have accepted and implemented both radical political and economic reforms. In other words, history would appear to be on the side of the radical reformers and should at least give them a second chance to debate over the characteristics of China's economic reform process in the future. That future should lie sometime in the coming decade and we can only hope the radical reformers have learned enough from their mistakes in the past to design a reform process that will give rise to an even more promising era in China's economic history in the future.

Notes

1. For a description of the traditional Soviet-type economic system, see Robert F. Dernberger, "The State-Planned, Centralized System: China, North Korea, Vietnam," in Robert A. Scalapino, Seizaburo Sato, and Jusuf Wanandi, eds., *Asian Economic Development: Present and Future* (Berkeley, CA: Institute of East Asian Studies, University of California, 1985), pp. 13–42. Some observers believe there exists among the leadership in China today a group that advocates a return to the economic system of the mid-1950s, i.e., a strict Soviet-type economy. I do not believe that is likely as those same people were arguing on behalf of reforming that system in 1956 as they had found it inappropriate to China's circumstances and needs. Other observers, mostly journalists, believe that those advocating reforms today wish to adopt market socialism in China, i.e., they label the introduction of markets in a Soviet-type economy as "market socialism." Economists should know better as the specific institutional framework for a "market socialist system" was well defined by its founder, Oskar Lange. See, Oskar Lange and Fred M. Taylor, *On the Economic Theory of Socialism* (New York: McGraw-Hill Book Company, 1964). There are those who do advocate market socialism in China and they are accused of having done so by the post-Tiananmen leadership. It would be incorrect, however, to say they represented the consensus "Deng leadership," even before the Tiananmen Square incident, as many members of that leadership had specifically ruled out that economic system as being inconsistent with "socialism with Chinese characteristics."

2. Janos Kornai, "The Hungarian Reform Process," *Journal of Economic Literature,* vol. 24, no. 4 (December 1986), pp. 1687–1737.

3. Ibid., p. 1734.

4. Throughout the discussion, the term Deng era economy and the Deng leadership are used to refer to the Chinese economy in 1979 through 1988 and to the collection of decision makers among the top levels of the party, bureaucracy, and economy that determined and implemented economic policy, strategy, and institutional changes in China over the same period. While Deng Xiaoping certainly emerged as the single most important political leader in China and individually has done much to assure the adoption and implementation of the economic reform program, our reliance on these simple terms does not mean to imply he deserves all the credit (or blame) for economic developments in China over the past decade, nor even to argue that the leadership group that should be included in the assessment of credit (or blame) should be restricted to a relatively few individuals at the top. Our purpose in this essay is not to analyze the policy-making process in China during the post-Mao period, but the effect of the policies that were adopted and implemented by the Deng leadership, whoever the members of that leadership may have been in the period 1979–88.

5. Because of changing definitions and coverage, changing methods of statistical estimation and reporting, and the ever-present problem of revisions of earlier released statistics, any attempt to utilize the statistics released since the draft essay presented at the conference would require a complete revision of most entries in each of the tables to make the statistics in a given table comparable, a recalculation of all estimates presented in the text to be compatible with the new tables, and even a rewriting of the entire text itself. I believe such an effort would not result in significant changes in the arguments made in the essay, but would require an effort well beyond that required of authors revising their papers for inclusion in a conference volume (i.e., preparing a whole new essay). Nevertheless, inasmuch as these new statistics are available to me, I have included them in the tables as addenda for the reference of the reader, who can judge the extent to which they may strengthen or weaken the arguments and conclusions presented in the essay.

6. We are well aware and appreciate the many problems of definition, coverage, comparability, and accuracy in the data used in our analysis of the Deng era economy. Our purpose here is to assess the statistical record provided in the official statistics, which we explicitly accept as a reasonably accurate picture of actual developments in the economy over the post-1978 period. It is not our desire, nor our purpose, to become engaged in a debate over the accuracy of Chinese statistics, either in regard to some abstract standard of absolute accuracy or in comparison with the statistics of other countries. On the other hand, we will mention those areas where we believe these statistical problems are important to our analysis throughout the discussion and how those problems are likely to affect our analysis.

7. The annual growth rate of national income in 1952–78 had a moment coefficient of skewness of 1.14 and a moment coefficient of kurtosis of 5.01. As will be pointed out in Table 10 below, the coefficient of variation of the annual growth rate of national income in 1952–78 was 159.64, but only 34.75 in 1979–86.

8. In the first round of official price increases (March 1979), the quota prices for grain, oil seeds, cotton, and hogs were increased by 20, 25, 15, and 26 percent, respectively, while the above-quota price was set above the 1978 price by an increase of 80, 88, 50 percent, and an unknown amount, respectively. Price increases in eighteen other categories of agricultural products ranged from 20 to 50 percent. See Frederic M. Surles and Francis C. Tuan, "China's Agriculture in the Eighties," in Joint Economic Committee, U.S. Congress, *China under the Four Modernizations, Part I* (Washington, D.C.: U.S. Government Printing Office, 1982), pp. 428–29.

9. As can be seen from the Addendum in Table 2, largely because of the relatively slow growth in agricultural sector output in 1986–88, agriculture's share of national income had declined by 1988 to a share below its share in 1978. Because of a surge in investment and because of price increases, the shares for construction and commerce increased well above their 1978 levels in 1985–88; but this hardly accounts for a successful restructuring of the economy.

10. State Statistical Bureau, PRC, *Statistical Yearbook of China* (Hong Kong: Economic Information and Agency, p. 32. In 1986–88, however, light industrial output increased by an annual average of 17.8 percent and that of heavy industry by 11.5 percent. Nevertheless, both growth rates were well beyond that of agriculture, and total output of heavy industry, in current prices, remained larger than that of light industry. State Statistical Bureau, PRC, *Zhongguo tongji zhaiyao, 1987* (Statistical abstract of China, 1987) (Beijing: Chinese Statistics Publishers, 1987), pp. 9–10.

11. As indicated in note 9 above, output in both the construction and commerce sectors increased relatively rapidly in 1986 and 1989, *in current prices,* and this increases the services' share in national income to 21.4 percent, when national income and sector shares are estimated in current prices, as they are in Table 2. Again, this result, largely due to price increases, exaggerates the success in restructuring the economy due to the economic reforms.

12. For my own analysis of how the Soviet-type economy was adopted and used to achieve high growth rates in China after 1949, see Robert F. Dernberger and Richard S. Eckaus, *Financing Asian Development: China and India* (Lanham, MD: University Press of America, 1988), pp. 20–27.

13. For a more detailed discussion of this argument, see Dernberger and Eckaus, *Financing Asian Development*, pp. 49–56.

14. In 1978, 37.4 percent of capital construction in state-owned enterprises was for the expansion and reconstruction of existing enterprises; in 1985, it was 48.6 percent. By 1988, however, the share of investment on expansion and reconstruction of existing enterprises had declined to 43.6 percent of the total. State Statistical Bureau, PRC,

Zhongguo Tongji Zhaiyao, 1989 (Statistical abstract of China, 1989) (Beijing: Chinese Statistics Publishers, 1989), p. 61.

15. Ibid., p. 60.

16. Based on data for foreign trade and national income from State Statistical Bureau, PRC, *Statistical Yearbook of China, 1986,* pp. 481 and 40, respectively.

17. It is important to qualify this statement with the "explanatory note" to these estimates, presented in Table 6.

18. For the 1985 statistics for foreign investment, see State Statistical Bureau, PRC, *Statistical Yearbook of China, 1986,* p. 499. For the cumulative debt at the end of 1988, "China Announces Foreign Debt for the First Time,"*Beijing Review,* vol. 32, no. 44 (October 30–November 5, 1989), p. 40.

19. Statistics to verify this statement are not readily available; industrial statistics are being reported by type of ownership or by size (large, medium, and small), but not by size within each form of ownership. If we assume that all large and medium industrial enterprises are state-owned, then there were 3,500 new large and medium and 6,500 small-scale state-owned, industrial enterprises created in 1978–85. New jobs created in the former, of course, could easily have exceeded those created in the latter.

20. The economic reforms in the agricultural sector are dealt with in greater detail in the essay by Nicholas Lardy in this volume.

21. Economic Reform Research Institute, Comprehensive Investigation Group, ed., *Gaige: Women mianlin de tiaozhan yu xuanze* (Beijing: Chinese Economics Publishers, 1986). The results of the survey presented here are taken from William Byrd, "The Impact of the Two-Tier Plan/Market System in Chinese Industry," *Journal of Comparative Economics,* vol. 11, no. 3 (September 1987), p. 299. (This issue of the *Journal of Comparative Economics* was a special issue devoted to the papers on the Chinese economic reforms presented at the Arden House Conference on Chinese Economic Reform, Harriman, New York, October 9–12, 1986. A summary of the CESRRI survey of 1985 is also included in this issue.)

22. These estimates are from Louise do Rosario, "Course Correction," *Far Eastern Economic Review,* July 16, 1987, pp. 69–71. A slightly different set of statistics, but one following the same trends, was published in a Chinese source: Gao Shangquan, "Progress in Economic Reform (1979–86)," *Beijing Review,* July 6, 1987, pp. 20–24. Gao presents the same statistics for the decline in the share of investment covered by unilateral budget grants, but adds that "sales of commodities with prices fixed by the state account for only 40 percent of the country's total sales volume."

23. According to sample surveys of peasant households, rice and wheat accounted for 50 percent of the peasants' per capita grain consumption in 1978; 81 percent in 1985. State Statistical Bureau, PRC, *Statistical Yearbook of China, 1986,* p. 585.

24. At an annual rate of increase of 8.7 percent, compared to 5.8 percent for nonagricultural residents, it would still take more than thirty years for the peasants' per capita consumption to become equal to that of the nonagricultural residents.

25. According to sample surveys in 1985, urban households contained 3.8 persons per household, while peasant households contained 5.1 persons per household. State Statistical Bureau, PRC, *Statistical Yearbook of China, 1986,* pp. 570, 582.

26. This was the most common response to my question as to what was the most serious problem faced by Shanghai that I asked of the people I met during my visit to that city in June 1987.

27. Specifically, this is the average annual rate of growth of gross domestic product in 1914/18–1933. Dwight H. Perkins, "Growth and Changing Structure of China's Twentieth-Century Economy," in Dwight H. Perkins, ed., *China's Modern Economy in Historical Perspective* (Stanford, CA: Stanford University Press, 1975), p. 117.

28. John K. Chang, *Industrial Development in Pre-Communist China* (Chicago: Aldine Publishing Company, 1969), pp. 36, 71.

29. Estimates for the peak period of China's foreign trade indicate a trade participation ratio as high as 0.17 in the late 1920s; see Appendix A, Robert F. Dernberger, "China's Foreign Trade and Capital Movements, 1949–1962," unpublished Ph.D. thesis, Harvard University, 1965, p. 363. The estimated ratio for 1952–59, from the same source (p. 108), is 11 percent.

30. See "explanatory note" in Table 6 for the problem involved, i.e., the estimate of national income in domestic prices, the estimate of foreign trade values (in either yuan or in dollars) in foreign prices, and an exchange rate that overvalues the yuan.

31. An extremely rough estimate of the ratio of foreign investment to national income in China can be made on the basis of C. F. Remer's estimate for foreign investment in 1914 (1.5 billion U.S. dollars), Ou Paosan's estimate for per capita income in the prewar period ($20 per capita), and Dwight H. Perkins' estimate of population in 1914/18 (429.8 million), resulting in an estimate of the ratio of foreign investment to national income of 17.5 percent. As indicated above, Dwight H. Perkins' estimates that GNP grew by 1.4 percent in 1914/18–1933, while Remer estimates that foreign investment increased by 4.6 percent a year in 1914–31; thus, the ratio of foreign investment to national income must have been greater than 17.5 percent in the 1920s and early 1930s. For the estimates of Remer, see C. F. Remer, *Foreign Investments in China* (New York: Howard Fertig, 1968), p. 69. For the estimates of Ou Paosan, see Yu-kwei Cheng, *Foreign Trade and Industrial Development of China* (Washington, D.C.: The University Press of Washington, D.C., 1956), p. 38. For the estimate of Perkins, see Dwight H. Perkins, *Agricultural Development in China, 1368–1968* (Chicago: Aldine Publishing Company, 1969), p. 216.

32. In addition, the surveys that produce these estimates, such as the Buck data, are based on samples that undoubtedly result in estimates that are upward biased, i.e., rely on better- than-average units of production.

33. For labor force participation rates (total labor force/population) derived from population estimates and total labor force estimates, see State Statistical Bureau, PRC, *Statistical Yearbook of China, 1986*, pp. 71 and 92, respectively. For unemployment rate, see ibid., p. 104.

34. The newly created China Social Survey System, which is charged with carrying out Gallup-type polls of public opinion, reports that 64.4 percent of the population questioned were satisfied with the economic reforms, but the published results were not differentiated as to rural and urban respondents.

35. For the resulting income distribution as the average level of per capita income grew in other developing countries, see Simon Kuznets, "Distribution of Income by Size," *Economic Development and Cultural Change*, vol. 9, no. 4, part 2 (July 1961); and Jeffrey G. Williamson, "Regional Inequality and the Process of National Development: A Description of the Patterns," *Economic Development and Cultural Change*, vol. 13, no. 4, part 2 (July 1965).

36. It is interesting that some outside observers cited the supposed growing equality of income distribution as a positive feature of China's economy during the Maoist regime, unaware of or choosing to neglect the stagnation in the rate of growth in the average per capita income. Now that there can be no question but that the average is growing rapidly during the Dengist regime, some outside observers are concerned that the distribution may be becoming more inequitable. Even if we were to assume both circumstances depicted above are true characteristics of the pre- and post-1978 Chinese economy, a logical argument could be made that everyone can benefit in the latter, while only a few gained and many lost in the former. The point being made in the text, however, is that until we gain access to more and better data, we cannot rule out the possibility that a growing

equality accompanied the rapid growth in average per capita incomes in the post-1978 poriod.

37. See George J. Staller, "Fluctuations in Economic Activity: Planned and Free Market Economies, 1950–1960," *American Economic Review*, vol. 54, no. 4 (June 1964), pp. 385–95; and Alexander Bajt, "Investment Cycles in European Socialist Economies: A Review Article," *Journal of Economic Literature*, vol. 9, no. 1 (March 1971), pp. 53–63.

38. See Dernberger and Edkaus, *Financing Asian Development: China and India*, Appendix Table A–2, pp. 65–66.

39. World Bank, *China: Long-Term Development: Issues and Options* (Baltimore: The Johns Hopkins Press, 1985), Table 7.1, p. 111.

40. Gregory Chow, *The Chinese Economy* (New York: Harper & Row, Publishers, 1985), pp. 119–31.

41. Gerald M. Meier, *Financing Asian Development: Performance and Prospects* (New York: University Press of America, 1986), p. 7.

42. Justin Yifu Lin, "Measuring the Impacts of the Household Responsibility System on China's Agricultural Production," unpublished paper, Department of Economics, The University of Chicago, April 1986 (mimeo.). In a more recent paper, Dr. Lin has used a different methodology to update and revise these estimates, showing a somewhat larger impact of the economic reforms on output growth.

43. Data in this and the next sentence are from State Statistical Bureau, PRC, *Zhongguo tongji zhaiyao, 1987*, p. 24.

44. State Statistical Bureau, PRC, *Statistical Yearbook of China, 1986*, p. 124, and State Statistical Bureau, PRC, *Zhongguo tongji zhaiyao, 1987*, p. 37.

45. In a study published very recently, a critic of previous studies of industrial productivity in China has produced estimates based on "adjusted" data that shows total factor productivity increasing by 5 percent in a year in 1978–85. The adjustments made are to remove all nonproductive capital and labor inputs, to significantly deflate capital stock estimates to remove the effects of price increases, and to weigh capital and labor inputs by the weights of their contribution to output as estimated in an econometric estimate of an aggregate production function for Chinese industry. Theoretically, each of these adjustments are required to estimate correctly total factor productivity, but the adjustments actually made, I believe, all serve to result in an upward bias to the estimates for total factor productivity growth. No matter, all studies quoted show that total factor productivity increased after 1978 and made a large contribution as a source of growth after that year. See Chen Kuan, Wang Hongchang, Zheng Yuxin, Gary H. Jefferson, and Thomas G. Rawski, "Productivity Change in Chinese Industry, 1953–1985, *Journal of Comparative Economics*, vol. 12, no. 4 (December 1988), pp. 570–91.

46. The grouping of the reformers into these three groups was suggested by Liu Guoguang, Vice President, Chinese Academy of Social Sciences, in his Eckstein Memorial Lecture, delivered at the University of Michigan, September 15, 1987.

47. This concept of "growing out of the plan" was first suggested by Professor Barry Naughton and was developed in an essay by William Byrd, "The Impact of the Two-Tier Plan/Market System in Chinese Industry," *Journal of Comparative Economics*, vol. 11, no. 3 (September 1987), pp. 295–308 (see especially the discussion on pages 299–302).

48. For a discussion of this argument by one of its leading proponents, see Stephen Haggard, "Korea from Import-Substitution to Export-Led Growth," chapter 3 in a manuscript being completed on the process of economic policy formation in the Newly Industrialized Countries (n.d., mimeo.).

49. When a member of a visiting delegation meeting with Vice Premier Yao Yilin, I asked when the new economic system would be created as a result of the reform process and what it would look like, i.e., what did "socialism with Chinese characterisitcs" mean?

He replied that the process of experimenting would probably continue for at least another fifty years and, therefore, the present generation of leaders could not know what the ultimate result will look like as it will be determined by a future generation of leaders.

50. The published report on the results of the Fifth Plenum can be found in "Communique of the Fifth Plenary Session of the Thirteenth CPC Central Committee," *Beijing Review*, vol. 32, no. 47 (November 20–26), 1989, pp. 15–18. This report, however, does not say very much. A report on the thirty-eight specific measures said to be contained in the unpublished "Three-Year Retrenchment Program" adopted at the Plenum can be found in Louise do Rosario, "Three Years' Hard Labour," *Far Eastern Economic Review*, November 30, 1989, pp. 68–69. The three years cover the period 1989–91. For a report on how the retrenchment program already has succeeded in stabilizing the economy and some of the problems this has caused, see Li Ping, "Initial Success for Economic Rectification and Improvement," *Beijing Review*, vol. 32, no. 48 (November 27–December 3, 1989), pp. 20–22.

Comments by Nicholas R. Lardy

I am in broad agreement with most of Professor Dernberger's paper and with the conclusions he draws about the Deng era. I particularly agree with what I see as his two main characterizations of the Deng era: first, that it is an era of somewhat more rapid and stable growth than the preceding period and, second, that the reform process has taken China quite far from the traditional centrally planned economy, yet falls considerably short of a fully market socialist system.

I would like to say more about productivity issues and efficiency issues. I have some minor disagreements with some of Professor Dernberger's numbers. I think if one wants to calculate what has been happening to productivity, one should use value-added measures for what is happening in terms of industrial output and gross value figures that are used; that tends to overstate the rate of growth of the value-added, particularly since 1978; even Professor Dernberger's own data in the second part of Table 12 show that the rate of material consumption per unit of output has increased by a couple of percentage points. This will knock down the growth of the value-added. By the time one subtracts other adjustments, the total productivity has actually declined since 1978, as I argued in my paper. Several calculations by the World Bank and other authors have indicated the same thing.

I would hasten to add, however, that there are substantial problems in carrying out this kind of calculation, primarily because we do not really know with much certainty what has happened to the rate of growth in the capital stock even in the state-owned sector, and this is largely because we do not have a constant price series for the capital stock in the sector. The only available data are current prices, and obviously prices have been rising over time; that series will overstate the rate that underlines the real growth of the capital stock. Were we to use them to calculate productivity and improvements, we would understate an improvement in productivity that had occurred. On the other hand, prices have been falling. For example, machinery prices have been falling substantially between the 1950s and the 1960s. Then the capital stock series would substantially understate the capital stock, and calculation of productivity would be far too optimistic. In other words, the rate of decline would be more rapid than the calculation I have cited would suggest. What is most interesting about this is that I do not think anyone in China has any answer to this question. I think the Chinese have a very good fix on what has happened to productivity in manufacturing. I do not think they have the data to calculate this easily, and in the published literature, there are no calculations of the type we would like to have to analyze the issue. I suppose one can rely on microdata from a specific firm to draw conclusions. But if one wants to post a question in the aggregate, can the State Planning Commission or some other organization tell Zhao Ziyang whether productivity has been going up or down in state-owned factories? I would argue that at the present time they could not answer the question, at least not in the way we would tend to answer the question. It is problematic how they would evaluate the results of reforms at least in the aggregate.

I agree with Professor Dernberger, however, that in looking at the longer term, we should really have expected much more substantial improvements to have occurred in these conventional measures of productivity, not just in the last decade, but even over a longer term. I say this for three reasons, the first being education. When one applies this kind of calculus to other countries, one finds that a major reason factory productivity goes up is because of enormous improvement in education, particularly in the spread of mass literacy. This is an area in which China has had success, yet I do not see educational advances resulting in the kind of improvements that it accounts for in other economies. The second factor is the extent to which China has significantly underexploited its natural resources. Consider the Soviet case. One of the conventional explanations why factory productivity has declined over the last decade or so is that the Soviet Union has to explore more and more expensive sources of raw material. China in a sense faces an opposite situation. They have in the last couple of decades had access to huge quantities of low-cost energy, and that should be feeding the economy, by conventional measures, very much better than has been the case. The third factor that has been helping them in the last decade, and perhaps longer, is the shift of resources out of the hare-brained Maoist schemes, such as the third front, which was rapidly pouring money into extraordinarily inefficient projects, roughly in the early 1960s and the beginning of the 1970s. That was terminated more than a decade ago and we should be seeing the payoff from presumable re-deployment of those kinds of resources in more rational and efficient projects. Yet in the aggregate data, one simply does not see this yet. So one has to wonder why, given this longer favorable trend in manufacturing, we do not see a more significant payoff at the aggregate level. I think we have to go back to political factors and recognize that the enhancement of authorities at the intermediate level of government administration under the reform programs has led to a new kind of resource misallocation, similar to those China suffered in the past, one that has resulted in little or no improvement in efficiency in manufacturing.

Comments by Louis Putterman[1]

We are all much indebted to Professor Dernberger for providing us with a broad and comprehensive survey of the major trends in the Chinese economy in the Deng Xiaoping era, and for putting these trends in the perspective of China's history, the performance of other centrally planned economies, and the experiences of other developing countries. I will focus my comments on a few conceptual points and on areas where I might add something at the margin (as we economists never tire of saying) to the material Professor Dernberger has presented.

First, let me go back over some ground I covered yesterday [November 5, 1987] in discussing Professor Lardy's paper, in which context I borrowed more than one point from the present paper by Dernberger. One of those borrowings concerned the statement that China has exhibited a high growth economy under a variety of policy regimes since 1949. This reminds me of a statement I once heard Dwight Perkins make. Tongue-in-cheek, I think, Dwight remarked that China had achieved agricultural growth in the 1950s through the gradual collectivization of its farms, and that it was now achieving agricultural growth in the late 1970s and early 1980s through the *decollectivization* of its farms. In other words, China sometimes appears to be capable of getting mileage out of rearranging its institutional furniture, more or less regardless of what the content of the changes may be. But the points I would personally draw from both the Dernberger and Perkins observations are, first, that an ideal, efficient set of institutions may either not exist or may simply not be crucial to China's economic growth. (I suggested some other conditions that may be more important yesterday.) Second, it is as unjustified to become a *gung ho* "Dengist" in the 1980s as it was to be a foreign "Maoist" in the 1970s in particular, to fall into the mistake of imagining that China's economy is only now taking off after a period of endless economic stagnation. Third, it seems to me that there may be an economic explanation, after all, for why decollectivization and collectivization both produced fruits when occurring in a certain sequence: namely, that the mobilization of "surplus" labor to build rural infrastructure, and of "surplus" products to build rural industry, in the collective era, laid much of the groundwork for the rapid growth under decollectivization in the 1980s.

Another part of Professor Dernberger's paper of which I made brief approving reference yesterday was his analysis of the nature of recent growth in China's rural sector. I think he is correct in pointing out that much of the growth in crop production is due to the injection of additional inputs, and that such growth as occurred through productivity change is probably attributable to the one-time effect of institutional change, especially with regard to production incentives and the microlevel organization of the production process more generally. He also, quite importantly, points to the fact that much recent growth in rural output is not due to agriculture at all, but rather to village and township industrial enterprises.

Dernberger raises this point partly as a way of suggesting there are limits to the success of the agricultural reforms, whereas the rapid growth in rural industry is one source of my relative optimism about both the reform process and the growth prospects of the Chinese economy.

A point made by Professor Dernberger on which I did not have occasion to comment before and which I find worth underscoring, is his remark that the fashioning of operating markets and marketlike institutions among certain reformers in China makes very little economic sense, so long as markets are not permitted to play a leading role in price formation. Unless markets help sort out the valuation of resources through the pricing process, there is no basis in economic theory for thinking a market a desirable allocative device.

A few of Professor Dernberger's statements struck me as open to critical comments. One of these is his statement that in the 1960s and 1970s, the Chinese used the Soviet-type system more effectively—that is, achieved higher growth through it—than did the social economies of Eastern Europe. The comparison seems unfair to me since China's initial level of economic development was so much lower. Given absolute increments to industrial output represent much larger percentage increases when applied to a smaller base. The Soviet Union and many nonsocialist economies have also exhibited patterns of slowing growth over the very long run due to this and related phenomena; it would be more appropriate to compare China of the 1960s and 1970s with Russia in the 1930s than to compare the two contemporaneously.

A minor criticism concerns Professor Dernberger's comparison of the variability in the rate of economic growth in China in 1952–78, with its variability in 1978–86. As he himself points out, the troughs of the earlier economic cycles centered on 1961, 1967, and 1978. Beginning in 1949, this makes roughly one major trough per decade. The period 1978 to 1986 may simply be too short for comparison, although I hope that the continuing trend sustains Dernberger's interim observation.

A third point to which some criticism might be directed is the listing of drawbacks of the reforms, such as its effects on employment security, price stability, and state budget balance. Real social costs these are—and intellectually respectable arguments against using markets in the first place have been built partly on them. I have no problem with the argument that China has failed to prepare itself to deal with the social by-products of its market reforms. Prof. Dernberger's motivation, however, for listing the woes of the new system, in comparison with the old, is sometimes hard to understand. Market economies are known to be prone to price instability, unemployment, job insecurity, and budget deficits; so it makes as much sense to view the appearance of these problems as a sign that real reform is taking place, and that the Chinese people are being reintroduced to the realities of the world of markets, as it does to treat their appearance as negatives. It goes without saying, of course, that the problems will give rise to antireform sentiments, and strengthen the hands of existing antireform elements. Has market economy ever found a way to avoid these "side effects," which are among the causes of antimarket revolutions in the first place? Can we really expect China to be the first society ever to extract all of the good from markets without suffering the bad? Surely China's reforms ought not to be seen as failing just for being unable to meet so high a standard.[2]

Having completed my nit-picking, let me now try to make my promised "marginal contribution" in an area with which I have some familiarity through my own research, China's rural economy. Here I have three comments to offer. The first concerns Professor Dernberger's discussion of the gap between rural and urban living standards, and the apparently puzzling perception by urbanites that they are falling behind. I would suggest that it is important in this context to look beyond the averages, to the great heterogeneity of rural incomes both intraregionally and, especially, interregionally, where a common and often very substantial difference is that between residents in the rural outskirts of cities, both suburban and in surrounding counties, and peasants in more remote areas having less access to urban contract work and markets. Thus, while the ratio of average urban to average rural incomes remains large, it seems likely that at the upper tail of the rural income distribution are a nonnegligible number of households having distinctly higher living standards than average urban dwellers. It is with reference to these rural dwellers that urbanites correctly drew unfavorable comparisons.

The great heterogeneity of rural incomes implies that while the average gap between rural and urban incomes has narrowed somewhat, there are substantial segments of the rural population for which the gap has not narrowed at all, or has widened. Furthermore, more or less the same gap exists between the very large number of still quite poor rural dwellers and the far more affluent rural populations around cities and especially in places like southern Jiangsu Province and the Pearl River Delta. The fact that affluent rural households are concentrated near cities goes a long way to explain why urbanites feel they are falling behind. Indeed, at the rural urban interface, the sharp class boundary associated with the longstanding household registration system can work to the advantage of households with rural registration (who may belong to long-since urbanized former suburban communes), since some activities that are permitted to members of the more marketized rural sector are difficult or illegal for urban residents to undertake.

My second comment more directly concerns the effects of the reforms on income distribution. Professor Dernberger mentions the possibility that income inequality may or may not have increased, and that even if it did, all households including those at the bottom of the income distribution may have gained in the reforms; he wisely adds that more data are required before conclusions can be reached. My own contribution is that of a small body of evidence from a single rural township (formerly commune), Dahe, in Hebei Province, located just outside the municipality of Shijiazhuang, the provincial capital.[3] There, the roughly

100 production teams belonging to sixteen brigades or villages provided extensive annual financial and production accounts for the years 1970 to 1985, while about 250 households, constituting the full populations of five of the teams in five separate villags, provided detailed economic data at the household level for the years 1979 (before decollectivization at Dahe) and 1985 (following it).[4] The average value of the intrateam Gini coefficient of inequality of per capita income across households over the five teams surveyed at the household level rose from .172 in 1979 to .254 in 1985, indicating significantly higher, although still modest, inequality among households within the same team.[5] At the team level, the Gini coefficient of per capita distributed income,[6] which fell in the range of .06 to .09 between 1970 and 1978, rose to an average of .178 during 1983 to 1985, again suggesting increased but still modest inequality. More significant, perhaps, is that of the households surveyed before and after the reforms (in 1979 and 1985), 14.5 percent experienced absolute declines in real per capita incomes, while 41.5 percent saw gains of up to 100 percent, 27 percent saw gains of 100 to 200 percent, and 16.8 percent experienced increases of greater than 200 percent.[7] While it is possible that these households would have seen falling per capita incomes also in the absence of the reforms, because of life-cycle changes, it seems noteworthy that most of the poorest households in the 1985 survey were peasants dependent on agriculture and lacking family members employed in industry, transport, commerce, construction, or other more remunerative activities. Both increasing inequality and the absolute impoverishment of some fraction of rural households appear to be associated with occupational specialization at Dahe, and the phenomena could hold widely within other Chinese townships and even more so interregionally.

My final remark concerns Professor Dernberger's conclusion that the reforms have had their principal impact on the rate of economic growth in China, and only a minor impact, in spite of the leadership's intentions, on economic structure. Without having been able to consult data to support my point, I can only state qualitatively my sense that this conclusion may be in error by way of underestimating the magnitude of the rapid occupational shift taking place in much of the Chinese countryside, wherein former and perhaps still part-time cultivators are turning into workers in rural industry, construction, and other trades.[8] The present decade may be witnessing such substantial movement out of agricultural labor that in hindsight it will be seen to have been a watershed in the history of the Chinese economy, and the shift of the labor force from agriculture to nonagriculture *within the rural areas* may well be judged to be among the most important, if not the single most important, result(s) of the Deng leadership's economic reforms. The changing structural distribution of labor has been a more or less universal hallmark of the economic development process that has thus far been largely deferred by China, after a false start in the Great Leap Forward period. The most significant result of the rural reforms may turn out to be not increased output from China's limited arable area, but rather that the effort levels of the population engaged in farming have risen so substantially as to make possible the freeing of the majority of those formerly engaged in agriculture to other productive pursuits, thus raising the society's output from the same resource (e.g., labor) base.[9]

Notes

1. I have chosen not to undertake major revisions of my comments on Professor Dernberger's paper in response to his updating and substantial addition to the paper. Although the reader should have no difficulty relating these comments to the revised version of that paper, it should be borne in mind that my remarks do not reflect my views on the events in China subsequent to the 1987 conference. A few notes added at the final revision stage will be distinguished by square brackets. L.P., January 1990.

2. The revised paper is much less susceptible to this criticism than was the original, but the point seems worth retaining on general grounds. For a recent exercise of my own contrasting the sins of the semireformed economy with those of the old system, see Louis Putterman, "Industrial and Agricultural Investment Coordination under 'Plan' and 'Market' in China," paper presented at the Conference on Investment Coordination in the Asia-Pacific Region, University of Hawaii at Manoa, January 3–5, 1990.

3. Information on this township will be found in Louis Putterman, "Entering the Post-Collective Era in North China: Dahe Township," *Modern China* (1989) 15:275–320. The data cited in this paragraph are published in Bingyuan Hsiung and Louis Putterman, "Pre- and Post-Reform Income Distribution in a Chinese Commune: The Case of Dahe Commune in Hebei Province," *Journal of Comparative Economics* (1989) 13:406–45.

4. Some teams at Dahe introduced a less radical form of production responsibility system (*lianchan jichou*) in 1980, 1981, or 1982. All of the teams adopted the full household contracting system (*baogan daohu*) in 1983.

5. The Gini coefficient has a minimum of zero, for perfect equality, and a maximum of one, representing the most extreme inquality.

6. This covers collective income only for the 1970s, collective and household-generated incomes together for the 1980s. Because there is evidence that collective incomes were in most cases more unequally distributed than combined collective and household incomes, the difference in coverage is unlikely to explain the apparent increase in inequality after the reforms. (See Keith Griffin and Ashwani Saith, *Growth and Equity in Rural China* [Tokyo: Maruzen, 1981]; and Hsiung and Putterman, "Pre- and Post-Reform Income Distribution in a Chinese Commune.")

7. These computations are sensitive to the procedure adopted for correcting for price changes. Using unadjusted nominal data, 8.1 percent of the households experience lower incomes.

8. This point is certainly supported for the local data from Dahe township. For recent research on these issues treating national trends, see Jeffrey R. Taylor, "Rural Employment Trends in China and the Legacy of Surplus Labor, 1978–1986," *China Quarterly* (1988) 116:736–66, and Louis Putterman and Calla Wiemer, "Reallocating Labor from Chinese Agriculture: The Intersection of Structural Change and Institutional Reform," paper presented at a joint session of the American Economic Association and the Chinese Economic Association in North America, Atlanta, December 29, 1989.

9. Three brief notes here: One, causality may also run in the opposite direction. That is, the greater freedom afforded rural dwellers to pursue noncrop producing activities may be a major cause of increased efficiency of agricultural work, in part because it has raised

the opportunity cost of time devoted to it. Two, there are structural conflicts between state industry and agriculture, and between the state sector and rural industry, that are now preventing change from taking place more rapidly (Putterman and Wiemer, "Reallocating Labor from Chinese Agriculture." Three, *even after* China's structural transformation with respect to the employment of its rural labor force, the country remains internationally atypical with respect to another major dimension, that of residence. Movement of labor out of agriculture has most often not entailed movement of workers from rural areas, although many of those areas are gradually becoming semiurban in character.

7

EDUCATIONAL REFORM IN THE 1980s:
A Retrospective on the Maoist Era

Suzanne Pepper

THE FIRST step in fulfilling an assignment to assess the post-Mao educational reforms in relation to their past requires a definition of the relevant past. The comparison lies obviously with the Maoist era which in turn begs the question as to the significance of those years. Hence, the first main part of this essay addresses the issue of historical relevance while the second part concentrates, within that historical context, on the educational reforms of the post-Mao order led by Deng Xiaoping.

The main aims of educational policy during the final decade of Mao's rule and the first decade under his successors can actually be compared without further elaboration. In few sectors did the Maoist innovations receive wider publicity; in few were they as quickly overturned after Mao's death in 1976. The Maoist innovations aimed at quantity over quality as conventionally defined. They aimed to expand the base of the pyramid, or mass education, at the expense of its pinnacle, that is, elite forms of schooling and the tertiary level. They were concerned also with equalizing the content and quality of education available to everyone. This is another way of saying that they tried to reduce the social inequalities that education helps to reinforce. And they aimed to break the power of professional educators over education. One of the reasons for this last aim was the "bourgeois" or nonproletarian background of China's educational establishment in a society ruled by a Communist party that still took seriously its antibourgeois objectives. Another reason for wanting to break the continuing influence of the educated elite was to remove the obstacles they were creating to radical innovations in education. These innovations developed over a twenty-year period, roughly from 1958 until Mao's death in 1976, but were most systematically pursued during the 1966–76 Cultural Revolution decade.

The radical innovations were contending with opposition on almost every point. That opposition has consequently been in the ascendancy since 1976, reversing all the Maoist priorities. Power was restored to professional educators and elite education became the overriding focus of attention. This was justified in the interests of technological and economic development while social inequalities were allowed to develop unobstructed as an assumed inevitable cost of the overriding aim.

Central to the shift between one set of priorities and the other, of course, was the Cultural Revolution, which was declared officially ended shortly after Mao Zedong's death in 1976. By 1980, the new official line decreed that "not one good thing" could be said of developments in education or anywhere else for that matter, throughout the entire 1966–76 Cultural Revolution decade. The new line refused to distinguish between the Red Guard rebellion that launched the Cultural Revolution in the late 1960s, the subsequent intensified application of political and social criteria in education, or the specific policies introduced in pursuit of what was called China's "education revolution." All alike were redefined as manifestations of the "ten-year turmoil" and unworthy of anything but the dustbin of history. Educators throughout the country professed themselves incredulous in 1980 that the outside world could have sought to learn from China's revolution in education in the early 1970s. Indeed, they were unable to identify even one feature that deserved to be retained or remembered from that experience, which was still being lauded internationally as the best of all possible solutions for the dilemmas of educational development.[1]

China's sudden reverse course raised several questions that are directly relevant to our assignment here. For example, how could so drastic a change be explained? Was there any substance to the claims made during the early 1970s, or were they all part of some grand illusion created by the force of Mao's aging political ego and a gullible foreign audience? But if there was substance to the earlier claims, why were the Chinese so systematically denying them? And if there was substance to the claims, what of their past and future? Where, in other words, did the 1966–76 Cultural Revolution episode come from? If it was, as the post-1978 rhetoric suggested, just another of the mistakes Mao committed in his dotage, then the episode might be successfully erased from the pages of history and the memories of its participants. But if the Cultural Revolution or at least its educational component was something more, then the experience must have had antecedents and roots of its own that could not be so easily extracted. The historical perspective elaborated in this essay derives from the foregoing questions.

Origins and Development of the "Two-Line Struggle" in Education

Following official Chinese discourse, it became fashionable during the late 1960s to trace the "two-line struggle" in education and most everything else back to the Yan'an decade. In fact, the documents from that time do verify a relevant dichotomy in the educational policy of the Chinese Communist Party (CCP) between 1938 and 1944—although not in any such clear-cut form, with Mao on one side and his adversaries on the other, as was later claimed.[2] More pertinent, what the historical records indicate is that the same controversies that existed in Chinese education circles generally at the time were reproduced in Yan'an as well, after the party's political and intellectual leaders made it their headquarters in the mid-1930s. They arrived in the new capital together with all of their conflicting commitments and built these into the "new" education policies they devised for the expanding Communist-led border regions.

The Anti-Establishment Backlash of the 1920s

The conflicting commitments had developed during the 1920s, as part of the critical backlash against the sudden rush to learn from the foreign Western world what had occurred in China during the first two decades of the century. The backlash appeared to draw strength from a variety of sources during the years following the May Fourth Incident of 1919. These sources included an underlying cultural conservatism that was only submerged but not extinguished during the rush to modernize, newly critical perspectives that returning students brought back from the West itself in the aftermath of World War I, the victory via the Russian Revolution of Marxism as the most self-critical Western perspective of all, and the growing nationalism of the post-May Fourth years. But whatever the source, this backlash as it developed among Chinese educators and erstwhile educational reformers aimed at a common target, namely, the uncritical imitation of foreign ideas in China's schools at the time.

This concern was perhaps most succinctly summarized in a 1923 statement by the liberal educator, Tao Xingzhi: "At first she (China) sacrificed everything old for the new. Gradually she came to a realization that the old is not necessarily bad and the new is not necessarily good. Thus our schoolmen have become much more criticial than in former years."[3] Tao Xingzhi had been educated at Columbia University Teachers College, was a liberal disciple of John Dewey, and headed the pro-American Chinese National Association for the Advancement of Education. He claimed that his own personal awakening occurred in the autumn of that year when he decided to buy a change of cotton peasant clothes and "rushed back to the way of the common people." Thereafter he devoted himself increasingly to mass education and nonformal schooling, eventually turning away from the formal educational system altogether to concentrate on the vast numbers who never entered it.

Having finally overcome their scruples against Western ways and ideas, China's educated elite had abandoned its Confucian learning, the ancient civil service examination system, and the imperial system itself, all with unprecedented revolutionary haste. Thousands left for study abroad after the examinations were abolished in 1905. On returning, these students established a modern school system for China patterned on those they had seen in Japan, the United States, and Europe. Successive waves of "returned students" imposed successive rounds of reform on the system. But it was this essentially foreign transplant that served as a lightening rod for the post-1919 critics. Reflecting their diverse intellectual and political orientations, the backlash against Western influence found adherents all across the political spectrum. Their interests and inclinations would ultimately take them in many different directions; but in the early 1920s, a common denominator of agreement crystallized quite suddenly and then hardened into a critical consensus against the new established school system. The consensus was such that budding Marxist Mao Zedong, cultural conservative Liang Shuming, and pro-American liberal Tao Xingzhi, could all share it. By the 1930s, the critique was so popular that virtually everyone was at least paying lip service to it including the Guomindang government, League of Nations experts, American missionaries, and even the Rockefeller Foundation.[4] The argument contained the following points:

The new schools in whatever form, that is, public, private, Chinese or foreign-run, secular or Christian, together with overseas study, had created an urban-oriented elite divorced by its learning and life-style from the rest of Chinese society.

The new intellectuals were estranged from the rest of society owing to their uncritical acceptance of the Western educational models to which they were indebted for their new learning.

But those models also acquired a formalistic and elitist nature that they did not necessarily have in their original settings, when transplanted into the alien Chinese environment still influenced in many ways by its Confucian heritage.

New and more appropriate forms had to be designed and the necessary sources of teachers and money had to be found to promote mass education and especially rural mass education since the great majority of China's people lived in the countryside.

One additional feature that the activist critics shared in common, however, was their ambivalent relationship with the chief object of their concern, namely, the established educational system. The dichotomy that later developed in Yan'an's educational policies arose directly from that relationship. Thus, despite its popularity, the backlash remained always too weak to inspire in practice anything more than experimental challenges to the modern school system. This appeared impervious to the changes that would have solved the problems everyone acknowledged. Exactly why that should have been so remained unclear, but the professional educators who staffed the system appeared by and large overwhelmingly committed to it. Once established during the early decades of the century, China's modern educational system continued to create the conditions for its own existence in terms of the interests and values of those associated with it. Thus when activist critics wanted to put their ideas into practice, they invariably had to take their experiments outside the established system because there was no place for them within it. But outside the system, the experiments inevitably failed after a few years for lack of adequate political support, financial backing, or military protection. Nor should the larger context of the controversy be obscured by the fact that some of the sharpest critics were themselves foreign-trained professional educators. Activist reformers, such as Tao Xingzhi and James Yen, won recognition because they were exceptions to the rule of the day, not representatives of it.[5] And their successes were undermined not only by the politicians and militarists, but also by their own fellow intellectuals. Because of that internal resistance, the reformers could not at the time have changed the system as a whole according to the prevailing critique even had they been given a politics-free environment within which to proceed.

Yet the returned students and professional educators presided over a system that was in fact hopelessly inadequate to the needs of Chinese society. Official statistics never claimed more than 25 percent of the age group in attendance at the elementary level during the pre-1949 era. Secondary and tertiary education was even more abbreviated. In 1949, China's secondary schools had an enrollment of 1.3 million, or about 2 percent of the relevant age group. Only 120,000 students were in college (0.3 percent of the age group). China's population was then about 540 million.[6]

The League of Nations' 1931 mission also found, however, that the system was overstaffed and buildings underutilized at all levels. The ratio between the cost of educating primary and college students was 1:200. Comparable ratios in European countries at the time did not exceed 1:10. Similarly, the difference between primary and college teacher's salaries was 1:20 or more in China, by comparison with no more than 1:4 in Europe—all indicating "extraordinary neglect" of basic-level mass education in China. It was estimated that given the existing resources, both human and material, at least twice the number of students could have been accommodated in the schools already existing at each level. Overall, the mission was most sharply critical of the people responsible for this system, namely, the new generation of Chinese intellectuals who equated modernization with expensive buildings, imported equipment, and the mechanical imitation of foreign learning. Toward that end, many richly endowed schools and colleges had been established. Yet no initiative had been made to integrate them into a coherent system of public education. The net result was a disjointed system emphasizing schools of higher standard. This had created an "enormous abyss between the masses of the Chinese people, plunged in illiteracy, and not understanding the needs of their country, and the intelligentsia educated in luxurious schools and indifferent to the wants of the masses."[7]

Yan'an: Regularization versus the Mass Line

In a fascinating example of social reproduction, this new generation of intellectuals—and the most Left-leaning among them at that—then proceeded to try to build an identical kind of system in the Communists' new Shaanxi-Gansu-Ningxia base area. This region lay at the nether end of the "enormous abyss" educationally and in most other ways as well. It was predominantly rural, poor, and sparsely populated. Towns were small provincial backwaters and social customs backward even for contemporary rural China. The illiteracy rate was the highest estimated for any region. There was no modern established educational system to speak of and therefore no interests to defend against the activist critics. Not, at least, until the new arrivals began creating them. By the end of the 1930s, many thousands of intellectuals (in those days the term was used for anyone with a secondary school education or above) with leftist inclinations had congregated in the Communists' new northwestern headquarters. Mao's old teacher from Changsha, Xu Teli, headed the Shaan-Gan-Ning government's education office which began immediately to promote mass education, as Xu had also done as acting head of education for the Jiangxi Soviet in the early 1930s. The number of elementary schools in northern Shaanxi grew rapidly, from just over 100 in 1935 to 1,341 in early 1940. Most of these were three-year junior primary schools that were easiest to set up and maintain at the village level. Student enrollments increased from about 2,000 to 41,458.[8]

By 1940, however, such statistics were being publicized to bolster the argument that primary schooling had been too precipitous in its growth. Probably it was no mere coincidence that Xu Teli was transferred to other work in 1938. From that year concern began to mount, at least as reflected in the education department's documents, over the low quality of the education being provided. Xu was succeeded as head of the department by Zhou Yang, communist cultural luminary recently arrived from Shanghai. What if anything Zhou had to do with the mundane details of elementary education has yet to be revealed. By the time this new concern for quality peaked in 1942, he too had been transferred to other work. But his arrival in the border region and in its education department coincided with the onset of the "regularization" drive that would dominate border region education during the next four years.

As the school system grew, a preoccupation with low standards developed accordingly. The newly arrived educators in charge of this burgeoning system interpreted its defects as being essentially quantitative, that is, too many schools set up too quickly. The "rural-ness" of the system also bothered them. Many of the new schools were little different from the old fashioned *sishu*, or private Chinese classes with a teacher and four or five students using the old Confucian primers. Investigations in many parts of the country had shown that rural people preferred this type of schooling because it was the only alternative they knew and because the curriculum in the new-style modern schools seemed irrelevant to the unchanged patterns of their lives and work. The old-style literacy classes, by contrast, were casual affairs. Students tended to drift in and out to accommodate family obligations and farm work. The teachers tended to enforce classroom discipline with corporal punishment—which the parents liked—and taught as the spirit moved them, often ignoring the modern subjects, newly issued textbooks, and fixed teaching plans.

Initially, in 1938, the education department cautioned that the method of 'merging" schools or closing some should be avoided in the drive to improve quality. Past experience had already proven that it meant a direct trade-off sacrificing quantity for quality. Parents did not like to send young children the longer distances to schools in other villages. When the number of schools declined, therefore, the number of students could not increase. This precaution was soon abandoned, however, as the movement to "regularize" (*zhengguihua*) the system escalated. In 1940, each county was authorized to close up to ten ordinary junior primary schools. The closure of schools that could not muster between 20 and 30 students was also authorized. By the time this trend culminated during the 1942–43 school year, the number of schools had been reduced by almost half, to 752; enrollments were down to 26,816.[9] Those remaining were ordered to follow the rules and regulations. Elementary education could not be improved unless all the "necessary systems" were established with unified texts, teaching materials, fixed standards, uniform teaching plans, regular schedules, students divided properly into grades and classes, and so on.

Finally, improved quality also required the "concentration of strength to run complete primary schools and create their central function of being model schools." Here were the innocent enough beginnings of an idea that, when eventually institutionalized nationwide, would become the controversial "key-point" school system of Cultural Revolution fame. Back in 1940–41, the Shaan-Gan-Ning Border Region could boast only forty-seven complete five-year primary schools and perhaps another fifty central (*zhongxin*) three-year junior primaries. These added up to a hundred model schools, although some of the five-year institutions were "very deficient" and therefore unable to perform their "model functions" as guides and pace-setters in their districts. The education department therefore instructed the counties to concentrate their resources on a few good schools, ensuring that they had more funds, the best teachers and administrators, complete furnishings, and followed all the rules. "Some people will say this is just putting on a show," said an education department official, "and it is just that," namely, to show everyone how schools should be run.[10]

The net effect of these efforts would have been to reproduce in the border region the same much-maligned educational system that existed in the rest of the country. Just as the critique of that system had adherents all along the political spectrum, so the instincts of professional Chinese educators were also essentially the same whatever their political inclinations. Economic considerations were mentioned scarcely at all as a justification for the school mergers, even though the border regions were experiencing financial difficulties at the time. Rather, the rationale was drawn on academic grounds appealing to conventional views among Chinese educators, namely, that quality of necessity meant a concentration of resources, both human and material, and that no school was preferable to low-quality schools.

The shift came in the spring of 1944. Again the documents are silent as to who actually made which decisions. At the time, the 1944 changes were attributed simply to the overall reorientation and radicalization that occurred in many sectors of border region public life following the 1942 party rectification campaign that Mao dominated. Thus, the later claim that the 1944 educational reforms represented "Mao's line" has some generalized substance in fact, although there is no direct evidence linking him to the specific policy changes implemented at the time. These essentially reversed the regularization drive that had overtaken the educational system between 1938 and 1942.

Two sources of inspiration were officially cited for the new direction.[11] One was the "new education" introduced around the turn of the century, or, more specifically, the ongoing debate it had spawned. The second was Marxist teachings on the role of education in society. Marxists advocated combining production with knowledge and Lenin had put that idea into practice. The border regions did not aim to transplant the practical proposals of Marx and Lenin, but only "to translate them into proper Chinese." The result should be a kind of education joined together with the people. Yet the life of border region people in the 1940s was dominated by war, economic difficulties, and revolution. Education remained largely divorced from those realities.

The main reason for the failing was the influence of the conventional system. It had an international background and was linked with the whole of human knowledge. Hence, "no matter how much it is criticized and attacked, to substitute another system for it is not something that can be done overnight." Yet its weaknesses for China lay in its very foreignness. It was the product of peacetime, city life, and a high stage of capitalist mechanized production. It was characterized in its European, American, and Japanese variants by a long period of study from first grade through college, with every grade rigidly demarcated and linked, dozens of compulsory subjects, and hundreds of technical courses. In Guomindang China, there had been a general copying of the "international" educational system and although many intellectuals had opinions against it all their efforts to reform the system had born little fruit. Meanwhile, the Communist-led border region had compounded the error by trying to develop that same conventional educational system.

The new slogans were "oppose the old-style uniformity" and "oppose regularity in education." At the secondary level, the earlier goal of transforming the border region's six middle schools into college-preparatory institutions was reversed. The recently standardized curriculum and enrollment procedures were revised to provide terminal education for students who could then fill the urgent personnel needs of the government, military, and production units in the region. The curriculum was redesigned with an eye to practical relevance given the war effort and economic needs. The nineteen courses that had formed the standardized curriculum were reduced to only eight. Flexibility was the hallmark of the new system.

The *minban* school, or school run by the people, was the answer to the problems of promoting universal mass education at the village level. The *minban* schools, financially supported and managed by the grass-roots localities themselves, were essentially an adaptation of the old privately run village school. The difference was that the village as a whole, rather than just an individual within it, had to assume responsibility for running the school. The full designation was actually *minban gongzhu*, or run by the people with public assistance. The latter meant higher-level government assistance with finance, the printing of educational materials, the introducing and training of teachers, as well as administrative and academic guidance. Otherwise, many of the rules and regulations were revised, such as the one that fixed the minimum number of students as a condition for keeping a school in operation. Under this new formula, most of the quantitative losses at the elementary level were regained. By the spring semester in 1945, the number of primary schools in Shaan-Gan-Ning had grown to 1,377 (of which more than 1,000 were the new *minban* variety), with a total enrollment of 34,000 students.[12]

The Yan'an experience is important to our story for several reasons. First, it provided a sort of controlled experiment that showed how instinctively committed Chinese educators were to the forms and structures of the established system. Given the opportunity, they immediately proceeded to replicate that same system regardless of its acknowledged defects and inappropriateness to the time and place.

Second, the Yan'an experience played an adaptive function between the past and future. This role was developed in the course of carrying out Mao's brief instruction for the party's rectification movement as a whole, namely, to "sinicize Marxism" or "translate it into proper Chinese." The then sympathetic observer, Michael Lindsay, wrote of the 1944 reforms: "[they] show Chinese Communist theory at its best, combining Marxist principles with strong common sense and concern for practical problems."[13] What he might have said more accurately was that while Marxist principles were being applied to the task of educational reform, at the same time the decades-old critique of China's modern educational system was being incorporated within the theory and practice of Chinese communism. This integration proved an important step in the growing status of the antiestablishment critique. Previously, it had always remained outside the system owing to lack of sufficient interest within. The critics never gained sufficient political protection, public financing, or direct support among educators as a whole. As a result, individual reform experiments rarely progressed beyond the pilot project stage. But with the 1944 Yan'an reforms, the antiestablishment critique acquired a much firmer foundation. For it had finally won backing within a new political establishment that was about to win national power.

The third point to highlight, however, is that the official recognition accorded the old critique in rural wartime Yan'an was by no means sufficient to establish its preeminence either within the CCP itself or the wider intellectual community responsible for running the educational system on a nationwide basis. The 1944

Yan'an reforms also did not progress very far. The civil war, loss of Yan'an in early 1947, and the simultaneous escalation of land reform throughout the Communist-led areas disrupted implementation of educational policy. But as soon as civilian life and social order began to resume in northern China in the late 1940s, the forces of regularization took up where they had left off in 1942. And it was that same conventional system that existed nationwide and had stood for thirty years impervious to the reformers' blandishments that the CCP inherited in 1949. Meanwhile, the contest between the pro-establishment and anti-establishment orientation has waxed and waned ever since.

The persistence might be owing to the Chinese penchant for creating new traditions and then trying to use them ever after as authoritative precedents. Or, more likely, the contest persists because the basic social and economic distinctions that gave birth to the controversy so long ago still exist. The main cleavages within Chinese society that have influenced educational development remain a combination of those that existed traditionally and others that developed during a century of "modernization." These are the distinctions between the educated and the unschooled, between mental and manual occupations, urban and rural life, and between people more receptive to foreign influence and people more inward-looking in experience and orientation. These distinctions were not grouped in mutually exclusive packages of illiterate, rural, and culture-bound laborers and literate, cosmopolitan, and urban intellectuals. But the patterns were consistent enough to create subcultures and self-perceptions within Chinese society that endure to this day. The bigger the city, the better the educational and job opportunities. The closer to the coast, the more likely to have "overseas Chinese" relations living in Hong Kong, Southeast Asia, or California, and therefore the more tolerant of foreign influence. Meanwhile, the inland rural areas still represent the obverse on all those counts. These were the distinctions that, on the one hand, provided the receptive host environment for imported Western learning, and, on the other, fueled the backlash against it.

Whatever the underlying causes, however, the regularization drive that followed Mao's last great effort between 1966 and 1976 to change China's entire educational system in conformity with the old reformers' goals has recreated, in turn, patterns and procedures in the post-Mao era that would have been entirely familiar to educators in Yan'an during the 1938–42 regularization drive. Seemingly independent of the economic consideration, conceptions as to what is necessary to promote quality education have endured unchanged. They include a preoccupation with fixed uniform standards, concentrating resources in a few elite schools regardless of the social implications, an unquestioning assumption that the children of the existing social elites constitute a "quality" resource that deserves to be educated accordingly, a consequent willingness to sacrifice quantity for quality even to the extent of closing down schools and sending children home, and related investment priorities that disporportionately emphasize tertiary and elite education at the expense of the lower mass levels.

Soviet Reinforcements:
Regularization and Cultural Revolution

Up to 1949, however, the contention had remained relatively benign. Its destructive potential was not fully tapped until it was integrated further into the class-based social revolution that began as soon as the CCP won power and culminated in Mao's 1966–76 Cultural Revolution. Unfortunately, the documents that might reveal more fully the nature of the CCP's debts to Stalin and the Soviet Union also remain shrouded in official secrecy. But Soviet influence now appears to have been used selectively by the Chinese over the years to reinforce both sides of their educational debate, and as the catalyst that ignited its destructive potential as well.

In the 1950s, that influence reinforced the "regularization" side of the debate with a vengeance. The best-known features of this development were the restructuring of Chinese higher education to conform in an almost carbon-copy fashion to the "Soviet model" and the concurrent thought-reform campaign among university personnel. But these two disruptive and unwelcome (for academics) features of the effort to "learn from the Soviet Union," overshadowed the rest of the package which found a ready host among Chinese educators. Centralization and uniformity—of standards, curricula, teaching plans, schedules, textbooks, and the teaching research group that ensured their uniform application—were all features of the Soviet-style system. But, in retrospect, and especially in light of the Yan'an documents with their demands for all the "necessary systems" needed to improve quality, many features of the Soviet import must have been well received, which helps explain why they are now so difficult to change. Indeed, we should probably question which of the Soviet "innovations" adopted in the 1950s were actually imports and which were Chinese designs proliferating in the newly compatible climate.[14]

The nationally unified college entrance examinations, introduced in the early 1950s, appear to be a case in point. They dovetailed nicely with the new Soviet-style manpower planning and state job-assignment system, also introduced at the time, to govern the size, majors, and destinies of the college student population. But the nationally unified examination system itself was never part of the Soviet repertoire. Instead, it bears great resemblance both in structure and function to the old imperial examination system.[15]

Nevertheless, the CCP found itself tied overall to an inappropriate model of economic and revolutionary development. Among other things, it required heavy industry that required in turn a well-trained scientific and technological elite. By contrast, the newly empowered CCP was still committed to its goal of revolutionizing Chinese society, a task that had scarcely begun. Meanwhile, the existing educated elite was not only bourgeois by reason of birth but, if the "one hundred flowers" episode was any indication, remained unreconstructed as well in the concerns and commitments that it was passing on to the younger generation.[16]

From 1958, therefore, class background was made an increasingly important criterion both for admission to college and for access to other life's benefits. Also that year, the Great Leap Forward included extensive educational reforms, initially introduced as a "cultural revolution." By unacknowledged coincidence, the reforms were almost identical in spirit, if not in intensity, to the "Khrushchev reforms" being introduced concurrently in the Soviet Union.[17] In China, there occurred a massive assault on the centralized, standardized Soviet-Chinese educational system. When the Great Leap Forward collapsed, of course, the forces of regularization inevitably reasserted themselves once more. But this time they did so in a deliberately disjointed fashion.

The opposition in 1958 had allegedly been "some bourgeois educators" and "some of our comrades" who agreed with them in proposing to restrict the extent and speed of educational development. They also advocated one type of school system only, that is, state run and funded with regular schools, teachers, and methods of instruction. These "erroneous suggestions" were opposed and Mao's strategy of "walking on two legs" adopted as the only means of popularizing education among the worker-peasant masses within a reasonable time, given the huge burden of state expenditure that would otherwise be necessary. Many different forms of schooling would be used to create this system of mass education: schools run by the state and by collectives, general education and vocational training, education for children and for adults, full-day schools, work-study schools, and spare-time schools. More specifically, the task of rapidly universalizing education for the masses and raising the technical level of industry and agriculture, was given to the "irregular" half-work, half-study and spare-time schools. This was because these schools could be run more or less on a self-supporting basis by collective units and local communities with a minimum of financial aid from the state. They also did not require a professional staff but could rely on "whoever could teach." It was conceded, however, even in 1958, that some of the already established regular schools should retain their status. They, too, were supposed to undertake curricular reform and introduce productive labor activities, but their duty was to maintain a more academic orientation and responsibility for raising quality.

Nevertheless, when the high tide of enthusiasm receded, the experiments to shorten the curriculum and increase productive activities in the full-day schools were curtailed. By the mid-1960s, Mao's "walking on two legs" slogan had been reinterpreted and formalized in Liu Shaoqi's "two tracks," or two kinds of education: vocational and half-work, half-study schooling for the masses, while the regular full-day system, and especially the model or key-point schools within it, stood restored and strengthened to provide college-preparatory education for the few. Indeed, the systematic development of the key-point stream dates from this period. At the same time, the entrance criteria for these elite schools (examination scores plus class background, politics, and personal connections, the relative emphasis of which varied from year to year) meant that their students were primarily the children of intellectuals and cadres or the existing educated and political elites.[18]

It was this two-track system, or rather the regular stream within it, that Mao's final 1966–76 Cultural Revolution assault was designed to break. Only this time, "cultural revolution" was redefined to mean not just radical educational reforms as in 1958, but a systematic confrontation with all the perceived enemies, both old and new, of the Chinese Communist revolution. The rationale was that the socialist transformation of the economy was not sufficient; the realm of the superstructure had to be revolutionized as well. To accomplish this aim, bourgeois ideas and the people who espoused them had to be changed. Otherwise, they might react in such a way as to threaten the continuing existence of the revolution itself.

As with the Soviet model of the 1950s and probably Khrushchev's educational reforms of 1958, however, it now appears that Mao was also indebted to the Soviet experience for this redefinition of cultural revolution. It was as if, looking back over the progress made in revolutionizing Chinese society to date, Mao decided that China had skipped a step in rushing immediately to impose the postrevolutionary "classless" Stalin model on a society as yet unreconstructed along revolutionary lines. It was as if Mao was looking back to a stage Stalin had created briefly in Russia as a prerequisite for the postrevolutionary order he would then create. Whether or not Mao actually knew about Stalin's 1928–31 cultural revolution is another secret of China's political history. But the similarities seem too great to be purely coincidental. Thus, either there is some such functional necessity built into Communist-led revolutions, or Mao knew about the earlier Soviet episode and used it as a precedent—translating it into "proper Chinese" to break the impasse he perceived developing within his own revolution forty years later. In any event, the aim in both instances was to reinforce the destruction of bourgeois economic power by attacking bourgeois influence in the political and cultural realms as well.[19]

One major difference apparently was that, unlike Stalin, Mao did not intend his Cultural Revolution to be only a brief interlude. Following the high tide of Red Guard attacks against the targets, the objective thereafter was to rebuild the superstructure with a new or at least chastened set of leaders who would institutionalize the Cultural Revolution's objectives on a more permanent basis. Stalin himself had ended his adventure in mass radicalism and class struggle, but did so without exonerating its chief political targets or discrediting the new proletarian intellectual beneficiaries who went on to become the pillars of his new postrevolutionary establishment. Mao, by contrast, tried to create a new revolutionary establishment and an educational system that would help to produce it among the successor generations to follow him. Translating this goal into Chinese practice, he simply reached back to update the Yan'an tradition and the old radical educational critique incorporated within it, added the class struggle component, and attempted to restructure the nation's entire educational system on that basis.[20]

To summarize, by the mid-1960s, Mao's aims for education were twofold, reflecting their dual origins. These latter were the radical critique of China's "new" Western-style educational system, and the class-based superstructural concerns of a newly victorious Communist-led revolution. Both traditions had their roots in the 1920s and both had developed and reinforced each other from one decade to the next until they merged finally in the 1966–76 Cultural Revolution. Certainly not everyone even within the ruling circles of the CCP stayed the whole course and remained committed to both goals during all that time. And despite its popularity, the radical critique of the educational system never succeeded in realizing lasting changes within it. The most concerted experiments along those lines, prior to 1966, had occurred briefly in Yan'an between 1944 and 1947 and again during the abortive 1958 Great Leap. Mao was also apparently fighting back from a minority position within the party when he launched his last attempt at superstructural renovation in 1966–76. But that attempt represented the commitment of the party he led to radical educational reform and cultural revolution. And both must be treated as integral parts of his legacy.

Along with the ideals from the old reformers' critique, however, the 1966–76 experience shared the same weaknesses that were responsible for the failure of all their experiments as well. In the pre-1949 era, the educational system as a whole had defied reform because the criticism conflicted with the interests and commitments of the academic professionals within it. Hence, individual reformers regularly moved outside the system to set up their various experiments. But there they fell victims to another danger, namely, lack of political protection and support.

The Communists initially seemed to represent a potential for success on this score since they both accepted the logic of the old reformers' arguments, and also understood the importance of political leadership. Yet, in the end, Mao's formula rendered antiestablishment educational reform as politically vulnerable as it had always been. If the leadership had remained united, a viable solution incorporating the old antiestablishment critique might have evolved. But the leadership polarized particularly after the Great Leap Forward and the issue of educational reform was one of many that divided it. Even then compromises might have been worked out. But once Mao decided he could only achieve his aims by escalating the conflict into open political warfare after 1966, policy differences, of necessity, hardened into two distinct lines. Indeed, that was his objective, namely, to articulate his line clearly in contrast to its opposite. By so doing, however, he both reified and defined the nature of his opposition. He thus ensured that his line would prevail only so long as he was able to retain power. When power was lost at his death in 1976, the enemies Mao had targeted included both the "capitalist roaders" within the party and the "bourgeois intellectuals" in academia. They united in repudiating both his line and those who had helped to implement it.

Two Lines Become One:
Restoration and Reform in the 1980s

Such is also the political context within which the significance of the post-Mao reform must be assessed, for they represent not only the alternative strategy of socialist development that the two-line struggle ultimately brought into being, but also an explicit political repudiation of the Cultural Revolution experiment. This in turn defined the new political parameters drawn around the post-Mao reforms, determining their choices and limiting their options. Hence everything criticized during that decade had to be exonerated, while whatever was promoted then had to be discredited and dismantled, including the goals for education. The entire Cultural Revolution episode was formally negated by the CCP in 1984, which meant that theoretically and politically there could be no compromises.[21] But by 1980, the two-line policy struggle had already ceased to exist. There was only one line, seriously disrupted during the 1966–76 "decade of disaster," but now restored to its rightful status. The process of restoring that line in every sector of Chinese life was designated as "reform," the people who promoted it were the "reformers," those who opposed them for whatever reason were re-christened "conservatives," and the Maoist or Cultural Revolution orientation formally ceased to exist.

The post-Mao educational reforms thus entailed the restoration of pre-Cultural Revolution policies, structures, names, and symbols—even on points where the educational value and social consequences had long been debatable. Among such latter points were, of course, those inherited from the pre-1949 critique related to foreign borrowing, urban-rural disparities, and elite-mass distinctions. Ironically, the logic of the political struggle removed them more effectively from the field of educational controversy than at any time since they were first raised more than half a century ago.

They were essentially banned not only from the realm of official policy but from public discourse as well. The "regular" educational system, recreated after 1976, would therefore have appeared curiously disembodied were it not for evidence that those issues had not disappeared but only retreated inward. Hence the attempt to negate such long-standing concerns raised questions from the start about the political wisdom and stability of the course adopted by post-Mao leaders. Had those concerns actually been eliminated or solved with the passage of time, they could have been safely consigned to the pages of history. Instead, it was only the public controversy over them that was more or less effectively suppressed, while the policies implemented in fact served to intensify related tensions at many points—tensions that were clearly apparent well before the events of May and June 1989.

The implications of the arrest of the Gang of Four were registered at once and professional educators knew what they had to do. They appeared to move almost instinctively in the fall of 1976, to begin purging the system of its "irregular" features. The first to go that autumn were manual labor and "open-door" education for university students. Rumors that the unified college entrance examinations would be restored the next year began circulating shortly thereafter. Changes in this sector did not need to await the Third Plenum of the Eleventh Central Committee in December 1978, which officially inaugurated Deng Xiaoping's reform administration. By that time, almost all the decisions necessary to recreate the regular educational system in its pre-1966 form had already been announced and implementation was well underway. By 1980–81, the formal educational system had been reconstituted in as close an approximation of that format as was possible, considering the changes in personnel and student bodies that had occurred during the 1966–76 decade. Also, by 1980–81, tensions were such that they could no longer be ignored or dismissed as interventions of recalcitrant Maoist troublemakers.

Without actually admitting that the faults perhaps lay within the newly restored system itself, education authorities began acknowledging the critical "opinions in society" it had aroused. This, in turn, resulted in a further stream of supplementary adjustments and reforms within reforms. These have clearly been designed to accommodate various "opinions" and "interests," while avoiding any direct mention of the mass-based, egalitarian, and work-oriented concerns that evidently continue to inspire them. In 1985, the Education Ministry was upgraded into the more powerful State Education Commission (SEDC) as a mark of official recognition that the wide-ranging problems apparent within the educational sector needed a stronger hand to resolve them. The debates and complications those problems provoked can be summarized as follows:

Elementary Schooling and the 1986 Compulsory Education Law

The weak link at the elementary level is the countryside. All Chinese governments since the 1920s have proclaimed their commitment to universal elementary education but it is only in the post-1949 era that this goal has been "basically" realized. The achievement is noteworthy because of China's large rural population for whom the circle of mass illiteracy and educational underdevelopment is typically difficult to break. Some countries, such as India and Pakistan, for example, adopt a laissez faire approach. Local elites look after their own as they always have, while for the rest the forces of economic development work to the advantage of some, and the majority of rural children continue to grow up illiterate like their parents before them. Since 1949, China has maintained a more interventionist approach working, in effect, with elaborations of the 1944 Yan'an formula. The essentials of that formula developed into an activist central government that kept up the pressure and became increasingly effective in enforcing its will via the collective structures at the grass-roots level. The central government set general policy, provided financial assistance in the form of regular budgetary allocations, fixed curricula or issued guidelines, and did the same for books and materials.

The all-important budgetary allocation came down the bureaucratic chain through the provinces and counties that apportioned funds for their commune elementary schools. Only city schools were fully state funded, however. The money was allocated in such a way that communes, or more specifically the production brigades within them, had to rely on their own resources to make up the difference between their small share of state funds and the total cost of maintaining their village elementary schools. The state money typically covered the construction costs of building the school, its relatively minuscule operating expenses, salaries for a few of the teachers and, by the mid-1970s, a small subsidy for the remainder of a school's teaching staff, most of whom were locally hired (called *minban* teachers for that reason). Other costs were met locally by a combination of collectively produced grain for the local teachers (who were paid in work points the same as the peasants, except for the small monthly state subsidy), collective labor power for maintenance and repairs, some student fees, and sometimes small-scale, school-run farms and enterprises.

This formula, according to official statistics, succeeded in bringing 85 percent of the relevant age group into elementary schools by 1965, and upwards of 95 percent a decade later (Table 1). However exaggerated the official figures might be, former rural school teachers and rural residents interviewed by myself and others in Hong Kong in the 1970s and early 1980s corroborated the high enrollment claims. These informants, despite their basically dissident orientation that had resulted in their common decision to leave China, nevertheless included the rural elementary school enrollment figures in their assessment of the Communist regime's achievements.[22]

For the ex-school teachers, it was their achievement as well since it had often been the teachers' responsibility to mobilize reluctant parents primarily through home visits and persuasive arguments. Interestingly, they all regarded "compulsory" (*qianpo*) education as an alien Western concept that would have aroused undue resentment. Reports of actual penalties for noncompliance were rare. But speaking primarily with reference to the 1970s, they recalled that such enforcement really was not necessary. Except for the few who had been teaching in national minority areas of Yunnan and Xinjiang, their mobilization efforts were directed mainly at bringing dropouts (more often girls than boys) back to the fold. Given the network of collective pressures and inducements that had grown up around them, rural people had by that time grasped the importance of learning to read and write and do simple calculations. A few of the teachers with longer memories could recall this as a mark of the difference between the 1970s and the 1950s, when mass mobilization efforts were just getting under way and the peasants still needed to be convinced. The circle had thus been broken. But the achievement was hard-won and based on a fragile balance. Regression was the price of failure to maintain the formula based on activism from the center, plus collectively supported enforcement, and local mobilization efforts.

The drag or pull exerted by the past was marked in turn by the dropout rates

Table 1

Elementary Schools and Enrollments

Year	Number of schools	Number of students in school (millions)
1949	346,800	24
1965	1,681,900	116
1966		103
1971		112
1972		125
1973		136
1974		145
1975		151
1976	1,044,300	150
1977		146
1978		146
1979	923,500	147
1980		146
1981	894,074	143
1982	880,516	140
1983	862,165	136
1984	853,740	136
1985	832,309	134
1986	820,846	132
1987	807,406	128
Six-year schools	458,671	75
Five-year schools	348,735	53
1988		125

Sources: (a) Official statistics issued in the 1980s for the Cultural Revolution decade are roughly similar to those given earlier in other sources. One source of confusion in the later official compilations is the failure to distinguish between the academic and calendar years. One major unexplained discrepancy appears in the figures for 1965. The World Bank figures (*China: Socialist Economic Development* 3:134) show 682,000 primary schools instead of 1,681,900 as shown above. The number of students in school is, however, the same in all sources that cite this figure.

(b) Number of schools from 1949 to 1979: *Zhongguo baike nianjian*, 1980 (China encyclopedic yearbook, 1980) (Beijing, 1980), P. 535.

(c) Number of students for 1949 and 1965: *Peking Review*, no. 5 (February 3, 1978), pp. 16–17.

(d) Number of students from 1966 to 1980: State Statistical Bureau, ed., *Zhongguo tongji nianjian, 1981* (China statistical yearbook, 1981) (Beijing: Zhongguo gongji chubanshe, 1988), pp. 873, 976.

(e) 1981 to 1987: State Statistical Bureau, ed., *Zhongguo tongji nianjian, 1988* (China statistical yearbook, 1988) (Beijing: Zhongguo tongji chubanshe, 1988), pp. 873, 876.

(f) 1987 breakdown between six-year and five-year schools: State Education Commission, Planning and Financial Affairs Bureau, ed., Zhongguo jiaoyu tongji nianjian, 1987 (China education statistical yearbook, 1987) (Beijing: Gongye daxue chubanshe, 1988), pp. 78–79.

(g) 1988: State Statistical Bureau, Communiqué for 1988, *Renmin ribao*, March 1, 1989.

and the 1982 census figures showing 235,820,000 (or 31.9 percent of the population) to be "illiterate or semiliterate" (that is, twelve years of age and over, knowing less than 1,500 characters).[23] Some questions might be raised as to why the illiterates and semiliterates were lumped together, and how the census-takers were able to ascertain that each person did or did not know 1,500 characters. Nevertheless, that number, used to define the category, is approximately what a person would retain from three or four years of elementary schooling, which is the sum total received by many village youth and thus the most basic qualification of the universal enrollments claim.

Beginning in 1978, the formula that had made all this possible began to unravel. The forces working against it came from two directions: (1) the regularization trend within the education sector itself, and (2) the decollectivization of agriculture. Deriving from the first, activist pressures from the center that had accelerated during the early 1970s eased almost immediately after 1976. Local governments and education authorities similarly ceased their active promotion of rural schooling, as all attention focused on rebuilding the regular urban-based, quality-oriented system. An officially inspired idea also began circulating that all rural schools would be regularized. This would have entailed the state assuming full responsibility for the cost of running the schools and transferring all *minban* teachers onto the state pay scale. Also, in deference to quality and the sudden disfavor into which labor and practical learning fell, many schools stopped running the various farms, workshops, and projects that had contributed to school budgets. Further, in the interests of quality, local teachers began to be tested. Some areas required refresher courses for those who failed; others simply sent them back to the front line of production. Millions of "sent-down" city youth also returned to their urban homes in 1978–79. Many of these had served as village school teachers and had left without knowing who their replacements might be.

The first steps toward agricultural decollectivization also began in 1978, with the campaign to "reduce the peasants' collective burdens." This meant, among other things, that peasants had to be remunerated for any labor they performed for the collective. The costs of rural schooling began to climb. The advantages of nonattendance also rose with the new household responsibility system. On the one hand, families were given more incentives and more opportunities to make money, while, on the other, their economic well-being suddenly depended solely on their own resources.

The result of these combined pressures were registered quickly in terms of closing or "merging" schools, declining enrollments, rising dropout rates, and the unmet payrolls of locally hired teachers. The number of students enrolled in elementary schools declined from a high of 150 million in 1975–76 to 139.7 million in 1982, and on down to 131.8 million in mid-1987. The number of elementary schools declined from just over 1 million in 1976, to 894,000 in 1981 (Table 1). Between 1979 and 1981, the number of students enrolled in the first grade declined from 37.79 million to 27.49 million.[24]

After the single-child family campaign was launched, the shrinking size of the age group became the standard defense. Thus, in early 1984, an authoritative presentation of educational statistics acknowledged that the number of elementary schools in 1983 was eighteen thousand fewer than the year before, and the number of students in school had fallen by 3.9 million during the same year. But the decline was dismissed as being due "mainly to the falling birth rate in recent years."[25] Earlier accounts, however, blamed the new educational and agricultural policies directly.

A report from Hebei Province complained that the number of primary and secondary school students in the province had declined by 700,000 during 1982. "We should seriously investigate this question and take steps," noted the report. "We cannot eliminate illiteracy, on the one hand, and produce new illiterates, on the other."[26] A complaint from Yunnan asserted that the rate of attendance at the elementary school level dropped for three consecutive years between 1979 and 1981.[27] Yunnan blamed the household responsibility system in the countryside. As a result, teachers were leaving their jobs, students were dropping out, attendance rates had declined, and some rural schools had been closed.[28] Out in Qinghai Province, where school attendance rates were among the lowest in the country anyway, more than a thousand rural schools closed down in 1980. Also, because of the new agricultural policies, locally hired teachers were not being issued their grain ration and work points (collective payment under the old system).[29] In Ningxia, the number of children enrolled in elementary school also dropped from 628,867 in 1977 to 553,900 in 1982, and there were "many more new illiterates."[30]

A survey of seven thousand production brigades conducted a few years earlier in Anhui Province suggested why the communes and brigades were finding it difficult to pay their teachers. Essentially, they lacked the means to do so. The problem was to find a reliable source of school funding when the local collective unit was losing control over local income. About a third of the brigades still retained some collective control with an assessment for brigade expenses, including the *minban* teachers' salaries, levied against every household contract. The amount was then withheld when the crops were sold to the state. This was the preferred method at the time, but it could only be used where local farm incomes were derived from growing government contract crops. Some 20 percent of the brigades were supporting their schools mainly by levying a tax on brigade-run enterprises but not all were well run, which apparently inhibited the widespread use of this method. Nevertheless, these were the two most reliable sources of funding. The other 50 percent of the brigades surveyed were using one of the two other unsatisfactory methods. One was to divide educational costs among all households in the brigade whether they had children or not, and send the teachers out door-to-door to collect, which the teachers did not like. The other way was to divide up costs only among those households with school-age children, which increased the dropout rates because many families could not afford the higher fees.[31]

The same decentralization/decollectivization process that precipitated these trends have also inhibited the search for alternatives. Toward that end, the central government has issued a steady stream of directives reiterating its commitment to universal elementary schooling and, given its other goals, has probably done as much as it can to promote solutions. Their systematic enforcement remains dependent on the institutionalization of a viable system of local township government and especially township financial administration to replace the now defunct collective. Official recognition and responses to the dilemma began in 1979 and culminated in the 1986 compulsory (*yiwu*) educational law.

First, in response to the anticipation of more state funds, an official clarification was issued in 1979. The state would not be able to take over responsibility for all rural schools immediately. The localities should therefore continue to run them in the interim.[32] In 1980, the CCP Central Committee and the State Council issued a "Resolution Regarding Certain Questions in Popularizing Elementary Education," which called for its realization by the end of the decade, *albeit* without specifying how the growing obstacles were to be overcome. Local officials responsible for implementation were caught in the middle. They were supposed to continue to keep their schools open. But they had also been ordered not to mobilize peasants for unremunerated labor or otherwise increase their burdens for collective undertakings. No one seemed to know who should be responsible or where to start. Official support was reiterated for school-run workshops and farms, primarily for income earning purposes rather than for labor education and practice as before. Newly rich peasants and others were encouraged to make voluntary private contributions. Soliciting contributions from overseas Chinese compatriots resumed, also with official blessing. This custom has sustained many rural schools in Fujian and Guangdong prior to 1966. But these were all *ad hoc* expedients, incapable of maintaining universal elementary education on a nationwide basis.

A 1982 article in *People's Education*, published by the Ministry of Education, pleaded for a solution to the dilemma: "Of course, in solving these problems we cannot rely completely on the state. So long as we are reasonable, the peasants will be happy to take on the burden. Moreover, for many years they have already been bearing the expenses of making needed repairs and maintaining the desks and chairs. In this matter it would be best to have some stipulated guiding principles, the better to be followed uniformly in the various areas."[33] Provincial leaders in Henan reached the same conclusion at a 1983 education work conference. The sense of the meeting was that "we cannot regard taking money from the peasants to run education as an increase of the burden on them."[34] In Hunan, local leaders simply broke the new rules. Commune and brigade cadres "launched the masses to contribute labor and material to repair the buildings and make some teaching equipment."[35]

In Sichuan, by contrast, local leaders blamed those at the provincial level: "Educational reform in our province started late and failed to make good progress. . . . Up to now, the provincial department of education has not yet been able to put forward any concrete reform plan and there has been no experience of experimentation gained at any selected point from which we can learn. Even if the lower levels want to carry out reform, they do not know how to start it."[36]

Yet in Shaanxi, the head of the provincial education bureau seemed totally at a loss. "In many localities," he wrote, "the desolate situation exists where they rely on a small number of people in the educational departments to run the schools. General education is an enterprise for local management, for our schools are found in nearly every inhabited locale. . . . How to arouse the enthusiasm toward running schools on the county and township level, particularly under the conditions of the current transformation of the rural economic structure, and how to reform the management system of rural education are the new problems facing education departments on every level, who should issue many articles on reform."[37]

The cause of the bureau chief's consternation was undoubtedly the increasing pressure on the localities to bear even more responsibility for funding rural schools. The pressure from the center increased during 1984, with the national publicity given to the Hebei experiment. By April, fifty-one counties in the province had reportedly converted to the new system with good results. It entailed the withdrawal of all state funds from all rural schools, including both elementary and junior secondary schools and the state subsidy for the *minban* teachers. The state money thus saved within any given country was to be concentrated in its "elite" state supported sector, that is, in its key-point schools, senior secondary and technical education, and to increase the salaries of the teachers therein. Limited and temporary state subsidies were promised to help out very poor districts. The official rationale was that state appropriations were scarcely adequate to maintain existing levels of education. Meanwhile, the peasants were growing wealthy because of the new agricultural policies. Hence they should be able to fund all their own schools locally from their own resources.[38]

It is impossible to ascertain, from a distance, whether the Hebei experiment actually meant to withdraw all state funds from all rural schools as published descriptions indicated; or whether the experiment was more in the nature of a publicity effort aimed at reviving local efforts in this regard, by giving the local authorities the guiding examples they were demanding. Or perhaps it really was an experiment, in which case the results should have been anticipated, namely, that such a measure, if actually implemented nationwide, would have dealt a major blow to rural education. In any event, the State Council issued a clarification in late 1984. It promised that "educational operating expenses allocated by the state will continue to be issued on the original basis, and be sent down from the country to the township; they cannot be reduced or held back." But, "henceforth any increase in educational appropriation issued by the state and local governments will be used primarily to develop teacher training education and subsidize poor districts. Rich districts must rely on themselves for any increase in township educational operating expenses." To facilitate the latter endeavor, the same circular also, finally, authorized the township governments to collect an educational surtax to be levied against agricultural and township enterprises. The circular did not suggest alternatives for localities without profit-making enterprises but the unpopular head tax and land tax methods were forbidden.[39]

Given such unsteady foundations, the plans for a compulsory educational law announced in mid-1985 appeared somewhat premature. The law itself was promulgated a year later and now stands at least as an official declaration of intent. As such it also plays an important political role in countering the charge that the new policies are one-sided in their pursuit of quality to the detriment of mass education. Publicity surrounding the law claimed it placed China among the many advanced nations that have ten to twelve years of compulsory education. The law formally institutes a nine-year compulsory educational system, that is, including both elementary and junior secondary schooling. According to the law, compulsory education is to be tuition free. Organizations and individuals are forbidden to employ school-age children. Local governments are authorized to take action against parents who do not send their children to school and employers who might hire them.[40]

Official explanations of the new law, however, place it more clearly within the context of Chinese realities. Commenting on the various provisions, He Dongchang (formerly Minister of Education, now a Vice Minister of the Education Commission) acknowledged that "in many rural areas elementary education is still not universal and new generations of illiterates continue to emerge." He also acknowledged further that unlike the cities, most rural elementary schools had not reverted to the (pre-Cultural Revolution) six-year format. Hence, combined elementary and junior middle school was only eight years at most in the countryside and should remain so for the time being. Indeed, the overall timetable for implementing the law remained very open-minded. Cities and certain developed areas of the hinterland were supposed to fulfill its provisions by 1990; less developed cities, towns, and rural areas by 1995; and "areas with poor economic and cultural background" as conditions permit. A similarly flexible interpretation was authorized for the "tuition free" regulation as well. Given the financial difficulties, schools can (and do) continue to collect "miscellaneous fees."[41]

Clearly, the central authorities have taken the initiative in trying to counteract the initial damaging effects of their reform policies on rural education. But for the time being, the current claim that primary school enrollments have now climbed to 97 percent of the age group remains to be substantiated. Vice Minister of the State Education Commission He Dongchang made this claim at a press conference in March 1989. He said that during the previous year, 97 percent of all school-age children were attending elementary schools and 97 percent of all such students completed their education. He did not clarify whether they completed five or six years of schooling. Nor did he explain how this figure could have been achieved given his subsequent admission that only 1,326 of China's

2,017 county-level administrative division have achieved universal elementary education.[42]

In fact, such clarifications must more realistically await further progress in the collection and use of the educational surtax as well as the developing township financial structure. These will have to guarantee stable funding in good years and bad, even when local enterprises are in a state of decline, and not just in the rich coastal provinces. These are the new prerequisites for popularizing rural education and overcoming the recent losses. In particular, it must be shown that the new township and village authorities, which replace local collective leadership at the commune and production brigade levels, have the will and the wherewithal to make up the difference between the small share of the state education budget that reaches a village school and the sum total of its expenses.

Education officials remained understandably vague on these points because the basic problems were rooted in the Deng Xiaoping administration's policy of agricultural de-collectivization which could not be directly challenged. Hence, solutions are dependent not just on the state education bureaucracy but on a rural political economy not yet sufficiently reconstructed to define, much less enforce, the new more limited scope of its public authority.

Minister of the State Education Commission Li Tieying could therefore say only that current thinking is still focused on the education surtax when reporters asked about current plans for solving rural educational problems at the March 1989 press conference. The aim, he said, is to "gradually set up a mechanism through which we have state appropriations and education tax in the main to be aided by the funds raised through various channels." On the contradiction between the provisions of the existing compulsory education law and the universally acknowledged realities of rising dropout rates, child labor, poor facilities, arbitrary school fees, and underpaid teachers, he replied similarly that "we should gradually introduce a legal regime so that laws can be used for developing education." Added He Dongchang, "The law governing compulsory education in China still has to be supported by other relevant laws, and our work in this regard is quite inadequate."

Secondary Education

Even an unqualified success in solving the rural elementary school problem would, however, only go part way toward defusing the charge that the new educational policies have been one-sided and elitist to the detriment of mass education. This is because the biggest case to answer on that score concerns their impact at the secondary level. It is at this level that the regularization patterns inherited from the past have been most faithfully reproduced, and also at this level that those patterns have provoked the most negative "opinions in society."

The patterns from the past concern the attempt to reimpose quality and order on the Cultural Revolution system, which contradicted the assumptions of professional educators about how schools should be run. In Yan'an, the newly arrived intellectuals sought to impose order on the region's nascent educational system; hence the impact was greatest at the elementary level. By 1976, the commitment to mass education at the elementary level was strong enough to withstand the anti-Cultural Revolution backlash, *albeit* with shaky foundations as we have seen. The secondary level has, by contrast, taken the full force of the regularization drive, complete with explicit directives to close schools, reduce enrollments, concentrate resources, and all the rest.

The basic tasks that should be performed at the secondary level are to provide education that will be terminal for most and college preparatory for some, in ways the economy can afford and society can accept as fair. An added challenge is to provide kinds of education that will realistically prepare young people for the lives they must lead after leaving school. During the early 1960s, as noted, the formula for fulfilling these tasks that emerged in the wake of the Great Leap Forward experiments was an increasingly stratified one with the urban-based, quality-oriented key schools emerging as the college preparatory stream. Other kinds of less regular work-study and vocational options were used to meet the inevitable demands for some kind of mass secondary schooling that grew on the base of the rapidly developing elementary school system. Liu Shaoqi is now credited with articulating this formula (as he was blamed for it during the Cultural Revolution) of "two kinds of education," which gave a different meaning to Mao's "walking on two legs" slogan.[43]

The "Maoist" solution, as it finally crystallized during the 1966–76 decade, was to break up the whole bifurcated system. Despite all the rhetoric, the net effect was not just to politicize education but also to popularize and vocationalize it—in the same way that the 1944 Yan'an reforms broke up the 1938–42 regularization trend. The aim was to popularize secondary schooling as quickly as possible, based on the shortened ten-year system (five years each of primary and secondary schooling, down from six years at each level). For the countryside, the immediate goal, which interviewees indicate was widely achieved, was to attach junior middle classes to production brigade elementary schools and establish one complete junior/senior middle school in every commune. By the end of the Cultural Revolution decade, the goal was to achieve universal senior secondary schooling in all cities and universal junior secondary education in the countryside by 1985.[44] Entrance examinations were abolished and instead of concentrating the best students, the key-point schools became ordinary schools attended by those who lived nearby. Everybody's physics, chemistry, and biology courses were revised to become classes in either industrial or agricultural technology. Two years of work experience after middle school became the new prerequisite for admission to college, along with the political/class background criteria.

This new system naturally appalled professional educators and worked against the interests of all those in the key-point stream whose route to college was thus disrupted. Having spent two years in the countryside or in a factory, one could then be recategorized as a peasant or worker for college admission purposes, so that of those who began making their way back to college in the early 1970s, many (although not all) were young people who would have been there anyway. Some interviewees recounted proudly how their communes were able to send local youth to college for the first time ever from their new middle schools. In at least two cases, youth from those schools even passed the national college entrance examinations when they were restored in 1977. But, by and large, the quality stream was destroyed; the lives of everyone within it disrupted; and conventional views about education turned upside down.

Interestingly, the new political and old intellectual interests that united in coalition to overthrow the Maoist legacy are the very same beneficiaries of the educational system they also immediately restored. The problem concerns the many millions excluded from it. The official argument is that the Cultural Revolution policies not only tried to universalize (*puji*) secondary schooling prematurely, but also sought to unify (*danyihua*) education in a manner inappropriate to China's level of economic development. The new post-Mao policies have therefore set about reversing the consequent equalization of quantity and quality that took place between 1966–76. As a result, the education system at the secondary level has been drastically reduced in size. It has also been retracked and streamed in a manner deliberately designed to exploit and reinforce the existing social divisions of labor.

Quantitative Declines

The reduced enrollments were enforced uniformly in city and countryside between 1978 and 1983. No direct or immediate effort was made to coordinate the declines either with demographic trends or with the expansion of vocational education (as shown in Tables 2, page 250, and 3, page 252). The quotas were never made public but they were imposed even on the largest cities that had achieved universal or near-universal ten-year schooling. These included Beijing, Shanghai, Hangzhou, and Guangzhou. In the countryside, the plan announced in the late 1970s was to close down the senior sections of the commune middle schools, leaving only one or a few complete secondary schools in each county. Also to be abolished were the junior middle classes attached to production brigade primary schools. At most, only one junior middle school was to be retained in each commune.

The secondary school system had grown overall from 14 million students enrolled in 1965 to about 68 million during the 1977–78 academic year, when the new line began to be implemented. When the decline finally stopped in 1983, enrollments stood at 43.9 million. During 1980 alone, more than 20,000 secondary schools were closed. The cutbacks were most drastic at the senior secondary level where, according to one claim, enrollments for 1981–82 fell by approximately two-thirds as compared to 1978.[45] The argument used to justify the

Table 2

Secondary Schools and Students:
General Secondary (Including Key-points)*

Year	Schools	Students (millions)
1949	4,045	1.04
1965	18,102	9.34
1966		12.50
1968		13.92
1970		26.42
1972		35.82
1974		36.50
1975		44.66
1976	192,152	58.36
		Jr.: 43.53
		Sr.: 14.84
1977		67.80
1978		65.48
1979	144,233	59.05
		Jr.: 46.13
		Sr.: 12.92
	(5,200)	(5.20)
1980		55.08
1981	106,718	48.60
		Jr.: 41.45
		Sr.: 7.15
1982	101,649	45.28
		Jr.: 38.88
		Sr.: 6.40
1983	96,474	43.98
1984	93,714	45.54
1985	93,221	47.06
1986	92,967	48.90
1987	92,857	49.48
		Jr.: 41.74
		Sr.: 7.74
	(2,243)	(3.08)

*Key-point schools are included in the category of general or ordinary (*putong*) schools. All in this category, whether keypoint or non-keypoint, are distinguished by being academic rather than technical or vocational in orientation. Separate figures for key-point schools are shown here in parentheses for the years 1979 and 1987 only.

Sources:(General Secondary) Schools: *Zhongguo baike nianjian*, 1980, p. 535; *Zhongguo baike nianjian, 1981*, pp. iv, 205–6; and *China: Socialist Economic Development, 3:134*.
Students: *Zhongguo baike nianjian, 1980*, p. 536; *Zhongguo baike nianjian, 1988*, p. 876.
Key-point schools and students: Figures in parentheses, for 1979 and 1987 only, from *Zhongguo baike nianjian, 1980*, p. 541, and *Zhongguo jiaoyu tongji nianjian, 1987*, pp. 58–59, 65, respectively.

reductions at this level specifically was that since such a small proportion of students were able to enter college, large senior secondary enrollments were unnecessary. Following this logic, ratios were "appropriately" adjusted. The number of senior middle school graduates declined from an all-time high of 7.2 million in 1979 to 1.96 million in 1985.[46]

The press, both national and provincial, was extremely cautious in publicizing the cutbacks and especially any public response to them. Probably the most forthright published criticism was that from the *Journal of the Dialectics of Nature* which argued that quality and quantity were two sides of the same question. The author calculated that out of the sum total of 322 million young people aged six to eighteen, given the existing level of education in 1980, 20 million would grow up illiterate, at least 133 million would have no more than a primary school education, and only 10 million would receive any kind of professional or tertiary schooling. "It is unthinkable," admonished the writer, "to rely on such a composition of the population to build a modern nation."[47]

The authorities have yet to implement an effective response to this challenge. Nevertheless, the slight increase in general secondary school enrollments since 1984 seems to reflect a recognition that the deflation should be halted. That year, localities were instructed not to continue reducing secondary enrollments. In some places where reduction had "gone too far," increases could be permitted, "in order to fulfill the demand of the broad masses of youth to continue their studies." In 1983, nationwide, 67.3 percent of the primary school graduates continued on to junior middle school, and only 35.5 percent of the graduates at that level were able to continue on to the next.[48] Pressures must have been intense in those "some places" if Beijing's experience is any indication. Three years later, in 1987, when the class that entered secondary school in 1984 was about to graduate, authorities in the capital had to cope with a junior middle graduating class of 150,000—up from only 80,000 the year before.[49]

Perhaps it was just coincidental that in 1987, as "conservative" political winds were rising in Beijing, publicity was directed more realistically at the basic cause of the problem, that is, the mass pressures from below for more schooling, in conflict with the curtailed opportunities at the senior middle school level. In 1986, the junior middle school graduating class in Beijing was 80,000 in Beijing, and 60,000 went on to the senior level. In 1987, room at the senior level was made for an expanded enrollment of 90,000. But with 150,000 junior middle graduates, reflecting the expanded enrollments permitted in 1984, four out of ten would be unable to continue their studies. About 40 percent of the graduating class was under the age of sixteen. When these figures were publicized as examination time approached, to prepare everyone for the ordeal ahead, many worried parents wrote letters of complaint challenging the city authorities to find ways of keeping their children off the streets.[50]

Similarly, the cities of Fuzhou and Guangzhou also acknowledged the mass pressures for more schooling in 1987. Fuzhou announced that it was shifting

Table 3

Secondary Schools and Students: Specialized and Vocational

Year	Professional (*Zhuanye*): technical and teacher training (*zhiye*) (*nongye*)		Vocational/Agricultural (*jishu*)(*shifan*)	
	Schools	Students	Schools	Students
1949	1,171	229,000		
1957	1,320	778,000		
1965	1,265	547,000	61,626	4,433,000
1976	2,443	690,000		
1979	3,033	1,199,000		
1980	3,069	1,243,000	3,314	453,600
			(390	133,600) vocational
			(2,924	320,000) agricultural
1981	3,132	1,069,000	2,655	480,900
			(561	213,100) vocational
			(2,094	267,800) agricultural
1982	3,076	1,039,000	3,104	704,000
1983	3,090	1,143,000	5,481	
1984	3,301	322,000	7,002	
1985	3,557	1,571,000	8,070	2,295,000
1986	3,782	1,757,000	8,187	
1987	3,913	1,874,000	8,381	2,676,000

Sources: 1949–1979: *Zhongguo baike nianjian, 1980*, pp. 535–36.
1980: *Zhongguo jingji nianjian, 1981*, pp. iv, 205–6.
1981: *Zhongguo baike nianjian, 1982*, p. 568.
1982–87: *Zhongguo tongji nianjian, 1988*, pp. 873, 876.

emphasis from concentrating on the college preparatory stream to "energetically raising the quality of the laboring people." The pass rate from elementary school on to the junior secondary level had been maintained "for a long time" at under 60 percent in the greater Fuzhou area. This meant that some 30,000 elementary school graduates each year were unable to continue on to middle schools in Fuzhou's eight suburban counties. In 1987, however, the city increased educational expenditure and expanded enrollments so that 16,180 of the 17,040 primary school graduates in the city proper were able to continue on to middle schools along with 76.7 percent of their counterparts in the surrounding counties. This proportion was up by 35 percent over the preceding year. Youngsters who failed to pass were allowed to repeat the final year of the primary school if they were under fourteen years of age. Those over that age could be channeled into vocational training classes.[51]

Vocational Education

A second major plank in the reform platform at this level is to create separate academic and vocational streams, claiming authority from Liu Shaoqi's "two kinds of education and labor systems" formulation. The intention was never to replace all of the closing general middle schools with vocational equivalents, although public announcements were often deliberately phrased so as to give that impression. Rather the announced objective was to build on and restructure the reduced base so that by 1990 there would be, at the senior secondary level, one student receiving some kind of technical or vocational education for everyone in the general academic stream.

In 1978–79, it was claimed that Cultural Revolution policies had deliberately destroyed technical and vocational education. Statistics published later (see Tables 2 and 3) indicate that such education was never very extensive. What the Cultural Revolution policies had opposed was the "two kinds of education" formula, which was criticized as a device for perpetuating existing social inequalities. Hence, the Cultural Revolution solution of a uniform kind of schooling that offered some kind of practical work-study combination for everyone, *albeit* within the structure of the existing general middle school.

In fact, the main problems with the two-track approach are lack of popularity and cost. People generally, both in town and countryside (and not just the professional educators among them), entertain the same assumption on this point. Everyone feels that a general academic education is more valuable than any other. This long-standing assumption has been reinforced since 1978, because academic secondary schooling once again leads directly to the tertiary level, and the relative benefits of a college education are greater in the post-Mao era than at any time since 1949. The current official argument, however, is that since most youths cannot aspire to enter that realm, they should be satisfied with practical and relevant alternatives. The logic of the argument cannot be faulted. School and job placement systems based on it would undoubtedly be the most efficient of all possible alternatives. It is nevertheless perceived by many as unfair and by many others as a waste of time. So much so that dropping out (especially if gainful work is available) is often elected as a more useful personal strategy than vocational training.

The full implications of the plan to resegregate academic and vocational training were not immediately apparent in 1978–79, perhaps because no one took it very seriously. Interviewees both in Hong Kong and China were amused by the idea and assumed it would be modified to accommodate realities once the early post-Mao rhetoric had eased. One typical report since 1980, noting that it had already taken three meetings of the entire leadership of Dehua County (Fujian) to reach agreement on collapsing the county's eleven middle schools into only five, continued, "If so much difficulty is encountered in modifying middle schools, even greater difficulty will be encountered in developing vocational and technical education."[52]

Nevertheless, the initial unenthusiastic response was countered by ever more determined directives from the center. The expense of converting ordinary schools was recognized at once as prohibitive by everyone. The only alternative solution was to introduce vocational subjects and "labor education" into the curriculum of the ordinary non-key schools at the senior secondary level. This practice was approved by the State Council in 1980 and remains the official solution.[53] To the extent that a general secondary school takes this assignment seriously, its students will not be able to compete successfully for admission to college—which is of course the official intention. It is also probably the main reason why general middle schools were so slow in setting up such courses, and why they keep the vocational students separate from the academic stream within the school. Even though non-key schools know their students cannot really compete with those in the key schools, everyone still wants to try.

Besides contradicting the carefully preserved legal fiction that every qualified person has the right to compete on the open and free college entrance examinations, and besides the added costs, a third major problem with vocational education is that it does not necessarily provide training that is vocationally relevant. The Chinese immediately encountered the same problem experienced by others who have tried to introduce vocational training at this level. The difficulty is to match teachers and specific training programs with the jobs available to the students on graduation. The first graduates of Hangzhou's vocational courses had trouble finding employment because the specialties they had studied were not those needed that year by work units with job openings.[54] Local education departments were advised to learn not only which subjects were needed but also which kinds of jobs were likely to become available, and synchronize this information with their course offerings. "The labor force that may be scarce today in a given occupational category may tomorrow be in large supply. Without a basic estimate and forecast of the need for a given labor force, vocational education will develop blindly and create passivity."[55] Essentially, this long-recognized problem concerns the extent to which schools can and should be expected to provide what is essentially job-specific apprenticeship training.[56]

For rural schools, the problem is further compounded by changes that are occurring owing to the agricultural reforms. Thus the challenge for urban education officials is to "correctly predict the kind of talent needed in various sectors with the same foresight that formed the open-door policy and made the economy more responsible." In the countryside, the difficulties entail predicting job opportunities and providing relevant courses for young people likely to "drift out of agriculture but not from the rural areas."[57]

In the countryside, moreover, the vocational school becomes the current equivalent of the old agricultural middle school, especially since the work-study idea has been promoted along with it to help finance costs. But agricultural middle schools have already failed on at least two pre-1966 attempts. Interviewees explained that rural people generally did not like to send their children to such schools for the same reasons that obtained in the early 1960s. If a child could not attend a regular school in the county town, then a similar school in the commune seat was acceptable. But to attend school to learn about agriculture, on a work-study basis, was regarded as a waste of time. Students could learn much the same from their elders, and begin contributing to the family income at the same time. The few such schools initially set up in the late 1970s were already declining in number by 1981 (Table 3).

Yet directives continued to reaffirm the central authorities' determination to establish agricultural middle schools. Primary schools were to begin the process of vocationalization, orienting their curriculum to agricultural production and rural life. Junior middle schools were directed to revise their curricula so that 30 percent of their courses were vocational. At the senior secondary level, the goal was to enroll at least as many students in agricultural vocational schools as in general schools by 1990 and vocational courses were not to be less than 30 percent of the total taught in the former. The directives also suggested that students graduating from rural secondary schools should be given preference in admission to agricultural colleges.[58]

Noting that "we have stressed the importance of vocational and technical education for years, but no significant progress has been made," the 1985 Central Committee decision on education reaffirmed the commitment to a bifurcated academic/vocational system. To counteract the "contempt" in which the latter continued to be held, the decision advocated the practice of requiring employers to give first preference in hiring to technical and vocational graduates.[59] The decision also held out the promise of continuing opportunities at the tertiary level for such graduates, to make the option appear fairer and more attractive. If actually implemented, of course, this practice would defeat the whole purpose of the vocational plan, which is to prepare the majority of students not for college but for work.

The promotion of vocational/technical secondary schooling nevertheless intensified in the late 1980s when yet another new plan was announced toward that end. Currently in the experimental stage, it entails further restructuring the regular system, with the elementary level again being reduced to five years in length and the junior secondary increased to four years. The fourth year is to be used for vocational training.[60]

The Key-Point College Preparatory Stream

The key-point stream now offers prospects so greatly enhanced by comparison with the alternatives that it once again dominates the entire school system as in the early 1960s. The key-point (*zhongdian*) schools thus stand at the apex of the secondary school hierarchy where they provide virtually the only route into a regular college program. Throughout the 1980s, a degree from such a program was, in turn, one of the few means of securing "iron rice bowl" state employment, or the new high paying joint-venture jobs, as well as the new prerequisite for leading cadre positions in the state bureaucracy, both civilian and military, and for study abroad. Next in popularity after the key-point stream are ordinary (*putong*) schools, to the extent that they have not vocationalized themselves. Specialized technical secondary schools (*zhongdeng zhuanye xuexiao*) rank third; their students graduate into lower ranking jobs on the state salaried cadre pay scale. Vocational schools are in last place; their students become skilled workers at best. Despite much controversy, this popular rank order stood virtually unchallenged for a full decade. The impact of the multiple economic and political crises during 1988–89 is noted in the following section on the tertiary level.

The key-point schools, which bore the brunt of the Cultural Revolution's anti-elitist wrath, were restored throughout the country at all levels from kindergarten through the university level in the late 1970s. Their specific task was to concentrate the best teachers, administrators, students, facilities, and learning conditions in a manner that would "guarantee quality." At the secondary level, there were usually one or two such key-point schools per county and one or two in each city district, plus a few additional super key points enrolling the very best students from a wider or all-city catchment area.[61]

Official concern with the social consequences of enrollment policies or the kind of education offered to different kinds of students was dropped. Both the earlier 1950s practice of giving preference to qualified working class youth, and the later Cultural Revolution bias in favor of candidates of "good" class background were accordingly dropped. Unified entrance examinations were restored in the late 1970s at the junior and senior secondary levels, and students were channeled into the hierarchy of schools on the basis of those examinations. Statistics on family background are not available, since this remains a sensitive point. But conventional wisdom among teachers and school administrators is that the children of cadres and intellectuals are most able to benefit from this system, and their competition for scarce college seats now proceeds unobstructed. A majority of students entering key-point middle schools originate in key-point primary schools, or the key-point classes of ordinary primaries. At the elementary level, teachers indicated that the parents' background is considered since it is a common-place that children of educated and economically secure parents perform better in school. Indeed, key schools are often located in the "better" neighborhoods with large concentrations of cadres and intellectuals.

Everyone also acknowledges the general criticism of the revived key-point school system that exists "in society." This led to an outburst against them aired briefly in the press in late 1981. The commentary echoed the Cultural Revolution critique of these schools and it was the first time that any such statements concerning them had appeared in the press since 1976. The thrust of the commentary was that the schools should be abolished because of the unfair advantages they gave to a small privileged minority and because of the damage they were doing to the "enthusiasm for learning" among the majority. The best "backbone" teachers and students were just then being transferred from ordinary schools into the re-created key-points. The reduction of secondary enrollments also peaked at this time. Tensions were such that at a National People's Congress (NPC) meeting in December, several delegates called for the abolition of the key-point schools at the elementary and junior middle levels.[62] The debate was then terminated abruptly at the end of the month with the announcement that, whatever their defects, key-point schools would be retained.[63]

The outburst against key-point schools in 1981 was actually part of a developing controversy then underway over many commonly acknowledged educational drawbacks of the newly rebuilt system. Probably given impetus by the cutbacks at the secondary level, the controversy nevertheless only skirted that issue concentrating instead on a number of specific pedagogical concerns. Besides the key-point stream itself, these were the related practice of streaming or segregating students within schools and teaching them separately according to ability, the inflexible rigors reimposed on the system by the need to pass entrance examinations at each level, and the ensuing competitive drive to achieve high pass rates. All sources agreed that the cramming and competition were, if anything, more intense in the late 1970s than ever before.

Teachers almost uniformly claim to prefer the "regularity" of the restored national unified curriculum with its clear standards and demands, fixed progression of lessons, enforced by the full panoply of quizzes, tests, and examinations. Yet the logic of the pedagogical arguments against most of these features has also been accepted generally. Streaming, for example, was specifically not permitted in the original Soviet-style system of the 1950s. But because that prohibition contradicted the traditional Chinese assumption that "special talent" deserves special training, the issue was widely debated at the time. Such training was then allowed in the early 1960s but forbidden again during the 1966–76 decade, leaving Chinese educators very familiar with the pedagogical arguments, pro and con. They generally agree, for example, that streaming benefits only the brightest students, leaving the others if not demoralized at least more intellectually passive. Hence, when such features of the system were allowed to develop unchecked in the late 1970s, there was a basis for criticism even among teachers otherwise instinctively committed to "regularity."

Yet correctives had to come from the central authorities responsible for fixing the centralized rules of the system, and, predictably, given the logic of the two-line struggle, the official correctives came not in the form of a rebuke for the new system but instead for that of its predecessor. Climaxing the 1981 controversy, Jiang Nanxiang, then Education Minister, conceded that the competition for college admission was being waged more intensely, with all the attendant evils than at any time in the past. The problem was not the restored college entrance examinations or the key-point stream, however, but that too many senior middle school graduates were chasing too few seats in college. He recalled somewhat wistfully how much more manageable the secondary school system had been in the mid-1960s, when it had an enrollment of only fourteen million. He seemed to be defending the reduction of enrollments then underway by suggesting that the tensions within the system would be alleviated once it had fewer students to worry about.[64]

In fact, as he and his successors have discovered, turning back this particular clock is more easily said than done. The tensions may be less at the college level, where only about two million senior secondary graduates are now competing annually for 600,000 college seats (by contrast with seven million vying for half that number in 1979).[65] Equally important in this regard, the number of officially recognized key-point secondary schools has also been streamlined (there were in 1987 only 2,243 such schools nationwide as shown in Table 2), so as to produce about 600,000 graduates each year, or a number more or less exactly the same as the annual intake of college freshmen.[66] But the competition, far from being eliminated, was only forced down the line where sixth-graders and ninth-graders are prepped and crammed in a valiant effort to push them into the key-point stream.

The radical arguments with their anti-elitist implications can also be kept out of the newspapers (and since 1981 have been). But it is not possible to eliminate the "interests" that the Cultural Revolution policies created in the form of a mass education base with all the upward pressures arising from it. And whether the old radical arguments are used, or the currently acceptable professional ones, the key-point stream loses out either way. Another upsurge of criticism, using the latter, occurred between 1984–86, when calls were again raised to abolish such schools at the elementary and secondary levels. The main points of critique in the mid-1980s were elaborated as follows:

1. Non-keypoint schools had lost all of the best teachers to their key-point rivals.

2. Keypoint schools were ignoring their junior middle sections while putting all their efforts into the senior level to achieve high pass rates into college.

3. As a result, students from key-point schools were not only arrogant but had no interest in politics or social activities.

4. Teachers in the non-key schools were demoralized because they knew their students were the rejects of the key-point stream.

5. Student morale was also low because they knew they had little chance of going on to college, and job opportunities for them were scarce.

6. The key-point system worked to the disadvantage of boys whose intellectual development was slower than that of girls. Female students performed better on entrance examinations, but "because of various social, historical, and psychological factors," their performance declined after the first year of senior middle school. Hence, "many promising male students are deprived of normal development because they have entered non-key schools that do not have . . . competent teachers, adequate teaching facilities, or enough funds."

7. Finally, the key-point stream worked generally to the detriment of intellectual

development. This was because, regardless of all the resolutions issued each year, everyone judged key-point schools by their main *raison d' être*, namely, the access they provided to the next level and especially to college. The key-point schools therefore had no choice but to base their teaching on the cram method in order to guarantee examination results and high pass rates.[67]

Such arguments were aired extensively in the national and provincial press between 1984 and 1986.[68] Unlike 1981, however, the critics of the mid-1980s were more careful to acknowledge the legitimacy of the key-point concept "in principle." But central decision-makers, on this matter too, were obviously caught between their "line" and the logic of the arguments against it. Hence, they steadfastly refused to repudiate the key-point concept or the system they had recreated with such determination in the late 1970s, while nevertheless responding with a series of gestures and measures aimed at mollifying the critics.

The gestures included a stream of increasingly defensive publicity designed to cast the key-point schools in a benign light by showing that they can correct their faults and work for the common good. More substantively, an "opinion" was issued by the Education Ministry in 1983 to the effect that unified junior middle school entrance examinations should "in principle" be abolished in cities which had universalized schooling at that level.[69] The aim was to eliminate the elaborate procedure whereby elementary school graduates were channeled into the hierarchy of key-point and non-key point schools within a city on the basis of unified entrance examinations scores. Key-point junior middle schools were then to enroll only children from their own immediate neighborhoods as was done during the 1968–76 period. This 1983 opinion was reaffirmed in a 1986 circular that continues to govern practice in this regard.[70]

At present, localities are in a "transitional stage" as they try to combine in practice the two contradictory concepts of neighborhood enrollment and key-point schools. These continue otherwise unchanged with all their concentrated resources, that is, with the best teachers, facilities, and pass rates on to the key-point senior middle level, while parents outside the school district naturally continue to demand access. The corollary to the neighborhood enrollment principle, therefore, is the promise now being made by many localities either "to abolish progressively" the key-point junior secondaries or "to reduce gradually" the qualitative differences between these and the non-key point schools.[71]

Meanwhile, the 1986 circular authorized schools to use recommendations, oral examinations, or "other enrollment methods" during this uncertain period of indefinite duration, leaving it to the local authorities themselves to decide. Except in the case of truly outstanding students, however, such methods leave open much room for maneuver—especially given the common assumption expressed by Chinese educators everywhere that children from "established," including intellectual and economically secure families, will perform better in school and therefore deserve access to better facilities. Stories also abound regarding the exchange of favors and money that occur at this point.

Obviously, central policymakers have made concessions both in principle and practice to the critical opinions in society that have been demanding the abolition of the key-point stream at the lower levels at least since 1981, and probably never accepted its reimposition in the first place. But whether the key-point schools themselves actually "disappear" is another matter, since the old ambivalence between the critics and advocates of "regular" education is also so clearly evident. SEDC Vice Chairman Wang Mingda identified the contradiction in remarks at a meeting of non-Communist party intellectuals called to discuss education problems at the start of the 1986–87 academic year. Wang told the gathering that "on the problem of key-point middle schools, we have already given notice that they should be eliminated at the junior secondary level. But in actually doing that, the larger the city, the greater the obstacles are, and the main one is the opinion of cadres and intellectuals since they all hope their own children will attend key-point middle schools."[72]

Hence, China's educational system at the present time has turned a full circle. The mass base may be very different from what it was half a century ago. But the regularization patterns reimposed on it are clearly identifiable, both in the precedents they evoke and the ambivalence these arouse. Because of the potential the regularized key-point stream represents, all parents want their children to enter it. At the same time, however, the critical consensus is such that almost everyone can also recite the system's defects by heart—including even many of the same people whose interests are tied to it.

Higher Education

At the elementary level and even more so at the secondary level, major tensions in the 1980s derived from the initial attempt to restore the "regular" patterns of China's educational tradition without much regard for the underlying popular critique in either its old or new manifestations. To reiterate, the concerns underlying that critique both before and after 1949 revolved essentially around the questions of whose children should receive how much of what kind of education. At the tertiary level, similar tensions are also evident. But they have been compounded by the new rush of direct influences from the West, as Chinese political and intellectual leaders abandoned the "appropriate technology" argument of the Maoist era to revive their quest for "advanced international standards." In the process, they have also revived in appropriately updated form the concerns associated with foreign borrowing and mechanical copying that were first articulated by critics during the early decades of the century. On this dimension also, therefore, China's educational system seems to have turned a full circle—although the old contest between Chinese foundations and foreign imports was, in the 1980s, further complicated as a clash between Chinese socialist ways and Western capitalist means.

The result as of 1987—when the then Minister of Culture Wang Meng published a prophetic warning about the dangers of superficial foreign borrowing, the one-sided obsession with wealth, and a need for real alternatives to iron rice bowl egalitarianism—looked like overall stalemate.[73] The reforms in higher education, interacting with those in other sectors, had created problems that no one seemed willing or able to solve. After the multiple economic and political crises of 1988 and 1989, the consequences of Deng Xiaoping's decade of reform for higher education, at least, could better be categorized as a major tragedy for all concerned.

By contrast, his decade began with great fanfare and high hopes. The Cultural Revolution priorities had included expansion at the mass level and vocationalization of the entire system. Higher education suffered the same fate but without the quantitative growth. The lower levels also reopened for business much earlier, in 1968–69, after the Red Guard phase of the Cultural Revolution ended. Institutions of higher learning did not begin enrolling new students on a regular basis until the early 1970s. College education was thus being rebuilt and enrollments were growing but in 1976 had not yet reached even their pre-1966 levels. Qualitatively, the "appropriate technology" aim prevailed and attempts to strive for international standards were deliberately rejected. According to interviewees, college curricula were essentially cut in half during the early 1970s. Socially and politically, the objective was to produce more worker-peasant intellectuals (by building mass secondary enrollments and using nonacademic criteria for college admission), and to turn existing intellectuals into workers and peasants as well (by recategorizing young people from nonworking-class families after a stint of farm labor or factory work).

Following the logic of the post-1976 era, all of these priorities were reversed. The regularization patterns reimposed on the system may have derived from old-fashioned assumptions among Chinese educators about how best to supply a quality product. But Deng Xiaoping's modernization strategy provided the demand and justification. He argued that China had to catch up with the rest of the world. Its first priority would be economic development. Since science and technology were the keys to economic modernization and since education in turn held the key to their development, education should be reconstituted to fulfill these tasks.[74]

Deng Xiaoping also, in the late 1970s, declared class struggle and mass movements to be at an end. Political labels from the past, such as "rightist" and "historical counterrevolutionary," were removed. The use of family or class background as criteria for college admissions, job assignments, and other of life's benefits was ended. Indeed, all the social consequences and implications of different kinds of education for different kinds of people were declared irrelevant to the overriding aim of education for modernization. In this respect, the system was freer of social and political constraints than it had been at any time since the founding of the People's Republic. Intellectuals were redesignated mental laborers in the service of socialism and the aim was to rebuild tertiary education by exploiting the existing social divisions of labor.

The older generation of university intellectuals referred openly to Deng Xiaoping as their "liberator" for the changes this reversal of priorities wrought in their lives. The university system that was reestablished between 1977–80 replicated the antebellum model of the 1960s, which was essentially the same as the Sino-Soviet compromise variation that had emerged from the early 1950s pro-Soviet period. Hence, all that system's centralized features that had been abolished during the 1966–76 decade were restored. These included the national unified college entrance examinations, unified enrollment and job assignment plans, unified curricula, and systematized rules and regulations for everything.

Probably, if left entirely as an island unto itself thereafter, China's university system would have settled back more or less comfortably into this mold. From it, the worker-peasant-soldier students, Cultural Revolution radical intellectuals, and other nonprofessionals were being purged or at least disempowered. Elementary and secondary education was being appropriately tracked and streamed all with the single-minded aim of producing talent for the tertiary sector. Educators consequently found themselves with greater freedom to pursue "quality" than at any time since 1949, and, as noted, the value of a college education was also similarly enhanced.

Finally, in the late 1970s, the cushion of socialist security was further inflated for university intellectuals as if to compensate for the deprivations of previous years. They continued to enjoy lifetime tenure, but now guaranteed in the kind of work for which they were trained. Cradle-to-grave security was also enhanced. For example, the special schools attended by and maintained for their children were exonerated and restored. Dependents of deceased university personnel could even continue to occupy scarce campus housing. College students, for their part, continued to enjoy free tuition, room, and board. They also graduated into similarly secure state-assigned jobs that now promised better prospects than ever before. Little wonder that in 1980, university intellectuals felt themselves on the threshold of a new "golden age" of peace and security while parents could think of no better guarantee for their children's future than admission to college.[75]

Deng Xiaoping's plans for everyone were only just beginning, however. Not only did he, just prior to his own trip to the United States in 1978, order ten thousand students to follow him as quickly as possible. He also is said to have ordered all leading cadres to make at least one trip abroad. Everyone would soon discover that his aim was not just to give them a glimpse of the outside world, or even to import Western capital and technology, but to try and graft the ways and means of capitalism onto China's socialist system in the hope of making it work more effectively. He aimed further to include China's institutions of higher learning in that experiment. Already aware of the new orientation, although not the extent to which they would be pushed to achieve it, university educators said in 1980 that China was now looking especially to the United States as a source of expertise precisely because of the latter's status as the most successful example of Western capitalism. Also being discussed were specific ways in which China's universities might learn from their American counterparts.

In fact, a single essay is scarcely sufficient to do justice to the changes imposed on China's institutions of higher learning during the 1980s. Here it is possible only to list the most important and highlight, in conclusion, those that contributed most significantly to the crisis of confidence that overtook China's universities at the end of the decade. That crisis developed, of course, in a complex interaction between the economic and political reforms and those within the education sector. Intervening at many points, however, were the contemporary versions of old contradictions clearly identifiable from the pre-1949 critique of Chinese education. Roughly in the order of their appearance the major reforms at the university level included the following:

Returning to China for the first time in thirty years, Western development experts advised, among other things, that a country China's size should have a college enrollment of about two million. Chinese leaders readily accepted this advice and fixed 1990 as the target for achieving it. As the following figures show, this was one target that was achieved ahead of time:[76]

Year	Institutions	Students
1965	434	674,000
1977	404	625,000
1985	1,016	1,703,000
1988	1,016	2,066,000

Another overfulfilled target was Deng Xiaoping's injunction to send ten thousand students abroad forthwith. According to one of the more authoritative compilations of Chinese government statistics on this point, China sent more than fifty thousand to some seventy countries betwen 1978 and 1988.[77]

Economic reforms, following those for the country as a whole, aimed to break up the overcentralization of economic power and socialist distribution. Universities and faculties had already been advised by 1980 that they must learn to supplement modest budgets and low incomes with their own collective and private profit-making endeavors. Students had similarly been told to prepare for the end of free state-financed higher education.

Deng Xiaoping himself announced in 1980 a further series of political and administrative reforms, without which, it was argued, the economic reforms could not succeed. These "reforms of 1980" were designed to correct the over-concentration of political power and other evils of bureaucratism. The aims included: (a) reform of the cadre or personnel system to entail the abolition of lifetime tenure, smashing of iron rice bowls, and tying job performance to rewards, punishments, and dismissals; (b) democratic management and popular participation in local government and enterprise administration; (c) the separation of political/party functions from professional/administrative work; and (d) decentralization or expanding local autonomy and the decision-making powers of individual institutions.78 Educators had been told by 1980 to anticipate the application of these aims to academic institutions where they would mean the breakup of the centralized Sino-Soviet model, including its unified entrance examinations, curricula, and teaching plans, changes in student enrollment and job-assignment procedures, in faculty selection and administrative appointment procedures, and in the power of university presidents and department chairmen relative to that of the university CCP organization.

Undoubtedly, one major fault was simply a surfeit of reforms. No other sector of Chinese society has been quite so overloaded as higher education—ordered to implement simultaneously major academic, economic, and political reforms as well as absorb the sudden impact of direct contact with the West. By the late 1980s, the issues of most immediate concern were, in simplest terms, too many students, too little money, and too few employment opportunities commensurate with expectations. It was at this point when the balance shifted and the reforms overall suddenly seemed to be creating as many problems as they were solving, that the patterns from the past reappeared. Thus, many of the explanations advanced by academics and policymakers during the crisis years, 1988–90, would have been as familiar to the educational system's pre-1949 critics as would the post-Mao regularization drive to the professional educators who tried to reproduce the system in Yan'an during the late 1930s.

In higher education, the step that marked the beginning of the shift was probably the SEDC announcement in early 1988 concerning the next phase of the student finance and job assignment reforms. Guangdong was selected as the trial point. Its tertiary institutions were directed to begin collecting tuition from freshmen students beginning with the fall semester. When these same students graduated, two to four years thereafter, depending on their study programs, the state job-assignment plans would not apply to them. They would be responsible for finding employment on their own. From 1988 on, these changes would be introduced for each new freshman class until they were extended to all college students in the province. The same set of reforms was to begin at the start of the fall semester of 1989 in the thirty-six institutions administered directly by the SEDC. All other tertiary institutions throughout the country were to introduce the reforms for their first-year students by the start of the 1990–91 academic year.[79]

The national reaction to this announcement was intense and immediate. When the popular *China Youth News* printed a critical comment from a reader, it prompted 1,361 additional letters in response. The paper did not report how many were for and how many against the measures. But the main argument against the measures in those it selected for publication was that fair competititon on the job market was not possible. "In finding employment," wrote one reader, "there is only equality on the surface but not underneath." Another demanded "legal guarantees of fair competition" as a precondition for forcing graduates to find their own jobs. The consensus of the controversy was that the best opportunities are in fact reserved for male students from big cities whose parents have many "well- connected" friends and relations.[80]

Indeed, the reaction was so great as to influence applications at the senior secondary level for the fall 1988 semester. Press commentators reported uniformly that the major reasons for the drop were the low remuneration for jobs filled by college graduates, plus the new regulations announced in early 1988, abolishing tuition-free higher education and guaranteed job assignments for college graduates. "This year," noted one correspondent, "in order to find work, many university and graduate students and their parents are going everywhere establishing connections and seeking the help of influential people, which has had a great influence on the parents of secondary school students. They feel that the burdens of sending their children to senior middle school and on to college are too great ... and the monetary rewards too small."[81] "Some say," wrote another commentator, "that this year the specialized technical middle school has become the last iron rice bowl."[82]

Beijing, for example, had planned to enroll 25,077 students in 1988, but only 13,779 wrote first-preference applications for ordinary senior middle schools there, a drop of 45 percent over the year before. The beneficiaries were the previously unpopular secondary technical and vocational schools that had 59,683 first-preference applications in 1988 for only 10,354 places. Even key-point schools were affected. Some 48 percent of the students graduating from Beijing's district level key-point junior middle schools applied to enter technical or vocational schools.[83] Presumably, if these figures from 1988 and those cited above for 1987 were both accurate, Beijing authorities should have been happier than the reports suggested, to win a respite from the upward pressures for more secondary schooling and acceptance of vocational education all at a single stroke.

Also in early 1988 the SEDC decided to publicize its new measures designed to induce students overseas to return home. Much discussed and applied piecemeal up to that time, the measures were apparently intended for more systematic enforcement.[84] Once again, protestations were intense and immediate, this time among Chinese students overseas. The scene then shifted to the annual meetings of the National People's Congress where university representatives were outspoken in their lobbying efforts to highlight the incipient "crisis" in higher education.

Beijing University President Ding Shisun emerged as the most prominent unofficial spokesman for this course after his remarks to a gathering of delegates received extensive publicity in the official Chinese press during the NPC meetings. "Some people ask me whether as Beijing University president I fear student protests," he said, "but I answer that what I fear most is not having enough money."[85] He then slipped easily back into the old professional educator's mode by blaming his budgetary problems on quantity at the expanse of quality. He lashed out, among other things, at the recent "blind" effort to increase tertiary enrollments. He argued that the billions of dollars used to build new colleges and universities would have produced better results had they been allocated instead to existing institutions. He explained further that the reason so many college graduates were unnecessary was that the more advanced sectors of the economy had not grown fast enough to accommodate them. Meanwhile, the main growth sector had been small-scale, county-level enterprises that needed middle-level technicians not college graduates.

Perhaps the most widely quoted of President Ding's comments, however, concerned the overseas study problem. "Don't blame students abroad for not returning home," he said. "The real problem is whether or not they are respected in their work." He declared himself opposed to the new restrictions being imposed on them, including the "thousand and one ways" of trying to bring them home. He argued that under present conditions, the real difficulty was not bringing them home but how to absorb those who did return. To illustrate this point, he told of a new Ph.D. who gave up a U.S. $40,000 a year job abroad to return to Beijing University. With great difficulty, they found housing for him and a laboratory, plus an associate professor's title that carried a basic monthly salary of RMB 122 (about U.S. $33, at the then rate of exchange).

From the perspective of educational development, one of its classic or at least most common dilemmas seemed to be at work. The growth of the economy had not kept pace with that of higher education which was therefore training large numbers of students for positions that did not exist. In formal statements, the SEDC also seemed to have accepted this interpretation. A spokesman interviewed in December 1988 emphasized the need to adapt higher education more closely to the developing need of Chinese society. He recalled that this problem was not formally recognized until 1983, but had become the subject of increasing corrective efforts since 1985. The current official view was that the structure of the newly restored system of higher education was inappropriately designed, producing too many four-year graduates in the general sciences both social and natural, and not enough intermediate-level technicians for which there was the greatest need. Consequently, the official objective was to continue restructuring higher education until the number of regular four-year college students was at least equaled by the number of students in two-year post-secondary programs.[86]

Underlying the SEDC's detached assessment, of course, lay all the endemic strains of twentieth-century China's educational development—banished from consideration when the system was being rebuilt in the late 1970s, but now returning inexorably to haunt everyone once more. University administrators, on the front line as they are of this reemerging dilemma, were considerably less clinical. For them it translated into the increasing difficulties they faced each summer in placing the annual crop of graduating seniors, difficulties that were being exacerbated by the concurrent reform aimed at allowing graduates to find their own jobs.

At one Beijing college, an elderly vice president, also interviewed in December 1988, commented on the universally acknowledged "contradiction between supply and demand," or the surfeit of college graduates trained for jobs that do not exist, while the needs of "basic level" and rural work units for trained personnel go unmet. But he ignored the official explanation of too many college students in an improperly structured tertiary system. Instead, he blamed the restructured system at the secondary level and the social origins of the students it is designed to serve. "The problem of job assignments for students is directly related to the problem of students' background and origins," he said. "All college students now originate from urban senior middle schools and it is only the children of cadres and intellectuals who can go to college." Because of their origins, he said, his students all wanted provincial jobs at least and were not interested in openings at the county level or below where needs were the greatest.

Others eschewed this view with all its ties to the radical critique of the recent Maoist past, reverting instead to older less controversial variations on the same theme to explain the current "brain drain"—from county towns to provincial capitals, from the latter to big cities, and from the nation's leading universities to those abroad. There was no dearth of jobs but only of graduates willing to take those available. The problem was not lack of employment opportunities but the unrealistic expectations of college students whose aspirations combined the inherited prejudices of Chinese intellectuals with the promises of Deng Xiaoping's modernization program.

Thus repeating the old reformer's axiom that "college educated intellectuals concentrate where culture is high," a university vice president in Guangzhou cited the example of Hainan Island, recently separated from Guangdong to become an independent province. Even within the island itself, he said, the brain drain was evident. "Students who graduate from Hainan Island senior middle schools go to colleges on the mainland and do not return. The best leave and the backwardness remains. If they do return, they want to work at Haikou, while the counties in the hinterland have a difficult time getting teachers and doctors."

Direct descendants of this self-critical educational tradition that they all are, decision-makers and intellectuals responsible for the reform policies might have anticipated such an end but evidently did not when they began in the late 1970s. Hence, the increasingly negative mood on Chinese university campuses a decade later, aggravated of course by the deteriorating economic climate and demands among intellectuals for faster political reform. The net result was the explosion of dissent that led to the massacre at Tiananmen Square in 1989, and also to the decisions for the education sector that were subsequently announced by the "new" conservative administration in Beijing.

Conclusion

Returning to the questions raised at the outset, this essay suggests that the Maoist "education revolution" was not illusory but that its substance was ultimately overshadowed by the political imperatives of the "two-line struggle" within which it was embedded. Education was an important component of that struggle and the arguments on both sides go back to commitments formed during the early decades of the century. These concerned how "modern" schools should be run, on the one hand, and the critical backlash they provoked, on the other. Mao Zedong actually began his career in Changsha as an erstwhile education reformer of the latter persuasion and carried the early commitments with him until he had won sufficient political power to think he could impose them on the entire country. But what he had also done in the interim was to integrate them with the larger aims of a newly victorious Communist party still intent on achieving social and cultural revolution.

In the process, however, this strategy ensured that Mao's line and everything associated with it could prevail only so long as he was able to retain power. When power was lost at his death, all the enemies Mao had created along the way united in repudiating both his line and those who had helped him implement it. Conversely, the post-Mao reforms in education must also be assessed within this political context because they represent both the alternative strategy for socialist development and an explicit political repudiation of the Cultural Revolution experiment as well.

Deng Xiaoping's solution accordingly was to reverse his predecessor's priorities on almost every point, ending both social revolution and radical educational reform. Repudiated also were the issues inherited from the old pre-1949 critique related to foreign borrowing, intellectual elites, and urban-rural disparities.

One of Deng Xiaoping's strategic errors thus followed inevitably from playing out the logic of the two-line struggle. Most significant for education, in this respect, was the refusal to distinguish either analytically or in practice between the class-based Communist revolution and the antiestablishment critique of the educational system that Mao had joined together. As a result, the "forces of regularization" reestablished themselves with the full support of the new administration in order to serve its modernization goals. Hence, the basic ideas and assumptions of Chinese educators about how to run modern schools in order to produce a quality product reemerged virtually unchanged from those of half a century earlier. The only thing missing seemed to be the old antiestablishment critique itself, which was banished from the realm of public discourse along with the leftist excesses of the Maoist era.

Education policymakers have consequently found themselves with "so many problems we never anticipated," to quote the SEDC spokesman cited above, and liabilities at every level: primary, secondary, and tertiary. Just as Mao overestimated his power to break the regular system, so the professional educators working under Deng Xiaoping's authority have discovered the truth of Wang Meng's warning. The interests and concerns underlying the old leftist arguments can be neither eliminated nor ignored, at least not yet. This is not because they have taken on an ideological life of their own, but because they are still tied to essentially the same divisions within twentieth-century Chinese society that inspired them in the first place. These are especially the distinctions between elites and masses, between city and countryside, and between the outward-looking coastal areas and the inward-oriented hinterland. Like a complex of enduring fault lines, these divisions represent the as yet unreconciled interests within Chinese society as a whole, along which the search for a new, modern consensus to replace the old has repeatedly broken. But at the same time those divisions and interests have become an important force contributing to the dynamic of the development process itself.

The most significant interests that developed around the Cultural Revolution educational strategy were those represented by the mass enrollments at the elementary and secondary levels, reinforced by a unitary structure that offered a similar kind of work-oriented education for all. The reimposition of clear-cut vocational tracks and elitist academic streams, together with the reduced enrollments, therefore gives contemporary relevance to the old arguments. These live on in the undercurrent of pressure and criticism that continued throughout the 1980s.

Clearly on the defensive, central decision-makers responded in the mid-1980s by promulgating a compulsory nine-year (elementary and junior secondary education) decree, as yet unenforced; by allowing a limited increase in secondary enrollments; and by agreeing "in principle" to eliminate key-point schools at the elementary and junior middle levels. For higher education, the consequences of producing too many college graduates all drawn from the same urban key-point middle school stream was not acknowledged until the end of the decade. Viable solutions will mean not only luring back the thousands from that stream who graduated into successful student careers overseas, but inducing those educated at home to work in "basic level" units for which neither their training nor their expectations are appropriate.

Given the endemic nature of the concerns underlying these issues, Deng Xiaoping's reform administration would evidently have been better advised to integrate them into its strategy from the start. Certainly, respecting the lessons of history rather than continually erasing them and then having to rediscover them the hard way would have reduced the costs to the nation and its young people. During the 1980s these costs have been registered in terms of new illiterates in the countryside, demoralized urban youth without jobs, schools, or futures, and a new generation of college graduates with aspirations that cannot be fulfilled, while the needs of society for trained personnel go unmet.

In a further ironic parallel with the Maoist past, a second strategic error apparent in the education sector by the 1980s concerned the damage being done specifically at the tertiary level. Unlike the 1966–76 era, the intention in the 1980s was neither deliberate nor politically motivated—at least not until the spring of 1989. But neither is the damage entirely the unintended consequence of inflation, corruption, and other problems afflicting the economy as a whole. The administration not only left the educational system unprotected from these adverse consequences of its market-oriented reforms, but even pushed forward with their direct application to institutions of higher learning at a time when those consequences were at their height. The sequence of events is all the more surprising in that higher education was initially a favored sector, so important for Deng Xiaoping's modernization goals in the late 1970s that it justified restructuring the entire educational system to concentrate resources at the tertiary level and within the college-preparatory, key-point stream. Perhaps the growing awareness of dislocations within that part of the system precipitated the increasingly cavalier approach toward it. But the announcement of further student finance and job-assignment reforms in 1988—when inflation-eroded university budgets and academic incomes were already major campus concerns—had an impact so immediate that it even led to reduced applications at the senior secondary level for the 1988–89 academic year.

After the violent suppression of the protest movement on June 4, 1989, of course, China's institutions of higher learning were locked irreversibly into the larger contradictions between economic and political reform that finally overtook the Deng Xiaoping administration at the end of its first decade in power. But applying the lessons of recent history, such an end should probably have been anticipated since education has, both intentionally and otherwise, been so regularly eclipsed by other priorities. In addition, however, the "error" of tying the old education concerns to the ongoing political power struggle is also being deliberately repeated. This is occurring as the next phase of the cycle begins under the leadership of a "new" Deng Xiaoping administration, dominated, after June 4, by the CCP's conservative leaders. Their rhetoric inevitably combines the official line denouncing the "counterrevolutionary rebellion" and the intellectual elitism responsible for it with antidotes that might be interpreted as a Maoist revival but that are also inherited from a much older tradition. Some people understand neither China nor foreign countries and "mechanically copy Western things," admonished a *People's Daily* writer. "Some people think of themselves as society's elite (*jingying*), feel much superior to the laboring people, and are neither willing to work hard on the front line of production at the basic levels, nor to merge with the masses and learn through practice."[87]

Specific measures announced in 1989–90 centered around the already revived theme of society's needs and grass-roots application, albeit with a heavy rhetorical flourish lacking in 1988. The new aim was to strengthen party building and political education, said Education Minister Li Tieying in the SEDC's first formal post-June 4 policy summation. "In principle," the immediate post-Cultural Revolution leadership formula of "university president responsibility under the leadership of the CCP committee" should be revived, he said, to enhance the authority of the latter by comparison with the former in a direct reversal of the 1980s trends. Political criteria should be similarly revived in assessing qualifications for student enrollment, job placement, staff promotions, and overseas study.[88]

Li Tieying also cited recent laxity in enrollment work. The 1988 planned intake of 640,000 had actually been exceeded by 100,000, he claimed. He did not mention that the expedient of enrolling outside the plan had been used by schools to earn extra income since they are allowed to keep fees paid by such extra self-financed students. But henceforth, he said, enrollment must adhere strictly to the state plans, and he defended the 1989 reduced intake as necessary to counteract recent excesses. The growth of tertiary institutions was also to be curtailed. He noted that in 1984 and 1985 alone, some two hundred schools had opened. The SEDC would no longer permit the establishment of new tertiary level institutions nor approve requests to upgrade, as from junior to regular college status. Those unable to meet stipulated standards should be improved, reorganized, or, if necessary, merged. Students for their part should adjust their expectations downward, "to the basic levels, the villages, the border regions, and bitter occupations." Qualified college graduates "should obey the state's requirements and the state should be responsible for assigning them appropriate work."[89]

When the admissions plan of 620,000 was announced for 1990, a SEDC spokesman said that intake would be reduced or curtailed "in those schools where political education work is weak and in specialties where the aim of study is unclear," as well as in specialties for which job openings were limited and in schools undergoing reorganization. The practice of accepting fully self-financed students was said to be still in the "experimental" stage and such students were not to exceed 3 percent of all those admitted. Recognized alternatives for unsuccessful candidates included the television university and correspondence courses.[90]

SEDC Vice Minister He Dongchang also revealed that henceforth key-point elementary and middle schools would no longer be regarded as an appropriate form of education and that other methods of promoting students in the lower grades were under consideration.[91] Accordingly, the SEDC is now "demanding" that localities that have universalized junior secondary education should allow youngsters to move directly to that level from elementary schools. By mid-1990, 116 cities had announced the abolition of their key-point enrollment systems for the junior midddle level and their reversion to the neighborhood school principle promoted in the early 1970s.[92]

In all of these ways, then, the recently rediscovered concerns about adapting higher education more appropriately to China's needs have been reinterpreted by the post-June 4 leadership not just as a social responsibility, or as part of a time-honored twentieth-century Chinese controversy, but also as a form of punishment to be imposed collectively on the country's rebellious intellectual elite. Hence, Ding Shisun would probably approve the reduced tertiary enrollments and school mergers—but not as retribution against those where political education was weak and certainly not at the cost of the presidential responsibility system that allowed him to publicize his demands in the first place. The key-point college preparatory stream has enjoyed a controversial existence at best throughout the 1980s and many of its critics would surely applaud its demise—were the government's motives not also inspired by the likely political aim of trying to undercut the pretentions and aspirations built into the college preparatory stream from elementary school upward.

Solutions are, in other words, being deliberately redefined as part of a leftist backlash against the urban-based, Western-oriented wing of China's political and intellectual establishment. However necessary, then, if actually implemented in the manner announced during 1989–90, such solutions will undoubtedly be eclipsed by yet another backlash against them—when the balance of political forces shifts once more and the logic of the two-line struggle proceeds to its next conclusion. In the process, we will be able to watch as yet another typical episode unfolds in the history of China's educational development—confounded again by the political imperatives surrounding it.

Presumably, these imperatives will wind down and their destructive impulses will also moderate over time. Eventually, it may be possible to objectify social interests and select reasonable policy alternatives from both sides of the Left-Right political divide. Successes in economic development might even render irrelevant contradictions such as those between college graduates' aspirations and society's needs. As the last decade of the century begins, however, such eventualities seem more like utopian visions of the century to come than a realistic conclusion for the one ending.

Notes

1. The reference is to three months of interviews conducted by the author in China in 1980 under the U.S.-China exchange program administered by the Committee on Scholarly Communication with the People's Republic of China. Not one administrator at any of the fifteen universities and eight secondary schools visited was willing to offer even one qualification to the new line that the Cultural Revolution was a ten-year disaster. World Bank economist John Simmons expressed a widely held view within the international development community when he wrote in a book published the same year that China's educational system (prior to the onset of the Deng Xiaoping era reforms) "comes closest to the World Bank's model program for a developing country." See "Introduction and Summary," in John Simmons, ed., *The Education Dilemma: Policy Issues for Developing Countries in the 1980s* (New York: Pergamon Press, 1980), pp. 9–10.

2. The fullest collection of old documents is the series, *Laojiefangqu jiaoyu ziliao* (Educational materials from the old liberated areas), Zhongyang jiaoyu kexue yanjiu so, ed. (Beijing: Jiaoyu kexue chubanshe, 1981, 1986), 3 vols. These recent compilations add much new detail but no startling revelations to the educational history of the CCP base areas. (See Peter J. Seybolt, "The Yenan Revolution in Mass Education," *The China Quarterly*, no. 48 (October/December 1971); Michael Lindsay, *Notes on Educational Problems in Communist China, 1941–1947* (New York: Institute of Pacific Relations, 1950); Mark Selden, *The Yenan Way in Revolutionary China* (Cambridge: Harvard University Press, 1971), pp. 267–74.

3. Quoted in Barry Keenan, *The Dewey Experiment in China: Educational Reform and Political Power in the Early Republic* (Cambridge: Harvard University Press, 1977), p. 91.

4. See, for example, Mao Zedong, "Hunan zixiu daxue chuangli xuanyan" (The founding announcement of the Hanan Self-study Univeristy) (August 1921); *Mao Zedong ji* (Mao Zedong's works) (Hong Kong, 1975) I: 81–84; Guy S. Alitto, *The Last Confucian: Liang Shu-ming and the Chinese Dilemma of Modernity* (Berkeley: University of California Press, 1979); James C. Thomson, Jr., *While China Faced West: American Reformers in Nationalist China, 1928–1937* (Cambridge: Harvard University Press, 1969); and the League of Nations' Mission of Educational Experts (C. H. Becker, M. Falski, P. Langevin, R. H. Tawney), *The Reorganization of Education in China* (Paris: League of Nations' Institute of Intellectual Cooperation, 1932).

5. Among interested foreigners, James Yen was the best known of the education reformers, particularly for his rural education and reconstruction work in Ding County, Hebei (Sidney D. Gamble, *Ting Hsien: A North China Rural Community* [New York: Institute of Pacific Relations, 1954]); also, Charles W. Hayford, *To The People: James Yen and Village China* (New York: Columbia University Press, 1990).

6. *China: Socialist Economic Development*, vol. 3 (Washington, D.C.: The World Bank, 1983), p. 134.

7. League of Nations' Mission of Educational Experts, *Reorganization of Education in China*, pp. 21, 45, 51–52, 62–64, 76–79, 80–84, and 90–92.

8. "Bianqu sinianlai xuexiao jiaoyu menglie zengjia" (The vigorous increase of schooling in the border region during the past four years), *Jiefang ribao* (Liberation Daily), June 5, 1941, reprinted in *Shaanganning geming genjudi shilaio xuanji* (Selection of historical materials from the Shaan-Gan-Ning Revolutionary Base), vol 4 (Lanzhou: Gansu renmin chubanshe, 1985), p. 451. These figures were for the Shaan-Gan-Ning region only. During those years the region itself grew in terms of population from about .5 million to an estimated 1.5 million. On education in the early 1930s during the Jiangxi Soviet period, see vol. 1 of the three-volume series, *Educational Materials from the Old Liberated Areas*.

9. Jiang Longji, "Guanyu minban gongzhu zhengce de chubu zongjie" (A preliminary summary of the people-manage public-help policy), n.d., mimeographed, reprinted in *Educational Materials from the Old Liberated Areas*, vol. 2, xia, p. 376.

10. Ding Haochuan, "Jinnian jiaoyu gongzuo de zhongxin" (Central tasks of this year's educational work), January 17, 1941, originally in *Xin Zhonghua bao* (New China news), February 2, 1941, reprinted in *Shaanganning geming genjudi shiliao xuanji*, vol. 4, pp. 417–20.

11. The rationale for the new direction was presented in two widely reprinted editorials from the *Jiefang ribao* (Liberation Daily) dated April 7 and May 27, 1944, which circulated with the reform directives. For example, *Shaanganning bianqu jiaoyu fangzhen* (The educational policy of the Shaanxi-Gangsu-Ningxia border region) (Shaanganning bianqu zhengfu bangongting, July 1944), pp. 31–53; translation in Michael Lindsay, *Notes on Educational Problems in Communist China, 1941–47*. The discussion here is based on these two editorials.

12. Jiang Longji, "Guanyu minban gongzhu zhengce de chubu zongjie," p. 376.

13. Lindsay, *Notes on Educational Problems*, p. 39.

14. Ronald Price asks a similar question in his essay, "Convergence or Copying: China and the Soviet Union," in Ruth Hayhoe and Marianne Bastid, eds., *China's Education and the Industrialized World: Studies in Cultural Transfer* (Armonk, NY: M. E. Sharpe, 1987), pp. 158–83.

15. For general similarities between China's post-1976 college enrollment system (which was essentially the same as its pre-Cultural Revolution predecessor) and the old imperial examinations, compare Suzanne Pepper, *China's Universities: Post-Mao Enrollment Policies*. (Ann Arbor, MI: Center for Chinese Studies, The University of Michigan,

1984), monograph No.46; and, for example, Ichisada Miyazaki, *China's Examination Hell: The Civil Service Examination of Imperial China*, trans. Conrad Schirokauer (New Haven, CT: Yale University Press, 1981).

16. Roderick MacFarquhar, ed., *The Hundred Flowers Campaign and the Chinese Intellectuals* (New York: Praeger, 1960).

17. On the Khrushchev educational reforms: Nigel Grant, *Soviet Education*, 4th ed. (New York: Penguin, 1979) pp. 102–4, 109–17; Mervyn Matthews, *Education in the Soviet Union: Policies and Institutions since Stalin* (London: George Allen and Unwin, 1982), pp. 15–33; Mervyn Matthews, *Privilege in the Soviet Union: A Study of Elite Life-Styles under Communism* (London: George Allen and Unwin, 1978), pp. 114–17, 126–30; George. Z. F. Bereday, William W. Brickman, and Gerald H. Read, eds. *The Changing Soviet School* (Boston: Houghton Mifflin, 1960), pp. 86–100, 290–91.

18. On these developments between the Great Leap of 1958 and the advent of the Cultural Revolution in 1966, see especially, Robert D. Barendsen, *Half-Work, Half-Study Schools in Communist China* (Washington, D.C.: U.S. Department of Health, Education, and Welfare, 1964; Stanley Rosen, *Red Guard Factionalism and the Cultural Revolution in Guangzhou* (Boulder, CO: Westview Press, 1982); Susan L. Shirk, *Competitive Comrades: Career Incentives and Student Strategies in China* (Berkeley: University of California Press, 1982); Jonathan Unger, *Education under Mao: Class and Competititon in Canton Schools, 1960–1980* (New York: Columbia Univeristy Press, 1982).

19. See Sheila Fitzpatrick, *Education and Social Mobility in the Soviet Union, 1921–1934* (Cambridge: Cambridge University Press, 1979); and Sheila Fitzpatrick, ed., *Cultural Revolution in Russia, 1928–1931* (Bloomington: Indiana University Press, 1978).

20. On the "educational revolution" component of the Cultural Revolution, see Theodore Hsi-en Chen, *The Maoist Educational Revolution* (New York: Praeger, 1974); Theodore Hsi-en Chen, *Chinese Education since 1949: Academic and Revolutionary Models* (New York: Pergamon, 1981); Jonathan Unger, *Education under Mao, part two*.

21. *Renmin ribao*, April 23, 1984.

22. My own interviewees include some sixty former teachers from China; more than forty were ex-rural school teachers from all parts of the country. The interviews concentrated on the 1970s and were conducted between mid-1980 and mid-1983 (write-up currently in progress). For rural Guangdong only, see William L. Parish and Martin King Whyte, *Village and Family in Contemporary China* (Chicago: University of Chicago Press, 1978), pp. 78–85.

23. *Zhongguo 1982 nian renkou pucha 10 percent chouyang ziliao* (10 percent sampling tabulation on the 1982 population census of the People's Republic of China) (Beijing: Zhongguo tongji chubanshe, 1983), pp. 316–17; also, *Beijing Review*, no. 14 (April 2, 1984), pp. 22–23.

24. The 1979 figure for the first grade enrollments is in *China: Socialist Economic Developmen* 3:205; the 1981 figure is from *Zhongguo baike nianjian, 1982* (China encyclopedic yearbook, 1982) (Beijing and Shanghai, 1982), p. 568.

25. Guojia tongji ju, Shehui tongji si (State Statistical Bureau, Division of Social Statistics), "Woguo jiaoyu shiye zai tiaozhengzhong fazhan" (The development of our country's educational enterprise during consolidation), *Tongji* (Statistics), no. 6 (June 17, 1984), p. 16.

26. Xinhua in Chinese for *Hebei ribao*, June 12, 1983, trans. in Joint Publication Research Service of the Foreign Broadcast Information Service, *China Report: Political, Sociological, and Military* (hereafter, JPRS, *CR:PSM*,) no. 437 (July 11, 1983), pp. 109–10.

27. Kuming, Yunnan service, February 17, 1983, trans. in JPRS, *CR:PSM*, no. 403 (March 21, 1983), p. 92.

28. *Guangming ribao* (Bright daily), October 8, 1980.

29. Xining, Qinghai service, January 8, 1981, trans. in JPRS, *CR:PSM*, no. 159 (January 26, 1981), p. 101.

30. Chen Li, "My Humble Opinion about Investment in Intellectual Resources in Ningxia," *Ningxia shehui kexue* (Social science in Ningxia), Yinchuan, no. 3 (August 1984), trans. in JPRS, *CR:PSM*, no. 89 (December 19, 1984), p. 80.

31. Ming Kecheng, "Renqing nongcun jingji xingshi; banhao nongcun jiaoyu" (Have a clear understanding of the rural economic situation; manage village education well), *Jiaoyu yanjiu* (Educational research), no. 6 (1981), pp. 18–19.

32. *Renmin ribao*, August 12, 1979; *Guangming ribao*, July 24, 1979.

33. Zhang Zhiyuan, "Putong jiaoyu gongzuo zhong de liangge tuqu wenti" (Two pressing questions in general educational work), *Renmin jiaoyu* (People's education), no. 10 (1982), p. 10.

34. Zhengzhou, Henan service, August 8, 1983, trans. in JPRS, *CR:PSM*, no. 457 (September 15, 1983), p. 29.

35. Changsha, Hunan service, September 4, 1982, trans. in JPRS, *CR:PSM*, no. 340 (September 24, 1982), p. 87.

36. *Sichuan ribao*, Chengdu, June 27, 1984, trans. in JPRS, *CR: PSM*, no. 071 (October 22, 1984), p. 38.

37. *Shaanxi ribao*, Xian, September 22, 1984.

38. Ten-part series by Zhang Tianlai and Mei Zhanyi, *Guangming ribao*, February 22–28, 1984; Gao Baoli, "Guanyu Hebeisheng nongcun jiaoyu gaige de lilun tantao" (A theoretical inquiry into Hebei's rural educational reform), and Zhao Qin, "Hebeisheng nongcun jizi banjiaoyu de kexingxing yanjiu" (Research on the feasibility of raising funds for rural education in Hebei Province), both in *Jiaoyu yanjiu* (Educational research), no. 9 (1984), pp. 39–43 and 44–46, respectively; Xin Xiangrong, "Peasants Run Their Own Schools," *Beijing Review*, no. 15 (April 9, 1984), pp. 4–5; Hubert O. Brown, "Teachers and the Rural Responsibility System in the People's Republic of China," *The Asian Journal of Public Administration* (Hong Kong University), vol. 7, no. 1 (June 1985), pp. 2–17.

39. "Guowuyuan guanyu choucuo nongcun xuexiao banxue jingfei de tongzhi" (State Council circular on raising funds for rural school operating expense), December 13, 1984, *Zhonghua renmin gongheguo guowuyuan gongbao* (Bulletin of the State Council of the People's Republic of China), no. 31 (December 30, 1984), p. 1046.

40. *Renmin ribao*, April 18, 1986.

41. See Table 1 for the year 1987, which shows the breakdown between five- and six-year elementary schools. He Dongchang's explanation was widely reprinted prior to the law's promulgation, e.g., *Zhongguo jiaoyu bao* (China education news), January 18, 1986. The same points were reiterated by Li Peng, then Vice Premier and Chairman of the newly created SEDC, in his formal explanation of the compulsory education law (*Renmin ribao*, April 18, 1986).

42. The press briefing was carried live on Beijing television, March 24, 1989, in SWB, FE/0420 C1/5, March 29, 1989. Only a portion of the briefing was printed in *Renmin ribao*, March 25, 1989. The same county-level figure was also given in the State Statistical Bureau's communique for 1988 (*Renmin ribao*, March 1, 1989).

43. "Bangong bandu, yigong yinong" (Half-work, half-study, in both industry and agriculture), August 1, 1964, *Liu Shaoqi Xuanji* (Selected works of Liu Shaoqi), vol. 2 (Beijing: Renmin chubanshe, 1985), pp. 465–69.

44. Hua Kuofeng, "Report on the Work of the Government," February 26, 1978, *Peking Review*, no. 10 (March 10, 1978), p. 28.

45. *Guangming ribao*, October 12, 1981.

46. *Zhongguo baike nianjian, 1980*, p. 538; *Zhongguo baike nianjian, 1986*, p. 433.

47. Song Jian, "Population and Education," *Ziran bianzhengfa tongxun* (Journal of the dialectics of nature), no. 3 (June 1980), translated in JPRS, *CR:PSM*, no. 178 (April 3, 1981), pp. 44, 47.

48. *Tongji*, no. 6 (1984), pp. 16–17 (see above, note 25); *Zhongguo jiaoyu bao*, October 16, 1984.

49. "Beijingshi dui 1987 nian chuzhong biyesheng ruhe anpai" (How to take care of Beijing's 1987 junior middle school graduates), *Liaowang* (Outlook), domestic edition, no. 7 (February 16, 1987), p. 48.

50. Ibid.; *Zhongguo jiaoyu bao*, February 24, 1987; *Beijing ribao*, July 5, 1987; *China Daily*, April 8 and 23, 1987.

51. *Zhongguo jiaoyu bao*, October 10, 1987; *Guangming ribao*, October 10, 1987; for Guangzhou, see *Nanfang ribao* (Southern Daily), Guangzhou, June 21, 1987, January 14, and July 12, 1988.

52. *Fujian ribao*, Fuzhou, November 8, 1980, trans. in JPRS, *CR:PSM*, no. 174 (March 25, 1981), p. 82.

53. "Guowuyuan pizhuan jiaoyubu, guojia laodong zongju guanyu zhongdeng jiaoyu jiegou gaige de baogao" (Report of the Education Ministry and the National Labor Bureau on restructuring secondary education, as approved and circulated by the State Council), October 7, 1980. *Zhonghua renmin gongheguo guowuyuan gongbao*, no. 16 (December 1, 1980), pp. 492–93. "Jiaoyubu, laodong renshibu, caizhengbu, guojia jihua weiyuanhui guanyu gaige chengshi zhongdeng jiaoyu jiegou, fazhan zhiye jishu jiaoyu de yijian" (Opinion of the Education Ministry, the Labor and Personnel Ministry, the Finance Ministry, and the State Planning Commission, on the Reform of the Structure of Urban Middle Schools and the Development of Vocational and Technical Education), May 9, 1983, *Zhonghua renmin gongheguo guowuyuan gongbao*, no. 12 (July 10, 1983), pp. 552–56; "Jiaoyubu guanyu jinyibu tigao putong zhongxue jiaoyu zhiliang de jidian yijian" (A few opinions from the Education Ministry concerning the progressive raising of the quality of education in ordinary middle schools), August 10, 1983, *Zhonghua renmin gongheguo guowuyuan gongbao*, no. 18 (September 20, 1983), pp. 839–44.

54. *Renmin ribao*, September 17, 1981.

55. Zhang Zhiyuan, "Putong jiaoyu gongzuozhong de liangge tuchu wenti" (Two pressing problems in ordinary educational Work), *Renmin jiaoyu* (People's education), no. 10 (October 25, 1982), p. 11.

56. The classic account of this dilemma in the educational development literature is Philip J. Foster, "The Vocational School Fallacy in Development Planning," reprinted in C. Arnold Anderson and Mary Jean Bowman, eds., *Education and Economic Development*, (Chicago: Aldine Publishing Company, 1965), pp. 142–66.

57. *Zhongguo jiaoyu bao*, August 25, 1984; also, Zhang Enhua, "Nongcun zhiye jishu jiaoyu bixu wei zhenxing nongcun jingji fuwu" (Rural vocational and technical education must serve the development of the rural economy), *Jiaoyu yu zhiye* (Education and occupation), Shanghai, no. 6 (1986), pp. 9–10.

58. "Zhonggong zhongyang, guowuyuan guanyu jiachiang he gaige nongcun xuexiao jiaoyu rogan wenti de tongzhi" (Notice by the party center and the State Council on some questions concerning the strengthening and reform of rural schools and education), May 6, 1983, *Zhonghua renmin gongheguo guowuyuan gongbao*, no. 12 (July 10, 1983), pp. 528–32.

59. *Renmin ribao*, May 29, 1985; also, "Jiaoyu jiegou he laodong renshi zhidu tongbu gaige jinzhande ruhe?" (How is the concurrent reform of the educational structure and the labor personnel system progressing?) *Jiaoyu yu zhiye* (Education and occupation), Shanghai, no. 5 (1986), pp. 15–19.

60. *Guangming ribao*, January 21 and August 12, 1987; *Zhongguo jiaoyu bao*, September 23, 1986, and February 10, 1987.

61. On the revival of this stream, see Stanley Rosen, "Restoring Key Secondary Schools in Post-Mao China: the Politics of Competition and Educational Quality," in David M. Lampton, ed., *Policy Implementation in Post-Mao China* (Berkeley: University of California Press, 1987), pp. 321–53.

62. Xinhua Domestic Service, Beijing, December 11, 1981, translated in JPRS, *CR:PSM*, no. 253 (December 30, 1981), p. 66; also *Guangming ribao*, December 5, 1981.

63. *Beijing ribao*, December 25, 1981. On the press commentary that preceded this statement, see *Zhongguo qingnian bao* (China youth news), October 31, November 21, December 5, 12, 1981; *Wenhui bao*, Shanghai, October 21 and December 12, 1981; *Guangming ribao*, November 7, 16, and December 5, 1981; *Beijing ribao*, December 12, 1981; *Renmin ribao*, November 12, 15, 17, 1981.

64. *Beijing ribao*, January 3, 1982.

65. *Zhongguo tongji nianjian, 1988*, pp. 878, 881.

66. *Zhongguo jiaoyu tongji nianjian, 1987*, pp. 58–59, 65.

67. The above points are from an article in *Guangming ribao*, September 6, 1984.

68. For example, in 1984: *Wenhui bao*, Shanghai, August 17, 25, 31, 1984; Liu Huo, "Shi peiyang rencai haishi yayi rencai?" (Nurturing talent, or suppressing talent?), *Xin guancha* (New observer), no. 18 (1984), pp. 14–15. In 1985: *Renmin ribao*, September 22, October 20, 1985; *Jiaoyu wenzhai* (Educational digest), Beijing, January 1, April 5, May 5, November 5, 1985; *Wenhui bao*, Shanghai, July 26, August 2, 9, 23, September 13, 20, 1985. In 1986: *Wenhui bao*, Shanghai, May 7, 15, 29, 1986; *Nanfang ribao* (Southern daily), Guangzhou, November 8, 29, 1986; *Renmin zhengxie bao* (People's political consultative conference news), Beijing, April 18, June 3, October 24, 1986.

69. "A Few Opinions from the Education Ministry Concerning the Progressive Raising of the Quality of Education in Ordinary Middle Schools," August 10, 1983. See note 53 above.

70. *Zhongguo jiaoyu bao*, March 8, 1986; May 30, 1987.

71. Such localities include: Shanghai: *Wenhui bao*, May 7, 1986; *Zhongguo jiaoyu bao*, April 26, 1986, February 24, 1987; *Guangming ribao*, November 10, 1987; Guangzhou: *Yangcheng wanbao*, May 11, 1988; Dalian: *Guangming ribao*, August 12, 1987; Shenyang: *Liaoning ribao*, March 6, 1987; Yingkou: *Guangming ribao*, February 13, 1989; Xiamen: *Zhongguo jiaoyu bao*, June 13, 1987; Henan: *Jiaoyu shibao* (Education times), May 5, 1988.

72. *Renmin zhengxie bao*, Beijing, October 24, 1986.

73. Wang Meng's signed article appeared in *Renmin ribao*, Septebmer 8, 1987.

74. Deng Xiaoping, "Zunzhong zhishi, zunzhong rencai" (Respect knowledge, respect talent), May 24, 1977, and "Guanyu kexue he jiaoyu gongzuo de jidian yijian" (A few opinions on science and educational work), August 8, 1977, both in *Deng Xiaoping wenxuan* (Deng Xiaoping's selected works) (Beijing: Renmin chubanshe, 1983), pp. 37–38 and 45–55, respectively.

75. The reference is to the 1980 research trip cited in note 1 above. The interviews with university administrators were written up in Suzanne Pepper, "China's Universities: New Experiments in Socialist Democracy and Administrative Reform," *Modern China*, vol. 8, no. 2 (April 1982), pp. 147–204; and in Pepper, *China's Universities*.

76. State Statistical Bureau, ed., *Zhongguo tongji nianjian, 1986* (Statistical yearbook of China, 1986) (Beijing: Zhongguo tongji chubanshe, 1986), pp. 723, 726; *Renmin ribao*, March 1, 1989.

77. Zhuang Yan, "Zhongguo liuxue renyuan gongzuo toushi" (A thorough explanation of work concerning Chinese studying overseas), *Liaowang zhoukan* (Outlook weekly), Beijing, Overseas edition, March 21, 1988, pp. 5–6.

78. "Deng Xiaoping zai zhongyang zhenzhiju kuoda huiyishang de jianghua" (Deng

Xiaoping's speech at the enlarged meeting of the Central Political Bureau), August 18, 1980, *Zhanwang*, Hong Kong, no. 461 (April 16, 1981), pp. 24–30; also, Liao Gailong, "Zhonggong 'gengshen gaige' fangan" (The Chinese Communist Party's "reform of 1980" program), *Qishi niandai* (The seventies), Hong Kong (March, 1981), pp. 38–48; and a two-part article by Feng Wenbin in *Renmin ribao*, November 24 and 25, 1980. Deng's 1980 speech was not officially published until 1987 (*Renmin ribao*, July 1, 1987).

79. The public announcement of this timetable appeared in *Zhongguo qingnian bao*, January 2, 1988, for the nation as a whole; *Nanfang ribao* Guangzhou, April 18, May 13, and June 23, 1988, for Guangdong Province; *Wenhui bao*, Shanghai, April 27, 1988, for Guangdong and Shanghai.

80. *Zhongguo qingnian bao*, April 19 and May 9, 1988.

81. *Renmin ribao*, July 25, 1988.

82. *Renmin ribao*, July 8, 1988.

83. *Guangming ribao*, July 8, 1988.

84. Zhuang Yan, "Zhongguo liuxue renyuan gongzuo toushi."

85. *Zhongguo qingnian bao* (China youth news), Beijing, April 5, 1988. Professor Ding's comments at the time were also reported in *Guangming ribao*, March 29, 1988; Zhongguo xinwen she (China News Service), Beijing, April 5, 1988; Xinhua, English, March 20, 1988, in *SWB*, FE/0110 B2/7, March 26, 1988; *China Daily*, April 13, 1988.

86. All references to information from interviews in late 1988 or the winter of 1988–89 refer to a series of formal interviews and informal discussions I conducted at the time in Hong Kong, Beijing, and Guangzhou with Chinese university and education administrators, and with foreign academic consultants in China. All of the interviewees spoke on the record for attribution at the time. But rather than worry about possible repercussions for these individuals in the post-June 4, 1989, Chinese political environment, which is very different from the one in which they spoke, for the most part I do not identify here either the individuals or their work units. The exception is the interview conducted in early December 1988 with the State Education Commission spokesman. Both questions and answers were prepared in advance and the resulting information was entirely uncontroversial. These interviews and discussions were conducted while I was on temporary assignment for *The Chronicle of Higher Education* (Washington, D.C.). The *Chronicle* is, of course, not responsible for the way the material is presented in this essay.

87. *Renmin ribao*, August 12, 1989.

88. Li Tieying's report to the National People's Congress Standing Committee, December 23, 1989, in *Renmin ribao*, January 3, 1990. The aim of reviving party leadership over universities by placing the presidential responsibility system beneath it was reiterated at a spring conference on party building in tertiary institutions. The conference also advocated reviving the tradition of central and local party leaders outside the education sector exercising an active supervisory role over institutions of higher learning (e.g., *Renmin ribao*, April 13 and 17, 1990).

89. Li Tieying in *Renmin ribao*, January 3, 1990. According to figures subsequently issued by the State Statistical Bureau in its annual communique, only 597,000 freshmen were actually admitted into regular tertiary-level programs in 1989, said to be down by 10.8 percent compared with the year preceding (*Renmin ribao*, February 21, 1990).

90. *Renmin ribao*, March 7, 1990.

91. He Dongchang's comments were made at a meeting on "joyful education" organized by SEDC in May according to *Yangzi wanbao* (Yangtze evening news), Nanjing, May 24, 1990. The *People's Daily* account of this Beijing meeting did not include He Dongchang's statement on key-point schools (*Renmin ribao*, May 24, 1990).

92. *Wenhui bao*, Shanghai, June 10, 1990.

Comments by Jerome B. Grieder

I approach this task as something of a *wai-hang*, since my specialty is not the study of the People's Republic of China (PRC), but earlier prenatal, prenascent twentieth-century history. I am inclined to fit what I have learned about the PRC into the framework of what I think I already know.

Professor Pepper's paper is a richly informative one. Most of the papers presented at the conference have concluded on a cautionary tone, warning that there are large, important, and complicated problems awaiting solution as the Deng reform movement continues, and warning that we should not expect too much too soon. Nor should we expect that what eventuates will conform to what we envision as the logical and preferable outcome. But none of the papers is more somber in its outlook and implication than Professor Pepper's, none conveys to me a clearer sense of political and social risk, ambiguities attendant on China's projected policies.

What she gives us here really is a penetrating examination of the dark underside of the bright prospect celebrated in the Thirteenth Party Congress. The moral I draw is that we will be ill served in trying to understand China's new turning today and tomorrow if we seize on the repudiation of Maoism as uncritically as was done twenty years ago as the key to understanding the riddle of Chinese policy. She makes it abundantly clear that dismantling the Maoist legacy is not only not a simple task, but is a process with many inevitable consequences, many of which may prove profoundly disruptive. Reduced to lamentably simplistic essentials, what Professor Pepper is arguing is that current reforms being implemented in primary, secondary, and tertiary education are, in a historical sense and a social sense, more reactionary than progressive. That is, they are essentially a reanimation of the educational policies she has already described here of the nascent communist regime in the 1950s and 1960s, down to the beginning of the Cultural Revolution, which were in turn reminiscent of the policies of the early Yenan years, which were themselves the product of educational debates dating back at least to the 1920s, if not to the very beginning of the century. In those earlier periods, as now again, perhaps even more emphatically now, the educational system was linked to the pursuit of nationalist, rather than socialist, objectives, that is, economic modernization rather than the restructuring of social relationships. This is, of course, the formulation that was reversed during the periods of proto-Maoism, or rampant Maoism, most conspicuously during the Cultural Revolution when education became one of the principal vehicles of social revolution, mass mobilization, and politicization of the masses. The differences between these two approaches are stark. Professor Pepper has outlined these differences in her remarks, so I will not go into them here. On the Maoist side, there are politicization of education, vocationalization of education, universalization of vocationalism as an educational value, the popularization of education, and the attempt to create a massive educational structure; on the other side, the emphasis on fixed uniform standards and the judgment of who is educatable, the channeling of resources to a small, in some ways increasingly small number of elite schools, the emphasis on quality over quantity, the preference given to the children of established social elites as being self-evidently more qualified to benefit from education, and the emphasis on higher levels of education, rather than secondary education that is mentioned. Professor Pepper's paper draws attention interestingly to what these very different approaches share in common, that is, each side justifies its policies and priorities in terms of a similar assessment of China's level of development: the Maoist claiming that in a backward society there is no need to educate a chosen few sophisticated in exotic arts, and the Dengist insisting that given China's backwardness, the development of high-level technical expertise is the urgent need. Recalling Ambassador Li's opening remarks at this conference about the accomplishments of the Chinese in recent years, such as researches into superconductivity, robotics, and so forth, I wonder, parenthetically, to what extent this reliance on the stages of development as a rationale arises perhaps from a sense differently felt at different times by different people, but by people with a similar sense of cultural nationalism or cultural uniqueness.

Other aspects of the reform program impinging in critical ways on educational policy include, for example, the impact of the responsibility system in agriculture, which, by placing a premium on productivity and family production, encourages the family to get their child out of school and into the sideline industries. More to the point, the dismantling of all the structures of collective responsibility in collective enterprises, and the state's reluctance, perhaps inability, to pick up the slack, have plunged China into a crisis in funding, especially in the countryside, that seems on the verge of bankruptcy. This Professor Pepper eloquently documents. Teachers go from door to door to collect the educational assessment from the locality. Parents withdraw children from school because they do not want to pay the assessed fees, and so on.

There are signs of change, which Professor Pepper has called our attention to, at least in the commandments that have come down from Beijing; but whether these will prove a feasible foundation for the funding of education remains to be seen. The picture that emerges is generally grim and deeply disturbing, whether or not one views it from the perspective of the Maoist egalitarian idealism in its uncorrupted sense. The picture that emerges is that of shrinking educational opportunities partly due to the deliberate policy decisions and partly to unintended consequences of other efforts of the reform movement. According to the calculations of one of the authors cited, if the school-age population of some 320 million 6–18 year olds, some 20 million will come to adulthood illiterate, 133 million will receive only primary education, and only some 10 million will receive higher education, that is, some kind of professional or university training. The conclusion of this author was that modernization in light of such estimates is an unthinkable aspiration. This was in 1980, and my impression is that the situation since then has deteriorated. It is hardly original to observe in conclusion that China is a society where status and privilege are not primarily assessed in terms of material wealth, but in terms of access to authority, the *guan-xi*, the ability to manipulate the sociopolitical environment in which one lives through nonmaterial means. In such a society a hundred years ago, or a thousand years ago, education was an extraordinarily valued commodity. It has been for centuries the path to preferment, and student demonstrations in the mid-sixties and mid-eighties remind us there is always the awareness and fear that education will become, if is has not indeed already become, an elite monopoly, manipulated by those in positions of authority, whereby the elites can perpetuate their privileges.

Comments by Suzanne Ogden

Professor Pepper's paper gives us a real sense of the obstacles that exist to reform. I want to focus on what I consider the three major variables that are the sources of problems of educational reforms. In my view, they are issues China has faced since 1949: the cultural variable, the political variable, and the developmental variable. Interaction of these variables have created irresolvable issues in China.

First, the cultural variable. The Chinese educators in the 1980s have been considering how to modernize their pedigogical techniques, content, and research system in ways that would encourage creative thought and greater knowledge, and would thereby advance China's development more rapidly. But it is not easy to abandon a style of education that is so deeply entrenched in Chinese ways of thinking. Included in these Chinese ways of thinking is the predisposition to think what one is told to think by people in positions of authority, and this is reinforced in the present period with the knowledge of the danger of thinking too independently. Furthermore, the school entrance examinations, especially national unified college entrance examinations, is, as Professor Pepper pointed out, really a Chinese system, not a Soviet approach to the educational system, not even one reinforced by the Soviet model. This system values the rote memorization of facts more than the ability to think. It is unlikely that the Chinese would rush into a Western-style education. In addition, in terms of educational values, there has traditionally been an educational elitism in China. This has been emphasized in the use of traditional pedigogical techniques, lecturing, student note-taking, and memorization and regurgitation of what the texts, teachers, and authorities have said without analyses. The state determines the tests and curriculum, rather than professors or teachers deciding what the most relevant curriculum could be for a particular time and place. And the emphasis is on teaching Chinese morality, sometimes disguised as political ideology—political ideology with emphasis on traditional Chinese values.

Second, the political variable is important. We have seen in all the areas of analysis during this conference that political reforms are essential to educational reforms, political reforms, for example, that will get the party out of the university administration and that will emphasize the importance of education for developing the ability to think and to be educated in and of itself, rather than being educated to serve the state or the desires of one faction or another. As long as these political issues go unresolved, it is likely that there will not be much accomplished in terms of educational reform than if there was a consensus, a consensus in terms of developing the educational system in a more modern way. There are many subsidiary goals, however, that need to be considered, for example, the issue of egalitarianism and the line-up of political forces, which, incidentally, is not as clear as might be expected. In fact, well-known intellectuals, not leftist radicals, with a more egalitarian set of values, are some of the most vocal supporters for basic mass education. So the discussion continues about how best to allocate basic educational resources, whether to train a small high-quality elite, or to broaden egalitarian objectives to eradicate illiteracy, or provide a sound basic education for all. One thing is clear, for the time being at least, economic experts, not politicals and redness, are in command in the educational sector, as in all sectors.

Education toward increasing China's productivity has now taken precedence over education as a means to achieve political goals. Although some of the constraints on modernizing the educational system have been created by developmental factors, I think this will be the third set of factors. I would say that most of China's unresolved issues in education have been created by policy choices at the top. It is the leaders' choices, based on ideological and political values, not China's low level of development, that are responsible for holding back the educational sector. In fact, even according to China's own admission, her allocation of funds to the educational sector is an unusually low proportion of the state budget. Generally, other countries allocate some 15–20 percent of their total state budget to education, while China's allocation hovers around 10 percent. In 1978 the UNESCO ranked China 130th among 149 countries in the order of size of allocation for education in proportion to the GNP, putting China not only far below countries of the First and Second Worlds, but also at the bottom of the list of most Third World countries. We can see that it has been a political choice to have only a few resources allocated to the educational sector. The question then is what to do with these limited resources, since one can only do so much. I think Professor Pepper argues that the Chinese have perhaps been wrongly concentrating resources in the primary and tertiary higher education sectors at the expense of secondary education. I would actually defend what the Chinese have done to a certain extent. I would say that basic mass education is a sine qua non for development and that the Chinese have put a significant amount of resources into primary education. Although it is hard to measure, they have certainly tried to bring about mass literacy. This is essential to modernize the country. On the other hand, there must be a technological and scientific leap, so the tertiary higher educational sector must be developed. On cannot expect the system to go very far when high school students are being taught by other high school graduates. It is hoped that college-educated people are the ones who will better lead the country and make better policy choices for the country as a whole. Further, I think that supporting only a million students in college as China is doing now is hardly an overcommitment of resources in the tertiary sector. As Professor Pepper notes in her paper, even the international development experts say that a country the size of China should have two million students in college. Again, the problem is not that China overemphasizes the tertiary sector at the expense of the secondary school sector, but rather that the country just does not have enough money to begin with for the educational sector.

China gets a lot of "bang for the buck" out of educational exchange. There are about thirteen thousand *gong-fei* students here, paid for by the government, and another six thousand who are privately supported. This is cheap for the Chinese government and a great way to get students into the higher education sector so they can then help educate other college students.

The Chinese have progressed in another area in the 1980s not mentioned in this paper and that is in the area of adult education. This is another dimension to the question of whom to educate, and the Chinese have discovered that with very little resources they can educate hundreds and thousands of workers. Indeed it is impressive how many workers have gone to the trouble to get a correspondence university degree, which is presumably equivalent to a college degree. Television and radio colleges are proliferating in China. There are literally hundreds of thousands of cadres who are self-taught and who have tested to be qualified in a single field of study. In this respect, the expansion of higher education in China meets the dual objectives of popularizing education at the primary level and increasing the level of scientific and technological expertise in higher education. The mistake is not so much in the sectors in which they concentrated their educational resources, but in how the already inadequate resources available for secondary levels are used. The perversity of the system is well documented, not only by Professor Pepper but also by Stanley Rosen in his study of how the key-point school classroom draws students, how students were basically bribed to stay in the normal classroom, how teachers are discouraged that the best students are taken out of the school system, and so on. There is the skewed allocation of resources in the secondary sector. Yet if one has limited resources to begin with and one wants mass literacy, as well as scientific and technological leaders at the top, then people must get to college so they can become leaders. There are really not many choices left for the Chinese. They have taken the most dynamic and most educatable students in the secondary school system and have concentrated their resources on them.

Finally, in terms of adopting features of the Western educational system, some have wondered whether China would adopt the worst of the Western educational system and synthesize these with the worst of the Chinese culture.

I also question why peasants in the countryside are so concerned about their children going to college. My understanding is that peasants have always found it difficult to imagine the benefits of even sending their children to high school. Moreover, if they are so against agricultural middle schools, and these have not worked out, why then are they so persistent in pushing agricultural middle schools? In conclusion, I want to point out how eclectic the Western education model is. In fact, there is no one model of Western education to look at. In my research I find it interesting that, without a plan, the Chinese are picking and choosing from a diversity of models and values in the Western system to enrich their own system.

8

THE INTELLECTUALS IN THE DENG ERA

Merle Goldman

UNTIL the Tiananmen massacre of June 4, 1989, and its aftermath, the position of the intellectuals under the Deng Xiaoping regime had improved considerably since the Mao years. The higher intellectuals, defined as those with university degrees or some university education, number about six million. Although proportionately small, about 0.6 percent of the population, the Deng regime regards these people as the key to China's modernization. This view, plus the fear of another Cultural Revolution, not only limited the political repression of intellectuals, but also enhanced their stature. They had more leeway and access to the outside world than at any other time since 1949. Characterized as indispensable in achieving modernization, they were shifted from the bourgeois and even reactionary classification to members of the working class. They enjoyed better working conditions, more responsibility, and opportunities to travel abroad. More significant, the party acknowledged that not only the anti-intellectual violence of the Cultural Revolution, but the party's monopoly over intellectual life, as well as over the economic and political structure, had led to stagnation. Thus, the party retreated somewhat from the intellectual realm and partially devolved authorities to the professionals, technocrats, and managers in specialized fields. Consequently, intellectuals gained some degree of professional autonomy.

Diverse opinions on a wide range of issues were expressed in the daily media, as well as in specialized journals and at conferences; the press was filled with debates on a variety of subjects and with suggestions for reform, even political reform. Whereas under Mao, except for the Hundred Flowers of 1956 and the first half of 1957, debate and criticism were permitted but only in a veiled form and with subtle inferences, under Deng, until June 4, 1989, there was open, lively public debate by professionals, intellectuals, and officials. Basic policies were discussed and challenged in public forums, and different newspapers and journals openly took sides on public issues. The official party newspaper, *People's Daily*, tended to express more reformist views; the official theoretical journal, *Red Flag*, more conservative views. At the same time there existed, until they were closed in June 1989, semi-independent papers such as the *World Economic Herald* in Shanghai and *Economic Weekly* in Beijing.

Similarities and Differences in the Treatment of Intellectuals Between the Mao and Deng Eras

Considerable as these improvements were, they did not occur steadily nor were they secure, as proven by the ease with which the Jiang Zemin-Li Peng regime were able to roll them back. Although the reform era of 1978 until mid-1989 was more flexible and provided some autonomy especially in private life, the party's control of intellectuals remained. Until 1989, the reform leaders Deng, Zhao Ziyang, and Hu Yaobang encouraged the intellectuals to participate in policymaking, a sharp contrast to Mao's hostility toward the intellectuals after 1957. They sought to change the relatively uneducated political elite into an intellectual-technocratic elite. Only 4 percent of the party had a college education and more than half were illiterate or had only a primary school education. But the more conservative leaders, the party elders and former Long Marchers—Peng Zhen, Chen Yun, Bo Yibo, Li Xiannian, Wang Zhen, Yang Shangkun, and their associates—sought to prevent any diminution of the party's authority in the intellectual realm, as well as in the political realm.

On the local level, officials were reluctant to give intellectuals responsibilities and appropriate positions and, in some cases, refused to make restitution from past abuses. Working under untutored, jealous cadres, many intellectuals endured poor working conditions, inadequate housing, and meager salaries. Even the reform leaders did not fully trust the intellectuals, as evidenced in the continuation of political campaigns against them. They were subjected to the cycles of relative repression and relative relaxation that characterized the Mao era. Although the cycles of relaxation were much longer and more frequent than in the Mao era, the Deng regime continued Mao's contradictory approach toward the intellectuals: on the one hand, it wanted them to be productive and creative in their professions in order to modernize China; on the other, it set limits on their ideas and indoctrinated them in the party line, whatever it may be at any given time.

As under Mao, the shifts in policy toward intellectuals also had a dynamic of their town. The party tightened its controls until the intellectuals appeared reluctant to produce; it then relaxed its controls, until its political authority appeared threatened. In intervals of relative relaxation, the party fostered or at least permitted intellectual debates, Western influence, and criticism of the bureaucracy in order to root out abuses and make the economy run more efficiently. It initiated and established the framework within which, at least in the beginning, intellectuals were to express themselves. But although the party limited the scope and fixed the terms in which the discourse was to be carried on, it could not fully control the response. Some intellectuals demanded individual self-expression in their own work; others demanded a voice on broader political issues. When criticism and discussion went beyond criticism of individual bureaucrats to criticism of the system and suggestions of alternatives, the regime cracked down with varying degrees of intensity.

The oscillations in policy toward the intellectuals under Deng, as well as under Mao, were also determined by political factors, particularly factional maneuvering and power struggles in top leadership. Once the remnant top Maoists were pushed out of power in 1980, divisions in the coalition that brought about their demise began to emerge. These divisions reflected policy as well as power differences. In post-Mao China, the conservative and reform leaders both advocated economic modernization, but the conservatives viewed party hegemony, unity, and stability as prerequisites for economic development and opposed fundamental systemic change. They also were against the disruption and chaos of the Cultural Revolution. Therefore, they opposed mass movements and spontaneous demonstrations. When they talked of legal reform, they did not mean legal checks on the abuse of power, but the regularization of party procedures and supervision over society. They wanted contact with the West in order to import selectively Western science, technology, and capital, but they did not want to import Western values and culture. They drew their support from the bureaucracy, fearful that change would reduce their prerogatives, and from a generally widespread anxiety that change may lead to open conflict and another Cultural Revolution.

The reform leaders were more willing to experiment with economic practices, such as the market and political procedures, by allowing more democratic practices on the local level. Most important, they formed a tacit alliance with the intellectuals, not only to gain their cooperation and support in economic reforms, but also in opposition to the conservatives. Hu Yaobang, as the head of the Organization Department from December 1977 to December 1978 and as the party's general secretary from 1981 until January 1987, oversaw the rehabilitation of thousands of intellectuals who were victims not only of the Cultural Revolution but also of the anti-rightist campaign of 1957–59. He gained a reputation as the official patron of the intellectuals. Along with Zhao, he was willing to tolerate intellectual diversity, even in the reinterpretation of Marxism-Leninism. He and Zhao may not have wanted genuine democratic reforms, but they were willing to tolerate discussion of them.

Their leader Deng, however, wanted administrative reforms, but was much less tolerant of demands of democratic reforms. He allowed the activists of the Democratic Movement of the late 1970s to criticize Mao and the Maoists in the top leadership, but once he purged the Maoists, he suppressed the movement and jailed its leaders. He asserted in March 1979 that all discussion must take place within the limits of the four fundamental principles: adherence to socialism, people's democratic dictatorship, the party, and Marxism-Leninism-Maoism. Although he wanted more scope for technical and managerial talent, he, like the conservatives, insisted on party hegemony. Deng was the leader of the reformists, but at certain times and in 1989, he joined with the conservatives not only because of the need to compromise with them in order to undercut their opposition and ensure implementation of economic reforms, but also because he agreed with their view on the party's monopoly of power. Thus, policy and ideological conflicts were intertwined with power interests.

One of the conflicts between the reform leaders and intellectuals, on one side, and the conservatives and sometimes Deng, on the other, revived the nineteenth-century debate over the *ti*, Chinese principle, and the *yong*, Western function. While the reform leaders may tolerate debate and the intellectuals suggest revisions of the *ti*, the conservatives, like their nineteenth-century predecessors, distrusted, resisted and even sabotaged efforts to change the *ti*, which in the twentieth century is Marxism-Leninism, rather than Confucianism. They realized that even a partial revision of the *ti* might loosen their monopoly on the exercise of power. Therefore, they staunchly opposed any introduction of the Western *ti*, specifically democratic practices and intellectual freedom, which they denounced as spiritual pollution and bourgeois liberalization. By contrast, the reform leaders were not against, and most intellectuals were for, importing some Western *ti* with the Western *yong* and modifying certain aspects of Marxism-Leninism in order to adapt it to the changing economy. The reform leaders were more in the tradition of the Hundred Day reformers of the late nineteenth century who radically reinterpreted Confucianism; some of their intellectual associates were more in the tradition of their May Fourth predecessors who sought to replace Confucianism with Western political and social institutions. Thus, there was even a tension between the reformers and some of their intellectual allies, as well as between the reformers and the conservatives.

As under Mao, political factions used and manipulated the intellectuals for their own political purposes. They attempted to seize the initiative by directing intellectuals to write articles, conduct debates, and hold conferences in order to influence elite public opinion. Because the reform leaders had a tacit alliance with the intellectuals, they had an advantage in this propaganda struggle, but the conservatives had a number of older intellectuals who were allied with them in the revolutionary period and in the 1950s who espoused their views. In what Carol Hamrin[1] has characterized as reform "surges," the intellectuals allied with the reform leaders provided positive reinforcement, but, as in the Mao years, they invariably went much further and asked for much greater changes than even their reform patrons desired, thereby weakening their patrons and provoking conservative "backlashes," in which the intellectuals allied with the conservatives retaliated against their more liberal counterparts. Although until June 1989 there were more genuinely intellectual debates on specific academic issues, the debates, reflecting conflicts among the top leaders over power as well as issues, still dominated the intellectual scene.

Because of the regime's commitment to economic and technological modernization, even the conservatives until June 1989 did not pressure intellectuals to conform to the point of producing an atmosphere that would altogether stifle their productivity and initiative. Without Mao's charismatic leadership and his particular animosity toward intellectuals and especially after the trauma of the Cultural Revolution, even if the regime wished to mobilize mass movement, incite fanaticism, and direct violence against the intellectuals as in the past, it would have been very difficult. Therefore, the emphasis until June 1989 was on relaxation rather than tightening of controls against intellectuals and the repressive phases were briefer and much less extreme than in the Maoist period. The approach was more moderate for fear of reviving the Cultural Revolution's repressive practices and disrupting economic modernization. The party still had the power to isolate, discredit, and coerce any intellectual it designated, but until the Tiananmen Square massacre, it was more selective, and did not condemn all their colleagues and families as under Mao. Moreover, the victims did not become nonpersons. After a time, they were able to return to positions somewhat related to their skills.

Differences in the Role of the Intellectual in the Mao and Deng Eras

Scientists and Engineers in Post-Mao China

That similar calls for far-reaching departures were also being heard in the Soviet Union and Eastern Europe in the 1980s suggests that the demands of Chinese intellectuals and reform officials for radical change were more than a reaction to the Cultural Revolution trauma. They, like their Communist brethrens, were also responding to the technological backwardness of their countries vis-à-vis the West and Japan. Thus, reforming science and technology became crucial to the reform process. China's opening to the outside world under Deng until at least June 1989 had been more extensive and lasted longer than at any other time in the People's Republic of China (PRC). The influx of Western ideas, learning, and methodologies and the exposure of China's intellectuals to the West engendered skepticism not only about Marxism-Leninism and the one-party state, but also about the party leadership and political system that had allowed China to fall so far behind scientifically and economically, especially with their East Asian neighbors who until modern times had followed China's lead.

When the party came to power in 1949, one of its major goals was to modernize China's science and technology. Like China's nineteenth-century self-strengtheners and their Soviet mentors, they regarded the development of science and technology as the means to achieving wealth, power, and status in the international arena. Despite the twists and turns of policies, this goal has remained quite consistent. The one exception was the ten years of the Cultural Revolution, after which China's leaders, as well as intellectuals, became increasingly aware of China's backwardness. This consciousness generated a sense of urgency to make up for lost time. To become an advanced scientific and technological society by the twenty-first century became an obsession.

Deng's China, however, is constrained by its emulation of the Soviet model in the 1950s.[2] Along with receiving considerable Soviet assistance in technological expertise, equipment, and training of Chinese students in the Soviet Union, China also received the Soviet system of scientific and technological organization. It was characterized by a deemphasis on research in universities and centralization of research in institutes under an Academy of Science, giving high priority to research related to military and heavy industrial needs. As in the Soviet Union, the scientific advances in the research institutes did not flow into industry and the economy. Research activities became isolated from production activities. Furthermore, achieving production quotas rather than quality goods was the measure of success. Power over activities related to science and technology and within the research institutes was determined by a handful of political leaders who had little understanding of science and technology.

Periodically, Mao shook up the encrusted Soviet model as in the Great Leap Forward and Cultural Revolution, in which he imposed his, rather than the Soviet's, criteria onto technological and economic activities. He emphasized mass participation, egalitarianism, self-reliance, and indigenous scientific and technological development. Maoist activists took over scientific and technological tasks from professionals who were sent to the countryside and factories to learn from peasants and workers. Political mobilization and ideological exhortation rather than scientific research and laboratory experiments were to achieve technological breakthroughs. Central planning of science and technology was disrupted and power devolved to institutes and ministries with even less interactions than before. More damaging were the political campaigns that demoralized and decimated several generations, particularly in the Cultural Revolution when most academic, professional, and scientific activities were stopped as scientists, along with writers and social scientists, were persecuted, reeducated, and sent away for labor reform.

The Deng regime attempted not only to rectify the abuses of Mao's policies, but, more important, to do away with the Soviet system which it regarded as obstructing China's entrance into the age of high technology. It decentralized resources and authority to lower levels in order to reduce stifling effects of the Soviet-style centralized control while, at the same time, it concentrated overall direction in the State Council Leading Group for Science and Technology. It also encouraged universities to engage in scientific research as was done before 1949.

Research centers and universities were also encouraged to participate in the market. They were to compete for projects and contract their services to economic enterprises. Supposedly as these practices took hold, institutes would become increasingly self-supporting and the central government would gradually decrease its direct funding of research except in high priority areas, such as defense. As the role of the party diminished in scientific and technological matters, scientific research became increasingly independent of political control. Some research institutes even formed joint ventures with economic enterprises and gradually merged with them. "Research development production alliances" were created in key industrial cities, such as Harbin, Shanghai, and Dalian. Because greater mobility is necessary to facilitate the diffusion of ideas, concepts, and a more rational distribution of skilled manpower, contracts, private consulting and moonlighting helped break the vertical rigidities and allowed some movement of technical personnel. Revision in ideology also buttressed use of the market in science and technology.[3] In Deng's China, science and technology were no longer treated as free goods, but as commodities that could be bought and sold. This revision was institutionalized in a patent system established in April 1985, which legally provided material incentives for scientific and technological innovation. For those engaged in basic research, as well as applied research, a Chinese Science Foundation, patterned on the United States' National Science Foundation, was established in February 1986 to allocate funds through peer review and competition rather than by administrative decree and party favors.

Another reform that helped insulate science and technology from political interference was the election of directors of institutes by their colleagues. In 1981, President Lu Jiaxi of the Academy of Sciences was elected by his peers, though when he was forced to resign in 1987, his replacement was appointed by the party. Still, the new president Zhou Guanzhao, is a highly respected physicist, trained in the Soviet Union, who became directly involved in advising the political leadership on scientific matters. Until Zhao Ziyang's purge in June 1989, economists at the Economic Institute of the Academy of Social Sciences, along with think tanks in the State Council and Central Committee advised on economic matters.

These reforms—decentralization of research, the introduction of a scientific market, private consulting, increased mobility, and peer evaluation—have the potential for a fundamental structural change because they undermine the party's monopoly of control over science and technology. Like the reforms in other areas, such as agriculture, they obviated the party's entrenched bureaucracy and lessened its authority to intervene in such critical areas as the selection of research projects, promotion of particular scientists, and distribution of financial resources. Equally important in undermining the party's power in the scientific and technological realm was the reestablishment of ties with the international scientific community that had been severed in 1949.

Precisely because the reforms and international contacts were a threat to the bureaucracy's vested interests, party officials in science and technology obstructed and in some cases even resisted their full implementation. Furthermore, their antagonism was exacerbated by the scientists' opportunities to earn additional income and study abroad, opportunities not readily available to bureaucrats. Ideological factors also stiffened the bureaucracy's resistance. The scientific bureaucrats were not against scientific and technological development per se, but some shared the concern Mao tried to redress in the Great Leap Forward and the Cultural Revolution—a concern that faces all modernizing societies: as science and technology modernize, they become the preserve of a core of apolitical experts engaged in specialized activities that exclude the masses, which inevitably increases inequalities. Perhaps it is impossible to create a modern science without a degree of exclusivity. Nevertheless, despite the destructiveness of Cultural Revolution policies toward science and technology, Mao was facing an important issue in a nation's development—can it truly be modernized scientifcally if the masses of people are excluded from the process? Thus the reforms in science and technology were only beginnings, most of which still remained more in the realm of intent than reality. As in other areas, there was a difference between enunciation of policies and their effective implementation, which have been thwarted by the very bureaucrats and cadres who were to carry them out.

The resistance of the entrenched bureaucracy was reinforced by the Deng regime's continuing use of political campaigns against the intellectuals. The campaigns were not against scientists; in fact, scientists were explicitly excluded from them. With the important exception of Fang Lizhi, most of the targets were nonscientific intellectuals, but the way in which the regime treated the nonscientists affected the scientists. If the nonscientific intellectuals were inhibited from learning from abroad and were subjected to arbitrary, repressive treatment, it intimidated scientists as well, especially those who from 1966 to 1976 were subjected to violence and humiliation just because of their Western orientation and expertise. Scientists need sustained effort and extensive, ongoing interaction with the international community. Periodic restrictions on the flow of experts, information, and initiative disrupt the continuity and contacts that transcend disciplines, institutions, and borders, necessary for modernizing science and technology.

True, even with the much longer and more drastic political interruptions under Mao, China was able to imitate and even modify some Western science and technology. While relying on the Soviet model and using a centralized system of direction, it developed rocket and space technology and made synthetic insulin, synthetic ribonucleic acid, germanium crystal, and state of the art advances in superconductivity at relatively high temperatures. Certain pockets of excellence may be created through a combination of trained manpower, local initiatives, and central government priorities. But China's aspirations are much higher—an advanced science and technology that requires experimentation, uncertainty, questioning, and alternative views. Even in science, the effort to break away from the Soviet and Maoist models ran into bureaucratic resistance and the overall restraint of the Marxist-Leninist ideology, which inhibits inquiry and schools of thought outside the established orthodoxy.

The sudden opening to the outside world, even the exaltation of Western science and technology as the panacea for all China's problems, may be as superficial and shortlived as in the May Fourth era, when the new orthodoxy of Marxism-Leninism replaced the traditional orthodoxy of Confucianism. There is no question that China has potential for modern science and technology. Even with the beginnings of structural reform in science and technology, the research improved and the professional quality rose quickly. The real problem is not the talent or even the age of the equipment in the laboratories; it remains the overriding weight of a political system whose controls, while lessened somewhat by the reforms, still do not allow this talent to express itself fully so as to attain the scientific and technological achievements the regime desires. Modern science requires the establishment of a relatively independent research community with its own norms and objectives. Its criteria for achievement, based on ability and scholarly attainment, conflict with the party's criteria based on seniority and political orthodoxy. A Leninist party state, even one that gives its scientists a degree of autonomy, stifles the ethos of wide-ranging scientific inquiry, tolerance of error, testing of new ideas, and open communication and free exchange with the outside world on a continuing basis required for scientific advancement. The scientific profession inherently challenges dogma. For these reasons, China's scientists have joined with their nonscientific colleagues to demand institutions and laws that will encourage and protect this ethos. Such an ethos ultimately challenges the party's authority, based on Marxism-Leninism.

The Hungarian writers, George Konrad and Ivan Szelenyi, in the book, *Intellectuals on the Road in Class Power*, argue that as communist regimes in post-Stalinist Eastern Europe abandoned their revolutionary goals and made concessions to technocrats in order to modernize, an alliance gradually formed between the political leadership and technocrats. This alliance opened the way for increasing wealth, status, and political clout of scientists and technocrats, who desire expensive equipment, foreign travel, and membership on important advisory councils. Thus, this alliance has not benefited and has even hurt nonscientific intellectuals.

The experience of scientists in China, however, suggests that it is difficult to isolate the scientists from the fate of other intellectuals. A number of talented scientists suffered in the anti-rightist campaign. In the Cultural Revolution, Mao tried to protect scientists from the violence of the Red Guards, but the dynamics of the campaign inevitably swept up virtually all the intellectuals. As in Eastern Europe, the scientists and technocrats have readier access to training, responsibility, study abroad, and influence on policies in their areas of expertise than intellectuals in the humanities and creative arts, but the split that Konrad and Szelenyi describe in Eastern Europe has not yet occurred in China. In fact, among the leaders of the 1989 student demonstrations, a disproportionately greater number came from the sciences, and members of the Academy of Sciences were active participants. Moreover, the dynamics of the opening to the outside world have affected the literary intellectuals, as well as the scientists.

Once the door is open, as China discovered in the nineteenth century, it is impossible to control what comes in and who is influenced by it. Western political and philosophical concepts flow in along with scientific ideas and technological gadgets. Li Honglin, an ideological spokesman for the reformers, has pointed out that it is impossible to exclude the nonscientific realm from foreign influence without hurting the scientific realm. He acknowledges that "decadent and degenerate ideology and culture will enter our culture along with Western science and technology and contaminate the air. But even if the door were closed somewhat, such 'dirty things' would enter anyway from outside through the cracks in the walls."[4] Thus, to give scientists and engineers access to the outside world inevitably allows access to nonscientific intellectuals as well.

Even if the regime should play off scientists against nonscientists, neither group may be willing to play the game. Not only would nonscientists like Li Honglin protest, but, more important, the periodic threat of repression and closing off of contact with the outside world, though primarily directed against nonscientists, also frightens scientists. They may be less directly affected, but they also were buffeted by shifts in the political line. Furthermore, with scientists more involved politically in post-Mao China, they, too, are bound to become scapegoats, as happened to Fang Lizhi in the campaign against "bourgeois liberalization in 1987 and in June 1989. Perhaps most important, scientists still remember their persecutions in the Cultural Revolution when their attackers made little distinction between writer and scientist. The threat of another Cultural Revolution unites all intellectuals as they had never been united before to resist an attack against any group among them. Because of the specter of another Cultural Revolution, scientists share with nonscientific intellectuals an interest in building institutions and establishing laws to protect themselves and their autonomy. Finally, as the scientific elite is expanded by students who have studied abroad, this elite, exposed to greater intellectual freedom and professional autonomy, will greatly strengthen the constituency for the right to engage more freely in one's professional work, unencumbered by political demands. Unfortunately, these processes had not gone far enough by June 1989 to protect scientists as well as nonscientists. Once again, the regime made no distinction between scientists and nonscientists in attacking those infected with "bourgeois liberalism."

The Nonscientific Intellectuals

The reform of the social sciences, at least until the Tiananmen Square massacre, also had the potential for challenging the party's political monopoly. As in the Mao period, scholarship still was subordinated to the political line, ideology, and factions, but there was greater diversity of the subject matter studied and techniques used. For the first time since 1949, Western approaches in the social sciences and humanities were considered objectively. More attention was given to factual accuracy and there was more willingness to engage in wide-ranging debates on doctrinal issues. The disciplines of anthropology, sociology, and political science were revived after twenty years of virtual suppression. As at the turn of the century, when thousands of Chinese students went abroad in search of political and economic theories to strengthen Chinese society, so, too, under Deng thousands flocked to Japan and the West in search of ways to reform Chinese society. Like their predecessors, they shared a commitment to making China wealthy and powerful.

Modern social sciences were introduced into China around the turn of the century through translations of Western books. From the onset they were meant to serve the political purpose of reforming China and facilitating its national survival. In addition to medicine, science, and engineering, Western style universities also taught history, literature, political economy, and political philosophy. Although they were turning away from the old traditions, they were actually building on the traditional subjects of study and shared the traditional concern with political issues. Even though many social scientists were educated in the West, their work was politically oriented especially to strengthening China.

With the reorganization of higher education along Soviet lines after 1949, the teaching of the humanities and the social sciences was done primarily in the universities and the research primarily in the Institutes of Philosophy and Social Sciences in the Academy of Sciences. When a separate Academy of Social Sciences was established in May 1977, the social sciences were given importance in their own right and were at least theoretically assured a degree of autonomy given to their scientific colleagues. In the slogans of the day, they were to "emancipate minds" and "seek truth from facts." Controversies were no longer to be initiated or resolved by political leaders and ideological doctrine, but with reference to empirical data and rigorous debate. All these activities, however, were ultimately political in that they contribute to China's modernization.

By August 1984, the Academy of Social Sciences had thirty-two research institutes, a postgraduate school, and a publishing house. It employed more than five thousand researchers and three thousand staff.[5] Its specific role was to advise on policy. Its economic institutes studied Western economic institutions, foreign investment, technology transfer, and theories of modernization. In addition to the think tanks under the State Council and the Central Committee, they were among a number of different sources contributing to policy formulation. The humanists were in charge of developing a modern culture and revising ideology in line with the changes in the economy. They were to inculcate social and political values deemed necessary for modernization.

Sociologists, political scientists, and anthropologists experimented with Western techniques, such as quantitative analysis, survey research, and opinion polls to ascertain the views of the population. These methods were to provide a quantified, more accurate sample on which the leadership could devise policies more responsive to the people's will than those based hitherto on the leaders' ideology, political interests, or whim. They could even provide a "truer" version of the people's wishes than the ones the critical intellectuals perceived and presented in their writings. It is unlikely that after the Tiananmen Square massacre the social sciences will be allowed to develop as an independent profession and carry on their inquiries unimpeded by political considerations at least until the party elders pass from the scene. They have the potential for providing the leadership with more objective sources of information on which to devise policies. Nevertheless, even if the social scientists are totally committed to their methodologies and have no desire to make political statement, if their work presents information that contradicts the party's view of society or the party's interest, it is unlikely that it will be listened to and can easily be suppressed.

Differing methodologies, as much as the differing content, also challenged the party and Marxism-Leninism. In 1985, for example, two major controversies arose over methodology. Ma Ting, a young scholar at Nanjing University, suggested that Western economic theories, econometrics, and quantitative techniques might be more helpful in developing the economy than the Marxist political-economic approach. The head of the Institute of Literature Liu Zaifu recommended Western literary theories, such as structuralism and deconstruction, as more instructive in understanding literature than socialist realism and the substitution of politics for art. It is not surprising that the conservatives were enraged at these recommendations because, as they rightly charged, the two scholars were rejecting the party's ideology and thereby its leadership. Without institutional protections, the social scientists' more variegated view of society will not be heard.

In the Deng era, literature, as in traditional times and under Mao, remains the principal means for expressing criticism of the regime. This criticism began with the "wound literature," stories, plays, and poems on the officially approved topic of persecution by the Gang of Four in the Cultural Revolution. But by the mid-1980s, writings on the Cultural Revolution were gradually being restricted because, as Deng pointed out, to criticize Mao's policies also meant criticizing party leaders like himself who had also supported Mao's policies. The genre of "the wounded" also became outmoded as the mood of the nation turned more to the present and was replaced by the genre of "exposure," which reveals the corruption and abuses of officials. This genre was not new. It existed in traditional times, during the May Fourth era, and even under Mao, especially during the Hundred Flowers when the writers Liu Binyan and Wang Meng exposed incompetent officials who were corrupting the system. A new trend in the Deng era, led by Wang Meng, who was to become Minister of Culture in 1985, and a number of younger writers, is that they write less about overt political issues and more about the emotions, frustrations, and relationships of everyday life. More important, they experiment with a variety of styles, intricate language, folk tales, and stream of consciousness to evoke memories, inner feelings, and random associations. They regarded these new techniques as more appropriate to their subject matter.

Even though the Deng regime initially encouraged greater leeway in style and content in an effort to win the support of the creative intellectuals, to be artistically apolitical in a society in which politics hitherto permeated every aspect of life expressed a rejection of political interference in one's creative work. It was a direct challenge to the party's politicization of culture. Some writers, such as Wang Meng, have become less political because they also believe that when literature is used for didactic purposes, it stifles the writer's ability to express genuine emotions and create artistic works. This apolitical trend was most noticeable among writers in their thirties and early forties who spent their formative years in the Cultural Revolution. Disillusioned, they were skeptical of all politics. For the first time in China, serious writers explicitly departed from the moral-political orientation of their traditional May Fourth and party elders, shunning political commentary for self-expression. Although the Deng regime periodically cracked down on what it called "obscure" poetry, unintelligible to the ordinary people, it treated apolitical writers less harshly than it did the critical intellectuals. Academic discussion of modernism was allowed periodically. There was greater tolerance of experimentation with style than with content because it less directly challenged the regime.

Although political control of high literary culture continued, the Deng regime showed greater restraint than Mao in coercing the whole literary profession. Individual writers were singled out as negative examples, but not the whole profession, as in the Great Leap Forward and the Cultural Revolution. Equally important, instead of insisting that literature serve politics and the political line, Deng asked it to serve the more general cause of socialism and especially modernization. Supposedly writers could write in any style they pleased and on any subject they wished as long as they assisted the cause of modernization. Furthermore, until June 1989 literature no longer had to cater only to workers, peasants, and soldiers, but to all social groups. While none of these injunctions provided autonomy, they made it possible to write less politicized literature. More important, breaking away from the realistic and socialist realist legacy and experimenting with styles led to experimentation with content as well. They explored new, hitherto "forbidden" topics. In reaction to the collectivist emphasis of the Cultural Revolution, some fiction in the Deng era dwelled on the individual consciousness.

The Critical Intellectuals

Whereas the scientists, engineers, professionals, and the relatively apolitical writers challenged the party's monopoly of power indirectly and potentially, the critical intellectuals challenged it directly and immediately until they were silenced in June 1989. As in the past, a tiny minority of intellectuals, the critical intellectuals, made political demands and exposed repression, bureaucratic privilege, arbitrary rule, corruption, and irrational practices. Most of them were Marxists who pointed out the difference between Marxist ideals and the realities of everyday life, even under the

Deng regime with which they were initially allied. Most sought change not by destroying the prevailing political order but by reforming it. In the initial period after Deng's accession to power in late 1978, they saw themselves as they had in the Mao years, as the conduit through which the "people's" views reached the political leaders and through which the leaders learned of the effects of their policies. They were the intermediaries who interpreted "the murmurings" of the people to the government. If the leaders listened to the voices of the people, as interpreted by these self-appointed spokespersons, and responded, then the relationship between the leaders and the led would be strengthened and their interests would be harmonized. They regarded the government as inherently good and wanted to ensure that it lived up to its benevolent image. This elitist view, which looks on the "people" as an undifferentiated mass and in whose names they speak, is in the traditional image of the literati's paternalistic responsibility for the common people. As with the literati, it gives the critical intellectuals a special status and implicitly accepts an autocratic polity.

By the second half of the 1980s, however, the critical intellectuals were no longer willing merely to accept concessions from the political leadership. In addition to their experiences in the anti-rightist campaign and the Cultural Revolution, the periodic attacks on them in the Deng era made them realize that even when rights were given to them by an enlightened leadership, they could be taken away. Thus, they began to demand institutional and legal guarantees of civil rights, freedom of expression, and the establishment of some form of representative government in order to check abuses of political power. They sought protection from the retribution they endured in the Deng as well as Mao period for expressing differing and individual views. They were no longer willing to rely merely on the good services of the party leadership, even when those leaders were their patrons.

They pointed out the gap between state and society that began with the alienation of the peasants in the Great Leap Forward and widened still further in the Cultural Revolution as the intellectuals and officials became the chief victims and virtually the whole population suffered from its violence and anarchy. As the famous writer Ba Jin declared, "Never before in the history of man nor in any other country have people had such a fearful and ridiculous, weird and tragic experience as in the Cultural Revolution."[6] One legacy was the willingness of some leaders, such as Hu Yaobang and Zhao Ziyang, as well as intellectuals, to question the political and economic system that had allowed such a tragedy to occur. For the first time, critical intellectuals also questioned the elitist assumption they had held in the Maoist era, in the tradition of their principled literati predecessors, that they spoke on behalf of the people or at least for the benefit of the people. They also questioned their previous assumption that leaders, when properly informed of the people's will would respond accordingly. An important departure in the Deng era is the critical intellectuals' realization that these assumptions may have contributed to the repressive system itself and that perhaps another approach, such as representative government and freedom of speech, might more effectively close the gap between the leaders and the led.

China's reform leaders and intellectuals recognized that the Cultural Revolution was not due merely to the abuses of a single leader, however tyrannical he was, but to the very nature of the system in which he operated. Consequently, they called for far-reaching departures from prevailing practices across all areas of life—the economy, society, culture, and even the political system. As in the past, when political leaders mobilized groups of intellectuals to articulate their ideas in the public arena, the intellectuals articulated their own particular demands, as well as those of their patrons, demands that sometimes differed from their patron's. Not only did the nature of their demands differ from the Mao era, their methods also differed. Because the Deng regime was less oppressive, they spoke out much more directly than in the Mao era and resorted less to the traditional use of the oblique, subtle criticism. Moreover, whereas under Mao most critical intellectuals were mostly literary intellectuals, under Deng their ranks were expanded with scientists and economists who also actively engaged in public debate.

The leaders of the critical intellectuals were primarily in their fifties and early sixties. Many of them were labeled "rightists" in the late 1950s. They had "lost" not only the ten years of the Cultural Revolution, but more than twenty years at the hands of the very same people, such as Deng Xiaoping and Peng Zhen, in power in the post-Cultural Revolution period. Their protests were against the people and system that had allowed such traumas as the anti-rightist campaign and the Cultural Revolution to occur.

While most of the critical intellectuals justified their actions in Marxist terms, their interpretations of Marxism drew on their Confucian heritage, the Western democratic concepts introduced into China in the early decades of the twentieth century, and Western Marxism. Their ideas and practices also resembled their Soviet and East European counterparts because of continuing contact with them and also because of structural similarities with their critical roles vis-à-vis the ruling Communist parties. Although some of their ideas overlapped with the ex-Red Guard democratic activists of the late 1970s and student demonstrators of the 1980s, the way in which they protested until the 1989 Tiananmen Square demonstration was more in the style of their literati predecessors than in the more Western-style of the democratic activists who expressed themselves through unofficial channels, self-printed pamphlets, wall posters, demonstrations, and in talks with Western journalists. Like their literati predecessors, they were well connected and, under Deng, connected directly and indirectly to Zhao Ziyang and especially to Hu Yaobang, for whom several of them had worked in the 1950s, when Hu was the head of the Communist Youth League. They published in the most prestigious newspapers and journals and held positions high up in the intellectual hierarchy.

In return for these positions, the reform leaders expected that the critical intellectuals would perform a practical function by lobbying for reform and attacking those opposed to reform. Like a number of enlightened emperors or Mao in the Hundred Flowers and Gorbachev in the Soviet Union, the Deng leadership not only encouraged criticism of officials who abused the system in order to make it run more efficiently, they also encouraged attack on their political opponents who obstructed the reforms. Similarly, as under Mao, the critical intellectuals used their access to the party's newspapers and journals to insert their own ideas. What is different in the Deng period is that the memory of the Cultural Revolution and desire to be accepted in the international community limited the party's repression of the critical intellectuals and, at the same time, impelled the critical intellectuals to speak out more persistently and more daringly than they had before the Cultural Revolution.

Under the Confucian system and Mao's rule, there was no distinction between the state and society. Most intellectuals, even the Western-trained ones, had accepted this undifferentiated view because at the time of the 1949 revolution, they believed the Communist party was the only political group that could unite and save the nation. Because of this unreflective patriotism, most of them went along with the party's persecution of the left-wing writer Hu Feng and his coterie in 1955 as "traitors." Many acquiesced and even participated in the condemnation in 1957–59 of more than half a million of China's brightest and best intellectuals as "rightists" who, at Mao's behest in the Hundred Flowers movement, had criticized bureaucratic abuses. Even those designated as "rightists" initially believed that their criticism of the party bureaucracy in the Hundred Flowers had hurt the nation. In addition to their feelings of patriotism, which justified closing ranks against officially designated scapegoats, intellectuals feared that if they did not acquiesce they, too, would be labeled "traitors" or "rightists," which could result in public disgrace, isolation, labor reform, and even imprisonment for themselves and their families.

As the regime increasingly equated loyalty to the nation with loyalty to the party, however, and in the Cultural Revolution to Mao himself, the intellectuals became more and more alienated. With the persecution of virtually all intellectuals in the Cultural Revolution, the tension between loyalty to their nation and people and loyalty to the party and its political leaders burst out into the open in the post-Mao period. The critical intellectuals, in particular, were no longer willing to equate loyalty to the nation with loyalty to the political leadership. They began to redefine the traditional and Maoist identity of government and society. If leaders ignore the people's cries and draw apart from the people as they did in the Cultural Revolution, then the people's spokespersons must choose between the government and the people. Their articulation of the grievances of the led increasingly took precedence over articulation of the will of the leaders. They no longer equated their support for their country, society, or even their view of Marxism with support for the party or even for a particular faction with which they may be allied. The government and the party they had served had turned against some of them in the anti-rightist campaign, against the peasants in the Great Leap Forward, and against virtually the whole population in the Cultural Revolution. Those experiences had made them realize that what the party or any leader decreed was not necessarily good for the nation or even for socialism.

These views were spelled out by the preeminent critical intellectual, the writer-journalist Liu Binyan, when he returned after twenty-two years in exile as a rightist. In his first major address at the Fourth Congress of the All-China Federation of Literary and Art Circles in the fall of 1979, appropriately entitled "The Call of the Times," he revealed that only when he was sent to the countryside for labor reform did he discover that the lives of the peasants were "exactly the opposite of what the higher levels were saying and what the newspapers were publishing." No matter how much he wanted to believe what the party told him, "I saw that the peasants wanted one thing, the leadership and newspapers something else." When the demands of the people and the demands of the party contradict each other, Liu insisted, "We should listen to the people; we owe allegiance to the welfare and needs of the people," because, as Liu observed, "the party is not infallible." Thus, "when this sort of double truth . . . appears in our lives, writers should obey their feeling of great responsibility to the people."[7] Liu called on his fellow writers to be independent spokespersons who, when confronted with a conflict between what the party decreed and what the people wanted, work with the people.

He deals with this conflict in reportage, *baogao wenxue*, a genre he had learned from the Soviet "thaw" writers of the mid-1950s. It is investigative reporting made into an art form. This conflict is most directly expressed in "In the Second Kind of Loyalty," published in the spring of 1985. He talks of various kinds of loyalties: the most common is the safe one personified by the Lei Feng model, who follows the party's orders, whatever they may be. Then there is the second kind of loyalty, the one Liu most admires. It is personified by two protagonists—Chen Shizhong, a mechanical engineer, and Ni Yuxian, a soldier enrolled in the Shanghai Naval Transport College, whose loyalty to their country and society is much more meaningful than Lei Feng's slavish loyalty to the political line. In the Maoist period, they risked death to point out the abuses of power or to defend others against injustice. Even in the Deng period, where at least in the early stage there was a closer relationship between the leaders and the led, they continued to point out unpleasant facts of party corruption, privilege and deceit. Their loyalty was to the led, not to the leaders.[8]

In the post-Mao period, Liu expresses less of an elitist view than in his earlier work, during the Hundred Flowers, when his heroes were educated party youth who fought against bureaucratic officiousness and incompetence. His protagonists, though somewhat educated and skilled, were marginal figures on the fringes of society, whose moral courage led them to condemn the Great Leap Forward, the Cultural Revolution, and even certain aspects of the Deng period, people like himself. They are isolated individuals, loners with little power, surrounded by the overwhelming majority who commit and acquiesce in abuses. His view is pessimistic, like that of Lu Xun in his early stories—their cries are no match for the evil around them. His only solution for the conflict between the leaders and the led is moral outrage, voiced by individuals like himself who investigate the incidents brought to his attention in letters, petitions, and visits. His reportage functions as remonstrations to the leadership, a traditional approach to redressing grievances.[9] In his belief, until the mid-1980s, that he could interpret the "murmurings" of the people, he is in the traditional literati mold, but in his distinction between the country and society, on the one hand, and the government and leaders, on the other, his views are revolutionary in the Chinese context.

Disillusionment because of the experiences of the anti-rightist campaign, the Great Leap Forward and the Cultural Revolution extended to the orthodox ideology—Marxism-Leninism-Maoism. Actually, the reform leaders themselves, most prominently Hu Yaobang, acknowledged the disillusionment in calls to revise the ideology in line with changes in China, as well as in the rest of the world. The controversial December 7, 1984, *People's Daily* editorial, supposedly based on notes of Hu Yaobang, stated that "We cannot expect the writings of Marx and Lenin of that time to provide solutions to our current problems." The next day, "all" was added to "our current problems," reflecting a disagreement over the editorial. Yet even with the revision, the conclusion is that the orthodox ideology was largely irrelevant. In 1979, the Institute of Marxism-Leninism-Mao Zedong Thought had been established to update the ideology. Su Shaozhi, who became its head in 1982, admitted in an October 21, 1985, article in *People's Daily*, written with the student Ding Xueliang, that "the Cultural Revolution seriously set back Marxism . . . because of all the vicious things done in the period under the guise of Marxism." Therefore, it is necessary "to adopt a creative attitude and developmental view toward Marxism so as to maintain its vitality." Equally subversive to the orthodox ideology was Su's assertion that the intellectuals, not the workers, will lead the way to an advanced industrial society. "Information has replaced material resources as well as man's labor to become the dominant resource for the growth of social wealth." Moreover, "the productive forces of knowledge have become the key factors in productivity, competitiveness, and economic success." He does not blame Marxism itself as the cause of irrelevance and points out its emphasis on the role of technology in transforming society. Rather, he blames "some of our comrades, ignorant of the latest trends of science and technology." This ignorance, he insists, is a consequence not only of the traditional legacy, but also "a rigidity in thinking resulting from years of autocracy and 'leftist' influence."[10] Implicit in his argument is criticism of the system that allowed these negative forces to gain ascendancy. Although his views and those of his colleagues were influenced by the European Marxists' reinterpretations, their analyses stem primarily from their awareness of China's backwardness in the aftermath of the Cultural Revolution.

Another ideological theorist, Wang Ruoshui, deputy editor of the *People's Daily* until he was dismissed in the fall of 1983, expressed the disillusionment of the survivors of the Cultural Revolution and previous campaigns when he pointed out that alienation can exist under socialism. Like the European Marxists, he used Marx's early writings on alienation under capitalism to substantiate his view of alienation under socialism. He began writing on this subject in the late 1970s as part of the outpouring of works that explored the tragic dimensions of the Cultural Revolution. He argued that the system had produced so much suffering and so much violence that it had given rise to the opposite of what was intended. Instead of enhancing man's worth, it had diminished it. Specifically, this alienation was caused by: (1) the cult of personality during Mao's leadership; (2) such irrational economic policies as the Great Leap Forward and emphasis on heavy industry; and (3) the party cadres, supposedly "the servants of the people, transforming themselves into the masters of the people." Merely to overthrow the Gang of Four and to be on guard against another Cultural Revolution are not enough to end the alienation. It was necessary to limit the power of "the high and mighty officials" who were "indifferent to the interests of the people."[11] Although he mentions the need to restrict official power by means of genuine democracy and a legal system, his emphasis, like that of his literati predecessors, is still on ideological rather than institutional change. To counter the oppressive, dehumanizing society that he describes, he calls for a revival of humanism, whose principles he says can be found in Marxism.

Until the mid-1980s, most critical intellectuals were more concerned with ideological means rather than institutional means to achieve their goals. But as the Deng era evolved, they and a number of critical intellectuals began to switch this emphasis, calling for new institutions, as well as humaneness in order to check abusive political power. Despite their courage and willingness to challenge injustice, their method of moral suasion certainly had not saved them under Mao and had not protected them from attacks under Deng. Nor had high political patronage saved them because their patrons could not protect them, not Hu Yaobang who was dismissed from office in 1987 nor Zhao Ziyang even when he remained in office.

The increasing attention the critical intellectuals gave to institutional political change and civil law as the Deng regime proceeded was not only because of China's increasing exposure to Western ideas, it also had to do with the fact that Chinese society in the post-Cultural Revolution period was no longer passive. Because Mao had desanctified the party and incited various groups to rebel against authority, it was no longer possible to impose a "single truth" or dictate to a "unified society." Moreover, the retreat from Mao's utopian visions in the Deng period engendered distrust of social engineering not only among the educated, but also among the peasants who no longer could be treated as mere objects of official policy. Despite the reform leaders' greater willingness to recognize a more diverse society and govern in a more conciliatory, flexible way, they still expressed the traditional and Leninist view that only a small elite can govern and be entrusted with the ideological truth which periodically they attempt to impose even on those intellectuals associated with them. Thus, the critical intellectuals' shift in the mid-1980s from emphasizing moral transformation to increasing emphasis on political and legal checks on power is not only because of Western influence, it was also because of their own treatment and the actions of the Deng regime, their supposed political patrons.

The Party's Response

While the party's reactions to the democratic activists of 1979 was harsh once they had served the party's purposes, it was not until mid-1981 that the Deng regime began to react to the writings of the critical intellectuals and initially was somewhat reluctantly pushed by the military. Still, 1981 marks the beginning of the regime's concern with "bourgeois liberalization," which it defined as a belief in excessive and unchecked freedom that undermines Deng's four fundamental principles. Although Liu Binyan and other writers were criticized behind closed doors, the writer Bai Hua was made the target of the 1981 campaign for his controversial scenario "Unrequited Love," about a well-known artist who returned to China from the United States at the time of the revolution to help his country, only to be persecuted and die fleeing from the Red Guards in the Cultural Revolution.

Although the scenario has some vivid scenes, symbolically suggesting that Mao's rule had been based on superstition, Bai Hua was one of the first publicly to distinguish between loyalty to one's country and loyalty to one's government. Like Liu Binyan and Wang Ruoshui, Bai Hua in this work shows that one can love one's country and countrymen, but be alienated from one's government. Michael Duke, in his book, *Blooming and Contending: Chinese Literature in the Post-Mao Era*,[12] points out that Bai Hua uses the word "Zuoguo" throughout the scenario to describe the artist's patriotism. "Zuoguo" means country and people, but not necessarily government and political party. The only departure from this usage is in the famous scene in which the artist's daughter asks her father, "You love this nation of yours. . . . But does this nation love you?" In this question, she uses the term "guojia," which means government as a geographic unit. That is the meaning of the title. Instead of the government "requiting" the artist for his love of country, it persecutes him. Like his critical intellectual colleagues, Bai Hua no longer equated his country, China, with its government.

The Bai Hua affair was also the first indication of growing tension between the reform and conservative political leaders who had joined together to get rid of the remnant Maoists in the leadership. The military criticized Bai Hua, who worked in the Wuhan Military Region cultural bureau, in order to express its disagreement with some of the reform leadership's laxity on ideological matters, specifically Hu Yaobang, who was in charge of ideology. Consequently, as the campaign, begun by the army's General Political Department, sought to move from the military realm into the civilian realm, Hu urged the civilian press to resist it. Although Hu became the party's general secretary in June 1981, Deng, not Hu, replaced Hua Guofeng as head of the Military Affairs Commission and sided with the military. By the summer of 1981, the party's main papers, especially *People's Daily* and *Wenyi bao* (The Literary Gazette) followed the army's line. Deng's periodic decisions to side with the conservative forces, in this case the military, against his own reform colleagues, was a strategy to co-opt the conservative military and party veterans in order to win their support for his economic reforms. At times he did it also because of conviction as well as tactics. But Deng's compromise with the old guard on intellectual matters, in this case the Bai Hua campaign, gave the conservatives the opportunity to reassert themselves. In early 1982, the conservative ideologist, Deng Liqun, took over the Propaganda Department, and the elderly reform cultural official Zhou Yang retired as its deputy director. At the Twelfth Party Congress, in 1982, the conservative official Hu Qiaomu joined the Politburo and Deng Liqun the Secretariat, respectively, as the members in charge of culture. With their ascension to power, a major campaign was begun to strengthen faith in Communist morality, which was equated with patriotism, a direct rebuke to Bai Hua.

Yet, as opposed to the Mao era when there was a virtual uniformity of views once a campaign was launched, while the Bai Hua campaign against bourgeois liberalism in favor of communist morality was underway, the discussion of alienation under socialism and the relationship between Marxism and humanism, which had been going on since the late 1970s, continued and reached a climax at the centennial celebration of Marx's death in March 1983. There, Zhou Yang reiterated Wang Ruoshui's views against deification of the leadership, irrational economic policies, and a self-serving bureaucratic elite that had ignored the people's needs and induced alienation. Although Zhou Yang had mentioned the existence of alienation in 1963, it was only after the Cultural Revolution that he spoke of it openly as a prevailing feeling. Thus, it was not only critical intellectuals but a prominent, highly respected official who pointed out the disparity between the actions of the party and government and the needs of the population. He also heralded humanism, which he too claimed was included in Marx, as the counter to alienation. His restatement of Wang's ideas and its publication in the *People's Daily* brought them into the political arena.

Suddenly, in October 1983, at the meeting of the Second Plenum of the Twelfth Congress, Deng warned against applying such concepts as humanism and alienation in the abstract. Rather, he insisted these concepts preach the bourgeois theory of human nature, love, individual emancipation, individualism, anarchism, and nihilism. He labeled them "spiritual pollution" and asserted that they provided the theoretical basis for doubting and negating socialism and the party. Deng was genuinely concerned about "decadent" Western ideas and pornography that had seeped into China along with Western science and technology, but he was also again doing a balancing act, compromising with the conservatives. Again, Deng Liqun and Hu Qiaomu used the campaign to confirm ideological orthodoxy, reasserting tighter controls over the intellectuals and attacking Hu Yaobang's tolerance of these matters.

Although Su Shaozhi's institute was saved from being closed down by Hu Yaobang's intervention, the chief public targets of the campaign against spiritual pollution were Zhou Yang, who at the end of October was forced to make a self-criticism for his views on humanism and alienation; Hu Jiwei, chief editor of *People's Daily*, for publishing articles on the subject; and particularly Wang Ruoshui, the deputy editor, who was held responsible for inciting the controversy. He was charged with introducing concepts as if they were applicable to all societies, thereby ignoring the fundamental differences between capitalism and socialism. Moreover, other Western ideas such as Freud's view of the unconscious, Sartre's existentialism, and Kafka's antiauthoritarianism, all of which had been translated and won an audience among intellectuals for their relevance to their own situations, were denounced as spreading pessimism, disorder, and anarchy, similar to that of the Cultural Revolution. Thus, the regime blamed society's malaise and alienation not on the system, leaders, or ideology, but on those who had revealed that such feelings existed.

As opposed to the campaign against Bai Hua, which was limited to the military and literary intellectuals, the campaign against spiritual pollution was carried out on a nationwide scale in all the media, factories, and youth groups, signifying the support of the top leadership. Like the Bai Hua campaign, this one also was involved in factional conflict. The conservative leaders, along with their ideological associates in the cultural realm, pushed the campaign in order to counter increasing ideological confusion and disenchantment, especially among the youth; the reform leaders Hu Yaobang and Zhao Ziyang sought to limit the campaign, fearing its negative effects on the reforms. Hu was vulnerable because it was under his auspices that the reevaluation of Marxism and infusion of Western thought took place. But when Maoists in some local areas tried to revert the Maoist practices in the countryside, and workers were taken from production to study political tracts, Deng then swung his support away from the conservatives and back to the reform leaders in an effort to bring the campaign to a quick conclusion. In January 1984, the conservative ideologue, Hu Qiaomu, signaled the end of the campaign with an authoritative statement in *People's Daily* in which he acknowledged that humanism had played a useful role in the past, but he insisted that any theorizing about "man" in the abstract is a bourgeois view that is opposed to Marxism.[13]

The campaign against spiritual pollution was supposedly over. While it was over in the economy and in science and technology, it was not over in the literary realm, where it continued against Freud, Satre, Kafka, and modernism, and lingered on against writers and artists. The generally passive resistance of the intellectual community in which most refused to criticize their designated colleagues or wrote perfunctory criticisms, in addition to Wang Ruoshui's setting a precedent by refusing to write a self-criticism despite great pressure, led to the gradual dying out of the campaign against the literary intellectuals and the retreat of the conservatives' cultural officials, Hu Qiaomu and Deng Liqun.

In the more relaxed atmosphere of the second half of 1984, references to spiritual pollution in the media virtually disappeared. The media called for academic freedom in all areas of intellectual life and criticized dogmatists for hindering implementation of this freedom. Hu Yaobang succeeded in depriving Deng Liqun of his post as head of the Propaganda Department, though Deng still remained in the Secretariat. Hu replaced Deng with one of his followers, Zhu Houze, head of the Guizhou party committee, and his disciple Hu Qili, a Secretariat member, assumed the overseeing of cultural affairs.

That the demands of the critical intellectuals may have had some influence on policy, at least briefly, is evident at the Fourth Congress of the Chinese Writers Association in December 1984–January 1985, where Hu Qili, with Hu Yaobang sitting behind him, called for "freedom of speech." Such calls had been heard before, during Mao's Hundred Flowers and at the 1979 Fourth Congress of the All-China Federation of Literary and Art Circles, as expressed by Deng Xiaoping himself. What was different this time was the use of a democratic process at a professional conference in the PRC for the first time.[14] With the encouragement of Hu Yaobang, units were able to vote for the individual who was to represent them at the conference by means of secret competitive elections. At the Congress itself, the representatives voted again in secret competitive elections. In other words, there were more candidates than positions for the officials who were to lead the association. The slate voted into office differed sharply from the one originally authorized by the party. Hu had called for these democratic procedures in order to retaliate against those who had been advocates of the spiritual pollution campaign. In addition, these procedures had brought to power intellectuals associated with him. Liu Binyan, for example, had not been on the original official list for a vice chairmanship, but he received the second highest number of votes, second only to Ba Jin. Bai Hua, who had not even been on the original delegation to represent the army, received the highest number of votes in his unit when his unit held secret competitive elections, as Hu Yaobang had ordered. Though Bai Hua was not allowed to head his delegation, he attended the Congress. At the Congress, with the support of Liu Binyan, he was elected to a seat on the Writers' Council. Thus, through these more democratic procedures, Hu Yaobang was able to weaken those who had participated actively in the spiritual pollution campaign and strengthen those who had been criticized by the conservatives. Although his purpose was not democratic, the use of democratic procedures gave a group of intellectuals the opportunity for the first time to vote on their own, rather than the party's, choices, and to experiment with democratic practices.

Hu Qiaomu and Deng Liqun were conspicuously weakened by Hu's maneuvers. When their telegrams of greetings to the Congress were read aloud, there was deadly silence. By contrast, when the telegram from Zhou Yang, who was in the hospital, was read, there was loud, sustained applause. Furthermore, public inquiries were made about writers who had become nonpersons. One of them, Ye Wenfu, whose poem "General, You Cannot Do That" attacked the privileges and corruption of high army officials and who had been personally condemned by Deng Xiaoping, was no longer published. In the past, no one had dared raise inquiries about a nonperson, but at this Congress, several delegates asked what had happened to Ye and other nonpersons. Subsequently, Ye's poems reappeared in the February 1985 issue of *Shikan* (Poetry), a prestigious literary journal.

Some of the delegates at the Congress demanded legal protection for writers, an echo of the demands of the 1979 democratic activists. Most eloquent was the screenwriter Ke Ling, who pointed out that "fundamentally, it is a matter of whether it is rule by law or rule by the individual. In regard to the rights and obligations of writers and artists, there should be explicit and rational regulations to allow for individual achievements and shortcomings, rewards and penalties, and the legality of their actions. . . . The aim is . . . to free them from bureaucratic restrictions." Ke Ling acknowledged, however, that laws alone could not truly protect writers if officials did not enforce these laws. "Of course, even if there are laws to follow, the problem of deviation in exercising the law may emerge."[15]

While the Writers' Congress was in session, a *People's Daily* editorial of January 3, 1985, expressed the view that democracy was necessary in order for economic modernization to succeed, an argument the democratic activist Wei Jingsheng made in his "Fifth Modernization," for which he had been imprisoned. Now the party's newspaper expressed this similar view officially: "The Four Modernizations must be accompanied by political democracy." The editorial, representing Hu Yaobang's views, pointed out that "forbidding people to speak out," "practicing rule by the voice of one man alone," "acting on the will of those higher up," "this kind of centralization cannot in the least push forward modernization. On the contrary, it can only impede modernization." It also adversely affects stability and unity, the editorial argued, because its "bureaucratic, authoritarian style suppresses the people's reasonable political and economic demands." Consequently, "a very important principle is to develop democracy, thus allowing people to speak out, criticize, and vent their anger, if they have any." This should not mean, as some comrades believe, that "I give you democracy and allow you to speak out, but you must not say anything I don't like to hear." Rather, "a range of differing opinions from the people is not something dreadful but something good. What is dreadful is that the party and government cannot hear any differing voices."

The editorial asserted that a strong, confident government allows people to speak; a weak, insecure government does not.

> Let the people say what they wish and the heavens will not fall. If we do not allow people to say things that are incorrect, that is just the same as

keeping everyone's mouth shut. If a person is to be punished for saying the wrong thing, no one will dare to say what he thinks. If this is the case, it is called "giving up eating for fear of choking." Then, there will be neither people's democracy nor democracy within the party nor a lively situation.[16]

A new journal, initiated by thirty famous scholars, writers, and journalists who were to guide its editorial activities, was established in early 1985 to push for greater democracy. Its very title, *Qunyan* (Everyone has a say), states its purpose. The theorist Li Honglin on the occasion of its first issue wrote that in order to change the practice of "one person alone has a say" to "everyone has a say," is not simply to change a "style, but a system." Like the *People's Daily* editorial, he explained that this change is necessary for economic moderniza- tion. "One person has a say," is unsuitable for an economy that is moving from a closed, self-sufficiency to an open commodity-type of economy. Similarly, he insisted that "everyone has a say" was necessary for a more stable govern- ment. He cited examples from Chinese history, such as Jing Li of the Zhou dynasty who "suppressed public opinion and this ended in his fall." One of the reasons why the reign of the Emperor Tai Zong of the Tang was so successful was because of "his readiness to listen to the opinions of his ministers," such as Wei Zheng who confronted him with straight-forward criticism. Only when everyone's views are "genuinely respected, welcomed, and urgently needed,"[17] will the government, Li Honglin concluded, be stable and strong.

The Writers' Congress, the establishment of *Qunyan*, and the *People's Daily* pieces unleashed a barrage of demands. In addition to freedom of literature and art, there were calls in the press and at forums for freedom of academic research, publication, and comment that grew louder and louder in the early months of 1985. Other intellectual groups demanded the right to use the same procedures for electing their officials and protecting their members as was used by the Chinese Writers' Association. Hu Jiwei, deposed as chief editor of *People's Daily* in the spiritual pollution campaign but subsequently made president of the Federation of Journalists, called for legislation to protect freedom of speech in the press. He traveled to Hong Kong to inquire about the journalistic practices there and was encouraged by Hong Kong journalists to demand more rights at home, an indication of the liberalizing effect of the Hong Kong contact. He asked the regime to define exactly what it meant by such charges as "spreading rumors" and "divulging secrets" so as to prevent journalists from being accused of such practices. He pointed out that the vagueness of these terms hindered the journalists in gathering news more freely.[18]

As in the past, when the regime loosened its reins and encouraged expression of diverse views, those who responded expressed views that went beyond the party's limits and evoked a reaction not only from the opposing faction but even from the reform leadership, as indicated in Hu Yaobang's tough speech at an inner party meeting of the Secretariat in February 1985. It is not clear whether

Hu's speech expressed his own concerns, was meant to placate conservative leaders, or was forced on him. It was not published until April 1985 at the time when Hu Qiaomu and Deng Liqun, who had lain low since the end of the spiritual pollution campaign, were becoming increasingly active, an indication of conservative pressure. Moreover, Hu Qiaomu had it published when he was out of the country. In the speech, Hu had unequivocally stated that there could be no freedom of the press because the press must be "the mouthpiece of the party."[19] Before reporting important news, permission must be sought from higher authorities. Consequently, only the party's view of the shortcomings in society is to be presented in the media. Given the widely heralded freedom for literature and the arts granted at the Writers' Congress, Hu had to explain that writers and artists were different from journalists. They were "indirect" rather than "direct" mouthpieces of the party. Therefore they could write whatever they wanted in any style they wished, but, he warned, this does not mean that their work will be published. "The editorial boards of publications, newspapers, and publishing houses can also make a choice and have the right whether or not to publish a work. . . . Writers can never use their freedom to deprive the editorial boards of their freedom.[20] Immediately following the publication of Hu's talk, another series of forums were held, primarily under the auspices of the more conservative groups, the People's Liberation Army (PLA) and the Propaganda Department, praising its message.

Another significant departure in the Deng era, however, is that well-known intellectuals openly challenged the view of political leaders, as seen in Hu Jiwei's response to Hu Yaobang's views on journalism in a "Special Commentary" in the first issue of a new journal *Xinwen xuekan* (Journalist Bulletin). This commentary was reprinted in the overseas edition of *People's Daily* on August 4, 1985, most likely to reassure overseas Chinese upset by Hu Yaobang's speech. Although associated with the reform political leaders, Hu Jiwei was unwilling to accept their view that journalism could only speak with one voice, the official voice of the party. He said these were the old rules of journalism used during the revolutionary period, but were no longer applicable in a period of modernization. More significant, he pointed out that these outdated journalistic practices helped produce the Great Leap Forward and Cultural Revolution disasters. Quoting Liu Shaoqi: "Even when *People's Daily* advocated wrong things, people believed it pronounced opinions on behalf of the central leadership." With the ingenuity of a survivor, Hu Jiwei asserted that journalism is a "branch of learning" and therefore should be allowed "the freedom" accorded to academic subjects. Hence, in journalists' seminars and journals, "comrades holding different opinions should be able to state their views freely and carry out comradely discussions on an equal basis. In these forums, they should have a free atmosphere where they can express a variety of viewpoints and where, through free discussion and debate, people can judge what is right and what is wrong."[21]

Intellectuals Demand Institutional Change

Even though there was another slight retreat at the time that Hu Yaobang's speech on the press was published, by 1986 it appeared that the party's loosening of ideological restraints and the intellectuals' own ideological explorations were finally provoking a change in the nineteenth-century dichotomy between the *ti*, Chinese principle, and *yong*, Western function. Not only were the functions influenced by the West, but also principles were being influenced by Western ideas. In reaction to the experience of the Cultural Revolution, Deng himself had led off the discussion on political reform in the party establishment in his August 18, 1980, speech "On the Reform of the System of Party and State Leadership." In the speech he sharply criticized the highly centralized Leninist system:

> Overconcentration of power means inappropriate and indiscriminate concentration of all power in party committees in the name of strengthening central party leadership. Overconcentration of power in the hands of an individual or a few people means that most functionaries have no decision-making power at all, while the few who do are overburdened.

In addition to blaming this phenomenon on the feudal legacy, the usual culprit, Deng also blamed it on the "high degree of concentration of power in the hands of individual leaders of the Communist parties of various countries." While granting that overconcentration is attributable to the styles of individual leaders, Deng put the major blame on "problems in our organization and working system." As he pointed out, "Even so great a man as Mao was influenced to a serious degree by certain unsound systems and institutions, which resulted in grave misfortunes for the party, the state, and himself."[22] Deng suggested several reforms to guard against overconcentration of power, such as three parallel central committees that will mutually supervise and constrain one another, a form of checks and balances, and called for separation of the party from the government and economy; this latter point became central to his view of political reform. In good Leninist fashion, he did not want external constraints on the party, only internal ones, but he did recognize the need to restrict political power.

Several intellectuals elaborated on Deng's speech in public forums shortly after it was given. One of them, Liao Gailong, at the time a member of the Policy Study Office under the Central Committee, at a seminar on party history on October 25, 1980, went much further than Deng. He, too, called for mutual supervision, primarily between the party and the various "democratic" parties, a reform that Mao had called for in the Hundred Flowers and that Zhao Ziyang and Deng revived in the late 1980s. The "democratic" parties, however, were much too weak to act as any check on the party. Where Liao differed from Mao as well as Deng was that his call for political reform was not merely meant to make the economy and the state run more efficiently. He recommended political reform as an end in itself and advocated some external supervision—concepts more akin to

Western democratic ideas. He called for a legal system that did not simply guarantee the proper functioning of the prevailing system, but that also "safeguards the personal freedom and other civil rights of all citizens."[23] Furthermore, when the judiciary conducts a trial, "no one will be allowed to interfere in the independent actions of the judicial officers in their work. In short, the judiciary must be independent. Even party committees will not be able to interfere in this independence."[24] How a society without the tradition and institutional separation of the judiciary from the government will be able to protect itself from government interference was not addressed. He went further than Deng in calling for the party's separation from cultural organs, mass organizations, and the media, as well as from the government and the economy. He also advocated freedom of the press. "We should permit, require, and encourage the media, journalists, and commentators to assume independent responsibility of reporting or publishing news, letters from the masses, and comments."[25] His proposals for reform resonated with the practices of liberal Western democracies.

Liao even went so far as to recommend independent labor unions, a suggestion that had the potential for creating China's own Solidarity movement. "The workers are not permitted to elect the officials of the so-called trade unions. The party arbitrarily appoints the officials. Thus, the unions do not represent the workers' interests." He urged these reforms to avoid the situation that led to the Solidarity movement in Poland. "We all know what happened in Poland. If we do not change our course, the same things will happen to us."[26]

These proposals for political reform differed radically from Deng's more limited proposals, especially on how to avoid a Chinese Solidarity, which became an obsession with Deng. He rejected any suggestion that workers elect their own leaders. Nevertheless, Liao's views were echoed by others. Among them, Yu Haocheng, an editor of the Masses Publishing Company, who repeatedly stated that an enlightened ruler's "acceptance of dissident opinions by his subjects is not democracy." It is just the traditional convention of placing one's faith in "sagacious rulers, virtuous prime ministers, honest and good officials." This view only reinforces the convention that leaders can grant their subjects permission to speak, which also means that they can also withhold the right to speak when they disagree with what the subject says. As Yu points out "Such a work style of course cannot be designated as democracy as it falls far short of really letting people act as masters and exercising their own freedoms and rights."[27] China's intellectuals can no longer use these traditional methods that stress ideological persuasion because, as Yu explained, they do not protect those who have the courage to protest abuse of power. "How many masterful article writers like Deng Tuo and Wu Han . . . have died miserably under the sword of the executioner!"[28] The Constitution that guarantees freedom of expression and press is no guarantee either because "reality indicates that these prescriptions were merely things on paper and not actualities." He called, therefore, for the establishment of institutions and laws to protect freedom of the press and buttress the constitution. He asked, "Why must newspapers' offices and publishing houses be run only by party committees and government organs, must be subordinated to certain party committees or government organs, and cannot be managed independently as long as they comply with pertinent laws and edicts?" His answer was that "everything is subjected to state monopoly."[29] He implied that until that monopoly is lifted there can be no freedom.

As the economic reforms took off in the first half of the 1980s, however, with China's GNP growing at 9 to 10 percent, the need for political reform became less pressing. It was not until the spring of 1986 that the discussion of fundamental political reform again became a major part of public discourse. As the pace of economic development began to slow, the reform leaders again concluded that political reforms, particularly separating the party from the government and reducing its role in the economy, were necessary to ensure continuing economic development. The Secretariat set up a working group to explore political reform. The group, headed by Hu Qili, included Wang Zhaoguo, Zhu Houze, and Xiang Nan, former head of Fujian Province, all of whom were associated with Hu Yaobang. In June and July Hu Yaobang urged cadres to study Deng's 1980 speech on political reform as the basic formula to be followed in discussions of political reform, and he and his colleagues promised not to retaliate against those who might propose other formulas. The major party media in editorials and commentaries created an atmosphere that encouraged pluralism and tolerance for dissenting ideas. The reform leaders' purpose was to bring pressure and prepare public opinion for some political reforms to be announced at the Sixth Plenum to be held in September 1986. The reform leaders wanted limited administrative and political reforms to stop the bureaucratic establishment from hampering economic reform, but their encouragement of political debate emboldened the critical intellectuals to call for far-reaching institutional reforms.

Their discussions began in the institutes of the Academy of Social Sciences associated with the reform leaders and then spread to the public media. The major difference between the speeches of the reform leaders calling for diversity and more autonomy is that whereas they saw this pluralism as a means to economic modernization, some of the critical intellectuals saw pluralism as an end in itself. As stated by the head of the Institute of Political Science, Yan Jiaqi, "the purpose of political reforms is not merely to ensure the smooth progress of economic reforms, but also to build a highly democratic socialist state, which is a greater goal."[30] The traditional approach of the principled literati and the critical intellectuals in the Mao period of "listening to the people's opinion," was rejected by those involved in these discussions because, as Su Shaozhi pointed out, "it sounds as if someone is supposed to be superior to others."[31] Perhaps, most important, it had proven ineffective in handling abuses of political power and had led to retaliation against the critical intellectuals who had articulated "the people's opinion."

Forums with participants from research institutes, universities, government agencies, newspapers, journals, intellectuals' societies, and student organizations discussed a wide range of proposals for political reform. At one of the earliest forums, April 28–29, convened by the Academy of Social Sciences, some merely reiterated Deng's proposals on separating the party from governmental and economic activities; others advocated, again in line with Deng's proposals, more grass-roots democracy with multiple candidates in the local party congresses and even in the selection of factory managers in order to spark the populace's initiative in economic modernization and ensure greater accountability of cadres within the existing institutions. Some very traditional proposals were made, such as competitive nationwide public examinations for government office. Others proposed Sun Yatsen's somewhat unrealistic program of election, petition, recall, and referendum.

There were others, however, who recommended Western democratic practices that would transform the system. Several took up the issue of freedom of the press and civil rights, discussed earlier by Liao Gailong and Yu Haocheng. In contrast to Deng's emphasis on internal constraints, they emphasized external constraints. They noted: "Even now people still entrust their hopes for resolving social problems to honest, upright officials and heightened ideological awareness, but do not attempt to impose external rules and regulations."[32] Therefore, they called for institutions and laws that supervise externally and control political power. Still others called for a system of checks and balances with legislative and judicial oversight and even for a multiparty system as in the West.

Participants in the debates on political reform were given a further boost by another official, Wan Li, vice premier, Politburo member and ally of Hu Yaobang and Zhao Ziyang. In a speech in August 1986, he acknowledged that China lacked adequate policy consultation, supervision, and feedback from the populace and urged a freer atmosphere in which this could take place. "Leaders must respect the people's democratic right of free expression. They should not be afraid of different opinions or even opinions opposing themselves."

Like the intellectuals, Wan Li advocated brain trusts, surveys, testing of policies, and consultancy in order to get the intellectuals' input into policymaking. But even though Wan's emphasis was on the need for cooperation with the intellectuals and accurate feedback so that policy might conform more closely to the "people's" wishes, he also was telling intellectuals that their views have relevance to politics. "We used to take political problems as having antiparty, antisocialist, and counterrevolutionary motivations . . . and only scholarly, academic problems can be debated while political ones cannot. But often these two kinds of problems cannot be separated." Although he did not propose institutional change, he declared, "We should let people really exercise their constitutional right of freedom."[33]

Several intellectuals attempted to exercise that right. Zhang Youyu, a jurist and Chairman of the Chinese Law Association and Political Science Association, declared, "It is impossible to separate academic studies, particularly social sciences, from politics, nor is it necessary."[34] In addition to social scientists, Tan Jian, of the Institute of Political Science, insisted, "Newspapers, radios, and television stations should have the right to report and expose all violations of the constitution and the law or abuses of power by any government or political organization."[35] To avoid another Cultural Revolution, "no government or political organization or leading cadres can override the constitution and law. They must be restricted by the law. Without supervisory institutions . . . major policy mistakes cannot be redressed or prevented in time."[36] Both he, Yan Jiaqi, and several others proposed the strengthening of the National People's Congress (NPC) as a source of external institutional control on party power, though the irony is that it was headed by the conservative Peng Zhen at the time, whose orthodox views were counter to restricting political power. Nevertheless, Peng had turned the relatively ineffectual NPC into a public forum for protesting party policies, though his purpose was to obstruct the reformers rather than restrict political power.

Several denounced the hitherto sacrosanct concept of democratic centralism. Su Shaozhi pointed out that "Marx never mentioned "democratic centralism." The concept was put forth by Lenin under the conditions of the Russian revolution. Later it was distorted and the emphasis was placed only on centralization. " 'Democracy' under centralized guidance means that the people are not the masters, but the ruled."[37] Not only does Su call for an independent legislature and judiciary, but also independent mass organizations as Liao Gailong had in 1980. Su declared that mass organizations should not be "conveyor belts," They should represent the interests of the masses and have the right to independence."[38] Whereas in traditional society the ordinary person may have in fact been left alone by the government, in theory the government controlled everyone. Under Mao, the state had control in practice as well as in theory. Therefore, Su's and others' contention that there should be independent communal, professional, and political bodies was revolutionary in the Chinese context. It represented the effort to separate state and society in institutional terms as Liu Binyan, Bai Hua, and Wang Ruoshui attempted to do in ideological terms.

In sharp contrast to the conservatives' denunciation of Western concepts as "bourgeois," several intellectuals publicly and unambiguously asserted that their model for political reform was "bourgeois democracy." As stated by Yan Jiaqi, "I feel that a complete cultural opening must not be limited to the introduction of Western science and technology, but must also include Western political and social theories, its doctrines on the separation of power and checks and balances, and its views and practices on the people's greater participation in politics."[39] Wei Haibo, a researcher at the Law Research Institute, stated that despite their limitation, bourgeois democracies "ensure citizens the chance of having a series of individual freedoms, including freedom of speech and the press, the right to be secure in their persons, the right of election, and the authority to supervise the government."[40] The widely expressed admiration for Western political and social ideas expressed in 1986 revealed that the Chinese *ti*, principle, as well as *yong*, practice, was changing, at least among politically oriented intellectuals.

Despite the attraction of Western institutions, it is clear that the experience of the Cultural Revolution more than anything else was the impetus for the search for a different political system. Yan Jiaqi explains that "only after undergoing the Cultural Revolution has China begun to discuss openly the reform of the political system. In the 1950s, it could not be mentioned; whoever mentioned it was labeled a rightist. Nor could it be mentioned in the 1960s."[41] It could be mentioned in the 1980s not only because of the trauma of the Cultural Revolution undergone by officials as well as others, but also because reform party officials were willing to allow such a search. But those officials might be purged, as was to happen to Hu Yaobang in January 1987 and Zhao Ziyang in June 1989, or the views of their official patrons might change, as happened periodically to Deng Xiaoping. Zi Mu, in the *World Economic Herald*, explained that all the talk about democracy is meaningless "without protection of a legal system. . . . It cannot withstand shock waves such as the Cultural Revolution." Moreover, "the leaders change or some leaders change their views."[42] Instead of principled literati or critical intellectuals speaking for the people, representatives should be elected to the People's Congress to "speak for the people and be responsible for their constituents." If the elected representative has ideas that differ from the party, "he should be able to talk about them freely in the People's Congress. Such behavior should not be considered inconsistent with the party, because the representatives are elected by the people and not by the party members."[43] They should be "immune from investigation and blame for any objections or publication of opinion."[44]

In this period, Yu Haocheng, who had called for freedom of speech and publication in 1980, talks about the need to back up freedom of speech, which he regarded as "a minimum condition for democracy," with laws that will enforce the right of freedom of speech and publication in the constitution. As he pointed out, "Based on our experience and learning from other nations' relevant statutes, it is imperative, in fact a top priority, that we draw up a press law and a publication law as soon as possible." He quoted Hu Yaobang's quotation of Montesquieu, "Freedom is being able to do everything the law allows."[45] As long as writers stay within the law, all opinions have the legal right to be published without any interference. The editors and editorial boards of newspapers, radio stations, TV stations, and publishing houses should "decide whether or not to publish a particular opinion or a particular piece of work. No organization or individual has the power to interfere in their decision-making. Any interference will be construed as breaking the law, as encroaching on people's freedoms." These procedures must be written into law, because "If we do not write these things into law and content ourselves with mere declarations by party and government leaders about relaxation, about encouraging free expression, about the toleration of dissenting opinions . . . then freedom will lack tangible protection.

If experience is any guide, when the leaders relax, they can also tighten; what is given can also be taken away."[46]

These impassioned pleas for institutional change excited the intellectual community, but several of the participants felt the need to point out how remote their possibility for implementation, even under the rule of "good" leaders. Yan Jiaqi, whom Zhao Ziyang had appointed to a committee to draw up plans for political reform at the Thirteenth Party Congress in October 1987, admitted that "it is still premature to discuss a two-party or multiparty system. Realistically speaking, besides improving the collective leadership system by means of inner-party democracy, another important thing today is to perfect the democratic mechanisms of the National People's Congress."[47] Aspirations were much higher, but most, like Yan, believed they had to begin to reform the existing system before they could introduce new institutions.

Not only were efforts to change the *ti* principle unprecedented in the PRC, but the participation of scientists in this discussion of political reform was also unprecedented. Chief among them was the famous astrophysicist, Fang Lizhi. As the nonscientists pointed out repeatedly, scientists were treated much more favorably than nonscientific intellectuals, even under the Mao regime. They were the first to feel the effects of a political relaxation and the last to feel the effects of a political campaign, that is, until the Cultural Revolution period when their scientific and technical skills marked them for condemnation. Actually, Fang Lizhi had been labeled a "rightist" in the anti-rightist campaign of 1957 for criticizing political interference in scientific work during the Hundred Flowers, as was true of other scientists joining him in demands for institutional political reform in the mid-1980s. One of the few Chinese scientists recognized by the outside world, Fang had been invited abroad to international conferences in Europe, Japan, and the United States where he not only imbibed scientific knowledge, he also was impressed with the political rights of those he met.

In 1985–86, he spoke at China's major universities on the need to introduce similar rights in China. Though he advocated Western political concepts, he held a traditional view of the role of the intellectual. He believed that by virtue of their superior knowledge and skills, intellectuals have the right to participate in government. In fact, the impetus for his demand for civil rights stems less from the experience of the Cultural Revolution than from his concern with ensuring that intellectuals exercised their talents fully without the interference of party ideologues, like Hu Qiaomu, whom, he charged, knew nothing about science and scholarly endeavor. Like his literati predecessors, he believed that intellectuals have a responsibility to speak out on political matters. Though he claimed that his faith in expertise was based on the Marxist view that whoever controls the "most advanced forces of production are the most progressive force in society," he rejected Marx and Engels' guidance in intellectual work, especially in his field, because it "can only lead to erroneous outcomes. It has never produced correct results. . . . None of the 'academic' criticism conducted since Liberation proved to be correct. It is a hundred percent wrong."

Fang's outright rejection of Marxism-Leninism differed from the other criticial intellectuals in that some still believed in their own interpretation of Marxism and others were not so bold. Unlike them, he was not content merely to ally himself with the reform leaders Hu Yaobang's and Zhao Ziyang's efforts to use established procedures, such as party conferences and party plenums, to work for political change. In a speech at Jiaotong University in Shanghai, November 6, 1986, he called on intellectuals and students to grasp democracy from below because, as he said, the government will not give it to them. Despite his traditional elitist approach, he believed that rights were unalienable, a Western view contrary to Chinese tradition and the Marxist-Leninist view that rights were given. And he urged intellectuals and students to use the mass media, meetings, and organizations to fight for their own rights. "One should strive for what is one's due. It is time we changed the characteristics of the obedient intellectuals of the 1950s."[48]

It is not surprising that the discussions on political reform and Fang Lizhi's instigation of students and intellectuals to fight for their rights provoked the conservative leadership. They wanted economic reform and even some administrative reform to make the economy run more smoothly, but not the radical institutional reforms that the critical intellectuals were proposing. The military was also unhappy with the radical nature of the discussion and was especially unhappy with Hu Yaobang who had not only tolerated such wide-ranging ideas, but had also called for the retirement of the elderly military establishment. At the policy review conference at Beidaihe held before the Sixth Plenum, the conservative leaders insisted that any political reform must retain party leadership and adherence to the Four Principles, which would make any fundamental political change impossible. At the Sixth Plenum it was clear that the conservatives had prevailed because instead of coming out with a plan for political reform, the plenum called for renewed emphasis on socialist spiritual civilization and denounced bourgeois liberalism, the code words for institutional reform and Western ideas. This switch in emphasis revealed that the conservatives had launched a counterattack against the critical intellectuals and their patrons, principally Hu Yaobang, who they believed not only rejected orthodox beliefs, but, more important, threatened their entrenched power in the one-party state. The Propaganda Director of the 1950s, the veteran party official Lu Dingyi, and Wan Li had called for the deletion of the phrase against bourgeois liberalization, but the conservatives, led by Peng Zhen, won out.

Despite this setback, the critical intellectuals continued to demand political structural reform, primarily representative government, and freedom of speech, with increasing insistence and eloquence in the fall of 1986. It is within this context that the student demonstrations of December 1986 took place. Some of the students protested for personal reasons—poor living conditions in the universities, bad food, youthful zeal—but others protested for political reasons. Their political protests reveal a symbiotic relationship between the critical intellectuals and student protest. The protests began at the University of Science and Technology in Hefei, Anhui, where Fang Lizhi was vice chancellor. Taking Fang's advice to work for their political rights, the students registered to vote for their deputies to the local People's Congress, but found that the local party cadres controlled the electoral process. Discovering that the supposed democratic process was a sham, the students on December 5 protested against the local authorities. Within four weeks, student demonstrations mushroomed in China's major cities. The students repeated the political slogans they had heard from the critical intellectuals and invoked symbols of Western democracies.

The accelerating student unrest provided the opportunity for the conservatives to discredit the critical intellectuals and insert themselves into the political process by calling for the dismissal of Hu Yaobang, who had not only tolerated the student demonstrations for a month but had also refused to respond to entreaties to crack down on them. A similar scenario would play itself out again in the 1989 student demonstrations and subsequent purge of Zhao Ziyang, who sought to respond in some way to the student demands. In each case, the party elders used the unrest generated by the student demonstrations to get rid of reform leaders who they believed were undermining the party's and their own authority.

Campaign Against Bourgeois Liberalization and the 1989 Repression

With the pressure from the conservatives and military, Deng again switched sides in late 1986 and launched the campaign against bourgeois liberalism following the forced resignation of Hu Yaobang on January 16, 1987. Three prominent critical intellectuals—Liu Binyan, Fang Lizhi, and the old Shanghai writer Wang Ruowang—were purged from the party and made the public targets of the campaign. A leftist writer from Shanghai of the 1930s, Wang, like others of his generation, had been the victim of campaigns since the 1940s. Whereas the others sought peace and security in their old age, only Wang and Ba Jin of their generation continued to protest. Wang, in good Marxist style, had insisted that China must go through its bourgeois stage of development before it could move on to socialism.

The campaign was a continuation of the 1983 campaign against spiritual pollution. At the time, Hu Qiaomu and Deng Liqun had tried to make Liu Binyan and Wang Ruowang, as well as Wang Ruoshui, the targets, but Hu Yaobang, for whom they had worked on the *China Youth Daily* in the 1950s, was able to protect them then. In 1987, with Hu out as general-secretary, the conservatives were able to make them the targets and widen the campaign. They claimed that if the campaign against spiritual pollution had not been interrupted, they would have been able to prevent the spread of bourgeois liberalism and the student demonstrations of 1986. Their charges against Fang Lizhi for fomenting the demonstrations had some validity. Fang's speeches in the fall of 1986 urging young intellectuals to participate directly in political affairs were a direct cause of the demonstration, particularly in Anhui and Shanghai, where students demonstrated when the authorities refused to publish Fang's speeches.

The three intellectuals had shared the fate of being branded "rightists" in 1957. Liu and Fang had planned a commemorative meeting in June 1987, on the thirtieth anniversary of the start of the anti-rightist campaign, in order to publicize the "evils" of the repression of intellectuals and to ensure that such persecution would not be repeated. Liu had interviewed victims and planned to publish a multivolume oral history. They believed that the Cultural Revolution had evolved from previous campaigns, particularly the anti-rightist campaign. Their view contrasted with the official one that the anti-rightist campaign was all right, though its scope had been "far too broad." Intellectuals regarded the anti-rightist campaign second only to the Cultural Revolution in its repression of intellectuals.

Because Deng and Peng Zhen had led the 1957 anti-rightist campaign, it is not surprising that they regarded the planned condemnation of the anti-rightist campaign as a thinly veiled attack on themselves. Thus, the animosities and vendettas of a handful of aging leaders made the campaign against bourgeois liberalism a factional, as well as ideological struggle. Furthermore, the implementors of the campaign, Hu Qiaomu and Deng Liqun, were the same implementors who had been stopped from expanding the campaign against spiritual pollution. They now thought they had their opportunity, but when they began to extend the campaign into the economic area, again Deng switched back to the reform side and the campaign began to subside in April 1987. A few more critical intellectuals were discharged from the party in the summer of 1987— Wang Ruoshui and the playwright, Wu Zuguang, who had denounced censorship. Su Shaozhi was removed as head of his institute. Zhao Ziyang had been unable to protect them, or perhaps he and Deng went along with the conservatives in dismissing these outspoken critics in order to win the conservatives' acceptance of administrative reforms and further economic reforms. Deng and Zhao may have felt they were sacrificing only a few party intellectuals in order to placate the conservatives and continue the reforms, but in the long run they undermined those very reforms because of the increasing intimidation and resentment of the intellectuals who must carry them out.

Yet the intellectuals have changed from the Mao era. Wang Ruoshui, the target of the spiritual pollution campaign, and the three intellectuals of the bourgeois liberalization campaign refused to make abject public confessions, perhaps as a result of the party's more lenient treatment and their greater courage. Moreover, while a few of their colleagues denounced them, most did not or made perfunctory criticisms. Their past bitter experiences and the exposure to the West, as well as the discussions in their own journals, may have encouraged them not to give in this time. Whereas most intellectuals joined in the attack on designated targets in the Maoist period in order to protect themselves and their families, in the Deng period they felt less pressure to do so. In fact, the pressure came from their intellectual colleagues not to participate in actions against their colleagues and the long-range interests of the intellectual community.

While there was a respite after the Thirteenth Party Congress in September–October 1987 where a program for administrative reform was announced, such as separation of the party from the government and the economy, and the establishment of a civil service examination for government administrators, little headway was made even in these areas. A number of fascinating discussions took place in 1988 on culture sparked in part by the controversial television program "River Elegy," which advocated learning from the West and rejecting China's traditional culture. It provoked opposition of the party elders who regarded it as another effort to inject Western values and attack the *ti*, principle, in this case the party, its ideology and leadership.

Another debate emerged in late 1988 on neoauthoritarianism, which was a concept of government advocated by a group of young technocrats associated with Zhao Ziyang. They sought to use the East Asian model of a strong leader pushing a market economy and using his authority to get rid of those who obstruct the reforms. A period of strong one-man rule was necessary to introduce democracy eventually. They were opposed by several of the critical intellectuals who argued that neoauthoritarianism was no different than the old authoritarianism. With so much of the economy still under state control and with such a small middle class, it was likely that China would retreat to a dictatorship rather than move toward democracy. This debate, waged in journals, newspapers, and forums in late 1988 and early 1989, served only to focus once again on the benefits that could be derived from the introduction of democratic practices.

Also in early 1989 the critical intellectuals began to organize themselves politically and publicly for the first time. As usual, the physicist Fang Lizhi led the way by writing a letter to Deng requesting pardon for Wei Jingsheng. In February, a petition signed by thirty-three famous literary intellectuals called for Wei's pardon and commitment to a universal code of human rights. This group included a number of very old, well-known apolitical intellectuals, signifying that age may make a hard-liner in the party leadership but not necessarily among the rest of the population. The next month, forty-two intellectuals, mostly scientists, organized by Fang's close colleague, the historian of science Xu Liangying, organized a similar petition to the leadership, demanding also democracy and freedom of speech as stipulated in China's Constitution. In April, forty-three of China's most talented, younger intellectuals sent a similar petition.

Even though the intellectuals were organizing themselves, they did not instigate the student demonstrations in Tiananmen Square from mid-April until the crackdown on June 4, nor did they play an organizing role. It was a spontaneous movement that arose among the students themselves. Nevertheless, they had helped create a pluralistic atmosphere and in their forums and articles had discussed slogans that the students used. Through most of the 1980s, they had been content to act, as had the literati of old, as advisers to the reform leaders, but as their ideas evoked increasing opposition from the party elders, some of them concluded that individual intellectuals remonstrating by themselves had no real power. They must join with other groups, such as the emerging class of private entrepreneurs spawned by Deng's economic reforms, the professionals, and students, in order to provide a broader social base for their demands. Thus when the student protests began, a number of prominent intellectuals joined the students, chief among them Yan Jiaqi, who since the early 1980s had been calling for limited terms of office and making the National People's Congress into a real rather than rubber stamp legislature; the ideological theorist Su Shaozhi; the writer of the controversial television program, "River Elegy," Su Xiaokang; and Yu Haocheng. Like the students, they also established their own independent organization, the Federation of Beijing Intellectuals. They were joined in the Square by professional groups and the new entrepreneurs, just as they had hoped, as well as by all segments of urban society.

Actually, the seeds for a participatory society were sown earlier, in the Cultural Revolution, when Mao mobilized the population against the party bureaucracy. Deng continued this process in the post-Mao era. Like Gorbachev in the Soviet Union, he and the reform leaders sought to stimulate the initiative of the population for reform, by giving intellectuals, students, businessmen, peasants, and even workers a degree of freedom, not only in economic life but also in their personal lives—in terms of life-style and reading matter. The wide support given the student protest against the government indicates how far the increasing autonomy of at least the urban population vis-à-vis the state has already gone. But whereas the 1989 demonstration revealed how much society had changed, it also revealed that the political system and some of its leaders, specifically the party leaders, had not changed.

Once again, in the summer of 1989, intellectuals were subjected to a campaign of intimidation, repression, and arrest. But their response was different than in the Maoist period. Whereas the targets in Mao's campaign confessed their "sins" and accepted their fate, because of Deng's opening up of China, they have contacts with the outside world to which they have sought to escape. With the help of Westerners, overseas Chinese, native entrepreneurs, and even sympathetic officials, some of them have made their way through South China to Hong Kong and Macao and then abroad, where they continue to exert pressure on their government. In the 1950s, and in the Cultural Revolution, those under attack could not choose this route, not only because of Chinese isolation, but also because they still had faith in the system and thought their criticism had truly done damage to the country. That faith in 1989 had been shattered. Nevertheless, while several student leaders and Yan Jiaqi and Su Shaozhi escaped, thousands of others, including Su Xiaokang, Yu Haocheng, Li Honglin, as well as other intellectuals not directly involved in the demonstration, have been arrested.

Implications for the Future

If history has taught anything, it is that nothing is inevitable; certainly reform is not inexorable nor is continuing loosening of controls over China's intellectuals. China faces another period of tightening control and emphasis on ideology. The elders may not have a program, but they can obstruct reform. Most likely, the previous reforms will have some limited residual effects. The post-June 4, 1989, atmosphere was less stifling than under Mao, but for a time the forces for change, the students and intellectuals, were silenced and withdrew to their private lives or overseas.

Because of the Cultural Revolution, it was thought that China's leaders would never again allow such a tragedy to recur. But after initially facing up to the horrors of the Cultural Revolution the regime gradually restricted its discussion because, as Deng himself has said, he and his colleagues had supported Maoist policies. Efforts of writers to bear witness in their writings, and even the writer Ba Jin's efforts to establish a museum of the Cultural Revolution, were frustrated. The denunciation of Mao has not been as thorough as the Soviet condemnation of Stalin. Consequently, the memory of the Cultural Revolution was not sufficient to prevent the June 1989 crackdown.

At present, political change appears illusory, but the fact that the students did not succeed has more to do with the Leninist political system, the internal dynamics of the power struggle, and the party elders' continuing control over the military than with any inherent obstacles to political reform. If the elders had already left the scene Zhao might have won out, and the demands of the students and intellectuals might have at least been given a hearing because the social forces for change and the desire to restrain political power is perhaps even greater than before. Just because China reverted to totalitarian practice does not mean that the desire for political reform is lacking. Ostensibly, the population appears to have fallen into line. In addition to the ubiquitous military and police presence, the party still controlled assignment of jobs, housing, ration tickets, medical treatment, and education of most of the population. But the difference this time is that there has been a popular uprising not just by students and intellectuals, but by people from all walks of life in defiance of the party for the first time since 1949.

Moreover, as in other communist societies, today even these societies need the tacit consent of the people in order to govern. Because of the Tiananmen Square massacre, Deng has lost the mandate he was given when he promised an end to the traumas of the Mao era. Historically, when intellectuals and segments of the population feel the mandate has been lost, it is almost impossible to retrieve it. But whereas in traditional China, when new leaders gained the mandate, they were able to govern effectively within the existing system, today that appears increasingly difficult. Since the fall of the last dynasty in 1912, China has not been able to find the political system appropriate for its needs. The seventieth anniversary of the May Fourth Movement, the first student demonstration demanding democracy, was celebrated by the 1989 demonstrators, making the same demand. Will the seventieth anniversary of the 1989 Tiananmen demonstration still be making the same demand? China will continue to endure cycles of autocratic rule interspersed with periods of reformist benevolence until that demand is in some way realized.

Jiang Zemin, the party general secretary replacing Zhao, has a record of tough treatment of the critical intellectuals, but, like Deng, he is in the self-strengthening tradition of wanting Western science, technology, and business, while rejecting the Western ideas that accompany them. But as Li Honglin observed, there is no way to block them "coming in through the cracks." As the conservatives could not stop Western ideas from undermining Chinese orthodoxy in the nineteenth century, they certainly cannot stop them from subverting their orthodoxy and power in the late twentieth century.

As long as the party's goal remains economic modernization, the critical intellectuals will resume their demand for fundamental political changes some time in the future. The party cannot repress them altogether without also hampering the scientists and engineers needed for modernization and jeopardizing its relations with the outside world. To crush the critical intellectuals alienates others needed for modernization. Yet until new political institutions are established that change the party-dominated state and separate the state from society, the age-old tradition of small numbers of intellectuals pointing out the government's misdeeds and demanding reform will continue. What makes the critical intellectuals of the Deng period different from those of the traditional and Mao periods is that what they propose—democratic institutions—makes their traditional rule as spokespersons for the people obsolete. If and when new political institutions emerge, it may be owing to the efforts of the critical intellectuals as well as to the forces of modernization.

Notes

1. Carol Hamrin, "New Trends under Deng Xiaoping and His Successors," in *China's Intellectuals and the State*, ed. Merle Goldman, Timothy Cheek, and Carol Hamrin (Cambridge: Harvard University Press, Council on East Asian Studies, 1987), pp. 275–304.

2. Robert Suttmeier, "New Directions in Chinese Science and Technology," China Briefing, 1985, ed. John Major (Westview Press, 1986), pp. 91–102.

3. Robert Suttmeier, "Impact of Modernization of Science and Technology on the Political System," in *China's New Technological Revolution*, ed. Denis Simon and Merle Goldman (Cambridge: Harvard University Press, 1989), pp. 375–96.

4. Li Honglin, "Socialism and Opening to the Outside World," *Remin ribao*, October 15, 1984, p. 5.

5. For a full discussion of the social sciences, see *New Directions in the Social Sciences and Humanities in China*, ed. Michael B. Yahuda (New York: St. Martin's Press, 1987), particularly pp. 114–30.

6. Ba Jin, *Random Thoughts* (Hong Kong, 1984), p. 16.

7. Liu Binyan, "The Call of the Times," in *Chinese Literature for the 1980s*, ed.

Howard Goldblatt (Armonk, NY: M. E. Sharpe), p. 104.

8. Liu Binyan, "Dierzhong Zhongcheng" (The second kind of loyalty), *Kaituo* (Exploration), no. 1 (1985), pp. 4–23.

9. For an excellent discussion of the traditional aspects of Liu Binyan, see Leo Oufan Lee, "The Tragic Vision of Liu Binyan," unpublished manuscript.

10. Su Shaozhi and Ding Xueliang, "China and the Coming Post-Industrial Society," *Remin ribao*, October 21, 1985, p. 5.

11. Wang Ruoshui, "On Estrangement," originally in *The Journalist Front*, no. 8 (1980); reprinted in *Selected Works on Studies of Marxism* (Beijing), no. 1–20 (1981).

12. Michael Duke, *Blooming and Contending* (Bloomington: Indiana University Press, 1985), pp. 128, 144.

13. See Stuart R. Schram, *Ideology and Policy in China since the Third Plenum, 1978–84* (London: Contemporary China Institute, SOAS, 1984), pp. 51–57.

14. Described by Liu Binyan in a private interview, July 1986.

15. Ke Ling, "Concentrate on Rooting Out Stubborn "Leftist" Disease," *Renmin ribao*, December 31, 1984, p. 7; FBIS, January 9, 1985, p. K9.

16. *Renmin ribao*, January 3, 1985, p. 1.

17. Ibid., April 22, 1985, p. 5.

18. Hu Jiwei called for protection for journalists in *Xinwen zishe* (Journalist), no. 1 (1985); Zheng Ming (Hong Kong), no. 1 (June 1985); FBIS, June 6, 1985, p. W6.

19. Hu Yaobang, "On the Party's Journalism Work," given February 8, 1985, and published in *People's Daily* on April 14, 1985; FBIS, April 15, 1985, p. K1.

20. Ibid., p. K3.

21. *Xinwen zishe* (Journalist), no. 1 (1985); *Zheng Ming* (Hong Kong), June 1, 1985; FBIS, June 6, 1985, p. W6.

22. Deng Xiaoping, "On the Reform of the System of Party and State Leadership," *Selected Works of Deng Xiaoping* (Beijing: Foreign Language Press, 1984): pp. 302–25.

23. Liao Gailong, "The Reform Program of China," Hong Kong *Chi-shih Nien-tai* (The seventies), 4th section, March 1, 1981, pp. 38–48; FBIS, China Section, March 16, 1981, p. U1.

24. Ibid., p. U4.

25. Ibid., p. U12.

26. Ibid., p. U13.

27. Yu Haocheng, "Achieving Freedom of the Press Is an Important Problem," *Dushu* (Reading), vol. 1 (1981), pp. 26–29; JPRS, No. 77495, p. 20.

28. Ibid., p. 21.

29. Ibid., p. 22.

30. "Yan Jiaqi Discusses Political Structure and Political Reform," *Chi-shih Nien-tai* (December 1986), pp. 40–47; JPRS, No. CPS–87–020, p. 35.

31. Su Shaozhi, "Preconditions for Reform of the Political System Is Getting Rid of Feudal Pernicious Influences," in *Reform of China's Political System*, ed. Benedict Stavis, *Chinese Law and Government* (Spring 1987), p. 64.

32. "China's Political Restructuring and the Development of Political Science—a Summary of the Academic Symposium on Political Restructuring Convened by the *Social Sciences* in China," by Le Kejing, April 28–29, 1986, *Social Sciences*, no. 3 (1986), p. 13.

33. Wan Li, "Making Decision-Making More Democratic and Scientific Is an Important Part of Reform of the Political System, *People's Daily*, August 15, 1986, p. 1.

34. Zhang Youyu, "Reform of the Political System and Division of the Work of Party and Government," *Guangming ribao*, October 29, 1986; Stavis, p. 40.

35. Tan Jian, "Reform and Strengthening China's Political System," *Jingji ribao* (Economic Daily), August 9, 1986; Stavis, p. 45.

36. Ibid., p. 46.

37. Su Shaozhi, "My Humble Opinions on Reforming the Political System," *Dushu* (Reading), September 10, 1986, pp. 3–9; *JPRS*, No. CPS–87–020, p. 27.

38. Ibid., p. 28.

39. "Yan Jiaqi Discusses Political Structure and Political Reform," p. 34.

40. Wei Haibo, "Reform of the Political System and Political Democratization," *Faxue* (Legal studies), no. 10 (1986), pp. 6–8; Stavis, p. 75.

41. "Yan Jiaqi Discusses Political Structure and Political Reform," p. 40.

42. Zi Mu, "Strengthening the People's Congress Is the Fundamental Way to Develop Socialist Democracy," *Zhijie jingji daobao,* August 11, 1986; Stavis, p. 86.

43. Ibid., p. 87.

44. Ibid., p. 88.

45. Yu Haocheng, "Legislation Needed to Safeguard People's Freedom," *Xinguancha* (New observations), no. 16 (August 25, 1986), pp. 2–3; *JPRS*, No. CPS–86–081, p. 44.

46. Ibid., p. 45.

47. "Yan Jiaqi Discusses Political Structure and Political Reform," p. 43.

48. All the quotes from Fang Lizhi's speech at Jiaotong University, November 6, 1986, are from a tape of a Chinese graduate student who was at the talk.

Comments by Jerome B. Grieder

Professor Goldman's paper is a knowledgeable and penetrating analysis of the politics of high intellectual life in the last decade, in which she examines with her usual skill what one might call the nonantagonistic contradiction between the Chinese government and the Chinese establishment intellectuals. She is, if I judge her tenor correctly, on the whole quite optimistic about the status intellectuals have achieved as a result of the current reform movement. She will probably concur, with a view that has been expressed by others at this conference, that a point of no return has been reached, and the bad old days cannot return again in quite the same magnitude of evilness.

I believe Professor Goldman is saying that as long as the leadership remains dedicated to its present objectives—economic and technological modernization—the situation necessitates that the role assigned to the intellectual elite will ensure a degree of tolerance of outspokenness, or even direct criticism of its management style. Although the base line is low, as the experiences of the older generation, with whom she is primarily concerned, so eloquently attested, the curve is rising in terms of intellectual expectation. I do not disagree on the basis of much less well-informed knowledge of this troubled history. Under the reform leadership and its policies, the regime has openly and frankly acknowledged its dependence on the intellectuals for its ambitious development program to succeed, acknowledged not quite unambiguously that this would necessitate certain restraint in dealing with its critics, and so forth.

Where I do differ with Professor Goldman is not in her assessment of the improved environment in which intellectuals operate today compared to what has gone before, but rather in her assessment of the change in their relationship to the government, on the one hand, and to the society at large, the culture, the masses, the people, on the other.

Professor Goldman herself has brought numerous parallels between the position occupied in traditional China by intellectuals, guardians of the moral probity of the regime they served, and China's high intellectuals of the 1980s, who, like Liu Pingyan, define the intellectuals' proper role as that of the ever watchful guardian against the abuse of power by an otherwise irresponsible state; certainly it is true, and Professor Goldman's paper offers ample documentation, that for China's intellectuals in the 1980s, the tradition of remonstrance is a lively and cherished precedent, even if it appears to be an inadequate precedent, as she has also indicated, in the current context. But I am not persuaded, as I think she may be, that China's contemporary intellectual critics, the higher intellectual critics at least, have gone conceptually much beyond the traditional perception of the intellectuals' moral and civic role and obligation.

In traditional China, the perennial source of frustration for the higher intellectuals, the literati, was the sense of denial of access to those in positions of political and social authority, denial of the right to be heard, to which their status entitled them by law and cultural tradition. So it seems to me that a similar sense of frustration motivates the intellectual critics of the present regime. Their demand is not so much a demand for direct participation for themselves, much less for the masses. They think the men who do make decisions should respect their judgment and heed their counsel somewhere along the line in their decision-making process, very much like their Confucian forebears and many of the so-called liberals in the May Fourth era. I think these intellectuals want to influence the public world without risking more than the absolutely necessary contamination that public responsibilities entail. This demand for recognition as persons of conscience and as members of the moral minority perpetuates essentially an elitist vision of the intellectuals in relationship to those in power, and I believe Professor Goldman makes an important point in stressing the significance of recent, that is autumn 1986 and spring 1987, demands of institutional and legal reforms that will give substance to the freedoms that are guaranteed in the Constitution. The opinions she cited of people like Fang Lizhi and Yan Jiaqi are incisive, and they are inspiring to anyone who is concerned with the issue of intellectual freedom. But I do not think this should be interpreted as a demand, a promotional campaign, either in its logic or in its substance, for democracy as a political system incorporates the self-perceived interest of the people as a whole, as the funding authority of political legitimacy. It remains the prerogative of the intellectuals to define popular interests and to articulate them, to promote them even at considerable personal risk when they perceive them abused by those in power.

I participated some years ago in a conference in New York to discuss the rather improbable or naive topic of the prospect for democracy in China. This was the period when one still, by huddling by the fire, could draw some warmth from the dying embers of the Democracy Wall phenomenon. It did not take long into the first session, however, to arrive at the recognition that when one talks about democracy one is talking about popular participation in the political process, popular participation carried to the extreme, one person one vote. In other words, power to the people. At that point, the Chinese participants in the conference, from Taiwan as well as from the PRC, came together and unanimously rejected the idea. No, they said, this is not what democracy means. This is not what we are talking about. We cannot talk about democracy if this is the way you are going to interpret the word. In other words, we in China are not in a position to contemplate the enfranchisement of the masses. Needless to say, the conference foundered on this rock. So, too, does any expectation that the increased vehemence and sophistication of the intellectuals' demands to secure the right of self-expression is the foundation on which we might hope to erect a politically and socially pluralistic order in China.

Mr. Li Miao, in his remarks, observed how difficult it is for Americans to understand a "centralized" society and how difficult it is, conversely, for the Chinese to understand a "pluralistic" society. I suggest that one of the sources of our difficulties is that when we hear students demanding democracy, we think,

"Ah, they are speaking our language, and we know what they mean." I do not think we know what they mean. I do not think that when they are demanding democracy they are demanding the kind of universalization of political participatory activity that we assume it to be. The elitism that is institutionalized in the educational system Suzanne Pepper writes about and the elitism that is perpetuated in the intellectuals' demand on their own behalf for a freer access to those who wield political authority and for freer rights to express their views are mutually reinforcing. I think that all we can realistically hope for at best is that elitism in the future will be a genuinely benign and morally conscientious one.

Comments by Susan H. Marsh

Professor Goldman's paper is very well written and extremely comprehensive. I have no disagreements with her. On certain points I am somewhat more optimistic than she, and on other points somewhat more pessimistic. I have three points to make:

First, in this paper and the papers so far presented, we too readily juxtapose leaders and intellectuals. Who are the leaders in China today? There are not many who do not fit the description of intellectuals broadly defined in Professor Goldman's paper. They are intellectuals who have made good in a certain chosen way. We tend to take the leaders to task. We concentrate our criticism on the leaders. But it is really from the ranks of intellectuals that most of the leaders emerge.

Second, we tend to juxtapose reformers and conservatives too neatly. Many people are reformers and many are conservatives; in between, however, there are even more who do not fit neatly into either category. There are many who are *qiqianpai*—I am not using the term pejoratively—people who literally do not know which way they should commit themselves. They could be reformers today and conservatives tomorrow, depending on a particular issue or on what their friends or the people they trust are advocating. Or it could be a matter of career consideration whether one joins the reformers or conservatives. So I think that perhaps we should not think in terms of reformers versus conservatives; it would be better to locate them on a continuum, some leaning more or less this way or that way, shifting their positions over time.

Third, so far we have rightly attributed the Cultural Revolution with the distinction of having prompted the reform and, in remembering the disastrous situation, people tend to unite to seek reform. Many of today's intellectuals really suffered during the Maoist days. They were not able to have input in policy matters. At best, they were policy servers and implementers. In the Maoist period, when they were characterized as intellectuals, most of them did not have an enviable time. When they achieved power and authority, however, they were no longer categorized as intellectuals. I also want to mention the 1950s because this was the time when all the unsavory practices had their rehearsals. Those who brought down the "capitalist roaders" with impunity and trumped up charges against others during the Cultural Revolution had seen such measures used in the 1950s on a smaller scale against different targets. When one reviews the cases of Liang Shuming and Hu Feng, one finds that many of the methods used and the twisted reasoning were later amplified in the Cultural Revolution. My question is why the intellectuals in the 1950s did not do something when bad practices were still in the budding stage and could have been diverted. Instead, these abusive activities and twisted reasoning were practiced again and again even by the intellectuals against each other until they reached a crescendo.

I am pessimistic about the intellectuals under the Deng reform program, despite the loosening of control in rural agricultural activities and in many other areas today.

Traditionally, people who were in positions of power wanted control, and those people were more or less intellectuals. I spoke with a number of college-educated cadres in China in 1978; they spoke of the freedom Americans enjoyed. At one point they all agreed and said, "In China, we are better off because we can tell who is where doing what." To what end? In fact, the Chinese have wasted a lot of energy and time just keeping tabs on people. I think this is still the case in China, a political culture where the elite equates governing with controlling.

The reform program has the tendency of creating a two-class society, a bifurcated society, in China. Some people have opportunities for higher education, and thus to become intellectuals; others are destined to be left out, as the paper on education has documented.

Another point, concerning popular culture: I know today, after the liberalization, that the songstress Deng Liqun's songs and voice are very popular. Back in the 1950s and 1960s, there was "Dong Fang Hong" (The East is red). When I first heard the words of that song I said to myself, "This is like praising a heaven-mandated emperor, like Zhu Yuanzhang." When one compares this song of extreme adoration with popular songs in China in the 1930s and 1940s, one can almost say there was a retrogression among the intellectuals as far as their sense of independence was concerned. In the 1930s and 1940s, China had popular songs that went like this: "Who wants to be a slave? Who wants to be a beast of burden? ... We want universal love, equality, and liberty. We're willing to pay the price for them, even to the extent of losing our lives ..." This was a song that originated in a Shanghai-made movie that became very popular among educated people. There were also songs like "Ye-ban ge-sheng" (Song after midnight), which protested oppression and inequality. There were songs of guerrillas, most of them of communist origins, popular among college students. One such song depicted the future paradise: "On the other side of the mountain, there is a good place, where the fields of rice are yellow, where people have plenty to eat as they cultivate their own land. Nobody uses you as beasts of burden. ... We practice democracy, and we love our place." When I was back in China in 1978, I asked the very people who used to sing such songs, "Do you remember those songs?" They were vague and evasive in their answers.

I am optimistic because today the leaders are talking about taking one step at a time. This reminds me of the intellectuals' debate in the 1920s: *Chuan-pan gai-zao* versus *i-bu i-bu gai-zao*, Li Dazhao versus Hu Shizhi. Today, people are less inclined to go for total transformation, because that would require an overarching ideology. Today, leaders are more pragmatic and I think this is better, because much common sense can be worked into their policies. Also, today there are many Chinese students and visiting scholars abroad, not only in the United States, but also in Europe, Australia, and Japan. These intellectuals, after they return home, will constitute a critical mass to have an impact on the policies of the regime. Five years ago I complimented a visiting scholar from the PRC, "When you get back, you will exercise some influence." The reply was, "After I return, I shall clam up." I think today the situation is more promising simply because there are many more intellectuals with experience in advanced industrial societies.

A high government official of the PRC once said to me in 1979, "I am envious of your system. Look at Henry Kissinger, he was the Secretary of State and powerful. But after he lost his job, he could go back to teaching and writing books; we do not have such options." I think the recent development in China seems to be pointing in that direction; with sufficient development and differentiation, politics may no longer be a zero-sum game; when one loses, one may not have to be a nonperson; one may have a viable alternative.

9

REORGANIZING AND MODERNIZING
THE CHINESE MILITARY

June Teufel Dreyer

THIS PAPER argues that not one but several models of the military existed at different times during Mao Zedong's tenure as head of the Chinese Communist Party (CCP). These are identified as the classical model, the functional specificity model, and the radical model. Mao seems to have been a guiding force at the inception of each, though dissatisfaction with certain aspects of the functioning of each led him to introduce new models or revert to the previous ones in accordance with his assessment of the needs of Chinese society at any given time.

This paper hypothesizes that Deng Xiaoping inherited a variant of the Maoist radical model that Mao himself could not have been completely happy with, and that Deng's military reforms represent a return to some aspects of the classical, and some aspects of the functional specificity, model. Rather than creating something fundamentally different, Deng has combined elements of these models in new and different ways. Problems similar to those that characterized each of these Maoist models are reemerging, and have led to certain adjustments in Deng's conceptualization of the military. It is possible that there will be more than one model of the military under Deng Xiaoping's leadership, just as there was under Mao's. Deng's need to turn to the military to resolve an internal political dispute during the demonstrations of the spring of 1989 may prove as much of a watershed for the People's Liberation Army (PLA) as Mao's similar action during a low point in the Cultural Revolution. Under none of these models is the PLA likely to approximate the professionalist model conceptualized by Samuel Huntington with its criteria of high levels of professional specialization, organizational differentiation, and political neutrality.[1] Deng's reputation as a pragmatist, derived from his economic reforms, would appear to extend to his views on military modernization as well.

Of Mao, Models, the Military, and Modernization

As succinctly summarized by Ying-mao Kau, the Maoist model of the military was characterized by multifunctionality, structural diffuseness, and politicization.[2] Exhibiting the classic form of this model in the late 1930s and early 1940s, the Red Army (subsequently renamed the People's Liberation Army, or PLA) performed many roles. In line with Mao's dictum that political power grows out of the barrel of a gun, the army had an important role in bringing the party's message to the masses. Military leadership was imperfectly distinguished from party and government leadership, with the same people often performing all three roles concurrently. In addition to training exercises and actual fighting, soldiers served in political, economic, and cultural roles. They were expected to propagandize the masses and help them with their economic and personal problems. Soldiers even put on plays and slide shows for the entertainment of the masses; typically these contained a political message. Soldiers were also held responsible for providing most of their own food, clothing, and housing needs, so as to minimize the cost of their upkeep to society as a whole.

Civil-military relations were considered of utmost importance, since the Chinese Communist leadership was aware that the support of the population was crucial to their continued existence. The local population was encouraged to think of the members of the Red Army as their children, and the military to regard the local population as kinfolk. A code of conduct for soldiers, the so-called three main rules and eight points for attention, warned soldiers against such civilian-antagonizing actions as appropriating anything without paying or taking liberties with local women. The lines between civilians and military were further blurred by enlisting adult civilians in a mass-based militia that played an important role in its own right, and even recruiting children, affectionately called "little devils," as couriers and spies for the army.

If the lines between the military and the nonmilitary roles of the army, and between the military and the civilian sectors of the population were blurred, so also were divisions of labor within the military. The Chinese Communist military was, prior to 1949, exclusively a ground force, with neither the knowledge nor the equipment to staff a navy or air force. The equipment possessed by the ground force was relatively primitive. Officers were typically not professional military men. Like the troops they commanded, most had received only rudimentary instruction in the ways of warfare. On-the-job training was the norm. Strategy and tactics attempted to use what meager resources the Red Army had to best advantage. Harrassment, hit-and-run tactics, and other techniques characteristic of guerrilla warfare were employed as much as possible.

Ideology encouraged the minimization of differences, with officers wearing no distinguishing bars of ribbons. Promotions often came from the ranks as a reward for meritorious service, and the commanders and those they commanded shared food and living accommodations of similar quantity and quality.

Poor though weapons and living standards might be, the ragtag Red Army was victorious over its Kuomintang (KMT) rivals in 1949. This allowed the Maoist military model to become synonymous with a formula for victory on the battlefield: people's war carried out by common folk whose political ideas were more important than the weapons they wielded would triumph in any confrontation. This formulation conveniently overlooked a number of other factors that also contributed heavily to the Chinese Communist victory. Following the war with Japan, a devastating inflation had hit China's urban areas, severely disadvantaging the KMT which, unlike the largely rural-based Communists, had its bases of strength in the cities. The KMT had been weakened as well by internal corruption and factional rivalries.

The Functional Specificity Model

Although it is more gratifying to think that one's victory has come against a formidable opponent rather than a weakened one, the extent to which the Maoist model of the military was dependent on the KMT's problems rather than on the strengths of the Chinese Communist model alone quickly became apparent during the Korean War. A major reorganization of the military was carried out to remedy deficiencies in weapons and training. There is no evidence that Mao Zedong opposed this; indeed, he is on record as favoring military modernization. The restructuring of the Chinese military was implemented with the help of the USSR and, not surprisingly, incorporated significant portions of Soviet military theory and practice. The military became more narrowly focused on training, to the detriment of the other functions it had performed in the society. Soviet weapons were introduced into PLA inventories. More sophisticated strategies and weapons called forth the need for more specialized training. Military academies were set up to train officers, lessening the average peasant recruit's chances of rising from the ranks. A more elaborate rank system was instituted, with new uniforms displaying insignia. Pay scales and standards of living became sharply differentiated in accordance with one's title. Those at the top of the hierarchy reportedly treated those at the bottom with increasing arrogance. The military in general tended to treat civilians highhandedly, leading to strained civil-military relations.[3] While there is little doubt that this reorganization produced a more capable fighting force, many Chinese Communist leaders, including Mao, came to feel that the disadvantages of this more functionally specific military model outweighed the benefits it conferred on the PLA.

The Radical Model

Revulsion against this more functionally specific and structurally differentiated (though scarcely less politicized) military model and those associated with it boiled over into the Great Leap Forward. The backlash, apparently strongly supported by

Mao, was characterized by policies that returned the military to many nonmilitary functions, including massive aid to the civilian economy, an officers-to-the-ranks movement aimed at reducing status distinctions, and a greater willingness to entrust China's defense to a mass-based militia rather than a professional standing army.[4] A model that could be described as derived from efforts to make the best possible use of the limited resources of the 1930s and early 1940s was now not merely reinstated but taken to new extremes, as a matter of ideology.

The efficacy of this model was never put to the test. The massive economic and social problems caused by the Great Leap Forward quickly became apparent and many of its programs, including those for the military, were abandoned. The problems lingered, however, in forms that affected military and civilians alike. Edema and other problems attendant on malnutrition were serious problems in the PLA from 1959 to 1961, as was loss of morale. A break in diplomatic relations with the Soviet Union meant that China no longer received Soviet weapons and technology.

Return to Functional Specificity

The return to a more functionally specific military was led by the newly appointed Defense Minister Lin Biao. Though seemingly at variance with his espousal of a highly politicized, rank-free, and multifunctional PLA during the Cultural Revolution, there can be no doubt of the devotion to professional standards that characterized Lin's actions in the immediate post-Great Leap Forward period. He is on record several times in the secret *Work Bulletins* of the PLA as saying that training must come first at all times, superseding political study, cultural activities, and labor projects.[5] China made efforts to copy Soviet weapons, and even to improve on their design. The efficacy of Lin's policies was reflected in the PLA's decisive win over Indian troops in the border confrontation of 1962. Though undoubtedly helped by the Indian side's inept political and military management, the PLA had fought well despite very long supply lines through difficult mountainous terrain occupied by a generally hostile Tibetan population.

Return to Radicalism

The advent of the Cultural Revolution caused another movement away from functional specificity and calls to return to features characteristic of the radical Maoist model. In May 1965, in the midst of a mass campaign wherein all Chinese were told to emulate the PLA, military ranks were abolished. The primacy of people over weapons was reemphasized, and military training exercises were deemphasized. The people versus weapons dichotomy that is implicit in Cultural Revolution pronouncements involves a radical reworking of classical Maoism. What Mao had originally done in his essay "On Protracted War" was to present a critique of what he considered the one-sided view that weapons alone are decisive in battle. His corrective was, "We see not only weapons but also people. Weapons are an important factor in war, but not the decisive factor; it is people, not things, that are decisive."[6]

The PLA, along with all other segments of Chinese society, became still more highly politicized. Political study meetings began to consume more and more time, as citizens and soldiers gathered to memorize and comment on the distilled wisdom of great leader Mao Zedong. This distillate, in the form of a small, red-covered book, had been commissioned by none other than Lin Biao. He soon became Mao's designated heir. The drastically different standards championed by Lin only a few years apart may have been undertaken partly at Mao's urging and, as hypothesized by Ralph Powell, partly because Lin was striving to make himself Mao's successor.[7]

One important feature of the classic Maoist model, multifunctionality, was conspicuous by its absence in this period. The military was told to intervene to support production only in February 1967, when administrative and social chaos had reached the point when many leaders feared the spring planting would not be done without the PLA's help. Radical pro-Maoists later denounced these actions as an "evil wind" designed to inhibit the proper development of the Cultural Revolution, and had the PLA withdrawn from these duties. During the next year, 1968, with chaos again spreading and the entire system close to immobilization, Mao himself ordered the military into schools and factories to ensure their proper functioning. This action seems to have been taken less because Mao considered it desirable than because he lacked other alternatives. Nevertheless, the PLA became more solidly entrenched in nonmilitary activities than it had been before. Soldiers ran study classes to reeducate unruly radicals and became a fixture on university campuses and industrial enterprises. The military's political power increased as well, with PLA men holding the top positions on revolutionary committees and, as party committees were reformed, in them as well. Frequently a PLA officer was concurrently the top party, government, and military leader in a province. As mentioned previously, the distinctions between party and military were typically blurred, especially at the top echelons of each. But a convincing argument can be made that during the late 1960s and early 1970s the PLA's many nonmilitary functions had reached a point where the army could be said to be controlling the party. The power of the military was further enhanced in 1969, when the Sino-Soviet war of words escalated into armed confrontation along the border and the threat of war seemed very real. Though continuing to affirm the primacy of people over weapons, China made serious efforts to upgrade its armaments. Defense production facilities, already seemingly large in proportion to the number of weapons produced, were further expanded during this period. And serious attention was paid to training.

Lin Biao's demise in late 1971, and the arrest of many PLA men associated with him, does not seem to have attenuated the influence of the military as such, but rather the influence of the radical faction within the military. PLA men continued to hold positions of power in the party and government hierarchies. The stronghold of leftist sentiment was now in the civilian sector, in the so-called Gang of Four, which was apparently backed by Mao Zedong. Not surprisingly, they distrusted the military and preferred to rely on the militia.

Subsequently, in December 1973, there was an unprecedented transfer of military region commands. Eight of the then-existing eleven military regions received new commanders; of the remaining three, two had received new leaders only a few months before. None of the newly appointed commanders held top party and government positions simultaneously. Mao's clear intent was to separate civil authority from military, and to reassert personal control over PLA leaders who, while loyal in the sense that they mounted no overt resistance to the transfers, could not necessarily be assumed to be in favor of radical programs espoused by Mao and many of his ardent supporters, including the Gang of Four. PLA officers who remained after the removal of Lin and his group included many who were acutely aware of the damage the Great Leap Forward and Cultural Revolution had done to the country in general and the military in particular, in terms of damage to its morale and war-fighting capability. They would therefore be apt to resist, or at least attempt to blunt, future attempts to implement leftist values. Removing these officers from civilian positions would attenuate their ability to offer such resistance.

This same period saw an attempt to build up the militia as a counterweight to the PLA.[8] Urban-based militia headquarters were established under left-leaning leaders and trained with arms that were, it was later charged, diverted from PLA storehouses. In addition to providing a support base for leftist policies, the urban militia was expected to be able to fight for a leftist leadership in the succession struggle that many anticipated would break out after Mao's death. The militia served as a left-wing shock force during the 1973–76 period and, among other activities, quelled the April 1976 demonstrations at Tienanmen Square. Radical forces succeeded in fixing the blame for the disturbances on Deng Xiaoping. He was summarily dismissed from all the positions he held, including that of head of the PLA's General Staff.

The military, however, retained many of the privileges that accrued to it during the Cultural Revolution, and continued to play an important part in the cultural and economic spheres of Chinese society. Mao's death later in 1976 was indeed followed by militia actions on behalf of the Gang of Four, but their units proved no match for the larger and better-equipped PLA. The Gang was arrested and the urban militia units were disbanded.[9]

Deng and Military Modernization

Deng was rehabilitated in 1977 and subsequently resumed his position as head of the PLA's General Staff Department. It is difficult to believe that either of these events could have occurred without the support of important elements within the military. Presumably these were elements that, broadly speaking, favored modernization and at least some aspects of functional specificity. Deng would thus, for reasons of his own as well as those of his support group, be expected to support these goals as well.

It would be tempting to juxtapose the classic Maoist model of a multifunctional, structurally diffuse, and politicized military with a Deng model characterized by professional specialization, organizational differentiation, and political neutrality. The military model that Deng inherited, however, had strayed not only from the classic model, but from the functional specificity and radical models as well in several important aspects. And the military model Deng seems to espouse involves elements of a return to certain aspects of both the classic Maoist and the functional specificity models. Basically, all the elements of Deng Xiaoping's military reforms were present at various times under Mao's leadership; rather than introducing something fundamentally new and different Deng has chosen to combine these elements in new and different ways.

The Chinese military in 1977 was *multifunctional* although there is evidence that the PLA did not perform its tasks on behalf of civilian construction with any great enthusiasm. Close civil-military relations, a touchstone of the classic Maoist model, had become quite strained. The peacekeeping activities the PLA had been assigned to during and after the Cultural Revolution had caused friction with those who felt they had been improperly treated. In addition, many of the military units that had been ordered to enter certain areas, such as university campuses, during the Cultural Revolution had become ensconced there, as well as in other housing belonging to civilians. They showed no intention of vacating it, much to the annoyance of students and ordinary citizens who wished to reclaim their residences. Civilians also resented other privileges accorded to military people and their families.

While *structurally diffuse* in the sense that ranks had been abolished, the status differences that accompanied them remained. No insignia were needed to know that an army commander was superior to the person who commanded a platoon. Salaries and the other amenities of life, such as a car and driver and access to housing, were distributed accordingly. Officers did not share "weal and woe" with their subordinates, many years of leftist propaganda notwithstanding. Moreover, the officer-to-soldier ratio was astonishingly high: 1:2.45.[10] This is considerably higher even than the militaries of advanced industrial states, which have the technologically more sophisticated equipment that generally elicits the need for larger proportions of officers. It was all the more surprising in the relatively low-technology environment of the PLA, with its ideological commitment to egalitarianism. Ideological commitment had not, however, been strong enough to resist constant pressures from within the organization for promotion. Since the PLA had not been a cost-conscious institution, it had little incentive to counter these pressures.

And while undoubtedly *politicized*, the military was also factionalized—another anathema to the Maoist canon. Differing ideological outlooks were to cause serious differences of opinion within the military on issues such as Deng's agricultural and financial reforms, the proper view of the legacy of Mao, new developments in literature and art, and military strategy and tactics. Failure to resolve these fissures within the military would affect not only the efficacy of the PLA as a fighting force but also the survival of Deng himself.

Deng probably saw his tasks more in terms of finding solutions in these problem areas—goals Mao himself could not have been philosophically opposed to—than in terms of overarching model-building. Yet the actions taken to remedy perceived deficiencies in the PLA, when taken in conjunction with the reforms Deng has introduced in other areas of society, will have profound consequences for the form and functioning of the Chinese military. As they concern the PLA, these reforms include the introduction of new strategic concepts and weapons, a streamlining and reorganization of the military, and a reworking of the relationship of the PLA to the rest of Chinese society.

Strategy and Doctrine

The techniques of People's War had been developed in an era where the highly mobile and lightly equipped Chinese Communist forces could afford to lure the enemy deep into their largely rural base areas and then disperse the opposing force and disrupt its supply lines. They had obvious deficiencies for the sort of invasion China would be likely to experience in the present day. While public pronouncements well into 1980 continued to threaten to "drown [the presumably Soviet] invader in a sea of People's War," there were subtle hints that the doctrine was being reworked. Some strategists argued that "luring deep" would involve surrendering a great deal of territory. In the case of a Soviet invasion of China's northeast—a highly likely route for such an invasion, since Manchuria is both an exposed salient and the most industrialized area in the PRC—luring deep would mean losing valuable assets that would compound the difficulties of successful resistance. More emphasis began to be paid to positional warfare, with the aim being to guide invading forces toward sites preselected for optimal counterattack. For example, a massive exercise held in September 1981 indicates that Zhangjiakou, approximately 90 miles northwest of Beijing, has been chosen as the position from which to defend the capital city.[11] This and subsequent exercises also show concerted efforts to coordinate the different service arms for joint action.

There was also a good deal of Chinese interest in developing their forces' ability to engage a front-line military offensive threat. In this regard, Chinese strategists showed keen interest in the U.S. Army's concept of the Air Land Battle. This strategy involves large-scale use of helicopters, some configured to destroy enemy tanks and others to land infantry behind enemy lines.[12]

There was a new interest in discussing strategic questions in general. Foreign military works, such as *On War* by Clausewitz and *The Reminiscences of Zhukov*, were translated into Chinese,[13] and the Beijing Institute of Strategic Studies, itself headed by a senior PLA officer, Xu Xiuquan, sponsored a "military salon" in which younger and middle-level officers were encouraged to exchange views.[14] Another change was toward increased interest in low intensity conflict, as opposed to the almost single-minded concentration on worldwide conflict that characterized past discussions of warfare.

Weapons and Equipment

Considerable progress has been made over the last decade in upgrading weapons and equipment, though starting from a low base level. Improvements have also been limited by constrained military budgets, scarce foreign exchange reserves, disagreements over whether to favor indigenous research and development or foreign imports, and a cumbersome procurement process. Additional problems have arisen in connection with transferring the results of theoretical research into serial production.

Domestic small arms production has been bolstered by the introduction of new rifle and submachine gun models since 1980.[15] The PRC has also purchased 155 mm-artillery shell technology from the United States.[16]

As for tanks, the Chinese have developed the Type 69, a follow-on to the Type 59, which had been copied from the Soviet Union's T–54 model. The new Chinese tank benefited significantly from Israeli help, that country having had several decades' experience in rebuilding and retrofitting captured Soviet tanks. Israeli contributions to the Type 69 include electronic fire control systems, nightsight scopes, and communications equipment.[17]

In terms of aircraft, China has developed the F–8 fighter as a follow-on to the F–7, which had in turn been copied from the Soviet MiG–21. The plane, a high-altitude delta-wing interceptor with twin engines, was a disappointment to aviation experts.[18] Its capabilities will be significantly improved, however, by the addition of radar and related equipment to upgrade the plane's fire control and navigation devices, purchased from the United States and Great Britain.[19]

In the maritime sphere, China has produced nuclear-powered and ballistic missile submarines, and in 1982 claimed to have successfully launched a missile from a submerged submarine.[20] In surface ships, however, a follow-on for the Luda class destroyer has been postponed indefinitely. Four LM 2500 gas turbine engines purchased from the United States will apparently be put on Luda class ships instead.[21]

The PLA's navy (PLAN) has taken modest steps toward acquiring a blue-water capacity. Its procurement of ocean-going supply ships has enabled the PLAN to sustain its warships at sea. In 1980, an 18-ship task force undertook a

35-day, 8,000-nautical mile mission into the South Pacific to police the target zone for China's intercontinental ballistic missile (ICBM) test. The flotilla also recovered the rockets' instrument modules and, not incidentally, showed the flag.[22] And, in November 1985, the PRC sent a guided missile destroyer and a supply ship on a two-month Indian Ocean "goodwill voyage." Their calls in Pakistan, Bangladesh, and Sri Lanka constituted the first visits by Chinese naval vessels to foreign ports since 1949.[23] While the voyage unquestionably demonstrated PLAN's ability to operate at such distances, there have been no port calls since then. Constrained budgets are the most likely reason.

Probably the PRC's most impressive progress to date has come in missile design and research. As in the case of other weapons systems, China first started missile production by copying Soviet designs. More recently, it has not only produced improved versions, but has designed, developed, and placed new missile systems in production.[24]

China also maintains a nuclear strike force. As mentioned above, its first ICBM was tested in 1980; it is believed that no more than twelve are presently deployed. In addition, the PRC has shorter-range missiles that are operational. Though small in numbers and not particularly accurate, the missiles are well hidden and give the PRC a credible second-strike capability or, as the PLA's official *Liberation Army Daily* recently described it, a "limited self-defense counterattack capability."[25]

This nuclear force, when taken together with the PRC's large standing army and huge number of potential recruits, means that China's capacity to defend its own territory is quite good. Poor logistics, inadequate roads and rail lines in border areas, and limited sea and air-lift capacities, however, mean that China has little ability to project power beyond its own borders. While improvements have been made in the last decade, the military capabilities of the PRC's neighbors have not been static either. Defense analysts believe that the gap between China's capabilities and those of its most likely adversary, the Soviet Union, has actually widened since Deng began his military modernization program.

Indeed, given the austere budget the PLA has operated under, it would be odd if this were not so. Military modernization has had the lowest priority of the Four Modernizations, and will likely retain it. The total investment in defense projects fell each year from 1985 to the time of writing in late 1989.[26] Both its austere defense budgets and its efforts to harmonize relations with the Soviet Union indicate that the PRC does not anticipate becoming involved in a major confrontation in the near future. As one analyst phrased it, the PRC has what is in essence a "no war" strategy.[27] PLA leaders have acknowledged that their backward technology is a major weakness and will continue to remain so. They have intimated that once the country's economy as a whole has been placed on a sound basis, the time will be appropriate for more serious efforts to improve military capabilities.[28]

Reorganization and Streamlining

There have been large-scale changes in military leadership, the most spectacular being the replacement of eight of the eleven Military Region commanders during the first two months of 1980—a feat reminiscent of Mao Zedong's actions in the closing days of 1973. Later, a reorganization of the eleven Military Regions into seven brought further changes: three new commanders and all seven commissars were new. The heads of the PLA's three General Departments have also been replaced since 1980. When Deng replaced the disgraced Hua Guofeng as head of the party's Central Military Commission—China's most prestigious military position—he named his protegé Yang Dezhi as chief of the General Staff. Though the need for leaders who were younger in age and superior in technical expertise was the stated reason for the personnel changes, one suspects that loyalty to Deng and to his programs was an even more important criterion: Deng himself is in his mid-eighties, the deputy chief of the Central Military Commission is eighty, and the heads of all three General Departments are in their seventies. Meanwhile, men in their fifties and sixties were being pushed into retirement.

Field armies, which were felt to be the foci of personalistic loyalties, were reorganized into group armies in 1985,[29] as new Military Regions were being formed. The new Military Regions were given the right to command the different service arms; in the past, these service arms had been placed under the command of the central armed forces.[30] A new conscription law and a new military service law were passed in 1984. Among other provisions, they established a military reserve force.[31] The militia, which had played an important part in purging Deng Xiaoping in 1976, has seen its grass-roots membership reduced by 60 percent, and of militia cadres by 80 percent.[32] The new laws also provided for the reinstitution of the rank system, though it took more than four years, until October 1988, to actually do so. High-level disagreement over who should get which ranks is believed to have been the most likely cause for the delay.

A major effort to force older officers to retire in favor of younger, more vigorous men succeeded in lowering the ages of commanders by an average of eight years.[33] And educational standards were instituted, with the aim of having all enlisted personnel literate and, eventually, all commissioned officers graduates of either universities or military academies.

A 25 percent cut in personnel has reduced the PLA by nearly a million persons. Partly, as will be seen in the following section, this involved the removal of certain nonmilitary tasks done by the PLA from PLA control. But the manner in which the cuts were implemented succeeded in reducing the officer-to-enlisted ratio from 1 to 2.45 to 1 to 3.3, with seventy-six kinds of positions formerly held by officers now staffed by ordinary soldiers.[34]

Relationship of the PLA to Chinese Society

Deng's reforms seem to have aimed at reducing the military's power in certain—
though not all—nonmilitary activities. To this end, the fourteen military divisions devoted to railway work were placed under the jurisdiction of the Ministry
of Railways, and certain units of the PLA's Capital Construction Corps were
civilianized as well. Together, these transfers reduced the size of the PLA by
500,000.[35] The military was also removed from internal security duties with the
formation of the People's Armed Police. The several hundred thousand PLA
members who had served in this capacity and as border guards were transferred
to the Ministry of Public Security, though the party Central Committee's announcement of the decision stated that "after reorganization, the armed police
will maintain the system of integrating compulsory military service with voluntary
military service, will enforce the rules and regulations of the PLA, use the standards
and supplies of the PLA, and enjoy the same treatment as the PLA."[36] Given this
continuity in organizational structure and training, the degree to which the PLA has
lost influence over these units is unclear. It is interesting to note that the major
address at the People's Armed Police conferences is typically given by leading PLA
figures rather than representatives of the Ministry of Public Security.[37]

In addition, only half a year before the internal security forces were removed,
at least in theory, from PLA jurisdiction, another very large paramilitary organization was revived and placed under its jurisdiction. Xinjiang's Production and
Construction Corps, which included several hundred thousand persons, was reconstituted under the jurisdiction of the Central Military Commission. Speeches
made at the celebratory rally noted that Deng Xiaoping himself had made the
decision to revive it.[38]

The PLA's role in the economy of China, important under Mao Zedong, has
remained large under Deng and is in certain ways even more important. The
army is still expected to strive for self-sufficiency in food production,[39] and has
been given a mandate to support economic modernization. This has included the
large-scale sharing of the PLA's facilities, including rail lines, airfields, and
docks, with nonmilitary users. The military has also been told to share its technology with civilian enterprises. An estimated 30 to 40 percent of the PLA's
defense facilities have been retooled to produce consumer goods.

Much of this is for domestic consumption, but goods are also produced for
shipment abroad. The scale can be immense. For example, Xinxing Corporation,
described as "the only army-controlled import-export corporation under the direct leadership of the PLA's General Logistics Department" was, at its inception
in 1984, "born strong." The army placed under its administration more than three
thousand factories, two thousand farms, and eight thousand enterprises, including scientific institutes, universities, and hospitals. Xinxing also controls dozens
of mines and sixteen large horse ranches. It employs 700,000 persons.[40]

The intent behind the founding of corporations like Xinxing was to better utilize the PLA's excess production facilities to support economic modernization in the civilian sector. But the PLA's defense production facilities have also been producing weapons, and not just for internal use. In the past five years China has become the world's fourth largest arms exporter, after the Soviet Union, the United States, and Great Britain.[41] The PRC has sold missiles, planes, tanks, and small arms to many Third World countries. It is reputedly Iran's largest supplier, but sells as well to Iraq, Egypt, Thailand, Brazil, and several African states.

The PLA is also engaged in less glamorous economic activities. It is expected to support civilian economic construction, participate in tree-planting campaigns, and help with crop-dusting. PLA men excavated a massive channel to divert the flow of the Luan River to chronically water-short Tianjin, and dug tunnels for the Beijing subway system. As part of the demobilization effort, the military instituted a large-scale program to produce "dual-use personnel." This aimed at teaching PLA members skills useful in the civilian economy, including such trades as gardening, tailoring, and small appliance repair.

The net effect of these actions has been to blur the distinctions between the civilian and military economies. And since PLA facilities and PLA resources are being used for nonmilitary purposes, they give the PLA a legitimate voice in influencing economic decision-making concerning areas not narrowly confined to the military.

As for the PLA's role in party and government, military representation on the Politburo of the Central Committee is now about 20 percent, down from higher percentages immediately after the Cultural Revolution, but still reflecting a substantial presence. New election laws give the PLA the right to elect 264 deputies out of a total of 2,978 members of the National People's Congress (NPC). Since the law provides that there shall be one deputy per 1.04 million rural dwellers and one per 130,000 urban residents, the PLA's three million members can scarcely be considered disadvantaged by this scheme. The law further provides that the PLA shall attend the NPC as a unit, and in uniform.[42]

With regard to its influence on Chinese culture, the PLA faced an important test in 1982. Certain military leaders, including some who had championed Deng's rehabilitation, were understandably concerned about the effect that less rigidly censored literature and art would have, both on the PLA and on society as a whole. Poetry, plays, and films satirizing military corruption began to appear, much to the annoyance of the officer corps. Military leaders also felt that the greater tolerance for the frailty of human emotions allowed under the new standards would have adverse effects on discipline and moral standards among the troops. Soldiers who preferred to watch pornography rather than training films and sing love songs instead of those with patriotic themes were not soldiers that they wanted to lead into battle.

These concerns were reflected in articles in the *Liberation Army Daily* and in a military journal called *Report on the Times*, criticizing "spiritual pollution" and "bourgeois liberalism" in literature and art. Deng's response was to sack the head of the PLA's General Political Department, to which both the paper and the journal were subordinate. This was no small matter: the incumbent, a certified hero of both the Anti-Japanese War and civil war, was virtually unique in having survived all previous purges of both the Left and the Right, and was in addition one of the very few members of a minority ethnic group to serve on the Politburo. He had been considered one of Deng's strong supporters. The newspaper made a public apology, with a new editor quickly appointed. The journal was completely reorganized and removed from control of the General Political Department.[43]

Deng had made his point forcefully. This action, however, did not diminish the role that the PLA plays in shaping Chinese culture. Through its movie studio, which produces films shown to the general public, and through its large contingent of literature and art workers, the PLA continues to play an important role. What Deng's actions did show was that he would not tolerate resistance to his reforms mounted by certain PLA leaders. As was revealed both in his conduct here and in his handling of the Tiananmen demonstrations, Deng has been authoritarian even in reform.

Deng has not always fared so well with the PLA on other matters. His 1982 attempt to create a State Military Commission with duties separate from that of the party's Central Military Commission were thwarted. Although the State Constitution that was ratified in that year did indeed set up such a commission,[44] its membership is exactly the same as that of the party commission, and it does not appear to have an existence of its own.

Even more important a setback was the failure of Deng's continuing attempts to resign as chair of the Central Military Commission and appoint his protegé, Hu Yaobang, in his place. Although Hu already held the highest position in the Communist party as a whole, the PLA refused to accept him as head of the Military Commission. Repeated attempts by Deng, including a personal visit to at least one ostensibly retired PLA leader, produced no results. When, in January 1987, Hu resigned as party secretary-general in the wake of student demonstrations, there were rumors that the PLA had been instrumental in his downfall. The only evidence to substantiate this charge is highly circumstantial. It is probably safe to say, however, that, at the very least, the PLA was able to successfully resist Hu Yaobang's appointment as head of the Military Commission until other influential segments of the Chinese decision-making elite came to share its view of his competence. Apart from PLA leaders' dim view of Hu's general abilities, the other reason for opposition to him was his lack of military experience. Deng's attempts to have him appointed to the country's top military position can clearly not be construed as motivated by professionalism or a desire for functional specificity. Communist youth work in the PLA was intensified rather than abated under Deng, and there were no noticeable efforts to dismantle the political commissar system.[45] Rather than depoliticizing the military, it would appear that Deng's changes aimed at ensuring that the PLA will share his particular political views.

This premise would seem to have been strengthened by the events surrounding the declaration of martial law in May 1989. In the Huntingtonian definition of professionalism, the military is politically neutral and would be expected to enforce the decree automatically. In fact, this did not happen, and the PRC's leadership seems to have anticipated that it would not. Immediately after the declaration, Deng Xiaoping reportedly convened a meeting of military region commanders to solicit their support. The session was said to have been contentious, with several of the commanders initially refusing to comply.[46]

In the Huntingtonian concept of professionalism, this would be tantamount to mutiny. In the context of the PRC, it was clearly not regarded as such. Mao Zedong's statement that political power grows out of the barrel of a gun implies a highly politicized military in the service of the party. Nothing that any of his successors, including Deng Xiaoping, has said would indicate that they view the military in any other way. When there is consensus with the party leadership on a course of action, the PLA's record of compliance has been exemplary. When there is a split within the top levels of the party, it is expected that this will be reflected in similar lines of cleavage within the military. Indeed, many officials hold top positions in the party and government, as well as in the military. Yang Shangkun, who is, as permanent vice chairman and secretary-general of the party Military Commission, in charge of the actual functioning of the PLA, serves simultaneously as president of China. Deng Xiaoping, widely regarded as China's paramount leader though he holds no important party or government position, is chair of the Military Commission. Because Yang, Deng, and several others occupy concurrent positions in nonmilitary and military hierarchies, lines of cleavage cannot be sharply drawn, either between those hierarchies or in decision-making processes affecting them. Given the Maoist conception of the military, the leadership is likely to argue that, for the good of the whole, such clear-cut distinctions should not exist. This is a major continuity between Mao and Deng that should not be overlooked.

Deng also tried to effect changes in the PLA's relationships with civilian society as a whole. These were intended to restore the "army is the fish and the people are the water" relationships that characterize the classic Maoist model. The military was ordered to vacate civilian premises it had occupied earlier, a process that seems to have had some successes and other instances of continuing resistance. During the early 1980s, the PLA was ordered to "perform good services for the people."[47] Approved examples of these services included sweeping streets, resurfacing roads, dredging sewers, and removing garbage. The PLA was also ordered to work with local areas to build so-called civilized villages, which would be models of amicable civil-military relations.

Attempts were made to curtail many of the PLA privileges that had caused civilian jealousy. For example, officers were told that when they traveled any distance in groups, they should use buses rather than convoys of individually chauffeured vehicles. And the practice of joining the army in order to give oneself a route out of the countryside was ended: regulations introduced soon after Deng returned to power stipulated that individuals should be demobilized in the same area that they had joined the PLA.

While Deng's reforms presumably had beneficial effects on civil-military relations, they caused other problems of morale within the military. PLA members resented the loss of perquisites they had enjoyed for many years. Moreover, Deng's reforms in agriculture had greatly increased rural incomes, making it more profitable to stay on the farm. In terms of neither of the overlapping categories of status and prestige, did a military career seem desirable any longer: for the first time in its history, the PLA had difficulty in attracting the sort of recruits it wanted.

Still other problems were caused by the stricter educational standards and the requirement that officers obtained higher education. Differences between officers and ordinary soldiers became more noticeable, as did frictions between the two groups. The army's official newspaper published complaints from soldiers that "nothing is successful without giving gifts [to officers]. Things that should be done according to regulations, such as visits home, educational leave, transfers, admission to the CCP, have to be done with wine, cigarettes, and personal connections."[48] While corruption was not unique to the military, it was exacerbated within the PLA by various factors that were specific to the military. For example, the greater authority that commanders exercised over soldiers as a result of the military's institutional requirement for discipline, played into the hands of corrupt commanders who wished to be given gifts. Also, enlistees often served in areas that were located at considerable distances from their homes. Therefore, the need for permission to leave for periods of time to attend to family emergencies or other personal reasons was more likely to arise.

In late 1986, Deputy Chief of the Central Military Commission Yang Shangkun described officer-soldier relations as "a major problem," and declared that they must improve.[49] One way in which this was attempted was the introduction of "eight prohibitions" as a supplement to the "three main rules for discipline and eight points for attention" that had been part of the code of ethics since the earliest days of the Red Army. Assuming that the military would not bother to ban practices that did not exist, it is instructive to examine the list of items prohibited:[50]

1. beating, swearing at, and corporal punishment for soldiers
2. receiving gifts from soldiers
3. cadres infringing on soldiers' interests
4. imposing fines on soldiers
5. alcoholism
6. gambling
7. reading pornographic materials
8. deception

A month later it was announced that the "eight no's" had been made into a song that was "easy to learn and remember," and was to be sung by officers and men together.[51]

In an effort to bolster corporate pride despite economic austerity, the military was also issued more attractive uniforms and encouraged to stage parades on national holidays. Newspapers continue to urge PLA members not to view military service as a hardship but a glorious duty, thus indicating that problems of morale continue to exist.

Civil-military relations seem to have been appreciably worsened by the PLA's role in putting down the Tiananmen demonstrations. According to Chinese newspapers, military facilities were attacked and military dependents set upon and beaten while soldiers were off quelling the disturbances.[52] Other civilians reportedly formed "dare-to-die" sniper squads, with the aim of killing soldiers with weapons stolen from the PLA during the demonstrations.[53]

Conclusions

Deng Xiaoping's military reforms do not fit neatly into any of the Maoist models delineated. His attempts to reinstitute the rank system and upgrade the PLA's weapons and training facilities resemble Mao's functional specificity model. On the other hand, his efforts to obtain better civil-military relations, involve the PLA in the civilian economy on a large scale, and install a politically reliable person with little military experience as head of the Central Military Commission more closely resemble the classic Maoist model. Others of Deng's reforms, such as the thus far unsuccessful attempt to set up a State Military Commission with a membership and agenda different from those of the party Military Commission, are less clear in their implications and may have more relevance for personal political survival than for model-building.

Indeed, it is unlikely that Deng set out with any well-defined model in mind. There are excellent reasons for trying to mitigate civil-military tensions, and for enlisting the PLA's support in civilian economic projects, quite apart from the fact that Mao championed both. Interestingly, though not surprisingly, the same kinds of problems Mao found growing out of the different models he espoused have reemerged. Greater functional specificity has had deleterious effects on officer-soldier relationships, and efforts to improve civil-military relations have had deleterious effects on military morale. Further experimentation with ways to alleviate these problems may be expected: Deng's reputation as a pragmatist rather than an ideologue, already noted in his approach to economic development, appears to extend to his military reforms as well.

Both successful resistance from the military and changing circumstances internal and external to China may modify Deng Xiaoping's present plans for the military. What effect the events of the spring of 1989 will have on Deng's military model remains to be seen. So far, there is no hard evidence that it has been modified. The Standing Committee of the Politburo contained no individual with strong military ties before the demonstrations, and the reorganized Standing Committee also contains no such individual. There have been no concrete rewards to the military in the form of pay raises or better living conditions. Indeed, the need for fiscal prudence in the face of rising inflation rates would seem to rule out such rewards, regardless of who is in charge in the Politburo.

Efforts to improve civil-military relations continue to be made, though effecting these improvements will be all the more difficult after the Tiananmen Square incident. And, as was argued above, the political decision-making involved in the PLA's behavior following the declaration of martial law is in continuity with Deng's previous understanding of military professionalism rather than representing a break with it. Given the PRC's present level of development and its perceived needs, the end of the Deng era is more likely to see the sort of "defense force with Chinese characteristics" the official media speak of than the model of Huntingtonian professionalism some U.S. analysts seem to anticipate.

Notes

1. Samuel P. Huntington, *The Soldier and the State* (Cambridge, MA: Harvard University Press, 1959), chap. 1.

2. Ying-mao Kau, *The People's Liberation Army and China's Nation-Building* (White Plains, NY: International Arts and Sciences Press, 1973), pp. xix-lvii.

3. Ellis Joffe, *Party and Army: Professionalism and Political Control in the Chinese Officer Corps, 1949–1964* (Cambridge, MA: Harvard East Asian Monographs no. 19; 1967), chap. 2, discusses the events of this period in detail.

4. John Gittings, *The Role of the Chinese Army* (London: Oxford University Press, 1967), chap. 6, summarizes major events during this time.

5. See, e.g., *Gongzuo tongxun* no. 15 (June 17, 1961), trans. in J. Chester Cheng, *The Politics of the Chinese Army: A Translation of the Bulletin of Activities of the People's Liberation Army* (Stanford, CA: Hoover Institution on War, Revolution, and Peace, 1966), p. 133.

6. Translated in *Selected Military Writings of Mao Zedong* (Beijing: Foreign Languages Press, 1963), p. 217.

7. Ralph Powell, "The Increasing Power of Lin Biao and the Party Soldiers" *The China Quarterly*, no. 34 (April–June 1968), pp. 38–65.

8. See the joint editorial in *Jiefang junbao* (hereafter *JFJB*) and *Renmin ribao* (hereafter *RMRB*), as translated in United States Department of Commerce, *Foreign Broadcast Information Service: China* (hereafter, *FBIS-CHI*) October 1, 1973, pp. B10–B12.

9. June Teufel Dreyer, "The Chinese Militia: Citizen-Soldiers and Civil-Military Relations in the People's Republic of China," *Armed Forces and Society*, vol. 9, no. 1 (Fall 1982), pp. 63–82.

10. Hong Kong, *Wen wei po*, May 4, 1981, in *FBIS-CHI*, May 5, 1987, p. K11.

11. *Wen wei po*, September 28, 1981, in United States Department of Commerce, *Joint Publications Research Service* (hereafter, *JPRS*) no. 79210 (October 15, 1981), p. 54.

12. See *Field Manual 100–5: Operations* (Fort Monroe, Virginia: Headquarters, Department of the Army, May 1986) for the official statement of the Air-Land Battle. The concept is also discussed in Boy Sutton et al., "New Directions in Conventional Defense," *Survival*, March–April 1984, pp. 50–70.

13. Beijing, *China Daily*, April 24, 1987, p. 5.

14. Hong Kong, *Liaowang*, November 25, 1985, in *FBIS-CHI*, December 5, 1985, p. K10-K12.

15. Beijing Radio, April 21, 1987, in *FBIS-CHI*, April 24, 1987, pp. K17–K19.

16. *Washington Post*, September 18, 1985, p. A33; Nayan Chanda, "A Technical Point," Hong Kong, *Far Eastern Economic Review* (hereafter, *FEER*), August 28, 1986, p. 27.

17. *Washington Post*, December 1, 1986, pp. C1, C4.

18. See, e.g., Kenneth Munson, "Fishbed, Finback, and the Chinese Future," London, *Jane's Defense Weekly* (hereafter, *JDW*), December 21, 1985, pp. 1367–69.

19. *New York Times*, April 7, 1986, p. 3; Beijing, *Xinhua*, December 9, 1986, in *FBIS-CHI*, January 5, 1987, p. G1.

20. Russell Warren Howe, "China to Develop Nuke Subs," *Washington Times*, October 28, 1982, p. 4.

21. London, *International Defense Review* (December 1986), p. 1737.

22. Richard Breeze, "The Wild Blue Yonder," *FEER* 11 (June 1982), pp. 21–22.

23. *New York Times*, November 17, 1985, p. 7.

24. Jim Bussert, "Chinese Missile Designs Increasing," *JDW*, November 8, 1986, p. 1098; Christopher Foss, "Missile Developments in the Chinese Army," *JDW*, January 17, 1987, pp. 64–69.

25. *JFJB*, March 20, 1987, in *FBIS-CHI*, March 26, 1987, p. K49.

26. See, e.g., *Xinhua*, March 31, 1987, in *FBIS-CHI*, April 3, 1987, pp. K9–K10.

27. Author's conversation with Professor Harvey Nelsen, University of South Florida, September 21, 1986.

28. *JFJB*, March 21, 1987, in *FBIS-CHI*, April 6, 1987, pp. K22–K23.

29. Hong Kong, *Zhongguo xinwenshe*, July 31, 1986, in *FBIS-CHI*, August 8, 1986, p. K1.

30. *Wen wei po*, October 17, 1985, in *FBIS-CHI*, October 22, 1985, pp. W1–W2. While the clear intent of this move was to increase operational efficiency, it may be seen that the change also increased the Military Region's ability to act autonomously—which might make it harder to erode the influence of personalistic loyalties.

31. *Xinhua*, June 4, 1984, in *FBIS-CHI*, June 6, 1984 pp. K1–K22.

32. Beijing Radio, December 16, 1985, in *FBIS-CHI*, December 18, 1985, p. K12.

33. *Liaowang*, October 7, 1985, in *FBIS-CHI*, October 30, 1985, p. K9.

34. *Wen wei po*, May 4, 1987, in *FBIS-CHI*, May 5, 1987, p. W2.

35. *Xinhua*, July 30, 1986, in *FBIS-CHI*, August 1, 1986, p. K11.

36. Cited in Hong Kong, *Ming pao*, January 29, 1983, *FBIS-CHI*, February 2, 1983, p. W2.

37. See, e.g., Yang Dezhi's speech in *Xinhua*, February 21, 1984, *FBIS-CHI*, February 23, 1984, p. K18.

38. Xinjiang Radio, June 1, 1982, in *FBIS-CHI*, June 3, 1982, p. T4.

39. *Xinhua*, March 31, 1987, in *FBIS-CHI*, April 3, 1987, pp. K9–K10.

40. *China Daily*, Business Supplement, April 8, 1987, p. 1.

41. *International Herald Tribune*, May 20, 1987, p. 7.

42. *Xinhua*, April 2, 1987, in *FBIS-CHI*, April 2, 1987, pp. K19–K20.

43. A summary of these developments is provided in Hong Kong, *Kuangchiao ching*, March 16, 1985, *FBIS-CHI*, March 22, 1985, pp. W1–W2.

44. *Xinhua*, December 4, 1982, in *FBIS-CHI*, December 7, 1982, pp. K15–K16, K21.

45. I am indebted to Professor Ying-mao Kau, Brown University, for this observation on the political commissar system. Conversation of October 14, 1987.

46. Beijing Radio, September 30, 1981, in *FBIS-CHI*, October 1, 1981, pp. K22–K25.

47. *Xinhua*, November 30, 1985, in *FBIS-CHI*, December 2, 1985, pp. K22–K25.

48. *Ming pao*, February 25, 1986, in *FBIS-CHI*, Febraury 26, 1986, p. W6.
49. Beijing Radio, October 10, 1986, in *FBIS-CHI*, October 14, 1986, p. K14.
50. Beijing Radio, August 8, 1986, in *FBIS-CHI*, August 11, 1986, p. K1.
51. *Xinhua*, September 27, 1986, in *FBIS-CHI*, September 29, 1986, p. K17.
52. Hebei Radio, July 15, 1989, in *FBIS-CHI*, July 18, 1989, p. 56.
53. *Hong Kong Standard*, July 19, 1989, in *FBIS-CHI*, July 19, 1989, p. 18.

Comments by Parris Chang

Professor Dreyer's paper is very succinct. She has emphasized different models, civil-military relations, and so forth. Of course we may ask, "So what?" Certain issues can be raised, however. First, has the development at the Thirteenth Party Congress in any way affected the paper's conclusion? Second, regarding Professor Dreyer's statement, "the current model of the PLA resembles the classic model during Mao's time," I would like Professor Dreyer to expound on this because with the opening to the West and increasing contact with the United States and all these sophisticated weapons, one would need much better-educated soldiers and officers. If there is some kind of resemblance on the surface, in reality there are many more differences. Certainly, China's weapons system today is much more sophisticated than in the 1950s.

There are two areas that Professor Dreyer did not discuss and that we may want to explore. One is that with a very modernized and reorganized Chinese People's Liberation Army, what is the implication? What is the policy input of the PLA? We want to know, for example, the PLA's role in the development of China's foreign policy. On the domestic side, Professor Dreyer mentioned the role played by the PLA as the veto group against certain reforms. That is true,, but what about the PLA's role in China's foreign policy and relations with other countries. What is the PLA's role in terms of Sino-U.S. relations and Sino-Soviet relations? What about arms sales? These are issues to be looked into.

Another area to be explored is the development of the Thirteenth Party Congress: Chairman Deng remained Chairman of the MAC, and Zhao Ziyang, First Vice Chairman of the MAC. Why? If we look at the relationship between the Party Chairman and the new Chairman of the MAC, what could his relationship be with the military? We can imagine a variety of scenarios: the party directs the gun, and this would have implications for politics. Another relationship might be some kind of coalition, checks and balances. Still another would be that the gun directs the party, a possibility that might occur after Deng dies. Can Zhao Ziyang or someone after him command the respect and obedience of the military? If Hu Yaobang fell, would a future party leader coming up do better? Professor Dreyer's discussion of what the military has done in terms of civil-military relations has not mentioned the role of the military in the process of a succession struggle, or the role it might play in the resolution of a conflict. Might this kind of role become more important in the years to come?

Comments by Michael Ying-mao Kau

The conceptual scheme developed by June Dreyer to discuss the process of development of the People's Liberation Army (PLA) is a very useful one. The scheme emphasizes three important analytical categories: the structural characteristics, the functional characteristics, and the patterns of political process. June has used the scheme to analyze the pattern of change, particularly from the era of Mao to that of Deng.

At the very general level of discussion, it is pertinent, first, for us to ask to what extent the Chinese PLA is different from other military establishments in other cultural settings, and then, to what extent Mao's approach to army-building is different from Deng's policy. If they are different, what are the independent variables that made such a difference: Was it because of personality and ideology, or due to other variables, such as the developments of new technology, weapon systems, or organizations that were essential to effective military operations.

Basically, I agree with Professor Dreyer that for the Mao period we did see the characteristics of the classical Maoist model as Mao articulated it in terms of the doctrine of "people's war" and "protracted guerrilla warfare." In the later period, one saw the emergence of a somewhat different model, which Professor Dreyer characterizes as the functional specificity model of military building. Then, for the Deng period, she suggests that the pattern resembles a combination of the classical model plus the emphasis on functional specificity model. As for the radical politicized model, it seems to be on the decline. Basically, her characterization makes sense.

My general question, however, is whether Professor Dreyer's approach is the best and only way to characterize the process of the PLA's change over time, or whether there are alternative ways that we can articulate its process of change. It is possible that were Chairman Mao here today, he might disagree with Professor Dreyer on some of the credit she tries to give him. For example, she suggests that Mao himself had introduced the functional specificity model in the later period (we have to blame the sociologists for all those Parsonsian jargons). Mao might disclaim that he introduced that model. He was interested primarily in a highly politicized model.

In various historical periods, one may indeed find that Mao argued strongly that the functional specificity model was in fact a deviation from his classical model. He did not really want the functionally specialized model to stand as a model per se. He always wanted the PLA to be properly balanced between political commitment and functional specialization. As he saw it, the functional specificity model represented a rightist deviation that paid too much attention to modernization, military training, and so on, at the expense of political involvement, support for the party, and so forth.

In the same vein, when the Cultural Revolution pushed the PLA to drift toward the extreme of military control and military intervention, Mao disclaimed that this was what he really intended. Mao might have allowed the kind of radicalism to develop at the beginning for the purpose of a power struggle, but at the end he quickly repudiated such a development in order to maintain the integrity of his model. So one can say that Mao insisted on his own classical model in terms of "people's war" and that all other models are really not his real intention; they are simply mistaken drifts from his pure model in the form of the rightist or leftist deviations. This is clearly shown in Mao's campaigns against Peng Dehuai's overemphasis on military modernization, on the one hand, and against Lin Biao's intervention in politics on the other. Here I am simply suggesting a different way of explaining the phenomena of the PLA's changing patterns of behavior: one can articulate it in terms of the alternation of three models or that of one model with two variants.

In this connection, one can ask further, has Deng really articulated his own model independently? Deng is a well-known pragmatist. According to the political tradition of the Chinese Communist Party, however, leaders always need to formulate some kind of theory or doctrine from which the country's policy lines can be derived. After considerable debate between the emphasis on people's war, on the one hand, and that of modern warfare, on the other, I think that a compromise, or a synthesis, as Professor Dreyer suggested, has emerged. It is known as the doctrine of "people's war under modern conditions."

Perhaps one can raise the question as to what extent it is a serious theoretical articulation. Or is it just a convenient mechanism to cover up the policy confusion? This is clearly related to the critical issue of the process of reform that we have been discussing in the past two days. At the Thirteenth Party Congress it is formally stressed that the current stage of development in China is the primary stage of socialism. I think there are certain similarities in the way military doctrine and ideological theory are handled by the leadership.

There could be two interpretations of Deng's articulation. One, as a pragmatist, Deng is just interested in modernization, including military modernization. The theory of the people's war under modern conditions is just a convenience to sneak in military modernization through the back door without bothering with the thorny issue of doctrine. The other interpretation is to see it as a serious attempt at formulating a new theory in which Deng tries to synthesize the old doctrine of guerrilla warfare and the PLA's new need for modernization.

In this connection, I think we can raise an intriguing question that is popular in the Western literature on the military: military technology tends to dictate military doctrine. The theory has the flavor of technological determinism: new weapons inevitably determine the organizational structure and operational style of the military. Hence, with Deng's emphasis on modernization, the PLA will have no choice but to change Mao's theory of people's war.

Let me add a little nitpicking here. Professor Parris Chang suggested earlier that Professor Dreyer should look into the policy statement of the Thirteenth

Party Congress and see what kind of new development, such as personnel change, one can find. It may be noted that as far as policy change is concerned, according to the newspaper account, Zhao Ziyang's political report contains thirty thousand words, but only thirty-four words are related to the military, saying only briefly that the Military Commission will make a separate report. Thirty thousand words versus thirty-four words is quite a contrast, and we want to know why? Does it suggest an ongoing confusion in the doctrine, policy, and power struggle?

Finally, let me raise a couple of factual questions. One is on Professor Dreyer's suggestion that probably 30–40 percent of the defense capabilities has been diverted for civilian, consumer goods production. She cited the Xingxing giant conglomerate. The question is why there is such a phenomenon. The official explanation is that the military should be mobilized to support economic development in accordance with the good old tradition of the PLA. There are speculations on other lines, however: the new policy of decentralization and decollectivization is bringing economic benefits to many people, but not the military. Therefore, unless the military is provided with opportunities for some economic satisfactions, it may be difficult to maintain the political loyalty of the military constituency. Perhaps a more specific political interpretation of the PLA's sideline activities is called for here.

The other factual question is on Professor Dreyer's assumption that Hu Yaobang's inability to assume the chairmanship of the party's Military Commission and to operationalize the State Military Commission, newly instituted by Deng himself, seems to be a setback for Deng. I just do not know if this is a correct interpretation. We need more information to answer the question. This is related to the whole issue of why Hu was booted out of power and what Deng's role was in that. Deng might have some reservations of Hu Yaobang to begin with, and he might have felt that Hu was good enough to be the party's general secretary, but not to be the head of the Military Commission because of his lack of proper connections in the PLA. The other related point is why the State Military Commission is not operationalized. Is it Deng's fault, or is it actually his deliberate design? All these questions deserve further attention.

10

CHINA BETWEEN THE SUPERPOWERS:
In Search of a Security Strategy*

Jonathan D. Pollack

THE REORIENTATION of Chinese security strategy ranks among the central achievements of the Deng Xiaoping era. From the time of Deng's political re-emergence in the summer of 1977, the enhancement of China's national security proved to be among his paramount policy goals. Through a highly resourceful combination of political, economic, and diplomatic means, Deng recast the framework of China's national security policy, subordinating its military dimension to larger political and diplomatic goals. A long-term geopolitical logic pervaded China's strategic calculations, but it differed appreciably from its Maoist antecedents.

The fully formed Dengist approach to national security presumed a prolonged period of diminished tensions, permitting China far more latitude and breathing space than in decades of confrontation with external adversaries or of international isolation. By deemphasizing the immediacy of military threats to Chinese security—in particular those that might lead China into armed conflict—Deng sought to accelerate the pace and scope of economic development, raise the living standards of the population, upgrade China's scientific and technological base, and reduce the size of China's military establishment.[1]

This less worrisome assessment of the international environment was premised on two principal factors: first, the constraints imposed on both superpowers by a highly competitive bilateral relationship, and, second, the readiness of Deng and other senior Chinese leaders to utilize the political opportunities presented by Soviet-American contention. According to Beijing's prevailing policy logic,

*The opinions in this essay are the author's alone, and should not be attributed to the RAND Corporation or any of its governmental sponsors.

neither Moscow nor Washington was capable of consolidating its strategic and political position in East Asia at China's expense; if anything, both sought to improve their regional position by wooing rather than ostracizing China. The People's Republic of China (PRC) therefore became the object of solicitation rather than the focus of political and military intimidation and encirclement. Under such conditions, Beijing sought to achieve a strategic position independent of both superpowers, but not in fundamental antagonism with either.

This strategic opportunity, however, depended on China's capacity to overcome major uncertainties in relations with both superpowers. At different times since the late 1970s, Deng was identified with three distinct national security concepts: (1) the "united front" strategy of the late 1970s that warned against American appeasement of Soviet expansion; (2) a reaction against a resurgently "hegemonic" United States in the early 1980s that threatened Sino-American rapprochement; and (3) an accommodationist posture toward both superpowers along separate bilateral tracks, with China thereby achieving a measure of strategic disengagement from the Soviet-American competition. The third strategy explicitly sought to reorient China's quest for national security away from primary threats and principal contradictions, with economic and technological factors superseding Maoist convictions about the struggle between imperialist and anti-imperialist forces.

It would be imprudent, therefore, to assume open-ended continuity in China's strategic course, especially with Deng's impending passage from the political scene. Although a broad consensus favoring strategic independence held for much of the 1980s, there are too many contingent elements to predict stability with any assurance. This judgment seems especially relevant in the aftermath of the Tiananmen Square events and the consequent reorientation in Sino-American relations. The incentives to maintain an incrementalist, low-risk posture seem self-evident, but the growing challenge to the party's legitimacy following the political crisis of 1989 suggests a different and far less certain dynamic in China's security strategy.

To consider the relevant prospects and possibilities, this essay will explore four principal issues: (1) Beijing's shifting calculations of external threat and their effects on defense and development priorities; (2) the implications of these trends for the Sino-American relationship; (3) the prospects and security consequences of Sino-Soviet accommodation; and (4) China's strategic alternatives in the post-Deng era.

Beijing's Shifting Calculus of External Threat

When Deng returned to power in 1977, he inherited a set of strategic concepts closely identified with Mao Zedong and Zhou Enlai, to which Deng had also contributed during his political ascendancy of 1974–75. The foremost assumption was the existence of a comprehensive Soviet political and military threat, aimed principally at the West and Japan and secondarily at China. According to this logic, the continuing aim of Soviet policy was to lull the West into complacency and appeasement, thereby enabling Moscow to heighten its pressure against China. Although in the near term Chinese leaders professed not to fear the possibility of Soviet military attack, there was mounting concern that the United States saw relations with China as subsidiary to the U.S.-Soviet relationship, quite possibly leading to compromises and concessions that would prove detrimental to Chinese interests. The Sino-American relationship had become largely stagnant by the mid-1970s, lacking a shared strategic design and unable to achieve significant headway on full diplomatic ties. To this extent, the value of a tacit strategic relationship with the United States seemed open to question, as reflected in the increasing frostiness in Sino-American relations during the Ford Administration.

At the same time, however, Deng saw no particular need to temporize in the face of a still ascendant Soviet geopolitical challenge. Although steps had been taken to stabilize the Sino-Soviet relationship and to avoid an outbreak of serious hostilities along the border, these actions did not alter the essence of the competition between Moscow and Beijing. As the Vietnam conflict neared its denouement, Deng recognized that Moscow was far better positioned to gain the upper hand in Hanoi, raising concerns about Soviet military encirclement to a much higher level.

The climactic political events of 1976 did little to alter China's near-term security calculations. If anything, attention to the Soviet military threat was heightened considerably in the months following Mao's death. Chinese military leaders, having proven essential to Hua Guofeng's consolidation of power, enjoyed their greatest prominence and visibility since Lin Biao's tenure as Mao's successor. Military interests were closely aligned with advocates of heavy industrial growth, both being premised on the supposed neglect of military preparedness under the Gang of Four. When Soviet leaders made overtures to Beijing in late 1976, they were sharply rebuffed on both ideological and security grounds. Sino-Soviet and Sino-American relations both seemed on hold, as the governments in all three capitals awaited the outcome of the succession struggle in Washington as well as Beijing.

Deng's return to power prior to the Eleventh Party Congress appeared to shift the parameters in Chinese debate, but only slightly. At first glance, his depiction of the global Soviet challenge seemed alarmist and confrontational. Subsequent reappraisals of the "inevitability of war" thesis attributed the overestimation of the likelihood of war and the incorrect appraisal of the international balance of forces to "leftist ideological trends" of the 1960s and 1970s.[2]

Deng's dire warnings to the West about Soviet hegemonism replicated earlier debates between Henry Kissinger and various Chinese interlocutors during the early and mid-1970s.[3] Kissinger had repeatedly asserted that a weak, divided, and vulnerable China was the grand strategic prize most coveted by leaders in the Kremlin, or at least the prize most readily within their grasp. Just as insistently, Mao, Zhou, Deng, and Qiao Guanhua countered that Western Europe remained the main focus of Soviet strategy, with East Asia a primary objective only after Moscow's domination over Europe had been achieved. Even as Soviet activities turned increasingly toward Southwest and Southeast Asia, Chinese strategists deemed Moscow's actions part of a larger design to gain a stranglehold over the economic lifelines of the West, thereby downplaying the implications of Soviet actions for the security of China.

These Sino-American strategic debates obscured the real issue: the relative value and priority placed by the United States on closer relations with the PRC, as opposed to sustaining the process of Soviet-American détente. Deng may well have regarded the United States as vacillating, irresolute, and inconsistent, but American support was a sine qua non for China to achieve its longer-term aspirations for national power and international stature. To Deng, further drift and delay in Sino-American relations suggested that officials in Washington did not consider closer ties with China a first-order policy objective. Deng's obsession with Soviet power was more comprehensible in this light: by describing relations with the United States as a strategic imperative, he sought to reshape opinion in the West about China's importance and potential strategic value. The prospect of a global antihegemony united front—including a tacit commitment to a strategic relationship with the United States—was a principal lure to a new administration still feeling its way in foreign policy.

At the same time, however, Deng was quietly laying the groundwork for a different Chinese security rationale. These initial shifts presaged the larger strategic reorientation of the mid- to late 1980s. By the time of Deng's return to power, the post-Gang of Four references to the risks of Soviet military subjugation had begun to diminish. In his political report to the Eleventh National Congress in August 1977, Hua Guofeng asserted: "The people of all countries of the world may be able to put off the outbreak of war."[4] In a meeting with a Japanese political delegation a month later, Deng for the first time put forward the slogan of China's need for a "long-term peaceful international environment," without which the comprehensive modernization of China's technological and industrial base would be incalculably more difficult.[5]

The hopes for realizing the goal of a more powerful and prosperous China therefore depended on the avoidance of war and the diminishing of the military competition with the USSR. Downplaying the urgency of China's near-term security requirements underscored the need for a credible relationship with the United States. Yet such a nonconfrontational approach did not preclude periodic initiatives toward the Soviet Union, provided such actions did not undermine primary ties with the United States. Gestures toward Moscow were necessarily more dependent on timing, sequence, and political context. Even prior to the normalization of relations with the United States, however, Deng sought to move away from the crisis-driven mentality of a "race against time." Such a concept (initially advocated by military planners during late 1976 and early 1977) seemed an effective rationale for increasing the defense budget, but could not help rebuild China's agricultural, industrial, and scientific base. China needed to buy time, not race against it.

China's "punitive war" against Vietnam, therefore, was somewhat anomalous in this context. It constituted the one instance since the Sino-Soviet border clashes of 1969 when there was a real possibility of major armed conflict with the Soviet Union. Had such hostilities broken out, Chinese forces would have been far more disadvantaged than in the firefights along the Ussuri a decade earlier. Deng appeared to recognize these risks, and sought to avoid actions that could have elicited Soviet retaliation. As Harry Gelman has observed, the massing of Soviet firepower to the north inhibited more forceful Chinese actions to the south.[6] Thus, the decade-long build-up of Soviet military might east of the Urals had changed the "rules of the game" in the Sino-Soviet conflict.

The sources and after-effects of the Chinese decision to go to war are of greater interest than the conflict itself. In many respects, the decision represents the last paroxysm of the long-entrenched approach to risk-taking and the use of force in Chinese foreign policy. This is not to suggest that China's leaders would be unwilling to contemplate military action should vital national interests again be judged at risk. But the 1979 events, although bearing Deng's imprint, seem the product of a different place and time: unambiguously initiated by Beijing, highly coercive, and utterly single-minded in planning, execution, and objective, regardless of political and human costs.[7]

Deng was pivotal to China's decision to intervene.[8] He believed that Chinese actions served three main purposes: as a forceful reminder to Vietnam that its occupation of Cambodia would not be cost-free, as a visceral expression of cumulative Chinese anger and frustration at Hanoi's ingratitude and defiance of leaders in Beijing, and as an opportunity for China's military commanders to test the mettle of their forces in combat. In addition, Deng probably calculated that senior American officials, many of whom shared his contempt and loathing for leaders in Hanoi, would not object to bloodying Vietnam's nose, and might even approve.

Trumpeted in Chinese media at the time as an unalloyed success, the attack on Vietnam ironically facilitated the shift to an alternative security strategy. Although Chinese actions compelled Hanoi to redeploy more than half its frontline troops to the provinces facing the PRC, they did not produce the anticipated pullback of Vietnam's forces from Cambodia. At the same time, Hanoi's dependence on Moscow for political, economic, and military support grew enormously. Moscow's compensation was the opportunity to augment its military presence at Vietnamese bases. The damage to China's military reputation was also severe, as reflected in the abysmal shortcomings in the PLA's military performance. Finally, and perhaps most important, Deng was chagrined by the lukewarm reception of senior Carter administration officials to his prewar briefing, indicating that Deng had misjudged Washington's readiness to act on China's behalf.

Although there is only scattered evidence of an "agonizing reappraisal" in the aftermath of the Vietnam conflict, the results were highly sobering to the Chinese, and perhaps to Deng personally. Major increases in Chinese defense expenditure occurred in mid-1979, as planners allocated additional resources to replace equipment lost or damaged in the war. These "out of cycle" expenditures were the decisive event in halting the 1978–79 spending binge, initiating the period of "reform and readjustment" that short-circuited the grandiose modernization package first presented by Hua Guofeng in the spring of 1978.

The consequences for Sino-Soviet relations were also significant.[9] In the aftermath of the brief war with Vietnam and only three months after the establishment of Sino-American diplomatic relations, the Ministry of Foreign Affairs notified the Soviet Union that China intended to let the 1950 treaty of alliance lapse. Nevertheless, China also unconditionally offered to open negotiations with Moscow on the full spectrum of interstate relations. Confronted by such an opportunity, Moscow agreed. Negotiations began in the Soviet capital during the fall. China's negotiators were more ardent suitors, with Soviet officials less eager to set a substantive agenda.

Prior to the invasion of Afghanistan in late December 1979, negotiations were scheduled to resume in Beijing in the spring. In mid-January, however, the Chinese Ministry of Foreign Affairs deemed further discussions "inappropriate," and canceled the pending second round of talks. The Afghan invasion thus delayed the onset of semiannual consultations by another three years, as well as injecting substantial momentum into the Sino-American relationship. But Beijing's actions signaled China's willingness to reactivate its long-dormant relations with the Soviet Union, thereby initiating its own version of "triangular diplomacy." The prospect of such ties did not presume equivalence or perfect symmetry in relations with Washington and Moscow, but they did reflect a more flexible and differentiated Chinese political and diplomatic strategy.

Three implications of this strategic reformulation were especially noteworthy:

First, China's long-term strategic interests were explicitly linked to a major expansion of political, economic, and technological relations with the industrialized world. National security concerns may have initially motivated these ties, but by themselves would not enable a more comprehensive Chinese engagement with the outside world. Absent credible, more diversified relations with the West, the sustainability of China's broader modernization strategy (in particular the acquisition of advanced technology from abroad) would have been called into serious question. Once relations with the West were solidified, however, Beijing would enjoy greater latitude in reducing tensions with the Soviet Union.

Second, the PRC's emergent security posture reflected the "indirect approach" long enshrined in Chinese strategy. Beijing would seek to avoid a frontal challenge to a militarily superior adversary. The goal was to deflect or redirect the enemy's efforts to other fronts, hoping that exhaustion or overextension would ultimately convince the opponent that the game was not worth the candle. There had long been a low-key debate among Chinese strategic specialists over Soviet capacities to sustain its internal and external empire, and the opportunity for "testing" differing estimates of Soviet power was far less risky once Beijing was more internationally engaged.

Third, there was a direct connection among China's larger strategic design, the degree of expressed external threat, and the allocation of institutional and budgetary resources within China. A politically oriented deterrence strategy assumed that the upgrading of Chinese military power could be safely deferred, and that any effort at a military "quick fix" would prove illusory. Placing China on a war footing would have proven highly destabilizing, risking misperception by enemies and friends alike.

This strategy began to reach fruition only in the mid-1980s, when the increasing diversification and institutionalization of Sino-American ties coincided with the efforts of Mikhail Gorbachev to initiate a much more comprehensive reduction of tensions with China. With China more fully engaged in global politics than at any point since 1949, leaders in Beijing believed that they enjoyed much more favorable circumstances in relation to both superpowers. An undiminished Soviet-American rivalry constrained Moscow from further enhancing its political and military pressure against China, and instead provided incentives for accommodation. Chinese officials hoped to achieve a partial respite from the international pressures that had long complicated their plans for economic and technological development. Deng in particular hoped that a more stable security environment and the removal of previous ideological inhibitions from China's development strategy would work to China's distinct advantage.

But latent contradictions and dilemmas still existed, and at times burst into full view. Chinese strategic observers continued to criticize the "hegemonism of the two superpowers," even as they also recognized that without such a rivalry Beijing's room for maneuver would be greatly reduced. Similarly, the People's Republic was a principal beneficiary of the resurgent American military challenge to the USSR in the 1980s, providing China with much needed breathing room. Relieved in some measure from increased Soviet political and military pressure and enjoying far fuller relations with the United States, China found itself with an unparalleled opportunity for economic and technological advancement, yet without incurring major political obligations to either superpowers.

By the close of the decade, however, this opportunity was imperiled, with China seemingly unable to maintain simultaneous nonantagonistic relations with both superpowers. Having reduced the ideological inhibitions that had previously constrained a more flexible development and defense strategy, the 1989 leadership crisis reinjected some of these considerations—at least to the extent that China and the United States were no longer able to sustain a working consensus on security relations. The larger backdrop of these changes, however, was the reconfiguration of the global strategic environment evident at the close of 1980s. To elucidate these developments and their possible consequences, we need to reexamine Chinese dealings with the United States and the Soviet Union in greater detail.

Sino-American Security Relations: The Elusive Search for Partnership

U.S.-China relations since the initial U.S. accommodation with Beijing have repeatedly experienced exaggerated expectations and abrupt worries about their fragility. At the close of the Reagan administration, however, the Sino-American relationship appeared on its soundest footing since the initiation of ties in the early 1970s. Having weathered various stresses and storms, both leaderships appeared to understand their mutual stake in closer relations, as well as the costs of a serious deterioration in these ties. There was also a much clearer sense of the opportunities and inhibitions affecting the potential scope of Sino-American security relations. Unlike the three previous administrations, all of which in varying degrees had pursued strategic alignment with Beijing, the security relationship with China had been operationalized by a conservative president, but without a pronounced anti-Soviet "tilt" to the policy.

These accomplishments, however, were unable to withstand the pressures induced by China's leadership crisis of 1989. Despite George Bush's election as president, neither cumulative personal ties nor complementary political and security incentives prevented a serious rupture in bilateral relations. The roots of the crisis were domestic, but external relations were also immediately embroiled in controversy. An embattled leadership in Beijing sought justification for its brutal crackdown on internal opposition through accusations of a hidden foreign hand, with the United States judged the principal perpetrator of a strategy of "peaceful evolution" designed to undermine socialist rule in China. As a consequence, China's security ties with the United States were among the principal casualties of the Tiananmen Square crisis, thereby undermining the PRC's international position and longer-term security prospects. The rapid unraveling of these relations raised the question of Beijing's capacity to sustain long-term collaborative ties with both superpowers. Perhaps most important, American policymakers, having begun to forge a qualitatively different relationship with the Soviet Union, no longer judged close U.S.-China ties a strategic imperative.

The 1989 reversal in relations afforded some parallels, as well as differences, with the near crisis in U.S.-China ties at the outset of the Reagan administration. In the earlier events, officials in Beijing had deemed President Reagan's initial stance toward the PRC needlessly provocative.[10] Chinese leaders (including Deng) made clear that there would be severe political costs to any upgrading of U.S. relations with Taiwan, even though the new administration's pledges to redress the "decade of neglect" in defense preparedness comported with Deng's repeated calls for a more forceful U.S. stance toward the Soviet Union.

There were also high level disputes within the Reagan administration, with

China's principal benefactor (Secretary of State Haig) losing far more battles than he won. Haig continued to insist that relations with Beijing were a strategic imperative, which the PRC leadership feared would necessitate Chinese acquiescence to enhanced U.S. relations with Taiwan as the price of expanded ties with Washington. In a relationship that was still more personal than institutionalized, American actions suggested a pattern of indifference toward ties with China. Under these circumstances, Deng and other leaders prepared for a "retrogression" in Sino-American relations, which probably would have entailed the withdrawal of the Chinese ambassador from Washington.

Although Deng Xiaoping was the leading exponent of the Sino-American relationship, tensions in relations with Washington did not seriously weaken his political position. Deng had sanctioned a much more permissive process of debate on foreign policy questions. To this extent, Deng may well have been open to adaptation and adjustment in China's security strategy; he did not appear reluctant to take issue with the United States.

In the immediate aftermath of Reagan's election, however, Deng had sought to leave the door open to heightened cooperation. When the outlook for Sino-American relations again soured, he provided the decisive impetus in moving away from the united front policy of the late 1970s. Deng took the lead in defining China's broad security and foreign policy options during the 1980s, including the shift away from Sino-American collaboration. Other top leaders contributed to this process, but never in a manner that challenged Deng's ascendance over Chinese security strategy.

The political and strategic uncertainties attending the deterioration of Sino-American relations slowed other political and institutional changes. In particular, Deng's efforts to restructure the Chinese armed forces met repeated resistance. To a very large extent, the agenda for military reform first proposed by Deng in 1975 remained unfulfilled a decade later. It was only in the summer of 1985 that Deng was finally able to secure the compliance of his aged military colleagues for a major reduction in Chinese troop strength and the consolidation of China's eleven military regions to seven. Indeed, 60 percent of the "one million man troop reduction" announced at that time consisted of superannuated officers, suggesting the depths of the problem Deng continued to face in seeking to transform the People's Liberation Army (PLA) into a professionalized military force.[11]

But the worst did not occur. The Reagan administration's January 1982 decision not to permit sale of a new air defense fighter to Taiwan was followed by the August communique limiting future arms sales to Taipei. Successive visits by Secretaries Shultz, Baldrige, and Weinberger in 1983 helped establish a floor to the Sino-American relationship in the three realms most vital to Beijing's security calculations (diplomacy, technology and trade, and national defense). The culmination of this process occurred with the early 1984 visits of Zhao Ziyang to the United States and Ronald Reagan to China. After voting for Nixon in 1972 and abstaining from the 1976 contest (Beijing did not even bother to register!), the Chinese cast their 1984 ballot for Reagan. Both states had recognized that stagnation or deterioration made sense for neither's interests, and could prove severely disadvantageous to their respective security calculations in East Asia.

The issues seemed especially acute for leaders in Beijing. China sought to reap the benefits of closer corporate and governmental relations with the United States, but without having to incur symbolic concessions that slighted China's pretensions to strategic independence. The readiness of Shultz and Weinberger to treat relations with China in a measured, almost routine manner contributed greatly to the continuity and predictability that Deng deemed vital. Both secretaries viewed relations with Beijing in a way that Kissinger, Brzezinski, and Haig had not—as an important relationship that presupposed collaboration and consultation, but without a "trip driven," crisis-generated character that imparted instability and uncertainty. In a real sense, Sino-American relations had finally been normalized.

The record of the second Reagan term bore out these judgments. The administration steadily liberalized export control criteria for China, including the specification of four military mission areas (antitank weaponry, artillery, air defense, and surface ship and antisubmarine warfare) where the United States was prepared to consider selected military sales to Beijing. When combined with U.S. technical and scientific assistance to the PRC and steady increases in high-technology trade, the cumulative accomplishments of the latter 1980s seemed striking.[12] Periodic grievances about restrictions and inconsistencies in licensing procedures still surfaced, and tensions over Chinese missile sales to Iran and Saudi Arabia marred the results of the process, but a more workable policy machinery for defense relations had evolved.[13]

There was also a routinization of dealings between the professional military establishments of both countries. Although not presaging an alliance, the network of leadership and institutional contacts enabled discussions of professional military development, regional security, and defense doctrine. An incremental, working-level logic had supplanted the far more politicized relationships of the 1970s, seemingly imparting a foundation for more durable relations.

Thus, the United States and China appeared disenthralled of the "deepest optimism and soaring pessimism" characteristic of the first decade of relations, helping to ease lingering regional suspicions about an underlying strategic design between the United States and China. A more broadly based relationship with the United States underscored Beijing's tacit endorsement of the U.S. regional presence, providing incentives for the Chinese military establishment—long the "odd institution out" in the Sino-American relationship—to engage gradually in interactions with the outside world.

These optimistic projections, however, proved premature. Following the Tiananmen Square crisis, U.S.-PRC security collaboration unraveled dramatically and abruptly. Within days of the bloodshed in Beijing, institutional ties between the military establishments of the two countries were placed on hold, and the major Sino-American defense technology collaboration effort (a $500 million project to upgrade the PLA's fighter-aircraft avionics) was interrupted and subsequently canceled. The Chinese decision in the spring of 1990 not to resume the avionics transaction can be explained partially by the daunting (and growing) costs of the project.[14] But Chinese political and security calculations were also very important. As the salience of shared Sino-American concerns about Soviet power eroded in the late 1980s, U.S.-Chinese ties were no longer animated by a subliminal strategic logic. At the same time, defense relations remained among the most sensitive aspects of Sino-American dealings in both systems, and they proved highly vulnerable once the fabric of collaboration was badly strained, especially in light of the PLA's central role in the bloody suppression of political protests in Beijing.

Quite apart from the Tiananmen Square events, it is possible that Sino-American security relations would have faced increasing difficulty. As shared U.S.-Chinese concerns about the expansion of Soviet power receded in the late 1980s, the existence of divergent American and Chinese interests (most notably, Chinese missile sales in the Middle East) was more starkly revealed. At the same time, defense collaboration had not proceeded to either side's satisfaction. U.S. officials judged the Chinese unprepared to move toward more comprehensive interactions between personnel and institutions, and some Chinese military figures appeared to regard U.S. policy as overly intrusive yet insufficiently prepared to proffer advanced technology. But the logic of cooperation—and selective instances of successful dealings—remained in place until Tiananmen and its aftermath.

Unlike the near crisis of 1980–81, however, neither side was especially inhibited in 1989 by the implications of a rupture in relations for their respective ties with the Soviet Union. Although the secret visit of National Security Advisor Brent Scowcroft and Under Secretary of State Lawrence Eagleburger to Beijing in early July 1989 suggested American anxieties about the direct damage of the Tiananmen Square crisis to Sino-American collaboration, the Chinese leadership (including Deng Xiaoping) proved unresponsive. A second visit by the same emissaries in December also failed to elicit anticipated results.

Although the Bush administration (including the President himself) initially appeared to believe that a strategic imperative could justify rapid resumption of high-level dealings, this assumption proved wanting. Despite the long identification and involvement of numerous senior U.S. officials in close relations with China (as well as repeated urgings by Nixon and Kissinger, the architects of the original accommodation with Beijing), the administration was unprepared to invest very heavily in resurrecting the relationship. The normalization of Sino-Soviet ties (to be considered below) and the stunning configuration of Soviet-American relations in the aftermath of the collapse of communist power in

Eastern Europe had recast the previous logic of Sino-American security collaboration. Even though the Chinese had far more developed and tangible ties in the late 1980s than at the outset of the decade, internal imperatives had become preeminent on the Chinese agenda, with external security preoccupations subordinate to the survival of communist rule in China.

Thus, the shifting geopolitical context had a decisive imprint on the dismantling of defense collaboration that had been painstakingly arranged over the latter half of the 1980s, although the sharp reversals in Chinese internal politics also contributed. In the aftermath of these changes, the prospects for China's pursuit of strategic independence seemed far more unsettled and problematic. To understand the implications of these shifts further, we need to turn to the reconfiguration of Sino-Soviet relations also underway in recent years.

The Sino-Soviet Accommodation: Sources, Prospects, and Security Implications

The reestablishment of Sino-Soviet relations offered vivid testimony to the increased suppleness and flexibility of Beijing's security and diplomatic strategy, especially during the latter half of the 1980s.[15] Despite uncertainties, complications, and conflicts of interest in both systems, there was sufficient leadership and bureaucratic support to sustain this process throughout the decade. In the aftermath of the rapid changes in Soviet-American and U.S.-Chinese relations at the outset of the 1990s, however, different opportunities and inhibitions have emerged more abruptly than either leadership previously thought possible. To understand these developments and their consequences, it is first necessary to retrace the changes of recent years.

At the outset of the 1980s, the Sino-Soviet confrontation remained in full bloom. Beyond the minimum requirements of diplomatic intercourse, intersocietal relations barely existed. The border negotiations were no longer active, and (as noted previously) the Afghanistan invasion had put further negotiations on interstate relations on hold. Most strategic specialists in Moscow and Beijing depicted the other's security strategy in an extremely threatening light, a phenomenon underscored by the increased pace of Sino-American relations at the close of the 1970s.[16] Both states seemed in a bidding war for the allegiance of the West, thereby dictating embellishment rather than moderation in their strategic pronouncements.

The frozen state of relations in the late 1970s reflected the militarization of the dispute and an incipient polarization in East Asia along the "fault lines of the Sino-Soviet feud."[17] Mao was interred but Brezhnev still lived, and showed no inclination to diminish the encirclement and intimidation of the PRC. Even allowing for political hyperbole, the prospect of a "U.S.-Japan-China military alliance" provoked Soviet nightmares about a two-front war of unimaginable proportions. If doubts existed about the costs and strategic wisdom of the steady movement of Soviet military power eastward, however, they were not readily detectable in Soviet strategic assessments at the time. The 1980s therefore seemed to augur more of the same. What happened? First, despite the worrisome pronouncements from both states, a measure of stability had been established in the relationship. Following China's Vietnam war, both sides sought to avoid an undesirable escalation of military tensions.[18] The war of words, although reflecting deep security concerns of both sides, also derived from inertial tendencies in the two systems: both leaderships seemed accustomed to resorting to inflammatory rhetoric directed at one another, irrespective of actual estimates of military threat. Despite the fearsome warnings issued from both capitals, a limiting process had been set in motion, including tacit restraints on the size and deployment of military forces along the Sino-Soviet border. This did not necessarily make the political and military environment propitious for change, but neither did it indicate that matters would become appreciably more unstable.

Thus, leaders in both states remained attentive to indications of change in the other's political and strategic stance. In his speech to the Twenty-Sixth Congress of the Communist Party of the Soviet Union (CPSU) in February 1981, Leonid Brezhnev took note of the internal changes that had already begun to take place in China (i.e., the dismemberment and disowning of Mao's political record), pronounced the trends encouraging, and stated the Soviet Union would follow future developments closely.[19] Brezhnev's observations reflected an ongoing debate among Soviet China watchers, with one school fearing the worst and the other being at least moderately hopeful that things were not as bad as they seemed and might with Mao's passage ultimately improve. (In this respect, the demotion of Hua Guofeng must have been viewed as an encouraging trend, although Deng was never perceived as a friend of the Soviet Union.) By the time of Brezhnev's early 1981 speech, the optimists saw the growing disagreements between Beijing and Washington as evidence that a Sino-American-Japanese alliance would not come to pass. China's economic retrenchment of 1979–80 also seemed cause for encouragement, since it implied a focus on internal tasks requiring a stable if not benign external environment.

In March 1982, Brezhnev delivered a major address on "the principled position of our party and the Soviet state on the question of Soviet-Chinese relations."[20] Speaking in Tashkent, the Soviet leader pledged noninterference in Chinese internal affairs, acknowledged the existence of a socialist system in China, supported Chinese claims to Taiwan, denied any Soviet territorial claims against the PRC, and offered to initiate without preconditions any measures designed to improve interstate relations. In essence, the Soviet offer to China was to "decouple" Sino-Soviet relations from the broader geopolitical competition that had developed between the two states. This offer remained intact throughout the 1980s, with the Chinese leadership ultimately proving more responsive to the political, strategic, and economic opportunities afforded by such an overture.

The timing and sequence of Chinese policy adaptations are worthy of note. Although the first appreciable increases in trade and other contact were discernible in 1981 and early 1982, the Chinese political-diplomatic agenda was still dominated by the uncertainties in U.S.-China relations. It was only in the aftermath of the signing of the joint communique on arms sales to Taiwan in August that Chinese officials began to explore more substantial initiatives toward Moscow. In October 1982, the PRC proposed in a low-key manner the resumption of the consultative process initiated three years earlier. Brezhnev's death shortly thereafter provided an opportunity for funeral diplomacy, with Foreign Minister Huang Hua (the highest Chinese visitor to Moscow since the 1960s) offering an expansive view of the prospects for improved relations.[21] China's near-term need was to present a rationale for improved relations flexible enough to test Soviet intentions but without appearing to yield ground on the larger national security differences that dominated the relationship. From the first, Deng and his colleagues were therefore attentive to two external audiences—one in Moscow, the other in Washington.

It was in this context that the "three obstacles" were enshrined as the central conditions that would govern the future of the Sino-Soviet relationship. Leaders in Beijing were desirous of more diversified relations with both superpowers (thus lending credibility to China's asserted claim to foreign policy independence), yet not in a manner that unsettled relations with Washington or convinced Moscow that Beijing was yielding on its core security concerns. Although the payoffs from this more differentiated strategy seemed real enough, the uncertainties and risks were also substantial. A review of these issues sheds light on some of the continuing dilemmas and choices confronting Chinese policymakers.

From the first, the logic of Sino-Soviet accommodation was incremental. Step by step and year by year, the modalities of a full bilateral relationship were laid in place. In view of the extraordinary leadership turnover in the Soviet Union following the death of Brezhnev, both leaderships may well have concluded that neither system could absorb a faster rate of change. There were fits and starts in the process, with Chinese officials acknowledging a "retrogression" during Konstantin Chernenko's brief tenure as CPSU General Secretary.

The pace of change accelerated dramatically under Mikhail Gorbachev, who was far more prepared than his predecessors to test the opportunities for a more comprehensive accommodation with Beijing. These relations advanced first from economic ties—one Soviet official privately observed that "we sell to one another what no one will buy from us"—to an increasing complementarity in development priorities. By the end of the decade, the logic of a much reinvigorated program of scientific and technological cooperation was also in place, although such collaboration still seemed to develop at a relatively slow rate, given infrastructural, technological, and financial constraints in both systems. Although some sectors (e.g., resource exploitation, metallurgy, chemicals, and power generation equipment) seemed "natural" areas for renewed Soviet assistance to China, the measured development of these ties may have reflected differences among Chinese planners over the appropriate mix of Western and Soviet technology. Sustaining the perception of a larger long-term potential to this collaboration nevertheless seemed important, especially at a time of growing economic weakness in both systems. Thus, more substantial projects seem likely in Beijing in 1987 and 1988; it was easier to argue that reform had assumed primacy for all socialist societies, and would also entail an appreciable and lasting change in Soviet political-military strategy toward China. Thus, the Sino-Soviet accommodation reflected the nonconfrontational, low-risk external course that Beijing deemed vital for its internal development.

Gorbachev's diligent efforts to conciliate the Chinese assumed increased momentum in 1988, as the Soviet withdrawals from Afghanistan and Soviet troop pullbacks from Mongolia became incontrovertible facts, as did Soviet pressure on Vietnam to remove its forces from Cambodia.[22] His simultaneous determination to remove the ideological inhibitions that had long blocked intersocietal and interstate ties also bore fruit, with the Soviet leadership openly endorsing Chinese reform measures and praising China's independent foreign policy line.

As Gorbachev's May 1989 visit to Beijing approached, the principal unresolved issue was whether Deng would assent openly to more active Sino-Soviet policy coordination, especially in the security and arms control arenas. On a visit to Moscow in late 1988, Foreign Minister Qian Qichen had offered China's "agreement in principle" to establish a channel for consultations among Soviet and Chinese "diplomatic and military experts" over force levels and confidence building along the Sino-Soviet border. Any Chinese decision to implement such arrangements more actively would represent an important symbolic concession to Moscow, which had long sought Chinese assent to negotiations over the Sino-Soviet balance of forces. Considered in a broader context, such steps would also have constituted an indirect endorsement of the validity of Soviet arms control proposals.

Yet the Chinese remained exceedingly reluctant to provide Gorbachev with any ammunition in his larger maneuverings with the United States in East Asia. From the time of Gorbachev's Vladivostok speech of July 1986, Soviet arms control proposals for Asia and the Pacific retained a highly self-serving aspect, for they sought above all to restrict the scope of American military activities in the region and, by extension, to deny the legitimacy of the forward deployment of U.S. naval and air power in the West Pacific.[23] Gorbachev not only returned from Beijing without any PRC endorsement of his arms control proposals, the Chinese pointedly arranged for ships from the U.S. Seventh Fleet to visit Shanghai at virtually the precise time when the Soviet leader would visit the city.

Thus, even though the logic of the strategic triangle seemed increasingly outmoded, the role of the United States in relation to both the Soviets and the Chinese still hovered over the summit deliberations. Deng was unprepared to put his far larger relationship with the United States at risk by endorsing Soviet positions criticizing the role of U.S. forces in Korea and other forward locations in East Asia. At the same time, there was a lingering unease within Chinese military circles about consenting unambiguously to a fully normalized Sino-Soviet relationship, as this presumed the conclusive passing of adversarial relations between the two states.[24]

But there was an outmoded element to thinking on both sides. Although the improvements in U.S.-Soviet relations had yet to approach their full extent (the breaching of the Berlin Wall and the collapse of socialism across Eastern Europe were still six months away), Sino-Soviet competition no longer had much political resonance in the eyes of American officials. Indeed, it is possible that Deng felt impelled to accelerate the pace of Sino-Soviet normalization prior to more definitive moves in Soviet-American ties, although his declining health and his desire to preside over the end of three decades of Sino-Soviet estrangement were also motivating factors.

Strategic calculations on both sides, however, were relegated to a background role amid the upheaval and subsequent carnage in Beijing. Gorbachev, having assiduously wooed leaders in Beijing on the expectations of complementary momentum toward political and institutional reform, saw his expectations dashed with the political humiliation of General Secretary Zhao Ziyang, his natural Chinese interlocutor. At the same time, the long-term Chinese goal of genuine strategic independence—i.e., simultaneous, nonantagonistic relations with both superpowers—was abruptly cast in disarray, as martial law and its violent imposition produced a sharp deterioration in Sino-American ties and renewed uncertainties about the predictability and value of Sino-Soviet accommodation.

Last, but hardly least, the postwar international order was on the verge of profound realignment. Although the Chinese desire for a peaceful international environment had produced regular endorsements of Soviet-American détente since the mid-1980s, leaders in Beijing and elsewhere did not anticipate the full consequences of the unraveling of the Soviet empire. The Chinese had always preferred and assumed a bounded superpower relationship, i.e., a sufficiently robust competition that avoided extreme tensions but also did not move rapidly to undue coincidence of American and Soviet interests. In the waning months of the decade, however, the latter outcome abruptly came to pass. Even worse, the rapid degeneration of Sino-American political, institutional, and security ties left China in a greatly weakened position, with the People's Republic no longer the object of earnest solicitation by either superpower.

Gorbachev's acquiescence to the collapse of socialism in Eastern Europe also provoked renewed deliberations within the Chinese leadership about the wisdom of sustaining and enhancing Sino-Soviet accommodation. A subterranean debate even contemplated resumption of public criticism of the Soviet leadership.[25] Despite Chinese grievances against Gorbachev, Deng avoided such a step, thereby sanctioning continued pursuit of measures initiated or agreed on at the time of the Sino-Soviet summit. These extended to the resumption of contacts between the Soviet and Chinese military leaderships. PLA participation in discussions among "diplomatic and military experts," to which the Chinese had assented in principle in late 1988, were initiated in November 1989. These and subsequent rounds of negotiations seemed a natural and appropriate response to the drawdown in Soviet military power deployed opposite China, but extending to the unilateral pullout in late 1989 of the bulk of Soviet airpower that had been deployed in Vietnam for close to a decade.[26] During Premier Li Peng's March 1990 visit to Moscow, an agreement on the reduction of forces along the Sino-Soviet border and related "principles for enhancing trust in military fields" were also ratified. Thus, notwithstanding renewed political differences between the two leaderships, both saw incentives to sustain efforts at force redeployments and tension reduction, formalizing understandings that had previously been declaratory.

There were larger prospective consequences to the two-week visit to the USSR of Liu Huaqing, secretary general of the Chinese Communist Party Military Commission, during June 1990. Liu's visit marked the official resumption of high-level Sino-Soviet military contact after a three-decade hiatus. According to subsequent reports, Liu's delegation also broached the subject of Chinese purchases of Soviet military technology, including prospective acquisition of advanced combat aircraft and related systems whose Western equivalents seemed an increasingly elusive prospect for the PRC military.[27]

The recourse to possible purchases from the Soviet Union would have been unthinkable prior to the normalization of Sino-Soviet ties, but it more immediately reflected the radically altered circumstances and opportunities confronting both military leaderships in the early 1990s. This seemed especially true for the PLA, whose senior leaders had long been highly doubting about the value and wisdom of resuming direct dealings with the Soviet armed forces. But the dismembering of Sino-American military dealings gave momentum to alternative approaches to upgrading the remarkably antiquated technological base of China's military forces, especially the PLA air force. These developments also graphically imparted the erosion of the logic underlying Sino-Soviet-American security interactions of the past decade. To consider Chinese security options in such an unsettled and unanticipated environment, we need to consider China's political and strategic prospects in the early 1990s.

Chinese Security in a New Era: Prospects and Implications

As the Deng Xiaoping era draws to a close, Chinese security strategy appears at a crossroads. By the late 1980s, an old agenda had been set aside, replaced by a less politicized and far more flexible set of policies and guidelines for the future. At the same time, Chinese thinking about international strategy seemed more "interconnected" among political, economic, technological, and military factors, lending far greater complexity to Chinese deliberations over national security. In the most basic sense, however, certain enduring issues persisted: How was China to avoid war and enhance its national power without yielding its claims to political and strategic independence? Would Chinese power remain sufficiently credible to deflect external pressure? And was China properly prepared should its expectations of long-term peace and stability prove invalid?

All these issues have assumed far greater urgency in the aftermath of the Tiananmen Square crisis. Opinions vary significantly on the magnitude and duration of the political changes induced by these events. Some see Tiananmen as a near-term perturbation whose effects will diminish rapidly, given the imperatives of China's modernization goals, the potential longer-term costs to China's international and strategic position, and the advanced age of those leaders who sought to stem or reverse processes of internal change. Others see a basic breakdown of the political arrangements operative under Deng Xiaoping, with a weak, divided leadership united only by fears of another crisis at the top of the system, and with Deng unable to cobble together again viable arrangements for the succession. Some believe that a weakened regime will somehow "muddle through," with a credible successor ultimately emerging following a struggle for power after Deng's death.

Regardless of one's estimate of China's future, the near to mid-term consequences are incontestable: China is a much diminished actor in larger political-military terms. These effects have been further magnified by the political and strategic alignment derivative of events in Europe in the late fall of 1989 and in the Persian Gulf in the summer of 1990. Rather than facing two highly competitive superpowers or (as widely predicted in Chinese strategic assessments) a genuinely multipolar world, the Chinese confront a world where Soviet power has been profoundly devalued, and where American political and strategic power (although in relative terms far less imposing than in the past) has assumed predominance on the global scene. Although these circumstances do not necessarily predict to a long-term "unipolar" world, there is at present no political or military actor able to assume or contest the role being played by American power.

Thus, the Chinese face an unsettled future with diminished credibility and standing in the international power equation. The weakening of China's international position has coincided with an intermittent but stunningly anachronistic Chinese retreat into political symbolism from the 1960s, replete with conspiratorial renderings of Western strategy toward China. Under circumstances where the Chinese leadership (including the military ranks) are preoccupied by averting a renewed political crisis, however, there are very substantial incentives to avoid any additional destabilization in China's broader security environment. But this judgment leaves largely unsettled China's future strategic position, and its implications for the global and the regional balance of power.

It is unsettling and potentially worrisome that there has been yet another turn in China's strategic clock, but it is premature to assume open-ended dissipation of China's capacity for accommodation with the outside world. To be sure, accommodation has been rendered much more difficult, reflecting China's shifting leadership priorities, i.e., the preeminent concern with regime stability and survival. This does not mean that portions of the leadership no longer desire collaboration with the United States; rather, their capacity to do so under prevailing political circumstances has been greatly diminished. As a consequence, China seems very likely to count for less, both in a geopolitical sense (given the transformative events in Europe and the ongoing crisis in the Persian Gulf, neither of which China is capable of influencing in a major way), and in view of the preoccupations of the authorities in Beijing.

At the same time, the Chinese have sought to avoid a decisive break in their external posture, and have repeatedly emphasized their continued desire for close collaboration with the West. But the Chinese cannot anticipate undiminished political, economic, and technological opportunities with the industrialized world so long as the authorities place major political limits on these dealings. It is possible that the Chinese envision much intensified relations with their prosperous capitalist neighbors (Japan, South Korea, Taiwan, Thailand, and Singapore), on the assumption that Confucian cultures are far more accepting of highly authoritarian political arrangements, and that regional actors have far greater incentives than distant superpowers to maintain accommodation with Beijing. Time will tell.

Although China may prove able to limit the damage to its economic interests, the psychic and political toll on its larger strategic pretensions could prove severe. The Chinese took great satisfaction that their country had begun to "count" on the world and regional scene over the past decade. The revisions in Chinese security strategy earlier in the 1980s reflected Deng Xiaoping's convictions about the need to acquire the requisite industrial and technological strength on which to stake China's long-term claim to world power standing. Speaking on the sixtieth anniversary of the PLA's founding in 1987, Yang Shangkun had even alluded to "China's status as a world power" *(shijie qiangguo diwei)* as the longer-term goal animating the modernization process.[28] It will therefore represent an enormous blow should China's political stature (like its currency) face a series of devaluations. Under conditions where China matters less, its incentives to collaborate with the outside world could also diminish. A less predictable, less accommodating China is not a welcome forecast, but it has become a far more likely prospect as a consequence of internal and external changes.

Thus, the Chinese leadership must yet come to grips with global strategic developments that it did not foresee, and that much degrade Beijing's expectations of an open-ended, Soviet-American competition. At the same time, there remains a profound Chinese ambivalence about the longer-term diffusion of power that finds Japan, not China, the only credible aspirant to superpower status in East Asia. Can China successfully accommodate to such emergent strategic realities? Will the Chinese devise means to sustain the nation's strategic relevance without seeking endlessly to manipulate rivalries among the world powers to their own advantage? Such questions seem likely to preoccupy Chinese strategists for years to come.

Notes

1. For the clearest statements of this policy line, see Deng's address to the Party Central Advisory Commission, October 22, 1984, in *FBIS Daily Report-China*, January 2, 1985, pp. K1–6; and his remarks to an enlarged meeting of the Central Military Commission, June 4, 1985, in *FBIS-China*, June 12, 1985, pp. K1–2.

2. See Chen Qimao, "Tentative Discussion on Postwar Changes in International Relations and the Possibility of Winning Lasting World Peace," *Hongqi* (Red flag), no. 13 (July 1986), in *FBIS-China*, July 28, 1986, p. A13.

3. For a more extended discussion, see Jonathan D. Pollack "The Opening to America," in Roderick MacFarquahar and John King Fairbank, eds., *The Cambridge History of China—Revolutions within the Chinese Revolution, 1966–1982* (New York: Cambridge University Press, 1991), esp. pp. 426–35.

4. Hua Guofeng, Political Report to the Eleventh CCP National Congress, August 12, 1977, in *The Eleventh National Congress of the Communist Party of China* (Beijing: Foreign Languages Press, 1977), p. 41.

5. Deng, interview with Delegation from New Liberal Club of Japan, *Asahi shimbun*, September 15, 1977.

6. Harry Gelman, *The Soviet Far East Buildup and Soviet Risk-Taking Against China* (Santa Monica: The RAND Corporation, R–2943-AF, August 1982), pp. 95–105.

7. See Nayan Chanda, *Brother Enemy: The War After the War* (New York: Harcourt Brace Jovanovich, 1987), especially pp. 356–62; and Robert S. Ross, *The Indochina Tangle: China's Vietnam Policy, 1975–1979* (New York: Columbia University Press, 1988), especially pp. 199–237.

8. Zbigniew Brzezinski's account is compelling. See Brzezinksi, *Power and Principle* (New York: Farrar, Straus, and Giroux, 1983), pp. 409–10.

9. For an invaluable account, see H. Lyman Miller, "From the Third Plenum to the April Adverse Current: The Domestic Politics of the Sino-Soviet Dispute," unpublished manuscript, October 1979. For my views, see Jonathan D. Pollack, *The Sino-Soviet Rivalry and Chinese Security Debate* (Santa Monica: The RAND Corporation, R–2907-AF, October 1982), pp. 46–48.

10. For an extended discussion, see my study *The Lessons of Coalition Politics: Sino-American Security Relations* (Santa Monica: The RAND Corporation, R–3133-AF, February 1984), pp. 73–124.

11. Interview with Chinese military researchers, Beijing, March 1987.

12. See Larry M. Wortzel, "U.S. Technology Transfer Policies and the Modernization of China's Armed Forces," *Asian Survey* (June 1987), pp. 615–37; see also the remarks of Edward Ross, in Martin Lasater, ed., *The Two Chinas* (Washington: D.C.; The Heritage Foundation, 1986), pp. 83–90.

13. Eden Y. Woon, "Chinese Arms Sales and U.S.-China Military Relations," *Asian Survey* (June 1989), pp. 601–18.

14. Jim Mann, "China Cancels U.S. Deal for Modernizing F-8 Jet," *Los Angeles Times*, May 15, 1990.

15. For more extended discussion, see Gerald Segal, *Sino-Soviet Relations after Mao* (London: International Institute for Strategic Studies, Adelphi Paper #202, Autumn 1985); and Jonathan D. Pollack, *The Sino-Soviet Summit-Implications for East Asia and U.S. Foreign Policy* (New York: The Asia Society, May 1989).

16. For a period piece that captures the flavor of these pronouncements, see Banning Garrett and Bonnie Glaser, *Peace and War: The Views from Moscow and Beijing* (Berkeley: University of California, Institute of International Studies, 1984).

17. See Richard H. Solomon, ed., *Asian Security in the 1980s* (Santa Monica: The RAND Corporation, R–2492-ISA, November 1979).

18. It is impossible to determine whether Moscow and Beijing engaged in private communication prior to the Chinese move into northern Vietnam, thereby achieving a measure of "crisis management." This topic is worthy of further investigation.

19. Leonid Brezhnev, Report to the Twenty-Sixth Congress of the CPSU, February 23, 1981, in *FBIS-Soviet Union-Supplement*, February 24, 1981, p. 9.

20. Leonid Brezhnev, Speech in Tashkent, March 24, 1982, in *FBIS-Soviet Union*, March 29, 1982, pp. R1–3.

21. There was speculation among Western specialists that Huang Hua's overly exuberant depiction of Sino-Soviet relations on his return to Beijing was partially responsible for his replacement later in the month. This hypothesis is not implausible.

22. For relevant details, see Pollack, *The Sino-Soviet Summit*, especially pp. 12–15.

23. For analysis and relevant texts, see Robert A. Manning, *Asia Policy: The New Soviet Challenge in the Pacific* (New York: Priority Press Publications, 1988).

24. The latter judgments derive from extended conversations between the author and Chinese military and strategic specialists on visits to the PRC during November 1988 and May 1989.

25. For a very useful review, consult Dieter Heinzig, "The Soviet Union and China: Headed Toward a New Conflict?" *Aussenpolitik*, III/90, pp. 258–67.

26. Ann Scott Tyson, "Sino-Soviet Border Talks Look to Future Military Cooperation," *The Chinese Science Monitor*, September 11, 1990.

27. Daniel Southerland, "China Seeks Technology from Soviet Military," *Washington Post*, July 17, 1990.

28. *Jiefangjun bao*, August 1, 1987, p. 2. I am unaware of any other statement from a senior Chinese leader staking such a claim.

Comments by Mark Garrison

As someone who works on U.S.-Soviet relations most of the time, I have found Professor Pollack's paper on the Chinese perception of their own security concerns absorbing and informative. I also find it somewhat one-dimensional, however, in the same way as I might a Sovietologist's analysis of Soviet security concerns. I will focus my comments on just what that kind of analysis might be missing. The intent is not to be critical of the paper, but to nudge all of us to a more integrated approach in this sort of analysis.

A case in point can be made that U.S.-Soviet relations are approaching the start of a qualitatively different arrangement. Whether that will in fact happen is open to question, and probably the odds are against it. It seems the probability is sufficiently live. The leaders of a third country, China, who, as I gathered, are inclined to think strategically and whose strategic thinking all along is to take full account of U.S.-Soviet relations, surely those fellows must be making some assessment on that score. Thus, I read Professor Pollack's paper with much interest, thinking perhaps to find out how China's leaders have factored the possibilities of U.S.-Soviet relations into their strategic thinking. The paper does not include much on this, undoubtedly partly due to the time pressure. In his remarks, Professor Pollack characterized the present stage as one of undiminished Soviet-American competition and he does give the Reagan administration credit for having stood up against the Soviets militarily and taken the heat off China. But nothing is said about where the Reagan administration is today: the Reagan-Gorbachev summitry, the Reagan-Gorbachev antinuclear rhetoric and impending arms control agreements, and so on. Of course all of that is the work of the formerly anti-Soviet Reagan administration, which, in any case, is in its final years. Who knows what will come next. I think most of the development of Soviet-American relations are largely the product of the Soviet side; so I also look for what the Chinese assessment is of those changes that are going on.

The paper has noted that both the Chinese and the Soviets have been attentive to the changes taking place in each of the societies. The illustrations are largely from the Brezhnev period, and mostly have to do with the Soviet Union's China policy, not societal changes. It would be extremely helpful, therefore, if we could get some clues about the Chinese assessment of the changes that began with Gorbachev coming into power and the radical changes that are being forecast. Gorbachev says that foreign policy in the Soviet Union has now taken a backseat to the need of domestic reform. Chinese leaders are familiar with that table of priorities. Do they see Gorbachev's priorities as sincere? Or do they see the Russians as merely looking for a breathing spell to regain their strength or to lure their opponents, and so on? Another question that may not be directly related to the security question, but one I would be curious to know the answer to, is how the Chinese feel about

Moscow's favorite interest in their own economic reform. Is it flattering? Or is there some concern? If the Soviets learn from the Chinese how to do it, maybe the Soviet economy can climb off the canvas? More important, Gorbachev is talking about a different foreign and security policy, just a reminder, shifting from military to political means for advancing and protecting Soviet interest, claiming recognition that national security can best be achieved through mutual security, apparently embracing the concept of reasonable sufficiency for both nuclear and conventional weapons, and then, in conventional weapons, calling for a shift not only to defensive doctrines, but also to defensive force structures. This is Europe, of course; then, too, in Europe, he is allowing that it may be necessary to have asymmetrical reductions in order to have parity at lower levels. This may not apply to China, but these are basic principles; maybe there is an application.

Gorbachev has also called for a system of comprehensive international security, which is in his article about getting the United Nations more activated in these matters. In that context, he talks not only of weapons questions, but also regional questions, which are of particualr interest. He also talks of human rights, which is not of interest to the Chinese. All these issues could be dismissed as pie in the sky; if this is what turns out to be, then there is no relationship to the security calculus. It seems to me, however, that prudent leaders, and I think the Chinese are, would be asking themselves: On which of these matters has the Soviet Union made good? Are the consequences for China positive, or are there some challenges and unpredictable terms that must be taken into account? I suppose from Beijing's point of view, worse yet would be that other major actors, particularly the United States and Japan, will be taken in by the new Soviet line and end up by helping the Soviets build their own technology while China stands on the sidelines crying foul. Then there is the possibility of another outcome, such as Gorbachev falling on his face and the chauvinists being reinvigorated; what would that mean for China? As the Chinese make their assessment, it would be helpful to know how they view all these things. I wonder if the time may not have come for all three players, the three points of the triangle, to sit back and reassess their overall view of the triangular relationship. Certainly circumstances have changed a great deal since we played our China card, and used it to help jolt U.S.-Soviet relations out of the rut we had been in. But the other two are learning how to play, to shuffle the deck, and, more important, it seems they both have turned their attention, in different degrees, to resolving their own domestic problems, and they both are demonstrating this calculated nonchalance about the threat posed by the other. It is not just the Chinese who are doing that, but also the Soviets.

Despite what one would call the "routinization" of U.S.-China military contacts and arrangement, one doesn't hear much about them. It seems, as I heard Tom Robinson say a year or so ago, there is a quiet interlude in prospect because of domestic concerns, not only in those two countries, but in our country as well. The question is what is that interlude to be used for? Will it just be for gathering strength so that eventually one can leap-frog ahead, or will it be to think through and talk about, and maybe even implement, mutual steps to keep future military threats to a minimum, and to maximize opportunities for stretching our respective economic and political possibilities?

Comments by Mark Kramer

My comments will concentrate mostly on China's relations with the Soviet Union. I do want to raise one quick point about relations with the United States, and that is the importance of the Taiwan issue and what it would attribute to the rapid deterioration of the Sino-American relations during the early part of the Reagan administration.

Regarding the Sino-Soviet relations, when this issue was discussed throughout the 1970s and 1980s, it was regarded as the Sino-Soviet conflict; for example, the article in Donald Zagoria's book on Soviet policy in East Asia is entitled "Sino-Soviet Conflict." The same applies to most articles on Sino-Soviet relations up to a few years ago. A positive aspect of Professor Pollack's paper was that it shed some light and showed why that conflict did not have to continue or be permanent. Toward the end of the paper, however, more could have been said about how that conflict may resume and how tensions might intensify again.

Professor Pollack also aptly pointed out the kind of wild fluctuation going on in Chinese policy—from the inevitability of a war doctrine ten years ago to the optimistic mood that exists today. Similarly, he was correct in pointing out that China generally has been the one that has changed. The U.S. and Soviet positions toward China have remained stable. The Chinese have changed, and changed radically. The improvement in Sino-Soviet relations has occurred despite the Soviet failure to act on the three conditions.

There are some points that I think could be added or modified in the paper. Too little attention was given to the role of ideology, particularly the fading importance of ideology, compared to its importance ten or fifteen years ago—such harsh ideological polemics were exchanged then versus today, when it really does not come up much any more. Similarly, why have the party-to-party relations advanced far more slowly than state-to-state relations? Why, despite the seemingly fading importance of ideology, are party-to-party relations more difficult? Further, Japan's role should be discussed, as well as the internal changes in the Soviet Union and China. How are reforms in one country being viewed by policymakers in the other countries?

I would like to comment on military relations before returning to the question of how the Sino-Soviet conflict might resume. On military relations, I think there is merit to the mood Professor Pollack described as the military threat from the Soviet Union, although there are contrary indications that the threat has diminished. I would point to the improved quality of the forces deployed along the Sino-Soviet border, although the quantity of forces has remained stagnant, still fifty-two or fifty-three divisions. What is important in looking at those divisions is that the level of readiness has remained as it was a few years ago, in the early 1980s. I do think, however, that it indicates a depletion of troops from some of those divisions. Similarly, Professor Pollack mentioned, but largely passed over, this question of the Soviet willingness to get rid of not only SS20s, but also

SS23s based along the Sino-Soviet border. I think this deserves more than just a fleeting reference. I am willing to grant that there are contrary signs, particularly the naval build-up, that work in the opposite direction.

In addition, I would say that the more important military threat comes from the fact that China has developed a nuclear deterrent, a much more capable nuclear force than, perhaps, even five or six years ago. In 1980 China tested its full range ICBM, and in October 1982 it tested its SOBM. Two years ago, in October 1985, it tested its first long-range, sea-launched cruise missile. More recently, the CIA has projected that the Chinese nuclear force will double by 1990. It is clear, then, that there has been the emergence of a genuine rather than a token nuclear deterrent force. Particularly important are the sea-based forces, which will be invulnerable, in contrast to the land-based forces, which, we know, the Soviet Union has contemplated taking out. I would like to mention a few other important points, as well as the sharp decline in Sino-Soviet competition in the world. Both China and the Soviet Union seem to have pulled back equally from increasing their involvement in the Third World. They do not seem to look constantly for opportunities there. Moreover, I think it is accurate that both countries are currently preoccupied with domestic problems. This does induce a greater degree of caution and a greater willingness to avoid military and extramilitary involvements.

Finally, I would like to mention a personnel change that I think is important. Dimitri Yazov and Ivan Traichev, as of a year ago, were the Commander in Chief of the Far Eastern Military District and Commander of the Far East Theater, respectively. Now Yazov is Defense Minister and Traichev is the Commander-in-Chief of the Air Defense Force. I think their transfer to Moscow suggests a greater concentration of forces arrayed against the West, and less concentration on the military threat posed by China.

Let me end by suggesting a few scenarios, in addition to those Professor Pollack mentioned in his paper: first, the possible resumption of the Sino-Soviet conflict; second, a serious escalation of war in Afghanistan, particularly if it brought in Pakistan and possibly the use of nuclear weapons; and, third, a serious escalation of the Indo-Chinese conflict—the one people have been talking about constantly. Those are possible external scenarios. Internally, I think there will be either a stagnation of economic reform in China or leadership instability that could lead to a more aggressive policy externally and an attempt to divert attention from internal problems.

11

REORIENTING CHINA'S FOREIGN POLICY: China and the World

Harold C. Hinton

ALTHOUGH they are not the sole concerns of China's foreign policy, the United States and the Soviet Union are its centerpieces. Much of the rest amounts to an effort to build for Beijing a constituency that can in theory facilitate the crucial task of coping with the superpowers. The current Chinese leadership, like its predecessors, perceives China as playing an important role on the world stage, potentially and rightfully, even if it is not actually able to do so at the present time. It is to this role, both in aspiration and in actuality, that the following analysis is addressed.

The Background: Deng Xiaoping and Zhou Enlai

By the beginning of the 1970s, as Mao Zedong aged rapidly and Lin Biao lost his influence because of his excessive radicalism, Premier Zhou Enlai emerged as China's de facto leader and policymaker.[1] There can be little doubt that Zhou intended Deng Xiaoping to succeed him as premier and de facto strongman, and a figurehead, Wang Hungwen, to become party chairman after Mao's death. Deng had served as Zhou's senior vice premier during the period of relatively stable government (1954–65) preceding the Cultural Revolution and as acting premier during an extended trip that Zhou took to Africa and South Asia in 1963–64.[2] Subsequently, Deng was rehabilitated from his Cultural Revolution disgrace by Zhou in April 1973, and, as Zhou's health failed, Deng rapidly took over most of his functions.

As Deng reemerged, certain changes in the style, and to a lesser extent the substance, of Chinese foreign policy and diplomacy made their appearance; these must be presumed to reflect Deng's views and personality to some extent, as well the objective circumstances of the period.

Deng being less patient and more acerbic than his mentor, there was a marked decline in the frequency of joint communiques issued at the conclusion of visits to China by foreign dignitaries and abroad by Chinese leaders; evidently the marginal value of most such documents now appeared not worth the considerable time and trouble that, as any diplomat knows, go into nearly all of them. The Sino-American relationship, which had been progressing rather smoothly for the year-and-a-half preceding the establishment of the liaison offices in the spring of 1973, was complicated soon afterward and exacerbated by the injection from the Chinese side of three conditions, not actually new but now formulated in a more obtrusive and uncompromising manner than before, for the normalization of relations. Apart from personality factors, Deng was—and is—less politically secure than Zhou was in his last years and therefore less able to take a relaxed view of the Taiwan issue. He also made little effort at the time of the Kissinger and Ford visits in October and December 1975, respectively, to conceal his opinion that the United States was not trying hard enough to cope with Soviet "hegemonism."

Dissatisfied with the state of China's relations with the superpowers, Deng made one of Beijing's most transparent appeals for sympathy and support from the Third World as a form of compensation. On April 10, 1974, at a special session of the United Nations General Assembly, Deng, actually representing Zhou Enlai but developing a theme piously attributed to Mao Zedong, divided the world, as Caesar had divided all Gaul, into three parts (or "worlds"). The first, consisting of the superpowers, he denounced as the "biggest international exploiters and aggressors of today." The second, composed of the developed countries (not identified by name) other than the superpowers, he described as a "complicated" case; some, like Portugal, were still colonial powers, and all were "in varying degrees controlled, threatened, or bullied by one superpower or the other." He clearly identified China with the Third World, which had "long suffered from colonialist and imperialist oppression and exploitation. . . . China is a socialist country and a developing country as well. China belongs to the Third World." China, he asserted, therefore, supports the other countries of the Third World in their supposed struggle against "imperialism" and "colonialism." This piece of rhetoric, throughly Maoist except for its Zhouist emphasis on "contention" (as against "collusion") between the superpowers, was clearly designed to curry favor for China in the Third World while grossing over the fact that China was still "tilting," if somewhat less markedly than two or three years earlier, toward the United States as a form of defense against Soviet pressures.[3]

Zhou's death on January 8, 1976, removed his shield and patronage from over Deng, whose unpopularity with the ultra-Maoist radicals led to his being purged again three months later and returning to the political wilderness for another fifteen months, approximately, after that. Once he was rehabilitated in 1977, his impressive qualities and formidable support soon gave him the edge over the unimposing Hua Guofeng. Since the celebrated Third Plenary Session of the

Eleventh Central Committee (December 1978), Deng can be considered to have been effectively in charge of Chinese foreign policy, in addition to being "more equal" than his colleagues in domestic politics as well.

Deng's Foreign Policy:
First Steps and General Considerations

Perhaps the centerpiece of Zhou Enlai's legacy to Deng Xiaoping, and to China, is the Four Modernizations (agriculture, industry, national defense, and science and technology), which were hoisted by Zhou a year before his death as a kind of national flag. Many Chinese have of course realized since the late nineteenth century that their country could be sure of enjoying security and influence only when and if it modernized, but never before the mid-1970s was this truism elevated to the top of the agenda as unambiguously as it has been since then. The connotations of this shift have been both important and non-Maoist: a virtual cessation of Maoist incantations and social upheavals ("mass campaigns") at home and an "opening" of the country to foreign economic contacts (especially inward technology transfer) to a degree unmatched since the last days of the "unequal" treaties.

This new, or at least significantly altered, approach came out rather clearly at the time of the Third Plenary Session just mentioned. The communique, as usual, was less informative than it might have been and was taken up largely with domestic affairs. Implicitly, the relative order of the last two "modernizations" was reversed, although the published order has never been authoritatively changed. This meant, or at least connoted, a minimization of expenditure on national defense (although not of the determination to get the biggest bang for the yuan), on the basis of a tacit gamble that the international environment would remain essentially nonthreatening, thanks, in large part if unadmittedly on Beijing's part, to the generally stabilizing role of the United States, and that China could make a useful contribution to keeping it that way. In fact, the Deng leadership has revived the approach of the late Marshal Peng Dehuai, purged in 1959 and rehabilitated in accordance with a decision taken at the Third Plenary Session: long-term balanced modernization, with emphasis on industry but not on defense industry per se, consequent gradual growth of China's military as well as economic capabilities, nonprovocative behavior toward the outside world, and reliance for security to a high degree on the friendly superpower (the Soviet Union in Peng's day, the United States now).

There was, however, a counterpoint at the Third Plenary Session that harmonized poorly with this overarching theme. Hanoi had "tilted" toward Moscow and was to invade Cambodia on Christmas Day, as it turned out, three days after the conclusion of the plenary session, in order to unseat the pro-Chinese if genocidal regime of Pol Pot. Foreseeing this, Beijing had announced its normalization agreement with the United States on December 15, partly as a means of helping to deter Soviet retaliation while China administered the "lesson" of which it had begun to warn Hanoi. Still another diplomatic ploy to shore up the international political position of the People's Republic of China (PRC) had been a visit by Deng to Thailand, Malaysia, and Singapore in November. This sort of thing was evidently not enough for the senior leadership of the People's Liberation Army, which felt that the Vietnamese had betrayed over the previous year or more the wartime comradeship-in-arms with China that had persisted down to about 1975. It is probable that Deng did not feel so strongly in favor of chastising the Vietnamese but went along in order to get military support for his own political position and for his incipient campaign to dump Hua Guofeng and other residual radicals within the party leadership. Accordingly, whereas Deng personally had been stressing—and continued to stress for a little longer—the threat from the north (the Soviet Union), the communique of the Third Plenary Session urged the country to "be prepared to repulse at any moment aggressors from any direction," an all-purpose Maoist clarion call that in this case was certainly intended to refer above all to the Vietnamese.[4] The "lesson" to Hanoi, an effective if inefficient one in the sense that it compelled Hanoi to maintain a large force of its best troops near the Chinese border and destroyed the myth of Vietnamese invincibility throughout Southeast Asia, began in mid-February 1979, shortly after Deng had further strengthened his international fences by visiting the United States.

   In the aftermath of four interrelated developments that followed each other in rapid succession—normalization of relations with the United States, the Third Plenary Session, Deng's visit to the United States, and the "lesson" to Hanoi— and partly as a consequence of them, there occurred a major, although by no means total, shift in Deng's strategic thinking and therefore in Chinese foreign policy. The primary concern was now China's long-term economic development, not its security in the short run. This strongly implied a judgment that there was no serious immediate (as contrasted with potential) threat from the Soviet Union, and therefore that the former Maoist/Zhouist "united front" strategy against Soviet "hegemonism," which Deng had ringingly endorsed on the eve of his American trip, was now more or less obsolete, at least under existing conditions. Moscow's failure to retaliate directly against China for its attack on Vietnam evidently eased Deng's concern in that direction, and the Soviet invasion of Afghanistan at the end of the year tended to confirm Beijing's impression, dating from about 1973, that the real thrust of Soviet "expansionism" was in the direction of Southwest rather than Northeast Asia. In any event, the Carter administration showed the exact opposite of interest in Deng's united front proposal while he was in Washington and disapproved of the attack on Vietnam; the invasion of Afghanistan worked a limited change in this American attitude in a direction favorable to "defense cooperation" (the Pentagon's term) with China, as Secretary of Defense Harold Brown's visit to China in January 1980 made clear, but not enough of a change to cause Deng to resurrect his united front concept. The new priorities remained in force.[5]

   Common sense suggests that a country that is not united tends to enjoy less international influence than one that is, other things being equal (as they never are). On top of that consideration, there is a powerful emotional, or nationalist, drive that has caused the Chinese Communist leadership to attach a high priority to territorial unification, although not high enough to tempt it into potential national suicide, for example, by hurling itself on the Seventh Fleet.

During the Deng era to date, there have been three areas that are relevant to the unification issue and therefore require discussion in this context. These are, obviously, Hong Kong, Macao, and Taiwan. Beijing draws a formal distinction among these cases, even while insisting that the famous Dengist formula "one country, two systems" (socialism and capitalism) is applicable to the future of all three as part of the PRC: Hong Kong and Macao, it holds, involve the recovery of sovereignty (from a foreign power), whereas Taiwan is a straightforward case of unification,[6] or, in other words, the termination by whatever means of the long Chinese civil war.

In practice, these two types of cases have indeed differed in every significant respect. Hong Kong and Macao are militarily indefensible enclaves on the PRC's doorstep, and their colonial possessors have long been ready to surrender them when Beijing got serious about demanding their retrocession. Taiwan, shielded by a hundred miles of blue water and held by a rival government able and willing to defend itself, is clearly a completely different problem for Beijing.

The case of Hong Kong was the first to become active, in the spring of 1982. The lapse of the lease on the New Territories, without which the rest of Hong Kong is not considered viable, in 1997, and the fact that the British authorities have customarily been granted land leases for a term of fifteen years, led them to inquire privately of Beijing whether the granting of further leases on those terms, after the spring of 1982, would be advisable. The answer, which was in the negative, alarmed official Hong Kong and started what turned out to be a rather rapid unraveling of the British position, notwithstanding Prime Minister Thatcher's abortive effort to use her recent victory in the Falklands (or the Malvinas, as Beijing prefers to call them in deference to Argentinian sensibilities) as a means of impressing Deng Xiaoping with London's determination. The result, announced on September 26, 1984, is well known. Sovereignty and jurisdiction over Hong kong are to pass to the PRC in mid-1997; for fifty years after that, Hong Kong is to enjoy "autonomous" status, and its social and economic systems are not to be disturbed.[7] The outlook for observance of this arrangement by Beijing is not very promising; already it exercises a virtual veto power over political trends in Hong Kong. The Xinhua office there has begun to assume the dimensions of a shadow government, and the confidence of the inhabitants in their future in Hong Kong has been eroding rather fast. Needless to say, the favorable impact on the chances of an agreement with Taiwan that Beijing had hoped would be a consequence of the Hong Kong settlement has not materialized.

Until recently, Macao has been shielded from a similar fate by Beijng's desire not to startle Hong Kong prematurely, but once the settlement for Hong Kong had been reached there was no longer any reason to delay pressing for a similar one for Macao. The Portuguese, who had yielded Beijing de facto over political developments in the colony during the Cultural Revolution, got only a slightly better deal than the British had gotten. The Macao arrangement, agreed to in March 1987, is modeled on the one for Hong Kong; in this case sovereignty and jurisdiction pass in 1999.[8]

The achievement of a Hong Kong settlement in 1984 spurred Beijing to work harder than ever for unification with Taiwan, but it did not really make the attainment of that goal any easier. Beijing's options are limited and have not changed essentially since 1950. They are: the use, or credible threat, of force, political approaches leading potentially to an eventual agreement, and efforts to bring the United States to reduce or eliminate its remaining ties (other than purely commercial) with the island, in the hope that Taipei would then throw in its hand.

To date (fall 1987), none of these ploys had produced more than a minimal observable effect in Taipei, where (from Beijing's viewpoint) movement needs to occur. Repeated semiofficial threats of force, especially a naval blockade, have worried Taipei but have not carried much conviction in light of the current military balance in the Taiwan Strait and the probability that Beijing would be blockading itself too, by driving foreign ships away from the "key economic area" extending from Shanghai to Guangzhou, inclusive. Beijing's repeated promises of "autonomy" for Taiwan after unification, reinforced by various elaborations intended to be encouraging, have achieved nothing tangible beyond a meeting in Hong Kong in May 1986 to arrange the return to Taiwan of a China Air Lines cargo aircraft and its crew (minus the defecting pilot). The Reagan administration's commitment to Taiwan's security has remained reasonably firm, within the mutually somewhat inconsistent parameters of the Taiwan Relations Act and the Sino-American joint communique of August 17, 1982, on the subject of American arms sales to Taiwan. The most that can be said on this last score is that the United States has felt some concern over the recent improvement in Sino-Soviet relations and accordingly a somewhat greater interest in conciliating Beijing; this was probably the source of Secretary Shultz's decision to break new ground, in his speech of February 28, 1987, at Shanghai, by publicly supporting the idea of contacts between Beijing and Taipei.

Just as Deng Xiaoping seems to have felt a sense of mission to preside if at all possible over the unification of China, so, as we have seen, he has associated himself with the proposition that China can and ought to play a role of special significance, although not necessarily one of actual leadership, in the Third World. In the latter sphere, the results to date have been if anything less impressive than in the former.

Despite its redundant pro-South and anti-North rhetoric and its continuing foreign aid program, the PRC is so atypical when considered as a Third World country that it has not acquired much usable influence there. It has no constituency or bloc at the United Nations and does not belong to the Nonaligned Movement. Its leaders no longer seem to feel the old Maoist certainty that communism is the wave of the future for the Third World, except perhaps in the very long run. For reasons apparently relating more to their intentions than to the obvious limitations on their capabilities, they have not been demonstrably active in supporting leftist insurgencies in the Third World; here they have fallen far behind the Soviet Union, Cuba, and even North Korea. They appear resigned to the need to work, to the extent feasible, with existing governments.

Accordingly, there is no discernible or significant probability that the PRC can build, in the "foreseeable" future, a base of power or influence in the Third World that might enable it to cope more effectively with the varying challenges presented by the superpowers.

China and Its Communist Neighbors

Beijing's ability to influence the policies and behavior of its communist neighbors is not very great, but its preferences in this connection are not difficult to determine. They are, in brief, that they should not constitute or reinforce a threat to China's security, and that their domestic policies should not be too far out of line with China's, which may be characterized as being comprised of significant economic reforms falling short to date of "market socialism" and of very modest political reforms.

On the first score, a direct threat comes, and can only come, from the Soviet Union; there can be no serious doubt that the Chinese leadership, and especially its military component, still regards the Soviet Union in this light. In an indirect sense, a threat can obviously result from a "tilt" by a neighbor toward the Soviet Union. This is clearly a problem in the case of Vietnam, and less obviously so in the case of North Korea. It is transparent in the case of Mongolia.

Among the various issues in Sino-Vietnamese relations, Hanoi's "tilt" toward Moscow and its effort to dominate Cambodia rank in Beijing's eyes approximately on a par, at the head of the list. The two problems are intimately interrelated; Moscow gives Hanoi economic and military aid without which it would probably not be able simultaneously to fight in Cambodia and maintain a strong blocking force near the Chinese border, and Moscow gets in return its important air and naval bases at Danang and Camranh Bay, respectively. To date, at any rate, the Soviets, in spite of their obvious desire for an improved relationship with China, have been unwilling to endanger these bases by putting effective pressure on the Vietnamese to withdraw from Cambodia. For its part, as is well known, Beijing rates Soviet support for Vietnam's operations in Cambodia as the most serious of the "three obstacles" to better Sino-Soviet relations; Chinese spokesmen, when queried as to the reason for this priority, answer that, unlike the Sino-Soviet border (including Mongolia) and Afghanistan, the other two "obstacles," Cambodia is an area where a hot war is going on in which China is actively involved in supporting one of the parties (i.e., the Khmer Rouge, and through it the anti-Vietnamese coalition headed more or less by Prince Sihanouk). This is true, although it is also true that Beijing has provided a modest amount of aid, on a covert basis, to the mujahidin in Afghanistan. By comparison with Cambodia, Beijing has publicly attached less importance to the Soviet bases in Vietnam, which, if a genuine position, presumably reflects a judgment that they are less of a problem for China than for other states in the region and for the United States.

Korea is an area of even greater strategic importance to China than Vietnam is. Accordingly, Beijing's relations with Pyongyang are in significant respects more sensitive and complex, although of course much less overtly hostile, than its relations with Hanoi.

The subject of North Korea is so sensitive from Beijing's point of view that Chinese sources do not discuss it frankly in public. There is probably no area of Chinese foreign policy where the real policy differs so markedly from the declaratory policy.

The real policy can be inferred, not from Chinese pronouncements but from China's behavior and from indirect evidence, such as the demonstrable North Korean perception of its neighbor's attitude. Beijing does not want Pyongyang to move either militarily against Seoul or politically toward Moscow. On the whole, it has handled the difficult task of optimizing these two goals, which are in considerable tension with one another, with some skill. The first requires the toleration, even the approval, of the American military presence in South Korea as a stabilizer and deterrent, an attitude that used to be conveyed confidentially to American officials in the early 1970s but has not been since then, presumably because of North Korean sensitivities. The second requires careful cultivation of Pyongyang, for example, by endorsing its call (since October 1983) for three-party talks on the future of the peninsula among the two Koreas and the United States; the message seems to be that although China does not deliver reasonably advanced military hardware to North Korea as the Soviet Union has been doing in recent years, it can provide something that Moscow cannot: a channel for United States-North Korea contacts and some political leverage on the United States in support of Pyongyang.

In a variety of ways, Beijing has sought to project an image of unconcern, even approval, over the improvement of Soviet-North Korean relations since the early 1980s, even though Soviet aircraft now overfly North Korea and reconnoiter targets on and around the Yellow Sea. Many non-Chinese observers have rejected this claim and, with some plausibility, have gone so far as to label the current mutual "tilt" between Moscow and Pyongyang as the unproclaimed "fourth obstacle" to better Sino-Soviet relations. This may be going too far, but probably not by very much. The writer has observed more than one informed Chinese grow instantly tense at the mention of the Soviet-North Korean relationship and then given an obviously rehearsed discourse to the effect that Beijing is not at all worried about it, that the United States and South Korea are the sources of tension in the peninsula, that the United States should accept the North Korean proposal for three-party talks and prod Seoul to do the same. This line of argument makes so little sense from an objective point of view that the aptest comment on it is probably one made by a distinguished American scholar-diplomat to the writer not long ago: Anyone who believes that will believe anything.

The truth appears to be that Beijing is extremely worried over the developing Soviet-North Korean relationship and sees it as a potential link in the Soviet "encirclement" of China and indeed as a de facto "fourth obstacle." The Korean peninsula is so strategically situated with respect to its neighbors, China emphatically included, that Beijing cannot willingly accept any possibility that North Korea might be drawn into an anti-Chinese combination, especially in time of war, with the Soviet Union. Accordingly, Beijing has gone to great, sometimes comical, lengths to conciliate and impress Pyongyang, especially the Great Leader Kim Il Song and his heir apparent Kim Jong Il. China, being weaker and less capable of dispensing concrete benefits than the Soviet Union, needs to be and is more energetic in wooing the prickly North Koreans. This perpetual Chinese smiling offensive does not deceive Pyongyang, which understands very clearly the rather stringent limits that Beijing imposes on its actual, as distinct from propaganda, support for North Korean policies and behavior, but at least the existing situation avoids giving Pyongyang an overt cause for taking offense at its Chinese ally and "tilting" even further toward its Soviet ally.

An important aspect of Beijing's behavior in recent years that has inevitably disturbed the North Koreans, both for emotional and for practical reasons, has been the Chinese "tilt" toward the United States in the security field. It is as though this policy of Beijing's, as well as its "unofficial" opening to South Korea (mainly trade), constitutes a mutually reinforcing cycle in connection with the growth of Soviet-North Korean security cooperation. One suspects that the North Koreans simultaneously object to the Sino-American relationship and find it useful as an argument to cite to the Soviet by way of support for the proposition that North Korea does not do things like that and is loyal to the Soviet connection. If so, both Beijing and Moscow presumably understand what Pyongyang is up to, and neither is much impressed by it. From the North Korean perspective, the most outrageous performance to date in the field of Sino-American security cooperation was probably the visit to Qingdao, for reasons that clearly transcended the excellent local beer, of three vessels of the United States Seventh Fleet in early November 1986; it is worth noting that Qingdao is located almost, although not quite, directly across the Yellow Sea from North Korea and had been substituted on short notice for the originally scheduled port of call, Shanghai, which of course is considerably farther from North Korea.

It is clear that when Soviet forces were introduced into the Mongolian People's Republic in the spring of 1966 they consisted mainly of offensive units (armor and airborne), not border guards, and were designed to pose a threat, whether aggressive or deterrent, to Beijing itself, which lies only about four hundred miles from the closest sector of the Sino-Mongolian border. Accordingly, Beijing has been eager to see those troops removed, and especially so since the Soviet Union drastically raised the level of its military threat to China as a direct result of the border crisis of March 1969. But the proximity of the Mongolian border to Beijing is by no means the only problem created for China by this situation. Far more than the Vietnamese or the Koreans, the ("outer") Mongols fear the Chinese, regardless of political persuasion, as a historic and unmanageable threat, their Colossus of the South, and have tended voluntarily to huddle close to Russia, first White and then Red, for protection. Even in the absence of the satellite status that the Soviet Union has imposed on Mongolia since the 1920s, this Mongolian attitude would create serious complications for China and would tend to lead the Mongols to welcome the presence of Soviet troops on their soil.

Accordingly, the recent Soviet withdrawal of one of the five divisions deployed in Mongolia, signaled by Gorbachev in his Vladivostok speech of July 28, 1986, has been welcomed by Beijing as at least a friendly gesture. Precisely because that is what it is, it has not disturbed the Mongols unduly. A delegation of Mongols recently visiting the United States made it clear that they could live with the withdrawal of the division, although they frankly admitted that they were still afraid of the Chinese and welcomed the retention of the other four divisions.

As for the second of its major concerns relating to its communist neighbors, Beijing appears to welcome, or at least logically speaking, ought to welcome, a trend toward economic reform, and possibly toward very limited political liberalization, to the extent that these may appear in its communist neighbors. It is clearly watching Gorbachev's innovations with positive interest and is presumably doing the same for the rudimentary reforms that have been instituted recently in Vietnam and North Korea. It is clear that in principle Beijing wants its relations with its communist neighbors to be good, or at least better than they are, and that broad correspondence in domestic policy can and generally does help to promote friendly interrelationships, among communist as well as among noncommunist states. It is equally clear that, as it showed in its own case by suppressing the student demonstrations of January 1987, Beijing does not want reform from above to be met from below by manifestations of that bugbear of all true Leninists, "spontaneity" (demonstrations, strikes, open intellectual dissent, and so forth). There is, fortunately for Beijing and unfortunately from the viewpoint of the noncommunist world, little likelihood of such tendencies on a large scale in the Soviet Union, Vietnam, North Korea, or Mongolia, or for that matter China itself, in the near future. The classic example of what Beijing hopes to see avoided in "fraternal socialist" countries, of course, is the developments in Poland associated with the emergence of Solidarity; Beijing refrained from criticizing the proclamation of martial law by General Jaruzelski in December 1981, which it clearly regarded as far preferable to either of the obvious alternatives, Soviet military intervention or an irreversible weakening of communist control.

China and Its Noncommunist Neighbors

The most important of China's noncommunist neighbors is obviously Japan. It is equally clear that the relationship between China and Japan is a complex one and that, in spite of or rather partly because of the fact that they trade heavily with one another, it is a relationship bedeviled by serious problems. There is no need here for an analysis of the Japanese side of this equation, but there certainly is of the Chinese side.

From an emotional and political point of view, the main problem on the Chinese side is a massive historical one: the escalating series of Japanese acts of aggression against China over half a century (1895–1945). All educated Chinese, even young ones, are well aware of this dark cloud over the past, and it does not take much, even when Sino-Japanese relations are seemingly on a smooth course, to bring this cloud to the forefront of their consciousness. A series of events in recent years has had this effect: various Japanese history textbooks that have condoned or even glorified Japanese aggression, the visit by Premier Nakasone to the Yasukuni Shrine (to Japan's war dead) on August 15, 1985, the fiftieth anniversary (July 7, 1987) of the Marco Polo Bridge "Incident" (which was commemorated in Taiwan with even greater outrage than on the mainland, inasmuch as the Kuomintang's headquarters would not be on the island if it had not been for the Japanese invasion).

Two other sets of forces are also at work on the Chinese side, one relating to the recent past, the other to the anticipated future.

The first is the fall of General Secretary Hu Yaobang in mid-January 1987. Before that time Hu had been prominently involved for more than three years in personal cooperation with Nakasone toward an improvement of Sino-Japanese relations, a logical concomitant of China's current "independent" policy of keeping a safe and comfortable distance from the superpowers (although in reality farther from the Soviet Union than from the United States). Naturally Hu's fall has tended to bring on a backlash of sorts against policies with which he had been personally and prominently identified, including his opening to Japan.

The Japanese appear to believe, or at least to hope, that the Hu affair is the main cause of the current frost on Sino-Japanese relations, and that the thing to do is "wait and see" on the theory that the whole thing will blow over and the shifting winds of Chinese politics will soon produce a warming trend once more. This may well turn out to be correct as an estimate of the future, but it is rather superficial as a piece of analysis. It tends to ignore both the considerations already mentioned and another negative factor at work, the expectations of many Chinese regarding Japan's future behavior.

As the writer was made aware during a recent (June 1987) trip to the PRC, these expectations tend to be pessimistic, at least in the form in which they are conveyed to visiting Americans. A synthesis of them would run approximately as follows: Japan has not confronted and tried to atone for its record of aggression to the extent that Germany has. Accordingly, Japan still has the potential for turning once more to millitary expansion. The problem is not acute at the present time, when Japan possesses nothing more than a limited self-defense capability, something to which its Chinese critics admit in principle it is entitled. The problem may become acute in the future, however, when and if Japan moves from a self-defense to a regional military capability; such a development would be very disturbing to the Chinese, because it could prove to be the immediate forerunner of a genuinely aggressive policy and posture.

This is not the place for a detailed analysis and evaluation of the validity of this argument. Two points may be made in passing, however. On the one hand, the argument appears to be sincere, at least to a degree. On the other hand, it is curious that Asians often criticize Japan when talking to Americans, as though to suggest that the United States really ought not to rate Japan as the main pillar of its regional interests and policy and that their own country is actually more reliable.

In spite of this anti-Japanese posture, it is clear that Beijing, at the highest levels at any rate, continues to regard the United States-Japan security relationship as the principal guarantee of regional peace and stability and therefore does not want it disrupted by arguments between Washington and Tokyo over military burden-sharing and the payments balance. From the Chinese point of view, as well as in reality, a viable United States-Japan security relationship not only helps to contain the Soviet Union in the region and discourage a Japanese-Soviet accommodation but also tends to restrain any tendency that might otherwise emerge for Japan to rearm on a large scale and on an independent ("Gaullist") basis.

The other main category of current Chinese objections to Japan is essentially economic, although it also has political and emotional overtones. Unlike the United States—but like everyone else—Japan is not actually transferring high technology to China on a significant scale. Instead, it is running large trade and payments surpluses through exports, although it is suspected of shipping its best goods elsewhere for currencies harder and more convertible than the yuan. This alleged situation is resented on obvious grounds of economic nationalism, and Americans are sometimes harangued on this subject as well. The writer has recently heard the United States asked the following rhetorical question by a Chinese speaker: "Have you no national pride? In other words, why do you not resent your deficit with Japan more and try to control it as we do?" It seems a fair question.

China's "unofficial" opening to South Korea since the beginning of the 1980s appears to have four main sources and motives: (1) A desire to benefit from the economic dynamism of the Fifth Republic through trade, and perhaps also through technological borrowing and study of the South Korean economic "model" (in this connection, the sizable Korean minority in the Northeast is ready and eager to act as an intermediary, to the extent feasible); (2) the enhanced diplomatic activity and influence of South Korea under the Fifth Republic, which is clearly not the American client state that its predecessors tended to be; (3) the wish to promote, or at least to see, a relaxation of tension in the Korean peninsula; and (4) a hope of balancing, and perhaps constraining, the mutual "tilt" between North Korea and the Soviet Union.

Like many other countries, China has found it necessary and expedient to take account of the fact that ASEAN has not only maintained its existence but has acquired a certain significance as an international organization.

ASEAN's current importance arises largely from its role more or less in the front lines of the Cambodian crisis. To date, Thailand has tended to set ASEAN's Cambodian policy, although this is coming less true. China's views on Cambodia appear parallel at first blush with those of ASEAN (or, more accurately, Thailand), since both demand the withdrawal of Vietnamese troops and a Cambodia free of Vietnamese domination. There is a considerable difference, however, over the means by which this is to be accomplished. ASEAN, understandably worried by Vietnam's million-man army, wants a negotiated settlement. Beijing, while paying lip service to this goal and to the tripartite Cambodian anti-Vietnamese coalition nominally headed by Prince Sihanouk, in reality prefers to see Vietnam "bled white," although not necessarily as the partial result of a second Chinese "lesson," which would create serious risks for China. As for the coalition, that the Khmer Rouge is its strongest component owes a good deal to preferential Chinese aid and support, at the expense of the other two components.

A few qualifications and observations are worth noting. One is that China's willingness to confront Vietnam directly over the Cambodian issue has been diminishing somewhat, although not yet dramatically, over the past few years, mainly because Beijing does not want to risk antagonizing Moscow unduly or unnecessarily over this or any other matter. Second, the United States claims to endorse the ASEAN view of the Cambodian issue, but in reality there is considerable quiet American sympathy, official as well as unofficial, for the Chinese position, both because of the past history of United States-Vietnamese relations and because of the greater importance of China, as compared with ASEAN, in the American scheme of things. Third, ASEAN is not really unanimous in support of Thailand on the Cambodian question; Indonesia, in particular, aspires to a leading role in ASEAN, regards China as a long-term threat to the region or at least as a rival for influence in it, and sees Vietnam as a valuable buffer against potential Chinese pressures on Southeast Asia.

Indonesia's anti-Chinese attitude, although tending to diminish slowly, is a major problem for Beijing, which would like to "normalize" relations with it but has met with minimal reciprocation from the military elite that has ruled the archipelago since the fall of Sukarno, with whom Beijing's relations had been very close in 1966–67. Beijing has no effective choice but to keep a low profile and bide its time, in the hope that eventually it will no longer be either feared as a threat or hated as a rival in Jakarta.

Near the other end of the scale, Sino-Thai relations are reasonably close, essentially on a common anti-Vietnamese platform. Deng Xiaoping did not create this situation, but he can claim considerable credit for fostering it through his important visit to Bangkok in November 1978. Thailand regards China and the United States as its two most important and useful friends, at least in the context of its security against Vietnam, and tends to perceive the former as probably more reliable than the latter. The question of reliability apart, current Chinese and American policies toward Thailand are parallel and compatible.

In Malaysia, Beijing's standing with the increasingly Islamic Malay elite that runs the country is basically poor. The root of the problem is the ethnic balance, unique in the world: a very large and economically powerful Chinese minority, which the ruling Malay majority not only wants to keep in its current second-class political citizenship but has been trying, without much success, to push toward second-class economic citizenship as well. This situation has an obvious explosive potential, and the Malay elite fears, on the basis of no observable evidence, that Beijing might at some point try to inject itself into the controversy on the side of its compatriots. Given this perspective, the Malays refuse to concede any present Soviet threat to the region but oppose American economic and technical support for China's modernization and anything else that might help Beijing to become such a threat some day. Again, Beijing has no choice, at least for the time being, but to keep its head down and hope for the best.

Ethnic compatibility has not been enough to ensure an easy relationship between China and Singapore. Prime Minister Lee Kuan Yew's socialist, but emphatically noncommunist, ideology and his effort to create a "Singaporean identity" in order to appease his Malay neighbors have led him to keep the PRC at arm's length, except in a commercial sense. He withholds diplomatic recognition of Beijing pending a restoration of normal relations between China and Indonesia. Under these conditions, Beijing welcomes Singaporean trade, investment, and managerial advice, but otherwise finds it advisable to maintain a low posture.

In the Philippines, Beijing again plays a minor role. There can be no reasonable doubt that it does not want the important American bases to fall into Soviet hands, as might well happen if the communist insurgency were to succeed, because of the probable drastic effect on the regional balance of power. Chinese policy, such as it is, appears to follow two parallel tracks: abstention from complicating President Aquino's problems by, for example, competing with Moscow in supporting the Communists (as the Soviets are apparently beginning to do); and private advice to the United States to establish a dialogue with the Communists in the hope that if they do come to power they will not then throw themselves into the arms of the Soviet Union, as Castro has done.

Except in the case of the Khmer Rouge, Beijing appears to be no longer in the business of supporting communist insurgencies in Southeast Asia. The last non-Cambodian exception to this rule, the Communist Party of Burma, was cut off a few years ago. From the perspective of the PRC's overall interests, it is much more important to oppose the growth of Soviet and Vietnamese influence in the region than to promote the unpromising cause of local Communists; this means, in general, support for local governments, or at least an avoidance of serious troublemaking for them. Still, the banner of Marxism-Leninism cannot be furled in public, and while he was in Southeast Asia in November 1978 Deng Xiaoping flatly refused to repudiate the principle of support for "wars of national liberation."

In addition to the local Communist parties, the other potential or suspected Trojan Horse for Beijing in the region is of course the Chinese communities (the "overseas Chinese," or *huaqiao*). At times when it was in a militant mood and objective conditions appeared favorable, Beijing has unquestionably tried to use one or another of these communities for its own political purposes, but such efforts have been more the exception than the rule. Like the local Communist parties, the Chinese communities have generally ranked lower in Beijing's scheme of values than the local governments. Furthermore, to a much greater extent than the Communist parties, the Chinese communities are potential hostages in the hands of local governments, political parties, armies, police forces, and mobs for Beijing's good behavior. As the events of 1978 in Vietnam showed, Beijing cannot protect the *huaqiao* when they are persecuted, regardless of its own feelings and the cause of any particular persecution. Again, a low profile for Beijing is clearly indicated and is generally maintained.

Unlike Southeast Asia, where two states, Vietnam and Indonesia, stand out as "more equal" than the others, in South Asia one power, India, of course, has clear preeminence, although not actual domination. Since the mid-1950s, Beijing's relations with this neighbor have ranged from uneasy to hostile. There are three basic reasons for this: (1) Chinese and Indians are on very different "wavelengths" in virtually every significant respect; (2) China and India have divergent, indeed basically incompatible, views as to the desirable situation in the border region between them, the Roof of the World; and (3) Beijing, unlike Moscow, has never accepted the principle of Indian "hegemony" in South Asia. Accordingly, since about the time of the Sino-Indian border war of October–November 1962, China has maintained very close relations with Pakistan, the only country in South Asia large enough and strong enough to constitute something of a counterweight to India.

For these underlying reasons, Beijing and New Delhi have been unable to reach agreement during their reasonably regular negotiations over their unresolved mutual border dispute. This failure is not necessarily critical of itself, but its effects have been compounded since 1986 by an increased Indian assertiveness apparently arising from India's internal problems and the activist personality of Rajiv Gandhi. This activism has been manifested toward most of India's neighbors, and China has not escaped it.

In late 1986 and early 1987, the government of India integrated the state of Arunachal Pradesh, which lies between the McMahon Line (approximately the main Himalayan ridgeline in that sector) and the northern edge of the Brahmaputra Valley, into the Indian Union, as it had done to Sikkim in 1973–74. China does not claim Sikkim, but it does claim the territory north of the Brahmaputra Valley (although not under that name) even though Beijing is apparently prepared ultimately to trade away its claim to that area, which it would have great difficulty in making good on a permanent basis across the main ridgeline of the Himalayas, for Indian recognition—not yet forthcoming—of China's claim to Aksai Chin, as the area at the junction of northeastern Kashmir, southwestern Xinjiang, and western Tibet is generally called.

In the spring of 1987, after the weather began to permit movement on the ground, the two sides resumed a game of "military chess" (Nehru's term) near the western end of the McMahon Line that had begun the previous summer. It involved forward troop redeployments on disputed territory by both sides, with the support of reinforcements moved up from rear areas; there appear to have been some clashes. It is worth noting that the military balance in the area has changed significantly since 1962, in favor of India.[9]

Obscure as the origins and course of this crisis are, the resolution is perhaps even more so. It looks as though both sides reached, independently, the common sense conclusion that events were moving toward a war that neither wanted. At any event, by the time the Indian Minister for External Affairs visited Beijing in mid-June, a modus vivendi of some kind had evidently been agreed on.

The Indian Army enjoys superiority not only over that portion of the People's Liberation Army that is deployed near the Sino-Indian border but also over the Pakistani army as a whole. In view of this, and in spite of occasional episodes of Indo-Pakistani détente, Pakistan appears to have been moving, as covertly as possible but not without occasional leaks of information, toward a capability at least to produce nuclear weapons. There is an equal probability, not quite amounting to a certainty, that Beijing has given some critical aid to this program, again as covertly as possible. If so, this does not necessarily mean that Beijing actively approves of the idea of its close friend "going nuclear," but rather that it chooses to support this Pakistani decision, as it did the disastrous one of 1971 to try to crush East Bengali separatism by force, in the interest of the overall Sino-Pakistani relationship. It seems, then, that Beijing's public position that it opposes the proliferation of nuclear weapons may be sincere when viewed as a general principle, but that it is ready to make exceptions in important specific cases—a policy more elastic than that of the other nuclear powers.

China and the World Outside Asia

There is no doubt that Beijing has ambitions, or perhaps more accurately aspirations, that transcend the status of a mere regional power. This is a difficult topic to analyze, partly because the idea appears to be only dimly formulated in the minds of the Deng leadership. It is reasonably clear that Beijing has given up the old Maoist utopia, which began to fade as early as 1965, of a world of revolutionary leftist states oriented toward Beijing as the source of their ideology and strategy. It is quite possible that Deng has a concept of China's future global role no more precise than the one he outlined at the important party conference of September 1985:

> By the middle of the next century, when we approach the level of the advanced countries, then there will have been really great changes. At that time the strength of China and its world role will be quite different. We shall be able to make greater contributions to mankind.[10]

In any event, for some time longer, China will remain essentially an Asian power, although one of increasing importance and one with interests extending well beyond Asia.

There are certain areas and countries outside East and South Asia where Beijing feels a particular interest, has a special policy, and may exercise some influence at least indirectly.

One of these is Iran. There is no serious doubt that this strategically critical country lies under a long-term threat from a combination of its own Tudeh Party and the ability of the Soviet Union to invade across the common border or through Afghanistan, if Moscow should ever decide to run the risk of general war that would inevitably ensue. Beijng's policy and behavior toward Iran, while not systematically explicated, can only be understood on the assumption that it finds the consideration just mentioned so overwhelmingly important as to throw all others into the shade. Thus, it is not especially concerned over matters that loom large in the eyes of other countries, such as the continuing availability of Iranian oil (China of course is an exporter, not an importer, of oil to date), and the antics of the Ayatollah Khomeini. Beijing opposes acts that might strengthen the Tudeh, weaken the Ayatollah, or (less likely) drive him closer to Moscow. Accordingly, it considered that the United States made entirely too much of the hostage crisis of 1979–81. There is no reasonable doubt that, its repeated denials notwithstanding, Beijing has been selling, and is committed to continue selling, large quantities of conventional arms, including Silkworm antiship missiles, to Iran, partly for the sake of foreign exchange but probably even more in consideration of the factors already mentioned.

China's support for Iran has become fairly widely known and is presumably having a negative effect on Beijing's image in the Arab countries. In turn, it is possible that Beijing has reduced its estimate, once rather high, of the importance of the Arab states to its interests, and that this is why it permitted a meeting between a Chinese and an Israeli representative at the United Nations in March 1987.[11]

Beijing's standing in Sub-Saharan Africa has been harmed by at least two things: revelations, or at least plausible assertions, that it not only trades with South Africa but has sold it nuclear materials of some kind, and demonstrations by African students in China in protest against alleged discrimination. The favorable impression that Beijing made in the 1970s by building the Tan-Zam (Tanzania-Zambia) Railway has largely evaporated.

As for Latin America, Beijing maintains normal diplomatic and commercial relations with the major states. It seems to have no active desire, and it certainly has no adequate capability, to compete with the Soviets and the Cubans in the field of "revolutionary" activity. There is no evidence that Beijing was involved in Grenada during its leftist phase or is supporting the Sandinistas. Indeed, it appears to have shipped some arms to the Nicaraguan Contras for a short time before 1985—evidently another testimonial to the practical genius of Oliver North.[12]

The recent increase of China's interest in détente between the superpowers and the decline of its efforts actively to manipulate the balance between them in "united front" or "triangular" fashion has been paralleled by a lessened Chinese involvement in Europe—Eastern and Western—where Beijing has been very active at times in the past, usually in an anti-American or anti-Soviet mode depending on its overall preoccupations of the moment. Accordingly, there is not much to report on this score. Beijing appears to believe that there is a basic balance of power in the European theater of confrontation, that the superpowers are working toward some form of arms reduction arrangement affecting Europe, and that their efforts should not be complicated by outsiders like China because such a trend is in the overall Chinese interest. In Eastern Europe, Beijing finds regimes that are ideologically and politically compatible, economically more or less complementary, and interested like China in maintaining a cooperative relationship with each other and with the Soviet Union without being dominated by Moscow in the process. Considerations such as these presumably underlay Premier Zhao Ziyang's trip to Poland, East Germany, Czechoslovakia, Hungary, and Bulgaria in June 1987.

One of the most constructive and potentially most important features of China's external relations under Deng Xiaoping has been the increasingly close and fruitful interaction with the major international economic agencies, the World Bank and the International Monetary Fund in particular. China has behaved responsibly in this context, by comparison with most other Third World countries, and in return has received a growing infusion of aid and useful advice from those agencies, as well as from other external sources.[13]

Conclusion

Like its domestic politics, China's foreign policy has changed significantly, although by no means totally, under Deng Xiaoping's leadership. The ideological drive and the eagerness for confrontation ("struggle"), verbal if not always actual, that were so conspicuous under Mao Zedong have declined. Modernization has clearly become the top priority, as it never really was under Mao. The late chairman's perennial glorification of actual or alleged "great upheavals" at home and abroad has given way to a preference for domestic and international stability as the condition most conducive both to security and to modernization. This attitude, which Gorbachev appears to share, has been a major force in the recent improvement in Sino-Soviet relations, cautious though it is. In Asia, China is not actively seeking confrontation with any state except Vietnam, and even in that case there has been a slight mellowing, mainly as a result of Beijing's interest in ameliorating its relationship with Moscow. The especially close ties with the Khmer Rouge and Pakistan, established under Mao, continue under Deng, as does the edginess toward India. Chinese political activism in the Third World beyond Asian and in Europe, often conspicuous under Mao, has declined under Deng in keeping with the primacy of modernization and the virtual lapse of "world revolution" as an operational goal of Beijing's foreign policy.

Notes

1. Mao told Edgar Snow during their last interview (December 18, 1970) that Zhou Enlai was running the country; Snow chose to omit that statement from his published accounts of the interview, probably at Zhou's request.
2. After Zhou's death his widow, Deng Yingchao, stated categorically to a Western correspondent known to the writer that her late husband had intended Deng to be his successor. This plan also seems to be a matter of fairly common knowledge among politically informed Chinese.
3. Deng Xiaoping, speech at the United Nations General Assembly, April 10, 1974; text released by Xinhua, same date (in Harold C. Hinton, ed., *The People's Republic of China, 1949–1979: A Documentary Survey*, vol. 5 (Wilmington, DE: Scholarly Resources, 1980), pp. 2430–34.
4. Communique of the Third Plenary Session of the Eleventh Central Committee of the Communist Party of China, December 22, 1978; text released by Xinhua, December 23, 1978 (in Hinton, ibid., pp. 2722–27).
5. Deng Xiaoping, interview in *Time*, February 5, 1979, p. 34.
6. Statement by Chairman Peng Zhen of the Standing Committee of the National People's Congress, September 7, 1985; text released by Xinhua, same date.
7. The text of the Joint Declaration, as Beijing styles it (because an agreement on a piece of Chinese territory made with another country is considered unthinkable), was released by Xinhua on September 26, 1984; the British side usually refers to it as an agreement (cf. *A Draft Agreement . . . on the Future of Hong Kong*, Comnd. 9352 (London: Her Majesty's Stationery Office, 1984).
8. Text of Sino-Portuguese "Joint Declaration" on Macao, released by Xinhua, March 26, 1987 (FBIS, March 26, 1987).

9. Pamela C. Harriman, "In China, Kremlin Watching," *The New York Times*, August 19, 1987.

10. Deng Xiaoping, speech at National Conference of the Communist Party of China, September 23, 1985; text released by Xinhua, same date (FBIS, September 23, 1985).

11. *The New York Times*, March 29, 1987.

12. *The New York Times*, May 2, 1987.

13. Cf. an important unpublished study by Harold K. Jacobson and Michel Oksenberg, *China and the Keystone International Economic Organizations*.

Comments by Thomas W. Robinson

Harold Hinton's paper is a sophisticated analysis. It covers almost all the water-front of Chinese foreign policy, and that is not easy to do in a short time. The only thing that is possibly needed is a somewhat broader framework for summing up and generalizing, on the basis of the statements, the analysis he has made. Let me offer a few thoughts.

Such a framework is essentially reduced to three words: development, balance, and participation. That is what I think Chinese foreign policy is today. It is development in the sense that what is going on at home is paramount: economic modernization. China is trying to subordinate what goes on abroad, or its involvement with what goes on abroad, to the need to modernize as rapidly as it can at home. We are all aware of that. What that means, of course, is that China wants somehow to arrange or fix the external landscape to have two things happen. First, China wants the external environment to be nonthreatening, which means nonthreatening militarily, culturally, and economically. It is not easy to have an external landscape that is nonthreatening in all three of those arenas, but that is what China is trying to do. Second, China wants the external world to be supportive of the modernization program at home. The problem here is that China has to approach the external world largely on the international system's terms, not on China's. And that is frustrating because although China has already met that problem many times in the last 150 or so years, still it is something China has difficulty with, as would any country with such ambitions and such a past. Indeed, parts of the two campaigns that we have seen since 1982 were reactions against this aspect of getting out into the external world on its own terms.

The second word is balance, and here I mean in the strategic triangle. Even last night a number of speakers were saying that China's policy still must center on its relations with the Americans and the Russians, although I think we are going to see more about the Japanese in the future. The trouble with the strategic triangle these days is that it is in flux. It is changing simultaneously on all three sides for the first time in a long time. Mostly those changes are on the Sino-Soviet and the Soviet-American legs, if not the Sino-American leg of the triangle. It is unusual for the Soviet-American leg to be changing as it is; usually that is, as it were, the base of the triangle, the fixed part, and what is left to vary are the other two. We see Soviet-American relations changing, largely, of course, because of the changes that have come since 1984 or 1985 in the Soviet Union. Regarding Sino-Soviet relations, I think the two countries are on the edge, in the next year or two, of a major change for the better. It has already been occurring bit by bit over the last several years, but I think there will indeed be an improvement in Sino-Soviet relations, militarily, and on economic terms. I think political changes will follow from that. Although I myself have not worried about party-to-party relations or the lack of them, probably that is not an important aspect to consider these days. The Soviet-American leg is a positive thing because of Gorbachev, and here I think we really ought to pay attention to what the Russians are doing and saying. I have recently been reading his speeches, both domestic and international, and they are indeed very different from what has been seen since before Lenin in the Soviet Union. Anyone who talks about interdependence, the integral world, the necessity to integrate the Soviet economy into a holistic international system in which national interests are legitimate on the part of all parties, that kind of attitude must be supported. I also believe that there will be a much more positive Soviet foreign policy in the future in terms of actions, as well as these nice declarations. The reason for this, of course, is that the Soviet Union, indeed like the United States, needs a decade's respite to solve the major problems it has at home. In terms of Soviet-American relations, largely for internal reasons to both countries, we are going to see a concentration on internal rather than external matters. This gives the strategic triangle itself a respite, and gives the Chinese, therefore, a chance to concentrate on their own internal developmental program. So the strategic triangle is largely in balance, and I think it is probably going to stay that way for at least some time.

Third, participation. The Chinese would like to participate in the international system, both in Asia and the Third World, and in the international economy. The two questions that are germane here are these: On whose terms will that participation occur? And how will it take place? For the Chinese this must be mostly on the terms of the three systems themselves, Asia, the Third World, and the international economy. That is a problem for China. How will they participate? Being a state with a number of instruments of policy, they have to use the available instruments at their disposal. The question is how are they going to do that. The problem for China is that by participating too fast and too far with the available instruments they have, they are getting themselves in trouble. The Persian Gulf problem, the Silkworms, and so forth, are indicative of this. The Chinese, indeed, like the Russians, lack the whole panoply of instruments of power in some balance and therefore have to depend on what they are best at. The trouble is that they have discovered around 1981–82 that they can sell military equipment and presumably gain influence in that manner and also earn money. They have been tempted and have done a lot of that. I think they have tried to divorce that activity from its foreign policy consequences. They presume they can go into the international arms economy and do these things and gain both influence and hard currency without having to worry about the consequences, and now we see that there are consequences. The Chinese, of course, have been caught red-handed in the Persian Gulf. We have the evidence and that is already affecting Sino-American relations. In other words, it affects the strategic triangle. There is a problem for China in that regard.

In fact, there are three problems for China in the coming several years. One is the problem of temptation, that is, the problem of becoming too participatory, too active too soon in these portions of the international system. That is a Chinese propensity, or at least a propensity under the Chinese Communist Party, indeed, since 1949. They have held themselves back under the present economic internal orientation, but they could well change that in years to come.

China's second problem is their lack of control over events. Events tend to take place, for example, in the international economy, in manners that they cannot greatly control or influence. Consider Taiwan, for example; what is going on in Taiwan is not within their control and they do not know what to do about it.

The third problem for China is emotion, something that usually does not come up when one talks about China. The Chinese are the product of their past, their history, and their culture; when one puts that together with China's temptations and lack of control, one gets an emotional aspect to their foreign policy that I think is probably going to be more important in years to come than it has been in the past.

To conclude, if China can combine the three basic elements of development, balance, and participation, then perhaps a degree of harmony may be achieved in China's foreign policy, certainly not overpushiness, for about four or five years in the future, perhaps to the early 1990s. The major question will be: Will the Chinese temptation to participate, that is, to project their power abroad too far too soon, contradict and ultimately corrupt the gains that have been provided by the combination of development and balance?

Comments by Lea E. Williams

I tend to look at Chinese foreign policy from a rather narrow perspective, usually Southeast Asian. One thing that struck me in this impressive paper was that such a presentation a few years ago would have heavily emphasized the *huaqiao* and what the Chinese were going to do about them. This is almost ignored, which suggests what is indeed the case, that China does not want to think about the *huaqiao* and does not want to be involved with them. This is a big change. For example, they are certainly not doing anything about the destructive pressure on the Chinese in Malaysia. The Chinese government, as far as I know, has done nothing about that. Perhaps there is really nothing they can do. But in Vietnam, for example, it became an important issue for the People's Republic of China. They certainly talked a lot about the *huaqiao* in Vietnam, but they are not saying a thing about those in Malaysia. This basically expresses the foundation of the Chinese foreign policy, that is, that in foreign policy, as in everything else, where possible, China tries very hard to be pragmatic. Will it work? If so, try it; if it will not work, keep quiet.

There is little mention in the paper of aid programs, which again is something that would have figured prominently not too many years ago, that is, attempting to assess China's foreign policy goals in terms of where China was investing its money. This is an area that is instructive. Nothing would have figured more prominently in such a paper a decade or two ago than Chinese support through interparty relations for wars of national liberation. It is not so long ago when a lot of attention would have been paid to the number of hours broadcast in what languages to parts of the world to stir up wars of national liberation or to express support for them. Now, there is no mention of that. I think that is very revealing.

What it comes down to basically is a change, summed up by two statements: first, by the last sentence of Professor Hinton's paper in which he says, "Chinese political activism in the Third World beyond Asia and Europe, often conspicuous under Mao, has declined under Deng in keeping with the primacy of modernization and the virtual lapse of 'world revolution' as an operational goal of Beijing's foreign policy." Put another way, as it was by Jonathan Pollack, to the extent that the PRC coyly depicts itself as somewhat peripheral to the global strategic balance, Chinese officials hope to achieve a partial respite from the international pressures that have complicated their plans for economic and technological development. In other words, China, in so far as any great power can do so, has put foreign issues on the back burner in order to deal with more pressing matters of internal development.

There was talk as to whether or not the PRC would send a representative to today's seventieth anniversary celebration of the October Revolution in Moscow, and then at the last minute they did send someone, as far as I know. It seems there is a message in this. In other words, what is happening in Moscow at this moment? This is another sign of what was spoken of earlier, that is, the shift in the third dimension in the three-way balance of power in the world, the Chinese move toward the Soviet Union.

In this paper, Professor Hinton mentions Secretary of State Shultz's speech in February of this year, in which it was suggested that the PRC and Taiwan might have a more useful exchange. Does his statement simply express American acceptance of what is becoming a reality? Professor Hinton talks about the Soviets' apparent reluctance to persuade the Vietnamese to withdraw from Cambodia. I wonder if that reluctance might not be borne of a shrewd assessment of reality, that is, the Russians know that they could tell the Vietnamese to get out of Cambodia, but that the Vietnamese for a variety of reasons, both historical and political, are not likely to do so, and therefore the Russians would just appear foolish. Perhaps the Russians have even told the Vietnamese to get out, and the Vietnamese have not responded.

Is it reasonable to believe that the PRC, in regard to Korea, is pleased to see a continuation of the American presence in the divided peninsula? As in Vietnam, the American presence may be something of a trip wire in case the Russians begin to do something frightening. Is it conceivable that North Korea would ever tilt totally toward China when the Soviet Union is so powerful and so able to help economically, perhaps more than Vietnam would ever tilt decisively toward China?

Does Professor Hinton imply that in its support at the moment for the Khmer Rouge in Cambodia, the PRC is motivated by a sense of ideological compatibility with the fraternal party? I cannot imagine that Professor Hinton believes that. It seems to me that the PRC's support for the Khmer Rouge is based precisely on the kind of cynical opportunism that our support of Vietnam was based on. I believe it has nothing to do with ideology.

12

DENG XIAOPING'S QUEST FOR "MODERNIZATION WITH CHINESE CHARACTERISTICS" AND THE FUTURE OF MARXISM-LENINISM

Stuart R. Schram

MANY things divide the China of Deng Xiaoping today from that of Mao Zedong two decades ago, but one thing has not changed a jot: the goal of learning from the West, and from Marxism in particular, in order to find a way of modernizing while remaining themselves. Despite this underlying continuity between Mao's utopian vision of collective salvation and Deng's experiments with market socialism, there are, manifestly, profound differences between the line in China under Mao, and that under Deng Xiaoping. How is one to characterize such a complex phenomenon as a line or model for socialist development? In an overview published in 1984, I noted four clusters of issues that seemed to merit attention in considering the relation between theory and policy in China:

1. patterns of rule, or the dialectics of leadership;
2. the ideological implications of economic policy;
3. the relation between thought or consciousness and the political realm, and in particular the methods used for inculcating "correct" ideology among the population; and
4. the relation between revolution and tradition, or more generally between Chinese and Western patterns of thought.[1]

As a checklist, or aide-mémoire, this classification proves useful, yet it does not evoke clearly enough the interrelationship between the various factors under consideration, nor does it indicate how they combine to determine the direction of change.

One logical anomaly in the above schema lies in the fact that the relation between revolution and tradition, and between Chinese and Western patterns of thought, cuts across each of the other three categories, and is thus not strictly parallel with them. I listed it last rather than first in 1984 because my aim was to examine recent trends in the explicitly Marxist ideology of the Chinese Communist Party (CCP), and I did not wish to overstress the importance of the cultural dimension. But while one should look at Marxist arguments in their own terms, the continuing influence of tradition is a palpable and important fact, which must be given due weight in any analysis.

To what extent can a framework for assessing the changes in ideology be derived from the Marxist standpoint adopted by the Chinese themselves? Broadly speaking, Marxism juxtaposes two basic approaches. On the one hand, history is read as the history of class struggles; on the other, it is seen as the record of humanity's increasing mastery over nature.[2] These two strands are ingeniously interwoven in Marx's own writings, and in those of his successors, but they are nonetheless quite distinct. A Marxist analysis of the relation between theory and policy must take account of both.

The perspective on all these matters has, of course, changed radically from Mao's day to Deng's. In the period of the Great Leap and the Cultural Revolution, economic policies were regarded as justified because they promoted ideologically correct ends. Indeed, it was even thought that policies would work because they were ideologically correct. In recent years, attitudes, such as the pursuit, within certain limits, of rational self-interest, have been encouraged because they would contribute to economic growth, and it sometimes appeared that anything that contributed to such growth was regarded ipso facto as socialist. The massacre of June 4, 1989, signaled, if not the end of any such outlook, the imposition for the time being of very strict limits on its application in practice. It can be argued that this change marked, not so much a return to Marxist orthodoxy, as a return to dogmatic attitudes of an earlier period in the history of Chinese communism, of which the roots are not necessarily or entirely Marxist.

In the end, while addressing some of the issues raised both by a Marxist analysis, and in my own list of 1984, I shall use a slightly different framework. Three variables were manifestly of primary importance in China during the decade after 1978: political reform, economic development, and ideological or cultural norms. That is not simply my judgment; the same factors loom large in the theoretical analyses of the Chinese themselves.

Each of these factors interacts with each of the others, but the resulting dualities are so closely intertwined that it would be confusing and repetitious to consider them one after the other. In this paper, I shall therefore take political change as the primary axis or theme. This will not exclude discussion, as appropriate, of economic reform, and its implications for the nature and theoretical basis of Chinese-style socialism, nor do I intend to neglect the cultural dimension of change.

Before embarking on an analysis of the issues as they have presented themselves in recent years, it is perhaps worth recalling here that Mao was not, in principle, hostile to economic development, nor did he object to the concept of "modernization." On the contrary, he freely used the term from the 1940s to the 1960s. During his last two decades, however, while he continued to stress the importance of economic progress, his increasing anxiety about the corrupting effects of prosperity and inequality led him to adopt a series of radical policies that, in the end, proved self-defeating. The Great Leap Forward resulted in economic disaster and starvation, and the so-called Great Proletarian Cultural Revolution tore the fabric of society apart. Thus, when he died in September 1976, Mao left China in a parlous state. His successors had to struggle with the problem of rescuing the country from this situation. Hua Guofeng's solution was to follow a "two-track policy." He pursued a grandiose program of modernization and import of foreign technology, before China was either ready to use it or able to pay for it. But he did this behind a screen of Maoist and Cultural Revolutionary slogans, thus trying to please both the "Left" and the "Right" of the party.

Even before Deng Xiaoping returned to a position of influence in 1977, he began undermining, and encouraging others to undermine, the ideological foundations of Hua's rule, symbolized by the slogan of the "two whatevers." A crucial role in this struggle against the "whateverists" was played by three great debates during the year 1978. The first, on the topic "Practice is the Sole Criterion for Testing Truth," meant, in effect, that results were more important than dogma. The second, about the appropriateness of the criterion of remuneration according to work in a socialist society, implied the negation of the egalitarianism that had prevailed since 1958, with Mao's personal support. The third, about the need to observe objective economic laws, contradicted Mao's view that the masses, when mobilized under the guidance of his thought, could do anything, overcoming all material difficulties.

By the end of 1978 the situation had progressed to such a point that at the Third Plenum in December Deng Xiaoping was able to obtain approval not only for the "responsibility system" in economic work, which has been the cornerstone of China's reform policies ever since, but for the abolition of "forbidden zones," and the "liberation of thought" from the shackles of the leftist dogmas of Mao's later years. Of all the ideological differences between Deng and Mao, most fundamental, perhaps, has been the contrast between "seeking the truth from facts" and the exaggeration of the people's capacity to change the world arbitrarily, which characterized Mao's last two decades. It is, of course, singularly ironic that this should be so, because the slogan *shishi qiushi* was not only put forward by Mao in Yan'an days, but corresponded to his practice at the time. Mao won victory in 1949 in large part because he had grasped that, given the real balance of forces in the 1920s and 1930s, the Chinese revolution could only be a protracted one, and rapid triumph through an urban uprising of the proletariat was impossible. Then, in an apparent paradox, after Mao had opposed his patience and realism to the impatience and doctrinaire illusions of the "orthodox" faction in the party, the roles were reversed. Now it was Mao who, unwilling to wait for the development of the productive forces, sought to leap into socialism, or even to communism, overnight.

All of the errors that Mao Zedong then proceeded to commit, in the Great Leap Forward and after, have been seen in China for the past ten years as a betrayal of his own principles of learning from practice and keeping a firm grip on reality. Whether or not Mao Zedong, as some have argued, regarded socialism as a mere way-station on the road to communism, he certainly believed that China, a decade or so after 1949, was already well launched on the process of creating a socialist society. Since 1978, in contrast, the view has come to be accepted that China still has a long way to go to build socialism, let alone communism. In 1979 the term "undeveloped socialism" (*bufada de shehuizhuyi*) was introduced to characterize China's current stage of development.[3] This concept was widely used for a year or two, and then rejected by the leadership because it appeared to cast too much doubt on whether socialism had taken root in China at all. Since June 1981 it has been said rather that China is in the "initial stage" (*chuji jieduan*) of socialism.[4] The meaning, however, is manifestly very similar. This point obviously has implications for the nature of Chinese society, and thereby for the shape of China's political system, and for the pattern of China's development as a whole.

The Issues Take Shape, 1978–1984

I do not believe that Chinese politics since 1978 should be seen in terms of tightly organized and unchanging factional alignments. There are, however, sharp differences of opinion within the leadership, and alliances have been formed and reformed on the basis of these differences. Such alliances are superimposed on personal links, or *guanxi*, based on various other criteria such as revolutionary experience or provincial origins. Though ideology may sometimes be thus used and misused, it is genuinely important in Deng Xiaoping's scheme of things. Both from a Leninist and a traditional Chinese perspective, the elaboration of correct doctrine is an essential attribute of political authority, and the internalization of such doctrine by the people is indispensable to the proper functioning of the political system. Deng is assuredly not, as he is sometimes called in the West, a "pragmatist." He is a veteran revolutionary who believes in the dictatorship of the proletariat, the vanguard role of the party, and a certain number of moral values he learned during the Yan'an period. Therefore, when these axioms appear to be under threat, he himself feels obliged (quite apart from what other leaders may think) to call a halt. The bloody events of June 1989 are only the latest in a series of words and actions on his part that have served to underscore the limits on his "pragmatism" or "liberalism," including the enunciation of the "Four Basic Principles" in March 1979, the campaign against "spiritual pollution" in 1983, and the overthrow of Hu Yaobang in the name of opposing "bourgeois liberalization" in 1987.

Under the dual influence of contradictions within the leading elites and within Deng Xiaoping himself, the ideological line has followed, for the past decade, a zig-zag course. The details have been chronicled in many books and articles.[5] In any case, so many different ideas have been put forward during these ten years that it would be impossible to deal with them here. I shall therefore merely point out a few of the key issues in the debate about democracy and political reform, before examining in more detail the trends from 1986 to 1988.

Perhaps the most incisive and cogent statement of the dilemma facing all Chinese rulers since the fall of the empire is that by Tang Tsou who argues that a vital society has been perceived as providing the indispensable ground for creating a strong and effective state, but at the same time as a threat to the state's control.[6] This problem obviously lies at the root of the question we must pose before we even begin to discuss the substance and ideological implications of the reforms: "Why have there been any political reforms at all?" It has, of course, been widely and indeed almost uniformly stated, since the Tiananmen Square massacre, that there has never *been* any political reform in China since 1978, and that Deng Xiaoping was unwilling even to countenance such an idea. This view is demonstrably false and absurd. Deng and the other old men called a brutal halt to reform when it threatened their own power, or their idea of what constituted the raison d'être of socialism, but that is no justification for rewriting the whole history of the 1980s.

Why, then, did Deng Xiaoping and his partisans undertake, even with many hesitations and reversals, to carry out significant changes in the party and state system, even though these involved considerable risks of instability? In essence, I would suggest it was because of what might be called the "Yan Fu argument." By this I mean a line of reflection analogous to that developed by Yan Fu at the turn of the century, according to which only by increasing the spirit of initiative of each and every Chinese citizen would the total energies of the population be maximized, thereby maximizing the capacity of the nation and of the state to survive and develop. There is a clear echo of this idea in Deng Xiaoping's statement, on the eve of the Third Plenum: "One thing a revolutionary party does need to worry about is its inability to hear the voice of the people. *The thing to be feared most is silence*."[7]

Mao Zedong, too, was deeply influenced in his youth by the ideas of Yan Fu, and continued to believe to the end of his days that the active participation of the people was indispensable to the creation of a new China. This concern finds an echo in his formulation of 1957 which Mao liked so much that he frequently quoted from it thereafter:

> Our aim is to create a political situation in which we have both centralism and democracy, both discipline and freedom, both unity of will and personal ease of mind and liveliness, and thus to promote our socialist revolution and socialist construction, make it easier to overcome difficulties, build a modern industry and modern agriculture more rapidly, and make our party and state more secure.[8]

The way in which Mao pursued this goal during the last nineteen years of his life assuredly ruled out the "silence" that Deng Xiaoping regards as so ominous. But was the din of gongs and drums, and of the denunciation of "class enemies," which accompanied the unceasing campaigns of Mao's last two decades, actually more meaningful than silence? Did it constitute a genuine response from below, or imply any real involvement by the people in political affairs? Though their voices were raised, were their feelings not numb, and their minds not closed?

The current view, at least until very recently, has been, of course, that such was indeed the case. To the extent that Deng Xiaoping, and the Chinese Communist Party under his leadership, recognized this fact, Deng may be accounted a better disciple of Yan Fu than Mao. But he has nonetheless followed Yan Fu, and Mao, in seeking to turn the energizing of the citizens above all to the service of the power and the dynamism of the state.

As I have already suggested, the tension between the desire to liberate, and thereby to energize the Chinese people, and the firm determination to maintain ultimate party control over their thinking and make sure they remain on the correct path, does not correspond simply to differences of opinion, or even the clash of factions, within the leadership. It represents a contradiction that lies at the very center of Deng's own thinking. Thus, on the one hand, it is he who has repeatedly used, and given currency to, the term "democratization" (*minzhuhua*). But at the same time he has raised the banner of struggle against "bourgeois liberalization" and "spiritual pollution."

The ambiguity of Deng Xiaoping's attitude is vividly illustrated by his changing stance during the first great upsurge of reform in the winter of 1978–79 when, after giving his blessing to the "Democracy Wall" in December 1978, he himself drew a line three months later by setting up the Four Basic Principles.[9] Commenting on this episode in 1981, Liao Gailong declared that the proclamation of the Four Principles had been necessary not only because some elements among the people had abused the call for the liberation of thought to attack Marxism-Leninism and the socialist system, but because

> those comrades whose thinking is ossified, . . . and who obstinately support the erroneous line of the 'two whatevers' took advantage of the opportunity to attack the correct line of the Third Plenum . . . , saying that the decisions of the Third Plenum had brought about a mad attack by the bourgeois rightists, and even that the party and the state were once again in the same situation as in the summer of 1957.[10]

In other words, it had been necessary to throw the young hotheads of the democracy movement to the wolves, in order to preserve the possibility for carrying out reforms in a systematic way, from above.

The most important document expressing the democratic half of Deng's views on this polarity—liberation/control—is, undoubtedly, his speech of August 18, 1980,

"On the Reform of the System of Party and State Leadership." This text attracted well-deserved attention as soon as it was released in Taiwan in 1981. It was first officially published in the Chinese edition of Deng's *Selected Works* in July 1983, and translated, with great fanfare, in *Beijing Review* later that year.[11]

The continuing seminal role of this speech is underscored by the fact that it has been described as the programmatic document for China's political reform both by Hu Yaobang in 1986 before his fall, and by authoritative spokesmen in the autumn of 1987, in the run-up to the Thirteenth Party Congress. Because this speech is both easily available and extremely well known, I shall not analyze it in detail here. The crucial points, from our perspective, are two in number. First, that Deng actually used, repeatedly, the term "democratization" on this occasion has provided, over the years, an unassailable defense for those intellectuals who, in relatively conservative periods such as 1981 and 1983, continued to use this word rather than the more innocuous expression "high-level democracy." Second, it is noteworthy that Deng blamed the "excessive powers" assumed by Mao Zedong in his later years not only on the old Chinese tradition of "feudal autocracy," but on patterns established by the Comintern.[12]

In his celebrated "Gengshen Reform Report," which was manifestly intended as an elaboration of the ideas Deng Xiaoping had put forward two months earlier, Liao Gailong pushed the responsibility for the authoritarian tradition of the Comintern back beyond Stalin to Lenin himself, and notably to the conceptions expounded in *What Is to Be Done?* Though I know of no similar statement by a top leader, it is noteworthy that when Liao's October 1980 report was published in book form in November 1983, this passage was left substantially unaltered.[13] It is hardly necessary to add that until the dramatic events of 1989 in the Soviet Union and Eastern Europe, no spokesperson for a ruling Communist party had ever thus explicitly criticized Lenin's theory of the party as insufficiently democratic, antithetic to the rule of law, and overly focused on the role of the leaders rather than on that of the masses. It is equally unnecessary to note that any such views have, since June 1989, been utterly repudiated in China. That they have now been condemned does not, however, efface from the historical record the fact that Deng Xiaoping long tolerated and encouraged such ideas.

Liao Gailong also directly contradicted Mao Zedong's dictum of 1957: "Democracy as such sometimes seems to be an end, but it is in fact only a means."[14] Hu Yaobang had already opened the way to such explicit criticism of Mao by declaring that democracy was "not only a means but an end, it is our basic system."[15] Deng Xiaoping has not said precisely that, but his speech of August 18, 1980, does contain criticism of Mao that points in the same direction.

The combination of "feudal" and Stalinist influences, Deng argued, led to a bad system, and when the system is bad, even great figures may be encouraged in evildoing rather than restrained by it:

When Stalin gravely disrupted the socialist legal system, Comrade Mao Zedong said that this kind of thing could not have happened in Western countries such as England, France, and the United States. But although he himself recognized this point, because the problems of the system had not really been solved . . . , there nonetheless came about the ten years of calamity of the Cultural Revolution.

Deng therefore gave it as his goal "to reform and perfect, in a practical way, the party and state systems, and to ensure, on the basis of these systems, the democratization of the political life of the party and the state, the democratization of economic management, and the democratization of the life of society as a whole."[16] The clear implication of this analysis is that despite all the talk in the 1980s about breaking with the Soviet model, Mao Zedong's approach to political leadership remained to the end marked by Leninist authoritarianism.

Quite apart from the prominence that long continued to be given to it in China, Deng Xiaoping's speech of August 1980 remains a remarkable document. But it must be read, as I have already suggested, in parallel, or in counterpoint, with Deng's utterances stressing not liberation, but conformity. And the starting point for considering this strand in his thinking must be the views he has put forward, beginning in 1981, regarding the threat of "bourgeois liberalization."

At a meeting called by the Propaganda Department of the Central Committee in July and August 1981, Deng Xiaoping declared in a talk of July 17 that the "kernel" (*hexin*) of bourgeois liberalization was "opposition to party leadership." Its social and historical background, he said, lay in the ten years of turmoil of the Cultural Revolution, though "corrosion by bourgeois ideology from abroad" was also a factor. The main problem, however, in Deng's view, was not so much the existence of this phenomenon as "laxity and weakness" (*huansan ruanruo*) in dealing with it.[17]

Deng Xiaoping's position in the ideological center of the party is well illustrated by the opinions expressed on this occasion. Hu Yaobang, while acknowledging the weakness of the Secretariat in dealing with erroneous tendencies, such as those reflected in Bai Hua's "Bitter Love," did not even mention the expression "bourgeois liberalization" when he spoke on August 3, 1981.[18] Hu Qiaomu, on the other hand, laid considerable stress on this concept in his long speech of August 8, defining it essentially in the same terms as Deng. When he came to revise this text in April 1982, however, Hu Qiaomu sharpened his attack considerably, declaring, in a newly added section on bourgeois liberalization:

We do not hesitate to wage resolute struggle against anyone who negates, opposes, or undermines China's socialist cause and the leadership of the Chinese Communist Party over it and demands that socialist democracy and the socialist system be replaced by the bourgeois liberal system, *no matter how much he denies that he is doing so.*"[19]

The ideological climate, and Deng Xiaoping's own stance, were nonetheless relatively tolerant and open before and after the Twelfth Party Congress in 1982. Then, suddenly, at the Second Plenum of September–October 1983, Deng Xiaoping and Chen Yun jointly put forward a demand to carry out extensive ideological work aimed at eliminating what was called "spiritual pollution," This "work" (it was not to be called a campaign) was to take place simultaneously with the "rectification of the party" (*zhengdang*), aimed in the first instance against those doctrinaire or careerist elements who had risen to positions of authority during the Cultural Revolution decade. Moreover, Deng Xiaoping, in his speech of October 1983 which laid down the framework for what soon became in reality a campaign against "spiritual pollution," clearly stated, after vigorously condemning the residual influence of the Cultural Revolution, and insisting on the importance of continuing to combat leftism: "We must point out clearly that at present on the ideological front, the problem which we must first of all apply ourselves to resolving is that of rectifying the rightist trend toward weakness and laxity."[20]

Why did Deng Xiaoping initially approve this campaign, and why did he subsequently call a halt to it? Undoubtedly he launched it in part because, as I have already said, he is a veteran revolutionary who genuinely believes in Marxist ideals, and in the "revolutionary spirit" inherited from Yan'an, and does not want them called into question by too much enthusiasm for "bourgeois liberalization," individualism, and other wrong ideas. But it is certainly no accident that this campaign was started simultaneously with the beginning of the "Rectification Campaign" in the party. At a time when he was attacking the Left, Deng did not want to be seen by those worried about this purge as "soft on capitalism."

The reasons for the abandonment of the campaign against "spiritual pollution" in March 1984 are even clearer. The political climate that had developed in this context, and especially the attacks on those who had "become rich first" and the confiscation of their wealth in some cases, was badly disrupting the work on the reform and development of the economy, which Deng Xiaoping regarded as of primary importance. He therefore refused to authorize the open publication of his September 1983 speech on "spiritual pollution," for fear of prolonging and intensifying the campaign, and stopped the whole thing abruptly.[21]

In this context there is great symbolic significance in his visit to Shenzhen in February 1984. On his return to Beijing, he talked with senior comrades, and expressed his enthusiasm for the "open policy" in general, and the special economic zones in particular. They were, he said, a window for importing both foreign technology and foreign techniques of management. He endorsed the slogan current in Shenzhen, "Time is money." (I do not know whether or not he was aware that this slogan had been coined originally by the American capitalist J. P. Morgan.) It was right, he said, for some areas such as this to become rich first. "Egalitarianism will not work."[22]

There followed, in March and April 1984, a shift in economic policy not only toward the reaffirmation of the responsibility system in the countryside, but toward its much more sweeping extension to industry and the cities. This went hand in hand with the redefinition of the main enemy as, once again, "leftism" rather than rightism or bourgeois influences. Hu Yaobang played a very important role in this respect; an editorial of *People's Daily* on April 1, 1984, which was in fact a summary of a talk by Hu, declared that, in the aftermath of the Great Leap Forward and the Cultural Revolution, it would take years of work to root out the leftist poison. The entrepreneur, whether he be the enterprising peasant who gets rich first in the countryside, or the manager of a collectively owned factory in the city, was hailed as the hero of the present age.[23]

Toward a Socialist Commodity Economy, 1984–1986

The seal was set on this new upsurge of reform at the Third Plenum of the Twelfth Central Committee in October 1984. Like the Third Plenum of the Eleventh Central Committee in December 1978, which had started the whole process, this meeting was important because of the political line it adopted rather than because of any precise and detailed policy decisions. The crucial point was that the Chinese economy was explicitly defined as a "planned socialist commodity economy."

Henceforth, theoretical discussions of commodities and of the role of the market would be regarded as completely legitimate, contrary to the situation in 1980–81, when Chen Yun's ideas of the market as a "bird" in the "cage" of the planned economy predominated. The Decision adopted by the Central Committee on this occasion called for devolving "decision-making power" to enterprises. It also spoke out once again against egalitarianism, and stressed that the open-door policy would be maintained.[24]

The end of the year 1984 was marked by a high tide of free discussion and of criticism of dogmatism in all its forms. The famous article of December 7, 1984,[25] which was widely interpreted outside China as a repudiation of Marxism, did not in fact say any such thing. It simply made the point, which had been made many times since the hundredth anniversary of Marx's death in 1983, that he had lived a long time ago, and that all of today's problems could not be solved merely by referring to his works on the shelf. The statement was, however, given added authority by the fact that this article, too, was a summary of Hu Yaobang's views.

At the same time, in late 1984, prices were rising steeply, the economy was "overheating," credit was being expanded recklessly, and above all the so-called evil winds or unrighteous winds (*buzheng zhi feng*) of corruption and abuse of privilege were beginning to blow. The main problems raised were polarization, the threat of the emergence of a new bourgeoisie, speculation and black market transactions, and, above all, the misuse of official positions to engage in business through intermediaries.

Deng Xiaoping sharply denounced these phenomena in February and March 1985, but at the same time he stressed that measures against such "unrighteous winds" were indispensable precisely because, if these negative side-effects were not eliminated, the reforms themselves, which he characterized in March 1985 as a "second revolution," equal in importance to 1949,[26] would be compromised. The September 1985 Party Conference saw what can only be characterized as a standoff between the two powerful old men, Deng Xiaoping and Chen Yun. Their speeches were not wholly contradictory, but the emphasis was quite different. Deng said, in effect, that while there were negative effects of the new policies, such as economic crimes, and so forth, and these must be combatted, the reforms themselves, and the opening to the outside world, must be pushed boldly forward. Chen Yun stressed rather the negative consequences of reform, and the need to strengthen ideological work, and to reinforce the prestige of the organs concerned with propaganda.[27]

During the half year following the Conference of autumn 1985, problems continued to manifest themselves. Inflation in prices for consumer goods, especially in the cities, was perhaps the most acute. Yet the impulse toward reform, and the key ideas accompanying the reform, survived. There was, however, little said about the theories or broad principles of the new society being shaped by the reforms.

In the spring of 1986, this situation suddenly changed, and the Chinese began speaking of the need for a comprehensive theoretical framework to define the nature of the new system that was emerging. It is important to underscore the difference in this respect between 1984 and 1986. On the former occasion, when the campaign against "spiritual pollution" was suddenly halted, the opponents of this witch-hunt did not launch a theoretical counteroffensive. Instead, they shifted the ground of controversy from theory to practice, and argued forcefully that the new policies based on material incentives, the decentralization of authority, and the negation of the egalitarianism of the Cultural Revolution would work, and would rapidly bring prosperity not only to a few successful entrepreneurs, but to the whole country.

In 1986, however, people high up in the Chinese Communist Party, beginning with Hu Yaobang, appear to have decided that the continuing uncertainty about the shape of the emerging new order was more dangerous than attacking the problem squarely, even if a frank statement of the plans for creating a "socialist commodity economy" might be misinterpreted as a move in the direction of capitalism. Some of the first new formulations were publicly advanced during the period when the Seventh Five-Year Plan was under consideration by the National People's Congress. From a political perspective, the first, and perhaps the most significant point in the Plan itself is the clear statement, in the opening section, that of the three tasks—reform, economic growth and technological progress, and improving living standards—reform is the most important.

In some respects, the content and even the language of the Plan followed fairly closely the Decision of October 1984, but in other respects the Plan marked a step ahead. For example, the call for turning enterprises into "relatively independent socialist commodity producers and dealers, with full authority over their own management, and full responsibility for their own profits and losses" echoes almost exactly the 1984 Decision, but the emphasis was placed even more strongly on extending the scope of the responsibility system, and above all on reducing the role of mandatory planning.[28]

Although these points relate explicity to reform of the economic system, it is evident that they have political implications as well. This is underscored by the term used, both in the Plan itself and in Zhao Ziyang's report, to characterize the next five years as "the period of replacing the old system by the new" (*xinjiu tizhi zhuanhuan shiqi*). Manifestly, the statement that the whole of the "old system" was in the process of being replaced by a new order, and the calls for the elaboration of a comprehensive theory defining that new order, were extremely worrying to those who felt that reform was going too far too fast, and threatened to get out of hand.

Early in 1986, influential figures in the leadership still devoted to Leninist doctrine as it has long been understood, such as Hu Qiaomu and Deng Liqun, were seeking to make of such ideological issues the main topic of discussion at the forthcoming Sixth Plenum of the Central Committee. By April 1986, however, the agenda for this plenum had been changed to deal not with "thought" or "ideology," code words for fidelity to Leninist dogmas, but with the vaguer and less controversial topic of building "socialist spiritual civilization."

Plainly, Hu Yaobang had this controversy in mind when, in April 1986, he addressed the problem of "contradictions within the party," thereby revealing the existence of divergences at the highest levels of the party:

> The contradictions within the party are for the most part the result of differing views about our work and about our understanding of the situation. Under normal circumstances, such contradictions are not antagonistic, and can very well be resolved. We should use the methods of exchange of ideas, democratic consultation, private talks, and mutual understanding and tolerance. If we use the correct methods, we need not fear trouble, and we need not fear democracy (*buyao pa mafan, buyao pa minzhu*).[29]

In raising the issue of contradictions within the party in this way, Hu Yaobang appeared to have two aims: to reassure and to warn. On the one hand, he signaled that there was to be no witch-hunt, and that the partisans of reform wished to unite all members of the leadership around an agreed-on policy line. But at the same time it was made crystal clear that in the last analysis reform *would* be pushed forward vigorously, and that those who had doubts about it would have to fall into line. This speech, and its publication, must have been seen by the leftists as a deliberate throwing down of the gauntlet.

On April 22, 1986, Zhu Houze, the new Head of the Propaganda Department who had replaced Deng Liqun the previous August, called on social scientists, while holding to the Four Basic Principles, to think for themselves, put forward different views and argue them in a relaxed atmosphere, and thereby to carry out theoretical "breakthroughs" (*tupo*), and put into practice the policy of "a hundred flowers and a hundred schools."[30]

At about the same time Su Shaozhi wrote that Marx himself had made extensive use of bourgeois economic works; the critical assimilation of ideas from all quarters was therefore an integral part of Marxism. The Chinese reforms were, according to Su, the first serious (even though as yet inadequate) attempt since Stalin put an end to Lenin's New Economic Policy to devise a method for building socialism different from the Stalinist model, which had been applied in China for more than thirty years, i.e., from 1953 until the Decision of October 1984. Reform itself, said Su, was a breakthrough, and must therefore involve constant theoretical exploration and ruptures with past dogmas.[31]

Debate on these issues was given further impetus in the spring of 1986 by the meetings and discussions that marked the thirtieth anniversary of the proclamation by Mao Zedong, in May 1956, of the slogan "Let a hundred flowers bloom, let a hundred schools of thought contend!" It was recalled that when he first advanced this slogan, Mao had remarked that at present the "hundred schools" amounted in fact to only two schools—the bourgeois school and the proletarian school.[32] In other words, the idea of genuine pluralism within the socialist camp was totally foreign to Mao. Now, Su Shaozhi pointed out that the abolition of the "hundred schools" slogan in Chinese history was the result of the action of the Qin autocracy, with its goal of "uniformity of thought" (*sixiang yizhi*). Thus, monolithic ideological unity, long held up as a socialist ideal, was stigmatized by implication as a "feudal relic."[33]

In the summer of 1986, the exploration of new ideas about the shape of China's political system became both more concrete and more official. In May, a "Committee on the Reform of the State Structure" was formed at a very high level,[34] and in early July a theoretical symposium on political structure was held at the Central Party School, at the instigation of Deng Xiaoping.[35]

It seemed then, to many (including myself), that victory was within the grasp of the partisans of political and ideological, as well as economic reform. The events from September 1986 on, and especially from the turn of the year 1986–87, were to show that the conservative leftists retained a great deal of strength, and above all that Deng Xiaoping himself remained, to be sure, a partisan of reform, but at the same time a centrist, committed to order and discipline as well as to "democratization" and the "liberation of thought."

Some described the changes of January 1987 as a coup d'état, concluding that Deng had lost such a large measure of his power and influence that he was unable to prevent the reversal of his policies by the partisans of doctrinal orthodoxy. In fact, it should have been evident even at the time that Deng's decision to support the removal of Hu Yaobang did not mark a complete reversal of his stance if viewed in the context of a balanced picture of his previous line. Far more dramatic evidence to this effect was to come two years later.

One Step Forward, Two Steps Back, 1986–1988

The two years from the end of 1986 to the end of 1988 saw not only dramatic shifts in the balance of power within the leadership, but an intense, even if muted, debate about ideological issues. This debate revolved explicitly around the limits to political reform, the threat posed by so-called bourgeois liberalization, and the link between reform, liberalization, and changes in the economic system. In the background could be perceived, however, shadows of all the major controversies of the previous eight years.

While no one, in the spring and summer of 1986, denied that it was necessary to develop Marxism in accordance with the new conditions prevailing in China in the era of reform, there were those who stressed the need to study and preserve the doctrine of the party rather than the importance of innovation.[36] It is well established that at Beidaihe, in the weeks before the Sixth Plenum of September 1986, a number of leading figures of this cast of mind exchanged ideas, agreed on a common strategy, and sought to ensure that the resolution that was to be adopted on that occasion corresponded to their viewpoint. A number of drafts were produced by various authors, and while the final text represented, on balance, a victory for the partisans of boldness and openness, it was a relatively narrow victory, obtained only after sharp discussion.

Not surprisingly, the Resolution of the Sixth Plenum, as finally adopted on 29 September 1986, stressed the need to take Marxism as a guide in building socialist spiritual civilization (or, as the new official translation of *jingshen wenming* has it, "a socialist society with an advanced culture and ideology"). But at the same time the resolution states that the party has already "abandoned a series of ossified concepts" in its interpretation of Marxism. While insisting that party leadership must be upheld, it also asserts that there can be "no socialist modernization without democracy," and that the "policy-making process" must be "democratized" and given a more scientific basis, in the context of the "two hundreds" policy. Finally, it is emphasized that "no country can progress if it refuses to accept elements of advanced science and culture from abroad."[37]

To balance this, there was a reference in the resolution to the need to carry out political reform "step by step and with proper guidance." Above all, there was the clear statement that "to engage in bourgeois liberalization, which means negating the socialist system and advocating the capitalist system, is in fundamental opposition to the people's interests and to the historical tide, and is firmly opposed by the broad population (*guangda renmin*)."[38]

At the time it was not generally known outside China that this particular passage had been included in the resolution following a direct personal intervention by Deng Xiaoping. Deng's remarks on this occasion were, in many respects, even harsher and more sweeping in their condemnation of "bourgeois liberaliza-tion" than his 1981 speech, quoted previously. This is above all the case of the flat statement that *all* liberalization is, of necessity, *bourgeois* liberalization.[39] Deng himself subsequently said that he had not originally intended to intervene in this debate, but had in the end felt obliged to do so.[40] Manifestly he did not like the tone of the discussions at the plenum. According to some accounts, his blast was provoked by a proposal, put forward by Lu Dingyi, that all reference to the struggle against bourgeois liberalization should be deleted from the resolu-tion.[41] There is no direct confirmation of this point available to me from an official source, but such an action on Lu's part would not be incompatible with what is known of his views and those of people associated with him. In any case, the episode underscores the reality of the "contradictions within the party" dis-cerned by Hu Yaobang, and confirms that regarding the contradiction between bolder and more moderate reformers, Deng Xiaoping leaned on this occasion toward the moderate side.

It is hard to believe that Deng's words at the Sixth Plenum were, as he complained on December 30, 1986, never disseminated within the party, or that they "had no great effect," but it was the case that they did not immediately put an end to ideological statements of which Deng disapproved.[42] In particular, Deng may have been alluding here to the work already under way in November and December 1986, under the guidance of Hu Yaobang, on the drafting of preliminary documents that would serve as the basis for the resolutions in vari-ous domains at the Thirteenth Party Congress. It appears that some relatively bold-minded reformers were playing a major role in preparing the draft on ideo-logical issues, and the desire to control the direction of this important activity must have provided a further spur to the efforts of those who had long felt that Hu Yaobang was not keeping a firm enough hand on the situation, and had allowed bourgeois and subversive tendencies to flourish.

Some of those involved in the events of late 1986 actually did praise Western ideas of democracy, including not only students, but Fang Lizhi, as reported by his admirers.[43] Most of the other leading Chinese intellectuals who were subject to sharp attack in early 1987 had always clearly placed their remarks in an explicitly Marxist framework but were caught in the trap set by Hu Qiaomu in 1982 when he denounced as "bourgeois liberalizers" all those whose formula-tions might be interpreted as giving aid and comfort to antisocialist arguments, even if such was not their intention.

It is curious that Deng Xiaoping should have offered tacit support to such a position by his statement that all liberalization is bourgeois liberalization. He cannot be unaware of the many eloquent passages in which Marx speaks of freedom, the most striking being that in volume 3 of *Capital*. The question might be raised whether there was not here a linguistic misunderstanding on Deng's part in some respects comparable to Mao Zedong's skewed perception of what is meant by the term "proletariat." It has often been suggested that, although Mao obviously knew intellectually that Marx used this word to designate in the first instance the urban working class, the Chinese equivalent, *wuchanjieji*, probably evoked rather in his mind, or in his feelings, its literal meaning of "propertyless class." Similarly, though Deng Xiaoping surely has some familiarity at least with the ways terms such as "liberty" and "freedom" have been used in the Western liberal tradition, his perception of this idea may well be colored by the literal sense of the Chinese compound *ziyou*, which carries overtones of doing whatever one likes. After Tiananmen, however, it is no longer possible to doubt that Deng's opposition to "liberalization," whatever this concept means to him, is pitiless and implacable.

The crucial point is obviously Deng's absolute determination to make sure that the transformation of the Chinese political system takes place in an orderly manner, under firm party control. This means, in effect, that for Deng Xiaoping Leninism is the *sole* valid or legitimate interpretation of Marxism, or in any case the only one suited to China at the present time. It has always seemed, to outside observers, something of an exercise in squaring the circle to pursue the democratization of the Chinese political system within a strict Leninist framework. In China itself, there are, as already indicated, those who, since 1978, have criticized some aspects of Lenin's political doctrine. Indeed, it had been suggested that the hyphen in Marxism-Leninism should be replaced by a comma, thus indicating that Lenin's interpretation of Marx was a link in the chain, but not the last word on the subject. The top leadership, including Deng Xiaoping, has never been prepared to accept this view. The Resolution of the Sixth Plenum refers only once to "Marxism-Leninism-Mao Zedong Thought," as against approximately twenty references simply to "Marxism," and, by endorsing this language, Deng appeared to be moving toward the view that Leninism was not necessarily sacred. If that was the case, he has changed his mind.

The acute concern of Deng Xiaoping (not to mention more conservative figures in the party) with the maintenance of political control from the top must be seen as reflecting not only the imprint of Leninism, but also the continuing influence of traditional Chinese ideas. To discuss this question is, by implication, to pose once again the problem of what Mao Zedong baptized the "sinification of Marxism."

It is almost exactly a half century since Mao Zedong first addressed these issues in October 1938. In the new situation created by the conquest of power, and the metamorphosis of the Chinese Communist Party into a "ruling party" (*zhizheng dang*), to use the terminology current today, the task of the adaptation of Marxism to China and China's needs became far more complicated. The party's theory and tactics were no longer simply a guide to action in the struggle for power, but the doctrine of the state, defining the nature and goals of the polity and society. In particular, the cultural dimension of this enterprise became, more than had been the case in the past, a matter of political culture, as the conditions which had to be taken into account came to include, in addition to the economic and social reality of a still primarily peasant country, the problem of the institutionalization of revolutionary power.

It is worth emphasizing again in this context that the inculcation of "correct" ideas is, and has always been in China, a crucial aspect of the art of statecraft, and of the vocation of the ruler.[44] The importance of traditional stereotypes and role models in analyzing Mao's rule has been frequently stressed.[45] It is apparent that Chinese politics of recent years remains marked by similar influences. Developments since January 1987 have further underscored the deep-rooted aspiration toward doctrinal unity, and the veneration for the top leader, which have long been traits of Chinese culture. At the same time, the ambiguity of Deng's role as, like Mao, both respected ancestor and party leader, is strikingly symbolized by the duality of form and content in the repeated reissuing of his speech of August 18, 1980. The form, or the medium, of this operation underscores his personal authority; the content, or message, stresses the need for institutionalization. Indeed, the paradox of a quest for institutionalization, maintained and guaranteed primarily by the personal authority of one old man, has been a central feature of the ongoing reform process. (This paradox has, of course, been carried to a wholly new level since the spring of 1989.)

If the crisis of January 1987 undoubtedly owed something both to forces beyond Deng's control, and to his own prudent and centrist instincts, the rapid reversal of his position nonetheless underscores a strong resolve to get on with the task of political as well as economic reform. In January Deng declared that rightism was a greater danger than leftism;[46] by April he had reverted to the view (formerly defended by Hu Yaobang) that leftism was more dangerous.[47]

Following his renewed change of heart on this issue, Deng elaborated a clear and consistent argument regarding the relation between reform and development, on the one hand, and "bourgeois liberalization," on the other. His position at that time can be summed up in four propositions:

1. China is still at the stage of a socialism marked by poverty, and will reach an economic level corresponding to real socialism only in the middle of the next century.

2. This means that there is a "market" for bourgeois ideas, created by the fact that although socialism will in due course bring abundance the capitalist countries (of which the Chinese people now have much greater knowledge) may appear superior in various ways.

3. Because of the time required to move beyond socialism marked by poverty, and the market for bourgeois ideas that will exist the while, the Chinese people cannot be trusted, at present, to vote wisely at national elections. Such elections will be possible only in the middle of the next century, when the citizens enjoy both a higher cultural level and a degree of prosperity that will enable them to make an intelligent comparison between capitalism and socialism.

4. Nevertheless, it is only by pressing ahead with reform and opening to the

outside world that "bourgeois liberalization" can be effectively combatted, for only thus can the productive forces be developed, the superiority of socialism be manifested in full measure, and the economic roots of liberalization be cut.

The first of these four points appears to have been put forward initially by Deng Xiaoping in a talk of April 26, 1987, with the Czechoslovak premier. The key passage, rapidly made public in a *People's Daily* editorial, reads as follows:

> We must support socialism, but we must move ahead in building a socialism which is truly superior to capitalism. We must first rid ourselves of the socialism of poverty (*pinkun shehuizhuyi*); although everyone now says we are creating socialism, it is only in the middle of the next century, when we have reached the level of the moderately developed countries, that we will be able to say with assurance that socialism is really superior to capitalism and that we are really building socialism.[48]

One might, incidentally, ask whether Deng's socialism of poverty represents a level of socialist development higher or lower than that characterized formerly as "undeveloped socialism."

Both the second and fourth propositions summarized above were first enunciated by Zhao Ziyang in a speech of May 13 to propaganda and theoretical workers. Citing Deng Xiaoping's words about the need to move beyond socialism marked by poverty, and introducing the metaphor of a "market" for bourgeois ideas created by China's backwardness, Zhao declared, in particular:

> If we do not reform, the productive forces will not be able to develop rapidly, and for a long period it will be impossible to improve the life of the people. The superiority of socialism will not be manifested in full measure, and socialism will not have much power of attraction. Will this not bring aid and support to the intellectual current of bourgeois liberalization?[49]

There can be little doubt that Zhao Ziyang was voicing here Deng Xiaoping's opinion as well as his own. This speech also introduced the formulation: "The extent to which the productive forces are freed should be the major criterion for judging whether something is progressive or retrogressive; practice is thus the sole criterion for testing truth." This idea was, as grasped earlier by some perceptive observers, implicit in the "practice criterion" as originally formulated in 1978, but to spell it out in this way was of considerable significance and represented a new trend.

While Zhao Ziyang demanded that, as stipulated in Central Committee Document No. 4, party members holding "systematically erroneous views" should, after being subjected to "comradely criticism," recognize and retract their mistakes, his main target was the dogmatists of the Left:

> Today a noteworthy phenomenon has appeared in the domain of research in economic theory. Some comrades characterize things which have been shown by practice to be conducive to liberating the productive forces . . . as capitalist,

and things which fetter the development of the productive forces as socialist. Productive forces and the relations of production must be examined as a whole. The idea of studying production relations separately without considering the development of the productive forces is not a Marxist viewpoint.

Indeed, the whole thrust of Zhao Ziyang's comprehensive ideological statement was directed against those who, since January 1987, had argued that "the source of bourgeois liberalization lies in the economic sector," and even that "a planned economy is socialist, and a commodity economy is capitalist, and promoting a commodity economy is tantamount to promoting capitalism and the root cause of bourgeois liberalization."

Reiterating the view put forward by Deng Xiaoping in 1985 that "reform, too, is a revolution," Zhao Ziyang noted: "At present, even the Soviet Union is engaged in reform. Reform has become the tide in the socialist countries. Without reform, there is no way out."

Despite the fact that "Comrade Xiaoping" had talked about the question several times, some people still thought that the struggle against bourgeois liberalization ruled out reform and the open policy, or regarded political reform as the negation of party leadership. It had therefore been agreed with Deng that his speech of August 18, 1980 should be reprinted yet again on July 1 for further study.

Finally, Zhao Ziyang's speech ends with an extraordinary passage praising Deng Xiaoping's theoretical contributions in terms almost identical to those used to speak of Mao Zedong from Yan'an days to the Cultural Revolution. Deng's thought, Zhao declared, "represents a model in the integration of the universal truth of Marxism with Chinese reality, it is a great development of Marxism in China." He stops short, however, of using the term "Deng Xiaoping Thought." The reference is rather to "these thoughts of Comrade Xiaoping" (*Xiaoping tongzhi zhexie sixiang*), i.e., to Deng's ideas on particular topics, such as building socialism with Chinese characteristics, combating bourgeois liberalization, reform of the economic and political structure, opening to the outside world, and building "socialist spiritual civilization." The echoes of Liu Shaoqi's eulogy of Mao at the Seventh Congress of 1945 are nonetheless striking.

From the Thirteenth Congress to the Tiananmen Square Massacre

If political reform was still on the order of the day as laid down at the 1987 Congress, and was to be pushed ahead even faster, as Deng Xiaoping had repeatedly said, what sort of political system was to be created by the reforms? This point relates to the third of the propositions with which I earlier summarized Deng Xiaoping's thinking, to the effect that the Chinese people were not yet ripe for elections on the national level. Such a view was advanced by Deng publicly and unequivocally in an address of mid-April 1987 to the Hong Kong Basic Law Drafting Committee Delegation:

> Take elections and democracy as an example. Western democracy consists of parliamentary elections. We are not opposed to parliamentary elections. So long as it is practicable in these countries, they may do so. But we, on the Chinese mainland, do not practice this. . . . As far as Hong Kong is concerned, will general elections be absolutely beneficial? Hong Kong in the future will be administered by the Hong Kong people. The criteria for those who will administer Hong Kong affairs are that they be patriotic and love Hong Kong. . . . General elections do not necessarily ensure that such people will be elected. . . . Even if general elections should be held, there should also be a gradual transition, one step at a time. I told a foreigner that general elections may be held on the mainland in the next century, half a century later. We are now conducting indirect elections. Direct elections are conducted only in grassroots units at or below the county level. This is because we have a population of one billion. Moreover, the people's cultural quality is also insufficient. We are not provided with the necessary conditions to practice direct elections. At least, our conditions are not ripe.[50]

Deng repeated some of the same arguments in remarks of June 12, 1987, to Stefan Korosec of Yugoslavia, adding a sharp critique of the confusion and paralysis resulting from the system of the separation of powers prevailing in the West. "The greatest advantage of the socialist system," he declared, "is that when the central leadership makes a decision it is promptly implemented without interference from any other quarters. . . . We don't have to go through a lot of repetitive discussion and consultation, with one branch of government holding up another. . . . From this point of view, our system is very efficient. We should neither copy Western democracy nor introduce the system of a balance of three powers."[51] Thus, to the argument about the political immaturity of the Chinese people, Deng added praise for the efficiency of a monolithic system. He thus appeared to repudiate the limited moves in the direction of the separation of powers in the Constitution of December 1982.[52]

Deng Xiaoping did not go so far as Chen Junsheng, the secretary general of the State Council, who, during the crisis of January 1987, had published an article pointing out that some countries in Asia that had achieved faster economic growth than China, such as South Korea and Taiwan, were governed by "autocracies" or "military dictatorships," and suggesting that too much emphasis on democracy in China was a disruptive side-issue that might lead to a new "warlord era."[53]

It is understandable, in light of the letter of Marx's writings and of the conditioning party members have undergone during the last two decades of Mao's rule, that there should be anxieties, especially among the cadres, as to where all this will lead. The appeal to "material incentives," in the cities as well as in the countryside, and the veritable cult of the entrepreneur as the hero of the present age that flourished in China for several years could not but create mental attitudes that reinforced and encouraged an emphasis on the individual seemingly analogous to that which prevails in the West. Above all, free choice in the realm of individual and family economic strategies encouraged people to think of intellectual and political freedoms as well.

Indeed, some authors who have written about these issues in the Chinese press see such a trend not as a threat but as a promise. The political and social order, they argue, should immediately be brought into conformity with the logic of a socialist market economy.[54] It is therefore not surprising that many articles should have appeared pressing home Zhao's view that neither the role of commodities and the market, nor any other aspect of the economic reforms, can be regarded as anti-Marxist or "capitalist."[55] All these arguments are linked to the basic assumption that China is still in the "initial stage" of socialism.

The Thirteenth Party Congress brought substantial confirmation of the trends announced in the speeches of Deng Xiaoping and Zhao Ziyang since April 1987. Most striking, perhaps, in Zhao's report, was the categorical reiteration of the new criterion for assessing truth, commonly referred to in China at that time as the "criterion of economic results" (*jingji xiaoguo biaozhun*):

> Whatever is conducive to the growth [of the productive forces] is in keeping with the fundamental interests of the people and is therefore needed by socialism and allowed to exist. Conversely, whatever is detrimental to this growth goes against scientific socialism and is therefore not allowed to exist.[56]

Zhao Ziyang also summed up concisely the then current view regarding the primary stage of socialism:

> To believe that the Chinese people cannot take the socialist road without going through the stage of fully developed capitalism is to take a mechanistic position on the question of the development of revolution, and that is the major cognitive root of Right mistakes. On the other hand, to believe that it is possible to jump over the primary stage of socialism, in which the productive forces are to be highly developed, is to take a utopian position on this question, and that is the major cognitive root of Left mistakes.

Finally, while insisting unequivocally on party leadership, and rejecting, like Deng Xiaoping, the separation of the three powers, and "different parties ruling the country in turn," Zhao called for more democracy within the party, and, more broadly, for a new political structure to replace that "which took shape during the revolutionary war years, was basically established in the period of socialist transformation," and "developed in large-scale mass movements and in the process of constantly intensified mandatory planning." In other words, Zhao Ziyang, too, wished to adapt the political superstructure to the new era of the socialist commodity economy. But at the same time he stressed and elaborated a point Deng had made repeatedly:

In the primary stage, as there are many factors making for instability, the maintenance of stability and unity is of special importance. . . . Because feudal autocratic influence is still strong, it is particularly urgent to build socialist democracy, but in view of the restrictions imposed by historical and social conditions, that can only be done step by step and in an orderly way.

One such "condition" that, in Zhao's view, counseled prudence was of course the heritage of the Cultural Revolution. "We shall never again," he declared, "allow the kind of 'great democracy' that undermines state law and social stability."[57]

Conclusion

During the past few years, seeking to sum up in a few words the distinction between the way Marxism was being applied in China and the way it was interpreted by Mao Zedong, I have suggested that while Mao was concerned above all with the dialectic between class struggle and building socialism, Deng Xiaoping took as the axis of his policy the dialectic between political reform and economic development. Mao believed that only unrelenting struggle in the superstructure could keep human beings on the correct course toward a new and selfless society, and that all the gains of the revolution since the bitter days of guerrilla warfare in the countryside could be forfeited in an instant if vigilance were relaxed before the goal was achieved. Deng, in contrast, argued that true socialism could only be built on a highly developed economy. In biblical language, Mao's view was "Seek ye first the kingdom of socialism, and riches shall be added unto you"; Deng's view appeared to be that he who builds on ideology alone builds on sand.

Today, the contrast between the two men does not appear so simple, or so stark. Yet even though Deng Xiaoping, like Mao, manifestly regards politics as central to socialist development, in his case it is politics guiding and shaping the economic basis, rather than politics and ideology taking precedence over everything and abrogating economic laws. A significantly different conception of Marxism is thus being applied today in China, but always with the same goal of making China rich and powerful and building a new society that will be both socialist and distinctively Chinese.

Notes

1. See Stuart R. Schram, *Ideology and Policy in China since the Third Plenum* (London: SOAS, 1984), pp. 5–6.

2. This dichotomy is related to, but does not simply overlap with, the distinction between history viewed as moral drama, and history as technico-economic progress, developed by Benjamin Schwartz in his contribution to the 1967 Chicago symposium, "China and the West in the 'Thought of Mao Tse-tung,' " in Ping-ti Ho and Tang Tsou,

eds., *China's Heritage and the Communist Political System*, vol. 1 (Chicago: The University of Chicago Press, 1968), pp. 365–79. (See also my comments on pp. 380–89 of the same volume.)

3. See Schram, *Ideology and Policy*, pp. 12–13. As indicated there, the most influential article on this theme was that by Su Shaozhi and Feng Lanrui, "Wuchanjieji qude zhengquan hou de shehui fazhan jieduan wenti" (The problem of stages in social development after the proletariat has taken power), *Jingji yanjiu*, no. 5 (1979), pp. 14–19.

4. The new formulation was laid down in par. 33 of the "Resolution on Certain Questions in the History of our Party since the Founding of the People's Republic of China" of June 27, 1981, in *Resolution on CCP History (1949–81)* (Beijing: Foreign Languages Press, 1981), p. 74. See also Schram, *Ideology and Policy*, p. 35, as well as my article "To Utopia and Back: A Cycle in the History of the Chinese Communist Party," *The China Quarterly*, no. 87 (September 1981), pp. 428–29.

5. My own account of the period down to 1984 is given in the pamphlet *Ideology and Policy*, already cited, and in briefer compass in my article " 'Economics in Command?' Ideology and Policy since the Third Plenum, 1978–84," *The China Quarterly*, no. 99 (September 1984), pp. 417–61. I have dealt with the period 1984–86 in my article "Ideology and Policy in China in the Era of Reform, 1978–1986," *Copenhagen Papers in East and Southeast Asian Studies*, no. 1 (1987), pp. 7–30. My analysis was further brought up to date in "China after the Thirteenth Congress," *The China Quarterly*, no. 114 (June 1988), pp. 177–97. Among other contributions, see in particular the book-length accounts by Lowell Dittmer, *China's Continuous Revolution: the Post-Liberation Epoch, 1949–1981 (Berkeley: University of California Press, 1987)* and Harry Harding, *China's Second Revolution: Reform after Mao* (Washington: Brookings Institution, 1987), both of which touch on the ideological dimension of events.

6. Tang Tsou, "Marxism, the Leninist Party, the Masses, and the Citizens in the Rebuilding of the Chinese State," in Stuart R. Schram, ed., *Foundations and Limits of State Power in China* (London: SOAS, and Hong Kong: The Chinese University Press, 1987), p. 258. This article, originally written for the conference on the foundations of the state held at Bellagio in May 1983, has also been published under a different title in Tsou's collected essays, *The Cultural Revolution and Post-Mao Reforms* (Chicago: University of Chicago Press, 1986). The version cited here has been updated to February 1987.

7. For a convenient summary of Deng's views at this time, see his speech on the eve of the Third Plenum, "Emancipate the Mind, Seek Truth from Facts, and Unite as One in Looking to the Future," in *Selected Works of Deng Xiaoping (1975–1982)* (Beijing: Foreign Languages Press, 1984), p. 156; Chinese in *Deng Xiaoping wenxuan (1975–1982)* (Beijing: Renmin chubanshe, 1983), p. 134. The italics in the above quotation are mine.

8. "The Situation in the Summer of 1957," *Selected Works of Mao Tsetung*, vol. 5 (Beijing: Foreign Languages Press, 1977), pp. 473–74. Mao used this formulation most notably in his talk of January 30, 1962; it was also incorporated into Article 5 of the Party Statutes adopted at the Ninth Congress in April 1969.

9. See, in particular, "Uphold the Four Cardinal Principles," *Selected Works of Deng Xiaoping*, pp. 166–91.

10. "Quanmian jianshe shehuizhuyi de daolu" (The road to the all-round edification of socialism), in Liao Gailong, book of the same title (Beijing: Zhongyang dangxiao chubanshe, 1983), p. 143 (Talks of October–November 1981 in Yunnan and Shandong).

11. See *Zhonggong yanjiu*, vol. 15, no. 7 (July 15, 1981), pp. 108–39; *Deng Xiaoping wenxuan*, pp. 280–302; *Selected Works of Deng Xiaoping*, pp. 302–25.

12. *Selected Works of Deng Xiaoping*, pp. 311–12.

13. Compare the text of Liao's October 25, 1980, report in *Zhonggong yanjiu*, vol. 15, no. 9 (September 15, 1981), pp. 108–77, with that later published: Liao Gailong, "Lishi de jingyan he women de fazhan daolu" (Historical experience and our road of development), in Liao Gailong, *Dangshi tansuo* (Explorations in party history) (Beijing: Zhongyang dangxiao chubanshe, 1983), pp. 308–65. The passages regarding Lenin are on pp. 143–44 and 333–34. For a longer discussion of the substance of Liao's report, see Schram *Ideology and Policy*, pp. 20–22.

14. Mao Zedong, "On the Correct Handling of Contradictions among the People." *Selected Works of Mao Zedong*, vol. 5, p. 388.

15. Hu Yaobang, speech of October 15, 1980 in *Dangfeng wenti* (The problem of party style) (Beijing: Zhongyang dangxiao chubanshe, 1981), p. 88.

16. Deng Xiaoping, "On the Reform of the System of Party and State Leadership," in *Selected Works of Deng Xioaping*, pp. 311–12, 316, 319. (Translation modified on the basis of the Chinese text.)

17. Deng Xiaoping, "Concerning Problems on the Ideological Front," *Selected Works*, pp. 368–69; Chinese in *Deng Xiaoping wenxuan*, pp. 345–46.

18. Hu Yaobang's speech has not been openly published; for the text see "Zai sixiang zhanxian wenti zuotanhui shang de jianghua" (Speech at the forum regarding problems on the ideological front), in *Sanzhong quanhui yilai zhongyao wenxian xuanbian*) (A selection of important documents since the Third Plenum) (Beijing: Renmin chubanshe, 1982), vol. 2, pp. 882–903.

19. For the original version of Hu Qiaomu's remarks, see "Dangqian sixiang zhanxian shang de ruogan wenti" (Some current problems on the ideological front), *Hongqi*, no. 23 (1981), pp. 2–22, and the summary in *Beijing Review*, no. 4 (1982), pp. 15–18. For the addenda, see *Hongqi*, no. 8 (1982), pp. 11–13, and *Beijing Review*, no. 23 (1982), pp. 20–21. (The italics at the end of the quotation are mine.)

20. Deng Xiaoping, "Dang zai zuzhi zhanxian he sixiang zhanxian shang de poqie renwu" (Urgent tasks of the party on the organizational and ideological fronts), in *Shier da yilai zhongyao wenxian xuanbian* (A selection of important documents since the Twelfth Congress), vol. 1 (Beijing: Renmin chubanshe, October 1986), pp. 411–12, 420–21. The first open publication of this text (which was, however, widely circulated for study within units in China during the winter of 1983–84) was in the volume of documents just cited.

21. For a more detailed discussion, see Schram, *Ideology and Policy*, pp. 42–56. I have dealt there, in particular, with the writings on alienation under socialism by Zhou Yang, Wang Ruoshui, and others, on the basis of the texts and of my conversations both with Wang Ruoshui, and with Deng Liqun about Wang. As already indicated, Deng Xiaoping's speech launching the campaign was finally published only in October 1986. That the delay reflected a conscious decision on Deng's part is implicitly confirmed by his remarks of December 30, 1986, when he declared: "I still haven't changed my mind about opposing spiritual pollution. I have agreed to have the full text of my speech at the Second Plenary Session of the Twelfth Central Committee included in a new collection of my works." See Deng Xiaoping, "Take a Clear-Cut Stand Against Bourgeois Liberalization," in Deng Xiaoping, *Jianshe you Zhongguo tese de shehuizhuyi* (Beijing: Renmin chubanshe, 1987); translated as *Fundamental Issues in Present-Day China* (Beijing: Foreign Languages Press, 1987), p. 164.

22. Deng Xiaoping, "On Special Economic Zones and Opening More Cities to the Outside World," February 24, 1984, in *Fundamental Issues in Present-Day China*, p. 164.

23. "Suqing 'zou' de liudu he jiaozheng ruanruo huansan zhuangtai" (Eliminate the residual "leftist" poison, and correct the situation of weakness and laxity), *Renmin ribao*, April 1, 1984. See, for more details, Schram, *Ideology and Policy*, pp. 57–58.

24. Text in *Beijing Review*, no. 44 (1984), inset, especially section 2, p. vi.

25. "Benbao pinglunyuan" (This paper's commentator), "Lilun yu shiji" (Theory and reality), *Renmin ribao*, December 7, 1984.

26. *Renmin ribao*, March 29, 1985.

27. *Hongqi*, no. 10 (1985), pp. 32–36; *Beijing Review*, no. 39 (1985), pp. 15–20.

28. Compare the Seventh Five-Year Plan (text in *Renmin ribao*, April 15, 1988), especially section 8, par. 44, with the Decision of October 1984 cited above.

29. Talks of April 17 and 19, *Renmin ribao*, April 24, 1986. Hu had originally put forward these ideas in a talk of April 9, published in *Renmin ribao*, July 1, 1986; translated in *Beijing Review*, no. 28 (1986), pp. 12–13, 32.

30. *Renmin ribao*, April 25, 1986.

31. *Shijie jingji daobao*, April 21, 1986, pp. 1–2.

32. Yu Guangyuan, "Shuangbai fangzhen tichu sanshi zhounian" (The thirtieth anniversay of the putting forward of the two hundreds policy), *Renmin ribao*, May 16, 1986.

33. Su Shaozhi, " 'Shuangbai' fangzhen sanshinian" (Thirty years of the "two hundreds" policy), *Wenhui bao*, May 15, 1986.

34. *Liaowang*, July 21, 1986; extracts in SWB FE/8317/BII/1, July 22, 1986.

35. *Dagong bao* (Hong Kong) July 16, 1986; summary in SWB FE/8315/BII/1, July 19, 1986.

36. See, for example, Deng Liqun, "Sige jiben yuanzi shi gexiang zhengce de jichu" (The four basic principles are the basis of policy in every domain), *Dang de jianshe*, no. 5 (1986), pp. 3–5.

37. For the text of the resolution, see *Hongqi*, no. 19 (1986), pp. 2–9; translated in *Beijing Review*, no. 40 (1986), inset, pp. i–viii.

38. *Beijing Review*, no. 40 (1986), inset, p. v.

39. Deng Xiaoping, "Remarks at the Sixth Plenary Session of the Party's Twelfth Central Committee," September 28, 1986, in *Fundamental Issues in Present-Day China*, pp. 154–55.

40. Deng Xiaoping, "Take a Clear-cut Stand Against Bourgeois Liberalization," remarks of December 30, 1986, ibid., p. 164.

41. *China Spring Digest*, vol. 1, no. 4 (July/August 1987), p. 44.

42. Deng Xiaoping, *Fundamental Issues in Present-Day China*, p. 164.

43. See, for example, his speech of November 15, 1986, at Jiaotong University, *China Spring Digest*, vol. 1, no. 2 (March–April 1987), pp. 27–34.

44. On this theme, see Schram, *Foundations and Limits of State Power in China*, especially the introduction by Jacques Gernet and the conclusion by Karl Bünger.

45. For the most recent account of my own views on this question, see Stuart R. Schram, "Party Leader or True Ruler? Foundations and Significance of Mao Zedong's Personal Power," in Schram, *Foundations and Limits of State Power in China*, pp. 203–56.

46. Deng Xiaoping, "Clear Away Obstacles and Adhere to the Policies of Reform and of Opening to the Outside World" (Talk of January 13 with Noboru Takeshita), *Fundamental Issues in Present-Day China*, pp. 168–69.

47. Deng Xiaoping, "We Shall Draw on Historical Experience and Guard Against Erroneous Tendencies" (Remarks of April 30, 1987 to Alfonso Guerra), ibid., pp. 183–84.

48. Deng Xiaoping, "We Must Continue to Build Socialism and Eliminate Poverty" (Remarks of April 26, 1987, to Lubomir Strougal), *Fundamental Issues in Present-Day China*, pp. 176–78. The editorial in question appeared in *Renmin ribao*, May 17, 1987, under the title "Ba fandui zichanjieji ziyouhua de douzheng yinxiang shenru" (Let the struggle against bourgeois liberalization penetrate deeply).

49. The full text of Zhao's speech was published in *Renmin ribao*, July 10, 1987; a

summary in translation appears in *Beijing Review*, no. 29 (July 20, 1987), pp. 34–35. The main substance of the speech was conveyed in an editorial, "Gaige kaifang buqin yao jianchi erqie yao jiakuai" (Reform and opening up must not only be persevered in, but speeded up), *Renmin ribao* May 22, 1987, which incorporated verbatim the paragraph I have quoted above. The idea of the "market" had already been publicized in the *Renmin ribao* editorial of May 17, cited above, manifestly also inspired by Zhao's speech.

50. This account, from the Hong Kong *Wenhui bao*, translated in SWB FE/8547/A1–3, is fuller than that in the Chinese press.

51. Deng Xiaoping, "We Shall Speed Up Reform," *Fundamental Issues in Present-Day China*, pp. 192–93 and 195–96.

52. See articles 65 and 103 of the Constitution, and my comments in "Decentralization in a Unitary State: Theory and Practice, 1940–1984," in Stuart R. Schram, ed., *The Scope of State Power in China* (London: SOAS, and Hong Kong: The Chinese University Press, 1985), pp. 121–22.

53. For a translation, see *Beijing Review*, no. 4 (1987), pp. 14–18. These views obviously correspond to the theory of so-called New Authoritarianism, developed especially in 1988 and 1989 by people close to Zhao Ziyang. There is no scope here for a discussion of this concept, and the controversy aroused by it.

54. See, for example, the article by Fang Gongwen in *Jingji ribao*, November 4, 1986, in SWB FE/8422/BII/1.

55. For a summary of views put forward on this question, see Zhang Kai, "Some Views of Theoretical Circles on the Initial Stage of Socialism," *Shijie jingji daobao*, August 10, 1987, translated in SWB FE/8652/BII/7–10. An earlier article justifying the existence of commodities under socialism, despite what Marx said, is He Jianzhang, "Shangpin jingji shi shehuijingji fazhan bukeyuyue de jieduan" (Commodity economy is an inevitable stage in socioeconomic development), *Renmin ribao*, May 23, 1986.

56. *Beijing Review*, no. 45 (1987), p. xxvi (inset).

57. Ibid., p. xxi, vi, xv (inset).

Comments by A. Doak Barnett

I wish to comment on what I view as the basic issues raised by the paper and by the central question of this session, which is the implications of Deng's experiment for the future of Marxism-Leninism.

I agree with almost all that Professor Schram had to say about the development of ideology. In fact, I would not have the intrepidity to challenge him on this. He knows much more about it than I. If there is any area of disagreement, it is the extent to which the role and influence of ideology may be changing and may change in the future in China.

In my judgment, the policies now evolving in China and the systemic changes taking place in the system have relatively little to do with Marxism-Leninism, whether in its original, its Stalinist, or its Maoist forms, or even in relation to the new ideological definition now being formulated. What is occurring in China is a dramatic decline and secularization of ideology—not simply another stage in its adaptation to changing local conditions.

I agree that the end result is not likely to be the end of ideology, which people proclaim periodically. But I do think the end result may be a major reduction in the roles and influence of ideology in China. China's reform leaders, having rejected both Stalinist and Maoist models, clearly are attempting—and I would say pragmatically, eclectically, and experimentally—to carry out far-reaching systemic changes that we have been discussing throughout this conference.

Professor Schram asserts that Deng is certainly no pragmatist because of his experience, his belief in Leninism, and so on, but I would argue that whatever one labels him, he is certainly acting like a pragmatist, even though he obviously is influenced by his revolutionary experience.

Professor Schram says at the start of his paper that Mao's and Deng's programs have been using Marxism as a guide, to guide the revolution in China, and at the same time adapting it to Chinese circumstances. It seems to me, however, that the ideological concepts have in fact provided almost no guidance to China's reform leaders as they have attempted to create a new kind of mixed economy and new and looser form of political authority. The impetus for reform in China is rooted in the leaders' recognition that both traditional Marxism and Leninism and Mao's adaptation of it failed to provide an effective guide to modernization, which is highlighted by the Cultural Revolution breakdown. The primary goal of the present leaders, as Professor Schram himself emphasizes at the end of the paper, represents a resurgence of the old Chinese goal of making China rich and powerful, and, as he stresses, for many of China's reformers, whatever works and promotes economic development is now considered desirable and compatible with socialism.

Undoubtedly, the system that will ultimately result will still be called socialist, but it almost certainly will be a hybrid that, in reality, will blur the distinction between the socialist and nonsocialist systems, and I think it will have very weak roots in ideology. In my judgment, moreover, few young Chinese today are true believers in Marxism-Leninism in any form; in fact in the eyes of many, there is something close to an ideological vacuum. That is not to say that the ideological differences of recent years have been unimportant. They clearly have had a major impact on political debates. But the majority of those Professor Schram calls conservative leftists are aging leaders and, as I see it, they have been fighting a losing rearguard action. They have no alternative program; essentially, they have argued for less and less rapid reform. Moreover, I do not think they will be able to reproduce themselves. What is likely, therefore, is that as the generational change continues, the trend will be toward more pragmatism and eclecticism in China.

Nevertheless, even though ideology in my opinion has provided neither the impetus nor guidance for reform, the reinterpretation of ideology, which Professor Schram analyzes better than anyone else I know could, has been important at this stage. The initial step in this process, popularization of practice as the sole criterion of truth, was essential to break down the shackles of dogma inhibiting change. Then the attempt in the 1981 party resolution to carry out systematic de-Maoization further rationalized the ideological basis of reform, and he has dealt with further steps since then. In actuality, though, the process of reform has surged way ahead of the process of ideological interpretation. To many of China's young reformers, in my opinion, ideology has appeared increasingly irrelevant, or at least decreasingly relevant. And many of China's youth have become increasingly agnostic.

It is not surprising, in the face of such trends, that some senior leaders have periodically argued for measures to combat unhealthy tendencies, promote spiritual civilization, combat spiritual pollution and bourgeois liberalization, and so on. Deng himself has put forward his Four Principles, that, in my opinion, except for the principle of party leadership, are still so undefined, ill-defined, and will probably remain so that they have little operational significance.

In the recent comprehensive attempt to reinterpret ideology, perhaps the ideas of initial steps toward socialism and planned commodity economy may provide a somewhat more acceptable ideological justification for some party members than previously developing a mixed economy with a larger role for market forces and varied forms of ownership. These efforts to define socialism with Chinese characteristics, however, will probably continue to be very general, plastic, and tentative and are not likely to prevent the continuing decline and secularization of ideology.

If this trend continues, and I think it will, what is the role of ideology likely to be in China in the period ahead? It will doubtless continue to be used to try to support the regime's claim to legitimacy and party leadership. It will also serve as a basis for rationalizing after the fact policies adopted for essentially nonideological reasons. Maybe to a limited extent it may impose some constraints on policy. But I do not think it will be a guiding force behind policy. It almost certainly will no longer be an effective instrument for mobilizing and indoctrinating the population as it was in the Maoist era. The driving forces that will continue to propel the reform process forward will be essentially nonideological. These include the imperatives inherent in the requirements for economic growth, improved productivity, managerial efficiency, the desire to raise living standards, the demands imposed by China's growing interdependency in the world economy, the impact on China of rapid advances worldwide in science and technology, and, at least to some degree, the pressures to tolerate limited political and social as well as economic pluralism as the Chinese economy becomes more complex.

Professor Schram argues that Deng sees the need for some political reform, but remains opposed to Western pluralism in a Leninist way. I basically agree. There is little doubt that as China modernizes, pressures for liberalization will gradually increase, but also little doubt that reform in the political field will lag behind economic reform. But above all, in my judgment, this is rooted in Chinese authoritarian traditions and concern for stability, order, and centralized control rather than ideology as such, even in its Leninist form. Professor Schram also stresses that from both a Leninist and a traditional Chinese perspective the elaboration of correct doctrine is an essential attribute of political authority and argues that the inculcation of correct ideas is and has always been in China a crucial aspect of the art of statecraft. The views are widely shared among Chinese I know, as well as among Western scholars. And in the past, I, as much as anyone else, have tended to argue that in light of its history and political culture, China appears to need a coherent, well-defined ideology as a unifying force. Therefore, the decline of Marxism and Leninism could create serious political problems, and if it does decline there would be attempts to revivify ideology or the political system might be seriously weakened. Now I am inclined to doubt this conventional wisdom. Clearly a country as large and complex as China with a tradition of ideological orthodoxy does need some kind of consensus on values and goals, but I am no longer sure that it needs an ideological orthodoxy such as Confucianism or Marxism-Leninism-Mao Zedong Thought.

Patriotism, national pride, a commitment to development and modernization, plus the pragmatic goals of raising living standards and improving the quality of life, can, I am now convinced, provide motivation for the population and a kind of national vision even if a rather vague one. Values and forces such as these, after all, are what help explain the dynamism of the most successful modernizing nations on China's periphery in East Asia, countries that belong to the Sinic cultural area and in the past have shared many traditonal values with premodern China. As the force of Marxism-Leninism weakens in China, my guess is that China, like these countries, will still increasingly be moved by powerful forces of modernization and nationalism. Even if the forces of Marixism-Leninism are greatly weakened, it will remain undoubtedly the official ideology.

The changes that have been taking place in China have not been taking place in a vacuum. The rapidity of change in China is clearly related to the domestic breakdown of the Cultural Revolution, but Chinese leaders have been influenced significantly in recent years by efforts at reform in other communist countries, particularly Eastern Europe. They have also been greatly influenced by recognition of the huge gap between China and the major industrialized countries, and, most important, by the realization that in the 1960s and 1970s China's nonsocialist neighbors were developing more successfully than China was.

Gorbachev, in his recent speech on the occasion of the seventieth anniversary of the Bolshevik Revolution, used the term "wind of change." I think clearly the wind of change is blowing strongly throughout much of the communist world where leaders have recognized the flaws of centrally planned economies and have increasingly feared the stagnation that would widen the gap between the communist and noncommunist countries. Reform in Eastern Europe unquestionably influenced China, and I believe China's reforms are now influencing the Soviet Union.

In my view, reform is now in many respects resonating throughout the communist world in a fascinating and little understood fashion. And internal pressures of reform have been reinforced also by increasing interactions among the communist nations and those with noncommunist systems, and, in China's case, especially those in East Asia and the Pacific.

The erosion of traditional Marxist-Leninist ideology, as I have said, does not necessarily imply a serious weakening of political, economic, and social systems in these nations. It may in fact be, and probably is, a prerequisite in many respects for any genuine revitalization of these systems. In sum, while Marxism-Leninism is not dead, in my opinion, it is not only being reinterpreted but is undergoing a steady decline in its power and influence certainly in China and in much of the communist world as well.

Comments by Lowell Dittmer

Because I agree with most of what Professor Schram has to say, I would like to begin from the particular and work to the general, begin with questions about various specific points and then present a few general questions.

Professor Schram begins by discussing the question of the West. I think a rectification of names is needed about what the West is. I think China today no longer thinks of Marxism as Westernization. Somehow Marxism-Leninism-Mao Zedong Thought is considered Chinese; it has become sinicized. The three debates in 1978—most people think in terms of one debate, which is the criterion of truth debate—included debates on the question of objective laws of economics and on remuneration according to work. Remuneration according to work was the principle of socialism. So that represents no change. The question of objective laws of economics does represent a debate, but not a public debate as far as I know; certainly it must have been an internal debate. We know there must have been some differences, but I think they were internal because the piece was not published until several months later.

Professor Schram sees a standoff between Chen Yun and Deng Xiaoping at the 1985 special Party Congress. I would differ with this. I think the general interpretation in the press at the time was that there was a standoff between Chen Yun and Deng Xiaoping. But I think it involved a somewhat contrived reading of Deng Xiaoping's speech. In my view, a straightforward reading would indicate that Deng was largely in agreement with Chen Yun at the time. In retrospect, I think this may have been the beginning of the differences between Hu Yaobang and Deng Xiaoping that we saw widening during the coming year, during the January conference on work that resulted in setting up the special committee on discipline. Deng Xiaoping played no role, whereas Hu Yaobang was there, so I think this was perhaps the beginning of the breach between the two.

What then follows is an account of the developments of the past year, which is fascinating. I think the reason the reformers focused their attack on the superstructure, whereas previously they had focused on the economic base, as Professor Schram correctly points out, was that the economic reforms had run into serious difficulties by the spring of 1986 and were put on hold at the time, so that if the reforms were to continue, they had to move to the superstructure. This was a departure for the reformers that did not turn out well.

Professor Schram's reporting on the Hundred Flowers was perhaps a bit tendentious because only the good guys are reported on and the bad guys remain invisible. This is a tendency in Western China-watching, to report only on the liberals. There were refutations of the liberals in the press and, in this connection, the whole notion of spiritual civilization deserves to be taken seriously, as some Chinese take it seriously. It is a serious intellectual construct; it is meant seriously, and it is surprising really that it has received little serious analysis by Western China-watchers.

The term "developing stage of socialism" is a mistranslation. I do not know who mistranslated it. I know that the Soviets, during the Brezhnev period, defined their socialism as a developed stage of socialism, not developing; but this is an interesting point and the reason I raise it is because if it is the Chinese who are mistranslating it, this indicates a certain amount of embarrassment that they are now behind the Soviets perhaps, that they are now in the first stage of developing socialism, and not developed socialism. Whereas earlier in the 1950s the Chinese were contending with the Soviets for being in an advanced stage of socialism, now there is this new formulation. While this more modest formulation has certain advantages, it does place the Chinese behind the Soviets, and I wonder if this mistranslation is a sort of clue that indicates a certain embarrassment about that.

The general themes that we see in Professor Schram paper are certain paradoxes. First, with regard to Mao, a paradox about his ideas of development: approval of development conflicting with late developments of Maoism that inhibited development. But the focus is on Deng Xiaoping and his ideas about democracy. Here the general theme is that the contradictions we have seen in the last few years are direct ramifications of contradictions in Deng Xiaoping's thought. Chinese politics is playing out on a broad screen, so to speak, of contradictions in Deng Xiaoping's thought. So the student movements in the fall of 1986, if we can draw implications from this, were not a result of the reformers, but contradictions within Deng Xiaoping's thought itself. I wonder if that would be the logical implication of what Professor Schram has said.

PART II:
PUBLIC ADDRESSES
AND COMMENTS

13

A DECADE OF REFORM
UNDER DENG XIAOPING:
An Overview and Prospects for the Future

Li Luye*

IT IS ALMOST a decade since China began its sweeping reform. Those of you familiar with modern Chinese history may still remember that there was a period of indecision after the smash of the Gang of Four in 1976. The country was moving haltingly and the people were anxious to see changes after the disastrous Cultural Revolution had been brought to an end. It was Deng Xiaoping, a great Long March veteran, who gave China at the crossroads a new direction, namely, to break away from the leftist trend of the past and build socialism with Chinese characteristics through economic and political reforms. It is no exaggeration to say that Deng Xiaoping is the chief architect of China's reform, which not only touches the life of every Chinese but perhaps bears significantly on the rest of the world. Today I shall focus on the ongoing reform in China.

In 1949 the revolution, led by the Chinese Communist Party, won a nation-wide victory, and the People's Republic of China was founded. For the first time in a hundred years China was unified under a strong central government and the Chinese people became masters of their own country. In the past thirty-eight years China has covered vast distances in its endeavor to build a nation. With only 7 percent of the world's arable land China is feeding 22 percent of the world's population. Its industries, which were almost nonexistent at the time of Liberation, have grown steadily to meet rising needs of economic reconstruction, the domestic consumer market, and a flourishing foreign trade. Its scientists have

*Li Luye was appointed Permanent Representative of the People's Republic of China to the United Nations in New York in 1985. He was president of the Security Council in January 1986 and May 1987.

successfully launched geostationary satellites and are making progress in such frontiers as superconductivity and robotics. All these testify to the fact that socialism has not only set China on its feet but has also promised it a bright future.

This does not mean, however, that it has all been smooth sailing. In fact, we have traversed a bumpy and tortuous road with many ups and downs. The detours we have made—the Great Leap Forward, the Cultural Revolution, just to name a few—not only caused deep suffering to our people but held back our economic growth for years, allowing the gap between us and the developed countries to widen further. In the wake of the downfall of the Gang of Four the Chinese people were pondering some important questions: How could this tragedy ever have happened? What must be done to prevent this from happening again? From such soul-searching a national awareness emerged. If China wanted to make up for lost time and eventually catch up with the advanced countries, it must break new ground and blaze a new trail in building socialism in light of its own realities. Thanks to the arduous work of our leaders, first and foremost Comrade Deng Xiaoping, the focus of our work, which had for years been on class struggle, was shifted to economic development. At the end of 1978, a fresh agenda calling for reform, opening to the outside world, and economic invigoration was formulated at the watershed Third Plenary of the Party's Eleventh Central Committee.

The rural reform got under way immediately after the plenum. It received an initial boost when the government decided to increase the purchasing prices of farm products, lift restrictions on multiple operations, and introduce incentives to make farming more profitable. Shortly after these measures were implemented, at the initiative of the peasants, the commune system was replaced by a contracted household responsibility system. While the land remains the collective property of the peasants, it is the household responsible for it under contract that decides how the production is operated. Once the quota for state purchase is met, the household can freely dispose the extras on its own. To increase their income and diversify its sources, the farmers are encouraged to engage in rural and township industries, commerce, transport, building, and other trades. As a result, the annual per capita income in the rural areas registered a 160 percent increase in real terms in eight years. In a country where 80 percent of its population make a living in the countryside, this change means more than just the improvement of the welfare of the peasants. Rural reform is still deepening. As more and more of the farming population shift to industries and other operations, timely adjustment in rural policies is needed. One area of such adjustment would be to allow the land allotted to households engaging in nonfarming trades to be transferred to those specialized in farming. Another area would be to give greater incentives to grain farmers so as to ensure steady growth in food grain in the years ahead.

Built on the success of the rural reform, a comprehensive economic restructuring centered around urban reform was introduced in the fall of 1984 nationwide. Its focus was to revitalize some 400,000 industrial enterprises in the country by expanding their decision-making power and creating a more favorable environment, so that they could truly become economic powerhouses instead of recipients of government subsidies. While promoting higher economic efficiency and technological transformation of the enterprises, efforts have been made to revamp the existing industrial structure and encourage interregional and interdepartmental associations. Particular emphasis has been given to the development of collective and private enterprises, especially in the tertiary sector of the urban areas. Special economic zones have been set up to serve as test grounds for new policies for closer economic ties with foreign countries. An increasing number of coastal regions and cities have been opened up for foreign investment and joint ventures. Work on economic legislation has made steady and remarkable headway. Earnest efforts are being made to create and flesh up a market system for commodity, labor, capital, technology, information, and real estate. As the role of the market increases, the government has gradually reduced its control over the economy from 100 percent nine years ago to only 50 percent today, and it will reduce its control even further as the reform deepens. Throughout China, a more open economic system, characterized by greater vitality and diversity, is gradually taking shape.

Although this reform has been set in motion for only a few years, its benefits to the country and people have been immense. During the eight years between 1978 and 1986, China's gross social product grew at an annual rate of 10.1 percent, its national income grew at 8.7 percent, foreign trade at 17.3 percent, and total turnover from retail, an indicator of the people's consumption level, at 15.5 percent. From 1979 to June 1987 China has absorbed a total of U.S. $31.9 billion in foreign capital and set up nearly eight thousand joint ventures, cooperative businesses, and wholly foreign-owned enterprises. In fact, this period represents the best in the history of the People's Republic in terms of political stability, economic growth, and real benefit to the people.

Yet there are changes more far-reaching than figures can illustrate. For decades China was beset with some tough problems: to feed, clothe, and shelter its growing population, to create enough jobs for the urban youth and surplus rural laborers, to ensure a well-supplied market for the consumers, and to strike a rational balance between the major sectors of the national economy. It seems a path has finally been found to solve these problems. Although still quite low in consumption level, the average Chinese man and woman can now afford a fairly decent living. Except for grain, all once-prevalent ration coupons have since been abolished as supply of daily necessities and consumer durables have become more abundant. Over the past eight years some seventy million urban people have found jobs, and eighty million rural workers started working on nonfarming jobs while remaining in the countryside. This indicates that China might avoid having millions of its peasants come to the cities in search of jobs, a common phenomenon of the industrializing nations. We have already taken an important step forward in our reform practices. In doing so, our understanding of scientific socialism, as laid down by the founders of Marxism, has further deepened, and our efforts to integrate their theory with our practices have achieved some progress.

During this process, it is only natural for us to discard some of their utopian conclusions, resulting from the limitations of historical circumstances, and reject some dogmatic interpretations of Marxism or mistaken views. The recently concluded Thirteenth National Party Congress has made a more detailed elaboration about these breakthroughs. Let me share some preliminary thoughts in this respect.

First, developing the social productive forces should be our fundamental task. The traditional concept of socialism tended to ignore the level of productive forces while emphasizing such artificial principles as excessive level of public ownership and egalitarianism in distribution. The new understanding, however, is that socialism, for all it superiorities, must manifest itself not only in elements of relations of production, such as public ownership and distribution according to work, but also in the elements of productive forces, such as higher productivity and growth rate. In a nutshell, it is the growth of social productive forces, not some abstract features imposed on it from the outside, that determines the development of socialism. As Comrade Deng Xiaoping told a visiting European leader earlier this year, at present we are practicing socialism, but only when we have reached the level of medium-developed countries in the middle of the next century will we be able to declare that our socialism is superior to capitalism and that we are practicing genuine socialism. His words are worth thinking about.

Second, China is still in the primary stage of socialism. Traditional theory held that socialism was only a short transitional phase leading immediately to communism. Here lies the very theoretical foundation for the leftist trend. We understand now that socialism may be a fairly long and relatively independent social formation. It might even have more than one developmental stage, and that China, having embarked on socialism for only thirty-eight years, and under conditions of backward productive forces and an underdeveloped commodity economy, is still in its primary stage. This new theory will allow us to formulate policies conducive to the development of social productive forces and pursue them for an extended period of time.

Third, different types of ownerships should be allowed to co-exist during the present stage of socialism. Traditional theory insisted that only public or collective ownership could exist under socialism. We understand now that types of ownership are also subjected to the level of social productive forces. By allowing collective, private, and even foreign sectors to play a part supplementary to the predominant public sector, China's overall economic development can only be accelerated. Even in state-owned enterprises efforts should be made to separate ownership from management through such systems as contracting or leasing.

Fourth, and finally, a socialist planned commodity economy should be a system that integrates planning with the market. The old thinking was that the commodity economy was irrelevant to socialism. As a result, defying the law of value and ignoring the market forces were commonplace. We understand now that ours is a commodity economy, and the essential difference between our economy and a capitalist commodity economy is that they are based on different ownerships. As far as macroeconomic control is concerned, the government's role should be to formulate policies and facilitate their implementation by applying economic levers. The economy, on the other hand, should be left on its own, allowing the enterprises to function as independent commodity producers in a competitive market. The basic economic structure as we envisage now would be a three-tiered framework in which the government regulates the market through planning, both mandatory and guidance, and legal and financial levers; the market, in turn, guides the economic behaviors of the enterprises through its supply and demand mechanisms.

While citing the achievements of the past decade we are by no means content with them. In fact, we are too aware of our problems to be complacent. As the largest developing country in the world, China lags behind the most developed countries like the United States by half a century if not more. Our goal of modernization is both ambitious and realistic. According to our development strategy, we intend to achieve our goal in three steps. First, we plan to solve the problem of meeting our people's basic needs for food and clothing by 1990; it is likely that this will be achieved ahead of schedule. Second, we plan to quadruple our 1980 GNP by the year 2000 so that the Chinese people can enjoy a comfortable standard of living with a per capita annual income between U.S. $800 and U.S. $1,000. Third, we will continue to work hard for three to five decades so that by the middle of the next century we will be able to rank China among the medium-level developed countries in terms of per capita annual income for our estimated 1.4 to 1.5 billion people. With an economy of such a size China's contribution to the world would be much greater.

As for the immediate future, our economic reform will continue to move forward in both the cities and countryside, and at a quickened pace along the established guidelines and priority areas. The reform of the current political structure, which is increasingly unable to keep up with the changes brought about by the economic reform, will have to be carried out in greater urgency. Such a reform will cover a wide range of issues from streamlining government institutions to protecting citizens' rights and freedoms. The Thirteenth Party Congress has come up with a relevant guideline for a nationwide political reform. As General Secretary Zhao Ziyang pointed out in his speech to the Congress, the long-range goal of reform is to build a socialist political system with a high degree of democracy and a complete set of laws, a system that is effective and full of vitality. To this end, he proposed the separation of the functions of the party and the government, the establishment of a public service system, the strengthening of the socialist legal system, and the introduction of a system of consultation and dialogue as a means to combat bureaucratism and unhealthy tendencies.

Our reform has all along enjoyed the support of the Chinese people. After seeing the initial real benefits, they have become all the more convinced that the future of their country and themselves lies in the reform. As the reform can only proceed in a step-by-step manner the old way and the new would have to function simultaneously. Frictions and conflicts between them are hardly avoidable, giving rise to complicated political, economic, as well as social problems. To carry out such a complex reform in a country of a billion people we must be sober-minded, confident and prudent, and do a good job in harmonizing the pace of change with the crucial need of maintaining stability. To this end we must, on the one hand, persist in the socialist orientation and, on the other, adhere to our general political line in the new era of reform—opening and economic invigoration. Only by upholding these two basic points can we ensure the success of our reform. In any case, there must not be retreat to the ossified past. After all, it is the Chinese people who will in the final analysis decide what they want.

To sum up, the reform we have been conducting in the past nine years is part of the self-improvement process of our socialist system, a revolutionary change aimed at doing away with the defects that are either inherited from our historical past or imposed on us by the mistaken interpretations of socialism. We will continue to surge ahead with our reform. We are confident that this great experiment will be crowned with success.

Comments by Lynn T. White

The timing of this conference could not be better, just a few days after the conclusion of the Thirteenth Party Congress. Nor could our topic here be more important; it is after all the future of more than a billion people. With people like Ambassador Li running the country the Chinese will be going places in the next few decades. Can you imagine a speech as practical, as circumspect, and as efficiency-minded as the one we have just heard, being given by a Chinese ambassador as little as a decade ago?

Today on the front page of the *New York Times*, the reporter Edward Gargan writes, "When Zhao Ziyang introduced the new Standing Committee of the Politburo, not one of the Chinese leaders on the new Standing Committee wore the familiar high-collared Mao suit." More important about Ambassador Li's being here is not the fact that he has a tie on, but rather the substance of his talk. The ambassador gives us not just a political statement, but an analysis that is practical and development-minded. He began appropriately with a statement about Deng Xiaoping. Journalists have been telling us that Deng has just retired; that is true. But as Ambassador Li told us, Deng is the chief architect of China's reform. Despite all the news about his retirement, this man has made China now a lively place, which allows the creation of institutions that may enable this trend to continue even after his death. Deng is more retired than he was last week, and Zhao Ziyang does look like he is in charge. But I am glad Deng is still with us and that the institutions he has created and the new people he has brought to the top of the Chinese political hierarchy will last.

Ambassador Li shows why Deng's system will survive him. The reason lies largely in agricultural economics. Early in his speech, the ambassador was not talking about ideology and philosophy, but about arable land, per capita income, robotics, and superconductors, practical and technical subjects. He cites statistics and talks about the benefits the new policies have brought to China's people.

What is ideology compared to all these matters? As the ambassador says, "it seems a path has finally been found." There is a sigh of relief, both at the national and local levels. By now people know that another Great Leap Forward or another Cultural Revolution is not about to be tried in China. The revolution is finally mellowing and settling down to longer-term work. When the ambassador does talk about ideology, especially the four major points at the end of his talk, he begins by saying that developing social productive forces should be our fundamental task. To say that development is the fundamental task in China and no longer class struggle is to reverse the emphasis of Mao Zedong.

Ambassador Li's second point concerns the so-called primary stage of socialism, suggesting perhaps that China is developing toward socialism, but is not there yet. The idea of China in a primary stage of socialism is, in an ideological way, inferring many things about policy, and I think the aspects that interest the ambassador and many leaders in China are the policy aspects. In economic policy there is little difference between saying that China is in the primary stage of socialism or is moving toward socialism and saying that China is emphasizing decentralization and efficiency in production. But there is a political difference between these two views because in socialism there is the continuing need of the party, suggesting the continuing need for order and stability, not just efficiency.

Ambassador Li's third point clarifies the earlier two points. It is about the ownership system. In the past the public sector was overwhelmingly important. Now, as he says, it should remain predominant, but supplementary ownership, private ownership, collective ownership, and even foreign ownership are permissible forms. The ambassador's third point represents some change from the traditional emphasis on the public sector that had at least been held by many Chinese politicians and leaders, politicians like Yu Qiuli, or the so-called Petroleum Group at the center, and politicians who emphasize the importance of heavy industry. The new view promises much more attention than in the past to light industry, especially to the service sector, whose productive contribution to China has long been undervalued. This service sector with light industry is where foreign, collective, and private ownership are likely to prove important, and where heavy industry is probably not very important.

The fourth point concerns the socialist market economy, or socialist commodity economy. Here, too, there is some change of emphasis from previous policies. Chen Yun, who retired on Sunday, talked about "the bird of the market in a cage of the plan" metaphor for the relationship between the market and the plan; the market was an active bird within the framework of the plan. But the ambassador talked about guidance and planning, not just mandatory planning, but about economic levers of the sort that are in fact used in many countries, including this one. I have the sense that Chen Yun's birdcage is a lot smaller than Zhao Ziyang's and Ambassador Li's. There is an emphasis on efficiency in the new viewpoint that is coming out of Beijing, which will emphasize the importance of more production. No one in China wants inflation, and everyone there, as here, would like to see a balanced government budget, in trade accounts and between supply and demand, so prices would remain stable. This was certainly the aim of Chen Yun's emphasis on the plan. But Zhao Ziyang's bird may live in a cage where some flying can be done, where efficiency is also a very important goal alongside economic stability.

Finally, the ambassador is specific on the question of time in his speech; he mentions working hard for "three to five decades," "the middle of the next century," "the inital stage of socialism will take some time." I could not help noticing that the middle of the next century is very close to the year 2047, which is fifty years after 1997, and, as we know, the Sino-British agreement on the subject of Hong Kong refers to that fifty years as being very important. Perhaps I am reading too much into these words, but there is another aspect to consider. After so long as half of a century, who knows what the situation will be like?

There is much more than a call for long-term planning in the ambassador's speech. There is also a call for long-term flexibility, a long-term search for different methods, to create habits of service and efficiency in China, especially in its bureaucracy. The bureaucracy is as much a target as a tool for the things the ambassador talks about explicitly in his speech. Of course it was a tool for Chairman Mao, too. But the ambassador has a much more realistic program than Chairman Mao did on how to change the bureaucracy. The ambassador makes two points at the end of his speech: persistence in the socialist orientation and no retreat to the ossified past. This is realistic, hopeful, and expressed in terms of a program that gives people incentives to escape from the past. And it is also honest to the size of the task in terms of the time frame in which the task is put, and in terms of the incentives that are implicit in so many of the policies that are described in the speech.

We can all be happy that a Chinese ambassador can give such a speech, and that people like Ambassador Li are currently running China. I believe their policies will over a period of long time benefit the people.

14

CHINA AND ITS ASIAN NEIGHBORS:
A Japanese Perspective

Kimio Fujita*

Development of Sino-Japanese Relations

ABOUT A MONTH ago, on September 29, 1987, Japan and China celebrated the fifteenth anniversary of the normalization of their relations in 1972. During the past fifteen years the two nations have developed relations in all sectors of the political, economic, and social fields.

At the end of 1978, under Deng Xiaoping, China began to implement an aggressive modernization policy and to open her doors to the outside world; since then development of Sino-Japanese bilateral relations has been greatly strengthened and expedited as a result of diligent efforts on the part of the Japanese government.

The late Prime Minister Ohira presented Japan's basic policy toward China in a speech delivered in Beijing on December 7, 1979.[1] The prime minister reaffirmed Japan's readiness to cooperate with the modernization efforts of the Chinese government and people, stating his conviction that "the emergence of a more prosperous China can be expected to contribute to shaping a better world." Prime Minister Nakasone expressed the same conviction in 1984 when he welcomed China's modernization policy and stated that Japan's "cooperation with China's modernization program is of vital importance, not only to relations between our two countries but also to the peace and prosperity of Asia and the world."[2] These statements reflect the Japanese government's view that a prosperous, stable, and open China will require greater international exchange and cooperation, and only then will China be able to

---

*A graduate of Tokyo University, Mr. Fujita was Director-General of Asian Affairs Bureau of the Ministry of Foreign Affairs in Japan at the time of the Conference. He is now Japanese Ambassador to the Netherlands.

452

play an essential role in the maintenance of stability and peace in Asia. At the present stage of development in China, the alternative to the pursuit of a modernization policy would be a nation of one billion people governed either by radical revolutionary ideologues or conservative party bureaucrats, neither offering much hope for a better standard of living. Therefore, it is safe to assume that China's modernization efforts will gain the support, at least within the nonmilitary economic field, of all countries in the free world.

This conviction of the Japanese government was shared by the United States. In 1984 when President Reagan was in Beijing, he announced to his Chinese host, Premier Zhao Ziyang,

> [In] your drive for modernization you have our best wishes. If you ask for our advice, we can only answer with truth as we see it. But let me assure you that we want you to succeed. Having one billion people—nearly a quarter of mankind—healthy, well-fed, clothed and housed, educated and given the opportunity for a higher standard of living, is in the interest of good and decent people everywhere. It is certainly in the interest of the American people, who wish to trade and be friends with the Chinese people.[3]

I would now like to describe the development of relations between Japan and China during the past fifteen years, especially the past decade, to give you an idea of the scope of that relationship.

In terms of official political relations, several treaties and agreements have been negotiated and signed, ranging from the Treaty of Peace and Friendship in 1978, to agreements on trade, aviation, navigation, fisheries, protection of trademarks, cultural exchange, science and technology, prevention of double taxation, and protection of migratory birds. Annual consultations at the cabinet ministers' level, subministerial level, and lower official levels have been carried out. Since 1972, Beijing has been one of the first capitals a new Japanese prime minister would visit. Top leaders of the Chinese Communist Party and government have reciprocated by visiting Tokyo.

Beyond those official political relations, a unique Japan-China Twenty-First Century Commission was set up in 1984; composed of eleven intellectuals from all sectors of society on each side, it is supported by the two governments. The purpose of the commission is to present recommendations to both governments on medium- and long-range problems and policy alternatives relative to bilateral relations.

In the economic field, since 1973 China's leading trade partner in both exports and imports has been Japan, which has accounted for close to 25 percent of China's trade volume. China, incidentally, represents less than 5 percent of Japan's total trade. The volume of trade between the two countries has expanded from U.S. $1.1 billion in 1972 to U.S. $15.5 billion in 1986, a rate of increase far exceeding that of Japan's overall trade.

The economic cooperation that China receives from both government and private sources of Japan exceeds that from any other country. Since 1982 China has been the largest recipient of Japan's Official Development Assistance (ODA)—extended in the form of soft loans, grants, and technical assistance, on both a commitment and a disbursement basis, the volume of which amounted to about U.S. $500 million in 1986.

In the area of tourism, the 290,000 Japanese who visited China in 1985 represent the largest group of foreign visitors to that country in the last decade. That same year more Chinese, 100,000 of them, visited Japan than any nationals from any single country.

In the cultural field, Chinese study the Japanese language more than any other language except English. Many Japanese television programs have achieved high audience ratings in the Chinese national television network.

Japan's Cooperation with China

The start of the Deng Xiaoping era in 1978 coincided with the launching of Japan's official economic cooperation with China. In the Development Assistance Committee (DAC) of the Organization for Economic Cooperation and Development (OECD) Japan was the initiator in 1979 to include China in the group of "developing countries," entitled to the Official Development Assistance (ODA) from the Western industrialized nations. The Japanese government began extending her ODA to China the same year.

Nonmilitary Cooperation

Prime Minister Ohira's 1979 Beijing speech, quoted earlier, was made when the Japanese government began its ODA to China and it enumerated three basic principles of Japan's policy in its cooperative relations with China. The first principle is that Japan will not extend cooperation in the military field to any country, and China constitutes no exception. This policy is not so much a reflection of strategic considerations as it is a consequence of the renunciation of the right to wage war, as stipulated in the Japanese Constitution. Under the Constitution there are several self-imposed limitations that any Japanese government must observe. One of these is the policy that no arms may be exported; this includes the nontransfer of military technologies. Another limitation is the strict interpretation of the state's right of self-defense.

Incidentally, the military factor is the point on which Japanese cooperation with China differs from that of the United States. Japan simply does not have the so-called China card to play in her military strategic thinking, whereas the advisability and extent of military cooperation with China seems to be at the center of the "China card" debate in the United States. Since Defense Secretary Harold Brown's visit to China in 1980 and the visit to the United States by the Chinese

Vice Premier Geng Biao in the same year, the U.S. government has made it known that six kinds of military support equipment are exportable to China. A visit by a U.S. fleet to Qingdao in May 1987 further demonstrates the military side of the relations between China and the United States. In this context, I would like to point out that while Mr. Ohira said that Japan looked forward to "a more prosperous China," President Reagan went further by mentioning that "a strong China dedicated to peace is in the interest of international stability and in the best interest of the United States." This difference in emphasis seems to differentiate the approaches the two countries take in their relations with China.

Another difference between Japan and the United States in their approaches to relations with China lies in the different manners of presenting the Soviet Union as a determinant of rapprochement. As early as February 1972, when the Shanghai Communique was issued, both the United States and China pledged to oppose any efforts to establish hegemony in the Asia-Pacific region. Later pronouncements of friendship between the two countries always referred to "the presence of a (Soviet) military threat" as an underlining motivation of their closer relations. President Reagan's aforementioned remarks in 1984 also stated that "our cooperation is based on more than simply the desire to improve our economies. Today the peace of the world is threatened by a major power that is focusing its resources and energies not on economic progress but, instead, on military power."[4]

Japan also has consistently acknowledged its awareness of the increasing threat of military presence of the Soviet Union in the Pacific. But at the same time there has been a noticeable tendency on the part of the Japanese government, at least in its public pronouncements, to treat the Soviet military presence separately from the need for closer ties with China. This tendency led to the controversy over the "hegemony clause," which I will describe in detail later in this speech.

ASEAN

The second principle stated by Prime Minister Ohira is that "Japan's economic cooperation with China will not be made at the expense of Japan's cooperative relationships with other developing nations, especially the ASEAN nations." As is well known, Japan has long occupied a predominant position in the external economic relations of each of the six ASEAN countries. With a few exceptions, Japan has always been the largest importer of their products and the single largest supplier of goods to them. Further, about 30 percent of Japan's total ODA flows to the ASEAN countries; in fact, Indonesia had traditionally been the largest recipient of Japan's foreign aid before China replaced it in 1982. From the standpoint of each of the ASEAN recipient countries, Japan is the largest contributor of foreign assistance.

Therefore, when the news of Japan's launching of economic cooperation with

China was reported in the mass media there arose voices of concern in the ASEAN countries about possible negative impacts of this new relationship on the development of Japan-ASEAN cooperation. The prime minister's second principle was intended primarily to allay anxieties throughout the ASEAN region.

What effect could the modernization of the Chinese economy have on the ASEAN countries? If there were adverse effects, would it be justifiable to allege that Japanese cooperation with Chinese modernization efforts was responsible?

A study commissioned by the Japanese Foreign Ministry and conducted by a private research institute on this problem was made public in 1980.[5] This study points out that neither China nor the ASEAN countries are suppliers of indispensable goods to each other and, in terms of the economic relations between them, they could be termed as marginal trading partners to each other. The study concludes that although certain negative elements may be anticipated whereby Chinese-manufactured goods, such as textiles and home electric appliances, would compete with the local industries in the ASEAN market or where competition might arise between China and the ASEAN countries for capital inflows from the West, the positive elements, such as an increase of ASEAN exports of raw materials to China and the complementary development of industries among them on a horizontal division of labor, would more than offset the possible impact of such negative elements.

In a wider context, however, there is more than the economic aspect of the triangular relationship between Japan, China, and the ASEAN countries. Since the Vietnamese invasion of Cambodia in 1978, and through the period of continuing tension between the Indochinese countries and the ASEAN, especially between Vietnam and Thailand, the relations between China and the ASEAN countries have been considerably ameliorated. There are of course differences among the ASEAN countries in their attitudes toward China. Thailand, as a frontline state facing a direct Vietnamese military threat and suffering heavy economic and social burdens caused by the flood of refugees from Cambodia, stands closest to China in its attitude toward the Cambodian problem. Indonesia and, to a lesser extent, Malaysia maintain a reserved position toward China. The existence of the powerful Indonesian Communist Party (PKI), which nearly overtook the government of Indonesia in the mid-1960s, and its close links with China still haunt Indonesian people. Malaysia's rigid domestic policies as they relate to the Chinese community reflected its detached relations with China.

In general, however, relations between China and the ASEAN countries have been better in the nine years since the outbreak of the Cambodian problem than during any time since the birth of the People's Republic of China. A long-standing issue between them, and the thorniest one, the Chinese support of insurgent forces in the respective ASEAN country, appears to have receded to the background. Even in the Philippines, where the NPA (New People's Army) guerrilla activity poses the most serious threat to the political life of the Aquino government, no reference has ever been made as to their links with China, and the governments of China and the Philippines have maintained cordial and friendly relations.

When the rapprochement between Japan and China was achieved in 1972 some concern was expressed in the ASEAN countries about the possible danger of a condominium of the two countries over the whole of Asia. It was no doubt to allay this concern as well that Prime Minister Ohira emphasized that Japan's economic cooperation with China would not be made at the expense of its relations with the ASEAN countries. In more recent years, however, the voice of concern over such a condominium appears to have faded away.

The Nonexclusive Nature of Sino-Japanese Relations

As the third principle of Japan's cooperation policy toward China, Prime Minister Ohira pointed out that "the relationship between Japan and China is not an exclusive one." This principle was presented obviously to dispel anxiety and suspicion in some quarters of the world that Japan's active economic cooperation and enormous volume of trade with China would lead to its monopolization of the Chinese market. Prime Minister Ohira asserted that this anxiety is unfounded and that the Chinese side would neither wish nor accept such a tendency.

This principle seems also to have been aimed at refuting the possibility of Japan's adopting a "Gaullist" policy of keeping its distance from the United States while seeking closer ties with China. Ever since the Meiji Restoration Japan has struggled with the opposing pulls of East and West, and at the turn of the century there were some who advocated stronger ties with China and Korea to create a grand federation. Foreign observers have pointed out that whereas political rapprochement between Japan and the USSR is inconceivable, that between Japan and China is a possibility under certain circumstances.[6]

At least from the Japanese viewpoint, however, adoption of a "Gaullist" policy in that sense is a remote possibility. Politically the Sino-Japanese rapprochement was made possible only after the Sino-U.S. rapprochement was achieved, thereby ensuring the compatibility of the U.S.-Japan Security Treaty and Japan's friendly relations with China. With respect to economic relations, it is evident that China would offer Japan no effective substitute for the highly developed markets of the United States and Western Europe.

As was made clear in the Joint Statement of 1972, normalization of relations between Japan and China was based on the understanding that "in spite of the differences in their social systems existing between the two countries, the two countries should, and can, establish relations of peace and friendship."

I am inclined to interpret the third, or "nonexclusive," principle enunciated by Mr. Ohira as an assurance by the Japanese government that it had no intention to try to monopolize China economically, nor to try to play a political game of "Gaullist" diplomacy.

Tension and Relaxation

No one could object to the assertion that the past fiften years has witnessed an impressive expansion and deepening of Sino-Japanese relations. If, however, one were to ask whether the trend has been a straight upward one, the answer would be a definite no. Bilateral relations between Japan and China since normalization have been through ups and downs both in their spirit and substance. Looking back over the past fifteen years I can count five occasions of tension. We are now faced with a sixth one. The first showdown came in 1974, one-and-a-half years after normalization, in the form of aviation talks, in which Japan was forced to choose either the opening of a new air route to Beijing or the maintenance of air links with Taipei. The crisis was overcome by the declaration of the government of Japan that it does not recognize the flag of Taiwan as the national flag of any nation, thereby forcing Taiwan to cut its air links with Japan.

The second tension occurred half a year later in 1975 on the controversial issue on "hegemony" in the negotiations for the Peace and Friendship Treaty I alluded to earlier. The Japanese government at that time did not want to invite unnecessary animosity from the Soviet Union by including in the negotiated draft treaty an article stipulating the opposition of both parties to any act of "hegemony," (implying that of the Soviet Union). China, on the contrary, took the position that without the inclusion of the antihegemony clause the conclusion of the treaty was "meaningless." The controversy continued for almost three years; only after Deng Xiaoping's second rehabilitation, followed by the relaxation of tensions between China and the Soviet Union, was the treaty agreed on with the inclusion of the clause in question, together with another clause negating the antagonistic nature of the former clause. The treaty was ratified by both countries in October 1978.

The third crisis occurred in 1981, in connection with the across-the-board cancellation by China of the bulk of business contracts with industrialized countries; the hardest hit among them was Japan. The cancellation was prompted by the shortage of local funds on the part of China resulting from the drastic increase of importation of equipment and machinery. The problem was settled by the agreement between the two governments that substantial portions of the needed local funds be covered by Japanese loans.

The fourth crisis, which involved the wording in school history textbooks screened by the Japanese Ministry of Education, began in the spring of 1982. This incident was started by a Japanese newspaper report that an official guideline on screening school history textbooks allegedly brought about alterations in the description of the Sino-Japanese War and the annexation of Korea. The report was immediately carried in the press in both China and Korea, and prompted the lodgings of protests from the two governments.

The official visit by the Japanese prime minister to Yasukuni Shrine, where the war dead were enshrined, triggered violent student demonstrations in China in the autumn of 1985.

The latest and still continuing tension is over a ruling by a high court in Japan on the property right of a student dormitory located in Kyoto. The ruling accorded the property right to Taiwan, rejecting China's claim to the dormitory. The news of the ruling angered the Chinese and outbursts of protests have been voiced by Chinese leaders.

Therefore, we could say that Japan and China have been experiencing tension about once every two or three years. Friction is probably to some extent inevitable between neighboring countries, especially between such nations as Japan and China, with their recent history of severe belligerency.

Problems Between Japan and China

Here I would venture to categorize the various problems between Japan and China into four groups.

The first category of problems may be termed "the historical questions," meaning particularly the problems related to the Sino-Japanese War of 1931–45. These include the first school textbook controversy in 1982, the official visit by cabinet ministers to Yasukuni Shrine in 1985, the second school textbook incident in 1986, Education Minister Masayuki Fujio's article in a monthly journal on the modern history of Japan's relations with China and Korea, which resulted in his dismissal from his cabinet post, and the issue of Japan's 1987 defense budget which slightly exceeded 1 percent of the 1987 GNP.

The Japanese government, especially Prime Minister Nakasone, has consistently given serious considerations to all the problems in this category. The government expressed its deep regret over the history of Japan's colonization of Korea in its Joint Declaration with the Republic of Korea in 1965, and over the sufferings of the Chinese people from 1931 to 1945 in its Joint Statement with the People's Republic of China in 1972.

Strictly adhering to the letter and spirit of those two pronouncements, new guidelines have been set in the examination procedures for the authorization of the school textbooks. Going against strong public opinion, Prime Minister Nakasone refrained from visiting Yasukuni Shrine on the Termination-of-the-War Day, August 15, both in 1986 and 1987. The prime minister in the autumn of 1986 went so far as to dismiss Education Minister Fujio, one of the most powerful members of his own party, to demonstrate to the public his dissociation from Mr. Fujio's views on the role and conduct of the Japanese military in the Sino-Japanese War and on his judgment of the annexation of Korea in 1910. For Mr. Nakasone himself and for the majority of the Japanese, this historical question is not only of a political nature but of a moral and ethical one. We do understand the emotions underlying the student demonstrations in China protesting the Yasukuni Shrine visit in 1985.

Nevertheless, it is at the same time interesting to note that for some time after the normalization of relations in 1972, this historical question had been treated in a low-key manner by the Chinese authorities. At one point, as late as in 1980, a Chinese deputy chief of staff of the army publicly suggested to a visiting Japanese political figure (Mr. Nakasone, then a Diet member without governmental portfolio) the advisability of expanding Japan's defense budget to at least 2 percent of the GNP as a deterrent to the increasing Soviet military threat. China's public reference and warning to the need of heeding the lessons of recent history of Japanese militarism, after a ten-year silence since 1972, resumed around 1982.

This timing might be interpreted as a reflection of the latest swing of the pendulum of China's foreign policy. With the development of its policy of openness, there is undoubtedly a feeling that what it considers "the spiritual pollution of foreign cultures," especially among youngsters, must be combated. More than half its population of one billion are under the age of twenty, without any firsthand experience of the Second World War. Chinese leaders might have been feeling that their youngsters who covet cassette recorders and other consumer gadgets imported from Japan must be taught the history of the Sino-Japanese war and made to realize that the Japanese should not be their models.

The second category of problems relates to the Taiwan question. As early as 1973, Japan's position toward Taiwan became the greatest bone of contention between Beijing and Tokyo in their negotiations for an aviation agreement. There was a period from the mid-1970s to the early 1980s when Beijing's attitude to Taiwan showed some flexibility. In the past few years, however, the attitude of Beijing on the Taiwan question seems to have become more rigid.

Taiwan is now one of the most prospering areas not only in East Asia but in the entire developing world. It is quite understandable, therefore, for China's leaders to feel frustration at the economic prosperity and political stability of Taiwan, which shows no inclination toward any "unification with the fatherland" in the near future.

In the suspicious eyes of Beijing there is political and military support from the United States behind the prosperity of Taiwan. China also sees the strong economic support from Japan as another factor behind the successful economic performance of Taiwan. Japan's trade with Taiwan amounted to $12.5 billion in 1986, approaching the volume of that with China. Figures for the first seven months of 1987 show a more than 50 percent increase in both exports and imports over the same period in the previous year. Japanese investment in Taiwan has been expanding rapidly, especially with the sharply appreciating yen. Japanese investment in Taiwan amounted to $254 million last year, to the chagrin of the Chinese authorities who have long been complaining about the lack of enthusiasm of Japanese business for investing in China. In 1986, 697,000 Japanese visited Taiwan and 300,000 people from Taiwan visited Japan. These figures far exceed those between Japan and China.

These factors, demonstrating the expanding and deepening relations between Japan and Taiwan, have no doubt contributed to the Chinese leaders' increasing irritation toward Japan.

In the view of the Japanese, the Taiwan question remains an issue to be settled among the Chinese themselves. In the Joint Statement of 1972, the government of Japan recognized the government of the People's Republic of China as the sole and legal government of China, and also expressed its respect for Beijing's position on the status of Taiwan. Although we of course are to observe strictly the letter and spirit of this pledge, we are at the same time in no position, nor do we have any legal power, to go further than what we promised in 1972. Therefore, the Taiwan question will remain a "problem" between the two countries until the day a final settlement is reached. The intensity, however, with which "the Taiwan question" is taken up as an issue between Japan and China would depend to a large degree on the general political climate between the two countries and perhaps also on the domestic political situation in China.

As a footnote to the Taiwan question, it should be noted that the emotional content that is often evident in China's attitude on the Taiwan question is attributable to the elderly generation of leaders who now govern China. For them, Taiwan is not an island inhabited by twenty million people, but rather the surviving (and prospering) archenemy, namely, the Nationalist Government and Army with which they had fought a life-and- death struggle for half a century. This emotional content does not seem to be shared by Chinese of the younger generation. Japan looks forward to the day when affairs with Taiwan can be discussed and treated in a more businesslike manner with its Chinese counterpart.

The third category of problems affecting Sino-Japanese relations is an economic one; it may be seen as another case of relations between an industrialized and aid-donor country and a developing and aid-recipient country. The continuing trade deficit, aggravated by the declining prices of primary commodities, including oil, has constantly been a topic of bilateral talks between the two countries. Dissatisfaction over the "insufficient" volume of investment and of Official Development Assistance has been voiced frequently by the Chinese policymakers. As long as those economic dissatisfactions remain, the two countries should jointly identify the problems and work to find solutions. In relations with China, however, the dissatisfaction over economic and trade problems are often presented consciously or unconsciously in the context of political or historical relations. Recent remarks made by Chinese leaders that China's renunciation of war reparations justifies their demands of expanded investment and ODA from Japan are examples of this attitude.

China has been the largest recipient of Japan's ODA loans since 1985, and one of the largest recipients of grant financial aid and technical cooperation. The capacity of China to absorb all forms of economic aid appears to be limitless. Because Japan's ODA is focused mainly on infrastructure construction, there are always numerous economically feasible projects in China. The only constraints are the donor's financial capability and the political need to keep appropriate balance with other recipient countries. It should be noted that China is the most efficient utilizer of ODA and other funds. Therefore, when the same amounts of funds are committed to China and other recipients, China is by far the speedier user on the basis of disbursement.

In the area of investment, the Japanese business world ranks China behind the newly industrializing countries (NICs) in Asia and most of the ASEAN countries in its evaluation of investment climate. Japan is the third largest investor in China, after the United States and Hong Kong. Chinese authorities have complained about the "lack of courage" or "timidity" on the part of Japanese business. Under the drastic appreciation of the yen, the amount of investment directed to China has shown a substantial increase during the past two years. But the figure is not as conspicuous as those of Asian NICs or Thailand (where the 1986 figure was ten times that of the previous year). China is clearly competing with other Asian countries for attracting Japanese investment.

The fourth set of problems involves the Soviet factor. In the several years following the establishment of diplomatic relations the Soviet factor played a predominant role in all the political contact between Japan and China. This consideration has in fact come to prevail over all of China's foreign relations. As I have mentioned, the first major political talks between the two countries, the negotiation of the Treaty of Peace and Friendship in 1975, were stalled because of China's insistence on the need of taking the strongest possible stand opposing Soviet "hegemonism."

With the development of modernization and open economic policy under Deng Xiaoping, however, Chinese animosity toward the USSR has diminished considerably. Professor Tatsumi Okabe of the Tokyo Metropolitan University traces this change in attitude to 1981 and 1982.[7] Up until the end of 1981, the Chinese were officially critical of the antinuclear movement in Western Europe, stating that it would only benefit Soviet military and political strategy toward Europe. In June 1982, however, Mr. Huang Hua stated in his speech in the United Nations Disarmament Conference that China shared the sentiment of, and supported, the antinuclear movement in the Western European countries.

In any case, the impact of the Soviet factor on China's relations with Japan and other Asian countries has substantially decreased in recent years.

Images of Each Other

With all the political and economic complications in the relations between China and Japan, what is the image of Japan and the Japanese held by the Chinese public? In the absence of public opinion polls, published statistical material is not available to substantiate the generally accepted view that the Chinese dislike the Japanese. A Japanese press agency recently conducted a market research in China, mailing questionnaires to 120 employees of government agencies and institutions. The result of the survey showed that more than 80 percent of the respondents valued Japanese products, because of their high quality, but only 18 percent felt friendly toward Japan versus 53 percent who had no friendly feelings toward Japan. (Incidentally, of the responses to questions on their preferences between American and Japanese cultures, 29 percent of the respondents chose Japanese culture versus 40 percent who chose the American culture.) From my personal experience of living in China and maintaining contacts with the Chinese people, the above-cited figures seem to reflect an attitude widely shared by the Chinese public.

This sense of dislike or lack of affection for Japan on the part of the Chinese people is in sharp contrast to the Japanese feelings toward China and the Chinese people. In any public opinion poll conducted in Japan, China is consistently the second most-liked country, after the United States. A British observer describes this phenomenon as "another classic case of unrequited love for Japan's collection."[8].

Taking this situation into account, the single item that occupies the highest priority in Japan's overall policy toward China is the promotion of exchanges of students and young trainees of the two countries. It is recalled that at the turn of the century as many as twenty thousand Chinese students were studying in Japan; their understanding of Japan and the Japanese people played a mitigating role at a time when the relations between the two countries were at their lowest ebb. The late Premier Zhou Enlai and the late Vice President of the National People's Congress Liao Chengzhi are just two examples of the many Chinese who had lived and studied in Japan.

Conclusion

I have reviewed China's relations with her Asian neighbors, especially Japan, in the years under Deng Xiaoping's leadership. Some of the factors influencing China's foreign policy toward Japan may be applicable to other Asian neighbors. I cannot but feel, however, that Japan occupies a peculiar status in China's relations with her Asian neighbors. China has experienced hostilities with India, Vietnam, and Korea, but they were not of the same magnitude as that with Japan. From China's standpoint, economic relations between developing and developed nations exist between China and Japan.

It is not easy to summarize Japan's relations with China. Taking a macroscopic view of the forty-year history of the People's Republic of China, one might be overwhelmed by the sharp and violent swings of its foreign policy during those years. China started with a lean-to-one-side policy with the USSR from 1949 to 1959. It then embarked on an anti-U.S. and anti-Soviet policy in the 1960s. In 1971, with the visit by Dr. Kissinger to Beijing, it entered a period of pro-U.S. and anti-Soviet policy, which lasted until around 1981–82. The current policy of modernization and reform was established in the Third Plenary

Session of the Eleventh Central Committee in December 1978. According to an official statement, it seems that, after a lag of a few years, China's foreign policy has begun to reflect a new orientation based on its domestic policy.

The current foreign policy of the Chinese government could be described as "multidimensional diplomacy" as Professor Okabe termed it, or "equidistance foreign policy." [9] The Chinese government calls it "independent foreign policy." Its substance is a realistic policy based on an objective calculation of national interests free of ideological considerations. China tries to use all the available "cards" in her dealings with foreign governments. We the Asian neighbors have started to face tougher negotiations with China than before.

We are inclined, however, to welcome this new trend on various counts:

First, because policy formulation appears to be more objective, the direction of that policy should be more predictable. Predictability is the single most important condition for the maintenance of peace and stability in international relations.

Second, foreign policy based on a realistic calculation of national interests allows for compromise. In the mid-1970s, during the final days of Chairman Mao, anti-Sovietism was not negotiatable. Now this stance is far less evident in China's conduct of foreign relations.

Third, departure from ideology-determined diplomacy leads to normalcy in the conduct of diplomatic relations. Because of the long absence of diplomatic relations between China and Japan until 1972, the handling of trade, fisheries, repatriation of respective nationals, and many other exchanges between the two countries had been carried out through various nongovernmental channels. The people at the Chinese end of the channels are in any case either members of the government or of the Communist party. Therefore, even after the establishment of diplomatic relations most of them have continued their functions, unaffected by the new situation. This was not the case with the people at the Japanese end of the channels. Most of the people have settled down in their respective occupations in trade, journalism, academic institutions, or politics. Some of them, however, still remain as the "friendly people" or sympathizers of China. Whenever a friction occurs between China and Japan, these "friendly people" start their activity in defense of the Chinese position, sometimes more vigorously than the Chinese themselves, and to the annoyance of all parties concerned. Similar groups of people exist in our relations with the Soviet Union and North Korea. The activities of these "friendly people" has proven to be of great disservice to the promotion of genuine friendly relations between the nations by causing ill feelings in the general public. From this viewpoint, the current attitude of the Chinese government to place stronger emphasis on normal governmental channels is welcome as a sign of returning to normalcy in the conduct of foreign relations.

In concluding, I would like to emphasize and repeat the thesis I put forward at the outset: By encouraging the successful implementation of China's reform policy the neighboring Asians have the most to gain through the realization of a more stable and prosperous China, which, in turn, can contribute to the peace and stability of Asia and the world.

Notes

1. Address by Prime Minister M. Ohira at the Great Hall of the Chinese People's Political Consultative Council in Beijing on December 7, 1979.

2. Address by Prime Minister Y. Nakasone at Beijing University on March 24, 1984, "Looking toward the Twenty-First Century."

3. Remarks by President Reagan at the welcoming banquet in the Great Hall of the People, Beijing, April 27, 1984.

4. Ibid.

5. *Modernization of the Chinese Economy and Its Impact on the ASEAN Countries* (in Japanese) (Nomura Research Institute, May 1980).

6. Dick Wilson, *The Sun at Noon: An Anatomy of Modern Japan* (London: H. Hamilton, 1986); Robert Christopher, *The Japanese Mind* (New York: Simon & Schuster, 1983).

7. Tatsumi Okabe, "China's Asian Policy: Chance or Challenge?" *Japan Review of International Affairs* (Spring–Summer 1987).

8. Wilson, *The Sun at Noon.*

9. Tatsumi Okabe, "Recent Trends in China's Foreign Relations" (in Japanese). *Asia Monthly* (August 1987).

Comments by Donald S. Zagoria

Fujita-san is one of those most gifted in the Gaimusho who are playing a critical role in guiding Japan's foreign policy, including relations with China, from whom I have learned. There is little I can add to Fujita's account of the evolution of the policy. Scholars should invite diplomats to conferences more frequently.

To provoke discussion and set a framework, I will comment on the strategic environment. Fujita alludes to this framework when he speaks of the Soviet factor euphemistically. Strategic consideration, however, is not central to his analysis, perhaps because he is a diplomat. As an academic, I am not so restrained. The relationship between any of the four great Pacific powers cannot be analyzed properly without putting the security issues up front.

Prior to the important watershed years of 1978–79, there was an effort on the part of Japan to maintain an equidistance between the Soviet Union and China; Japan was reluctant for three years to sign a peace treaty with China that included the antihegemony clause. Similarly, when the Carter administration came to power in 1976, the secretary of state was determined to pursue an even-handed policy between the Soviet Union and China. By 1978–79, however, Secretary Vance was losing out to Brzezinski, who wanted to tilt toward China. Why? Here we must introduce the Soviet factor. It was, I would suggest, Soviet intervention in Ethiopia, the Soviet support of the Vietnamese invasion of Kampuchea, the Soviet invasion of Afghanistan, along with Soviet development of the SS20 in Siberia and the Soviet decision to militarize the disputed northern territories of Japan, along with unprecedented nuclear build-up, that ultimately drove Japan, China, and the United States closer together in the late 1970s and early 1980s.

The key element was Moscow's determination to alter the strategic balance to its advantage and to use Soviet power for that purpose. Japan reacted to this Soviet military expansion by signing a treaty with China, by staking out economic sanction against the Soviet Union after Afghanistan, by stepping up its own military cooperation with the United States, and by increasing its own military budget. China reacted by calling a united front with the United States against Soviet hegemonism. The United States reacted with a six to seven year-long military build-up, the longest in American postwar history, including the addition of several carrier forces to the Seventh Fleet in the Pacific. I would suggest that Japan's tilt toward China and America's tilt toward China, like China's tilt toward the West in the late 1970s and early 1980s, cannot be separated from the strategic environment in which all three powers felt threatened by the Soviets.

In addition to the Soviet factor, another factor that explains the tie between the three countries was the death of Mao Zedong. As a result of Deng Xiaoping's effort to introduce the market to China's economy and to open the door of China's economy to the outside, there has been a gigantic leap in China's trading and economic relations with the entire Western world. Nicholas Lardy, a participant of this conference, has pointed out that China's foreign trade has grown from fifteen billion to seventy billion in the space of a few short years. A considerable part of that trade is with the United States and Japan. So the two basic factors that in combination explain to me a good deal of the new Sino-Japanese and Sino-U.S. relations are, first, the Soviet factor, and, second, China's opening to the West.

If this analysis is correct, two questions arise. The first is the basic strategic situation. Is China's open-door policy likely to change? I leave it to the eminent China specialists of this conference to answer this question. I am confident, however, that the great majority here would predict continuity rather than dramatic changes in China's open-door policy. China simply does not have a realistic alternative if it wants to reach the level of a modern industrial power by the middle of the next century. Autarky is simply not an answer in the modern world.

On the question of whether the basic strategic situation is changing, first, since 1982, China has stopped calling for a united front in anti-Soviet hegemony. It has stopped using the term Soviet hegemony. It has stepped up economic and cultural relations with the Soviet Union, and it has pursued a more balanced relationship with both superpowers. As a weaker party in the triangle involving the Soviet Union and the United States, China is pursuing exactly the policy that Hans Morgenthau would have predicted. China indeed has played its card so skillfully that both superpowers are optimistic about their relations with China. Both are supplying it with technology and trading with it. Neither is so concerned any longer about the alliance of China with its superpower rival. This new triangle of balance has introduced a new stability and new realism into power relations in the Pacific.

The second important change concerns Soviet policy. Mr. Gorbachev is clearly concentrating his energy in correcting the deficiency of the technologically stagnant Soviet economy. To do this he needs a prolonged period of breathing space with the United States and Japan, as well as with China. For this reason, the Soviet Union is trying to improve relations with China and Japan, to reach a new arms agreement with the United States, and to join a variety of international economic organizations. Gorbachev has also come to the realization of some of the limits of military power.

The third strategic situation may be in the making. After the melt-down of the stock market, the United States may also be entering into a period perhaps like that of the Soviet Union and China. We need to keep our own house in order or face continuing decline as a great power. I would suggest that the present pattern of power relations among the powers in the Pacific is unprecedented in history and, for the first time, hopeful. For the first time there is no odd man out. Over breakfast this morning, Mr. Fujita told me that in the 1930s and 1940s, it was Japan who was the odd man out. We all know the disastrous consequences of that. In the 1950s, it was the United States that faced a Sino-Soviet alliance. This led to a cold war and indeed several hot wars involving China. And in the 1960s, China was the odd man out. It developed a case of paranoia. In this period the USSR and China fought along their borders, and China and the United States confronted each other in Vietnam. In the early 1980s, the Soviet Union was the odd man out as China and Japan moved toward a united front to check Soviet military expansion.

In the period we are now entering we are seeing small, fragile, but encouraging signs of great power accommodation. The USSR and China have entered into a period of détente, which is likely to continue. China and the United States, and China and Japan, have developed a flourishing cultural and political relationship. This is likely to continue. The Soviet Union and the United States are about to sign an agreement eliminating a whole class of nuclear weapons, setting the stage for a subsequent agreement, to reduce by half long-range nuclear weapons. I hope I am not being overly optimistic in suggesting that this new major-power accommodation is likely to produce a more stable equilibrium among what some would call a Pacific quadrille. The U.S.-Japan Pacific alliance, though fraying at the edges over economic difficulties, will remain. China will continue to balance between the superpowers; relations with the Soviet Union will improve, but there is no return to the Sino-Soviet alliance of the 1950s. Such a strategic environment will provide the framework for a new equilibrium that will give all four powers flexibility and maneuverability within well- defined parameters.

As polarization declines, flexibility will increase for all the powers. It is already interesting to notice some movement in U.S. relations with India as Sino-Soviet relations improve. Of course it would be unwise and naive to expect too much from these developments. There is no end to great-power rivalries, to mutual suspicion, to conflicts of interests, or even to arms races. The U.S.-Soviet rivalry will remain the center of international rivalry in the Pacific. Millenium is not yet at hand. But we could be entering into a period when all the great powers in the Pacific have a common interest in reducing tension and in finding new rules of the game in managing their competition peacefully within basically this stable four-power equilibrium.

The one potential wild card could be Japan. Already Japan has the sixth largest military budget in the world and, within a few years, the fourth largest. That is why in China, in the Soviet Union, and increasingly, in the United States, the future role of Japan is being questioned. I personally believe that the resurgence of Japanese militarism is greatly exaggerated so long as Japan remains allied with the United States. Only an insecure Japan, threatened by the great powers and cut loose from the United States, will be a real danger to the power equilibrium in the region. That is why it is in the interest of all members of the Pacific quadrille for Japan to remain allied to the United States. I note with interest that China no longer criticizes the U.S.-Japan alliance, and I await the Soviet Union to adopt the same wise policy.

Let me pose two questions to Mr. Fujita: (1) What kind of China would be in Japan's interest in a decade or more? What would be the worst kind of China for Japan then? I would like to hear his assessment of the recently concluded Chinese Party Congress and its implications for Sino-Japanese relations. (2) What are Japan's realistic strategic options in the years ahead, regarding not only China, but the United States and the Soviet Union as well? One of the leading Japanese strategists, Okazaki, has recently published a book on which he argued that over the past 150 years, given the power realities of the Pacific, Japan's basic choice has been an Anglo option and a Slave option. Japan went off the track when it quit the Anglo-Japanese Alliance of the 1920s, and it got back on the right track by establishing an alliance with the United States in the 1950s.

Fujita told me that this view is widely accepted in the Japanese establishment, even though from time to time, as he has said in his speech, some Japanese and foreign observers may think Japan has a Chinese or a Gaullist option. I would ask him whether there are any circumstances he can foresee that might be tempting Japan to abandon this Western option, or any circumstances in which there might be a realistic alternative for Japan.

15

REFORMS IN THE
PEOPLE'S REPUBLIC OF CHINA:
A Russian Perspective

Yevgeniy V. Afanasyev*

LET ME briefly discuss what the distinguished economist Professor E. A. Konovalov would like to say here. His topic is "Reform in the price-making system in the People's Republic of China," one of the key elements in the reform. The resolution of the Central Committee of the Chinese Communist Party (CCP) in 1984 on the reform of the economic system stated that the reform of the price system was the key. For a long time the price-making system in the People's Republic of China (PRC) favored subjective administrative decisions; on the whole, commodity prices did not reflect the costs of production. Transformation of the price system was made urgent by great deficiencies. As I studied the professor's paper I noticed many similarities with what Ambassador Li had said today. Until 1978, for almost thirty years, the PRC was dominated basically by a one-channel system of fixed state-established prices. This centrally fixed price system, without feedback, was considered an advantage of the planned economy.

Now that I have summarized Professor Konovalov's paper, let me present a

*In the program of the conference Professor E. A. Konovalov of the Institute of the Far East, USSR, was scheduled to give the talk. He had submitted a paper entitled "Reform of the Price-Making System in the PRC" for the conference, but was unable to leave Moscow to attend the conference on November 4. Mr. Y. Afanasyev was asked to take his place. Mr. Afanasyev, trained at the Moscow State Institute for International Relations, was posted in Beijing in 1970–75, and in Washington, D.C., in 1976–84. A member of the First Far Eastern Department and assistant to the Deputy Foreign Minister in charge of Asia from 1984–87, he has been Counselor in charge of Asian Affairs at the Embasssy of the USSR in Washington, D.C., since 1987.

few remarks of my own. First, I want to say that we in the Soviet Union pay a great deal of attention to what is going on inside China and to changes in China's domestic and foreign policy. This is because China is a great nation; without China's participation we cannot solve any great international issue or achieve lasting peace. It is also because China is our largest neighbor; our common border is more than 7,000 miles, the longest border in the world. So we will live forever side by side with China. For our interest and for the interest of China, despite our differences, we must find ways for better and stable relations, for accommodation, and for cooperation. Disagreements that have existed in some areas between the Soviet Union and China do not have long-term objective bases; they are the results of historical development, of some subjective steps made by the two sides, and they can be considered as some of the difficulties in the creation of new socialist forms in the world. In principle, socialist countries—both China and Russia are socialist—can and must have good friendly relations.

As you know, from 1979 China is carrying on a big economic reform; China is taking steps to develop her economy by using forms and methods of management related to the commodity-money relationship and the development of individual enterprises. This reform is a major component for the overhaul of Chinese society. At the same time, in the Soviet Union, we also have changes in our society: economic and political. We call them reconstruction (*perestroika*). We can see how *perestroika* is parallel to the Chinese reform. For example, in many areas we use the same principle and method; we use an economic method, not an administrative one: the rights of individual enterprises and the decrease and decentralization of planning. China is doing the same. The difficulties we have encountered are similar to what China has experienced. In some areas China is ahead of us, having started its reform earlier than we.

Certainly the levels of development are different. For example, we see that, despite the reform since 1979, there is still a problem of the central departments' interference in individual enterprises and there is no real independence at the lower levels of the economic mechanism. This reflects real Chinese conditions: Chinese socialism with specific Chinese characteristics. Economically, we see in China such specific conditions: a work force with low technical skills and the development of private individual enterprises necessitated by the enormous task of feeding and housing a billion people. The government of China may be credited with many successes; however, differences between different branches of industries and regions are acute, and there is deficiency of arable land. Ambassador Li mentioned that China has 7 percent of the world's arable land but is feeding more than 20 percent of the world's population. All these dictate specific approaches of China toward reforms of its economic and political systems. These reforms do not touch the substance of Chinese society; the main goal of China is to turn the country as quickly as possible into a modern, powerful country. We think, in China, solving the question of continuity in pursuit of this line is a prerequisite to achieving the goals. At the same time there are difficulties that hamper this development.

In general, changes in China toward more realistic domestic and foreign policies started in the 1970s. We understand that the last Party Congress undertook to eliminate the party's role in the economic sphere and to concentrate its active role in policy decisions, as well as in raising the skills of the cadres. All these reforms are necessary for China. We see many things in China that we can study. But China has also profited from the experience of the Soviet Union and other socialist countries. Basically, despite differences, socialist countries have similarities.

We have seen some changes in China's foreign policy and we think that the basis of these changes to a large degree lies in changes inside China. Because building socialism requires peace, China needs better relations with the outside world. This does not mean that China will be developing relationships only with Western countries, but with the Soviet Union and other socialist countries as well. Zhao Ziyang, General Secretary of the CCP Central Committee, stated clearly that to achieve social modernization, China should pursue a policy of peace and independence, and strive for a peaceful international situation for a long period of time. This is a very important statement of China's foreign policy.

We do not close our eyes to the problems we have with China; we have problems. Despite this, we feel that we and China see many things in this world in the same way. We try to overcome these difficulties and in doing so, we do not want to harm in any way China's relationship with other major powers, with the United States or Japan, or others. This relationship is dictated by the interests of China. We in the Soviet Union fully respect the independent Chinese policy, and we fully understand the striving of China to have better relationships with other countries. We would like to see China as a prosperous country having an active input to the preservation of peace in the world and to the development of international cooperation. In the future, the Soviet Union and China may differ in views on international issues; the important thing is to learn how to discuss and solve the problems in a spirit of mutual respect and cooperation.

In general, we are optimistic about our relationship with China. The optimism results from our analyses of China's internal and external development. In the future, of course, China's relationship with the West will undergo development, but we hope there will also be development in China's relationship with the Soviet Union. This will benefit not only the Soviet Union and China, but also the entire region.

Comments by Lucian W. Pye

The diplomat has to step in to pinch-hit for the scholar who is not here, but whose paper is here. Let me say that it is important to take seriously the views about China of Soviet scholars and Soviet government officials. In the past we tended to assume that these were statements of propaganda and could therefore be dismissed. The truth is, since 1949, Soviet views of Chinese developments are probably more accurate than many views of some scholars in the West. Indeed, it might have been propaganda, but it was also the truth. There were times when the Soviets were talking about Mao's policies as being disastrous policies. They were pointing out the Great Leap Forward as being great foolishness. I regret to say there were Western scholars at the time whose analyses and interpretations of what was going on in China at times bordered on sophisticated idiocy. They elaborated views and rationalized views that even the Chinese themselves have rejected.

This raises an important question: How did we get so far off the mark? How did we miss out on the Great Leap? There was a disastrous famine taking place. We now know in retrospect how serious that was. How did we miss it? I have a colleague at Massachusetts Institute of Technology who was talking to a Harvard-trained PRC economist. He asked him, "How is it possible that you people were able to convince the world that so many good things were happening when so many bad things were happening?" This Harvard-trained man, who is now a very important person in Beijing, responded, "Yes, we do a little bit of that. But you must know there is something called cognitive dissonance. People who want to believe things believe them." That is interesting about Western interpretations. What is interesting is that the Soviets had no reason to have cognitive dissonance during this period, yet, indeed, even the Soviets were not telling us how bad things were at certain times in the Cultural Revolution and the like. What is holding them back?

I also think it is interesting when we compare notes with Soviet views and perspectives about developments in China. I happen to be one who thinks it is rather good that we do not share the same views. I expressed this view at a conference that Bob Scalapino organized about a year-and-a-half ago. After one of the Americans who had spoken quite enthusiastically about how it was desirable for Americans and Russians to arrive at common understandings and to share views and look at China in the same way, I suggested that maybe this was not the best thing to do. It turned out that both we and the Russians who heard the speech are convinced that we had the inside track to the Chinese; the Chinese really loved us better than the others. And this is a good thing, and each of us has gotten along better with the Chinese as a result. Americans are quite convinced, for example, that Moscow cannot get too close to Beijing, because, after all, there are the three obstacles: Afghanistan, Kampuchia, and the troops on the border. The Soviets, on the other hand, have their three Ts, maybe four Ts by now:

Taiwan, technology, textiles, and now, Tibet. They are convinced they have the inside track. May be it is better they see the world their way.

Actually, in terms of serious thrusts, it is important to listen carefully to how the Soviets view the PRC, not only because of questions of factual accuracy and the like in scholarly discussions, but also because this is a profound indicator of where thinking is going in terms of Marxism-Leninism and doctrinaire thinking. Let us not forget that most of the tensions that developed between the Russians and Chinese, between Moscow and Beijing, and between Khrushchev and Mao Zedong, revolved around the questions of interpretations of Marxism and Leninism, questions about stages of advancement toward communism. When Mao said that China was ahead of everyone else moving to the sacred land of communism, he of course provoked reactions in Moscow. The question is not one of the so-called monolithic control coming out of Moscow. Rather, the question should have been a perception of the world in world history, a perception that is developed authoritatively in events by the Soviets.

Today, it is significant that the Soviets have not reacted with shock and horror at the idea that the Chinese are advancing their socialism with Chinese characteristics. I think this is a major step in the transformation of Marxism and Leninism. In the past, historically, there was always a denial of cultural differences as being relevant and significant in the evolution of societies; there was always the assumption that there were certain universalistic qualities, stages, and dynamics that peasants, workers, and the bourgeoisie all shared in common universally. To accept the idea that there is indeed socialism with Chinese characteristics is to open up a whole new idea about the stages of evolution of communism. This raises questions about whether the Soviet Union is evolving a socialism with Russian characteristics or universalistic characteristics.

Of interest to me, listening to the papers tonight, is that, first, the scholar Professor Konovalov chose the topic that was most esoteric for most Americans who followed the newspapers. American newspapers have not been talking about the problems of price or price structure in all the reforms. Yet in some respects, the problem of price and price reform does get to the core, maybe the very vulnerable core. It is interesting that the Soviet scholar, in writing about price reform, treated this entirely in terms of supply and demand and the market. We in the West have been singing praises about the market and that the Chinese are moving toward the market. What has not been pointed out is that this is a market with some very false prices in it; they can lead to disastrous decisions, irrational allocation of resources, and the like. The Soviet analysis has pointed out that until the Chinese correct these prices, there will be serious problems. The Chinese do not seem to be going back to administrative controls. It is rather, as any classical liberal economists would say, one has got to be in to get one's price right. One must face the problem of inflation. The Chinese are nervous about a 20 percent inflation. How are they going to cope with this? Professor Konovalov also pointed out the problem of corruption. Interestingly, he does not play it up as much as the Chinese. What is the definition of corruption and what is maximizing profit?

Moving on to the diplomat and his remarks. I also find them significant and interesting. One has a feeling, as he speaks, that both Russia and China today are in the same boat, and therefore should be more harmonious. I am not sure that people in the same boat should necessarily be happy with each other. He does seem to suggest that the very fact that China is going through with reforms and that Gorbachev is going through with reforms somehow makes them have something in common and, therefore, Americans should step aside and analyze from afar. I think what he is saying is that what the Chinese are doing in a sense legitimizes what the Soviets are doing. He is ambivalent about who is ahead and who has gone further. He seems to suggest that in some ways the Soviets are ahead, in other ways the Chinese are ahead. It is interesting that he even raises the question as to who is ahead. I think it is significant that they are moving into the area where no one knows what is going to come out. There is still the tendency to put down the Chinese. The Chinese problem is big, bigger than ours. But at the same time there is also a legitimate sympathy.

I never understand the issue of the relationship of the party to the government and the separation of the two. Somehow, in the Soviet mind, there is the idea that if one separates the party and the government one achieves democracy, and if one mixes them, as Mao did, one destroys democracy. Both the Soviets and the Chinese today agree that the task is to separate somehow the party, the government, and the bureaucracy. I find this interesting, but I do not understand what this means in the end. There is the situation in which Zhao Ziyang is going to be the head of the party, not the government. There is the situation where much of the talent has been in the party. There is also the case of a lot of local control. It seems to me that without going back to central planning, the only way to get rid of inefficient industries and the like is to allow the party to play a role in this. I can see that a stronger party is positive, yet the Chinese speak of it as being a negative factor. It is also interesting that the Russians seem to agree with the Chinese on this.

Finally, with respect to foreign policy, I will be brief. Obviously we all welcome the idea that any foreign policy is in favor of peace. I think the Soviets are sincere in wanting better relations with Beijing, and I expect they are going to achieve this. I expect this is one of the issues that may cause a certain amount of tension within certain elements in the United States as improved relations between Moscow and Beijing are taking place. What I am puzzled about is how Mr. Afanasyev's speech would read in Hanoi if it were published there. How would they react in Hanoi? Actually, in terms of getting back to the three obstacles the Chinese have raised, I have a feeling they are in a sense synthetic issues. Regarding Afghanistan, why should China be more on the front? The scholars in the Beijing Institute of Strategic Studies raised this question. They asked also about Hanoi and Kampuchea. They said the Soviets must get out of Kampuchea. I said, if you want the Soviets out of Kampuchea, is the tactic you should follow not the same one you used when you invited Henry Kissinger and Richard Nixon to come to Beijing while we were still fighting against Hanoi? If you could improve your relations with Moscow, would you indeed damage Hanoi? I wonder if this is beginning to take place both from Beijing's point of view and Moscow's.

16

DENG'S REFORM MOVEMENT AND THE WEST:
An American Perspective

J. Stapleton Roy*

THE THEME of this conference, "A Decade of Reform under Deng Xiaoping," has, in a sense, also been the central theme of the just concluded Thirteenth Congress of the Chinese Communist Party. The issue of reform has been at the center of the major policy debates that erupted in China in the wake of the December 1986 student demonstrations and the subsequent fall of Party General Secretary Hu Yaobang. While the Party Congress has strongly reaffirmed China's commitment to go forward with its reform program, we can be certain that the internal debate over how far and how fast implementation of the policies should go will continue through the years ahead in one form or another. The boldness of the course on which Deng has set China is one of its most intriguing features. Franz Kafka's short story, "The Great Wall of China," contains a parable that speaks to the historical difficulties of change in China. It tells of a courier at the imperial palace who receives the emperor's dying instruction and sets forth in the full idealism and vigor of his youth to speed the word across the empire. But as he emerges from the inner chambers he finds himself enmeshed in the dense throng that has gathered in the garden and in the courtyard beyond. Though he strainsto free himself from the entanglements and to race forward on his mission, his progress is labored and slow.

Modern Chinese history has in many ways reflected Kafka's metaphorical

---

*Deputy Assistant Secretary of State in charge of East Asian and Pacific Affairs at the time of this conference, J. Stapleton Roy served in Beijing from 1978 to 1981, and was U.S. Ambassador to Singapore. He is now U.S. Ambassador to the People's Republic of China.

image. As far back as the mid-nineteenth century, successive generations of Chinese—the Taiping movement, the Self-Strengtheners, the late Qing constitutionalists, the Nationalists, the present communist government—have sought the key to modernizing the country. China's current reformers have roots going back at least a hundred years to the late nineteenth-century reform movement, guided by such figures as Kang Youwei and Liang Qichao, who were attracted to Western liberal ideas not for their uniquely Western celebration of democratic individualism and political freedoms but because they hoped to find in the experience of the West a road map for building up China's own wealth and power. This mind-set of the early reformers has much in common with Beijing's current drive to raise living standards and to enhance China's role in world affairs.

Each of these earlier efforts in turn discovered the harsh truth that conceptualizing change is easier than implementing it. Each eventually foundered, as did Kafka's messenger, on the enormous obstacles to change that China has presented: its massive population, entrenched bureaucracy, impoverished economic base, traditional family and social structures, and stubborn resistance to innovation and adoption of foreign political and economic forms. Throughout China's modern history, Chinese reformers have struggled to draw distinctions between modernization and Westernization, a struggle still seen in the antibourgeois liberalism campaign and in the insistence of China's leaders that they must have socialism with Chinese characteristics. Dissatisfaction over the introduction of objectionable foreign practices into the country has all too often provoked violent, nativistic responses.

Undeterred by these earlier examples, China has again embarked on an ambitious course of political and economic reform, which Deng Xiaoping has characterized as a "second revolution." It is tempting to quibble with this phrase, which has been adopted as the subtitle of this conference, and to question whether Deng's reforms can properly be counted as only the "second" of China's various revolutions. We are dealing, after all, with a country where the concept of "permanent revolution" or "unending revolution" was a subject of lively scholarly debate in the not so distant past. Nevertheless, however one chooses to periodize China's revolutionary process, the changes envisoned under these policies are certainly revolutionary in their implications.

The goals of this movement are none other than to restructure, reorient, and rejuvinate the political leadership, expand the economy, and remove social and political controls that stifle creativity and initiative. If carried through to conclusion, Deng's reform plans will see major alterations in the current economic system and in the role of the party, a dramatic rise in the standard and quality of living for the Chinese people, systemic revisions in the relationship between local and central authority, and a new conceptual framework for dealing with the outside world.

Success achieved in some sectors, such as agriculture, have already enhanced the authority of China's leaders. Nevertheless, difficulties remain in extending the reforms into the more complex urban industrial and marketing sectors. The prospect for further political reforms is also fraught with difficulties. Indeed, the reformers themselves would be the first to concede how great a distance lies between their conception and the final goal. The degree to which they are successful in moving toward this goal will have profound implications for China domestically and internationally, and for the rest of us as well.

It is to the international implications of reform that I have been asked to speak tonight. Specifically, I have been asked to provide an American perspective on how Deng's reform movement relates to the West. The particular American perspective I shall provide is not that of a scholar but of a government China specialist. As such, my remarks will focus on the relationship between the normalization of U.S.-China relations and China's turn toward the West, which has been an integral part of the reform movement.

I will leave it to the historians and political scientists here to establish the precise relationship between U.S.-PRC normalization and China's opening to the West. Clearly, both developments bore the personal stamp of Deng himself. In retrospect, it seems hardly coincidental that the successful conclusion of the secret negotiations that led up to the establishment of U.S.-PRC diplomatic relations coincided with the Third Plenum of the Eleventh Central Committee in 1978 at which Deng, who had just recently reemerged as the most powerful political figure in China, introduced his ideological and programmatic reforms. The rapid development of Sino-American relations that followed was no longer based simply on common strategic concerns, but rather on a shared perception of potential mutual benefits across a broad spectrum of economic, commercial, cultural, and political areas.

U.S. Attitudes Toward China's Reforms

The United States has welcomed China's reform policies for a variety of reasons. The first is our own self-interest. China's reform program and opening to the outside have meshed well with our own policy objectives, which have sought to develop a relationship with China that will encourage it to be a force for regional stability, to give priority to improving the well-being of its people, to see benefit in expanding ties with the industrialized democracies, and to pursue a foreign policy course independent of the Soviet Union. In turn, China's quest for rapid modernization has reinforced the rationale for developing closer relations with a technologically advanced country like the United States. This has brought benefits to both of us in areas such as trade, scientific and technical cooperation, and scholarly exchange.

Our favorable view of the reforms has also been influenced by the progress China has made over the last decade in the area of human rights. China's current leadership has launched a reform of the legal system, mitigated some of the harsher aspects of its "one child" policy, and relaxed restrictions in such areas as emigration, domestic travel, and the practice of religion. The United States has welcomed Chinese moves toward a more open society with increased economic and political liberalization, looser controls over enterprises and individuals, and greater exposure to the outside world and foreign ideas.

In addititon, Americans have responded positively to the spirit of pragmatism that has marked China's current effort to speed up the development process. One manifestation of this spirit can be seen in the effort to elaborate such concepts as the "initial stage of socialism," which has been used to define more precisely the Dengist slogan of "building socialism with Chinese characteristics." By giving legitimacy to such concepts, China's leaders have loosened ideological constraints on what techniques can be used, which models can be followed, and which ideas and systems may be imitated so that methods can be adopted on the basis of their applicability to China's needs, not ideological purity.

The Impact of the Reform Movement on U.S.-PRC Relations

These factors help to explain why China's reform program has played such an important role in facilitating the development of the mature and stable relationship that now exists between China and the United States. This does not mean that we always agree with each other, either on goals or methods. There will always be differences of opinion between countries with radically different political and economic systems. Rather, the pragmatism with which we both approach our relationship allows for constructive interaction in dealing with problem areas and in exchanging views on issues in a frank nonpolemical way, regardless of whether we agree or not.

Our leaders now exchange regular visits, our businessmen trade in a variety of commodities, and our bilateral scientific and technological exchanges are the largest we have with any country. Some nineteen thousand Chinese students now study in the United States, while roughly two hundred American institutions have established exchange programs with Chinese counterparts. Where a decade ago the United States did not have a single signed agreement with the PRC, we now have agreements in areas ranging from nuclear cooperation, taxes, and trade to culture and education.

These developments have far-reaching implications. The number of Chinese being trained in the United States has already surpassed the number trained in the Soviet Union in the entire decade of the 1950s; by 1990 it will surpass the number trained in the West between 1840 and 1949. Some have already returned and been promoted to high offices. Reflecting the current friendly but nonallied status of U.S.-China relations, we have also moved cautiously and deliberately to develop military cooperation in selected areas, as symbolized by the visit in the fall of 1986 of U.S. navy ships to Qingdao for the first time in nearly forty years.

On the economic front, China's opening of the door to Western trade and investment has resulted in an enormous expansion in our bilateral economic relations, with significant benefits for the United States. If China remains committed to the path of reform, we foresee substantial opportunities for expansion of U.S. trade to China during the next few years, especially with respect to industrial modernization and major infrastructure projects in the energy and transportation sectors. We have sought to encourage development of U.S. exports through a variety of means, such as increased investment, liberalized technology transfer consistent with national security interests, and assistance from the Trade Development Program and the Overseas Private Investment Corporation.

The Foreign Policy of the PRC

In the realm of foreign policy, the United States and China have both derived enormous benefit from the convergence in their approaches to key international problems. On many Asian issues, where the interplay between our respective interests has the greatest policy relevance, our views are similar and we are working in parallel. We each want to reduce tensions in the Korean peninsula. We both believe that the conflicts in Cambodia and Afghanistan should be resolved through the withdrawal of foreign occupying forces.

We naturally have differences with the PRC on a variety of international issues, especially in areas such as Africa, the Middle East, and Central America, which are more remote from China's vital interests. In these regions, China often takes a more critical view of our policies and has been prone to adopt Third World rhetoric at odds with our approach. This provides a useful reminder that China's "opening to the outside" is not synonymous with the opening to the West. Our relationship with China is not based on some mystical affinity for each other that somehow transcends other considerations. On the contrary, our relationship has matured and stabilized because both sides have recognized that we can each advance our national interests more effectively through friendshp and cooperation than through confrontation and hostility.

This healthy pragmatism has enabled us to weather perceived shifts in attitude on the other side and to prevent minor irritants from hobbling the relationship. For example, the enthusiastic development of Sino-U.S. relations during the period immediately following the establishment of U.S.-PRC diplomatic relations in 1979 was followed by a period of adjustment on both sides. The PRC reoriented its foreign policy in 1981–82 toward a more "independent" stance and reverted toward a view of the world that in some respects reflected prenormalization attitudes characteristic of the mid-1970s.

The lesson is clear that neither side is comfortable in too close an embrace between the world's leading capitalist power and a country whose leaders are determined to keep adherence to the socialist road and leadership of the Communist party among its cardinal principles. At the same time, it is a sign of growing mutual confidence that both Washington and Beijing are now less concerned than before at being manipulated by the other within the great power triangle. This is because both of us are coldly realistic in our assessment of Soviet policies. Each judges Moscow by its actions rather than its words, and each is interested in exploring possibilities for relaxing tensions if Soviet policies change. This is a sign of the degree to which we have moved beyond the narrow focus on the Soviet threat that first brought us together fifteen years ago.

The question of Taiwan, of course, remains an issue that requires our attention. Chinese officials continue to refer to the Taiwan problem as a cloud that hangs over our bilateral relations. And they remain concerned over our arms sales to Taiwan. For our part, we recognize that this cloud is not likely to vanish until there is a peaceful resolution of the Taiwan question. In the meantime, the United States remains firmly committed to a "one-China" policy and will continue to adhere to the mutually acceptable framework we have established with the PRC for dealing with this problem in the form of the three communiques that define the principles on which we base our relations. Firm commitment to these principles will enable both sides to deal with differences as they arise. While this is a problem to which the Chinese themselves must find a solution, the success of China's reform program is not irrelevant to this process since reducing the tremendous disparities between living conditions in Taiwan and on the mainland could affect attitudes on both sides.

Deng Xiaoping—The Man and the Model

To a significant degree, the flexible, nonideological spirit that has enabled China's current leaders to experiment with new systems and ideas draws its inspiration from the character of Deng himself, especially from his celebrated pragmatism. Ideologues made him pay dearly for this characteristic during the Cultural Revolution, when he was accused of caring less about the color of a cat than its ability to catch mice. Ten years later, during the last hurrah of the Gang of Four, they launched a nationwide campaign to discredit him as an out-and-out "capitalist roader" because of his disdain for the ideological economics that had marked the Cultural Revolution years.

Deng himself has never been ashamed of his pragmatism. On the contrary, for a number of years he has been fond of telling visitors that he is a reformer if this means that he supports China's reform program, and that he is a conservative if this means that he believes China must adhere faithfully to the "four cardinal principles," but that in reality he is a person who "seeks truth from facts." It is this quality of tactical flexibility combined with underlying convictions that is Deng's most distinguishing characteristic—one that has enabled him to motivate and give direction to China's reform program.

Despite his role in launching China on the path of reform, Deng shares certain viewpoints with conservative party elders. Like them, he believes strongly that

China cannot tolerate challenges to the two "cardinal principles" that he considers most relevant to China's current circumstances, i.e., the leadership of the Communist party and adherence to the socialist road. Nor has he had compunctions in supporting crackdowns on intellectuals who have gone too far in expressing doubts about the ultimate realization of communism, or who, like Bai Hua, have harshly criticized sacred cows such as the People's Liberation Army.

Moreover, to a degree that sets him apart both from other Long March veterans and from many Chinese intellectuals, Deng has always adhered to the view that balance must be maintained between initiative and experimentation on the one hand, and discipline and order on the other. As a result, he has displayed impatience with intellectuals who have succumbed to skepticism because of the party's many errors or yielded to the attraction of Western social and philosophical ideas. To him, such persons lack practical knowledge of the requirements for running a massive country like China. Whether or not Deng was in total agreement with the conservative campaign against "bourgeois liberalism," he undoubtedly saw merit in using the campaign to keep his modernization program from being transformed by overzealous reformers into a thinly disguised form of "total Westernization."

While he has skillfully used outpourings of popular sentiment for his own purposes, as during the Democracy Wall period in 1978, Deng has never considered Western-style democracy suitable for China. Although he has called for greater democratization as part of political reform, in essence this has meant broadening inputs into party decisions at lower levels as a means of revitalizing the party and loosening the dead hand of cautious and unimaginative bureaucrats.

Deng's Reform Program

As we near the end of the first decade of reform under Deng Xioaping, it is too early to provide a definitive assessment. Overall, the authors of China's reform programs can boast a remarkable record of achievement. Moreover, Deng's success at the Thirteenth Party Congress in rejuvenating China's leadership, in providing an ideological justification for the reform program, and in confirming the main direction of the country's policies, represents a historic accomplishment.

In looking to the future, however, China's reformers face daunting obstacles. These constraints are by no means unique to China, but they represent a formidable challenge for China's new leaders as they seek to instill the efficiency and dynamism needed to modernize a nation of a billion people with a per capita income of roughly $300. These constraints include, first, the difficulty of energizing China's lethargic and ponderous bureaucracy, a problem that has stymied many an administration in Washington on a much smaller scale; second, constantly shifting economic policies, as leaders argue about and experiment with methods of arriving at the proper balance between administrative controls and market forces, centralization and decentralization, military and civilian expenditures, and investment in heavy industry, light industry, and agriculture; third, continuing pressures to limit contacts with foreigners and the influx of foreign influences, to make China more self-reliant. As the "spiritual pollution" campaign of the early 1980s and, to a lesser degree, the "antibourgeois liberalism" campaign in 1987 have shown, the problem of xenophobic reactions to unwanted foreign influences is a continuing one; and, fourth, widespread cynicism, lack of confidence in the party, and the spread of corruption and resort to "backdoor" deals. Problems like these are one of the "inevitable consequences" of loosening internal discipline and controls, but they are no less troubling to China's rulers for that reason.

We must also be under no illusion that China's continued adherence to reform will be a panacea for all the difficulties in our bilateral relationship. We must recognize that there are limits to the changes that are possible in modern China, and that Chinese socialism, however flexible, will not tolerate some ideas that Americans hold dear. Positive developments in the human rights area notwithstanding, no communist government in China is likely to display tolerance for fundamental dissent, such as criticism of the Communist party or of China's socialist system. Prohibitions on free speech, freedom of the press, and complete freedom of religious expression will continue to place limits on the closeness of our ties with each other. Moreover, the intrinsic relationship between economic modernization and political modernization appears blocked despite the optimistic pronouncements of Chinese leaders. To the degree that U.S. ideals conflict with the Chinese regime's view that it needs to crack down to maintain order, there will always be friction.

Other factors beyond the control of China's leaders could also place limits on the reform process. The health of the international economic situation will continue to affect China, along with the rest of the world. Domestically, the reform program is running up against problems engendered by its own success, such as balancing the need to overhaul China's pricing system against the country's historical fear of inflation. Other such tough choices lie ahead.

Prospects

The key question is whether China's current reformers will succeed where earlier reformers failed. Is China in danger of reverting to the radicalism of the Cultural Revolution era? Will the reforms survive their chief architect, Deng Xiaoping? Behind these questions lies our acute consciousness of the instability of Chinese politics in the modern age.

The historians among you will doubtless recall that the Qing dynasty's great nineteenth-century reformer, Kang Youwei, grew frustrated over China's lapse into reaction following the collapse of the brief "hundred days" of reform. Confronted with a weak and disintegrating China, Kang eventually found refuge in propagandizing impractical utopian ideals. After encountering similar frustrations, Kang's brilliant disciple Liang Qichao concluded in despair that "in China today only cunning, crooked, vile, and ruthless people can flourish." As Benjamin Schwartz has documented in his study of Yen Fu's long fascination with Western ideas, the vision of Yen Fu's youth ultimately gave way to the discouragement of old age, his rejection of Western concepts, and his return to the traditional values of Confucianism and the mystical strain in Lao-zi and Zhuangzi . Will this pattern repeat itself?

In our search for the answer to this question, one indicator can be found in the success of the reforms themselves. For the first time in three decades, China has known a protracted period of internal stability. The high growth rates achieved in both agricultural and industrial sectors over a period of years, combined with the loosening of restrictions on cultural, literary, and artistic expression, have imroved both the standard of living and the quality of life for all sectors of China's population. In short, in relative terms China has become a more open, prosperous, and tolerant society over the past ten years. Judged by this standard, the Chinese people have nothing to gain and much to lose by a return either to the radicalism of the Maoist past or to a more orthodox Marxist approach.

Moreover, as China is drawn further into the global economy, it will become increasingly difficult for it to revert to isolationism and autarky. China has clearly benefited from the opening to the outside, and its leaders understand the importance of continued access to the technology, management techniques, and business practices of foreign countries. Resistant as they are to transposing Western solutions and value systems to China in toto, they recognize the relevance to China's problems of foreign experience in areas such as economic theory and scientific practice. They have seen the benefits their neighbors have derived from developing lucrative trade markets in developed countries, and they have gained confidence in their ability to follow a similar course. According to this line of analysis, as long as pragmatism works, China's leaders are not likely to revert to ideological solutions. Not surprisingly, China's pragmatic leaders belong to this school of thought and contend that the very success of the reforms is the best guarantee that they will continue.

Or perhaps the answer should be sought in the character of Deng Xiaoping himself, as the first leader in China's reform history who has combined the political strength, the intellectual vision, and the tactical flexibility to launch a sustained drive for national wealth and power. For what distinguishes China's present reformers from their nineteenth-century predecessors is that they are in a position to implement their ideas. Ninety years ago, China's reformers had to deal with leaders and institutions that either failed to share their vision or were incapable of translating their concepts into reality; confronted with an unsolvable dilemma, they lapsed with time into frustration, despair, and irrelevancy. In contrast, it has been Deng's success in motivating, implementing, and giving direction to China's reform program, and in passing that task on to his chosen successors, that has enabled him to remain optimistic and forward-looking at the ripe age of eighty-three.

It may be one of the great ironies of the modern world that a life-long Communist, a man who worked his way up through the party apparatus, who was elevated to the position of General Secretary of the Party more than thirty years ago, should have become responsible for such a thorough-going reshaping of China's domestic and foreign policy course. Nevertheless, it is undeniable that this transformation has been beneficial, whether from China's own standpoint, from the standpoint of United States relations with China, or from the standpoint of the West in general.

Earlier in this speech I referred to the cautionary parable of the messenger from Kafka's short story, "The Great Wall of China." The story also contains a more positive metaphor of what can be accomplished through the persistence of human endeavor. The author describes a river in the spring that "grows mightier and nourishes more richly the soil on ... its banks, still maintaining its own course until it reaches the sea." This metaphor of steady movement until a goal is reached is an apt one both for our Chinese friends in their quest for modernization and for ourselves in seeking to build a stronger relationship with China.

Development of friendly, stable, and enduring relations with the People's Republic of China has been a foreign policy objective of four consecutive American administrations. President Reagan has stated that, "such a relationship is vital to our long-term national security interests and contributes to stability in East Asia." This view is predicated on the belief that a stable and prospering China can be a force for peace, both in Asia and in the world. Thus far, the results of China's reform program have been compatible with that goal.

Comments by Li Miao

Shortly after I arrived in Boston less than a month ago, I took part in a panel discussion at the Kennedy School Forum; the topic of the forum was "China on the Road to Capitalism?" The question mark was bigger than the letters. That was the state of mind of most Americans in Boston. They had the euphoric feeling that China was on the road to capitalism, and this panel discussion was attended by more than four hundred people. A lot of people expected us to say that China was on the road to capitalism. I thought it would be good to the relations of the two countries to disabuse the American audience. Therefore, I told them unequivocally that China was not on the road to capitalism and gave them a number of reasons; thus started the conversation that lasted for the entire length of my stay in Boston. It was not a matter of whether I liked or disliked China embarking on the road to capitalism. It was a fact that China was not on the road to capitalism.

Watching the American media report on China is to see that they grasp certain things, certain rhetoric, that the American audience understands and that feeds the news and kind of rhetoric of the American audience. Then they try to gauge Chinese events by the standards that the American audience would like to see, and they therefore arrive at judgments that are entirely out of sync with the actuality in China. Therefore, what I want to do today is again tell you some things I know that I think would be conducive to your understanding of the Chinese reality, instead of commenting on Ambassador Roy's brilliant speech.

One point I want to underscore is that after a period of uncertainty starting from last December, we are now reassured after the Thirteenth Party Congress of the Chinese Communist Party (CCP) that China will be continuing with the reform. Despite the fact that Ambassador Roy stresses the difference between a China opening to the outside world and a China opening to the West, I should point out that funds and technology come mainly from the West, and the Chinese leaders are pragmatic people.

I was fortunate enough to be among the first group of Chinese that negotiated China's return to the International Monetary Fund (IMF) and the World Bank. After I arrived at the Ministry of Finance in 1980 I discovered from the files that China had been contemplating to return to these two world economic organizations as far back as 1978, which coincided with the new policy set by the Third Plenary Session of the Eleventh Central Committee of the CCP. So I read the files and knew what was happening. China even sent a delegation to Rumania and Yugoslavia to learn how to deal with the World Bank and the IMF. It was at the end of March that an IMF delegation came to China. When the delegation arrived in Beijing, it discovered that the Chinese were eager to return to the IMF. It was in the course of about five days of continuous negotiation that a final agreement was reached, and China was finally admitted to the IMF. When the delegation returned to Washington, D.C., it told MacNamara, then President of the World Bank, about China's willingness to return to the two world economic organizations. That was on a Saturday, and on Sunday the World Bank mission, headed by Bob MacNamara, started their China trip. It was on the plane that Bob MacNamara revised the entire itinerary. He redrafted everything. Originally, he thought it would be high-level meetings first, trying to convince the Chinese to return to the World Bank. But now he revised it. So the day following his arrival in Beijing, we sat at the table at the State Guest House with Bob MacNamara and hammered out a statement, which we signed; then he met with Deng Xiaoping and a number of Chinese senior officials. I am telling you the story simply to illustrate China's willingness to return to the two keystone world economic organizations. China's commitment to opening its economy and to reforming its economy to bring prosperity and wealth to the country was started at that time. I think this is an important and positive example.

Another point I want to make is that China began its reform in the countryside by disbanding the commune system, which all of you know no longer exists. According to the 1986 statistics, the total output value of the rural enterprises exceeded the total value of agricultural enterprises. This is important. In agriculture, like in many other fields, China has reached a point of no return. China will no longer be able to return to the old commune system. Earlier, after the disbanding of the commune system, the peasants were allowed to contract land from the state and sell a portion of the produce to the state; the remaining part would be sold on the free market. The percentage they were obliged to sell to the state was reduced last year.

From a Hong Kong newspaper I have learned that at a press conference during the Thirteenth Party Congress Du Rensheng, head of the agricultural research committee, made the announcement that the state now allowed the peasants to sell the right to use the land to others. Some 70 million of the peasants in China (out of the 800 million) had left farming and taken up rural enterprises. He expected another 100 million to leave farming and to engage in rural enterprises by 1995. He said these peasants would sell the land to others, and if they had improved the land, they could ask for compensation as well. I read this as another step toward decentralization in the Chinese countryside. I have not gotten hold of the full text of the general secretary's report to the Thirteenth Party Congress. The Hong Kong papers cited him as saying that at the present moment about 50 percent of the Chinese economy is planned, and he envisaged only about 30 percent of the whole economy to be planned by the end of this century. I see this as an improvement—continuous reforms and continuous decentralization, which again are points of no return. I have heard many senior Chinese officials remark to World Bank officials saying we would not embark on the old road again; we have suffered tremendously by imitating the old Soviet model. China has nothing to gain by reverting to the old ways of managing the economy.

In 1983 several friends gathered in my home. One asked the question whether it is possible to have an open economy and economic reform without having an open society. Would economic reforms be successful in a closed society? The collective answer to that question was a definite no.

I am glad that political reform was on the agenda of the Thirteenth Party Congress. How it was laid out in the prime minister's report I do not know. But it seems to have been discussed at the meeting. Whatever is said in that report, I think we should not expect the reform to follow the Western democratic model. As a first step, so far as I understand it, it needs streamlining of state apparatus, making it efficient, cutting away the dead flesh. Ambassador Roy mentioned the ponderous bureaucracy. He is perhaps expressing a scholar's academic understanding of it. My understanding is actual, having lived in a ponderous bureaucracy. I welcome the first step. I think this first step will help in the progress of economic reform. In turn, economic reform will then promote more political reforms. Again, this is a point of no return, in which one reform promotes the other.

I would like to mention some of my personal academic points of view: I hope to see a situation in which the Chinese media would play a greater role in the decision-making process. The media are now a party organ, a party mouthpiece. I would like to see the Chinese media play a more active role in exposing the corruption and the bureaucracy and leading different schools of thought in discussing future prospects of China. Here in America there is a special way of rating movies, such as G, PG, R, and X. PG stands for parental guidance. I think the Chinese literary and artistic communities and some of the news media would do better if parental guidance were softened or lessened to a certain degree.

Ambassador Roy spoke of the many obstacles that loomed on the path of China's economic reform. I would like to mention one briefly. I must first state, however, that I am plagiarizing the academic viewpoints of my Soviet colleague as well as Ambassador Roy when I say that the Chinese price system is out of date; it is a system that neither reflects market supply and demand nor the value of goods. Actually, the Chinese, in calculating with the World Bank about loans and about the Chinese economy, used a shadow price, that is, an international price. The World Bank simply said that it was unable to calculate the Chinese economy on the prices the Chinese quoted. On the other hand, recently, a senior World Bank official was talking to a Chinese official about changing the Chinese price system, and the senior Chinese official told him that we would have to go very slowly because inflationary consequences would lead to political instability. He said we would have to go at a snail's pace. I think something will have to be done about this in the future.

Another very irrational system is the Chinese wage and salary system. It must be changed; otherwise, there is no incentive for doing better work. As an intellectual, I want to make one more point, that is, that the Chinese intellectuals have been treated shabbily for nearly thirty years after 1949. This is not to say that they were not in a deplorable condition before 1949. There is a saying in China, actually a joke, that the Chinese intellectuals are like commodities or goods; the goods are good and the price is cheap, and the goods are even durable. In other words, the conditions of the Chinese intellectuals were bad. They have been improved since 1978, after the end of the Cultural Revolution. But that does not mean that after the improvement nothing else could be done and that we intellectuals are in the best of conditions. There is still much more to be done to improve the conditions of the Chinese intellectuals, both academically and in their living standards. Contrary to the frustration expressed by one of my American colleague's, I am glad the Chinese intellectuals now have good access to their Western counterparts. This American colleague's frustration was that America had something like twenty thousand Chinese scholars and students here and that they were showing no results. I think it is short-sighted to expect immediate results from these intellectuals studying in the United States. What Ambassador Roy said in his speech reflects the actual true idea of the Chinese studying in America.

Finally, for the development of good relations between China and the West, it is important that they understand each other well. From my more than one-year stay in America, studying the U.S. news media, I have discovered that few Americans understand the Chinese situation. The Boston panel discussion was an example. I think it is also the case in China. Very few Chinese understand the complex political mediation process in America. Many Chinese think that, in America, once one's candidate is elected into office everything will be fine for two years, four years, or six years. It is actually not that simple. Rather, it is a continuous process in which different interest groups and parties interact with each other with the media playing an important role. Most Chinese would not understand why the Iran-Contra affair would figure so importantly in American politics. Nor did they understand the Watergate affair.

I think it is also fair to mention that few Americans understand the position of China on Tibet and Taiwan. Few Americans understand the national emotions involved on these two issues. One cannot talk about these two issues as only involving the sovereignty of China. I was rather disappointed with my two friends from the *Christian Science Monitor*, presently stationed in Beijing as reporters. They wrote a piece on Tibet that catered very much to the American taste, but was out of sync with reality in Tibet.

Just yesterday I had a luncheon meeting with a group of professors at the University of California at Berkeley; to my great surprise, the point emphasized at the luncheon was the so-called peaceful succession that took place at the Thirteenth Party Congress. I told them I never expected a bloody succession. This came up simply because one of the networks was talking about a peaceful succession; even professors picked that up and repeated it without thinking. It is difficult for a pluralistic society like America to understand a centralized society like China. It is equally difficult for a nonpluralistic, centralized society like China to understand a pluralistic society like America, that is, to understand each other's ethics, values, and traditions. There is a tremendous amount to be studied and understood if we are going to have good relations with each other. The Chinese should also understand that when an American president stands up to speak, or a certain senator stands up to speak, he is talking not only to a certain country related to his speech, he is talking to the interest groups that surround him, to the secretaries, the White House, the Congress. To conclude, I wish to reiterate that it is very important to promote better understanding between our two countries.

INDEX